W9-DJP-179

Assessment
and Treatment
of Childhood
Problems

A Clinician's Guide

Assessment

and Treatment

of Childhood

Problems

A Clinician's Guide

Carolyn S. Schroeder
University of North Carolina
  at Chapel Hill
Chapel Hill Pediatrics

Betty N. Gordon
University of North Carolina
  at Chapel Hill

THE GUILFORD PRESS
NEW YORK   LONDON

© 1991 The Guilford Press
A Division of Guilford Publications, Inc.
72 Spring Street, New York, NY 10012

Printed in the United States of America

This book is printed on acid-free paper.

Last digit is print number: 9 8 7 6 5 4 3

Library of Congress Cataloging-in-Publication Data

Schroeder, Carolyn S.
    Assessment and treatment of childhood problems : a clinician's
guide / Carolyn S. Schroeder, Betty N. Gordon.
        p. cm.
    Includes bibliographical references and index.
    ISBN 0-89862-565-3
    1. Behavior disorders in children—Diagnosis. 2. Behavior
disorders in children—Treatment. I. Gordon, Betty N. II. Title.
    [DNLM: 1. Child Behavior Disorders—diagnosis—handbooks.
2. Child Behavior Disorders—therapy—handbooks. 3. Child
Development Disorders—diagnosis—handbooks. 4. Child Development
Disorders—therapy—handbooks. 5. Mental Disorders—in infancy &
childhood—handbooks. WS 39 S2381a]
RJ506.B44S37 1991
618.92′85′8—dc20
DNLM/DLC
for Library of Congress   91-20201
                                                          CIP

*To all parents, who have the awesome responsibility for raising
the next generation and, most especially, to our own parents,
Margaret and Evan Stineman and Alma and George Nye,
whose love, support, and encouragement
has given us the freedom to grow.*

PREFACE

*T*his book is an outgrowth of over 18 years of work in a primary health care setting where our focus is on enhancing children's development, preventing problems, and helping parents to manage stressful life events and common but often persistent and troublesome behavior problems. The primary health care setting provides a unique opportunity to follow children as they develop from birth through adulthood. We view this development as a function of a dynamic interaction between the child, the environment, and chance events, and view psychopathology as normal development gone awry.

The child clinician's role is multifaceted, including that of educator, advocate, service provider, and case manager. Parents, however, have the primary and ultimate responsibility for their children's development, and it is through our work with parents that we are able to enhance or change the trajectory of a child's life. The clinician provides expertise based on an understanding of developmental processes and the empirical literature related to children's problems, while parents bring unique knowledge about their child and family. We work together with parents to help them deal more effectively with the tasks of parenting and to enable them to help their children cope successfully with the stresses of growing up in an imperfect world. This approach results in a consultative relationship in which the clinician collaborates with parents to identify the strengths and weaknesses of the child, the family, and the larger environment and helps them plan and implement effective and manageable solutions to problems and concerns. A hallmark of the collaborative clinician–parent relationship is the open and frequent sharing of information related to the parents' concerns. This book reflects our belief that this consultative relationship with parents enhances the clinician's ability to intervene in most child-related problems.

Our approach to intervention is based on behavioral principles; we have been strongly influenced by behavioral, social learning, and cognitive–behavioral theorists. For each problem area presented, we have tried whenever possible to describe treatment approaches that are developmentally sensitive and have documented efficacy for the specific problem in question. For many childhood problems, however, the clinician is forced to be creative in developing innovative intervention strategies that have not yet been empirically validated for the majority of children with a specific problem but may be effective for an individual child or family.

The first section of the book sets the stage for understanding specific problem areas. Chapter 1 provides an overview of child development with an emphasis on the areas of development that seem most related to childhood problems. We believe that this information is fundamental to understanding "where things can go wrong." Chapter 2 describes factors that can enhance development or cause children to be more vulnerable to life stresses. In this chapter, the focus is on prevention of childhood problems by minimizing the effects of risk factors and maximizing protective factors. The Comprehensive Assessment-to-Intervention System (CAIS) described in Chapter 3 is used throughout the book as the framework by which clinicians can systematically gather the information necessary to understand and intervene in the problem areas covered in later chapters. The second section of the book covers sources of considerable stress for many children and parents during the course of growing up: siblings, divorce, and death. The third section deals with problems that often occur in childhood: enuresis, encopresis, sleep difficulties, sexual abuse, negative behavior, fears and anxieties, and habits and tics. For each stressful event or problem area, we provide a brief review of the literature, a guide to comprehensive assessment, specific treatment options, and a case example that illustrates the central features of the problem. The final section of the book consists of a chapter that describes the pediatric psychology practice developed at Chapel Hill Pediatrics. The focus of this practice has been on service (prevention, assessment, treatment, community consultation) and training; research and activities in each of these areas are described. We were also fortunate to have the administrator of the pediatric psychology practice, Judy Mann, contribute to this chapter. Judy provides a blueprint on how to set up and run such a practice. Her expertise is offered in the hope that our readers will sense the challenges and satisfaction that are part of working in a primary health care setting and will be inspired to develop similar practices. Finally, in the appendices we have included clinical forms, questionnaires, and descriptions of published instruments. One section provides a brief description of books for parents and children that can be used either preventively or as adjuncts to treatment. We have also included business forms that we have found helpful in setting up and running the practice, and consumer satisfaction questionnaires that give us feedback on how well we are meeting our clients' needs.

Who do we hope will read this book? Our aim is to reach all professionals who provide services to children. This includes not only child psychologists but also pediatricians, child psychiatrists, nurses, social workers, guidance counselors, and trainees in all of these fields.

This book provided us with the long anticipated opportunity to describe the work that we have been fortunate to do over so many years and gave us the chance to review the burgeoning literature relevant to children. We have gained a new appreciation for the work of Michael Rutter, Norman Garmezy, Michael Roberts, Eugene Walker, Alan Kazdin, Susan Campbell, Russell Barkley, and many other outstanding developmental and clinical child professionals. It was especially gratifying to discover the beginning integration of the work of basic researchers in developmental psychology with that of child clinicians who test the credibility of various theories and hypotheses in the context of real life settings and situations. We owe a very special acknowledgment to Sheila Eyberg, who as a first-rate clinician, researcher, and writer gave us the benefit of her expertise by critically reading the entire manuscript and gently pointing out inconsistencies and flaws. Sarah Kennedy, our production editor, did an excellent job of moving the book through the production process, and Marie Sprayberry of editing the manuscript; we thank them both.

There are many other people who by their very presence greatly influenced our work: the parents and children in Chapel Hill, North Carolina with whom we have been most fortunate to work; our colleagues at the pediatric office and the University of North Carolina at Chapel Hill who so ably "held the fort" as we wrote; and our wonderful husbands, children, and families who tolerated our unavailability with good grace (usually!). We did most of the writing at a cottage on Emerald Isle where the beauty of the ever-changing ocean, the birds, sea life, and an occasional young family on the beach kept us inspired to complete the task. A special thanks to Clark Wylde of Busy Bee Fix-it, whose help allowed us to work at Walden III through the winter and spring.

The person who has had the greatest influence in making this work possible is Dr. Charles I. Sheaffer, a pediatrician at Chapel Hill Pediatrics and the University of North Carolina at Chapel Hill. Charlie is a tireless advocate for children who sees beyond the possible and continually provides us with the opportunity to do more. He has been a mentor, colleague, friend, physician, facilitator, and, above all, a model for child advocacy that has changed the way we think about our professional roles. Thank you Charlie!

CONTENTS

PART I

THE BASIS FOR

ASSESSMENT

AND TREATMENT

Chapter 1

Development

◼◼◼◼◼◼◼◼◼◼◼◼◼◼◼◼◼◼◼◼◼◼

*M*ost children, in the process of growing up, will have emotional and behavioral problems that are transient in nature and result from the stresses of development and adaptation to family and societal expectations. The major parenting task is to enhance children's development by helping them gain control over normal developmental events such as toilet training, sexuality, being told "No," fears, and dealing with siblings and peers. Children and parents must also cope with life circumstances such as poverty or unemployment, and stressful events such as hospitalization, divorce, death, or the birth of a sibling. For all of this pressure to cope and adapt, it is heartening that epidemiological studies find rather consistently that over the course of any one year, only 5–15% of children suffer from an emotional or behavioral problem that is severe enough to interfere with their day-to-day functioning (Rutter, 1975). The goal of the child clinician is not only to help this group of children who have major mental health problems, but also to help the other 85–95% of children and their parents manage the stresses of normal growth and development, and consequently to enhance their opportunities to live, love, and work with a sense of well-being.

Because of their rapid growth and development, children represent a unique population. Previously, the importance attributed to changes in any aspect of development depended to a great extent on one's theoretical perspective. Psychoanalytic theory, for example, emphasizes the emergence of independence and psychosexual development, whereas social learning theory focuses on the development of self-control and self-efficacy. However, the failure of any one theory to explain the full complexity of development across ages and areas has led to general acceptance of a transactional and/or ecological perspective, which attempts to account for factors within the child, family, and society that influence development either directly or indirectly (Campbell, 1990). Within this perspective, developmental gains in each area (social, cognitive, motor, language, etc.) are thought to be related to progress in other areas. Furthermore, competence or problems in any area of development early in life are seen as setting the stage for later development.

Thus, developmental change (both positive and negative) is the result of the transactional dialogue among each child with his or her unique biological/genetic makeup, the physical and social environment, and the cultural milieu into which he or she is born. As Mash and Terdal (1988) point out, "it is critical to recognize the ebb and flow of this developmental dialogue because it has critical implications for the manner in which child behaviors are conceptualized, measured, classified, diagnosed, changed, and evaluated" (p. 22). Behaviors common at one age may be considered significant problems at another age, and many childhood problems may change both qualitatively and quantitatively with age. Likewise, the impact of stressful life events may vary with the child's stage of development, parent characteristics, and the social support system available to the family at that time.

Knowledge of developmental norms is clearly essential for the clinician to recognize which behaviors are excessive or deficient for children at a given developmental stage. An understanding of normal development is also important to the child clinician in choosing appropriate intervention techniques. For example, treatment of the school-age child would rely more heavily on cognitive and language skills, while use of concrete, situation-specific tasks and developmentally appropriate play activities would be more appropriate for the preschool child. The clinician must also have knowledge of the normal sequence of acquisition of skills in order to plan appropriate treatment for problems such as social skills deficits.

In light of the importance of a developmental perspective for clinical work with children, this chapter focuses on normal developmental milestones of the young child (ages 2–10 years) and their influence on the child's later development. (See Campbell, 1990, for an excellent discussion of theoretical issues of development and behavior problems.)

DEVELOPMENTAL MILESTONES:
GENERAL COMMENTS

The developmental tasks of children obviously change with age, and each stage of development presents unique challenges to children and parents. Child psychologists consider the preschool years (ages 2–5) to be one of the most important developmental periods, because it is during this time that the foundation for later competence in many areas is laid. The emergence of language, self-awareness, peer relationships, autonomy, and independence, as well as the increased complexity of cognitive, play, social, and motor skills, also sets the stage for new and often intense interactions between the child and the environment. As a child's capacity to interact with the environment increases, so do the problems and concerns of parents. Although most of these problems are transient, significant problems in any one developmental area can affect the development of other skills. For example, difficulty with language can affect cognitive development, or problems with self-control can affect self-esteem and social relationships.

The developmental tasks for children ages 6–10 involve the consolidation and refinement of skills necessary for meeting the expectations of society. It is during this period that children develop new and more complex cognitive and language skills, refine their fine and gross motor and attending skills, and confront the social and emotional challenges of interacting with increased numbers of adults and children in structured and unstructured settings. Self-concept and the perceptions of others become increasingly abstract and consequently more accurate, leading to the development of social support networks outside the immediate family. The ways in which significant adults help children through these difficult periods can have implications for children's later development. A child who is having trouble with separation and individuation, for example, may have more trouble with social skills if the parents deal with separation issues in an angry or rejecting manner.

In considering developmental milestones, the clinician should keep inter- and intraindividual differences in mind. Individual differences in the rate of development are clearly apparent during the preschool years, and these differences persist into the school years. Some children, for example, begin to develop language before the age of 1, whereas other "normal" children have not acquired extensive language by age 3. Differences in physical growth become dramatically apparent in the elementary and early adolescent years, although each child may be developing along a normal continuum. At school age, academic standards reflect differences among children.

An individual child's rate of development within various areas can vary as much as the rate of development among children. A child may be speaking in sentences at age 2 years, but may not begin hopping or skipping until much later than expected. Likewise, a child may be at the top of the class in reading, but may have difficulty participating in group play activities. Some of these inter- and intraindividual differences are primarily the result of genetic/organic factors; others seem to be more the result of environmental influences. It is, of course, the unique interaction of these two factors—the child and the environment—that ultimately determines each child's developmental progress.

Because many types of learning take place rapidly and simultaneously during the childhood years, it is common for children who are not developing normally to be identified at this time (particularly during the preschool years), often because they fail to achieve an expected developmental milestone. It is usually the general pattern of development rather than slower development in any specific area that alerts one to potential problems. For example, toilet training may be slower and more difficult; the child may be slower to learn to dress and eat independently; and constant supervision may be needed at a time when most children are becoming independent, helpful family members. If developmental problems are not noticed during the preschool years, they will almost inevitably be identified as the child enters school, when there are increased expectations to sit quietly, pay attention, process more complex language, read, do arithmetic, and deal with difficult social situations.

PHYSICAL AND MOTOR DEVELOPMENT

There is a steady growth of both height and weight during the preschool years; by age 5 weight is double that of 1 year, and height has doubled birth length by age 3. Most remarkable, by age 5 the brain has reached 90% of its adult weight (Rutter, 1975). The relevant brain maturation, along with adequate stimulation, sets the stage for developing important physical and motor skills and for learning about the physical and social world.

Most children have accomplished the gross motor skills of climbing, balancing, jumping, running, pushing, and pulling by 5 years of age. By age 6 years they can hop, throw and catch a ball, bounce a ball four to six times, tie shoelaces, skate, and ride a bicycle. Motor development is essential for active exploration and mastery of the environment; yet as children develop gross motor skills, activity level increases (Routh, Schroeder, & O'Tuma, 1974) and parents often become concerned about overactivity (Campbell, 1990). Although individual differences in activity level are believed to have a significant genetic component (Buss & Plomin, 1984), environmental factors such as types of toys (O'Brian & Huston, 1986), parental modeling (Sallis, Patterson, McKenzie, & Nader,

1988), and home or classroom environments can also influence activity levels.

Fine motor skills move from scribbling at age 2 to copying a circle by 3, a square by 4, and a triangle by 5; by 5½ years of age, most children are able to print their own names (Rand, 1973). Although still crude and with little detail, the drawings of 5-year-old children are usually recognizable as pictures of houses or people (Rutter, 1975). Understanding drawing rules such as "start at the left," "start at the top," and "draw horizontal lines from left to right" seems to occur in a developmental sequence (Goodnow & Levine, 1973). By age 6, children can print a few words and numbers and can draw a person with at least six body parts, as well as depict the figure wearing clothes.

COGNITIVE DEVELOPMENT

The area of cognitive development is so complex that only a brief discussion is possible in this chapter. The reader is referred to Gelman and Baillargeon (1983), Shantz (1983), and Wolman (1985) for reviews. The work of Piaget has greatly influenced our understanding of cognitive development. Piaget (Piaget & Inhelder, 1969) proposed that children progress through a universal sequence of stages in their understanding of the physical world. According to Piaget, cognitive development consists of qualitative changes in the ability to reason about environmental events and is driven by an inherent motivation to explore and experience the environment (Flavell, 1977). Preschool children are described as "preoperational." They are beginning to think symbolically and to understand cause-and-effect relationships; yet they lack the ability to take another's perspective (this lack is called "egocentrism"), have trouble coordinating information from more than one source, and cannot attend to more than one dimension of a stimulus array at a time. As Campbell (1990) points out, these constraints on preschoolers' thinking skills can lead to faulty logic and errors in understanding the world. Current work, however, suggests that Piaget may have underestimated the capabilities of preschoolers (Gelman & Baillargeon, 1983). When tasks and materials are familiar and do not require sophisticated language skills, preschoolers appear less egocentric and better able to reason.

Children gradually develop increasingly mobile, flexible, and reversible thought processes, and move into a cognitive developmental period termed the "concrete operational" stage by Piaget (Gruen, 1985). By 7 or 8 years, children are able to use representational or internalized cognitive strategies in a systematic fashion to organize and order objects, numbers, and events that are concrete and manipulable (i.e., that exist in the here and now). Later, the adolescent will be able to think of possibilities that do not exist in reality and to see that reality is just a special case of what is possible (Gruen, 1985).

In the area of perceptual development, Gibson's (1969) early work identified important prerequisites for reading. She indicated that most 4-year-olds can differentiate letters according to closure (e.g., O vs. C), but they still have trouble with line-to-curve transformation (e.g., V to U) and rotational transformations (e.g., b to d). Preschoolers also have trouble remembering the names, and, more importantly, the sounds that go with each letter (Caldwell & Hall, 1970). From ages 4 to 8, the most common orientation errors are mirror-image reversals; next are inversions, then inverted reversals, and finally rotations. Word reversals are infrequent, but there is a tendency to transpose letters within words, a common occurrence for children up to 9 years of age.

Memory development is thought to proceed through a process of increased knowledge about the world and increased reasoning skills, which allow for better organization of information in memory and the use of memory strategies (Ornstein, 1978). A preschooler's demonstration of memory skills depends to some extent on how important the event is, how familiar the child is with the context, and how the child is asked to recall the event. DeLoache, Cassidy, and Brown (1985) found some evidence for use of memory strategies in 18- to 24-month-olds, while Bauer and Mandler (1989) have reported immediate and delayed (2 weeks) recall of familiar and novel events in 16- to 20-month-olds. Moreover, preschool children have demonstrated behavioral memory (in contrast to verbal reports) of very traumatic events that occurred during infancy (Terr, 1988). With their increased ability to organize and manipulate internalized thought processes, most children have memory abilities comparable to those of adults by age 9 or 10. Their knowledge base has broadened, and this facilitates the organization of information in memory. Furthermore, they are increasingly adept at using memory strategies such as rehearsal or association. Actually, much of what goes on at school is teaching and practicing memory skills (e.g., learning spelling words, number facts, etc.).

Children who evidence slower cognitive development are commonly referred for evaluation during the preschool years because of problems in other areas (e.g., slow or atypical language development, poor motor skills, or behavior problems). As children approach school age, parents may be concerned that the child is not ready to start school, and school-age children may be referred because they are not doing well in school. The resulting diagnosis may be mental retardation or, more commonly, learning disability.

According to the revised third edition of the *Diagnostic and Statistical Manual of Mental Disorders* (DSM-III-R), children with learning disabilities evidence deficits in one or several academic areas (reading, writing, arithmetic, etc.) in spite of average or above-average intellectual abilities, and in the absence of physical or neurological disorders, mental retardation, or deficient educational opportunities (American Psychiatric Association, 1987). In contrast, Cruickshank (1977) argues that average intelligence should not be required for a diagnosis of learning disability. He suggests that learning disabilities involve a perceptual processing deficit that results in learning problems, and that this deficit can occur at any level of intelligence. Nevertheless, learning disabilities are most often diagnosed by documenting a "significant discrepancy" between intellectual and academic functioning.

DSM-III-R estimates the prevalence of specific reading disorders at 2–8% of school-age children. No prevalence data are given for arithmetic disorders, although these are estimated to be less frequent than reading disorders. Children with learning disabilities are thought to be at high risk for associated behavior problems. Neeper and Lahey (1983) indicate that a diagnosis of hyperactivity is most commonly associated with learning disability. Other associated behavior problems include aggression, social withdrawal, depression, and poor self-esteem. Children with learning disabilities also tend to be rejected by their peers and thus are vulnerable to the long-term consequences of social rejection, including delinquency, dropping out of school, and psychiatric disturbances (Neeper & Lahey, 1983).

Mental retardation is defined as significantly below-average cognitive and adaptive behavior skills (see Matson & Mulick, 1983, for a review of this area). Children with mental retardation are more likely to exhibit deviant behavior than are children in the general population (Jacobson, 1982a, 1982b). Jacobson (1982a) surveyed more than 8,000 children with mental retardation who ranged in age from infancy to adolescence. He found that 9.8% of these children had significant psychiatric problems. The presence of behavior problems was related to age (younger children had fewer problems), degree of retardation (there were fewer problems among children with mild or profound retardation), and living context (there were fewer problems for children living at home). Work by Crnic, Friedrich, and Greenberg (1983) suggests that the parents and siblings of a child with mental retardation and the family as a unit are also at risk for significant problems. Thus the impact of the child with mental retardation on the family, as well as the impact of a particular family on the child with mental retardation, should be assessed when planning intervention programs for this population.

At the opposite end of the spectrum from the child with mental retardation, but no less exceptional, is the gifted child. Gifted children are usually identified because they go beyond our developmental expectations (Roedell, Jackson, & Robinson, 1980). Current definitions of giftedness have been broadened from a unitary concept of general intelligence to include measures of intellectual, scholastic, and psychomotor ability, as well as creativity, leadership, and artistic or athletic talent (Roedell et al., 1980). Moreover, it is generally accepted that gifted children differ from one another in many areas of development as much as average or handicapped children differ from one another. Even within the same child, the variation in different skill areas can be tremendous. It is not uncommon to find children gifted in one area and average or even below average in another.

Extremely gifted children have been thought to be at risk for adjustment problems, in part because of the wide gaps between levels of intellectual, physical, social, or emotional development. In addition, gifted children may be isolated from peers or seen as different or peculiar because of their extraordinary abilities. Chamrad and Robinson (1986), however, report that young gifted children often have higher self-esteem, and more energy, enthusiasm, and curiosity, than average children.

LANGUAGE DEVELOPMENT

The development of language skills during the preschool years is astounding! Rice (1989), in an excellent summary, states that expressive language appears at about 1 year of age, followed by a rapid spurt in number of words at about 18 months, when word combinations begin to occur. Between 2 and 6 years of age, children acquire as many as 14,000 new word meanings! Children at first draw heavily upon the salience of objects and actions upon objects in mastering language, in a way that closely parallels Piaget's ideas about cognitive development (Brown, 1973). Later, children begin to be able to use language to develop cognitive skills, to facilitate their understanding of the world, to aid their remembering, and to organize their thoughts (Rice, 1989). Rice (1989) suggests several environmental factors that can enhance language development. These include (1) speaking "motherese," which consists of such features as simple sentences focused on present events, slow rate of speech with pauses at significant words, and paraphrasing of the child's utterances; (2) semantic contingency, which involves immediate responses to the child's utterances and conversing about what the child is presently interested in; and (3) reading to the child. Factors that may impede language development include a controlling style of interaction with the child, which involves many commands, directives, and questions (Nelson, 1973).

It is important to note that there is a great deal of variability in the rate with which individual children meet the developmental milestones for language (see Vetter, 1980, for a table of milestones). Lillywhite, Young, and Olmsted (1970) have compiled a list of 20 guidelines useful for determining when a child has a significant problem needing referral or when he or she is developing normally (albeit at his or her own pace) and is best left alone (Table 1.1).

The importance of language development is demonstrated by studies indicating that language mediates cognitive and social development (e.g., Simon, Larson, & Lehrer, 1988). Thus delays or disorders of language will impede development in other areas as well. Any of the major categories of speech and language disorders can be seen in children as young as the preschool years, including disorders of speech (articulation, voice quality, and fluency); disorders of language (understanding the symbol system, and production of words, meanings, and grammar); and disorders of communication or pragmatics (social uses of language as a communication system) (Vetter, 1980).

TABLE 1.1. Guidelines for Referral to Communication Specialist

Refer if any of the following conditions exist:

1. Child is not talking at all by age 2.
2. Speech is largely unintelligible after age 3.
3. There are many omissions of initial consonants after age 3.
4. There are no sentences by age 3.
5. Sounds are more than a year late in appearing according to developmental sequence.
6. There is an excessive amount of indiscriminate irrelevant verbalizing after 18 months.
7. There is consistent and frequent omission of initial consonants.
8. There are many substitutions of easy sounds for difficult ones after age 5.
9. The amount of vocalizing decreases rather than steadily increasing at any period up to age 7.
10. The child uses mostly vowel sounds in his speech at any age after 1 year.
11. Word endings are consistently dropped after age 5.
12. Sentence structure is consistently faulty after age 5.
13. The child is embarrassed or disturbed by his speech at any age.
14. The child is noticeably nonfluent (stuttering) after age 5.
15. The child is distorting, omitting, or substituting any sounds after age 7.
16. The voice is a monotone, extremely loud, largely inaudible, or of poor quality.
17. The pitch is not appropriate to the child's age and sex.
18. There is noticeable hypernasality or lack of nasal resonance.
19. There are unusual confusions, reversals, or telescoping in connected speech.
20. There is abnormal rhythm, rate, and inflection after age 5.

Note. From *Pediatrician's Handbook of Communication Disorders* by H. S. Lillywhite, N. B. Young, and R. W. Olmsted, 1970, Philadelphia: Lea & Febiger. Copyright 1970 by Lea & Febiger. Reprinted by permission.

Middle-ear disease, which is often accompanied by fluctuating hearing loss in preschool children, is associated with language delays (Simon et al., 1988; Wallace, Gravel, McCarton, & Ruben, 1988). This is a significant problem when one considers that as many as 40% of preschoolers' visits to the pediatrician involve middle-ear disease (Teele, Klein, & Rosner, 1984). Wallace et al. (1988) have reported delays in expressive language in children as young as 1 year who had chronic middle-ear infections. Furthermore, a longitudinal study by Feagans, Sanyal, Henderson, Collier, and Appelbaum (1987) indicated that middle-ear disease in the preschool years was related to attentional problems in elementary school, in spite of the fact that the language delays had resolved.

Language problems must always be assessed relative to a child's developmental status and environmental circumstances. For example, stuttering can be a major problem for older children, but it is not uncommon for preschoolers to hesitate and stutter because they do not yet have the vocabulary to express all that they know. Pressure by anxious parents only creates more difficulty. In fact, most serious cases of dysfluency in older children have their origins between the ages of 2 and 5 (Lillywhite et al., 1970).

It is through language that we are able to communicate and socialize with those around us and to learn to internalize the values, customs, and rules of society (Piacentini, 1987). It is thus not surprising that delays or deficiencies in the development of speech and language in children have been associated with behavioral, emotional, and social disturbances (Baker & Cantwell, 1985; see Piacentini, 1987, for an excellent review of language dysfunction and childhood behavior disorders). Studies have shown that as many as 50% of speech- and language-disordered children also evidence some form of psychopathology (Piacentini, 1987).

SOCIAL DEVELOPMENT

Social development is dependent on many other aspects of development. Reasoning about the physical world, for example, provides the basis for reasoning about the social world. Social competence is in part a function of the development of specific cognitive skills, such as representational or symbolic thinking and social perspective taking (Howes, 1987), as well as language skills. In contrast, behavioral genetics suggests that some aspects of social competence, such as sociability and extroversion, have a substantial genetic component (Plomin, 1989).

Developmental research has shown that children's experiences in early caregiving relationships provide the basis for the development of social competence (Jacobson & Wille, 1986; Park & Waters, 1989). For example, Jacobson & Wille (1986) demonstrated that the quality of the mother–child attachment bond was related to the quality of the child's peer relationships; securely attached peers had happier, more harmonious and less controlling relationships than did insecurely attached peers. In an excellent review of the development of social relationships, Hartup (1989) describes the importance of having both vertical relationships (i.e., attachments to individuals with greater knowledge and social power) and horizontal relationships (i.e., relationships in which individuals have equal amounts of social power). Whereas vertical relationships provide security and protection, horizontal relationships allow children to elaborate skills with individuals more or less similar to themselves. These relationships are seen as bidirectional, because both the child and the relationships change as a result of the interaction. For example, as a child gets older, the form of parent–child interactions changes from primarily physical to the parents' giving verbal instructions to the parents' sharing information. It is within the context of these relationships that the complexities of cooperation and competitiveness are mastered, and "intimacy" in social relationships is first achieved (Hartup, 1989).

Studies have also shown that early social relationships can affect the course of the child's development in other areas. Main, Kaplan, and Cassidy (1985), for example, found that children who were securely attached at 12 months were characterized as more emotionally secure and better able to express their feelings at age 6; 6-year-olds who were not securely attached at 12 months had great difficulty discussing their feelings and had few strategies for dealing with separation. Furthermore, children with secure attachments to their caregivers, as compared to children with less secure attachments, show more appropriate social adaptations (e.g., they are more popular, make more social contact, and are more helpful to others) over time (Hartup, 1989). Patterns of cognitive functioning, including more symbolic play, more internal control, and better problem-solving skills (Matas, Arend, & Sroufe, 1978), as well as increased task mastery (Baumrind, 1971) and higher school achievement (Estrada, Arsenio, Hess, & Holloway, 1987), are also associated with early secure attachment to caregivers. Early relationships have likewise been found to be important in emotional development, influencing popularity, number of social contacts, ability to offer support to others, and self-esteem (Cassidy, 1988; Sroufe & Fleeson, 1986). Hartup (1989) suggests a number of ways in which these early affective relationships may influence cognitive functioning:

(a) Mothers who have good relationships with their children may be especially encouraged to engage them and support them in solving problems. (b) Children in these relationships may also be more competent and, hence, more willing to accept tutelage and maternal assistance. (c) Finally, children who have warm and flexible relationships with their mothers may use them more readily as a stable emotional base for exploring the wider world and learning from these experiences. (pp. 123–124)

Children's friendships, as defined by reciprocity and commitment between individuals who are more or less equal, usually begin to develop after age 2 with the onset of parallel play. Gradually play becomes more cooperative and reciprocal between 3 and 5 years of age (Howes, 1987), and by middle childhood competition becomes an important part of social relationships, especially for boys (Berndt, 1981). Children's friendships are primarily same-sex at all ages from the preschool years through adolescence. They are based on common play interests and the attraction that emanates from similarities between self and others.

Evidence suggests that friends are "developmental advantages" in socioemotional development (Hartup, 1989). Because of their intensity and equality, friendships provide optimal contexts for learning certain social skills, such as cooperation and intimacy. Hartup (1989) points out that although close relationships with other children may not be developmental necessities, being disliked by one's companions is a risk factor, because social rejection in childhood is consistently found to be related to later adjustment problems (Parker & Asher, 1987). Achenbach and Edelbrock (1981) report that 30–75% of children referred to guidance clinics are reported by their parents to have peer difficulties. Given the importance of parent–child relationships in the socialization process, Putallaz (1987) suggests that intervention efforts for children who have peer relationship problems should be directed at parent behavior as well as child behavior. She states that the parent–child interaction easily becomes cyclical, and if the parent does not change along with the child, the child's original maladaptive behavioral repertoire will continue to be elicited in interactions with peers.

PERSONALITY DEVELOPMENT

Temperament

"Temperament," or the behavioral style of a child's interaction with the environment, is an important aspect of early personality development. The work of Thomas and Chess (1977) demonstrated individual differences in temperament as early as the first few weeks of life, and current research in behavioral genetics suggests that many aspects of temperament/personality may be inborn (Plomin, 1989). Whereas Thomas and his colleagues (Thomas, Chess, & Birch, 1968) assessed temperament in terms of nine categories, McCall (Goldsmith et al., 1987) recently synthesized various conceptualizations of temperament and proposed four dimensions: activity, reactivity, emotionality, and sociability. Thomas et al. (1968) also derived a cluster of traits (irregularity of biological functions or rhythmicity, withdrawal from novel stimuli, slow adaptation, intense responses, and predominantly negative mood) called "difficult temperament," which was thought to be clinically significant. Current work has shown that the "difficult" child is harder to parent and is at higher risk for developing behavior problems (Goldsmith et al., 1987). McDevitt and Carey (1978), in a sample of 350 children (ages 3–5) from a pediatric practice, found almost 19% to be difficult. Carey and McDevitt (1978) found that the temperament characteristics regarded by parents as difficult to manage changed with age. At ages 1–3, all characteristics of the difficult-child cluster (as defined by Thomas et al., 1968) were troublesome. At ages 3–7 years, rhythmicity decreased in importance, while low persistence and high activity level were perceived as most troublesome. Thomas et al. (1968) also introduced the idea of "goodness of fit," which accounts for the interrelationship between the child's characteristics and environmental demands and expectations, and can serve to facilitate or interfere with optimal development. Thus difficult infants born to highly stressed, unresponsive mothers would be considered at higher risk than difficult infants born to responsive, sensitive, calm mothers (Campbell, 1990).

Although various aspects of the construct of temperament (stability, measurement, definition, etc.) continue to be debated, considerable research has demonstrated the relationship between specific dimensions of temperament and other aspects of later development. Fussy infants, for example, have been found to be more noncompliant at age 4 (Himmelfarb, Hock, & Wenar, 1985). Earls and Jung (1987) found that children characterized as having greater intensity of emotional expression and less adaptibility at age 2 were more likely to have behavior problems at age 3. Significant relationships have also been found between temperament characteristics and concurrent measures of social and cognitive development. Brody, Stoneman, and Burke (1988), for example, found that temperament characteristics of 4- to 6-year-old children who had not been referred for mental health services were related to parents' perceptions of their children's adjustment: Children who were less persistent, more emotionally intense, or more active than older or younger siblings were seen as less well adjusted. Others have found that temperament is related to adjustment to preschool (Parker-Cohen & Bell, 1988) and kindergarten (Skarpness & Carson, 1987), to peer relations among preschoolers (Keogh & Burstein, 1988; Parker-Cohen & Bell, 1988), to preschoolers' helping a stranger (Stanhope, Bell, & Parker-Cohen, 1987), and to IQ scores and academic achievement (Palisin, 1986)! Thus, consideration of temperamental characteristics in young children is clearly important to understanding many aspects of their development. Very little has been written on temperament in the middle childhood years, but questioning parents about their child's early temperamental characteristics may shed light on current behavior and interpersonal relationships.

Self-System

Another important aspect of personality development is the development of the "self-system," which includes self-concept (one's view of what one is like), self-esteem (the discrepancy between one's actual self-concept and the ideal self), and self-control (the extent to which one directs the course of one's own behavior and activities) (Harter, 1983a). Consistent with their cognitive-developmental level, the self-concept of preschool children consists primarily of concrete attributes such as physical characteristics and possessions. Preschoolers also tend to think of themselves in either–or terms—for instance, as "nice" or "mean," "good" or "bad" (Pope, McHale, & Craighead, 1988). As children get older, they begin to describe themselves in terms of more abstract qualities. Development of self-concept from the school-age years to young adulthood proceeds from terms describing character ("honest," "neat") and emotional attributes ("happy," "angry") to labels describing interpersonal traits ("friendly," "popular") and finally to terms describing psychological makeup (values, beliefs) (Pope et al., 1988). So the nature of an individual's self-concept develops from ideas about the bodily self to ideas of the inner or moral self. Also, increasingly with age, self-concept is derived from comparisons with peers rather than feedback from parents.

Self-esteem, an evaluation of the information contained in the self-concept, plays a critical role in social–emotional development. Low self-esteem is associated with a number of psychiatric diagnoses (American Psychiatric Association, 1987) and also with poor academic achievement. High self-esteem, on the other hand, has been shown to buffer the effects of stress (O'Grady & Metz, 1987). Self-esteem is derived from a child's feelings about all the things he or she is (Pope et al., 1988). Self-esteem is based on a combination of objective information about oneself (perceived self) and subjective evaluation of that information (ideal self). When the perceived and ideal selves are a good match, the self-esteem is positive. For example, when children who value being good athletes are good athletes, then they should have positive evaluations of their actual characteristics. However, if there is a discrepancy between perceived self and ideal self, then there can be problems with self-esteem. Pope et al. (1988) say that children generally value themselves across five areas: social, academic, family, body image, and global self-esteem (an evaluation of all parts of oneself).

Clearly, early in development a sense of mastery over environmental events contributes to self-esteem, and interactions with important adults mediate the experience of mastery. Campbell (1990) states that adults can provide or thwart opportunities for children to explore the environment and consequently experience mastery, and they can reward, punish, or ignore successful experiences. Successful coping with stressful events may also foster a sense of mastery and thus enhance self-esteem (Brazelton & Yogman, 1986). So allowing children to experience and cope with mild stress can contribute to positive self-esteem.

Self-control is related both directly and indirectly to self-esteem (Pope et al., 1988). Direct effects are exemplified by the fact that children who have good self-control feel better about themselves and also get more positive feedback from adults. Indirect effects include parents' behavioral expectations for the child, their own styles of control, and the child's characteristics, all of which play a role in the development of self-control (Campbell, 1990; Harter, 1983a). Kopp (1982) outlines a developmental progression for the development of self-control. In infancy, self-control is a function of the child's ability to regulate arousal and the parents' abilities to provide regular, predictable routines; to respond to the child's signals appropriately and quickly; and to prevent the child from experiencing overwhelming frustration. From 12 to 24 months, self-control depends to some extent on increasing cognitive skills (e.g., object permanence) and memory skills, and to a greater extent on external structure (i.e., parental control). At this age, children can comply with simple requests in familiar, predictable situations, but do not understand the rationale for compliance and do not generalize to new situations. Kopp (1982) states that by 24 months of age, true self-control begins to emerge as the child has less need for external constraints. Self-control at this age is still largely external, however, and tied to concrete and specific situations; parents provide control either by manipulating the child's environment or by providing consequences for the child's appropriate or inappropriate behaviors (Pope et al., 1988). By 3–4 years of age, children are more able to generalize rules from situation to situation and can recognize when other people are behaving inappropriately. They also begin to exercise more control by talking out loud about their behavior, and by 5 or 6 years this verbal control begins to be internalized. The child then tends to control his or her own behavior by following the rules to get approval or disapproval from others. At about age 6 the beginnings of moral behavior appear, with the child's own conscience controlling behavior to avoid personal guilt rather than the condemnation of others.

Individual differences in personality or temperament mediate the development of self-control. In infancy, for example, irritable and easily aroused infants have more trouble regulating impulses and tolerating frustration than those who are more placid (Campbell, 1990). But parenting practices are also critical, particularly parents' own ways of exercising self-control or resolving conflicts with the child or others. The importance of the development of adequate self-control cannot be overemphasized, because deficits in self-control, as well as low self-esteem, are associated with many childhood disorders and with most conceptualizations of psychopathology (Achenbach & Edelbrock, 1978; Pope et al., 1988).

EMOTIONAL DEVELOPMENT

Expression of Emotions

The expression of emotion during the preschool years is intially uninhibited, because the child is in the process of learning how to express emotions in a socially acceptable way. Anger is often expressed physically by biting, scratching, or kicking, and boys are commonly more physical than girls (Rutter, 1975). Anger is usually expressed in response to an immediate stimulus and is short-lived. The increased interaction with peers and family also increases negative behavior and temper outbursts, which occur most often at 2–3 years of age and then gradually diminish during the later preschool years (Mesibov, Schroeder, & Wesson, 1977).

Kopp (1989) provides a developmental framework for the regulation of negative emotions. She states that in the preschool years, the development of language "offers young children a multipurpose vehicle for dealing with emotions and moving toward more effective ER [emotional regulation]" (p. 349). Children's ability to label emotions, to talk about emotions, and to use language about emotions to guide their own behavior increases rapidly during the preschool years (Kopp, 1989). Although 4- and 5-year-olds become quite distressed in the presence of adult anger and show different styles of coping (Cummings, 1987), the ability to interpret others' emotional expressions accurately does not appear to develop until later in childhood. Covell and Abramovitch (1987), for example, found that 5- and 6-year-olds attributed their mothers' anger and happiness only to themselves. Strayer (1986), in a study with children ages 4–5 years and 7–8 years, found that both interpersonal and achievement explanations for emotions increased with age; that fantasy contexts for fear decreased with age; and that girls used more interpersonal explanations for emotions than boys. Rotenberg (1988) studied the causes, motives, intensity, and consequences of reported anger in children from first, third, fifth, and seventh grades. He found similar causes and intensities of anger across the different ages with physical assaults by siblings and peers being the most frequent reason for anger, and verbal insults and parent behavior being less frequent causes. A common cause for anger given by older children was trying to get others to see their point of view. Rotenberg also reported age differences in how children handled their angry feelings: Younger children used more physical aggression, while older children used verbal responses, engaged in indirect retaliation or did nothing. Overall, the development of emotional regulation is clearly tied to cognitive, social, and language development, as well as the experiences the child has with others' reactions to emotionally arousing situations.

Coping Skills

Another important aspect of emotional development is the means children use to cope with distress. Children use a variety of ways to comfort themselves. One of the earliest is the use of a "transitional object," such as a favorite blanket or stuffed animal. A retrospective study of 230 young adolescents (ages 13–14) revealed that 88% of girls and 71% of boys reported using a transitional object at some time during the first 5 years of life (Shafii, 1986). Most of the children had given up the transitional object by age 5 or 6, but surprisingly, 21% of girls and 12% of boys reported that they continued to use their transitional objects as adolescents!

Kopp (1989) proposes that the use of transitional objects can function as a mechanism for young children to gain control over stress and emotional arousal. Passman (1987) suggests that transitional objects serve to reduce anxiety or arousal for the child because they are associated with positive consequences. Although there is a higher incidence of sucking habits among children attached to objects (Mahalski, Silva, & Spears, 1985), it is generally accepted that use of transitional objects is not associated with maladjustment or insecurity (Passman, 1987).

Empathy

The development of empathy has been studied extensively. Children ages 2–4 demonstrate some empathic behavior—that is, a vicarious emotional response to others in distress—but young children often fail to do anything to help the other person or act inappropriately (Caplan & Hay, 1989; Zahn-Waxler, Radke-Yarrow, & King, 1979). Children respond more empathically to others of the same sex or race, most likely because their cognitive-developmental level allows them to perceive these others as more similar to themselves (Hoffman, 1979). Guilt, a person's ability to be aware that he or she is the cause of distress and to feel bad as a result, is thought to be related to the development of empathy (Hoffman, 1977). There is evidence that some 2-year-olds have the beginnings of this response, and a definite guilt response appears in children as young as age 6 (Thompson & Hoffman, 1980; Zahn-Wexler et al., 1979).

SUMMARY AND CONCLUSIONS

Understanding the processes of normal development during childhood is critical for the child clinician, because it is during the course of this development that the foundation for later competence in many areas is laid. Each developmental stage presents unique stresses for parents and children, and many problem behaviors are common among normally developing children. Fortunately, these problems are transient for most children and studies have shown that developmental status and behavior problems during these years do not necessarily predict the future behavior of the child (Campbell, 1987, 1990; Kazdin, 1989). As Campbell (1990) states, the current debate is concerned not so much with prediction of future development as with issues of risk and resilience—understanding which factors place children at risk for problems and why some children are able to overcome early negative experiences while others are not. It is clear that early development is a complex process of organism–environment interaction that changes over time in a reciprocal fashion (Campbell, 1990; Sameroff & Chandler, 1975). Current work in behavioral genetics suggests that many if not most characteristics of human beings (including intelligence, personality, attitudes and beliefs, and psychopathology) are strongly influenced by inheritance (Plomin, 1989). There is also, however, clear evidence for the importance of environmental factors in determining development. In the preschool years, child-rearing styles and parent–child interaction have been noted as being particularly important for development in general (Clarke-Stewart, 1988) and behavior problems in particular (Campbell, 1990; Pettit & Bates, 1989).

Many of the common problems of childhood originate or are associated with particular periods of development. For example, many cases of enuresis and encopresis can be traced back to faulty toilet training. Negative behavior (e.g., temper tantrums, noncompliance, aggression, or defiance) typically first appears at about age 2 with the child's increased needs for autonomy and independence. How these problems are handled by parents will in part determine whether they continue to interfere with the child's functioning or are simply transient annoyances. Moreover, how the child learns to cope with the stresses inherent in the normal course of development will in part determine that child's developmental trajectory. The clinician must understand the developmental course of each child who presents with problems, in order to determine the unique etiology of that child's problems and to implement effective treatment. Understanding what typically happens during the course of children's development and what factors have a significant impact on development also has important implications for the prevention of severe problems.

Chapter 2

Enhancing

Children's

Development

*I*n addition to providing services for parents and children who present with significant disorders, child clinicians have an important role to play in enhancing the development of "normal" children and in preventing emotional and behavioral problems. To be effective in this role, the clinician must understand the issues that have been delineated by researchers in the field of prevention, and must also have knowledge of the factors that make children more or less vulnerable to mental health problems. In the latter area, a multivariate perspective is essential. Whereas parents were once thought to be the primary means of influencing developmental outcomes in children, there is now agreement that children play a major role in determining their own as well as their parents' behavior, and that factors in the environment have both direct and indirect effects on the parent–child relationship and, consequently, on the child's development.

Research on infant attachment serves as a good example of these changes in our thinking about development. Ainsworth's original work on children's attachments to primary caregivers indicated that a secure attachment was fostered by parenting that was sensitive and responsive to a child's signals and needs (Ainsworth, Blehar, Waters, & Wall, 1978).

Current work (summarized by Clarke-Stewart, 1988) demonstrates, however, that a secure attachment is dependent not only on the mother's sensitivity, but on the child's temperamental characteristics (thought to be largely biologically determined) and on the social–emotional context of the family. Thus, determining ways in which child clinicians can help parents enhance children's development necessarily involves a broad perspective, which considers how to work not just with parents but with all the many factors that impinge on an individual child and his or her family.

This chapter reviews the recent work on factors that clinicians must understand in order to provide services aimed at enhancing the development of children and preventing emotional and/or behavioral problems. The areas of research reviewed include the factors that contribute to the vulnerability or resilience of children; the determinants of individual differences in parenting practices; specific parenting practices that are associated with optimal child development; and the efficacy of parent education programs. Models for prevention, early intervention programs, and prevention of accidental injuries are also discussed.

VULNERABILITY AND RESILIENCE

Our society views children as simultaneously extremely vulnerable and wonderfully resilient. Given their cognitive, physical, and social limitations, children are thought to be especially vulnerable to adverse environmental conditions and as such are protected by laws against abuse, neglect, and exploitation. On the other hand, children are also seen as behaviorally and emotionally resilient, in part because of the developmental processes that characterize childhood. At this point, we might ask, "What makes some children more vulnerable or at risk for developmental and/or emotional/behavioral problems?" or, conversely, "Why do some children develop normally despite having experienced conditions and stresses that are known to have adverse effects?"

The answers to the questions above are difficult. We know that children with similar histories will have different outcomes and that children with similar outcomes may reach them by different developmental pathways (Sameroff, 1985). This suggests that a multivariate, cumulative, and dynamic approach to vulnerability and resiliance, in which various factors interact to exacerbate or moderate the effects of adversity at any given time, may be most helpful (Gordon & Jens, 1988). This approach acknowledges that the presence of any one known risk or protective factor contributes little to our understanding of individual cases. Rather, the accumulation and interaction of factors, and the identification of areas of strength and vulnerability at a specific point in time, are the critical foci for assessment and treatment.

Risk and Protective Factors

The new field of developmental psychopathology merges our knowledge of normal development with that of clinical child psychology in order to give us a better understanding of the interplay of risk and protective factors during the course of children's development. Risk factors present in persons or environments result in a heightened probability for the subsequent development of a disease or disorder (Garmezy & Masten, 1986). Conversely, protective factors are "those attributes of persons, environments, situations and events that appear to temper predictions of psychopathology based upon an individual's 'at risk' status" (Garmezy, 1983, p. 73).

Recent research in developmental psychopathology has identified many factors that directly or indirectly affect children's resistance to stress (Cicchetti, 1984; Masten & Garmezy, 1985; Sroufe & Rutter, 1984), and these are presented in Table 2.1. The clinician must, however, also understand the complex interplay between and among these risk and protective factors. O'Grady and Metz (1987), for example, found that stressful events were highly correlated with increased adjustment problems among biologically high-risk children, but that stressful life events had little effect on adjustment among a contrast group of biologically low-risk children. Furthermore, stress was associated with increased emotional and behavioral problems for children with low social support, but there was no relationship between stress and problems for children who had high social support. Most interesting was the finding that children with an internal locus of control orientation actually seemed to benefit from life stresses; that is, a negative relationship between stress and school problems was found for these children. On the other hand, for children with a more external locus of control, social support was very important: Increased social support resulted in fewer problems and an increased sense of social competence. To summarize, a little stress may actually enhance the development and use of effective coping strategies for some children, and in the process may enhance their sense of competence and self-esteem in a positive cycle, whereas for others, when faced with stress, an external source of support may be essential for competent functioning.

The social context of growing up also plays an important role in determining the vulnerability or resilience of children. Socially disadvantaged children, for example, are exposed to more negative life events such as repeated hospitalizations, and also are more adversely affected by these negative life events (Kopp, 1983; Rutter, 1979, 1983; Wilson, 1985). On the other hand, a number of child characteristics help buffer the effects of stressful events, even for those children who grow up in homes of lower socioeconomic status (SES). General intellectual ability, for example, is associated with more successful adjustment, fewer behav-

TABLE 2.1. Risk and Protective Factors in Child Development

Risk factors	Protective factors
Child characteristics	
Medical problems	Good physical health
Genetic disorders	
Birth complications	
Being male	Being female
Difficult temperament	Easy temperament
Low intelligence	High intelligence
Uneven development	Even development
Extremes of activity level	Moderate activity level
Attention deficit	Adequate attention
Language disorder or delay	Normal language development
External locus of control	Internal locus of control
Physical unattractiveness	Physical attractiveness
Being first-born	Being later-born
Poor coping strategies	Flexible coping strategies
Social skills deficits	Good social skills
Insecure attachment	Secure attachment
Poor academic achievement	High academic achievement
Poor self-esteem	High self-esteem
Family/environment characteristics	
Single parent	Two parents
Many children	Fewer children
Marital conflict	Family cohesiveness
Disagreement over child rearing	Consistent discipline
Chronic poverty	Higher socioeconomic status
Poor social support network	Good individual and agency support
Unemployment or underemployment	Stable employment
Low parent education	High parent education
Inadequate child care resources	Adequate child care resources
Limited financial/material resources	Adequate financial resources
Stressful life events	Low stress
Urban environment	Rural environment

(*continued*)

TABLE 2.1. (*continued*)

Risk factors	Protective factors
Parent characteristics	
Depression or schizophrenia	Good psychological adjustment
Low intelligence	High intelligence
Fewer years of education	More years of education
Teenage mother	Mature mother
Insensitive/unresponsive	Sensitive/responsive
Unavailability	Availability
Low self-esteem	High self-esteem
Poor parenting models	Good parenting models
Avoidance coping style (denial)	Flexible coping style
Hypercritical	High nurturance/warmth
Inappropriate developmental expectations	Knowledge of development
Overly harsh or lax discipline	Authoritative discipline
Poor supervision of child	Close supervision
Poor physical health	Good physical health

ior problems, social competence, and school achievement (Garmezy, 1985; Wilson, 1985). Furthermore, there is strong support for the fact that girls are at lower risk for biological, learning, and behavior problems than are boys (Rutter, 1983; Werner & Smith, 1982). Garmezy and Rutter (1985) found that girls were also at lower risk for poor adjustment following major stressful events such as parental divorce or natural disasters. Being female seems to be protective with respect to problems of adaptation in early and middle childhood, although this difference between the sexes diminishes in late adolescence (Gelfand & Peterson, 1985). Taken together, research in the area of vulnerability and resilience indicates that successful prevention necessitates assessment of both risk and protective factors. Better understanding of the interaction between these two types of factors should lead to the development of programs aimed at minimizing the adverse effects of risk factors in part by capitalizing on and strengthening those protective factors present in the lives of individual children.

Day Care as a Risk Factor

Concerns about the effects of day care on the development of children have soared as increasing numbers of mothers join the work force. These concerns are being debated in the popular press (e.g., Brazelton, 1989) as well as in professional journals (e.g., Fein & Fox, 1988), and revolve around the question of whether day care should be considered a risk or protective factor for children's development. That is, have negative or positive effects of day care on children's development been documented? If so, what areas of development are affected, and what factors mediate or moderate these effects?

Research on the effects of day care has focused primarily on children's emotional, social, and intellectual development. With regard to emotional adjustment, Clarke-Stewart (1989) concludes in a recent comprehensive review of this research that there is little consistent evidence for detrimental effects of day care on children's emotional adjustment. She argues that studies showing that children in day care are less securely attached to their mothers have failed to consider that Ainsworth's Strange Situation (the method most commonly used to assess attachment) may not be a valid assessment method for children of working mothers (they may not perceive it as a very stressful situation and thus may not exhibit attachment behaviors). Other reviews concur with this reasoning (Hoffman, 1989; Scarr, Phillips, & McCartney, 1990) and point out the need for more ecologically valid measures of attachment.

Research that focuses on the effects of day care on children's social adjustment has consistently documented increased levels of aggression and noncompliance in day care children when compared with children raised at home (Clarke-Stewart, 1989; Haskins, 1985; Scarr et al, 1990). The results of other studies, however, have suggested that these behaviors may be primarily a function of the curriculum content of the day care program. Thus, when the curriculum is changed (e.g., by teaching prosocial behaviors), levels of aggression and noncompliance decrease (Finkelstein, 1982).

With regard to cognitive development, Clarke-Stewart's (1989) recent review concludes that day care may give intellectually average children a "head start," but that children reared at home quickly catch up when they enter school. Among economically and socially disadvantaged children, however, the day care experience may serve to prevent a decline in intellectual functioning that results from a lack of early intellectual stimulation (Ramey & Campbell, 1984).

To summarize, Scarr et al. (1990) state that "there is near consensus among developmental psychologists and early childhood experts that child care per se does not constitute a risk factor in children's lives; rather poor quality care and poor family environments can conspire to produce poor developmental outcomes" (p. 30). Day care may even function as a protective factor for children from highly-impoverished environments. Similarly, with regard to maternal employment, Hoffman (1989) states that "maternal employment is not so robust a variable that it can be related to child outcomes. It operates through its effects on the family environment and the child care arrangements, and these are moderated by parental attitudes, family structure, and other variables" (p. 289).

The effects of day care on children's development thus seem to be mediated by many of the same familial and environmental factors that mediate the development of any child (Howes, 1988). These include the mother's attitudes, beliefs, and perceptions of child rearing; her general sense of well-being; the support she receives from her spouse and/or family; her level of education; and her child-related behaviors. Factors unique to working mothers and day care that influence children's development are mothers' feelings about working and about their child care arrangements, and, most important, the quality of the care provided (Peterson & Peterson, 1986).

The quality of day care is a critical factor. Scarr et al. (1990) specify four criteria for high-quality care: (1) low caregiver–child ratio, which is related to increased safety and increased cognitive and language stimulation; (2) smaller group size, which is related to less caregiver time spent in management tasks and more spent in social, educational, and cognitive activities; (3) caregiver training and education, which has been associated with increased sensitivity, responsiveness to the children's needs, and provision of stimulating activities; and (4) stability of care or low staff turnover, which gives children the opportunity to form emotional attachments with their substitute caregivers. Child clinicians can provide an important service for parents by informing them of these empirical findings and assisting them in evaluating various child care options.

In thinking about vulnerability and resilience among children, we turn now to consideration of the broad context of the parent–child relationship. This context consists of characteristics of the child, such as sex, intelligence level, temperament, locus of control, and biological status, which interact with parental, familial, and environmental characteristics to predict the path of development for individual children. The child-rearing practices of parents are certainly an important component of this configuration: Parent behavior can set the stage for children to develop and use coping skills that make them more resilient, or, conversely, can place children at increased risk for problems (Blount et al., 1989). The next section reviews the work in this area.

PARENTING PRACTICES

Determinants of Parenting

Current work in the area of parenting practices has focused on the determinants of parenting styles and, not surprisingly, suggests that multiple factors influence how parents behave with their children.

Belsky (1984) describes three possible sources of influence on parenting: (1) characteristics of the parents, including their genetic and environmental origins and personal psychological resources; (2) characteristics of the child, especially his or her unique temperamental profile; and (3) characteristics of the environmental context of the parent–child relationship, including sources of stress or support, such as the marital relationship and social networks. Others (Abidin, 1989; Clarke-Stewart, 1988) argue that it is also important to understand parents' attitudes and beliefs about child rearing, because these can be critical motivational factors; that is, they can explain *why* parents behave toward their children in a particular manner.

Parents' Developmental History

The influence of the developmental history of parents, especially their own parenting histories, on parenting styles is demonstrated most clearly in studies of abusive parents; these show that parents who were mistreated during childhood are more likely to mistreat their own children than nonmistreated parents (Belsky, 1984). But the influence of parenting history has also been demonstrated for "normal" parents (e.g., Crockenberg, 1987). Parenting history may have a direct effect on current parenting behavior through modeling (we treat our children as we were treated by our parents) or inverse modeling (we are determined not to do to our children what our parents did to us). Belsky (1984) argues that the influence of parenting history is more likely to be indirect. He states that "in general, supportive developmental experiences give rise to a mature healthy personality, [one] that is then capable of providing sensitive parental care which fosters optimal child development" (p. 86).

A recent study by Crockenberg (1987) illustrates how parenting history influences current parent behavior. She found that adolescent mothers who had been rejected as children were more angry and punitive with their own children than were nonrejected adolescent mothers. The relationship between early rejection and punitive parenting practices was, however, moderated by current levels of social support, so that rejected mothers with good support were less punitive than those with low levels of support. Crockenberg concludes that parenting history has an important but not necessarily a determining role in the way mothers care for their children; early negative experiences of parenting can be overcome by current supportive relationships.

Parents' Psychological Resources

Research on the effects of maternal depression on parenting behavior illustrates the importance of parents' mental health status in determining how parents interact with their children. This work demonstrates that maternal depression is associated with negative parent behaviors such as increased criticism, physical punishment, and aversive responses to children (Panaccione & Wahler, 1986; Webster-Stratton & Hammond, 1988); avoidance of confrontation and lack of success in controlling child behavior (Kochanska, Kuczynski, Radke-Yarrow, & Welsh, 1987); and perceptions of increased child behavior deviance (Schaughency & Lahey, 1985). The process by which maternal depression may influence children's behavior and/or development is theorized to be indirect: Depressed mothers perceive their children more negatively, which leads to increased criticism and punishment, resulting in child behavior problems (e.g., Forehand, Lautenschlager, Faust, & Graziano, 1986). Egeland, Kalkoski, Gottesman, and Erickson (1990) suggest that maternal depression may indirectly affect the child's development through the home environment: Depressed mothers may be less organized and provide less stimulation than nondepressed mothers. It may also be the case, however, that the effects of depression on children are direct. Depressed mothers simply may not have the psychological resources necessary for effective parenting, and child behavior problems may develop as a result. In a longitudinal study of preschool children with behavior problems, Egeland et al. (1990) have provided evidence for this direct link. They found that mothers whose levels of depressive symptomatology decreased over time had children whose functioning improved; conversely, mothers whose depression increased had children who functioned more poorly. Egeland et al. also cite substantial research literature that links maternal depression with non-nurturing caretaking behavior (e.g., emotional unavailability, poor communication, inconsistency, hostility, and overinvolvement).

Child Temperament

The fact that children's characteristics have an important impact on their relationships with their parents is well accepted. Of all the characteristics of children that might influence the parent–child relationship, temperament has engendered the most research. Not only are "difficult" infants more difficult to parent and "easy" infants easier to parent, but children with different temperamental characteristics also respond differently to the same environment. Crockenberg (1987), for example, demonstrated that irritable infants with angry, punitive mothers were more likely to be angry and noncompliant and to have lower self-confidence as they grew older than were easy infants with angry, punitive mothers.

Child temperament alone, however, does not determine parent–child relationships. In fact, Clarke-Stewart (1988) provides evidence that parents may have some role in shaping their children's temperamental characteristics, although this appears more likely to be the case with children in the midrange of temperament than with those at the extremes. Rather, it is the "fit" among the unique characteristics of the child, the parent, and the environment that is the critical factor in developmental outcomes. Thus, for clinicians, the critical issue for prevention and/or intervention is the interplay between the unique temperamental characteristics of the child and the capabilities of the parents and broader environment to support the child's development within this context.

Social Support Networks

The extent of parents' social support networks—or, more precisely, the match between the support desired by parents and the support they actually receive—has also been shown to influence how parents care for their children. Perceptions of social support are associated with parents' physical and mental health, which, as discussed earlier, also affects parenting behavior (Cutrona, 1984; Heller & Swindle, 1983). Belsky (1984) argues that social support can have both direct and indirect effects on parenting behavior. Social support can have a beneficial effect on parents' mental health and sense of well-being in general (which in turn influences parenting behavior) in addition to providing concrete resources (financial help, child care, etc.) that directly enhance their abilities to parent. Moreover, contact with friends and family members that is desired and is positively perceived functions to moderate the stresses of parenting (Crockenberg, 1987).

Marital Relationship

The marital relationship can be considered either a source of support for parents or a source of stress. In separated or divorced families, ongoing conflict between parents may provide a significant source of stress that interferes with their abilities to care for their children adequately. Many studies have documented the relationship among marital conflict (in divorced or intact families), negative parenting behaviors, and child problems (e.g., Shaw & Emery, 1987; Stoneman, Brody, & Burke, 1989). Other work has shown that in intact families, spousal support may be a critical factor influencing parenting behavior (Brody, Pillegrini, & Sigel, 1986; Crnic, Greenberg, Ragozin, Robinson, & Basham, 1983; Crockenberg, 1987). Most interesting is a recent study by Howes and Markman (1989), which shows that the quality of the marital relationship *before* the birth of the child influences the child's functioning 3–5 years later!

Abidin (1989) suggests that the only aspect of the marital relationship relevant to child rearing is the alliance of the parents in regard to child-rearing issues. Belsky (1984), however, points out that the marital relationship may also affect the general psychological well-being of parents, and as such may exert an indirect (albeit important) influence on parenting skills.

Optimal Parenting Practices

Despite the knowledge that many other factors influence children's behavior, we know that parents remain a critical avenue through which child behavior and development are influenced. With the interrelated factors described above in mind, an important question for clinicians is "What can parents do to ensure the optimal development of their children?" Considerable research has addressed this question. Baumrind (1967) first identified an association between "authoritative" parenting (warm, reasonable, nonpunitive, and firm) and positive child behavior. Conversely, overcontrolling or authoritarian discipline, and undercontrolling or permissive disciplinary styles, were associated with negative child behavior. Building on this work, Belsky (1984) describes the kinds of parenting at different ages that are thought to promote optimal child functioning. In infancy, cognitive and motivational competence and healthy social–emotional development are promoted by parents' attentive, affectionate, stimulating, responsive, and nonrestrictive caregiving. For preschoolers, high levels of nurturance, affection, and control foster the development of good social skills, resourcefulness, and achievement motivation. By school age, inductive reasoning, consistent discipline, and expressions of affection are positively related to self-esteem, internalized controls, prosocial orientation, and intellectual achievement.

Pettit and Bates (1989) suggest that proactive parent behavior—characterized by monitoring children's activities, providing anticipatory guidance, expressing affection toward the children, and teaching—may function to prevent children's misbehavior and thus reduce the need for parents to react punitively when the children behave inappropriately. They found that in families where children had behavior problems, mothers exhibited less proactive behavior than in families with children who did not have problems.

Martin (1975), in a review of research on parent–child relationships, summarizes ways in which parents can positively influence their children's behavior. These include (1) consistently enforcing rules, (2) discussing and providing a rationale for the rules with the child, (3) reinforcing appropriate behavior more often than punishing inappropriate behavior, (4) accepting and nurturing the child, (5) assigning responsibilities to the child, and (6) modeling desired behaviors.

Taken together, this research provides guidelines for planning family intervention or prevention programs that are focused on enhancing children's development. In these programs, the assumption is made that if families are reached early enough, the life course trajectory of children can be significantly changed.

PREVENTION OF PROBLEMS

Children are prime targets for prevention programs, because many have not yet experienced significant damage from threats to their mental and physical health (Peterson & Ridley-Johnson, 1983). Although the term "prevention" is often used indiscriminately to describe a variety of programs and services, it may more productively be differentiated into three levels (Offord, 1987; Peterson & Ridley-Johnson, 1983):

1. "Primary prevention" is aimed at reducing the numbers of new cases of a disorder (incidence) or preventing a disorder before it occurs. Sex abuse prevention programs for children are examples of primary prevention, as is the Head Start program for disadvantaged youngsters, which focuses on prevention of learning problems.
2. "Secondary prevention" aims at reducing the number of existing cases (prevalence) by early identification and remediation. Screening programs for preschoolers designed to identify early learning and/or behavior problems that will interfere with progress in school are examples of secondary prevention.
3. "Tertiary prevention" aims to reduce the sequelae or the severity of the disability that might result from a particular disorder. Special education programs for mentally handicapped children are examples of tertiary prevention.

Child clinicians can play an important role in all three levels of prevention, although the focus of this chapter is on services for purposes of primary prevention.

Primary prevention services for children can be targeted toward everyone in a community (e.g., programs to increase seat belt usage), toward specific populations known to be at risk for a particular disorder or disorders (e.g., children of divorced parents or of parents with schizophrenia), or toward children at specific ages (e.g., immunizations provided at regularly spaced well-child checkups). The literature contains descriptions of a wide variety of primary prevention programs for children, including programs to prevent child abuse, accidents, or fears of medical and dental procedures; programs to prevent emotional and behavioral problems for children of divorce or chronically ill children; parent education programs; and educational programs for disadvantaged children (Peterson, Hartmann, & Gelfand, 1980). The critical issues in every primary prevention program are (1) demonstration of the program's effectiveness in actually preventing the targeted disorder(s), and (2) its cost–benefit ratio.

Price, Cowen, Lorion, and Ramos-McKay (1989) reviewed 300 prevention programs and concluded that prevention programs can be effective. They summarized the components that the programs with demonstrated effectiveness had in common. Effective programs (1) targeted a specific group of people; (2) were designed to alter the life course trajectory of the participants (i.e., they aimed for long-term rather than short-term effects); (3) strengthened the support systems available in the family, community, and school; and (4) provided extensive, carefully designed research to document their success. Price et al. (1989) state that cost–benefit analyses are rarely done in evaluating prevention programs, but this is a critical consideration for policy makers and taxpayers. They note two factors to consider in doing such analyses: First, benefits may not be apparent in the short term, but rather may increase over often lengthy periods of time; second, policy makers and taxpayers want to know *who* will gain or lose from the program, as well as the *size* of the gain or loss. Finally, Price et al. note that although some programs may never be completely cost-effective, they may have great value in promoting human dignity or relieving human suffering.

The need for prevention programs for children is highlighted by the American Psychological Association task force on prevention, which cites the increasing discrepancy between the number of children who need mental health services and the number of providers of those services (Price et al., 1989). Despite increasing interest in prevention among professionals, Rickel and Allen (1987) argue that competition for scarce resources between providers of prevention and direct services, particularly funding and staff time, has inhibited the development of primary prevention programs to the extent thought to be necessary. This situation will change only when professionals concerned with the welfare of children bring knowledge from the research community to the attention of legislators and others who shape public policy (Rickel & Allen, 1987). Child clinicians can play an important role in this process by advocating on a local, state, or national level for the needs of children. Chapter 14 describes some ways in which this has been done within the context of a private psychology practice.

Parent Education Programs

In an attempt to prevent the common problems of childhood from persisting and/or becoming increasingly severe, efforts of professionals have focused on providing parents with information about child development and training in behavior management techniques. Parent education or parent training programs have become increasingly popular, and the child clinician plays an important role by offering these programs to parents in their communities. A distinction is made between "parent education" and "parent training": Parent education focuses on prevention of the development of dysfunctional child behavior, whereas parent training attempts to resolve serious child disturbances (Schaefer & Briesmeister, 1989). Thus parent education is seen as primary prevention, whereas parent training is viewed as secondary or tertiary prevention. The two types of programs, however, share such techniques as providing information, teaching behavioral and learning principles, building parenting and communication skills, and developing problem-solving skills. Parent training programs can be viewed broadly as the primary focus in the treatment of young children's maladaptive behavior. It is, in fact, the parents who must carry out a sleep program or a habit reversal program, or who must change their behavior or the environment to support the child's learning of new skills or decreasing of negative behavior. Moreover, many of the parent training programs that focus on teaching specific management techniques also provide parents with techniques that can foster optimal development in many areas. For example, teaching parents how to use reflective comments can foster a child's language development and self-esteem. Teaching parents how to use time-out contributes to an authoritative parenting style (warmth with firm limits). Learning to apply contingent reinforcement provides the child with opportunities to develop self-esteem.

Parent education classes have received increased attention from child clinicians, and the content and theoretical views of these classes are as varied as the qualifications of the persons who do the educating (Dangel & Polster, 1984). What should be the focus of parent education programs? As previously stated, it is difficult to identify specific causal mechanisms in the development of childhood disorders, and equally difficult to delineate the specific factors contributing to or mediating outcome (Campbell, 1990). We can, however, share with parents our knowledge about factors that increase vulnerability or resilience in children, including specific parenting styles and practices. As discussed above, a warm and supportive parent–child relationship; firm, reasonable, consistent, and flexible child-rearing practices; and a generally positive emotional atmosphere are important factors in optimal child development. Conversely, a conflicted parent–child relationship; arbitrary, punitive, and/or uninvolved parenting; and a conflicted family atmosphere are associated with the development of behavior problems. In addition, the absence of positive parental behaviors is as important in the development of behavior problems as is the presence of negative parental behaviors (Pettit & Bates, 1989). Thus, teaching parents specific parenting practices that increase positive parent–child interactions, and that assist parents in setting limits and providing consistent consequences for inappropriate behavior, would be a reasonable approach to parent education programs.

To be effective, parent education programs should not only focus on specific information about child development and management techniques, but must also take into account the broader personal needs of the family members. We know, for example, that maternal depression or anxiety, a poor social support network, and marital discord are associated with the development of behavior problems among children (Bush & Cockrell, 1987; Panaccione & Wahler, 1986; Stoneman et al., 1989). Moreover, the child's characteristics are also important to consider in planning for effective parent education, because children respond differently to different techniques. Thus, parent education programs should provide information on the relationship of these "risk factors" to child behavior and guidelines for when parents should seek professional help.

Clarke-Stewart (1988) calls for clinicians to provide parent training programs for non-clinic-referred parents that are similar to those designed for parents of behavior-disordered children, and Webster-Stratton (1981) presents evidence that such programs can be effective in changing mothers' attitudes and behaviors in a cost-effective manner. Conceptualizing parent education more broadly, Bijou (1984) advocates comprehensive programs for prevention of behavior problems in high-risk families; such programs would provide services for parents and children from birth through fourth grade, focusing on developing and maintaining prosocial, ethical, and moral behaviors. Although the expertise is available to design and implement more and better parent education programs, studies are needed to examine the relative efficacy of different contents, teaching methods, and instructors for different samples of parents and children. Our approach to providing parent education groups as one of the services offered in a private psychology practice is described in Chapter 14.

Prevention of Accidental Injuries

One form of prevention that is receiving increasing interest is the prevention of children's accidental injuries. The normal developmental characteristics of children (e.g., mouthing objects, high activity levels, curiosity, and exploratory behavior) place them at high risk for injuries (Garbarino, 1988). This is reflected in the very high incidence of injuries among preschoolers. Christophersen (1989) cites data from the National Center for Health Statistics indicating that nonintentional injuries are second only to physical illness in causing death during the preschool years; one-half of all deaths of young children are the result of accidental injuries. Together, intentional and nonintentional injuries account for more childhood deaths than the next six most frequent causes of death combined. Christophersen notes that there has been a dramatic increase in the number of childhood deaths due to accidents and violence over the last 50 years, in part reflecting a general increase in violence in our society. Indeed, Christoffel and Liu (1983) report that child homicide rates in the United States are among the highest of the 23 developed nations studied (second only to Northern Ireland!), and that children 1–4 years of age are at particularly high risk, with almost 3% of the deaths reported for that age range due to homicide.

Whether a child's injury is considered accidental or intentional is often difficult to determine; thus, the relationship between physical abuse and childhood injuries is complex. Garbarino (1988) classifies childhood injuries on a continuum from random accidents to preventable accidents to negligence and finally to assault; he acknowledges that there is some overlap between these categories (e.g., injuries resulting from automobile accidents would once have been considered random accidents, but now are considered preventable). Moreover, whether or not an injured child is reported for physical abuse seems to be related to socioeconomic and racial factors. Daniel, Hampton, and Newberger (1983), for example, found that blacks and low-SES whites who sought medical attention for their children's injuries were more likely to be reported for child abuse than whites from higher-SES backgrounds.

Injuries that occur in the home are responsible for the majority of childhood deaths, and boys are more vulnerable to these injuries than girls, presumably because of behavioral differences (Christophersen, 1989). In a study by Matheny (1986), however, characteristics of the mother and the environment were found to be more closely related to injuries than child characteristics were. Toddlers whose mothers were more emotionally stable, more active, more energetic, and better educated, and who lived in organized, less cluttered homes, were less vulnerable to accidental injury. Garbarino (1988) also suggests that inappropriate parenting—in particular, a lack of appropriate supervision—plays a critical role in the occurrence of childhood injuries.

Christophersen (1989) outlines approaches to injury control, which include passage of laws requiring people to change their behavior (e.g., laws requiring use of seat belts) and passive control by redesign of products and the environment (e.g., safety caps for medicine bottles). Other successful approaches to prevention of accidental injuries have utilized principles of reinforcement. Roberts and Turner (1986), for example, rewarded parents with lottery tokens redeemable for prizes for using child safety seats and reported significantly increased usage during a 2-week period. Still other approaches have taught parents to use standard behavior management techniques to decrease dangerous behavior in their children (Matthews, Friman, Barone, Ross, & Christophersen,

1987). Of most relevance to the child clinician is research cited by Christophersen (1989), which demonstrates that information given to parents *before* the birth of a child is more effective in changing parents' child-safety-related behavior than information given when the child is a preschooler. Parents are apparently more receptive to child-related information during pregnancy than after the child is born. This suggests that other types of prevention programs for parents should begin prenatally, at which time parents could be given information designed to prevent a variety of childhood problems.

Early Intervention Programs

Another form of primary prevention of interest to child clinicians is the early intervention program. Early intervention programs have primarily targeted children through educational programs such as Head Start; through model programs such as the Abecedarian Project (Horacek, Ramey, Campbell, Hoffmann, & Fletcher, 1987; Ramey & Campbell, 1984); and through intervention in the family system (Heinicke, Beckwith, & Thompson, 1988). Of most concern to child clinicians is family-focused early intervention.

Early intervention in the family system is directed at changing parental functioning so that permanent negative effects on the child are minimized (Heinicke et al., 1988). Intervention can be directed at developing positive child-rearing techniques, improving parents' abilities to cope with stress, and/or promoting children's adaptive behaviors. The goal is not only to forestall events that are harmful to a child's development, but also to enhance the child's ability to cope with difficulties that occur in the normal course of development (Wolfe, Edwards, Manion, & Koverola, 1988). Christophersen, Barrish, Barrish, and Christophersen (1984) describe a comprehensive "anticipatory guidance" program for new parents. Parents are given information on normal growth and development; general behavior management skills; strategies for handling specific problems such as mealtimes, dressing, and bedtime; and health and child safety. Although the effectiveness of this program in preventing child problems has not been evaluated, parents have generally expressed considerable satisfaction with it.

In a review of 20 early intervention studies with high risk families, Heinicke et al. (1988) found that 75% of the studies showed at least one significant positive effect. The studies reviewed included work with parents during pregnancy, immediately after birth, and (in ongoing sessions) from the age of 1 month to school entrance. The number of sessions varied from 1 to over 1,000 contacts. Those programs producing a more pervasive effect—that is, those that influenced functioning in a greater number of areas—had 11 or more contacts with a family that began before or shortly after the birth of the child and continued for up to at least 3 months of age. Heinicke et al. (1988) concluded that there was an optimal length of time needed to develop a trusting relationship with these high-risk families and to help them identify and resolve core issues. Although this in no way means that the direct impact on the parent–child relationship is not significant, it does indicate that intervention is primarily leveraged through the relationship between the intervenor(s) and the family rather than through direct work with the child. Others support this view (Belsky, 1986; Haskins, 1989). In summary, parental involvement in the intervention process is important, and increased contact with parents increases the likelihood of their becoming and remaining involved, thus increasing the chances for significant positive outcome effects.

The success of early intervention programs that focus primarily on the child has also been linked to parental involvement. Sprigle and Schaefer (1985) compared two federally funded preschool programs, Learning to Learn and Head Start/Title I, and found significant differences in favor of the Learning to Learn groups on academic performance, special education placement, and retention in grade. In addition to differences in the quality of materials, teacher education, and the structure of the academic program, Learning to Learn emphasizes extensive parent contact through structured parent groups at regularly scheduled intervals as well as whenever the need arises. Haskins (1989), in a review of the efficacy of preschool education programs, concluded that although model programs (those included in a national consortium of outstanding early intervention programs) and the Head Start program both have immediate positive effects on the intellectual performance and social competence of children, this effect declines for Head Start children in the first few years of public schooling. In contrast, the evidence for improvement on long-term measures of school performance, such as special education placement, is substantial for the model programs. There is also provocative evidence that model programs may also have positive effects on "life success" measures such as teen pregnancy, delinquency, use of welfare, and employment; there is virtually no evidence linking Head Start attendance with any of these variables. One of the outstanding features of the model programs, which no doubt accounts for some of these differences, is parent involvement. Haskins (1989) describes one program that included 90-minute home visits by teachers each week!

SUMMARY AND CONCLUSIONS

Given the increasing discrepancy between the number of children needing mental health services and the number of providers and funds for these services, child clinicians and researchers must begin to focus on prevention programs. These programs not only should attempt to forestall harmful effects on the child's development, but should also enhance the child's ability to cope with the difficulties that occur over the normal course of development. This presents a challenge, given the complex interplay between risk and protective factors, wherein multiple risk factors may combine and potentiate each other while certain protective factors may buffer the effects of risk and stress. Biological factors, child characteristics, the social and environmental context, and characteristics of the parent all must be weighed in the assessment of risk and protective factors. Children, however, are of necessity reached through parents. Current early intervention programs have suggested that parental involvement in the intervention process is critical to the effectiveness of these programs in preventing child problems.

Although there is much to be learned about the processes involved in parent–child interaction and the factors causing and mediating positive outcomes for children, we have the methodology, knowledge, and experience to implement more and better preschool, parent education, and family intervention programs to enhance the development of children. In doing this, however, the quality of the programs and qualifications of the intervenor(s), as well as documentation of outcome, must be carefully considered.

Chapter 3

Assessment

In dealing with children's behavior problems, assessment is a critical and complex component of the treatment process. The clinician not only must directly observe and record the child's behavior, but also must take into account social, cultural, biological, and developmental influences on the child. In choosing methods to assess clinically significant childhood behaviors and the potential influences on these behaviors, the clinician often feels like a juggler balancing an ever-increasing number of objects of different shapes and sizes! Behavioral psychologists, recognizing the complexity of human behavior, have defined assessment as "an exploratory, hypothesis-testing process in which a range of specific procedures are used in order to understand a given child, group, or social ecology and to formulate and evaluate specific intervention strategies" (Ollendick & Hersen, 1984, p. 6). Thus, treatment strategies depend on accurate assessment of the behavior of concern and the conditions that maintain it (Bornstein, Bornstein, & Dawson, 1984). This view of assessment is consistent with our approach to childhood problems.

Mash and Terdal (1988) suggest that because of the complexity of human development, behavioral assessment is moving more toward a "problem-specific" approach—one that focuses on areas important for a specific problem, yet that assesses certain factors that are relevant for all cases (e.g., marital conflict, parent–child relationship). Mash and Terdal (1988) further state that the clinician needs three kinds of information in order to provide adequate assessment: (1) knowledge of general theories and principles of psychological assessment, including how to evaluate and select assessment methods, conduct an assessment, and communicate findings; (2) knowledge of normal child and family development, such as that presented in Chapter 1 of this volume; and (3) information about the incidence, prevalence, developmental characteristics, biological influences, and other characteristics of specific problems. In this chapter, we briefly cover the general prevalence of child problems, present a system for comprehensive assessment that will be adapted to specific problems as they are covered in later chapters, and discuss methods of assessment that we have found most useful in our clinical practice.

PREVALENCE OF PROBLEMS

Issues of Classification

The prevalence of disorders in children is difficult to determine because of the variety of nonstandardized criteria used to identify the presence of a particular problem, as well as the varying labels and definitions of problem behaviors. Currently, no one classification system for children's behavioral problems is accepted and employed by all health care professionals. The system most commonly used in the United States at present is the revised third edition of the *Diagnostic and Statistical Manual of Mental Disorders* (DSM-III-R; American Psychiatric Association, 1987). DSM-III-R lists nine diagnostic categories that apply to infants, children, or adolescents, and also indicates the adult diagnostic categories that are appropriate for children because the essential features are the same for children as adults (e.g., Schizophrenia, Mood Disorders). The DSM-III-R disorders that usually appear during the first 10 years of life, and the age of onset for each, are listed in Table 3.1.

The DSM-III-R classification system is relatively new and thus has not been thoroughly critiqued for its usefulness. Earlier versions of the system, however, have been criticized for using behavioral criteria that do not correspond well to empirically derived clusters of behavioral symptoms, particularly for children under age 7 (Achenbach, 1980; Cantwell, 1988). On the positive side, DSM-III-R is widely used to classify children for research purposes, and thus provides a basis for determining the comparability of children across studies.

A number of behaviorally oriented mental health workers use a dimensional rather than a categorical approach to classification (Achen-

TABLE 3.1. Age of Onset and Prevalence of DSM-III-R Categories of Disorders Relevant for Children from Birth to 10 Years of Age

Disorder	Age of onset	Prevalence
Developmental Disorders		
Mental Retardation	Birth	1%
Pervasive Developmental Disorder	Before 3 years	10–15 per 10,000
Autism	Before 3 years	4–5 per 10,000
Academic Skills Disorders		
Developmental Arithmetic Disorder	6–10 years	Unknown
Developmental Expressive Writing Disorder	7–10 years	Unknown
Developmental Reading Disorder	6–9 years	2–8%
Language and Speech Disorders		
Developmental Articulation Disorder	3–6 years	10% <8 years; 5% >8 years
Developmental Expressive Language Disorder	Before 3 years for severe forms	3–10% of school-age children
Developmental Receptive Language Disorder	2–7 years	3–10% of school-age children
Motor Skills Disorders		
Developmental Coordination Disorder	Preschool	6% of 5- to 11-year-olds
Disruptive Behavior Disorders		
Attention-deficit Hyperactivity Disorder	Before 4 years	3%
Conduct Disorder	Prepubertal	9% of males, 2% of females
Oppositional Defiant Disorder	Precursors in preschool years	Unknown
Anxiety Disorders		
Separation Anxiety Disorder	Preschool to 18	Common
Avoidant Disorder	2½ to early school years	Uncommon
Overanxious Disorder	Unknown	Common

Disorder	Age of Onset	Prevalence
Eating Disorders		
Anorexia Nervosa	12–18 years	1 in 100–800
Bulimia Nervosa	Adolescence	4.5% of females, 0.4% of males
Pica	1–2 years	Occasional
Rumination Disorder of Infancy	3–12 months	Very rare
Gender Identity Disorders		
Gender Identity Disorder of Childhood	Before 4 years	Uncommon
Tic Disorders		
Tourette's Disorder	1–14 years	0.5 per 1,000
Transient Tic Disorder	2 years to adolescence	5–24% of school-age children
Chronic Motor or Vocal Tic Disorder	Before 21 years	Unknown
Elimination Disorders		
Functional Encopresis	4–8 years	1% of 5-year-olds
Functional Enuresis	5–8 years	5-year-olds: 7% of males, 3% of females; 10-year-olds: 3% of males, 2% of females
Speech Disorders not Elsewhere Classified		
Cluttering	After 7 years	Unknown
Stuttering	2–7 years	10% of school-age children
Other Disorders		
Elective Mutism	Before 5 years	<1%
Reactive Attachment Disorder	Before 5 years	Unknown
Stereotypy/Habit Disorder	Infancy	Unknown

Note. From *Diagnostic and Statistical Manual of Mental Disorders* (3rd ed., rev.) by the American Psychiatric Association, 1987, Washington, DC: Author Copyright 1987 by the American Psychiatric Association. Adapted by permission.

bach, 1985; Quay, 1979). This approach does not lead to a statement that a child has a particular disorder, but rather describes the degree to which one or many characteristics are evident (Kazdin, 1987a) and allows the clinician to identify clusters of problems. A dimensional approach avoids the problem of deciding how severe a problem has to be before it is considered a psychopathological disorder, and also allows the clinician to deal with children who present with mixed clinical pictures (Rutter & Tuma, 1988). On the other hand, the dimensional approach assumes that symptom labels have the same meaning throughout the distribution (which might not be true). Moreover, classifying individuals is often difficult because they can have symptoms that fall on a number of different dimensions. As Rutter and Tuma (1988) point out, the distinction between the categorical and dimensional approaches is not always clear, with dimensions being translated into categories and vice versa. In reality, a combination of these approaches is probably most useful. For example, the categorical distinctions between severe and moderate mental retardation, and between both of these and normality, are useful for planning services and determining etiology and prognosis. The dimensional aspect of the intelligence level, however, is a very useful indicator in both the normal and abnormal ranges for planning specific educational and rehabilitation programs.

We have found both the categorical and dimensional approaches to classification useful in our work. Our assessment system (to be discussed later in this chapter) uses a variety of assessment methods to get a picture of the child; his or her family and important social/ecological factors; the child's behavior, compared to that of other children the same age; and the ways in which that behavior is viewed by the child's family and others in the child's environment. This leads to a judgment about the significance of the behavior problem and, if necessary, the appropriate areas to be considered for treatment. It can also result in the classification of a specific disorder.

Estimates of Prevalence

Various epidemiological studies have led to a general consensus that from 5% to 15% of all children (or between 3 and 9.6 million children in the United States) have problems that require mental health services (Goldberg, Roghmann, McInery, & Burke, 1984; Kazdin, 1989; Richman, Stevenson, & Graham, 1975; Rutter, Tizard, Yule, Graham, & Whitmore, 1976; Starfield et al., 1980). As Kazdin (1989) and Chapter 2 of this book have pointed out, however, prevalence figures are influenced by many factors, including age, sex, geographic region, socioeconomic status, and so on. For example, prevalence of problems is greater for boys than for girls, for children living in urban than for those in rural settings, and for children from single-parent than for those from two-parent families. Estimates of prevalence are also influenced by the perceptions of the referral persons (Kazdin, 1989). Children's problems are most often identified by parents; yet parents' perceptions of deviance are clearly influenced by their own characteristics (depression, marital conflict, self-esteem, etc.).

Despite these problems with estimates of prevalence, it is important to have some idea of the types of problems that are typically seen in young children. Table 3.1 above shows the estimated prevalence rates of DSM-III-R diagnoses. In contrast, Table 3.2 shows the percentage of concerns expressed by parents of non-clinic-referred children from birth to 10 years of age. One group was comprised of parents from a pediatric primary care practice who sought brief telephone consultation from psychologists over a 9-year period; the other was a random sample of 140 parents from the same pediatric practice who did not use this service (Schroeder, Gordon, Kanoy, & Routh, 1983). The table indicates that parents had similar concerns, whether or not they consulted the psychology staff. Negative behaviors (defined as noncompliance, temper tantrums, bossy and demanding behavior, crying, whining, and aggression) were the most troublesome for both groups of parents, supporting what others have found. Guidance of a talented child, specific fears, bad habits, sibling/peer problems, other family concerns/problems, food/eating problems, and concerns about death all caused considerable worry for the random sample of parents, particularly when one considers that parents' use of the telephone consultation service for these areas was relatively low. Toileting, school problems, and divorce-related problems were more often reported as concerns by the service users.

For both groups of parents, different problems seemed to peak at different ages. Table 3.3 illustrates the areas of concern to parents of children of a particular age. Problems with eating, sleeping, and toileting, as well as developmental delays, were reported as concerns more often in the preschool years; problems involving socialization were of greater concern in the school years. Negative behavior did not appear to center around the "terrible twos," but rather was a concern of parents of children at all ages. The greatest number of problems were reported for the 2- to 4-year-old group, with the ages of 5 and 6 being relatively calm, and another peak of problems reported between the ages of 7 and 10.

Another interesting question is the extent to which problems early in childhood are likely to persist. Earls (1983), for example, reported that 25% of the children in his sample with problems at 3 years also had problems at age 6. Externalizing problems (e.g., discipline problems, hyperactivity, and aggression) have predicted problems persisting beyond the preschool years (Bates & Bayles, 1988; Campbell, 1987; Fischer, Rolf, Hasazi, & Cummings, 1984; Gelfand & Peterson, 1985). For

TABLE 3.2.   Definitions of Problem Categories and Percentage of Parental
Concerns of a Random Sample and Users of Brief Psychological Consultation

Problem category and definition	Random sample $(n = 523)^a$	Service users $(n = 2,008)^a$
Negative behaviors	12%	15%
Noncompliance, temper tantrums, bossy and demanding, cries, whines, aggression.		
Toileting problems	2%	10%
Toilet training, enuresis, encopresis.		
Personality or emotional problems	6%	10%
Lacks self-control, no motivation, won't assume responsibility, lies, steals, dependent, difficult temperament.		
School problems	2%	9%
Hates school, poor achievement, learning problems, aggressive behavior, getting appropriate services, teacher–child relations.		
Sleep problems	4%	8%
Won't go to bed, wakes in night, nightmares, night terrors.		
Developmental problems	4%	7%
Slow development, perceptual–motor problems, school readiness, speech/ language problems, overactive.		
Sibling/peer problems	6%	7%
Won't share, no friends, aggression, fights a lot, sibling rivalry.		
Divorce/separation	1%	7%
Custody, visitation schedule, adjustment, how to tell child.		
Family problems	6%	4%
Parents disagree on discipline, depressed/ isolated mother, marital conflict, child abuse.		
Infant management	1%	3%
Feeding/nursing, cholic, postpartum depression, difficult temperament.		
Specific bad habits	6%	3%
Nail biting, tics, thumb sucking.		

(continued)

TABLE 3.2.   (*continued*)

Problem category and definition	Random sample $(n = 523)^a$	Service users $(n = 2,008)^a$
Specific fears	7%	2%
Dogs, dark, trucks, etc.		
Sexuality	3%	2%
Cross-sex dressing, lack of sex-appropriate interests/friends, gender confusion, sexual abuse.		
Physical complaints	4%	2%
Headaches, stomachaches.		
Parent's negative feelings	4%	2%
Don't like child, no enjoyment in child.		
Death	6%	1%
Understanding concept, adjustment, how to talk to child.		
Eating problems	6%	1%
Picky eater, too thin, obesity.		
Moving	3%	1%
Preparation, adjustment.		
Adoption/foster care	5%	1%
Advice on placement, what to tell child.		
Guidance of gifted child	8%	1%
Special services, appropriate stimulation, parenting.		

Note. From "Managing Children's Behavior Problems in Pediatric Practice" by C. S. Schroeder, B. N. Gordon, K. K. Kanoy, and D. K. Routh, 1983, in M. Wolraich and D. K. Routh (Eds.), *Advances in Developmental and Behavioral Pediatrics* (Vol. 4, p. 69). Greenwich, CT: JAI Press. Copyright 1983 by JAI Press, Inc. Reprinted by permission.
[a]These numbers refer to the total number of problems reported by parents.

example, in a follow-up study of 3-year-olds referred by their parents as hard to manage, Campbell, Ewing, Breaux, and Szumoski (1986) found that at age 6, one-half of the sample had persistent behavior problems and one-third of the sample met DSM-III criteria for Attention Deficit Disorder. Sixty-seven percent of those children who had problems at age 6 met DSM-III criteria for an externalizing disorder at age 9 (Campbell & Ewing, 1990). Campbell and Ewing (1990) also found that earlier child

TABLE 3.3. Problems as a Function of Age: Percentage of Parents with Children of a Particular Age ($n = 10$ in Each Age) Who Had Concerns in Each Problem Area, 1977–1978 Random Survey Data

Problem category	0-3 months	3-6 months	6-9 months	9-12 months	1 year	2 years	3 years	4 years	5 years	6 years	7 years	8 years	9 years	10 years
Infant management	10	20	20	10	0	0	0	0	0	0	0	0	0	0
Toileting	0	0	0	0	10	60 [a]	0	0	20	0	20	10	10	0
Developmental delays	0	10	10	10	0	20	50	20	0	20	30	0	30	30
Sleeping	20	10	0	0	0	50	0	40	20	10	10	20	10	20
Food/eating	0	10	10	0	10	60	30	50	30	20	20	10	40	20
Specific fears	20	0	30	0	20	70	40	40	40	30	40	0	20	10
Specific bad habits	30	20	20	0	30	30	20	40	20	40	20	0	20	10
Sex-related	0	0	0	10	0	30	30	20	10	20	0	20	0	10
Physical complaints	10	0	30	10	10	20	0	10	20	0	30	10	20	40
Negative behaviors	40	30	10	10	30	70	50	80	30	30	60	70	60	50

Category														
Death	0	10	10	0	0	20	40	40	10	30	30	30	30	**40**
Emotional	0	10	10	10	10	20	20	30	20	0	40	30	**50**	40
Sibling/peer	0	0	0	0	10	10	20	**40**	10	30	**60**	40	30	**60**
Adoption/foster/guardianship	10	0	20	20	10	**50**	10	0	10	0	20	**50**	30	20
Family	10	0	10	10	20	30	0	20	10	20	30	**50**	**50**	**50**
Parents' negative feelings	10	10	0	30	20	20	0	20	0	0	**40**	**40**	30	20
Guidance of talented child	10	10	10	20	20	**70**	20	30	20	20	**50**	**80**	30	**50**
Parents' school concerns	0	0	0	0	0	0	**40**	0	0	30	20	**50**	40	30
School problems	0	0	10	0	0	0	0	10	0	30	20	10	20	20
Divorce/separation	0	0	0	0	10	10	0	10	0	10	10	0	10	10
Moving	10	10	0	0	20	0	30	20	0	20	20	10	20	20

Note. Columns do not add to 100 because more than one problem could be checked on the Parent Questionnaire. From "Managing Children's Behavior Problems in Pediatric Practice" by C. S. Schroeder, B. N. Gordon, K. Kanoy, and D. K. Routh, 1983, in M. Wolraich and D. K. Routh (Eds.), *Advances in Developmental and Behavioral Pediatrics* (Vol. 4, p. 70). Greenwich, CT: JAI Press. Copyright 1983 by JAI Press, Inc. Reprinted by permission.

[a]Boxes indicate ages at which specific problems were of greatest concern.

behavior, maternal behavior symptom ratings, and ongoing family stress predicted which children would evidence later behavior disorders.

In summary, it is important to note that estimates of the prevalence of children's behavioral and emotional problems depend upon the classification system used and the characteristics of the population studied. Overall, however, it seems that at any point in time up to 50% of children will evidence at least one specific but transient problem behavior, such as fears or bedwetting; that 5–15% will evidence a cluster of specific behavior problems requiring mental health services; and that fewer than 1% will evidence a severe psychological disorder. Furthermore, children's behavior problems are often associated with a particular developmental period. These problems are transient for most children, but there is a certain group of children for whom problems persist. Biological vulnerability, environmental instability, the quality of the parent–child relationship, the number and frequency of problems, and the type of disorder all appear to contribute to prediction of the outcome.

PURPOSE OF ASSESSMENT

In clinical practice, assessment can have multiple purposes; depending on the case in question, these can be interrelated. We suggest that psychological assessment has three primary functions: (1) determining the nature and cause(s) of a disorder; (2) classifying, or grouping cases on the basis of distinguishing characteristics; and (3) providing guidelines for intervention (Gordon & Schroeder, 1990). It is important for the clinician to be aware of the potential purposes of assessment, because these will influence the focus and conduct of the assessment, choice of methods, and so on.

In clinical practice, most cases referred for assessment involve some combination of purposes, and many complicated cases involve all three. For example, a 6-year-old girl was described by her parents as impulsive, moody, and having difficulty in school. The parents sought an understanding of the problem, specific guidance to help their daughter make a better adjustment, and behavior management suggestions. In the process of assessment, the parents indicated that several male relatives on the mother's side of the family were mentally retarded. One of these relatives had been recently diagnosed as having a fragile-X chromosomal disorder. In reviewing the literature on this disorder, the clinician discovered that females are the carriers of the defective gene and that there is a phenotype for these females. As the assessment process progressed, the child's profile was found to have many of the characteristics of the female fragile-X carrier. After discussion with the parents, the child was referred for a genetic evaluation, which indeed indicated that she was a fragile-X carrier. The assessment also revealed a child with a learning disability and Attention-deficit Hyperactivity Disorder, who was functioning cognitively in the high average range. Socially, she had many friends and age-appropriate activities. Emotionally, she felt loved, but recognized that her impulsive behavior often created problems for herself and her family. Thus, the nature and cause of this child's problems were determined and classified (fragile-X carrier, Attention-deficit Hyperactivity Disorder, and a learning disability), and the assessment process gave specific information for intervention strategies. These included class placement, supportive work with the family in regard to the diagnosis, specific behavior management techniques for the parents, and individual work with the child to help her understand and cope with her strengths and weaknesses.

A COMPREHENSIVE
ASSESSMENT-TO-INTERVENTION SYSTEM

Clearly, many factors must be taken into account when identifying the emotional and behavioral problems of children. Some method of systematically collecting and organizing information during the assessment process is critical. We and our colleagues (Schroeder, Mesibov, Eastman, & Goolsby, 1981; Schroeder & Gordon, in press) describe a behaviorally oriented system for the assessment of children's behavioral problems that is based on Rutter's (1975) work (see Table 3.4). This system is referred to in this book as the Comprehensive Assessment-to-Intervention System (CAIS). It focuses on the specifics of the behavior of concern, as well as taking into account other characteristics of the child, family, and environment that influence the behavior. It also provides a framework for choosing instruments or techniques for gathering information, and for summarizing the assessment data. Specific methods are discussed later in the chapter.

I. Clarifying the Referral Question

Although clarification of the referral questions seems an obvious step in the assessment process, its importance cannot be overemphasized. The clinician and the referring person (whether it is a teacher, parent, or someone else) must agree on the issues to be addressed before assessment procedures can be selected. It is often the case that parents or teachers have questions that are not well articulated or of which they are not even aware. Once the issues are clarified, the clinician must then decide which questions he or she can adequately or appropriately address, and these must be agreed upon by the parents. The information gathered in the

TABLE 3.4. Comprehensive Assessment-to-Intervention System (CAIS) for Child Behavioral Problems

I. *Clarifying the referral question.*

   After the parent has described the problem, the clinician should be certain that he or she and the parent are thinking about the same problem. This can be done by simply reflecting what the parent has said: "It sounds like you are concerned about your child getting up in the night, as well as the different ways you and your husband are handling the situation."

II. *Determining the social context.*

   A child is referred because someone is concerned. This does not mean that the child needs treatment or that the child's behavior is the problem. The clinician should ask: "Who is concerned about the child?" "Why is this person concerned?" "Why is this person concerned now as opposed to some other time?" The parents' affect in describing the problems is significant: Are they overwhelmed, depressed, nonchalant?

III. *Assessing general areas.*

   A. Developmental status

      1. Physical/motor
      2. Cognitive
      3. Language
      4. Social
      5. Personality/emotional
      6. Psychosexual

   B. Parent and family characteristics

      1. Personality characteristics
      2. Psychopathology
      3. Marital status
      4. Availability and use of social support
      5. Parenting styles and techniques
      6. Sibling relationships

   C. Environmental characteristics

      1. Recent stressful life events
      2. Socioeconomic status
      3. Subcultural norms and values

   D. Consequences of the behavior

      1. Past and present management strategies
      2. "Payoff" for child
      3. Impact of behavior on child, parents, and environment
      4. Prognosis with and without treatment

(continued)

TABLE 3.4. (*continued*)

   E. Medical/health status

     1. Family history of medical/genetic problems
     2. Chronic illnesses (e.g., otitis media)
     3. Medications
     4. Prenatal history, birth history, and early development

IV. *Assessing specific areas.*

   A. Persistence of the behavior
   B. Changes in the behavior
   C. Severity of behavior
   D. Frequency of behavior
   E. Situation specificity
   F. Type of problem

V. *Determining the effects of the problem.*

   A. Who is suffering?
   B. Interference with development

VI. *Determining areas for intervention.*

   A. Development

     1. Teaching new skills to the child
     2. Providing appropriate stimulation
     3. Changing the behavior by increasing or decreasing it

   B. Parents

     1. Teaching new parenting techniques
     2. Changing the emotional atmosphere
     3. Treating marital problems or parent psychopathology
     4. Changing parental expectations, attitudes, or beliefs

   C. Environment

     1. Changing the cues that set off or prevent the behavior from occurring
     2. Helping parents build support networks and deal with daily living problems
     3. Helping child/family cope with life events

   D. Consequences of the behavior

     1. Changing parent's responses to the behavior
     2. Changing others' responses to the behavior
     3. Changing the payoff for the child

   E. Medical/health status

     1. Intervening in the cause of the problem
     2. Treating the effect of the problem

assessment process will be useful only to the extent that there is agreement on what is being asked.

II. Determining the Social Context of the Problem

As Furman (1980) states, child behaviors must be viewed in the wider context of societal attitudes and values, which vary both by culture and with the age of the child. In some cultures and subcultures, for example, aggression may be sanctioned for survival purposes. The goal for a child from this culture would be to learn to discriminate inappropriate and appropriate settings for aggression, rather than to decrease the level of aggression. On a more narrow scale, the accepted or common behavior in one social setting may be considered deviant or atypical in another social setting. For example, aggression on the streets of an inner-city neighborhood may be common (and may even have survival value), whereas in the classroom it is very inappropriate.

III. Assessing General Areas

In assessing a child's behavioral problems, it is important to keep in mind the general areas that influence the development of behavior problems (see Table 3.4): (A) the child's developmental status, (B) characteristics of the child's parents and extended family, (C) environmental characteristics and events, (D) the consequences of the behavior in both a narrow and a broad sense, and (E) the child's medical or health status.

Developmental Status

Knowledge of the child's developmental status allows the clinician to evaluate the behavior in comparison with that of other children of the same age or developmental level. Behavior that may be considered a significant problem at one stage in development may be quite normal at another, and the job of the clinician is to judge whether the behavior of concern is more or less than one would expect of any child at that age and in that environment. A 3-year-old child who wets the bed, for example, has a problem that may be considered "normal" or common for that age, whereas a 10-year-old who wets the bed is viewed as having a more significant problem. Also, the frequency of problem behaviors changes developmentally, and some behaviors change in the appropriate or desired direction without any intervention. Physical aggression, for example, reaches a peak during the preschool years and then naturally declines (Feshbach, 1970). Although physical aggression may be considered a problem at any age, its significance increases with age. Thus, the time when a behavior occurs in a child's life is as important as the behavior itself. Furthermore, as previously mentioned, the preschool years are a critical time for identification of and intervention with children with developmental problems. It is obvious that knowledge of normal development is critical in the assessment of these children.

Characteristics of the Parents and Extended Family

Although it is difficult to identify causal mechanisms in the development of childhood disorders, and equally difficult to delineate the specific factors contributing to or mediating outcome, the child development and child clinical literature do provide evidence for certain parent characteristics and parenting practices that facilitate development, as well as those that make the child more vulnerable (Clarke-Stewart, 1989). These are discussed in Chapter 2.

In assessing this area, it is important to gather information about various members of the family and their relationships with the child and the parents. Parenting history and models, and the presence of psychopathology in parents or other family members, are especially important areas to assess. Sensitivity to the affect expressed by parents is also important. Two mothers, for example, described their 3-year-old daughters as being anxious and fearful. One mother was calm, was in control of herself, and was using good judgment in attempting to deal with the problem. The other mother, however, was extremely upset and fearful, and was unable to view the problem objectively. Each parent presented a different focus for the assessment/intervention process.

Environment

The child's environment provides the setting conditions for the behavior in question and may be a more appropriate target for intervention than the behavior itself. The setting conditions can include very specific antecedents to the behavior (repeated commands, teasing, criticism, or hunger) or major events such as parental divorce, a death in the family, or an impending move. Setting conditions can lead to the appearance of behavior problems in young children, which may then persist and become increasingly severe because of environmental conditions.

In addition, it is important to remember that children rarely refer themselves for assessment or treatment. Rather, a child is referred because someone (usually an adult) is concerned about his or her behavior, and the perspective of the referring person must be taken into account. The referring person may lack information about children's development, may have emotional problems, or may be experiencing stress, all of which can distort his or her perception of the child's behavior. Forehand, King, Peed, and Yoder (1975) found that low parental tolerance, high expectations for child behavior, marital stress, and family problems influenced parents' perception of their child's behavior. Furthermore, Wahler's (1980) work shows that a mother's perception of her child's behavior is highly correlated with the type of environmental interaction (positive or coercive) she has just experienced.

Consequences of the Behavior

Assessment of the consequences of the behavior includes finding out the ways in which parents are currently managing it, the techniques that have been tried in the past, and the "payoff" for the child. Lack of careful assessment of these factors usually leads to parents' responding to suggestions regarding management of the child's behavior by saying, "Yes, but we've tried that and it didn't work." Assessment in this area can also involve looking at the consequences of the behavior for parents and others in the child's environment. Some behaviors may be totally acceptable to the family but may interfere with the child's functioning outside the home. For example, a child who is not toilet-trained because the parents do not want to "pressure" the child is likely to suffer negative consequences when he or she starts school.

Medical or Health Status

The clinician must be aware of the child's current medical or health status, as well as his or her medical history. Assessment of problems in this area requires that the clinician have some knowledge of the emotional and behavioral effects of physical conditions. For example, a 2½-year-old boy was referred by his parents because of noncompliance, irritability, and sleep problems; his parents felt incapable of parenting him appropriately. In the course of the assessment, it was found that his language skills were delayed and he did not always attend to language directed toward himself or others. Questioning the parents about the child's medical history revealed that he had had recurrent bouts of otitis media since 13 months of age, and that medication had not been effective in controlling the infections. Furthermore, the family's pediatrician did not believe in elective surgery for young children. After discussing the potential negative effects of otitis media on the child's development, the parents sought a second medical opinion, which resulted in surgical insertion of tubes. The child's emotional lability improved immediately, and a brief course of parent training resolved the remaining parent–child problems.

IV. Assessing Specific Areas

In addition to the general areas mentioned above, specific areas to consider (see Table 3.4) include (A) the persistence of the behavior (how long has it been going on?); (B) changes in the behavior (is it getting worse?); (C) severity (is the behavior very intense or dangerous, or "low-level" but annoying?); (D) frequency (has the behavior occurred only once or twice, or many times?); (E) situation specificity (does the behavior occur only at home or in a variety of settings?); and (F) the type of problem (is the problem a discrete behavior or a set of diffuse problems?).

V. Determining the Effects of the Problem

It is important to note who is suffering from the referral problem. It may be that the child's behavior is bothering one parent but not the other, or is annoying to the teacher but is not a problem for the parents. In other cases, although the behavior may be interfering with some aspect of the child's development, it may not be seen as a problem for the parents or other adults.

VI. Determining Areas for Intervention

Given our behavioral orientation, we attempt to apply the science of human behavior to teach new behavior, decrease inappropriate behavior, and increase desired behaviors. A clinician cannot be prepared to answer every question and/or to intervene effectively in every situation. If, however, the clinician looks systematically at the developmental status of the child and the emotional as well as the physical context in which the child lives, ideas for intervention follow naturally from the assessment. For example, interventions in the developmental area may include teaching new responses; increasing or decreasing behaviors; or changing parental expectations, attitudes, or beliefs. Environmental interventions may involve changes in the specific cues that elicit inappropriate behavior or prevent appropriate behavior from occurring, in the emotional atmosphere of the home, or in the physical setting where the problem behavior occurs most often. Focusing intervention on the consequences of the behavior may entail changing the responses of the parents or other significant people, or changing the payoff for the child (e.g., providing reinforcers). Intervening in the medical/health area may involve referral for treatment of the cause of the problem (e.g., persistent ear infections), or treating the effect of the problem (e.g., teaching relaxation skills to a child with cerebral palsy).

The CAIS framework should not be seen as rigid. Rather, it is offered as a logical and systematic way to generate and test hypotheses and to plan intervention for children's problems. The information can be gathered from a variety of sources via many different methods. The system is useful for complex cases, but also works well to assist the clinician in gathering essential information very quickly for brief assessment cases. The approach taken for a parent call-in service is a good example of a brief (15- to 20-minute) assessment-to-intervention process that incorporates the steps of the framework presented (Schroeder, Gordon, Kanoy, & Routh, 1983). The parent call-in service is discussed in detail in Chapter 14. Table 3.5 illustrates the use of the CAIS framework in assessing the case of a 6-year-old girl who was disrupting her class in school. As demonstrated in the table, most of the necessary information can be gathered quickly by listening carefully and asking specific questions, following the guidelines presented above.

METHODS FOR GATHERING INFORMATION

It should be clear from the CAIS framework that assessment of children's behavior problems necessitates a multimethod approach. It is also essential for the clinician to choose methods for assessment that are empirically based and developmentally sensitive (Mash & Terdal, 1988; Ollendick & Herson, 1984). The number of possible methods for gathering information is vast. This section presents a description of some of the instruments and techniques that we have found most useful with children. The clinician should, of course, select methods that will provide information appropriate to the nature of the presenting problem. In almost all cases, however, we have found two items to be essential: (1) a general parent questionnaire providing demographic information and the parent's perception of the problem, and (2) a normed behavior checklist. The reader is referred to Weaver (1985) and Rutter, Tuma, and Lann (1988) for more comprehensive reviews of available instruments. Descriptions of instruments we have found useful are provided in Appendix A. The CAIS provides a framework for ensuring that the pertinent areas for assessment of childhood problems are covered and that the assessment process proceeds in an orderly, stepwise fashion. The following outline illustrates the order in which various assessment methods may be used.

Step 1: Initial Contact

The initial contact is most often a telephone conversation during which the behavior or behaviors of concern are described and the referral question clarified. At the time of the initial contact, parents are informed

TABLE 3.5. The Assessment Process in a Brief Case Example

I. *Clarifying the referral question.*

A father called at the request of his daughter's first-grade teacher, who was concerned that the 6-year-old girl, once or twice a week, became distraught, walked in circles, and cried inconsolably. The clinician stated, "It sounds like Jane is disrupting the class and her teacher is not able to give her or the other children the attention they need. You're also wondering why she seems so genuinely distraught one or two times a week."

II. *Determining the social context.*

The father indicated that he and his wife were separated and that Jane was living with him.

   A. *Listening to affect*

   "I had so hoped this wouldn't happen again in Jane's new school. I don't know what I can do to help her."

   B. *Who was concerned?*

   The teacher was concerned for both Jane and the other children. The father stated, "I have been worried about Jane for the last 2 years, but generally her teachers and I have been able to calm her down."

   C. *Why now?*

   Jane just started in a new school.

III. *Assessing general areas.*

   A. *Developmental status*

   "Jane is a very bright child who rarely gives any problem at home. She has friends in the neighborhood and generally likes going to school. Recently she started wetting herself during the day and having nightmares."

   B. *Parent and family characteristics*

   "Her mother and I have been divorced for 3 years and went through a terrible custody battle. We still fight a lot over Jane."

   C. *Environmental characteristics*

   Jane visited her mother every Wednesday and every other weekend. She hated to go, reported being left alone, and was afraid of some of her mother's friends.

   D. *Consequences of the behavior*

   The father described the ways in which he had tried to deal with Jane's upset: "I tell Jane that the court says she has to visit her mother, that she should love her mother and have a good time. I also have told her not to act up in school because it gets me in trouble."

   E. *Medical/health status*

   "Although Jane has generally been healthy, in the last 3 months she has been to the doctor because of her wetting. She has complained of stomachaches and has had nightmares. I also should tell you that the

(continued)

TABLE 3.5. *(continued)*

department of social services investigated my ex-wife's charges against me for sexual abuse, which were not substantiated. Recently, Jane's doctor called the department because Jane had a number of bruises when she came home from a visit with her mother."

IV. *Assessing specific areas.*

A. *Persistence of behavior*

"Jane has been upset since the divorce, 3 years ago."

B. *Changes in behavior*

"She has never liked to visit her mother, but in the last 3 months it has gotten to the point where I have to force her to go."

C. *Severity of behavior*

"The night before she goes to visit her mother, she becomes very upset, doesn't listen to me, and has a very hard time getting to sleep. Sometimes she has nightmares."

D. *Frequency of behavior*

"These problems only seem to occur when she has to visit her mother."

E. *Situation specificity*

"She used to be upset only at home, but now it's happening at school too. I also think she looks sad a lot of the time."

F. *Type of problem*

This child's behavior was indicative of significant emotional distress. She was beginning to exhibit a variety of problematic behaviors both at home and at school. The extent of her upset was likely to have serious consequences for her functioning and development unless immediate intervention took place.

V. *Determining the effects of the problem.*

A. *Who was suffering?*

The child, the parents, the teacher, and other children in school.

B. *Interference with development*

The behavor was already interfering with Jane's adjustment at school. Most importantly, the child's emotional needs were not being met. Furthermore, she had few appropriate alternatives available to express her feelings.

VI. *Determining areas for intervention.*

The severity of this child's behavior and the complexity of the situation warranted further evaluation and treatment. In the meantime, the father and teacher were advised to work together to provide more emotional support within the school environment on the days Jane visited her mother. The father was also advised to tell the child, "It's OK for you to act upset if you're feeling bad on those days." The father and teacher were told to give her specific ways to express her feelings, such as drawing, working with clay, or simply talking to them.

that several questionnaires will be sent for them to complete and return before they come to the clinic. Since some of these questionnaires cover areas that parents may not perceive as directly related to the presenting problem (e.g., the marital relationship), the questionnaires are described and the importance of this information for our understanding of the child's problem is discussed. Parents are always given the option of not providing this information if they are uncomfortable doing so. Information from these questionnaires sets the stage for an interview with the family and allows the clinician to begin to develop various hypotheses about the nature of the problem and possible interventions. Descriptions of questionnaires and information about where they can be obtained are included in Appendix A. The questionnaires we most frequently use are the Child Behavior Checklist (Achenbach & Edelbrock, 1983), the Eyberg Child Behavior Inventory (Eyberg & Ross, 1978), the Parenting Stress Index (Abidin, 1990), and the Conners Parent Rating Scale (Goyette, Conners, & Ulrich, 1978). A copy of the Eyberg Child Behavior Inventory is included in Appendix B. The Conners Parent Rating Scale, the Child Behavior Checklist, and the Parenting Stress Index are described in Appendix A. We also use two instruments developed in our clinic (the Parent Questionnaire and the Daily Log), which are described below.

Parent Questionnaire

Our Parent Questionnaire provides information on the family's socioeconomic status; the child's developmental milestones, day care and school history, and medical history; and the parents' perception of the child's problem, its causes, and what they have done about it up to this point. A copy is included in Appendix B.

Daily Log

Daily records can be useful in providing information about the actual day-to-day functioning of the parent and child. The format can be quite variable, depending on the behaviors of interest. On our Daily Log (see Appendix B), parents record appropriate and inappropriate behavior on a daily basis and give their child a rating from 0 ("dreadful") to 10 ("fantastic!"). On the reverse side (the Specific Events Causing Concern form; see Appendix B), parents record the antecedents and consequences of behaviors identified as specific problems. This record helps the parents and clinician determine what the child is actually doing (in contrast to what the parents *think* the child is doing). The Daily Log also can be used during treatment to help the parents and clinician monitor progress.

Step 2: Parent and Child Interview

Information gained from the completed questionnaires permits the clinician to generate preliminary hypotheses about the nature and causes of the problem, as well as to plan for and focus the initial session with the parents and the child. In our work with preschool children, we routinely include the child in the initial parent interview. Although some clinicians may find this difficult, we have discovered that the information shared is rarely new to the child, and the opportunity to observe the child and the parent–child interaction at first hand far outweighs the drawbacks. Later interviews can be conducted with the parents alone, to go over more sensitive information or to provide information to the parents without the distraction of a particularly disruptive child. Parents of school-age children are typically interviewed alone, before the child is seen; adolescents are first seen with parents or alone depending on the nature of the problem.

Parent Interview

The parent interview provides a vehicle for understanding the parents' perception of the problem and the ways in which it has affected both the child and the family. The CAIS framework guides the interview, helps the clinician decide what questions need to be asked, and ensures that essential information is gathered quickly and efficiently. The parent interview also provides an opportunity to follow up on information gathered from the previously completed checklists and questionnaires. The clinician can also begin to test his or her hypotheses about the nature of the problem by asking parents for further information, and can determine what other areas need to be assessed, as well as the methods to be used. There are a number of structured parent interviews available; the reader is referred to Edelbrock and Costello (1988) for a review of these instruments.

Child Interview

The child interview (typically, the child is age 6 or older) provides valuable information on the child's perception of himself or herself (wishes, fears, interests, self-concept), the environment (peers, school, family), and the presenting problem, as well as on how the child attempts to cope with and solve personal and interpersonal problems. Much has been written recently about interviews with children (Bierman, 1983; Bierman & Schwartz, 1988; Boggs & Eyberg, 1988; Eyberg, 1985; Gross, 1984). Knowledge of the cognitive-developmental characteristics of children at different ages is essential to conducting a successful child interview.

Eyberg and her colleagues (Boggs & Eyberg, 1988; Kanfer, Eyberg, & Krahn, 1983) provide guidelines for organizing interviews with children, as well as techniques for maximizing rapport and information gathering. These include (1) using language that is at or just above the child's cognitive/language level (shorter, less complex words and sentences); (2) recognizing that children interpret silences as disapproval and interpret many direct questions as demanding, which can lead to increased resistance; and (3) introducing topics of interest to the child that are developmentally appropriate (TV shows, games, cartoon characters, etc.). General communication techniques that can be useful with children include (1) statements that describe the child's clothing, demeanor, or activity; (2) comments that reflect or restate what the child has said; (3) verbal and physical praise; and (4) structured, concrete questions ("Tell me one thing you like about your brother" vs. "What do you like about your brother?"). Providing age-appropriate, unstructured materials (crayons and paper, Legos, Play-Doh, etc.) for the child to play with while talking helps the child to feel more comfortable.

Several structured and semistructured interviews exist. As examples of these, descriptions of the Child Assessment Schedule (Hodges, Kline, Stern, Cytryn, & McKnew, 1982) and the Semistructured Interview for Children Aged 6–11 (McConaughy & Achenbach, 1990) are included in Appendix A.

Step 3: Observation of Behavior

Play

Obtaining useful information from interviews with young children is challenging, to say the least. Observation of a young child's play, however, can be a valuable source of information about how the child perceives his or her world. There is general agreement that play provides more reliable and useful information from preschool children than do verbal interviews (Gelfand & Peterson, 1985). Play is an extremely important part of development in the preschool years, and observation of the child's play can give information about intellectual and language development, feelings, thoughts, social relationships, and current concerns and anxieties.

It is useful to provide the child with opportunities to interact with a variety of age-appropriate toys and to vary the degree of structure during the play observation; this allows assessment of the maximum number of strengths and weaknesses. For example, providing the child with Legos enables the clinician to observe fine motor skills, frustration level, distractibility, persistence, creativity, and use of help (e.g., appropriate requests for help). Puppets allow observation of language skills, symbolic and "pretend" play, emotional expression, and coping skills. A doll house allows the child to demonstrate organizational skills, perceptions of family interaction, and role play. Simple rule-governed games reveal cognitive skills, compliance, frustration tolerance, and interactive play skills. The overall patterns of behavior in play are more important than any specific behavior (e.g., aggression only during puppet play vs. aggression with all types of materials).

Parent–Child Interaction

In the assessment of child behavior problems, observation of parent–child interaction is extremely important. Various methods for structuring and recording these observation sessions have been proposed (see, e.g., Barkley, 1981, 1987; Barton & Ascione, 1984; Eyberg & Robinson, 1983; Forehand & McMahon, 1981; Mash, Terdal, & Anderson, 1973; Patterson, Ray, Shaw, & Cobb, 1969). These methods vary in their complexity, but there is general agreement that the important dimensions of the interaction are (1) the extent to which the parent gives the child positive versus negative feedback, and whether that feedback is contingent on the child's behavior; (2) the number of demands placed on the child; (3) the number of questions asked; and (4) the child's compliance or noncompliance to parental demands. Most observations typically last 10–20 minutes and include both structured and unstructured time. With younger children, for example, parents might be provided a variety of toys and asked to "play with your child as you would at home." After 5 or 10 minutes they can be instructed to "have the child pick up all the toys." Older children and their parents can be asked to play a game, draw a picture together, or solve a family problem (e.g., where to go on vacation, how to spend a windfall).

Step 4: Further Assessment

By this point in the assessment process, the clinician should have a good idea about the nature of the problem and what other information is needed. For example, the child may be observed at home or at school. Permission to contact the child's teacher may be obtained, and questionnaires related to school behavior and academic progress sent. Measures of parent and/or child personality, a standardized test of intelligence, and/or a test of academic achievement may also be administered. For a discussion of standardized tests of intelligence and achievement, the reader is referred to Sattler (1988). Adaptive behavior, personality/emotional status, and school behavior can be assessed via the measures described in Appendix A. We most frequently use the Elementary School

Questionnaire developed in our clinic, a copy of which is sent to the child's teacher. This questionnaire is described below, and a copy is included in Appendix B.

Elementary School Questionnaire

Our Elementary School Questionnaire provides information on the child's academic progress and any behavior problems that occur in the school setting. The teacher's responses enable the clinician to screen for attention problems or hyperactivity, and also indicate specific academic areas in which the child may be having difficulty. The child's behavior in school can be further assessed by a number of standarized teacher rating scales: The Teacher Version of the Child Behavior Profile (Edelbrock & Achenbach, 1984); the Sutter–Eyberg Student Behavior Inventory (Sutter & Eyberg, 1984); A Behavior Rating Scale for the Preschool Child (Behar & Stringfield, 1974); and the Conners Teacher Rating Scale—Revised (Goyette, Conners, & Ulrich, 1978). Description of these instruments can be found in Appendix A.

Home and School Observation

Observation of the child's behavior at home or in school is important, as children often exhibit very different behavior in these two environments. Although the same recording methods used in the clinic could be used in the naturalistic setting, home and school observations usually go on for longer periods of time, so that the child can be seen engaging in a variety of activities. A good manner in which to begin the observation process is simply to keep a running record of the behavior as it occurs in 1-minute segments of time. In this way the clinician can quickly determine the salient behaviors of the child, his or her peers, and/or the adults in the situation. The clinician can then record the frequency and duration of those particular behaviors. It is also helpful to record the behavior of a sibling or randomly selected peer every other minute for about 20 minutes. This allows some comparison of the behavior of the referred child to at least one other child in his or her environment.

Step 5: Referral to Allied Health Professionals

If the nature of the problem is not yet completely understood at this point in the assessment process, the clinician may need to refer the child to an appropriate allied health professional (pediatrician, pediatric neurologist, occupational therapist, physical therapist, communication disorders specialist, or special educator) for further evaluation.

Step 6: Communication of Findings and Treatment Recommendations

Communicating the findings of the assessment and the clinician's interpretation of those findings provides the critical link between the assessment and intervention processes, and sets the stage for intervention. It can do these things in either a positive or a negative way: It can motivate parents, teachers, and others to obtain or provide the services required to meet the needs of the child effectively, or it can function to immobilize or overwhelm parents to the extent that the child's needs become secondary to their own. Information can be communicated to any number of individuals involved with the child (parents, teachers, social workers, lawyers, the child himself or herself, etc.), and this communication can occur through oral means (feedback conferences), through written material (reports and letters), or both.

Feedback Conference

The purpose of the feedback conference is not only to share information, but to engage with parents in problem solving that is focused on how best to meet the needs of their child. Preparation for the feedback conference really begins when the child is referred for assessment. At this time, the clinician can set the stage for the feedback session by carefully listening to and clarifying parents' concerns about the child (Shea, 1984). This, coupled with explanation about the nature and course of the assessment, can help to engage parents and others as active participants in the assessment process and can convey a sense of control over how the assessment proceeds. Conversely, when parents feel that their concerns and observations are not being taken seriously, they are more likely to be defensive and/or to question the clinician's conceptualization of the child's problem at the feedback conference.

It is reasonable to assume that the feedback conference constitutes a crisis of sorts for parents, regardless of the nature or severity of their child's problem (Schnell, 1982). The clinician may perceive the assessment results as "good news" (e.g., the child has a learning disability rather than mental retardation), whereas parents may perceive the same results as "bad news." The clinician's role is one of facilitating expressions of feelings about the information presented and promoting good coping responses on the part of parents by being supportive—that is, being empathic yet objective and truthful (Schnell, 1982; Shea, 1984). When the clinician is successful in this task, the parents will be ready to move to the next step: deciding what to do about the problem.

At this point, it is important to recognize that parents and professionals often have different values and priorities regarding services (Bailey,

1987). Parents, for example, may feel the best intervention is the one that requires the least expenditure of time, effort, or money on their part (Piersel & Gutkin, 1983); they may resist, ignore, or sabotage intervention programs that require their active participation. Bailey (1987) suggests that engaging parents in collaborative goal setting is an effective way to avoid this pitfall. In collaborative goal setting, the parents are asked to specify and prioritize their goals for their child. Then the clinician adds and prioritizes his or her goals. A process of negotiation between the parents and the clinician determines which goals will be addressed first (usually a combination of parent and clinician goals).

Written Reports

The purpose of written reports is to summarize the data gathered in the assessment, to interpret the data in order to answer the referral question(s), and to make recommendations for intervention. There are many sources of information about the content and organization of psychological assessment reports (see, e.g., Knoff, 1986; Sattler, 1988) but it is important to note that recent work has demonstrated that many parents and teachers have difficulty understanding these reports (Weddig, 1984). This is not surprising when one considers that the average reading level of psychological reports has been found to be about grade 14½ (Weddig, 1984)!

Written feedback to parents need not take the form of a formal report. Parents often benefit more from a letter summarizing the discussion that occurred at the feedback conference. Reports sent to community agencies (e.g., the school, the department of social services, or lawyers) may include more specific information on the test results, but the report should contain no information or interpretations that have not been shared with the parents. Many parents request a copy of the formal report for their records, in addition to the summary. Parents have a legal right to any information pertaining to their child; indeed, the collaborative relationship between parents and professionals would dictate their having easy access to this information.

On a broader scale, written reports provide a permanent record of the assessment process; they should also be used at a later date to provide a permanent record of the intervention methods used, as well as the response of the child and significant others to these methods. In some cases, it may be essential to provide a written summary of each session held with the parent or child. For example, in a recent case involving parental conflict over visitation following their divorce, the therapist summarized the areas discussed and the intervention plans agreed upon in each session, and sent this information to both parents as well as to both lawyers. This helped prevent miscommunication and promoted follow-through on the part of both parents. In addition, the court asked for a written summary and recommendations after 1 year of treatment. This gave the therapist and the parents an opportunity to reassess the current situation and the effectiveness of the intervention.

Although it is common practice to provide written feedback to parents about the initial assessment, it is equally important to give them a written summary of the intervention process and the changes that have been made. To this end, it is important to readminister the pretreatment assessment measures and, in a posttreatment session, to review the changes that have occurred. When possible, the review of pre- and posttreatment videotaped parent–child interactions can serve to make the parents more aware of changes that may have occurred gradually throughout the treatment process, and thus may increase generalization of the new parental responses.

PART II

MANAGING
STRESSFUL
LIFE EVENTS

Chapter 4

Siblings

Adjustment to the birth of a sibling and issues of sibling rivalry are among the most common concerns expressed by parents of young children (Brody & Stoneman, 1987). Eighty percent of children live with at least one sibling (Stillwell & Dunn, 1985), and it is within the often intense and close relationships between brothers and sisters that children learn important social and cognitive skills. Many argue that sibling relationships are a major influence on the development of individual differences in antisocial and prosocial behavior, as well as aspects of personality, intelligence, and achievement (Stillwell & Dunn, 1985). Research in this area has shown that various factors within families and within individual children influence how well children adjust to new siblings, as well as the quality of the relationship that develops between children and their brothers and sisters. Siblings influence each other's development both directly (by modeling or differentially reinforcing appropriate or inappropriate behaviors) and indirectly (by causing stress for parents, which in turn affects parenting skills).

Sibling relationships are quite different from peer relationships, in that they are "vertical" (the participants have unequal status) rather than "horizontal" (the participants have equal status) (Brody & Stoneman,

1983; Hartup, 1989). Research has shown that there is little relationship between the behavior of children with their siblings and with peers (Berndt & Bulleit, 1985). Incidents involving conflict, for example, occur with similar frequency between siblings and between peers, but those involving physical or verbal aggression are much more frequent between siblings (Dunn & Munn, 1985, 1986a; Shantz, 1987). This chapter reviews the research on how children adjust to the birth of a new sibling and presents suggestions for intervention/prevention with parents. Next, issues of sibling rivalry are discussed; the critical assessment issues for sibling problems are outlined; and suggestions for prevention and intervention are presented.

ADJUSTMENT TO THE BIRTH OF A SIBLING

The birth of a new sibling is clearly a major stressful event in the life of a young child, and the child's reactions to this event reflect his or her efforts to cope with the stress. As Stewart, Mobley, Van Tuyl, and Salvador (1987) note, "the birth of a sibling represents a complex period of adjustment for the firstborn child" (p. 341). The relationship between young children and their new siblings is best viewed as ambivalent, because most children evidence both positive and negative reactions (Campbell, 1990). Typical negative reactions of the older child include increased confrontation, anger and aggression, clinginess, separation distress and other anxious behaviors, more problems with toileting, and demands for bottles (Stewart et al., 1987). In contrast to most parents' perceptions, the child's overt negative behavior is more often directed toward them rather than toward the new baby (Dunn & Kendrick, 1982). Aggression in fantasy play, however, which also increases after the birth of a sibling, is more often directed at the infant (Field & Reite, 1984). Dunn and Kendrick (1982) argue that "regressive" behaviors on the part of the older sibling are best viewed as a form of imitation or mimicry—that is, a problem-solving or strategic approach by the older child to ensure that the parent will continue to care for him or her as well as the new baby. On the positive side, other studies note that increased maturity, independence, and empathy, as well as intense interest in and curiosity about the new baby, occur along with more negative reactions (see Campbell, 1990, for a review).

Research has also documented significant changes in the relationship between mothers and their first-born children following the birth of a second child. Dunn and Kendrick (1982) not only report decreases in the amount of time mothers spend in play or conversation with their older children, but also note that these children become the primary initiators of interactions with their mothers and that these interactions are largely confrontational. Mothers also begin to place increased demands for maturity and independence on their older children, presumably for very practical reasons.

Factors That Influence Adjustment

It is not surprising, given these changes in the mother–child relationship, that young children almost inevitably show some negative reactions to the birth of a sibling. For most children, however, these behaviors typically decrease by 4 months after the birth of the sibling (Stewart et al., 1987). Following this initial adjustment period, there is considerable stability in the quality of the older child's behavior toward the younger sibling (Stillwell & Dunn, 1985). The question of clinical importance is why the initial negative reaction of some children persists. Thus the factors that influence children's adjustment are important to understand.

The factors that have been shown to influence a child's adjustment to the birth of a new sibling include the child's temperamental characteristics, the existence of management problems prior to the birth, the child's age at the time of the birth, the mother's psychological well-being, and the manner in which the mother handles the child's involvement with the new baby. Dunn and Kendrick (1982) found that children (especially boys) with difficult temperament characteristics (negative mood and intense emotional reactions) were more likely to show anxious, withdrawn reactions to the birth of a sibling. This reaction tended to persist over time, indicating that temperamentally difficult children may have a harder time adjusting to a new sibling than children with easy temperaments (Campbell, 1990). Parents also report that when a child is difficult to manage prior to the birth of a new baby, these problems persist and are often exacerbated by the introduction of an infant into the family (Campbell, 1990). The intensity of the child's initial reaction to the birth of a sibling, which may be mediated by temperament, is also related to adjustment (Dunn & Kendrick, 1982). Surprisingly, however, children who react most explosively have been found to make a better adjustment than those who become withdrawn (Dunn & Kendrick, 1982).

Vandell (1987) cites considerable evidence that younger children (especially those under 18 months) have more trouble adjusting to the birth of a sibling than do older children. Older children are more likely to be interested in helping to care for the baby and to be involved with activities and interests outside the immediate family. Thus they are less dependent on their mothers for nurturance and support. Campbell (1990) cites inconsistent evidence for the effect of the gender of the older child on adjustment. Although girls are thought to be more nurturing toward a new baby than boys, these sex differences do not appear to hold up over time (Dunn & Kendrick, 1982).

Dunn and Kendrick (1982) suggest that children whose mothers are greatly fatigued or depressed after the birth of the baby have more trouble adjusting to the birth of a sibling. This probably reflects the extra lack of availability of these mothers for their older children. Finally, Dunn and Kendrick (1982) suggest that mothers can foster a positive adjustment on the part of their older children by involving them in the care of the infant (thus making it a shared experience rather than a responsibility), and by modeling respect for the infant as a person with needs and feelings.

Intervention Strategies

Helping a young child adjust to the arrival of a new brother or sister is best viewed as preventive work, because the quality of the relationship between siblings shows some consistency over time, and children who make a good adjustment in the early months may have less trouble with sibling rivalry later on. Furthermore, there are several things parents can do before a new baby is born to help prepare the older child and facilitate a good adjustment. After the baby is born, parents are most concerned about aggression directed toward the infant or regressive/imitative behaviors on the part of the older child; they often wonder whether the reactions the older child is showing are normal or whether they should be worried about them. Along with this, parents typically want help in managing the older child's behavior. Strategies for helping children cope with a new sibling must be extrapolated from the research literature, as there are few if any studies testing the efficacy of one approach versus another. In our practice we take a behavioral approach, liberally laced with common sense!

Preparation

Parents should prepare the older child for the birth of a sibling well in advance of the expected date. How far ahead to prepare will, of course, depend on how old the child is. Toddlers (ages 12–18 months), who have little sense of time (past or future), may need only a few days' or a week's notice. Preschoolers, although still tied to present experience, are very curious about their environment and are likely to have noticed and asked many questions about the physical changes in their mothers. This, in turn, is likely to lead to questions such as "Where do babies come from?" These questions give parents the opportunity to begin to prepare a child for the new baby. Simple, concrete, but honest factual information is appropriate for even very young children, and parents should provide this information even if their child has not asked any questions. Many very good books have been written for young children about sexuality, childbirth, and welcoming a new baby into the family, and we have listed some of these in Appendix C. Preschool children respond especially well to information in books; they enjoy the illustrations, and the text often sparks more questions and discussion. It is important for parents to recognize that young children cannot be prepared for the birth of a sibling (or for anything else!) in one session. For preschoolers especially, preparation is an ongoing process that should occur over many weeks in small doses.

Minimizing Stress

Recognizing that the birth of a new sibling is a major stressful event for children should alert parents to minimize other sources of stress in the child's life, so that his or her coping skills are not overwhelmed. Legg, Sherrick, and Wadland (1974) recommend keeping to the young child's regular schedule and routine as much as possible during the time just before and after the birth. Changes such as sleeping in a bed rather than the crib, moving to a new room or a new house, or starting a new preschool should be accomplished well in advance of the birth date, so that the older child has a chance to become used to the new routines. The child should be left with someone familiar and in a familiar place while the mother is in the hospital, and should be told ahead of time who will care for him or her. Furthermore, because parent–child conflict existing prior to the birth tends to escalate dramatically after the birth (Dunn & Kendrick, 1982), parents should be advised to seek help for any such problems before the new baby arrives.

Many parents ask about the advisability of having the older child visit the mother and new baby in the hospital. There is evidence that these visits have at least short-term benefits in alleviating the child's distress at separation from the mother (Vandell, 1987). There is no evidence, however, that visiting the mother in the hospital has long-term effects on the sibling relationship. Nor is there evidence that breast feeding versus bottle feeding of the new baby influences adjustment of the older child (Vandell, 1987).

When the Baby Comes Home

After the new baby comes home, extensive involvement of the father in the care of the older child can facilitate the child's adjustment (Vandell, 1987). The father's involvement probably has both direct and indirect effects on adjustment. His increased involvement can provide the older child with a substitute for the care and nurturance once provided by the mother, as well as easing the stress experienced by the mother as a result of her new responsibilities. Even a very young child can be involved in the care of the new infant by fetching diapers, holding the bottle, checking on the baby, and so on. Parents can also describe the interaction of the baby and older child in a way that emphasizes the "individuality" of the infant, as well as the infant's responsiveness to the older child. At the same time, appropriate behavior on the part of the older child can be reinforced. For example, a parent may say, "The baby is watching you and likes the way you are holding her so gently," or "Look, the baby is smiling at you. He likes the way you are holding his bottle."

It is essential that parents schedule time for the older child during which they can give the child their undivided attention. Even 10 or 15 minutes a day goes a long way toward fostering adjustment. A parent handout for maximizing this "quality" time (called "Child's Game") is provided in the chapter on negative behavior (see Chapter 11, Table 11.2). Special treats or events that emphasize the older child's capabilities (in contrast to the infant's relative lack of abilities) can help to eliminate the "regressive"/imitative behaviors. For example, going out to eat with Mom and Dad while the baby is left with a sitter provides an opportunity to reinforce grown-up behavior.

Behavior Management

Parents should provide clear consequences for aggressive behavior, whether it is directed at the parent, the infant, or both. If parents are not already using a procedure for time out by isolation, this is a good time to begin. How time-out is implemented will depend on the developmental (primarily language and cognitive) level of the child. The idea, however, is to remove the child from the situation quickly and briefly, without any discussion on the part of the parent, so the child can learn that physical aggression is inappropriate and will not be tolerated. Very young children can be placed briefly (e.g., for 1 minute) in a playpen (without toys) or an area of the floor (preferably in a corner) marked out with masking tape. Parents should completely ignore the child during time-out. At other times, parents should be taught to watch for appropriate interaction and to comment on it as it occurs. In this way, they are teaching the child what they like as well as what they do not like. Time-out procedures for children over 24 months of age are described in the "Treatment" section of Chapter 11.

Aggression expressed in fantasy play is often a concern for parents, particularly because it often is directed toward the infant. Parents may be worried that the child will begin to act out his or her fantasies and actually hurt the baby. This is not usually the case, and fantasy play provides an excellent way for the older child to express his or her very real feelings. Furthermore, young children use play to experience mastery over environmental events that they cannot really control; as such, it functions as an adaptive coping mechanism. Parents should be advised to allow aggression to be expressed in fantasy play and to provide other outlets for the appropriate expression of angry feelings (draw a picture of the baby, tear it into little pieces, and throw it in the trash!).

SIBLING RIVALRY

The Quality of Sibling Relationships

By the end of the first year after the birth of the new sibling, as the younger child becomes more mobile and curious, conflicts between siblings increase dramatically (Campbell, 1990). At first the older sibling is likely to assert his or her dominance in the relationship, but by the end of the second year, the younger child is likely to retaliate with aggression as well as to instigate conflict by teasing and provoking the older child. Observational studies of the interaction of preschool children with toddler siblings indicate that conflict occurs about seven or eight times an hour (similar to the frequency of conflict in peer interactions), and that verbal or physical aggression occurs in about 25% of these incidents (Dunn & Munn, 1985, 1986a). Furthermore, mothers have been found to intervene in sibling quarrels 50–60% of the time (Dunn & Munn, 1986a). It is no wonder that parents express concern about sibling rivalry!

Children perceive their relationships with siblings much more positively than observational studies would suggest. In a unique study conducted by fourth-grade children, the frequency of fights between siblings was estimated by fourth- and fifth-graders to be only 4.7 per day, with an average duration of 8.1 minutes per fight (Prochaska & Prochaska, 1985). The number of "fun times" was estimated to be 9.2 per day. The most common reasons for fighting given by the children were being in a bad mood, getting even, or protecting possessions or territory. In contrast to the commonly held belief that children are rivals for their parents' love and attention, the *least* common reason for fighting given was gaining parental attention!

There are certainly large individual differences in the quality of sibling relationships; some relationships are entirely positive, some are both positive and negative, and some are 100% negative (Dunn, 1988; Dunn & Kendrick, 1982). Furthermore, the extent to which siblings engage in cooperative, prosocial, friendly behavior appears to be independent of the extent to which they fight and argue (Dunn, 1988). On the positive side, older children often become objects of attachment for their younger siblings, offering comfort and reassurance during times of distress and serving as a base for exploration in the absence of the mother (Stewart & Marvin, 1984). Whether or not older children are nurturant toward their younger siblings seems to depend in part on the social-cognitive skill of being able to understand the perspective of another person (Stewart & Marvin, 1984); in fact, mothers are more likely to ask more cognitively mature youngsters to care for their younger siblings.

Dunn and Munn (1986b) found that sharing, helping, comforting, and cooperation were more often shown by older siblings toward their younger brothers and sisters than vice versa. More interesting, however, are the findings that prosocial behavior on the part of the older siblings was related to the development of more mature behavior in the younger children, and that friendly behavior on the part of younger children was also related to increased frequency of prosocial behavior by the older siblings. Cooperative, friendly behavior on the part of one sibling thus appears to encourage cooperative, friendly behavior on the part of the other.

Just as friendly behavior begets friendly behavior, so does aggressive behavior lead to increased aggression in sibling relationships. Patterson (1980) has shown that younger siblings of aggressive boys at first submit to aggressive attacks, thus negatively reinforcing the aggression and increasing its frequency of occurrence. Later the younger children learn to retaliate with aggression, and this leads to further aggression on the part of the older children. Thus, although the older child is responsible for the initial tone of a sibling relationship, both children contribute equally to the frequency and escalation of conflict. In summary, as children increasingly engage in social behavior between 12 and 24 months of age, the expression (prosocial or hostile) of this behavior in younger siblings is dependent, in part, on the behavior of older siblings toward the younger ones. Over time, however, younger children become increasingly able to shape the behavior of their older siblings.

Factors Influencing Sibling Relations

Again, the clinician is led to ask what factors are important in the development of positive versus negative relationships between siblings, and considerable research has been devoted to answering this question. Table 4.1 summarizes the factors that have been found to influence sibling relationships.

Stocker, Dunn, and Plomin (1989) report that when a wider age difference exists between siblings, the relationship is more likely to be positive than when siblings are closer in age. Furthermore, same-sex sibling dyads tend to have more positive relationships than opposite-sex dyads (Stocker et al., 1989). Other factors that are related to the quality of sibling relationships include differential maternal behavior toward the younger child, parental intervention in sibling conflicts, temperamental characteristics of the children, quality of the marital relationship, and parental adjustment. Stocker et al. (1989), for example, found that sibling

TABLE 4.1. Factors That Influence the Quality of Sibling Relationships

Source	Factor
Children	Temperament
	Age difference
	Gender differences
	Level of social-cognitive development
Parent–child relationship	Differential treatment
	Parent intervention in child conflict
	Lack of clear rules and expectations
	General child management problems
Family	Marital distress
	Parental maladjustment
	Life and environmental stress
	Emotional climate in home
	Family functioning

relationships were more negative when mothers were more affectionate, responsive, and controlling toward the younger sibling than toward the older sibling. Most mothers show differential behavior toward their younger children, and this probably reflects the children's relative developmental status. Support for this is provided by other work that has shown remarkable consistency in mothers' behavior toward each of two children at the same age (Dunn, Plomin, & Nettles, 1985). Thus, the important factor in how differential parental treatment influences the quality of sibling relationships may be children's *perceptions* of unequal treatment (Brody & Stoneman, 1987; Dunn, 1988). An older child finds it very difficult to understand and accept that the mother's differential treatment of the younger child is in large part due to the age and developmental differences of the siblings.

More negative temperamental characteristics of children, including high intensity of emotional response, activity level, impulsivity, and low persistence, have consistently been associated with more negative sibling relationships (Brody & Stoneman, 1987; Brody, Stoneman, & Burke, 1987; Stocker et al., 1989). Moreover, more conflict should be expected when both children in a sibling dyad possess difficult temperamental characteristics (Brody & Stoneman, 1987). Marital distress also is related to increased conflict between siblings; perhaps this connection reflects parental modeling of conflict behavior, children's anxiety over witnessing the parents' conflict, or an indirect effect of marital conflict on parenting skills (Dunn & Munn, 1986a). Finally, some types of parental intervention in sibling conflicts have been shown to increase the frequency of conflict (Brody & Stoneman, 1987) and use of physical aggression. On the other hand, use of time-out for fighting and positive reinforcement for appropriate interactions can successfully decrease sibling conflict (Brody & Stoneman, 1987). Moreover, when parental intervention involves teaching conflict resolution strategies, children increase their use of these more mature strategies (Dunn & Munn, 1986a).

ASSESSMENT OF SIBLING RIVALRY

When parents are concerned about and seek professional help for sibling conflict, certain factors are especially important to examine during the assessment of the problem. The present discussion follows the steps for gathering information in accordance with the Comprehensive Assessment-to-Intervention System (CAIS), presented in Chapter 3. The emphasis here is on those factors most related to sibling rivalry as outlined in Table 4.1.

Step 1: Initial Contact

The first step in the assessment process is to gather information from questionnaires and checklists completed by the parents. The following should be included in assessment of sibling rivalry:

1. A general questionnaire, such as the Parent Questionnaire developed in our clinic (see Appendix B). This gives information on the age and sex of all children in the family, who cares for the children, and parents' perceptions of the problem.
2. The Parenting Stress Index (PSI; Abidin, 1990; see Appendix A for a full description). The PSI includes parents' perceptions of the child's temperament and information about the marital relationship, parental depression, and life stress, all of which have been shown to influence sibling relationships. Both parents should be asked to complete the PSI, and it is also useful to have the child domain completed with reference to each child about whom the parents are concerned. Hypotheses about differential parental perceptions and treatment of the children can be developed from this information.
3. The Child Behavior Checklist (CBCL; Achenbach & Edelbrock, 1983) and/or the Eyberg Child Behavior Inventory (ECBI; Eyberg & Ross, 1978). These measures should be completed with reference to each child involved in the conflict. Information about the existence of other problems with any of the children is provided.
4. The Dyadic Adjustment Scale (Spanier, 1976; see Appendix A for a full description). This measure is particularly important in the assessment of sibling rivalry, because marital conflict has been shown to affect

sibling relationships, both directly and indirectly. The existence of serious marital problems should lead the clinician to work to resolve these before dealing with the referral problem of sibling rivalry.

5. The Beck Depression Inventory (Beck, Ward, Mendelson, Mock, & Erbaugh, 1961). This measure is particularly important to administer to parents who are concerned about the adjustment of their older child to a new baby. Postpartum depression is quite common and may need to be treated before the parents will be able to deal effectively with their older child's adjustment problems. Information on parental depression can also be obtained from the PSI.

6. The Daily Log. Parents should be asked to monitor and note all instances of sibling conflict on the Daily Log (see Appendix B). This gives the clinician excellent information about the frequency and duration of fights (are they more frequent than expected?); the instances that involve physical and/or verbal aggression; and parents' perceptions of who is at fault, how fights are resolved, how often and in what manner parents intervene, and so on. These data will also provide an excellent baseline for monitoring the effectiveness of any treatment program.

Step 2: Parent and Child Interview

Parent Interview

Interviewing the parents is the second step in the assessment of sibling rivalry. During the interview, in following the CAIS framework, the clinician should be particularly careful to gather the following information:

1. How do parents handle sibling conflict currently, and what methods have been tried in the past? Reviewing the data on the Daily Log with parents can help to clarify this. Having parents go over a "typical day" will reveal any particularly troublesome situations (e.g., fighting over TV, the predinner "combat hour," etc.).

2. How did the sibling relationship develop? Parents should be asked to describe how the older child or children were prepared for the arrival of the new baby and what the adjustment period was like. Any steps parents took to ease an older child's adjustment should also be described.

3. What kinds of behavior do the parents model for their children? Because parents are important models for their children, the parents' style of interaction with each other should also be observed during the interview. We have been amazed at the number of parents who are quite comfortable with a combative/argumentative interaction style in the marital relationship, and at the same time complain that their children

exhibit the very same style! Conveying information about modeling effects on children's behavior to parents during the feedback conference is an important part of the treatment program for these cases.

4. Do the children have problems with aggression/conflict in areas other than sibling interactions? Parents should be asked about the children's peer relationships, school progress, and other activities and interests. Data from the CBCL can provide the basis for gathering further information in these areas. Children who are having problems in other areas of their lives are, of course, of greater concern than those whose problems occur only in the context of sibling interaction. Furthermore, a child who does not have individual interests and activities outside the family may need to be helped to develop these in order to improve his or her sense of uniqueness, as well as to keep occupied and out of trouble.

Child Interview

Interviewing children in cases involving sibling rivalry is often not necessary. When done it is best left until after the clinician has observed the children's behavior. Children are usually unable to describe the problem in any but very global terms (e.g., "I hate him; he's always bugging me"). Observation enables the clinician to ask more specific questions regarding the sibling interaction.

Step 3: Observation of Behavior

Observation of the children together, both in the presence of parents and alone, is the next step in the assessment process. Although many clinics provide facilities for observation, observation in the home also provides useful information, because children may feel more comfortable and behave more naturally at home than in the clinic. In the parents' absence, instances of cooperative, friendly interaction between siblings may be observed; these will enable the clinician to give parents feedback about their children's strengths. Observing parents interacting with the children can provide information about management strategies, as well as reinforcement patterns. Parents often complain that clinicians do not actually witness instances of fighting when observing, because the children are on "their good behavior" in the presence of a stranger. Although this is often the case, valuable information about the emotional climate of the home and family relationships, potential for building positive relationships, differential parental treatment of children, and potential effective management strategies can be gained. It is a good idea to have a list of target behaviors in hand before going to the home, and then to record observations during or *immediately* after the visit.

Step 4: Further Assessment

For many cases of sibling rivalry, Steps 1, 2, and 3 will complete the assessment. The clinician should, of course, be aware of the possibility of more serious problems among the children, parents, and/or family that would require further psychological assessment.

Step 5: Referral to Allied Health Professionals

Referral to another professional should be considered for problems co-existing with sibling rivalry, and the need to treat any such problems prior to treating the sibling problems should be assessed.

Step 6: Communication of Findings and Treatment Recommendations

Prior to beginning treatment, the clinician should discuss his or her understanding of the nature and etiology of the sibling problems and provide a rationale for the proposed treatment program. The implications of sibling problems for the children's development in other areas and their impact on family life should be discussed. As for any child problem, the parents' understanding of the clinician's view of the sibling problems will influence their motivation to cooperate with the treatment recommendations. We next look at treatment methods for sibling rivalry, followed by specific areas on which to focus treatment.

TREATMENT OF SIBLING RIVALRY

Research Findings

There has been surprisingly little research on effective treatment methods for sibling rivalry. Studies that have examined the efficacy of various interventions in reducing the frequency of sibling conflict have been primarily based on one of two theoretical perspectives. The first, an Adlerian approach espoused by Dreikurs (1964), suggests that sibling conflict is best ignored by parents because its primary function is to gain parental attention. Allowing children to solve their own fights may also have the benefit of providing opportunities for children to learn important conflict resolution skills (Brody & Stoneman, 1987). Behavioral theory suggests that ignoring would be effective in reducing sibling conflict through the principle of extinction, and work reviewed by Brody and Stoneman (1983) indicates that this is indeed the case.

An operant approach to intervention advocates the use of differential reinforcement of other behaviors (e.g., reinforcement of not fighting), reinforcement of specific alternative behaviors (e.g., reinforcement of cooperative play), and/or use of time-out for fighting. Brody and Stoneman (1983) indicate that each of these methods is effective in reducing fighting. Olson and Roberts (1987) compared the use of time-out with skill-building sessions (teaching problem-solving and assertiveness skills to parents and children) in reducing sibling fighting. Overall, use of time-out was more effective than skills training, but these results were confounded by socioeconomic differences in the treatment groups. Nonetheless, the authors conclude that skill-building approaches may be more effective with families from higher socioeconomic backgrounds.

When children are asked what parents can do to stop their fighting, the results are discouraging! Prochaska and Prochaska (1985) found that even the methods mentioned as most effective by fourth- and fifth-graders were judged by these youngsters to decrease fighting only slightly. These methods were (1) rewards for being good; (2) being sent to room, spanked, or scolded; and (3) being kept busy with fun things. Parental ignoring was judged by these children to *increase* fighting!

When one child in a family is referred for treatment of aggressive behavior, training parents in strategies for managing the behavior of the target child often results in improvements in the behavior of other siblings as well (Brody & Stoneman, 1983; Eyberg & Robinson, 1982). This is important, because observations of the target children and their siblings usually reveal few differences in their behavior. It is not known why parents seek help for one child as opposed to another in these cases.

Studies have also examined the inclusion of siblings in the treatment process when one child is targeted for intervention. This approach makes sense when one recognizes that children interact more and engage in significantly more cooperative and prosocial play in the absence of parents than in their presence (Brody et al., 1987). Siblings have successfully been taught the use of behavior management techniques such as differential reinforcement and extinction (Brody & Stoneman, 1983). This type of intervention is most successful when both parents and children are consistent in their use of behavioral techniques and when parents are careful to focus equal attention on both children.

In our clinic we employ a variety of behaviorally based treatment strategies for sibling rivalry, the choice of which depends on our assessment of the problem. The treatment process begins with a feedback session with parents (and sometimes also with the children), during which they are given information about sibling rivalry in general and our assessment of how it operates in their particular family. Various strategies for treatment are discussed in the context of the CAIS framework, although some strategies clearly cut across the areas on which one can focus treatment.

Specific Treatment Strategies

Intervention in Development

In many cases it is clear that the children do not have adequate problem/ conflict resolution skills, and these must be directly taught. These skills include ignoring, negotiating, compromising, expressing angry feelings appropriately, and (when all else fails) walking away from the situation. Parents can be involved by actually doing the teaching or by reinforcing use of these skills at home.

If sibling conflict occurs because one or both children are bored or do not have enough ways to express their individuality, then the parents need to help the children develop outside interests and activities. Children should be encouraged to go their separate ways much of the time; parents should not insist, for example, that the older child include the younger in all his or her activities. Similarly, the older child should not be expected to provide regular child care for the younger sibling(s). If parents need a babysitter, they should hire one or pay the older child for accepting this responsibility. Nor should an older child be allowed to criticize or feel it is his or her responsibility to correct a younger child. A reminder that this is the parents' job may be needed.

Many children referred for sibling rivalry have good interaction skills in their behavioral repertoires. The treatment issue in these cases is increasing the use of these skills, or, conversely, decreasing the occurrence of inappropriate behaviors with siblings. This is most effectively accomplished through use of behavioral techniques. Using time-out for physical or verbal aggression, regardless of who did what to whom, is always appropriate and effective. Providing rewards for appropriate behavior or the absence of negative behavior is also important. For example, children may be given a certain number of points (or a sticker, for younger children) for playing cooperatively for 30 minutes (or a longer or shorter period of time, depending on the clinician's or parents' assessment of what is possible).

Intervention with Parents

Many parents who are concerned about sibling rivalry already possess good general child management skills. These parents simply need to be helped to apply these skills to the problem of sibling rivalry. Other parents must be taught basic skills, such as how to provide contingent reinforcement and how to implement time-out procedures, before they can begin to deal with sibling conflict. Parents must also model appropriate interaction. "Do as I say, not as I do" simply does not work with children.

In some families, the sibling conflict is only one aspect of the conflict that consumes the entire family. In these cases, it would be futile to try to eliminate sibling rivalry before working to improve the emotional atmosphere of the household. Similarly, if the marital relationship is distressed or either parent is experiencing significant psychological problems, treatment should focus on these problems before (or at least concurrently with) treatment of the sibling problem.

Changing parents' expectations, attitudes, or beliefs can be an important aspect of treatment for sibling problems. Many parents have unrealistic expectations for their children's relationship; they may expect sharing, helping, consideration, and so on 100% of the time. These parents may be too quick to intervene in squabbles, and consequently inadvertently reinforce fighting. Teaching them to ignore low-level conflict and to allow the children to work things out by themselves (assuming that the children have the appropriate skills) is often effective in these cases.

Parents must also be clear with their children about their expectations for their behavior and the household rules (Brody & Stoneman, 1987). Telling a child, for example, to "play nicely with your brother" is not specific enough. Schaefer and Millman (1981) suggest that parents hold regularly scheduled "family councils" when everyone sits down together to clarify rules and expectations, deal with transgressions, and plan family activities.

Other parents may have trouble appreciating one or both children and thus inadvertently favor one over the other. Schaefer and Millman (1981) recommend that parents periodically ask their children whether they feel that the parents have a favorite. Parents need to recognize that each child is different and that treating children equally does not mean treating them exactly the same. Rather, parents must find ways to meet each child's unique needs for time, attention, and family resources. Older children, for example, are entitled to privileges (later bedtimes, larger allowances, etc.) that are not appropriate for younger children.

Intervention in the Environment

Assessment should reveal whether there are specific times of day or situations in which children are particularly likely to fight. In many cases, simple interventions such as rearranging the family's schedule (e.g., having dinner an hour earlier) or taking away a particular toy can decrease fighting. Children are entitled to some privacy and should have a few personal possessions that they are not expected to share. If children have separate rooms, other children in the family can be prohibited from entering without permission. If children must share a room, then providing each with his or her own cupboard (with a lock, if necessary) in which to store "nonsharable" possessions can help. If prized possessions are left out of a child's room or cupboard, then they may be declared "fair game" for the other children.

In some cases, sibling rivalry is exacerbated by the degree of stress the family is experiencing. Preschool children are particularly adept at engaging in their worst behavior when parents are least able to manage it. One aspect of treatment for these families may be to help them find better ways to cope with stress, and at the same time keep the children under control. For example, giving parents permission to hire a sitter and have an evening out from time to time (perhaps even "prescribing" that they do this) can help.

Intervention in the Consequences of the Behavior

Several ways to intervene in the consequences of the behavior of individual children have already been described. Some parents have found group rewards and punishments to be effective in decreasing sibling conflict. For example, if children persist in fighting, all can be sent to time out or the TV can be unplugged until they can decide which programs to watch. Conversely, all children can be rewarded for playing together cooperatively for a specified period of time. If fighting occurs, no matter who starts it, no one gets the reward. Whatever method is adopted to handle fighting, everyone who cares for the children (babysitters, grandparents, etc.) should be familiar with the procedures and asked to use them consistently.

Intervention in Medical/Health Aspects

Intervention in medical or health aspects is most appropriate for parents who are concerned about the adjustment of the sibling of a handicapped or chronically ill child. Parents should be made aware of the unique challenges faced by children with handicapped siblings and should be encouraged to develop a special relationship with the nonhandicapped child. Although meeting the needs of a sick or handicapped child is inevitably difficult and time-consuming, parents must also recognize and meet the needs of their older child(ren). Many of the suggestions provided above are equally relevant for parents with both handicapped and nonhandicapped children. This may mean scheduling special time with the nonhandicapped child when the handicapped sibling is cared for by someone else, encouraging the nonhandicapped child to develop interests and activities outside the home, and facilitating his or her participation in these activities.

────────────── *CASE EXAMPLE* ──────────────

Step 1: Initial Contact

Mrs. Battle, the mother of three boys (ages 6, 8, and 10) and a girl (age 3), sounded very desperate when she called for an appointment to discuss sibling rivalry. Her oldest two children had recently caused physical harm to each other, with one sustaining a broken foot. Questionnaires (the Parent Questionnaire, the ECBI, the CBCL, and the PSI) were sent out for all four children, and both parents were asked to complete these for each child.

Child Behavior Measures

Mr. Battle's ratings of all the children on the behavioral measures were well within normal limits. He did, however, note that the 6-year-old was more hyperactive and impulsive, was less attentive, and had some difficulty understanding directions. Mrs. Battle's ratings, conversely, indicated major conduct problems for all of the children except the 3-year-old.

Parenting Stress Index

Both parents' PSI ratings for the 6-year-old indicated a child with a difficult temperament, who nevertheless was quite acceptable and reinforcing to each parent. The other children's scores were within normal limits, and Mrs. Battle noted that in viewing each child independently, she found them quite acceptable and reinforcing. Mrs. Battle's responses on the parent domain of the PSI indicated scores on the Depression, Relationship with Spouse, and Parent Health scales all over the 90th percentile. (High scores on the PSI are problematic.) Mr. Battle's scores on the parent domain were all below the 40th percentile.

Parent Questionnaire

Mr. Battle was a university professor and was well known and respected in the community. He was often involved in evening meetings, worked on Saturdays, and therefore had only limited child care responsibilities. Mrs. Battle was a homemaker who found little time for personal activities other than church. Her days and nights were totally devoted to the care of the children.

According to Mrs. Battle, school and preschool reports indicated that the children were well behaved, compliant, and socially appropriate. The 6-year-old's teacher did, however, indicate some problems with attention and following directions. The older children (the three boys) were involved in a number of community activities, including organized sports and church children's choir, and each had his own special friends. The youngest child, the 3-year-old girl, was described as beloved by everyone in the family and never involved in the sibling squabbles.

Step 2: Parent Interview

Mrs. Battle appeared as a pleasant woman in her early 30s, who was dressed in a casual manner (including running shoes). Her husband had decided not to come for the interview because he did not feel the children's problems were significant and attributed the latest "accident" to overly rambunctious behavior. Although Mr. Battle did not approve of such behavior, he did not see it as abnormal. Mrs. Battle, on the other hand, clearly felt responsible for her children's behavior. Mrs. Battle said that her husband was quite supportive of her seeking help and learning more effective management techniques.

The mother described the three boys as being intensely loyal to one another (e.g., they fiercely stood up for one another when in group settings with other children, and often dubbed themselves "the Battle boys"). They were also described as being able to play with each other for several hours without any major upset, especially if only two of the three older children were present. School vacations, however, were described as nightmares, with the mother constantly organizing activities, refereeing squabbles, and praying for the end of each day. Mrs. Battle's management of the sibling rivalry included reasoning with the children, acting as judge, separating the children, screaming at them, and trying to provide separate activities for them outside the home. None of these methods were used consistently; they varied with her mood, the time of day, and the situation. Fighting was particularly bad in the late afternoon, and she had started to feed the children earlier and earlier in the day. At the time of this appointment, the children were fed and put to bed no later than 6:30 P.M.! Consequently, her day usually began at about 5 A.M. She felt, however, that after a night away from the children she was in better shape to deal with them.

The home environment was described as quite pleasant, with a bedroom for each child, a large family room, and a large outside play area (with room for swings, as well as ball playing and other activities). Mrs. Battle had help with housework and had occasional babysitters, but was primarily responsible for the running of the household, car pooling, and the social life of the family. The latter was limited primarily to activities involving the children, and there was little time or energy left for the parents to be alone. Mrs. Battle said she loved her husband (who was a childhood sweetheart) very much and felt that he also loved her, but the lack of support from him with regard to the children was causing considerable stress on the marriage. She excused her husband's lack of involvement because of his many university and community responsibilities, which were seen as ultimately benefiting the family. Although money was not overly plentiful, there were certainly enough financial resources to meet all of their needs. Mrs. Battle had elected not to have more child care because she felt the children were her responsibility.

Mrs. Battle indicated close connections with and support from both the maternal and paternal sides of the family, but the recent illness and subsequent death of her mother was causing her great distress. She described a very close relationship with her mother and sorely missed her support. Mrs. Battle's significantly high score on the PSI Health scale related to difficulties with sleep, headaches, and major problems with ulcers. The sleep problems had started after her mother's death. Although sibling squabbles were the norm in this family, they had become significantly worse in the last year and a half, which coincided with the period of her mother's illness and death.

Step 3: Observation of Behavior

A home visit began 30 minutes before dinner and lasted through the dinner hour. The children were told that the clinician was helping their mother figure out ways to have their family run more smoothly and happily. This observation revealed a well-organized environment with ample materials to stimulate development. The children were all bright eyed and very interested in the observer. They made reassuring statements that things were not as bad as they seemed and that they were happy with their family. Soon, however, the normal pattern of interaction surfaced, with squabbles over who got the most milk, who got their story read first last night, and rough-housing that ended in tears. Mrs. Battle used no consistent management techniques, nor did the children respond to any but her most vociferous efforts.

Step 4: Further Assessment

After further discussion about the 6-year-old's behavior, it was agreed that questionnaires should be sent to the school, and the therapist was given permission to talk directly with his teacher. Through subsequent evaluation, it was determined that this child had a mild learning disability and Attention-deficit Hyperactivity Disorder. His behavior was felt to have an impact on the two older children's behavior, and vice versa.

These problems were treated simultaneously with the sibling rivalry problems.

Step 5: *Referral to Allied Health Professionals*

Referral to other professionals was not necessary in this case.

Step 6: *Communication of Findings and Treatment Recommendations*

This family had many strengths, including financial security, a pleasant and adequate home for the children, a supportive and caring extended family, and children who were functioning well with peers and in school. The 6-year-old's difficult temperament, mild learning disability, and Attention-deficit Hyperactivity Disorder negatively influenced his and the other children's relationships with each other. The stressful life events of the maternal grandmother's death and the mother's health problems, plus the life circumstances of the father's work schedule and the mother's responsibility for the four rambunctious children, set the stage for maternal depression, marital conflict, child management problems, and sibling rivalry. In the process of filling out questionnaires, keeping the Daily Logs, and talking to the child clinician, Mrs. Battle became aware of the negative factors influencing the family. Assessment of the 6-year-old's problems also helped both parents understand and arrange to meet this child's needs.

When the child clinician discussed sibling rivalry in a developmental context, with an analysis of what factors were most likely eliciting and maintaining negative interactions in their home, the parents readily agreed to the recommended treatment. It was interesting that while they saw their 6-year-old son's problems as adding to the conflict, they did not feel that this was a major component of the overall problem. They indicated that they had always tried to meet his special needs; they just had not realized that there were other ways to help him. They understood and accepted that some of the recommended treatment strategies were geared toward indirectly decreasing the sibling conflict.

Course of Treatment

Based on this assessment of the problem, treatment was implemented in the following areas:

1. *Development.* Mrs. Battle was given a copy of Elizabeth Crary's series of books on problem solving for children (see Appendix C). These skills were explained to her, and she was instructed to read the books to the children at times when they were not fighting.

Sibling Chart

Date: _____

Behavior	Total Possible Points	Saturday	Sunday	Monday	Tuesday	Wednesday	Thursday	Friday
MORNING								
1. All chores completed	0 or 3							
2. Positive statement	1–3							
3. No TOs for fighting	0 or 3							
AFTERNOON								
1. All chores completed	0 or 3							
2. Positive 30-minute activity	1–3							
3. No TOs for fighting	0 or 3							
EVENING								
1. Positive dinner talk	1–3							
2. Share family quiet time	1–3							
3. No TOs for fighting	0 or 3							
TOTAL	Daily–27 Weekly–189							

1st Prize (151–187 points) = _____
2nd Prize (132–150 points) = _____
3rd Prize (114–131 points) = _____

From *Assessment and Treatment of Childhood Problems: A Clinician's Guide* by Carolyn S. Schroeder and Betty N. Gordon. © 1991 by The Guilford Press.

Key

I. MORNING = the time the child gets up until he goes to school, or, if school is out, then from the time the child gets up to lunchtime

1. All chores completed = all three children's chores must be completed or the score is 0. The score is 0 or 3 points.

2. Positive statement = add 1 point for each child who says something positive to another child (e.g., "John, thanks for helping me feed the dogs"). A maximum of 3 points is possible.

3. No time outs (TOs) for fighting. The score is 0 or 3.

II. AFTERNOON = the time the child arrives home from school to dinnertime, or, if there is no school, from lunch to dinnertime

1. All chores completed = same as in the morning.

2. Play a game or do an activity together for 30 minutes without fighting = A point for each positive interaction, up to a maximum of 3 points.

3. No TOs for fighting. The score is 0 or 3 points.

III. EVENING = dinner to bedtime

1. Dinner talk = 1 point for each child who shares a positive interaction with a sibling (e.g., "I had fun playing ball with George today"). A maximum of 3 points is possible.

2. Share a quiet time (e.g., reading or TV) with family without fighting. A point for each child, with a maximum of 3 points.

3. No TOs for fighting. The score is 0 or 3 points.

Points

Total possible points per day	=	27
Total possible points per week	=	189
1st Prize (80–100% of points)	=	151–187
2nd Prize (70–80% of points)	=	132–150
3rd Prize (60–70% of points)	=	114–131

Prize Options

These were selected by parents and children. Each week they must choose the prizes they are working toward and receive the prize by 5:00 p.m. Sunday. The prizes for the week are listed on the front.

1st Prize Options
 Saturday morning breakfast out
 Go to movie
 Family picnic at park
 New game (one of four selected by children)

2nd Prize Options
 Rent video and popcorn
 $2.00 each to spend at video arcade
 Stay up 1 hour later on Saturday night

3rd Prize Options
 Dad rides bikes with them for 30 minutes
 Frozen yogurt
 $1 for Dollar Store

FIGURE 4.1. Sample sibling chart.

2. *Parents.* Mrs. Battle was referred for individual therapy to work through her grief over her mother's death. She also joined the women's group at her church, which involved one night out per week by herself. Mr. and Mrs. Battle agreed to participate in one social activity each week without the children. Finally, Mrs. Battle attended evening parent groups focused on sibling rivalry. These groups reassured her that other families were dealing with similar problems and that her children were not terribly abnormal. She also learned much general information about sibling rivalry and how other parents handled it.

3. *Environment.* The therapist worked with Mrs. Battle to reorganize the family's schedule. The children's bedtime was moved to 8 P.M., and Mr. Battle agreed to come home at 6 P.M. every night to help put the children to bed. Mrs. Battle hired a woman to come in every day at noon and stay until Mr. Battle arrived home. This woman helped with car pooling, child care, and other household jobs. The boys' possessions were divided into those that were private and those that were to be shared. Possessions left out of their respective rooms were automatically shared.

4. *Consequences.* Because Mrs. Battle was afraid the boys would kill each other if she ignored their fighting, she was instructed to use one response for every squabble. This was time-out by isolation for each child involved, regardless of who did what to whom. Negative comments, procrastination in going to time-out, and so on were dealt with by requiring additional time in isolation for that child. A chart system was implemented for the family, wherein the boys had to work together to earn a reward (see Figure 4.1). Points were given for cooperation between the children and accumulated over a week, at the end of which they were exchanged for the reward.

Mrs. Battle was supported in carrying out this program over the next month by one face-to-face interview and weekly telephone contacts. The children initially increased their negative interactions, but Mrs. Battle, with the help of her husband, was able to be consistent in her expectations for their behavior and in providing consequences for their appropriate and inappropriate behaviors. Within a 2-week period, Mrs. Battle reported that the household had calmed down considerably. She realized that in order for things to run smoothly, she would have to continue to provide a high degree of structure and consistency in her interactions with the children.

Chapter 5

Divorce

With the rapid increase in divorce rates over the last 20 years, clinicians and researchers have begun to recognize the significance of this stressful event for the development and adjustment of children. Substantial numbers of children experience parental divorce before they reach age 18; the National Center for Health Statistics (1985) reported that in 1982 alone, parents of 1.1 million children were divorced. Longitudinal studies have clearly documented that most children are negatively affected by their parents' divorce, at least in the short term (Hetherington, Cox, & Cox, 1978; Wallerstein & Kelly, 1980); these children have also been found to be overrepresented among clinic populations (Felner, Stolberg, & Cowen, 1975; Kalter, 1977). Furthermore, the 10-year follow-up study of children of divorce reported by Wallerstein (1985) suggests that many children continue to experience their parents' divorce as a significant influence in their lives well into adulthood.

Not all children, however, experience lasting negative effects as a result of their parents' divorces. Many cope amazingly well with the stresses that occur in the aftermath of divorce, and function extremely competently in all aspects of their lives. Research has thus shifted from focusing on the negative effects of divorce to determining the factors that mediate children's adjustment to the stresses of divorce and play a role in determining which children will adapt and which will continue to evidence problems. This chapter reviews the literature on the effects of divorce, with particular attention to factors that make children more or less vulnerable to negative effects of divorce. A brief discussion of the effects of various custody options is included. Finally, an outline for assessment and treatment for children of divorce is presented.

EFFECTS OF DIVORCE ON CHILDREN

Felner and Terre (1987) suggest that divorce is best viewed as a "transitional event," in that it is not the divorce per se that affects the child and family, but the often prolonged process of change and adaptation that precedes and follows the divorce. Thus the focus for clinicians is on understanding the broader context of the divorce. As Felner and Terre state, "the adaptation process required of family members may extend over a prolonged period during which they are confronted by a complex set of personal and environmental stressors, changes, and 'adaptive tasks'" (Felner & Terre, 1987, p. 110). Furthermore, these factors will interact with the characteristics of the child and family to determine how well each family member adapts.

Rutter's (1983) conceptualization of the cumulative effects of stress on coping and adaptation is applicable to the issues of divorce, because divorce almost inevitably results in multiple stressors for the child and family. This approach indicates that in dealing with a child affected by divorce, the child clinician must understand all the potential sources of stress that have been identified in the research literature and then assess each of these for the individual child and his or her primary caregiver. Some factors, such as the well-documented lower socioeconomic status of women following divorce, have multiple effects and account for much of the difference found in the adjustment of children of divorce versus those from intact families. Lack of adequate financial resources, for example, often leads mothers to return to work; they thus become less available to their children, typically just at the time when the children most need their support. Studies that statistically control for income level differences between children from divorced, single-parent families and those from intact families find that differences in child adjustment are no longer significant (Blum, Boyle, & Offord, 1988; Guidubaldi & Perry, 1985).

Among the other sources of stress that have been identified as being important to children's adjustment following parental divorce are the following: ongoing parental conflict; the child's personality characteristics; parental adjustment, especially adjustment of the custodial parent; contact with the noncustodial parent; remarriage of the custodial parent; age and gender of the child; and quality of parent–child interaction. Research relevant to each of these areas is briefly reviewed.

Parental Conflict

It is now well known that the conflict between marriage partners that precipitates the breakup of the couple often does not end with the divorce. In fact, many families evidence an increase in conflict following separation and divorce; for some parents, this becomes a characteristic of their interaction that may persist with undiminished intensity for years after the divorce is final. Ongoing parental conflict has been clearly demonstrated to have adverse effects on children's adjustment, both among those whose parents have divorced and those whose parents remain married, although the relationship between conflict and adjustment is stronger for boys than for girls (Reid & Crisafulli, 1990). Children in divorced families where there is little conflict after the divorce do not differ in adjustment from children in low-conflict intact families (Felner & Terre, 1987; Forehand, McCombs, Long, Brody, & Fauber, 1988); this indicates that many of the problems evidenced by children following divorce are a result of the circumstances of the divorce rather than the divorce itself. Children's adjustment is influenced by parental conflict prior to the divorce (Kurdek, 1986), as well as conflict that continues after the divorce (Shaw & Emery, 1987).

Long and Forehand (1987) suggest several mechanisms by which parental conflict may influence the adjustment of children: (1) Parental conflict serves as a model for children of an aggressive problem-solving style; (2) parents' abilities to discipline their children may be disrupted by the ongoing conflict, resulting in increased behavior problems in the children; (3) parent conflict may be a source of stress for children, so that as the amount of stress increases, so does the incidence of problems; (4) parents who engage in conflict may be genetically predisposed toward aggressive behavior and may transmit this predisposition to their children; and (5) children may engage in inappropriate behavior in order to distract their parents from the ongoing arguments. It is most likely that all these explanations are true, but that some operate in some families and not in others. Clinicians need to be aware of each, however, in order to understand the dynamics operating in individual families.

A final explanation for the association between parental conflict and child maladjustment is that the child's behavior problems cause the parents' conflict. Although the evidence is stronger for the idea that parental conflict causes child maladjustment, it is likely that a reciprocal relationship exists between the two and that child behavior problems exacerbate parental discord (Long & Forehand, 1987). Indeed, much of the conflict evidenced by divorced couples with children centers around child-related issues such as visitation, custody, discipline, and child support (Hetherington, Cox, & Cox, 1976; Johnston, Campbell, & Mayes, 1985; Johnston, Gonzalez, & Campbell, 1987).

In light of the extensive evidence for the adverse effects of parental conflict on children's adjustment to divorce, Long and Forehand (1987) recommend that parents who are concerned about the potential adverse effects of their separation and divorce on their children be advised to minimize the conflict to which their children are exposed, and to seek professional help if they find themselves unable or unwilling to reduce the amount of conflict.

Parent-Child Relationship

From the child's point of view, the most salient and painful aspect of parental separation is the perceived loss of one beloved parent, usually the father. For many children, this loss is real; various studies have found that between 9% and 14% of noncustodial fathers do not maintain contact with their children after separation and divorce (Kurdek, 1986). In addition, many fathers decrease contact with their children over time, often because of ongoing conflict with their former wives. For the typical child, however, parental separation results in considerably less time spent with the noncustodial parent, and often less time (because of increased stress and other demands) with the custodial parent. Thus the nature of the child's relationship with his or her parents following divorce is a key factor in how the child adjusts to the divorce.

Early work (Jacobson, 1978; Wallerstein & Kelly, 1980) suggested that the extent to which a child had access to the noncustodial parent was related to the child's adjustment. More recently, however, it has become clear that quantity of contact with either the custodial or the noncustodial parent is not as important as quality of the relationship and the context in which the relationship occurs (Hodges, Buchsbaum, & Tierney, 1983; Kanoy, Cunningham, White, & Adams, 1984; Kurdek, 1988). For the noncustodial parent, frequent, regular visits that occur in a conflict-free context, and the visiting parent's freedom from serious psychopathology, appear to be associated with good child adjustment (Felner & Terre, 1987). Conversely, when frequent contact occurs under less than optimal circumstances, the child's adjustment is likely to be compromised.

The child's relationship with the custodial parent is, of course, central to the child's adjustment. A warm, supportive, authoritative parenting style has been shown to promote optimal adjustment in children of divorce as well as in children of intact families (Hetherington, 1989; Hodges et al., 1983). Although the parenting relationship after the separation/divorce is important, research demonstrates that there is considerable continuity in parent–child interaction prior to and following the divorce. In a prospective longitudinal study of family interaction during which some families divorced, Block, Block, and Gjerde (1988) found that ineffective and unsupportive parenting of children existed as long as 11 years before the parents actually divorced and differentiated parents who divorced from those who did not. Thus, some children are exposed to negative parenting practices for long periods of time and it would not be surprising to find that the adjustment of these children was compromised regardless of whether or not their parents eventually divorced.

One factor that will affect the custodial parent's ability to provide appropriate child care and meet the child's needs is the extent to which that parent is able to cope adequately with the stresses of the divorce. Negative changes in the parent–child relationship following divorce are not inevitable, but often result from the parent's changed life circumstance. Felner and Terre (1987) point out several factors that have been found to influence the custodial parent's adjustment. One is the extent to which the divorce is perceived as desirable. Other stresses include decreased financial resources, conflict with the other parent, and the number of children in the family. Custodial parents may become less available to their children both physically and emotionally as they juggle the increased demands of work, single parenting, social life, and so on. It is also not uncommon for parents to experience significant depression following marital separation and divorce, and this is known to have an adverse impact on their ability to parent.

Although it may take several years for caregiving and discipline patterns, and family routines and relationships, to stabilize after the disruption of divorce, longitudinal research indicates that most families reach a new equilibrium within 2 years after the divorce, and that at this time many child behavior problems will decrease (Felner & Terre, 1987). Taken together, the research on parent–child relationships suggests that it is important for clinicians to determine the parenting styles that preceded the divorce, as well as current practices and the current emotional status of the custodial parent. Many children have clearly lived in a negative, aversive atmosphere for many years, while others may be experiencing the deterioration of parenting only in the aftermath of the separation and divorce. Treatment and prognosis for these two types of families will, of course, be quite different.

Personality of the Child

Given the extensive work on the relationship between temperament and the development of behavior problems, it should not be surprising that the personality characteristics of the child have been found to be related to the child's adjustment following divorce. Kurdek (1988) found that characteristics of easy temperament (low rhythmicity and low reactivity) measured 1 year after separation predicted children's adjustment 2 years after separation. He suggests that these children were better able to withstand the disruptions in routine and the many life changes brought about by the divorce. Hetherington (1989), however, argues that the relationship between temperament and adjustment may be more complex. She found that temperament interacted with levels of stress and adjustment in custodial mothers to predict parent–child interaction. When these mothers were emotionally stable and under low levels of stress, there was no difference in their reactions to temperamentally easy versus difficult children. Under conditions of high stress and/or when mothers had significant emotional problems, they interacted more negatively with difficult children. For difficult children, a linear relationship was found between stress and coping: The more stress, the less adequate coping. For easy children, the relationship was curvilinear, so that moderate amounts of stress promoted better coping than small or large amounts of stress.

Although temperament characteristics are thought to be in part genetically determined and to have some stability over time, there is evidence that the behavior of parents in the years prior to the separation may shape the personality development of their children. Block, Block, and Gjerde (1986) found that among boys whose parents later divorced, evidence of undercontrolled behavior (irritability, high activity, impulsivity, aggression) was present years before the parents separated. Thus the negative reactions and behaviors often seen in children (especially boys) after the divorce appear to have their origins in the predivorce period and are probably related to the negative parenting behaviors that have been documented during this period.

When the custodial mother remarries, an entirely new set of relationships is added to the family. Hetherington (1989) found that for the first 2 years after remarriage, both boys and girls had difficulties adjusting, but that after 2 years boys appeared to adapt well (and appeared better adjusted than boys whose mother's had not remarried), whereas girls continued to have difficulties accepting their stepfathers. Furthermore, in contrast to intact families, a close marital relationship between mothers and stepfathers and active involvement in parenting on the part of stepfathers were associated with increased parent–child conflict, especially between girls and their stepfathers. Hetherington (1989) concludes that it can be extremely difficult for stepfathers to integrate themselves into families with preadolescent girls. The best strategy for a stepfather may be initially to make no attempt to control the child's behavior, but rather to establish a good relationship with the child and support the mother in her discipline. Later, the stepfather should adopt an authoritative parenting style.

Sex Differences

On the basis of considerable research, it is commonly believed that boys are more vulnerable than girls to the negative effects of divorce, and that they are more likely to react with externalized or undercontrolled behavior (aggression, negative behavior, temper tantrums, etc.). However, there is substantial inconsistency in the research literature regarding this issue, with some recent studies reporting significant differences in adjustment between boys and girls (e.g., Hetherington, Cox, & Cox, 1985) and others reporting no differences (Allison & Furstenberg, 1989; Johnston et al., 1987). Felner and Terre (1987) for example, suggest that gender may be more closely related to the *pattern* of response to divorce than to the *severity* of the reaction. They argue that boys and girls are socialized differently, and that as a result they develop different coping styles and abilities that may lead to the appearance of differential effects of divorce on their adjustment. There is certainly evidence for differences in parents' interaction with sons versus daughters in intact families, and considerable evidence for more negative interaction of custodial single mothers with their sons than with their daughters (Hetherington, 1989).

The inconsistencies in findings of differential effects of divorce for boys versus girls appear to result from methodological factors and a failure to allow for the complexity of the divorce process (different custody and visitation arrangements, remarriage) (Zaslow, 1988, 1989). Zaslow (1988, 1989) accounted for these factors in a review of the research and concluded that there is evidence for boys' being more vulnerable to adverse effects of divorce than girls when they are in the custody of their mothers and when the mothers have not remarried. These adverse effects have been shown to persist as long as 6 years after the divorce (Hetherington et al., 1985). The adjustment of boys appears to improve when their mothers remarry, whereas the adjustment of girls worsens under these conditions (Hetherington et al., 1985). There is also evidence that older girls have more problems related to dating and heterosexual relationships than do boys (Zaslow, 1989).

Taking a developmental approach, Kalter, Riemer, Brickman, and Chen (1985) argue that these differential reactions to divorce are not surprising when one considers the role of fathers in the development of sons and daughters. Whereas fathers provide important models for boys throughout early development and buffer their relationship with their mothers, they are particularly important for girls just prior to and during adolescence in terms of developing a sense of sexual identity and self-worth, as well as positive attitudes toward men and marriage. The addition of a stepfather to a family may imperil the close relationship between a daughter and her mother and threaten the daughter's sense of independence, whereas it provides a son with a substitute for the missing role model (Hetherington, 1989).

Age Differences

Psychoanalytic theory and the idea of "critical periods" in development have often led writers on the subject to suggest children may be more vulnerable at certain ages to the adverse effects of divorce than at others. Specifically, preschool children and adolescents are thought to be at higher risk for problems than school-age children (Wallerstein & Kelly, 1980). The evidence for this is inconsistent, however, with some studies finding age differences in adjustment (although not always the same ages) and others none.

Felner and Terre (1987) argue, much as they do with regard to the relationship between a child's gender and postdivorce adjustment, that the age of the child at the time of the divorce may have more to do with the *pattern* of response to divorce (particularly as it relates to the coping strategies available to and utilized by the child) than with the *severity* of problems manifested by the child. There has been little research on the different coping strategies used by children of divorce at different ages. Kurdek and Sinclair (1988) found that adolescents who tended to use externalizing coping strategies (ventilating feelings, using drugs or alcohol, or smoking) were less well adjusted than those who used outside support strategies (talking with friends, clergy, or professionals). Johnston et al. (1985) examined how children coped with their divorced parents' disputes and found that younger children (ages 6–8) tried to control the fight by actively intervening or trying to distract their parents. These younger children were also likely simply not to cope; they displayed a variety of symptoms of acute distress, including hyperventilating, stomachaches, headaches, crying, asthma attacks, and so on. On the other hand, older children (ages 9–12) were more likely to take a strong stand in the fight or to take the side of one parent or the other. Two-thirds of the children at both ages coped by avoiding the argument (blocking eyes and ears, retreating to their rooms, disappearing, etc.). Avoidance was judged to be the most adaptive response. In contrast to these results, avoidance as a style of coping with parental divorce (as opposed to parental conflict) was found to be related to poorer adjustment, whereas active cognitive responses (changing the way one feels about something) and active behavioral responses (doing something about the problem) were associated with good adjustment in a study of adolescent girls ages 12–16 (Armistead et al., 1990).

Other work has examined children's understanding of divorce and, not surprisingly, has found age-related differences. McGurk and Glachan (1987), for example, found that children ages 4–6 from intact families were more likely to insist that both their parents would remain parents after a divorce, regardless of which parent a child lived with or whether the parents remarried; children from divorced families were more likely to believe that parenting was not continuous after divorce, but was contingent on whether the parents lived with the child, remarried, or continued to love the child. In contrast, older children in both groups clearly differentiated marital from parental relationships (i.e., spouses can be divorced but children cannot) and biological from caregiving parental relationships (i.e., parents remain parents even if they have little or no contact with the child). These results imply that older children may be able to cope better with parental divorce because of their greater understanding of the inviolate nature of parenthood.

Custody and Visitation

Determining custody and visitation arrangements for divorcing families can be one of the most stressful aspects of clinical work with these families. The basis on which custody has been determined has varied enormously over the years, depending on the cultural and societal values and attitudes in existence at a given time. Wyer, Gaylord, and Grove (1987) provide an excellent summary of the legal context of child custody decisions. At first, custody was determined solely on the basis of the sex of the parent: Fathers had absolute rights over their children, who were viewed as property. In the late 19th and early 20th centuries, the emphasis shifted to consideration of the "best interests of the child," and a presumption in favor of mothers was established. Awarding custody of children to their mothers was based on the "tender years" doctrine, which assumes that the mother is the appropriate custodian for young children and for girls of any age. Adolescent boys were often awarded to their fathers. Currently, the emphasis in determining custody continues to be on the best interests of the child, but with less importance given to the "tender years" doctrine and without a presumption for either parent. Unfortunately, most states do not provide adequate guidelines for determining the best interests of the child, leaving considerable discretion in the hands of judges. The Uniform Marriage and Divorce Act (cited in Wyer et al., 1987) states that the following should be considered in determining the best interests of the child:

1. the wishes of the child's parent or parents as to his custody;
2. the wishes of the child as to his custodian;

3. the interaction and interrelationship of the child with his parent or parents, his siblings, and any other person who may significantly affect the child's best interest;
4. the child's adjustment to his home, school, and community; and
5. the mental and physical health of all individuals involved. The court shall not consider conduct of a proposed custodian that does not affect this relationship to the child. (Wyer et al., 1987, p. 10)

More specifically, Rohman, Sales, and Lou (1987) suggest that the child's physical, emotional, and developmental needs be specified, and that the court attempt to satisfy those needs in determining custody. Weithorn and Grisso (1987) argue that many factors should be considered in determining custody. These include (1) child factors (age, sex, physical and psychological functioning, individual needs, and preferences regarding custody); (2) parent factors (age, sex, physical and psychological functioning, and history of meeting and current capacity to meet the child's needs); (3) environmental factors (characteristics of the environment and resources offered by each parent); and (4) relationship factors (relationships of the child with each parent and other important persons, such as siblings, grandparents, etc.).

There is clearly a role for the child clinician in providing information to the court concerning these areas and the specific needs of the individual child. However, a lengthy discussion of the methods of conducting custody evaluations is beyond the scope of this chapter. The reader is referred to Gardner (1982) for a "cookbook" approach to child custody evaluations, and to Weithorn (1987) for consideration of the relevant ethical and professional issues.

From the child's point of view, legal custody is far less important than physical custody (or the person with whom the child lives) and visitation arrangements. Increasingly, parents and the legal community are considering joint legal and physical custody as viable and even desirable options for divorcing families. Proponents of joint physical custody argue that this arrangement most closely resembles an intact family, fosters a continued relationship between the child and both parents, eliminates acrimonious custody disputes, and meets the parents' needs by alleviating one parent's feeling of being overburdened and the other's sense of loss (Felner & Terre, 1987). On the other hand, opponents of joint physical custody contend that this arrangement forces parents to continue to interact and may actually exacerbate conflict. Furthermore, joint physical custody usually involves complex child care arrangements and frequent disruptions in the continuity of care, especially if the parents live some distance apart, and this may be very stressful for the child. Finally, the child may be prevented from forming and maintaining a close attachment based on day-to-day ongoing care by one parent (Felner & Terre, 1987).

Research examining the influence of mother custody versus father custody versus joint custody has clearly demonstrated that no arrangement has inherent benefits over another (Fidler & Saunders, 1988; Kline, Tschann, Johnston, & Wallerstein, 1989). Steinman (1981) reported that while parents were generally satisfied with joint physical custody arrangements, children were significantly less positive. They expressed confusion, anxiety, fears, and feelings of being overburdened concerning their schedules and living arrangements. This was particularly true for younger children; adolescents felt that joint physical custody simply did not meet their needs. It is also important to note that most (if not all) of the studies of joint physical custody have involved families who have chosen this arrangement and are committed to making it work. Thus these parents represent a very different population from parents with sole custody arrangements. As Felner and Terre (1987) conclude, "no particular custody arrangement is 'best.' Arguments in favor of a presumption of one form over another are ill suited to the realities of family life and child development" (p. 140). They further state that "joint custody, under the most favorable of conditions, does not emerge as clearly superior to sole custody" (p. 140).

ASSESSMENT

As a whole, the research on children's adjustment to divorce provides useful guidelines for clinicians, but indicates clearly that the circumstances and needs of individual children and families must be carefully assessed in order to provide appropriate advice and treatment. Divorce is inevitably a difficult and painful process for children no matter what their age, and parents can expect a period of adjustment lasting up to 2 years after the divorce. Nonetheless, several factors stand out as being centrally related to children's ability to adapt:

Low parental conflict
Warm, supportive, consistent relationship with both parents
Authoritative parenting style (custodial parent)
Good adjustment and coping (custodial parent)
Low levels of life stress
Few changes in daily routines
Use of active coping strategies (child)
Easy temperamental characteristics (child)

The assessment process outlined below sets the stage for intervention and is not designed for determining custody in the legal sense. However, careful attention to the assessment process and the information gathered therein can provide the clinician with the tools necessary to help parents make good decisions regarding their children's well-being.

Step 1: Initial Contact

To keep the focus on the best interests of the child(ren), it is important to include both parents in the initial interview. It gives each parent the opportunity to share his or her views and concerns, and the clinician can more readily clarify the appropriate focus of the clinical contact. Furthermore, neither parent is seen as having "an advantage" with the clinician, and the final recommendations are more likely to be seen as impartial. The parent who calls for the initial interview often wants to give the clinician his or her view of the problem on the telephone or initially see the clinician alone. Thus, the clinician must clarify quickly how he or she proceeds with issues of separation or divorce, and what services he or she can offer (e.g., setting the stage for telling the children of an impending separation, providing information on children's reactions to separation, assisting in the determination of living arrangements, providing treatment for families and children of separated or divorced families, and/or doing custody evaluations for the court). For example, if parents want a custody evaluation for the court and a clinician does not offer this service, the parents should immediately be referred to someone who does this work.

Sending each parent a general questionnaire (e.g., our Parent Questionnaire; see Appendix B) that provides demographic information, as well as information on their reasons for seeking help and their perceptions of the problem, gives the clinician important data for the initial interview. In addition, having each parent complete for each child the Child Behavior Checklist (CBCL; Achenbach & Edelbrock, 1983), the Eyberg Child Behavior Inventory (ECBI; Eyberg & Robinson, 1978), and the Parenting Stress Index (PSI; Abidin, 1990) will give a wealth of information on each child's overall emotional and behavioral status, involvement in activities, temperament, and compliance to daily routines, as well as the parents' stress level. Fathers and mothers do not always have the same view of their children's behavior, and in the case of a separation, this information is especially important as a starting point in assessing each parent's relationship with each of the children.

Reviewing these questionnaires prior to the initial interview gives the clinician information on the potential problems or issues for the family. We have the found that parents are increasingly seeking guidance prior to separation; this is ideal, because it allows the clinician to provide information and guidance that has the potential to decrease greatly both the immediate and long-term adverse effects of the separation and divorce on the children.

Step 2: Parent and Child Interview

Parent Interview

The setting for the interview with the parents is important and should allow the parents to sit apart from each other. Because the clinician has already gathered a lot of information from both parents, it is good to begin the interview with a summary of the clinician's understanding of the reason for the session and to ask each parent to clarify this information, as well as what they hope to receive from the contact. The clinician should also let the parents know what he or she feels can be accomplished in the first session. Any conflict in regard to these points can be dealt with immediately. After hearing the concerns of each parent, it is important to gather information about the following areas:

1. Living arrangements. Where is each parent currently living? How is the children's time spent with each parent? How is this working? Are there plans to change the living arrangements? If so, when will these changes occur? These issues can be sources of conflict between the parents, and getting their views on what they want and why they think a particular arrangement is or is not appropriate is important. It also enables the clinician to determine whether the focus is primarily on the children's needs or on those of the parents.

2. Reasons for the separation. The reasons and events leading up to the decision to separate are very important in determining the past, current, and potential future level of conflict. Each parent's view of these events and reaction to them will give information on the emotional atmosphere surrounding the separation, as well as on how each parent is likely to share this information with the children.

3. What do the children know? What the children know or have been explicitly told about the separation is crucial to understanding how they are adjusting or will adjust. Parents sometimes think that a child does not have any idea that a separation is being considered, and others who are already separated have never given a full explanation because they feel the child "already knows" or would not understand. If there is more than one child in the family, have the parents shared information with some of them and not others?

4. Who knows about the separation? The people whom the parents have told about the separation, and the reactions of these people, are important in terms of the support the parents feel they have for making this decision. These people, in turn, will have an influence on a child's perception of the separation. Will the child be able to turn to them for support? Is there a chance that the child will lose contact with particular extended family members?

5. Lawyers. It is helpful to know how far the parents have gone in the legal process and who their lawyers are. This may have a direct bearing on the current and future level of conflict.

6. Financial arrangements. The current financial resources of the family, and the ways in which these will be divided or changed, are crucial to understanding children's adjustment to separation and divorce; financial arrangements are often a significant source of stress and conflict for divorced parents, and such conflict usually affects the children as well. The clinician should determine whether a child will have to change schools (e.g., from private to public) or decrease activities because of the changing financial situation. It is also important to know whether one or both parents are using or have used the issue of child custody or visitation as a threat or bargaining factor in determining property settlement, alimony, or child support.

7. Conflict between parents. On the basis of the parents' interaction in the interview, the clinician should be able to make some judgment about their level of conflict and the ways in which they are handling this with the children. Finding out when and how they talk about their own personal issues will shed light on the extent to which the children are exposed to parental conflict and the effects of the conflict on them. The PSI gives information on the level of stress each parent is experiencing; further exploration of this information is best left to a future individual session with each parent.

8. Perception of children's adjustment. The parents should be asked how they think their children are adjusting to the separation and/or what problems they perceive in their adjustment. They should also be asked what they think would help the children adjust better to the realities of the separation. Do they feel that their interactions with their child(ren) have changed since the separation or divorce? Again, gathering specific information on the parent–child relationships, the child(ren)'s daily routines, parenting styles, and discipline techniques is usually best left to future interviews with both or each parent.

Child Interview

The child (or children) is almost always seen in a separate session from the parents, although the interview should begin with the child and one or both parents present to clarify the reason for the contact and the ways in which the information gathered from the child will or will not be used. The child should be assured of confidentiality. If information is to be shared, the child is informed that he or she will first be told what, why, and with whom something will be shared. To this end it is best *not* to talk to parents immediately after seeing a child; rather, they should be seen at a separate time, or concerns should be discussed by telephone. It is often very hard for parents who are separated or divorced to wait to talk to the clinician, because they are usually very concerned about the information shared by their child(ren). Furthermore, the child should be told that he or she has a choice about sharing information from the sessions with the parents and that the child also has permission *not* to talk about the sessions. Saying these things to the child in the presence of the parents is important, because children of separated parents often feel pulled between the parents, and parents have been known to pressure children to divulge the content of their sessions with the clinician in order to gain "ammunition" to use against the other parent.

The child should be told the clinician's general understanding of the family situation. It is also important to let the child know that the clinician has seen other children whose parents are separated and knows that this can be a difficult time for everyone. As in other child interviews, the child should be told what to expect in the session (e.g., "Today I would like to hear about your school, your dance classes, and what you like to do. I'm also going to ask you to answer some questions which will help me better understand your likes, dislikes, and feelings about things. We should also have time to play a game, if you like"). For preschool children, the focus will be more on gathering information through play or drawing activities, but it is equally important to let them know what to expect. Specific information gathered during this session includes the child's general level of coping; his or her perception of why the parents separated; the child's understanding of what is happening or going to happen with regard to living arrangements; the child's perception of the living arrangements; and his or her worries or concerns about the separation and/or its effects on his or her life.

Step 3: Observation of Behavior

Direct observation of each parent's interaction with each child (and, if there is more than one child, with all the children together) is very important for answering specific questions about the best living arrangements or for understanding a parent and child's relationship. See Chapter 3 for more information on techniques to do this. A home visit is often an important and necessary way to gather data about the child's environment and family interactions. Specific focus should be on parent–child communication: For example, does the parent attend or listen to the child? How is information shared with the child? What kind of feedback is given to the child? And, likewise, how does the child interact with and respond to the parent? The clinician should also determine whether current interactions are similar to those prior to the separation.

Step 4: Further Assessment

In-depth assessment will depend on the nature of the questions being asked and the presenting problems or associated problems of the child(ren) or parents. This could involve formal psychoeducational assessment and/or further assessment of a child's emotional and social status. Problems present prior to the separation are certain to be exacerbated with the stress of separation, and further assessment of these problems is warranted.

The assessment process for questions surrounding separation or divorce usually involves at least one individual session with each parent and several sessions with the child(ren) in question. The parents' interviews should focus on their emotional status, social support network, stressors, and parenting ability.

Step 5: Referral to Allied Health Professionals

Parents who are having significant psychological problems or who are having significant problems with the separation or divorce should be referred to an appropriate professional. If the parents are having difficulty resolving their conflict, they should be referred for joint counseling sessions or for divorce mediation sessions. Most schools offer divorce groups for children, and these can be very supportive to the child(ren).

Step 6: Communication of Findings and Treatment Recommendations

Findings and recommendations should be communicated to both parents at the same time. Information about children's adjustment to divorce, and especially the effects of ongoing parental conflict and the quality of the child's relationship with both parents, should be shared with parents. This information provides a basis for ensuring the cooperation of both parents with the proposed treatment plan. If lawyers are involved, they should be given the information at the same time, with or without the parents' being present. Enough time should be allowed to answer parents' questions, and they should be given an opportunity to meet individually with the clinician after a joint feedback conference.

TREATMENT

The breakup of a family is always difficult, and the task of the child clinician is to help parents and children deal effectively with this painful process. In many ways, helping children deal with a divorce is like helping them deal with death (see Chapter 6), and as with death, there is an inevitable grieving process that must culminate in accepting the situation and learning to live with the life changes. This work is often preventive in nature; it involves offering information and advice on the factors affecting adjustment, as well as helping parents and children develop the skills necessary to cope with the changes in their lives. Groups for children and parents on separation and divorce appear to be a good way to help them deal with the feelings and problems associated with this event.

Given the individuality of each family's situation and needs, the focus of treatment will vary from family to family. Various intervention strategies are discussed here in the context of the Comprehensive Assessment-to-Intervention System (CAIS; see Chapter 3).

Intervention in Development

A primary intervention strategy for children of divorced parents is to provide honest information about the separation and divorce that is appropriate to the children's developmental level. Although the age and ability level of a child, as well as the family circumstances, will determine the specifics of this information, some general principles cut across all ages and circumstances. If possible, each child should be told by both parents a few days before the actual separation occurs. This allows the child to work through some feelings and reactions before the actual separation takes place. Preschool children are not able to appreciate future events as well as older children, so they are more likely to understand what is happening only after the separation actually occurs. Having both parents tell the child communicates the fact that this is a joint decision. Moreover, it decreases the likelihood that the child will take sides, and lets the child know that both parents will continue to be available after the separation (if this is true). Parents are going to be understandably upset during this time; although their emotional reactions should not detract from the specific information shared, they should be honest about their feelings. The expression of emotions (even crying) can facilitate the child's expression of his or her own feelings. The expression of rage or uncontrolled anger by parents is not helpful, however, as it makes it more difficult for the child to feel free to express his or her feelings of sadness or anger.

Children have wonderful imaginations, and their fantasies can often be more frightening than the truth about the separation. It is important for them to know the causes for the separation, so that they can deal with the facts yet continue to trust the parents. The details of the causes of the separation do not have to be shared, because children are likely to obsess over details, but the major causes should be addressed. For example, if the father is in love with another woman this should be stated, but giving the details of the relationship (when they met or why he loves her) is not needed or helpful. Children can cope with honesty and truth, but secrets are not manageable. Specifically telling children that nothing they did, said, or thought had anything to do with the separation is important, because a common response of children is to assume that it is their fault. Similarly, they need reassurance that they will have a home, will be cared for, and will be loved. It is also helpful for a child to know that the parents have told or will tell significant people in the child's life (e.g., relatives, neighbors, and teachers) about the separation. This relieves the child of the burden of telling these people and allows the child to seek support from them.

Children need to know specifically what is going to happen in the days immediately following the separation, what their living situation will be, when they will see both parents, and what will be expected of them. Even if there is some uncertainty about these arrangements, what is known should be shared with the children. The children should be told that these are things that the parents will take care of and share as soon as decisions have been made. Being able to ask questions as often as necessary, and to get specific information, is an important way for children to begin to cope with this major disruption in their lives. Honest answers from the parents allow each child to begin to trust that the parents will look after the child's needs and continue to care for him or her.

It is often hard for children to understand that other families or children have felt the way they do, or to believe that they will ever be happy again. Thus, the opportunity to talk with other children whose parents have separated, or to hear that other children have experienced separation, allows them to begin thinking creatively about their own situation and ways in which they can help themselves. Therapeutic groups in schools, which allow children to identify with peers, have become a popular way to help mitigate the behavioral and emotional problems that are the sequelae of separation or divorce. There is some empirical support for the effectiveness of group intervention programs in schools for children in second to sixth grades (Alpert-Gillis, Pedro-Carroll, & Cowen, 1989; Pedro-Carroll & Cowen, 1985; Pedro-Carroll, Cowen, Hightower, & Guare, 1986). Pedro-Carroll et al.'s groups emphasized a supportive environment to help children identify and express divorce-related feelings, clarify divorce-related concepts and misconceptions, develop relevant coping skills, and promote positive perceptions of self and family. Although all of the groups had 16 sessions, the groups that met once a week over a period of 4 months proved to be more effective than those that met twice a week for 2 months.

King and Kleemeier (1983) suggest a similiar focus for individual treatment, with an emphasis on providing a safe and supportive environment for the child to grieve openly, express fears, feel free to express rage and anger at both parents, and then begin learning skills to cope with the situation. Bibliotherapy is another widely used intervention strategy; there are many books that identify divorce-related feelings, issues, and coping skills for children. Books can be used in a preventive way by parents to explain divorce to their children, or as resources for treatment. Appendix C includes a list of books for parents and children about divorce.

Intervention with Parents

The role of the child clinician is to be an advocate for the child(ren). It is important that the clinician not be viewed as "taking sides" between parents, but rather as a person who shares information and advice related to the best interests of a child. Parents need information about the effects of separation and divorce on children, as well as help in determining how best to minimize the negative effects. Although parents can be supported in their own feelings about the separation, they must also be helped to understand what their child(ren) will need in order to adjust to the situation. Most important, although a child may have been exposed to parental conflict before the separation, it is important for the parents to understand the deleterious effects of continued conflict and the need to insulate the child from this conflict. This often involves great control and self-sacrifice on the part of parents, and they will need support to behave appropriately. Parents may need individual treatment to accomplish this.

Each parent will have to be responsible for his or her own relationship with each child. Even if one parent cannot support the child's relationship with the other parent, he or she should not criticize or condemn that parent; to do so only places the child in a conflicted situation. Similarly, a parent does not have to defend or excuse the parent who is unreliable or irresponsible. Rather, the child should be helped to express his or her angry or hurt feelings.

Parents often must be encouraged to establish new social support systems that enable them to meet their own personal needs. Children should not be responsible for taking care of parents, and parents should be helped to separate their own needs from those of the children.

Parents often find that supportive groups can be a therapeutic way to share feelings and concerns, and to begin to cope with the realities of their situation. Cebollero, Cruise, and Stollak (1986) have described concurrent groups for mothers and children experiencing the long-term negative effects of divorce. Although the report was descriptive rather than empirical, the parents indicated that the groups were very supportive and gave them new problem-solving skills; in addition, serving as cotherapists for the children's group gave them a better view of the divorce from their children's perspective.

Bibliotherapy is also very useful for parents as an adjunct to treatment for problems related to divorce. A number of excellent books give helpful information on living arrangements, strategies for resolving conflicts, and so on. A list of books for parents is included in Appendix C.

Intervention in the Environment

Familiar surroundings can help a child utilize established social support systems to begin coping with the separation (King & Kleemeier, 1983). Thus, if at all possible, the added stress of changing homes, schools, neighborhoods, caregivers, and so on should be avoided. Likewise, daily routines, activities, chores, and expectations should be kept as normal as possible. This allows the child to learn what parts of life will remain the same and what parts will be different.

Visitation schedules and living arrangements should take into account a child's developmental level and needs for stability, as well as the child's relationship with both parents. Preschool children need environmental stability because of the challenges of developing independence and a sense of mastery and control; school-age children need stability because they are moving out into the world and experiencing the stress of meeting new social and academic challenges. Although shared living arrangements are becoming more common and appear to meet the needs of the parents, these shared arrangements can be confusing and stressful for children. Each family situation is unique, and a careful review of how a particular arrangement will meet a child's needs apart from those of the parents is an important part of the treatment process.

Introducing significant new people in the parent's lives to the children is usually an inevitable part of the divorce process. Young children often resent sharing the time they spend with a parent; or, if they like the new person, they may feel that they are being disloyal to the other parent. For these reasons, it is often best to allow the child to establish a relationship alone with each parent before including new people in shared activities. It is, however, important for the children to understand that their parents have lives separate from them.

Changing the Consequences of the Behavior

An emotionally supportive environment with clearly established rules sets the stage for children to become increasingly competent and independent. It is thus important for parents to maintain expectations for each child's behavior and to continue to set limits for inappropriate behavior. Changing the expectations and consequences for appropriate and inappropriate behavior when the family is itself changing can create feelings of insecurity among children and decrease their ability to cope effectively with the situation. Children are likely to express a lot of their concerns and worries through inappropriate behavior or emotional lability. Thus, it is important for parents to acknowledge a child's feelings as they put limits on the behavior ("I know that you want to help me, but, as the parent, I am the one who will discipline your younger brother," or "I can understand that you might be angry with Mom for being late, but you may not hit your brother").

Intervention in Medical/Health Problems

Children whose parents are separating may have increased psychosomatic complaints; they may state, for example, that they don't feel well enough to go to school or that they want to sleep with Mom or Dad. Although it is important to have a physician attend to these physical complaints, it is often the case that such children are worried or upset about what is happening in the family. These complaints will usually decrease if the children are helped to identify and communicate openly about their feelings and anxieties.

─────────────── *CASE EXAMPLE* ───────────────

Step 1: Initial Contact

Mr. May, a city councilman and town businessman, requested an interview to discuss the current living arrangements of his 10-year-old daughter, Sarah. He stated that he was concerned that his former wife's emotional instability was having negative effects on Sarah, and that indeed the department of social services had investigated the mother on charges of neglect (instigated by Sarah's school). Sarah had been living with her mother since the parents had separated, 10 months earlier. In clarifying the referral question ("What is the best living arrangement for Sarah?"), the clinician indicated that the mother should be involved in this process, and that if at all possible she should be present at the initial interview. The father agreed to tell the mother of his contact with the clinician and to request her attendance at the interview.

When the father called back to confirm that the mother would be coming, the Parent Questionnaire, the ECBI, and the CBCL were sent to both parents. The responses to the ECBI and CBCL indicated that both parents perceived Sarah as a rather withdrawn and quiet child who was experiencing high levels of anxiety. The Parent Questionnaire responses indicated that legal custody had not yet been finalized and that neither parent had consulted a lawyer. Ms. May was concerned that Sarah, as an only child, was "overly close" to her and worried too much about her mother's well-being. Mr. May felt that Sarah's problems centered around the mother, who was depressed and an alcoholic. He also indicated that the mother used Sarah's visits with him as a weapon to vent her anger toward him. Sarah was living primarily with her mother; although there was no visitation schedule with the father, he saw her approximately every other weekend. He was currently living with another woman, who had joint physical custody of her two boys, ages 6 and 9.

Step 2: Parent and Child Interview

Parent Interview

The parents came separately to the session, and it was apparent in the waiting room that there was a great deal of tension and hostility between them. The father rarely made eye contact with the mother, and the mother talked about her husband as though he were not present. Mr. May stated that he had left the marriage because his wife's drinking had destroyed their relationship. He clearly stated that his current relationship with another woman had begun several months *after* he had left the home. Ms. May indicated that she was very angry at her husband for leaving her and that this anger was exacerbated when he moved in with another woman. She felt that given his work schedule with evening appointments and weekend work, he had never been available to her as a husband or to Sarah as a father. The fact that he was now willing to take time off for Sarah's school functions and to spend time with her made Ms. May even angrier, although she fully acknowledged the benefits of this relationship for Sarah. She described Sarah as a very loving and caring child and felt that perhaps she herself sometimes relied "too much" upon Sarah. Ms. May added that she had been under a great deal of stress, was seeing a psychiatrist, was on medication for depression, and was also having trouble controlling her drinking. She noted that she was herself the daughter of an alcoholic and that life had always been difficult for her. She was angry at Sarah's teacher for reporting her to the department of social services, and felt that she had done nothing wrong in allowing Sarah to stay home from school for a few "mental health" days.

Mr. May readily admitted to being out of the home a great deal prior to the separation and "not being the father he should have been" to Sarah when he and his wife were living together. He stated that he had come to realize how important appropriate parenting was through observation of the woman he currently lived with. He stated that his greatest fear was that the court would take Sarah away from both him and Ms. May. Mr. May described himself as a rather serious and intense person, who up to this point had been reluctant to share his feelings or give emotional support to people for whom he cared. He stated that he was aware of needing specific help on how best to interact with Sarah. Although money was not plentiful, finances were not a major point of dispute between Mr. and Ms. May. Mr. May stated that he was interested in doing what was best for Sarah and that it was not his intention to "take Sarah away" from the mother. Ms. May concurred with a desire to do whatever would be in Sarah's best interests. Neither parent had specifically asked for a custody evaluation from the courts, but the clinician had informed the father at the initial contact that she did not do such evaluations. When the clinician restated this restriction in her services, both parents indicated that they were not asking for a custody evaluation, but rather recommendations about the best living situation for Sarah at this time. They fully understood that living arrangements were ultimately their decision, but that the clinician would offer them some recommendations.

Sarah's daily routines included school, ballet lessons once a week, and close relationships with paternal and maternal grandparents. Both parents saw Sarah as easy-going and almost too adaptable to their needs. She had been told that her father was leaving the home, but no other explanation by either parent had been given to her, nor had she asked for further information.

Child Interview

The father and mother came with Sarah for her initial interview. With all three present, the clinician reviewed the purpose of the visit, assured Sarah of confidentiality, and briefly talked about the reasons for the separation and the mother's seeking help for her depression and alcoholism. The father further acknowledged that he had not always been available to Sarah or her mother when he lived with them. Sarah was told that the clinician would be meeting with Sarah, her parents, and the woman who was living with the father several times over the next month in order to determine what Sarah needed and to help the parents meet her needs.

The purpose of this first interview was to develop a relationship with Sarah and to help her feel comfortable about talking about her parents' separation. Given the parents' description of Sarah as quiet and withdrawn, a structured game that allowed for expression of feelings was played with Sarah. This game is called "The Talking, Feeling, Doing Game" and is available from Creative Therapeutics, 155 County Road, Cresskill, N.J. 07626. Sarah was initially reticent in expressing her likes, dislikes, and coping strategies for problematic situations, but she soon relaxed. After the game, Sarah was told that the clinician had talked with many children whose parents had separated, and that she could understand that Sarah might have questions or concerns about many things concerning the separation.

Step 3: Observation of Behavior

Each parent was observed interacting with Sarah while playing a game and planning a trip. Sarah tended to follow the mother's lead and readily agreed to all of her suggestions. The father tended to follow Sarah's lead and encouraged her to make suggestions. Sarah seemed to enjoy being with both parents, who were physically affectionate with her.

Step 4: Further Assessment

With the parents' permission, questionnaires were sent to Sarah's teacher, and phone contact was made with the teacher and the department of social services. The teacher described Sarah as a well-liked child who, however, was very quiet and not performing to her potential academically. Sarah had missed 13 days of school in the last grading period and was late for school about 50% of the time. The teacher's contacts with the mother had not changed this pattern, and the teacher had decided to call the department of social services when Sarah cried one morning, saying she was worried because her mother had passed out from drinking and had not yet recovered when she left for school. Representatives of the department indicated that although they did not want to remove Sarah from the mother's custody, they had insisted that the mother get into a program for alcohol abuse. They were monitoring the situation closely and were pleased to hear the parents had sought help for Sarah.

Step 5: Referral to Allied Health Professionals

Sarah was referred to the divorce group for children at her school. Ms. May was already receiving appropriate help for her problems.

Step 6: Communication of Findings and Treatment Recommendations

The findings and recommendations were given simultaneously to both parents. Sarah was described as an easy-going, loving child who was very confused about the current family situation and very worried about her mother's emotional and physical well-being; she felt that if she did not stay with her mother all the time, something terrible would happen to her mother. Although Sarah enjoyed being with her father, this made her feel disloyal to her mother. At this point, she was not able to freely express her feelings (in fact, she could not even fully identify them). The clinician felt that Sarah was desperately in need of a united front on the part of the parents; a living arrangement that provided her with consistent care; and emotional support from, and regular contact with, both parents.

Although the goal might ultimately be for Sarah to move easily between her parents, at the current time it was recommended that Sarah live with her father and visit her mother regularly. The purpose of this would be not only to provide Sarah with stability, but also to give the mother an opportunity to engage in and benefit from her treatment. This arrangement would allow Sarah to see that her mother would indeed be able to take care of herself. Ms. May agreed to this arrangement almost with relief and suggested that seeing Sarah two afternoons a week until 8 P.M. would be the best visiting schedule. It was also decided that the mother would call three times a week on set days, but that Sarah would not be told when the mother would be calling. This was to avoid Sarah's worrying about her mother if she did not call. The parents agreed for Sarah to begin treatment with a focus on identifying feelings, learning to express them, and developing coping skills. The mother agreed that the clinician could keep in regular contact with her therapist and the department of social services. The father agreed to attend an evening parent group focusing on developmental issues in the elementary school years and parenting techniques.

Chapter 6

Death

One of the most stressful life events faced by children is the death of a loved family member or their own impending death from a life-threatening illness. Death is not an uncommon problem for young children and their families, with approximately 4% of children in the United States losing a parent before they reach age 18 (U.S. Bureau of the Census, 1985). Furthermore, as survival rates for children with life-threatening illnesses improve, many young children must deal with the possibility of their own deaths, and at the same time must live with tremendous uncertainty as they undergo stressful medical treatment for their illnesses.

Understandably, parents (and many professionals) have great difficulty knowing what to say to children about death, how to help them deal with the aftermath of a death in the family, or how to help them cope with life-threatening illnesses. Efforts to help children deal with death have been influenced by the widely held assumption that children cannot fully comprehend the concept of death, and that even if they do, it may be harmful for them to be exposed to information about death (Kastenbaum & Costa, 1977). Consequently, professionals and parents have felt it best to shield young children from the experience of death. Children

often are not told how or why a person died, are not allowed to participate in family functions surrounding the death, and are encouraged to
deny the finality of death. Even terminally ill children have faced their
own deaths without help. Koocher (1983) rightly states that the assumption of childhood naiveté regarding death probably reflects the discomfort adults have with death, rather than the reality of children's ability to
understand and cope with death.

Children are routinely confronted with death in their day-to-day
lives through the deaths of pets, television programs in which people die
(often quite violently), dead animals by the roadside, and stories and
fairy tales. All children think about death, and concerns and questions
about death are a normal part of growing up. How children react when a
death occurs depends to a large extent on how parents and other family
members react to the death and how they respond to the children's
questions and expressions of feeling. It is important for clinicians to be
aware of the empirical literature in this area, so that they can be prepared
to help children and parents cope with death should the occasion arise.
This chapter reviews the literature in the following areas: (1) how much
children understand about the concept of death; (2) how they cope with
and adjust to the death of a family member; and (3) how terminally ill
children cope with their own illness and possible death. Suggestions for
assessment and intervention strategies are also provided.

CHILDREN'S UNDERSTANDING OF DEATH

The assumption that children have a limited understanding of death is
based on research that ties children's conception of death to the Piagetian
theory of cognitive development. Children in the preoperational stage
(approximately ages 2–6), who are egocentric, tied to present experience,
and unable to take the perspective of others, have been shown to have an
incomplete understanding of three central components of a concept of
death: (1) Death is irreversible (the physical body cannot be made alive
again); (2) death is universal (all living things die); and (3) all living
functions (eating, feeling, knowing, etc.) cease at death. Furthermore,
because the understanding of these young children is dependent on their
own experience, death is typically conceived of in terms of sleep, separation, and injury—experiences common to all preschoolers (Koocher,
1983). Children in the concrete operational stage (approximately ages 7–
10) are beginning to have an understanding of the permanence of death,
although it is not thought to be personally relevant; that is, they believe
that only old people die (Stambrook & Parker, 1987). Children this age
also tend to see death as externally caused, the result of a disease or
injury, rather than a biological process that affects all living things. By

adolescence, with the onset of formal operational thought, death is understood completely, and abstract theological ideas may be included in conceptions of death (Koocher, 1983).

In a review of studies of children's concept of death, Speece and Brent (1984) outline the cognitive capabilities thought to be necessary for a complete understanding of death. These are the ability to (1) classify objects and events on the basis of common characteristics, (2) focus on transformations as well as states, (3) understand time, (4) perform reversible operations, (5) take the perspective of another person, and (6) apply rules universally. Speece and Brent (1984) point out that although these skills are identified as necessary for an understanding of the concept of death, the rationale for their inclusion is not always clear. Nonetheless, because preoperational children possess none of these skills, they should not be able to understand death at all, and concrete operational children should have the beginnings of understanding. Studies show, however, that this is not necessarily the case (Koocher, 1973; White, Elsom, & Prawat, 1978). Many preoperational children demonstrate concepts of death that include irreversibility, universality, and functionality, and many concrete operational children do not. Even some children under 2 years appear to understand the finality of death (Stambrook & Parker, 1987). Furthermore, some would argue that because all of us have some level of anxiety about separation, during times of stress or when a loved one has died our thinking about death may regress to less mature levels.

Not surprisingly, children who have had experience with death appear to have a more mature understanding of the construct. Reilly, Hasazi, and Bond (1983) compared children (ages 5–10) who had experienced the death of a parent, a sibling, a close relative, or a peer with children who had no experience with death; the experienced children were found to have an understanding of personal mortality that indicated a more advanced understanding of death than that of the inexperienced children. Furthermore, the children who had experienced death often elaborated their understanding with specific examples from their experience. Jay, Green, Johnson, Caldwell, and Nitschke (1987) report that experience with death appears to have more impact on the death concepts of younger children than on those of older children. These researchers found that understanding of universality, irreversibility, and personal mortality was associated with the experience of death of a loved person among 3- to 6-year-old children, but not among older children.

To summarize, in the absence of experience with death, the development of a mature concept of death seems to depend to some extent on cognitive development. Children's understanding of death varies systematically with age (and presumably with cognitive-developmental level). However, the relationship between specific cognitive-developmental skills and death conceptualization has not been specified (Speece &

Brent, 1984). Furthermore, for young children particularly, experience with the death of a loved family member or pet can serve to accelerate the understanding of death. Thus it seems clear that even young children are capable of understanding information about death if it is presented in a concrete, simple fashion that takes into account their characteristic patterns of thinking.

CHILDREN'S ADJUSTMENT TO DEATH

Research Findings

The relationship between children's understanding of the concept of death and their adjustment to a death in the family is not clear, and this question has received little attention from researchers. Younger children (who have not experienced death) generally appear to show less anxiety about death and treat death more matter-of-factly than older children, perhaps because they often have a less complete understanding of its finality (Halpern & Palic, 1984). On the other hand, very young children are thought to be more vulnerable to adverse reactions to the death of a family member because of their natural dependency, although this has not been empirically demonstrated. Studies that have investigated the relationship between adjustment and age at the time of a parent's death have obtained conflicting results. Ragan and McGlashan (1986), for example, found that in a population of mentally ill adults, those who had lost a parent during their adolescent years (when their understanding of death was more complete) had more severe symptoms than those who were younger at the time of the loss. Others have found that loss of a parent, particularly prior to age 12, is associated with suicide attempts (but not with completed suicides) among adolescents (Sheras, 1983). In any case, it is not clear whether the experience of loss or the resulting disruption in family functioning is the key factor in the development of psychopathology. The patients who had experienced the death of a parent in the Ragan and McGalshan (1986) study, for example, had also experienced more chaotic family environments.

Children who experience the death of a parent or other close relative are believed to be at higher risk for behavioral or emotional problems, particularly for depression. Indeed, early studies of clinical populations reported a higher incidence of depressed mood among children who had lost a parent (Caplan & Douglas, 1969). More recently, however, Ragan and McGlashan (1986) found that death of a parent prior to age 18 was related to the severity of psychopathology, but not to the specific diagnosis, in a sample of severely mentally ill patients. In other words, affective disorders were no more likely to be diagnosed among patients who had lost a parent than among those who had not. Ragan and McGlashan

(1986) also found, however, that patients who had lost a parent had particular difficulty with intimate relationships and social functioning.

Although loss of a parent appears to contribute to the development of later emotional or behavioral problems, whether the loss of a parent inevitably leads to significant psychopathology is not clear. Death of a parent is clearly associated with increased psychological disturbances in almost all children in the weeks immediately following the death. Black and Urbanowicz (1987) found that 92% of the children in their sample showed signs of behavioral disturbance. Typical reactions can include high anxiety, crying and moodiness, overdependence, separation problems, increased aggression, nightmares and other sleep disturbances, fear of injury, toileting problems, loss of appetite, restlessness, lack of concentration, and learning problems (Kaffman & Elizur, 1983). Some children show symptoms of clinical depression (Black & Urbanowicz, 1987). Although these symptoms typically decrease over 6–12 months, many children continue to evidence significant problems. Kaffman and Elizur (Elizur & Kaffman, 1982; Kaffman & Elizur, 1983) followed Israeli children who had lost a father in the Yom Kippur war. Eighteen months after the death, 50% of the children had symptoms of sufficient severity to interfere with their functioning, and 39% continued to have significant problems requiring professional help at a 42-month follow-up. The nature of the problems of the younger children included frequent denial of the finality of the death, nightmares, separation anxiety, and overly dependent and demanding behavior. Older children showed emotional restraint and social withdrawal, restlessness, increased aggression, and unexpected "exemplary" behavior. Kaffman and Elizur (1983) noted that children who continued to show signs of upset had mothers who were also not coping well with the death or had not given the children help in understanding the death. Thus, the idea that "time will heal all wounds" appears not to have validity, at least for some children.

In addition to the mental health and coping ability of the surviving parent, recent research suggests that the gender of the child and the deceased parent may mediate the occurrence of later problems. Lyon and Vandenberg (1989) found that loss of a father was not associated with neuroticism in adult women. These authors suggest, however, that loss of a mother may cause more disruption of family functioning and communication and more distress for children than loss of a father, or that loss of the same-sex parent may be more upsetting for children. However, these issues remain to be examined.

Children who have experienced the death of a sibling appear to have only a slightly lower risk for behavioral disturbance than children who have lost a parent. McCown and Pratt (1985) in a review of the literature, report that from 30% to 50% of children show behavior problems after the death of a sibling. They studied 65 children from 2 to 13 months after the death and found that the behavior of 38.3% of the children was reported by parents to have worsened following the death. Children ages 6–11, and children whose deceased sibling was older than 2 years, had more problems. Other factors found to be related to behavior problems were the place of death (the home was better than a hospital), diagnosis of the deceased child (cardiac conditions or sudden infant death were better than cancer), and number of surviving children (more was better).

Funeral Attendance

One question of great concern to parents is the extent to which children should be involved in the events that follow the death, and specifically whether or not children should attend the funeral. The clinical literature indicates some consensus that children should be given the opportunity to attend the funeral but not forced to go, and that funeral attendance can actually help a child make a good adjustment to the death. A few studies (Furman, 1976; McCown & Pratt, 1985; Schowalter, 1976), however, have reported adverse reactions from children who attended funerals, although there has not been much controlled empirical work in this area. Moreover, the question of the relationship between funeral attendance and children's long-term adjustment has not received much attention. Weller, Weller, Fristad, Cain, and Bowes (1988) reported a study of 38 children (ages 5–12) who had recently experienced the death of a parent. Almost all of the children (92%) attended the funeral, and the majority of parents and children reported that they were expected to and wanted to attend. Twenty-one percent of the children reported having an adverse reaction (e.g., excessive crying) during the funeral. However, neither attendance at nor reactions to the funeral were associated with poor adjustment 2 months later. Interestingly, there was little agreement between parents and children on ratings of adverse reactions; that is, parents were not always aware of when their children were feeling unusually upset. Although older children were expected to go to the funeral more often than younger children, age was not a factor in determining actual attendance or adverse reactions.

Koocher (1983) suggests that parents should make sure that a child's attendance at the funeral will meet the child's needs and not just their own. Children can be asked whether they wish to attend in a way that truly gives them a choice ("Some children want to come to the funeral and some children do not want to come. Which would you like to do?"). Children should, of course, be told what to expect at the funeral home or memorial service, and someone who will not be excessively upset should be available to them to answer questions and/or manage their behavior.

THE TERMINALLY ILL CHILD

The adjustment of children with terminal illnesses has become a concern for clinicians in recent years because of dramatic increases in survival rates. Although cancer, for example, continues to be a leading cause of death among children, in 1976 55% of children with acute leukemia had lived 5 years or more beyond the diagnosis of their disease, and these figures continue to improve (Stehbens, 1988). Whereas professionals' efforts in the past were directed toward helping families cope with the death of children, the current focus is on (1) understanding how children with life-threatening illnesses perceive death; and (2) finding ways to help them cope with the invasive, lengthy, and often painful medical treatment of their disease and with the possibility of death.

Understanding of Illness and Death

Just as bereaved children were formerly assumed to be naive about death, children with terminal illnesses were thought to be unaware of the seriousness of their illness. Recent work, however, has clearly shown that children as young as 5 or 6 years have a very real understanding of their illness, and even younger children are sensitive to and react to the upset of their parents as they deal with the children's life-threatening illness (Koocher, 1983). As an example, the anxiety levels of children with cancer, in contrast to those with non-life-threatening chronic illnesses, have been shown to increase with an increase in visits to the clinic (Spinetta & Maloney, 1975); this suggests an awareness of the severity of their illness.

The idea that terminally ill children have more mature concepts of death (presumably because of having to face the possibility of their own deaths) has not been substantiated. Jay et al. (1987) looked at differences in specific aspects of the understanding of death among children with cancer as compared with healthy children. They found that among the youngest children (ages 3–6), healthy children were more likely to under-stand the concept of personal death than were the children with cancer (75% and 33% respectively). Jay et al. state, however, that it was not possible to determine whether the children with cancer had actually not developed the concept of personal death or whether admitting this possi-bility was too anxiety-provoking for them. In the cancer patients, the understanding of personal death, universality, and irreversibility was associated with the experience of death of a friend, parent, or other family member. Thus, as is true for healthy children, experience with death accelerates the death concepts of children with life-threatening illnesses. On the other hand, Jay et al. found that healthy children (ages 3–12) were more likely to think of death as punishment for wrongdoing than were the children with cancer (38% of healthy children vs. 0% of cancer patients). None of the older children (ages 13–16) in either group believed this. Jay et al. conclude that children with terminal illnesses do not necessarily have more advanced concepts of death than healthy children do.

Adjustment of Terminally Ill Children

It would not seem surprising to find increased symptoms of psychopathology among children with life-threatening illnesses. At the very least, these children are at high risk for emotional disturbances because of the stresses with which they must cope. Although some studies have found evidence of adjustment problems (e.g., greater anxiety or lower academic achievement) among terminally ill children, others have found few differences between these children and healthy children. As an example, Allen and Zigler (1986) compared children with cancer and a group of healthy children matched for age, and found no differences in self-concept or self-esteem, behavior problems, or an optimistic outlook. As Spinetta (1982) states, the responses of children with life-threatening illnesses are better thought of as reactions to extremely stressful circumstances than as evidence for psychopathology. These reactions are a function of many factors, including the age and sex of the child, the number of children in the family, family functioning and relationships, the religious orientation of the family, financial resources, the type of medical and psychosocial care provided, and family communication patterns (Stehbens, 1988).

The extent to which children and families are able to cope with the stresses of ongoing medical intervention and the possibility of death is a critical factor in determining the children's adjustment. Spinetta (1978) has defined the following behaviors as evidence of good coping: (1) nondefensive personal posture; (2) closeness to parents; (3) happiness with oneself; and (4) freedom to express negative emotions. He reports that open communication on the part of the parents is directly related to evidence of good coping among the children. Other research has clearly supported this view, indicating that open communication is also related to a family's adjustment following the death of a child (Stehbens, 1988). Kupst and Schulman (1988) found that factors (other than open communication) that enhance coping include the quality of the marital relationship, lack of concurrent stresses, and level of family support. The existence of emotional or behavioral problems prior to the onset of the disease is also related to coping, as these are likely to become more severe as the child and family experience the stresses of the illness (Kupst & Schulman, 1988). Interestingly, the medical status of the child and duration of the child's illness do not seem to be related to coping.

Helping Children Cope

In light of the fact that honest and open communication has been related both to a child's ability to cope and the family's adjustment before and after the child's death, providing the child with information about his or her disease seems essential. Stehbens (1988) suggests that the child should be told the name of the disease, the treatments that will be necessary, and the reasons why they are necessary, in language that is appropriate to the child's developmental level. Rando (1984) indicates that the child's understanding of this information depends less on age and intellectual ability than on the experience of the child with his or her illness. Thus, assimilation of information about the disease is likely to occur over the course of the illness rather than all at one time. At first the child learns that the illness is serious and that sometimes people can die from it. Next, the child learns about the various treatments, the means by which they will be administered, and their side effects. Then the child experiences various treatments in the cycle of remission and relapse, and finally the child comes to understand that the treatments are finite and death is a possibility. As is true for any stressful event, helping children cope by providing them with information is a process that is carried out over time, rather than in a one-time intervention.

Stehbens (1988) also recommends that children be given a sense of control over the disease. Information about why certain treatments are necessary is one way of doing this. Children can also be given choices about some aspects of their treatment, and this can foster a sense of control. Finally, Stehbens (1988) advocates helping the family maintain a future-oriented and optimistic point of view. As Rando (1984) indicates, children must be prepared for their further development as much as if not more than for their possible death. Maintenance of home and school activities is strongly encouraged, although this is often difficult for parents to accomplish. Overprotection and overindulgence are common among parents of terminally ill children (Rando, 1984; Stehbens, 1988), in spite of the fact that maintenance of appropriate limits on behavior is important to a child's sense of well-being and security. Rando (1984) advocates ensuring that the child continues with schoolwork during the course of the illness, either at home, in the hospital, or at school. Parents should be counseled regarding the importance of the child's returning to school as soon as possible. School personnel should be helped to understand changes in the child's functioning that result from treatment of the illness. Moreover, the child's frequent absences from school should be acknowledged, and ways to help the child cope with missed schoolwork should be discussed with the child's teacher.

Preparing children for invasive medical treatments by giving them information about the procedures can be effective in helping them cope with a serious illness. Jay (1988) describes preparation as including both sensory and procedural information. Sensory information includes a description of the sensations (noises, smells, physical sensations) the child will experience during the process; procedural information involves explaining the steps of the procedure. Information about medical procedures can be provided in a number of ways that are appropriate to a child's developmental level, including doll play, hospital tours, puppet shows, books, and modeling films. It is important to note, however, that children have been found to have different coping styles; some actively seek out information, while others appear to avoid it (Peterson, 1989). Although children categorized as "active copers" have been reported to experience less anxiety and to make a better adjustment to medical procedures, research has not evaluated the effectiveness of one method of providing information over another, or the issue of attempting to provide information to those children who actively avoid it.

Jay (1988) describes a variety of techniques that have been used to help children cope with invasive medical procedures. These include hypnosis, behavioral strategies (desensitization, modeling, contingency management, relaxation), and cognitive–behavioral techniques (selective attention, distraction, stress inoculation, cognitive restructuring, and coping skills training).

When death is imminent, the clinician must focus on helping the child and family adapt to that reality. The "stages" of adaptation to death (denial, anger, bargaining, depression, and acceptance) derived by Kübler-Ross (1969) from her work with adults appear to apply to children as well, although these are currently not thought of as fixed stages as much as various reactions to the realization that one is dying. As such, their expression can occur in any order and at any time during the process of adaptation. If given the message that it is OK to talk about their feelings, children will express denial, anger, bargaining, depression, and acceptance both verbally and through play. Some children are very open about their fears and concerns, while others continue to deny the seriousness of their illness, at the same time showing signs of great anxiety. Koocher (1983) suggests that for these latter children it is appropriate to treat the symptoms of anxiety, leaving the children's defenses intact. For example, for young children especially, anxiety is most likely related to fears of separation; therefore, a dying child should never be left alone. Spinetta (1982) suggests that children be given the following messages: (1) "You will not be alone at death or after death"; (2) "You have done all you could do with your life"; (3) "Death will not hurt"; (4) "Parents and others will always remember you and the happy times"; (5) "You can say goodbye to friends and family members if you want to"; (6) "We don't understand why children die, and we cry because we are sad about it"; and (7) "It's OK to cry and feel sad and angry, and it's OK not to want to talk about it too."

ASSESSMENT OF DEATH-RELATED ISSUES

Given that almost all children over the age of 2 or 3 show signs of grief at the death of a family member, an important issue for parents and clinicians is to determine whether the reaction is normal or pathological and to differentiate normal grieving from clinical depression. Koocher (1983) provides some guidelines for making this distinction. He states that it is important to assess the duration and intensity of the child's reaction (although there are no real guidelines about the length of time grieving should last). Typically, reactions decrease over several weeks after the death, but anniversaries, holidays, and other events can trigger renewed grief reactions (these should be less intense and of shorter duration than the original reaction). Other critical factors to consider are the presence of anxiety, feelings of guilt or personal responsibility, denial of feelings, and an inability to talk about the death. Koocher (1983) also warns that the reactions of young children are strongly influenced by behavioral contagion and social learning, as well as by the extent to which the child receives support from family members. Thus it is important to assess the reactions of parents and other family members who have contact with the child at the time of the death.

Kuperman and Stewart (1981) offer guidelines for determining whether normal grief has become clinical depression. They suggest attending to the duration and intensity of grieving, and point out that grieving children will continue to enjoy pleasurable activities from time to time, whereas children who are depressed typically do not. Furthermore, they state that depressed children often express feelings of self-worthlessness, which are not usually seen in children who are grieving normally.

When parents seek professional help for their children concerning issues of death, assessment will vary depending on whether the situation is an emergency (a parent or other family member has died suddenly) or one in which parents are anticipating an impending death. In the former situation, the clinician may not have the opportunity to send out parent questionnaires or checklists prior to the interview, but may request that parents complete them at a later time. Regardless of the methods used, certain factors are important to examine during the assessment process. The assessment outline presented below follows the steps for gathering information in accordance with the Comprehensive Assessment-to-Intervention System (CAIS), presented in Chapter 3; the emphasis here is on those factors most related to concerns about death.

Step 1: Initial Contact

If the clinician has the opportunity to do so, a general questionnaire such as our own Parent Questionnaire; the Parenting Stress Index (PSI; Abidin,

1990) for children under 12 years; and behavior rating scales such as the Child Behavior Checklist (CBCL; Achenbach & Edelbrock, 1983) or the Eyberg Child Behavior Inventory (ECBI; Eyberg & Ross, 1978) should be sent to parents to complete prior to their first appointment. Unless one child is the focus of the parents' concerns, they should be asked to complete a behavior problem measure for each child in the family. The PSI gives information about sources of stress for the family apart from the death, as well as indications of depression in the parent(s). The CBCL and ECBI alert the clinician both to child behavior problems that may be unrelated to the death (pre-existing) and to those that are reactions to the death; they also provide guidelines for judging the seriousness of these problems, relative to the behavior of normal children.

Step 2: Parent and Child Interview

Parent Interview

We typically begin the parent interview with the parents alone. During this time, the clinician can gather facts about the death and clarify the parents' specific concerns. In addition, the following information should be gathered:

1. How are the parent(s) (or the surviving parent, when it is a parent who has died) handling the death? Because parental functioning is clearly related to child adjustment following a death, questions should be asked regarding the parents' feelings about the death. High scores on the Depression scale of the PSI should alert the clinician to assess this possibility more fully. Other sources of stress (financial, family relationships, etc.) and the availability of emotional and other types of support for the parent(s) are also important to assess. A parent who is isolated or who is experiencing many other worries apart from a child's reactions is likely to have more difficulty in dealing with the death.

2. What questions about the death has the child asked? Information in this area will alert the clinician to the concerns of the child. Questions indicating feelings of guilt or personal responsibility, or the absence of any questions, should be noted.

3. What has the child been told regarding the death? Assessment of this issue can lead to discussion of parental beliefs and perceptions of the death. Religious beliefs in particular must be understood and appreciated by the clinician, because treatment will need to take these into consideration. Misconceptions about children's abilities to understand death can also be cleared up.

4. What was the relationship between the child and the deceased? Obviously, a child who had a very close relationship with the deceased

person will have a more difficult time adjusting to the death. A child who had a conflicted relationship with the deceased person, however, may feel quite guilty.

5. What unusual behaviors has the child exhibited? Responses to the CBCL and ECBI will provide clues as to the child's specific problems. Further information on the frequency, intensity, duration, antecedents, and consequences of the behaviors should be gathered by questioning the parent(s). If it is suspected that the child might be depressed, questions should address this issue specifically.

After the clinician has gathered this information, the parent or parents are told that the child will be invited to join the discussion and that the clinician would like the parent(s) to repeat some of what was said in front of the child. If a parent does not want the child to know about certain aspects of the death, the clinician can discuss the benefits and disadvantages for the child of not sharing this information openly. The parent or parents are asked to describe the course of events leading to the death (or, if the death is impending, the situation as it currently exists) and their concerns about the child. If a parent is not able to do this, the clinician supplies the words and asks the parent periodically whether he or she is in agreement. The purpose of this is to set the stage for open communication with the child and to relieve the child of the burden of providing the clinician with details about the death. The clinician is then free to explore the child's feelings and worries about the death, because all the facts are out in the open.

Child Interview

At this point, the parent or parents are excused, and the clinician talks with the child alone. The purpose of this first session with the child is to get to know him or her better, to express sympathy about the child's loss, and to gather information about the child's perceptions of the death and his or her current worries or concerns. The interview will, of course, vary considerably, depending on how able or willing the child is to talk about his or her concerns. It is appropriate to begin with a genuine expression of sympathy ("I know this is a very difficult time for you, and I am so sorry this happened"). Because the parent or parents (with the clinician's help) have talked about the death in the child's presence, the clinician can discuss these concerns openly with the child ("Your mother is worried about how you are handling the death of your father. What are you most worried about?"). If the child does not respond, the clinician can say, for example, "I have talked with other children whose fathers or mothers have died, and lots of them are worried that they might have done something to cause the death. Does this ever worry you?"

It is also important to gather information about other aspects of the child's life (school, friends, activities). This will provide the clinician with guidelines about how much support the child is likely to need. Children with lots of friends and activities are likely to have developed an extensive support network and will require less from the clinician than will isolated children.

Step 3: Observation of Behavior

Observation of the parent–child interaction or the child's behavior outside the clinic setting is generally not necessary in the assessment of death-related concerns unless there are specific questions regarding these areas. In the case of a terminally ill child, observation of the child in school might lead to suggestions for intervention regarding problems in that setting (peer relations, withdrawal, etc.).

Step 4: Further Evaluation

In most cases, the previously described steps will complete the assessment, although further evaluation may be indicated for a child who evidences problems that existed prior to the death.

Step 5: Referral to Allied Health Professionals

Parents who are experiencing significant depression should be referred to a mental health professional for counseling and/or medication. The child clinician should also be aware that siblings may also need to be seen.

Step 6: Communication of Findings and Treatment Recommendations

Prior to beginning treatment and often at the end of the initial interview, the clinician should provide the parent(s) with general information about children's understanding of death and how this applies to the child of concern. The clinician should also discuss his or her understanding of the current situation and present a rationale for treatment.

Intervention strategies for concerns about death are reviewed next, followed by specific areas on which to focus intervention.

TREATMENT OF DEATH-RELATED ISSUES

Intervention with bereaved children is preventive, in the sense that many of the strategies are aimed at preventing serious problems. Because death is such an integral part of life, talking with children about this topic should not be delayed until a death has occurred. Young children present us with many opportunities for conversations about death and dying, and it is at these "teachable moments" that children's understanding of death can be enhanced. Parents who respond openly to their children's questions about death communicate to their children that it is OK to discuss this topic.

Research Findings

There has been little research on effective methods of intervention with bereaved children. Koocher (1983) states that children typically have several concerns that are important but often unarticulated. These include (1) "Could it happen to me? Or to my parent(s)?"; (2) "Who will take care of me?"; (3) "What is expected of me?"; (4) "Did I cause it?"; and (5) "Why did he die?" (i.e., by what means). Koocher suggests that parents and other concerned adults simply talk to children openly about the death and address these concerns by talking about how people cope with death, what happens at funerals, what people feel when someone close to them has died, and so on. For children who are having trouble coping with their grief, the task of the therapist is to help the child differentiate his or her fate from that of the deceased and to come to some closure about the death.

Masterman and Reams (1988) identified several issues that surfaced during the course of support groups for bereaved preschool and school-age children. These were (1) the stresses that resulted from the death, such as the surviving parent's unavailability to the child and financial problems; (2) anger over disruptions in their lives, as well as anger toward the deceased parent; (3) fear of their own death; (4) use of fantasies or denial to explain the absence of the deceased parent; (5) physical symptoms similar to those of the parent before death; (6) a desire to be reunited with the deceased parent and suicidal ideation; and (7) a fear of being perceived of as different by their peers. Anger was often expressed in behavior problems, whereas fears were expressed through exemplary behavior, separation anxiety, and school refusal.

The sessions for school-age children described by Masterman and Reams (1988) lasted 1 hour each and were held once a week for 8 weeks. Each session was divided into four parts: (1) a 15-minute discussion of the previous week's events ("Tell me about your week"); (2) a 10-minute discussion of previously assigned homework (e.g., a letter or poem to the deceased person); (3) a 25-minute discussion of a planned topic (e.g., describing the person who has died, telling about the funeral, etc.); and (4) 10 minutes spent in a closing game or activity (making and throwing paper airplanes was the favorite!). Sessions for preschoolers were divided into five parts, including (1) a 5-minute beginning discussion (show-and-tell); (2) 15 minutes of free play (structured through the provision of specific toys, such as a doll house, crayons and paper, puppets, a baby doll, etc.); (3) 15 minutes of therapeutic stories and role plays (how parents die, fears of dying, what it is like to be dead, etc.); (4) 15 minutes of free play; and (5) 10 minutes of closing discussion about eventual termination (each week a child crossed off one of eight houses drawn on a blackboard) and a cooperative game (e.g., rolling a ball around the circle of children). Although the effectiveness of the Masterman and Reams (1988) groups was not formally evaluated, these authors report that parents noted a decrease in behavior problems at home and in school, as well as increased communication with their children concerning death-related issues. The children were observed to be less angry and better able to cope with their feelings about the death.

Black and Urbanowicz (1987) evaluated the effectiveness of an intervention program designed to provide support for the surviving parent and children in families where one parent had recently died. Each family was provided with six therapy sessions spaced 2–3 weeks apart; these were focused on promoting mourning (by having families describe events that led up to the death, talk about the deceased parent, show pictures, etc.) for both the children and the surviving parent, and on improving communication among family members (by modeling appropriate verbal behaviors and responses to the children's comments and questions), especially about the death. Follow-up at 1 and 2 years indicated fewer behavioral problems among the children who received treatment, as compared with a control group of children who did not receive treatment. Parents in the treatment group also had fewer problems (continued grief, worrying, depression, suicidal thoughts, and physical health) than controls, and parental well-being was associated with fewer problems in the children.

In the next section, various intervention strategies are discussed in the context of the Comprehensive Assessment-to-Intervention Systerm (CAIS; see Chapter 3), with emphasis on five areas: development, parents, environment, consequences of behavior, and medical/health aspects.

Intervention Strategies

Intervention in Development

One of the primary intervention strategies for death-related concerns is providing children with factual, honest information about death that is appropriate for their developmental level. For young children, this means crafting the message in terms that are concrete and related to the child's experience. Schaefer and Lyons (1986) offer excellent suggestions on how to explain death to children. They suggest an initial simple statement including the following elements: (1) The person has died; (2) this is very sad, and it's OK for children to talk about how they feel; (3) the person died because something happened to his or her body (this should be clarified as appropriate); (4) "dead" means that the body stops working and no longer does any of the things it used to do; and (5) it's OK for children to ask questions, and an adult will try to answer them. Children also need to know what will be happening in the days immediately following the death and exactly what is expected of them (who will take care of them, when and where the funeral or memorial service will be, etc.). Schaefer and Lyons (1986) also suggest avoiding the use of euphemisms such as "gone away," "passed on," "lost," "left us," or "died in his sleep," as these can be very confusing for young children. Furthermore, they state that religious concepts can also be confusing to children unless they are presented within the context of ongoing religious experience and instruction. Regardless of a family's religious beliefs, children should also be told the fact of death as a biological process.

Because children need to experience the finality of death very concretely, helping young children to grieve often involves allowing them to do things that make adults uncomfortable. Take, for instance, the case of a 2½-year-old girl (see Case Example 1, below) who, when taken to see her mother's body at the funeral home, repeatedly opened and shut the coffin lid while saying goodbye to her mother. Older children may act silly or laugh inappropriately because they are embarrassed or do not know how to act. For all children, it is important to keep in mind the concerns that they are likely to have as outlined earlier in this chapter, and to address these concerns directly, even if the children do not verbalize the questions. In particular, children who have experienced a parent's death are usually worried about what will happen to them if the other parent should die, and will often ask repeated questions about this. The surviving parent needs to be prepared with a plan that can be shared with the children ("Aunt Mary will take care of you if anything happens to me").

Intervention with Parents

Because the manner in which parents handle the grief process so clearly affects children's adjustment, it is important for the clinician to understand and support parents in their own grieving. Parents should be given permission to express a range of emotions in front of their children, as long as they provide an explanation to the children ("I am crying because I am sad that Daddy died"). The explanation is important because young children so easily misconstrue adults' expression of emotion, typically blaming themselves for the adults' tears or anger. In some cases, parents will need to be referred for individual treatment before they can deal adequately with their children's needs. For these parents, it may be necessary to have another adult (someone the children know and trust) be responsible for the children until the parents are better able to function.

Providing parents with information about the grieving process among children is another important intervention strategy. In many cases, helping parents understand how children at different ages understand death and what their typical concerns are, and giving them suggestions for the words to use to explain death, may be all that is needed. Parents need to be warned that the grief process in children is different from that in adults, and that as a result their children may behave as if nothing has happened (laughing, playing, running around). Although this often makes parents angry ("She doesn't seem to care that Grandpa died"), it is normal and simply reflects the fact that children cannot focus their attention on grief for long periods of time. Furthermore, it is through play that children come to terms with the fact of death. Thus playing out death scenes or funerals, and acting as though the deceased person is still alive (e.g., talking to Grandma on the telephone), are common activities among grieving children. Parents should be encouraged to talk about the deceased person, both as he or she is remembered and as things come up in the present that remind them of that person. At the same time, it is important to remind children of the finality of death ("It's OK to pretend to talk to Grandma, but she is really dead and we can't see her any more").

Intervention in the Environment

As part of the assessment, the clinician should have gathered information about the child's daily routines, and the parent(s) should be encouraged to maintain these routines as much as possible. Although it is appropriate to include children in the functions that occur following a death, it is also important to have them return to their normal activities as soon as possible. Parents often ask, "How long should I keep my child out of school?" We believe that it is in a child's best interests to return to school as soon as possible, within a few days at most. This reassures the child that life does indeed go on. Parents or another family member should inform the child's teacher (and other important adults who have contact with the child) about the death, so that they can be prepared to answer questions or help the child deal with any upset.

Changing the Consequences of the Behavior

It is important that the parent(s) maintain their expectations for appropriate behavior and continue to set limits for a child's inappropriate behavior. Changing the rules and expectations during times of family turmoil can be very unsettling for a child and can increase feelings of insecurity. Household rules can be enforced and consequences provided for inappropriate behavior while the parent expresses concerns for the child's feelings ("I know you are upset/angry that Daddy died, but I cannot let you hit your sister"). Children who exhibit specific problem behaviors such as fears or sleep problems may be operating under misconceptions about the death, which will then need to be clarified. Often the behavior of concern will decrease as the child gains a better understanding of the death, but if this is not the case, then the problem behavior will need to be dealt with directly.

Intervention in Medical/Health Aspects

Parents often ask whether a child should be given a sedative to calm him or her down, or sleep medication to help with sleep problems. It is rare that such medications are helpful for children, although some parents may benefit from sedation themselves. Generally, it is best to attempt to manage a child's upset by providing honest information, encouraging expressions of feelings, and providing clear consequences for inappropriate behaviors. Children sometimes present with psychosomatic symptoms following a death in the family, and these should be attended to by a physician. Often, however, these symptoms are related to unresolved anxiety and decrease as a child is allowed to communicate openly about his or her concerns.

CASE EXAMPLE 1

Step 1: Initial Contact

Mr. Graves called early on Sunday morning and said that his wife had died unexpectedly 24 hours after giving birth to their second daughter. He wanted to know how to tell his 2½-year-old daughter, Annie, about her mother's death and was concerned about her participation in the funeral. He said that the maternal grandparents were quite religious and that public grieving was part of their belief system but that his family was uncomfortable with this. The clinician offered to meet with Mr. Graves and the maternal and paternal grandparents, as well as the maternal aunt who had lived with the family during the first 2 years of Annie's life. There was no time, nor was it appropriate, to gather extensive background information prior to the meeting.

Step 2: Family Interview

Mr. Graves, the paternal grandmother, and the maternal aunt attended the session with the clinician. Mr. Graves, in a state of shock, described the death of his wife during the previous evening and indicated that his greatest concern was to help Annie understand and accept her mother's death. He had made arrangements for the baby to remain in the hospital until after the funeral. Annie was described as a strong-willed, precocious child, who had been well prepared for the birth of a sibling but who had already shown some regression in toileting and sleep habits. Currently, she was sleeping with her father and was having occasional daytime toileting accidents. The maternal grandparents had been staying with the family for the past 2 weeks and had planned to remain for at least a month to help care for the new baby. The maternal aunt had lived with the family for 2 years, as noted above, but in the last 6 months had moved into her own apartment. She said she would be able to move back into the family home immediately and to care for the two children.

Mr. Graves described conflict over the funeral arrangements. The maternal grandparents wanted an open casket and an opportunity to share their grief with friends. The paternal grandparents and Mr. Graves felt that it would be in everyone's best interests to have a cremation and a simple memorial service.

Step 3: Observation of Behavior

Step 4: Further Assessment

Step 5: Referral to Allied Health Professionals

These steps in the assessment process were not relevant to this case.

Step 6: Communication of Findings and Treatment Recommendations

Given the family's understandably intense emotions and the clinician's lack of familiarity with the family members, they were offered the opportunity to hear about children's understanding of death in general and ways in which this information might be applied to handling the current situation with Annie. They were quite open to this and understood the need for concrete, simple explanations regarding the mother's death. After this sharing of information relevant to Annie's understanding and acceptance of death, the family engaged in problem solving with the clinician on how best to meet both Annie's and their own needs. It was agreed that Annie would be allowed to see her mother's body in the funeral parlor and that she would attend a brief church ceremony. The family did not feel it was necessary for her to go to the cemetery, and the maternal aunt offered to stay home with her.

Although the paternal grandmother was concerned that open discussion and viewing of the body would make matters worse for Annie, she was able to understand that Annie would have many questions and concerns that could only be answered by seeing her mother's body. They were especially concerned that Annie not associate going to the hospital with death. Giving the child an opportunity for some grieving prior to the new baby sister's being brought home was felt to be important in distancing the mother's death from the sibling's birth. The family members were advised that after their initial adjustment to the mother's death, they would need to consider their own feelings about the new baby's arrival home.

The family was given several books appropriate for children Annie's age to review. They chose *Lifetimes* (see Appendix C), which describes death in terms of the beginning, middle, and end of life and explains that everyone has his or her own special lifetime. It was agreed that Mr. Graves and the maternal aunt would tell Annie about her mother's death and that everyone would be available to answer her questions in an honest and straightforward manner. Furthermore, they agreed to rely on each other when a response was too difficult for one of them or they did not have a ready answer. Mr. Graves requested that the clinician be available at the funeral parlor in case he or Annie needed her assistance.

Two days later, Mr. Graves took Annie to the funeral parlor to see her mother's body. Annie arrived looking happy and chatting nonstop about a new teddy bear her mother had given to her before she went to the hospital. Mr. Graves held her in his arms so that she could see her mother. After an initial silence, Annie stated, "But this isn't my mother. My mother always laughs and talks with me." Mr. Graves explained that this was only her mother's body, and that the mother she knew had died and was no longer able to laugh or talk with her. Annie asked to touch the mother's face, kissed her, and then asked, "Will she get awake like Sleeping Beauty?" Mr. Graves again explained that the body would never be able to move, nor would her mother become alive again. Annie then proceeded to close the casket and reopened it, with the obvious expectation that her mother might speak to her as if in hide-and-seek; she did this a number of times. Finally, her father indicated that it was time for them to say goodbye to the mother's body. The child waved goodbye to the body and closed the casket. Although Mr. Graves had tears streaming down his face, he indicated that it was clearly helpful for his daughter to have said a final goodbye to her mother.

The clinician had the opportunity to continue to work with this family from time to time over the next 2 years. Although adjustment was difficult for everyone, especially the father, the family warmly welcomed the new child. Annie continued to talk openly about her mother and her death, but eventually in a matter-of-fact way. On a home visit, for example, she showed the clinician her room and her toys, and explained that the pictures on the bulletin board were of her mother who had died.

———————————— *CASE EXAMPLE 2* ————————————

Step 1: Initial Contact

Mr. Finelli called from out of state indicating that his 5-year-old daughter, Gina, had been killed by a car the previous evening. He wanted advice on how to deal with his 10-year-old daughter, Mary, who had witnessed the accident. Mr. Finelli explained that Gina had run out into the street and that when she was called to come back, she darted in front of a car. She was taken to the hospital, where she later died. The body was severely disfigured and the family did not plan to have an open casket. The burial was to occur in the home town of the maternal and paternal grandparents, where the family was visiting.

Step 2: Parent and Child Interview

Parent Interview

Given the time factor, the parent interview was conducted on the telephone. Mr. Finelli said that Mary not only had witnessed the accident, but had been at the hospital with the family when Gina died. He said that Mary was aware of the meaning of death, but was having difficulty expressing any emotion about the event. The parents and grandparents were openly expressing their sadness; at these times, Mary tried to reassure them that it would be all right, and quietly disappeared to play or read by herself. Mr. Finelli indicated that this was a typical response from Mary when she was upset or under stress. He described her as a rather serious young lady who did well in school, had friends, and had enjoyed her 5-year-old sister. He was quick to add, however, that they had had their battles. They were concerned that Mary was not responding in a way that would help her adjust to Gina's death.

Mr. Finelli requested an appointment for Mary when they returned in 3 days, and also asked that the clinician offer assistance to Mary's and Gina's teachers and classmates at the private school the girls attended. Mr. Finelli had already informed the school, the local church, and several neighbors about the death.

Step 3: Observation of Behavior

Step 4: Further Assessment

Step 5: Referral to Allied Health Professionals

These steps in the assessment process were not relevant in this case.

Step 6: Communication of Findings and Treatment Recommendations

Mr. Finelli was assured that we all must deal with death in our own way and that Mary was handling it in the most effective way for her at this time. She was not avoiding the reality of the death, and she was able to offer solace to her parents, but she could not openly express her feelings. They were encouraged to include her in family rituals surrounding the burial; to continue expressing their feelings openly; and, while allowing her to be part of this process, not to force any grieving responses from her.

When the clinician contacted the principal of Mary's school, the latter indicated that she would have the girls' teachers talk with the clinician. The principal added that the school had already planned a memorial service for Gina and that this would be held after Mary returned. The parents had agreed to this plan.

The teachers' concerns centered around telling the children about the circumstances of Gina's death and finding ways to help all the children in the school and their parents adjust to this tragic loss. The books *How Do We Tell the Children?* and *Lifetimes* (see Appendix C) were taken to the school. In discussions with the teachers and the principal, it was determined that the children and the parents would be told the circumstances surrounding Gina's death: She had been playing in the front yard of her grandmother's house, had run into the road to get a ball, and when called to return had not looked both ways and had run in front of a car. She had been unconscious from that time until her death several hours later and had not felt any pain. It was agreed that this factual information would decrease the number of questions to Mary and her family, as well as rumors about how the death occurred. The teachers were able to think of things that each grade could do to express sympathy. They planned to ask the children what they would like to do, but had several projects in mind in the event that the children could not come up with ideas. Not surprisingly, the children were very creative in finding ways to express their sympathy (e.g., drawing pictures, writing poems, and talking about and engaging in many of Gina's favorite activities). Both Mary and her parents appreciated the outpouring of love and

TABLE 6.1. Example of Problem Solving with a Bereaved Child

Problem-solving steps	Example
1. Define the problem.	"The kids want to be nice, but their sympathy and questions make me upset."
2. Generate alternative solutions.	1. "I could change schools."
	2. "I could stay home."
	3. "I could tell them I appreciate their help, but it makes me sad to talk about Gina right now."
	4. "I could ask the teacher to tell the kids not to talk about Gina."
3. Evaluate the alternatives.	1. "I like my school, and it would make me even sadder if I left."
	2. "I would miss my friends and not be promoted."
	3. "It would let the kids know how I feel without hurting their feelings."
	4. "It's not that I don't want them *ever* to talk about Gina, just not all the time."
4. Choose a solution and practice it.	Mary chose solution #3.
5. Evaluate the results.	"I'll start telling, the kids on Monday, and we can talk about how it is going when I see you on Thursday."

support for them, and indicated that it was very helpful in their acceptance of Gina's death.

Child Interview

When Mary was seen by the clinician, she readily described what had happened to Gina and indicated that she was sad, but it was clear that she did not want to talk further about it.

Several weeks later, the parents called to say that Mary was complaining of stomachaches and headaches and did not want to go to school. When they allowed her to stay home, however, it was obvious that she was entirely well. A visit to the doctor found no medical reason for her physical complaints.

When Mary was seen by the clinician, she said that everyone at school was being very nice to her, but they were treating her as if she were "made of glass." She found the children's and teachers' continued expressions of sympathy very difficult to deal with, and she wished things would get back to the way they were before her sister's death. The clinician engaged Mary in a discussion of the different ways in which people express their grief. She was able to describe how each of her parents, her grandparents, and she herself were expressing their grief, and could also see that people were handling the death in very different ways. The children at school were handling it by telling her how sorry they were and trying to make her feel better by being "overly kind." The clinician and Mary then discussed how she might let the children at school know how she felt and what she needed without hurting their feelings. Through problem solving (see Table 6.1), Mary decided on several statements that could be used in a variety of situations (e.g., "We're sad but we're going to be OK," "Thank you for your concern, but I'm finding it hard to talk about Gina's death"). She also decided she would show the children that she was all right by actively participating in her regular activities. Mary's physical symptoms immediately decreased, and over the next 3 months she made a good adjustment in school.

PART III

MANAGING
COMMON
PROBLEMS

Chapter 7

Toileting:

Enuresis

Studies have consistently found that toileting is a major concern for parents of preschool children (Chamberlin, 1974; Mesibov, Schroeder, & Wesson, 1977), and, next to crying, incontinence has been reported to be the second most commonly stated reason for nonaccidental injury to children (Kempe & Helfer, 1972). Parents typically do not ask for toilet training advice from mental health professionals unless they happen to be in a pediatric health care setting (Christophersen & Rapoff, 1983; Schroeder, 1979; Stephens & Silber, 1974). This is understandable when one considers that even when children have elimination problems such as enuresis or encopresis, emotional and behavioral problems are not generally significant issues. When emotional or behavioral problems are present along with enuresis, they are primarily due to situational stress such as family disruption and stressful life events (Douglas, 1973). Furthermore, problems such as enuresis or encopresis are not usually due to bad (overly punitive) training practices, but rather to the inconsistent and infrequent use of good practices. Our goal in this chapter is to alert child clinicians to normal developmental issues relevant to toileting, to describe a toilet training program, and to present the procedures that have been effective in the treatment of nocturnal enuresis. Chapter 8 covers encopresis.

TOILET TRAINING

Although toilet training is a much-discussed topic among parents, friends, and relatives of preschoolers, there is actually very little scientific literature that compares different methods of training. Cultural and societal attitudes seem more important than data when it comes to deciding when a child is "ready" to be trained and choosing a training method. One early cross-cultural study found that the median age of starting regular toilet training in London was 4.6 months, in Paris 7.8 months, and in Stockholm 12.4 months (Hindley, Fillozat, Klackenberg, Nicolet-Meister, & Sand, 1965). In the United States, the suggested age at which to start training has varied from 1 (!) to 24 months, with current support for 18 months and preferably 24 months (Brazelton, 1962; Christophersen & Rapoff, 1983). In general, the older children are when toilet training is started, the faster the time to completion. If toilet training is begun when the child is older than 26 months, for example, it is accomplished twice as fast as if it is started when the child is younger than 2 years (Azrin & Foxx, 1974; Butler, 1976).

The developmental and scientific literatures, although limited, do give us some general guidelines for toilet training. To achieve mature bladder functioning, children have to gain cognitive control over the micturition reflex, and both developmental and psychological factors play a part in this learning process. Brazelton (1962) states that the physiological criteria for readiness include reflex sphincter control (which can be elicited as early as 9 months) and myelinization of pyramidal tracts (which is completed between 12 and 18 months). Furthermore, the ability to control urinary flow involves several component tasks that are generally achieved at different ages: Awareness of micturition occurs between 1 and 2 years; by 3 years, most children can consistently postpone urination; by 4 years, most children can voluntarily urinate upon command; and by 5 or 6 years, they usually can voluntarily withhold urination with any degree of bladder distension (Crawford, 1989). Although these are mean ages, and these tasks have not been proven to be necessary prerequisites for toilet training, they do support the fact that by the age of 36 months most children have achieved bladder and bowel control during the day, yet can have occasional accidents through the age of 5 years (Simonds, 1977).

Psychological and physical readiness criteria, according to Brazelton (1962), include the following: the ability to sit and walk, some verbal understanding, a desire to please, imitation of parents and others, and the desire to be autonomous. Azrin and Foxx's (1974) suggested readiness criteria include bladder control (the child consistently empties his or her bladder and stays dry for several hours); physical readiness (the child picks up objects easily and walks without assistance); and instructional readiness (the child understands and complies with one- and two-step directions).

Brazelton (1962) suggests a child-oriented, indirect approach to toilet training that is gradual and begins after the child is 18 months old. First, a potty chair on which the child sits fully clothed is introduced. Some weeks later, the child is encouraged to sit on the potty without diapers. Then the child is taken to the chair once a day to empty dirty diapers into it. Next the potty chair is placed in the child's play area, diapers are removed, and the child is told that he or she may use the potty. Then if the child begins to urinate in the potty, he or she is put in training pants and encouraged to use the potty. Brazelton reports that in a sample of 1,170 upper-middle-class children who started toilet training after 18 months, the average age for daytime bladder and bowel training was 28.5 months, and for nighttime training 33.3 months. He also reports that these children had very few problems with encopresis or enuresis.

Foxx and Azrin (1973) described a step-by-step approach for toilet training in less than a day that was first successful with people who were mentally retarded. It was then adapted for normally developing children, and a manual for parents titled *Toilet Training in Less Than a Day* (Azrin & Foxx, 1974) was written. Modeling (with a baby doll), repeated practice (increased liquid intake), reinforcement, mild punishment (help clean up accidents), and stimulus control (distended bladder is associated with the potty) are the main features of this program.

Several studies indicate, however, that parents have trouble using the manual without supervision and that children may show emotional side effects to the suggested program, including tantrums and avoidance behaviors (Butler, 1976; Matson & Ollendick, 1977). Other researchers have criticized the 1-day approach as being too intense and too demanding for parents to carry out alone (Christopherson & Rapoff, 1983; Kimmel, 1974). Nonetheless, Azrin and Foxx have very nicely laid out the component parts of the toilet training process, and one can learn a great deal about toilet training from reading their work.

The fact that most children are successfully toilet-trained during the preschool years testifies to the effectiveness of many different approaches. The goal of parents and clinicians should be to help children accomplish this important developmental task in a way that enhances their sense of mastery and self-confidence. Methods that take into account a child's individual characteristics and developmental status, and use learning principles to help parents approach the toilet training process in a systematic, positive, and unpressured manner, are recommended.

Working in a pediatric primary care clinic for over 18 years has given us the opportunity to work with many parents on toilet training issues. Although we do not have data to support the efficacy of our approach, parents have given it strong endorsement, indicating that for children 22 months and older the average toilet training time is 2–4 weeks (with occasional accidents up to several months following the initial training). This approach is summarized below.

Step 1: Determining Readiness

To be successful at toilet training, a child must be able to do three things: (1) voluntarily control the sphincter muscles, (2) communicate needs verbally or by other means, and (3) desire to control the impulse to urinate or defecate. Most children, when they are ready to be trained, show a fairly regular pattern of urinating four to nine times a day. Bowel movements may occur at varying intervals from once every other day to twice daily, and at different times each day. The first step in toilet training is to determine the times at which a child normally empties her or his bladder or bowels. This gives information on the child's ability to control the sphincter muscles (increased time between wets) and alerts the parent to the times when the child's bladder is usually full. Parents should be instructed to check the child's diaper every half hour and record D (dry), W (wet), or S (soiled) on a chart such as that shown in Figure 7.1. Parents should comment matter-of-factly to the child by saying, "Oh, good, you're dry," or "Oh, yuck, you're wet." After 3–5 days of checking, a regular pattern should be evident. If the child does not show a regular pattern or is wet every hour, he or she may not be physiologically ready for training.

Step 2: No More Diapers

The next step in the training process is to stop using diapers (except for naptime and at night). Toilet training involves helping the child unlearn certain behaviors that were acceptable in the past, as well as learning a

———————————————————————→

FIGURE 7.1. Use the following directions for the dry pants chart for baseline data in toilet training: (1) Set a timer for 30 minutes. When it rings, check the child's pants or diapers. (2) If dry and clean, say "Oh, dry, good," and mark a D on the chart. (3) If wet or soiled, say "Oh, wet (stinky), yuck," and mark a W or S on the chart. (4) Do not act upset. Take your child to the bathroom and change the soiled clothes. (5) In 3–5 days you should see a regular pattern of times your child wets.

Dry Pants Chart

Record data for any 5 consecutive days during usual waking hours.

Child's Name: _____

Times	Sunday	Monday	Tuesday	Wednesday	Thursday	Friday	Saturday
6:30 A.M.							
7:00							
7:30							
8:00							
8:30							
9:00							
9:30							
10:00							
10:30							
11:00							
11:30							
12:00 noon							
12:30 P.M.							
1:00							
1:30							
2:00							
2:30							
3:00							
3:30							
4:00							
4:30							
5:00							
5:30							
6:00							
6:30							
7:00							
7:30							
8:00							

From *Assessment and Treatment of Childhood Problems: A Clinician's Guide* by Carolyn S. Schroeder and Betty N. Gordon. © 1991 by The Guilford Press.

complex set of new behaviors. Diapers serve as a cue to the old behaviors (urinating or defecating in a diaper); even periodic use of diapers during the day is confusing to the child and will make it more difficult to break old habits and learn new ones. The child should wear thin training pants which will make the consequences of wetting or soiling very evident ("Yuck!"). In addition, clothing that is easy to take off and put on will allow the parent to respond quickly to the child's signals and will make it easier for the child to use the toilet independently. We have found that eliminating diapers initially during waking hours and then, when the child is dry during the day, eliminating them for naps and at night gives the child the opportunity to participate actively in gaining control over urination without setting the expectations too high. When the child is dry during the day and begins to have occasional dry nights, it is time to stop using diapers for naps and nights.

Step 3: Regular Sitting

Parents should be advised to use a potty chair or a toilet seat ring on the toilet (one without a cup in front prevents the child from hurting himself or herself when getting on and off the toilet), to decrease the child's realistic fear of falling in. If the child sits on the regular toilet, the parents should provide support, such as a stool or a pile of books, for the child's feet. If a potty chair is used, it should be kept only in the bathroom.

The parents should have the child sit on the potty chair or toilet for up to 5 minutes at the times when he or she is most likely to urinate or defecate. (This information should be evident from the daily dry pants record; see Figure 7.1.) Use of a timer will help parents and child keep track of the time, and let the child know when it's OK to get off the potty chair or toilet. A special "potty toy" that the child plays with only while sitting on the toilet can be used to help the child sit happily. The parents should reward the child for sitting with praise and a star drawn on a reward chart (Figure 7.2). If the child urinates or defecates in the toilet, he or she should be rewarded with more praise and a special sticker. The reward chart helps to record progress as well as to reward successes. Later, the chart can be used to reward the child for dry, clean days.

Step 4: Handling Accidents

Because toilet training is a learning process, there are bound to be accidents. At first the child may wet her or his pants soon after getting off the potty chair or toilet, or may do some in the potty chair or toilet and then, shortly afterward, do some more in the pants. Accidents should be handled matter-of-factly by saying, "Oops, you're wet (or dirty). Let's change. You'll make it to the toilet next time." The child should help the

Sitting Chart

Time to Sit	Sits Quietly - 5 Minutes	Urination
	SAMPLE	
As soon as awake	(star)	(sticker)
10:00 A.M.	(star)	

FIGURE 7.2. Sitting chart for toilet training. Key: star for sitting; sticker for urination.

parents to clean up and change his or her clothes, and all of this should be done in the bathroom. The child should then sit on the potty chair or toilet for 5 minutes to "finish up."

Some children are very resistant to toilet training or persist in having frequent daytime accidents (wetting or soiling their pants) for a year to 2 years or more after starting the toilet training process. Depending on the age of the resistant child, it may be best to stop the training process until a later date or to review the parent–child interaction carefully. In the absence of a physical problem, significant emotional/behavioral difficulties, or stress, resistance to toilet training or frequent accidents are best handled by teaching good toileting habits. Such problems are discussed in the next section on enuresis and in Chapter 8 on encopresis.

ENURESIS

Although no fatal case has ever been reported, the involuntary discharge of urine, or enuresis, has been a nuisance for literally hundreds of years. Treatment remedies predate modern civilization; there is a discussion of enuresis in the Ebers Papyrus of 550 B.C.! Enuresis is also listed as a disease in the first book of pediatrics written in English, in a section titled "Of Pyssying in the Bedde" (Glicklich, 1951).

Despite early recognition of the problem and a voluminous professional and lay literature, our understanding and effective treatment of this disorder have been very slow to develop. Treatments have included everything from potions of berries and animal parts, to sleeping on spikes and using electrical shock (Glicklich, 1951). By the early 20th century, the study and treatment of enuresis was profoundly affected by psychodynamic theory, which considers urinary incontinence to be a symptom of underlying emotional dysfunction, psychological conflict, and anxiety (Pierce, 1971). There is no evidence to support this theory, and psychotherapy has not proven helpful for the majority of children with enuresis. In the last 20 years, however, a learning theory approach has resulted in very effective methods of treatment. More recently, medical research has found that many enuretic children do not have a normal diurnal rhythm of antidiuretic hormone secretion, which would normally reduce the nocturnal urine output to a volume less than the functional bladder capacity. Following from this, treatment with desmopressin, a chemical analogue of the antidiuretic hormone vasopressin, is promising. The remainder of this chapter briefly reviews the definition and prevalence of enuresis, and then focuses on effective assessment and treatment methods for nocturnal enuresis, with a brief discussion of diurnal enuresis. (For an extensive review of enuresis, see Walker, Kenning, & Faust-Campanile, 1989.)

Definition

Enuresis is defined as the involuntary discharge of urine; daytime wetting is called "diurnal enuresis," and wetting during the night "nocturnal enuresis." When a child wets both night and day, it is called "nocturnal–diurnal enuresis" or "mixed enuresis." Although boys are twice as likely as girls to be nocturnally enuretic, daytime frequency of urination and wetting tend to be more common among girls (DeJonge, 1973). A voiding dysfunction can be either functional or organic in origin. "Functional enuresis" is defined as a continued pattern of involuntary or intentional voiding of urine in the clothing or bed, beyond the age when children are typically toilet-trained and in the absence of a physical disorder (Walker et al., 1989). Organic causes of enuresis are discussed later. Enuresis can be primary or secondary: "Primary enuresis" exists when a child has never achieved consistent dryness for at least a year or more, and "secondary enuresis" describes the child who has achieved dryness for at least a year and subsequently loses bladder control. DeJonge (1973) reports that 85% of all nocturnal enuresis is primary enuresis. The distinction between primary and secondary enuresis is made largely for classification purposes, since there is no reported difference in response to treatment (Walker et al., 1989).

According to the revised third edition of the *Diagnostic and Statistical Manual of Mental Disorders* (DSM-III-R; American Psychiatric Association, 1987), a diagnosis of Functional Enuresis requires the following:

(A) Repeated voiding of urine during the day or night into bed or clothes, whether involuntary or intentional.
(B) At least two such events per month for children between the ages of five or six, and at least one event per month for older children.
(C) Chronologic age at least five, and mental age at least four.
(D) Not due to a physical disorder, such as diabetes, urinary tract infection, or a seizure disorder. (p. 85)

Although DSM-III-R uses the age of 5 years, there is disagreement on the chronological age at which the diagnosis should be made, varying from 3 years to 6 or 7 years (Walker et al., 1989). Normally developing children usually achieve nighttime control a year or two later than they do daytime control, and control over urination is achieved earlier by girls than by boys. Therefore, we agree with MacKeith, Meadow, and Turner (1973) that the diagnosis of enuresis should be reserved for wetting beyond the ages of 5 years for girls and 6 years for boys.

Prevalence

Prevalence studies in the United States report rather consistently that 15–20% of 5-year-olds, 5% of 10-year-olds, and about 2% of 12- to 14-year-olds experience nocturnal enuresis (Oppel, Harper, & Rider, 1968; Perlmutter, 1985). Approximately 15% of bedwetters will spontaneously achieve control each year, so that by age 15, only 1-2% remain enuretic (Forsythe & Redmond, 1974). Other work has found that the spontaneous remission rate for girls is higher than for boys, especially between ages 4 and 6, when it can be as high as 44-71% (Verhulst et al., 1985). Bedwetting is, thus, not common for girls after age 11 and for boys after age 13 (Verhulst et al., 1985).

Walker et al. (1989) report on studies showing that diurnal enuresis is far less common than nocturnal enuresis, with estimates reported at only 3% of 6-year-olds in Great Britain and Sweden (Blomfield & Douglas, 1956; Hallgren, 1956). Furthermore, 50-60% of children with diurnal enuresis also have nocturnal enuresis (Hallgren, 1956).

Genetic factors appear to contribute to nocturnal enuresis. According to Bakwin (1973), when both parents have a history of enuresis, 77% of the children have enuresis; when only one parent has a history of enuresis, 44% of the children are enuretic; when neither parent have a history of enuresis, only 15% of the children have enuresis. These data, however, do not take into account toilet training methods or potentially high tolerance levels for wetting in parents who were themselves enuretic.

Most children with enuresis do not have emotional or behavioral problems, but enuresis is more frequent in children who do have emotional disturbance (Shaffer, 1973). Heightened stress such as family disruption or stressful life events may cause enuresis in children, but the presence of enuresis is not necessarily a sign of psychopathology in itself (Douglas, 1973). Stress that occurs during ages 2-4 years, when children are in the process of being toilet-trained or have just completed training, can often result in incomplete training and thus in enuresis (Walker et al., 1989). Enuresis is more prevalent among developmentally delayed youngsters and institutionalized children, whether they are of normal or subnormal intelligence (Moffatt, 1989).

Etiology

Two etiological theories of enuresis, organic and learning, are briefly reviewed here because of their direct bearing on the assessment and treatment of the problem.

Organic Theories

The actual incidence of organic urinary incontinence is very low in children, with estimates of 1-3% (Forsythe & Redmond, 1974). Organic causes that have been clearly identified include a variety of acquired and congenital central nervous system lesions, as well as disorders in the neural innervation of the bladder; structural problems of the genital–urinary system; bladder or urinary tract infections; and chronic diseases such as diabetes mellitus, diabetes insipidus, seizure disorders, sickle cell disease, and possible food allergies (Walker et al., 1989). In addition, a number of theories about the pathogenesis of nocturnal enuresis have resulted in three targets for medical treatment: sleep mechanisms, the bladder or urinary sphincter, and diuresis (increased or excessive secretion of urine) (Norgaard, Rittig, & Djurhuus, 1989).

Norgaard et al. (1989) conducted extensive investigations of enuretic children and found that (1) these children had normal daytime bladder capacities, (2) a full bladder was necessary for enuresis to occur, (3) enuresis did not occur in any specific sleep stage, and (4) there were no specific sleep patterns before or during the enuretic episode. Thus there is no rationale for the use of sleep-lightening drugs (e.g., amphetamines), or, in the absence of physical evidence, for the use of drugs directed to a spastic bladder. Imipramine, a drug commonly used for depression, is frequently prescribed for nocturnal enuresis; in fact, the *Physicians' Desk Reference* (PDR, 1990) lists enuresis as the only indication for using it with children. This is remarkable, given that the rationale for its use for enuresis is not at all clear. It may have been based at one time on the observation that urinary retention occurs as a side effect in some adults who were taking imipramine. However, urinary retention rarely if ever occurs in children who are being treated with imipramine for depression (L. O'Quinn, personal communication, November 28, 1990). It is disturbing then that imipramine continues to be listed in the PDR as a treatment for childhood enuresis and that physicians continue to prescribe it, given the abundance of empirical evidence demonstrating its ineffectiveness in treating enuresis and the unclear rationale for its use.

The findings of Norgaard et al. (1989), plus the fact that many nocturnal enuretics report several involuntary voidings during one night, have led to diuresis studies. This research indicates that enuretic children have stable antidiuretic hormone (arginine vasopressin) secretion, whereas normal children have an increase in this hormone during the night (Norgaard et al., 1989). Children with nocturnal enuresis evidence a high urine output, exceeding bladder capacity during sleep. This high output of poorly concentrated urine seems to be produced by the lack of an increase in the secretion of vasopressin during the night. Desmopressin, a chemical analogue of vasopressin, has been used to reduce the amount of urine produced during the night. Several studies have demonstrated that desmopressin will diminish nocturnal enuresis, and no serious side effects have been reported (Klauber, 1989; Norgaard et al., 1989). In a study of 34 patients treated with desmopressin intranasal spray, 24 (70%) became totally dry during the treatment, 4 improved, and 6 did not respond at all. In general, a 20- to 40-μg dose is given intranasally at bedtime, regardless of age and body weight. Relapse rate after discontinuation of the drug is high, especially if the desmopressin is not gradually tapered (Miller, Goldberg, & Atkin, 1989). It is suggested that desmopressin therapy may be especially helpful for short-term use or for emergency or special occasions (Klauber, 1989).

Learning Theory

Learning theory suggests that habit deficiency, inadequate learning experiences, and inappropriate reinforcement contingencies result in the failure to learn to control the complex urination reflex. This reflex involves, in part, contractions of the detrusor muscle within the wall of the bladder, along with relaxation of the internal and external sphincter muscles located between the neck of the bladder and the beginning of the urethra (see Figure 7.3). Treatment focuses on teaching the correct response(s) and prerequisite skills, such as recognizing when the bladder is full and undressing. Interventions based on learning theory have been shown to be the most effective long-term treatments for nocturnal enuresis, with success rates of 70–90% (Walker et al., 1989). These constitute the focus of our section on treatment of nocturnal enuresis. Prior to an indepth discussion of these treatment approaches, we focus on the assessment of nocturnal enuresis.

ASSESSMENT OF NOCTURNAL ENURESIS

The assessment process for nocturnal enuresis (hereafter referred to simply as enuresis) follows the steps for gathering information in accordance with the Comprehensive Assessment-to-Intervention System (CAIS; see Chapter 3); the focus, of course, is on gathering information specifically pertinent to understanding and treating enuresis.

Step 1: Initial Contact

When a parent refers a child for enuresis, the clinician should first determine whether there has been a recent medical evaluation of the problem; if not, a referral should be made for such an evaluation. Although the incidence of organic or physiological difficulties resulting in enuresis is low, the possibility of such difficulties must be ruled out before beginning further assessment and treatment.

When there is no organic basis for the problem, then the clinician should rule out the presence of significant emotional or behavioral problems. This can be done by mailing parents a general questionnaire (e.g., our own Parent Questionnaire; see Appendix B) and such screening

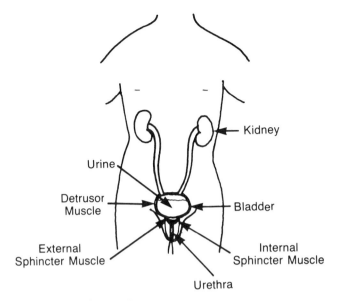

FIGURE 7.3.   Urinary tract system.

instruments as the Child Behavior Checklist (CBCL; Achenbach & Edelbrock, 1983), the Eyberg Child Behavior Inventory (ECBI; Eyberg &
Ross, 1978), and the Parenting Stress Index (PSI; Abidin, 1990). (See
Appendix A for descriptions of these three instruments.) Parents should
also be asked to keep a record of the time the child goes to bed and arises,
as well as the number of wet and dry nights. During this baseline period
the child should be taken out of all protective clothing, including diapers,
thick underwear, or rubber pants. The parents should check to see
whether the child is wet before they go to bed and, if possible, every 2–3
hours throughout the night. We have found that a 7-day record is usually
sufficient. Sending parents a form (Figure 7.4) on which to keep this
information ensures that the appropriate data will be obtained. All of this
information should be returned to and reviewed by the clinician prior to
the initial interview.

Step 2: Parent and Child Interview

We recommend including the child, regardless of age, in the initial interview with the parents. Treatment of enuresis involves a great deal of
cooperation on the part of the child, and the child's level of interest in a
treatment program must be determined. In addition, children often share
information about the problem that is not known by the parents (e.g., do
they wake up right before or after they urinate, or do they feel the

Nighttime Wetting Chart
Baseline

Child's Name: _____   Age: _____

Address: _____

DATE/DAY	BEDTIME	TIME UP IN A.M.	TIME OF WET(S)	SIZE Small Medium Large	WHAT DID YOU DO?	COMMENTS

From *Assessment and Treatment of Childhood Problems: A Clinician's Guide* by Carolyn S. Schroeder and Betty N. Gordon. © 1991 by The Guilford Press.

FIGURE 7.4. Nighttime wetting chart for enuresis baseline data.

bladder pressure indicating the need to void?). Butler, Redfern, and Forsythe (1990) give support for interviewing children about their perception of bedwetting, the value of stopping bedwetting, and their resistance to changing the behavior. In a study of 55 children ages 6–14 years, successful treatment was associated with the perception of bedwetting as having psychological implications (i.e., social, emotional, and parent affective response) and with an absence of resistance to changing the behavior. In contrast, treatment was less successful with children who perceived bedwetting as having predominantly nonpsychological implications (e.g., bad smell, changing sheets) and who were resistant to change. Developmentally, the ability to take a psychological perspective increases with age, so that the older the child, the more likely it is that treatment will be effective. These data, however, should not be construed as meaning that treatment should not be offered to the 6- or 7-year-old child who cannot yet take a psychological perspective. If the child is not resistant to change, would like to stop bedwetting, and has a supportive family, treatment has a good chance of being successful.

During the initial interview, the clinician should be particularly careful to gather the following information:

1. Are there other behavioral or developmental problems? The presence of other problems can be determined from the screening instruments. Problems such as oppositional behavior and noncompliance can interfere with treatment of enuresis and should be treated first. Doleys (1978) also encourages the clinician to be alert to problems such as fear of the dark or of the toilet, which may be causing the child to avoid using the toilet at night. If there is indication of serious psychopathology, then it is recommended that treatment of enuresis be postponed until these problems are further evaluated and possibly treated.

2. What is the history and current status of the child's urination habits and incontinence? Questions on the nature of these behaviors should include (a) information on daytime as well as nighttime voiding (frequency, time, and volume of wets); (b) intermittent or daily incontinence (frequency, antecedents, and consequences); (c) primary or secondary status (if previously dry, the time and circumstances when wetting began); and (d) age, methods, and circumstances of the initial toilet training process. If the child has never been dry, special attention should be given to whether the child has learned the prerequisite skills. Information on the child's ability to retain urine after he or she has the urge to void during the day (e.g., "When you have the urge to go to the bathroom, can you hold it for 5–10 minutes or do you have to rush to the toilet?") and daily frequency of voiding, as well as quantity and type of liquids consumed on a daily basis, is often very helpful in determining whether there is a bladder capacity problem.

3. Is there a family history of incontinence? This question is important, given the increased frequency of enuresis among children with a positive family history of the disorder. A positive family history does not preclude treatment, but it may affect the parents' attitude toward treatment and the methods previously used in treating the problem (e.g., are they overindulgent or exasperated?).

4. What is the environmental context of the problem? Environmental circumstances—including recent, unexpected, or ongoing stressful life events; bedtime rituals; sleeping arrangements; the child's proximity to the bathroom; temperature in the house; and what the child wears to bed—give information on the potential cause of enuresis and potential problems in carrying out a program.

5. How have the parents handled the problem? Information on the previous attempts at treatment should be gathered in great detail. Often these attempts are made for brief periods of time and in an unsystematic fashion. It is important to give parents information about the usefulness of previously used techniques, as well as why some techniques might not have been successful. The parents' attitudes about the toileting process, conflict over how it should be handled, and their willingness to follow through on a treatment program should be assessed at this time.

6. Why are the parents' seeking help now? Finding out why the parents are seeking help now rather than at some other time provides information on their attitudes toward the problem and potential compliance with treatment. The parents are a critical factor in the success or failure of a treatment program for enuresis, and their attitudes, beliefs, and acceptance of a treatment approach must be carefully considered before embarking on treatment (Doleys & Dolce, 1982).

7. How does the child feel about the problem? The child's interest in resolving the problem should be assessed, because, again, his or her cooperation is as crucial as that of the parents in the success of a treatment program for enuresis. Butler et al. (1990) used a series of question to determine a child's understanding of the benefits of stopping bedwetting: (1) "What are the bad things about bedwetting?"; (2) "What are the good things about being dry?"; (3) "What difference would being dry make to you?"; and (4) "What do you imagine might change if you become dry every night?" Questions to determine resistance to change included "Could you see any problems in being dry?" and "What might be good about bedwetting?" They reported that one child responded to the latter question with "The smell will frighten off burglars!"

Step 3: Observation of Behavior

Observation of the parent–child interaction during the interview is useful in determining the support that will probably be given by the parents to the child during treatment. In addition, observing how the child reacts to the discussion can give information on the child's interest in treatment and/or steps that may be needed to elicit his or her cooperation with the treatment plan.

Step 4: Further Assessment

Further psychological assessment is only necessary if other problems become evident during the assessment process.

Step 5: Referral to Allied Health Professionals

A medical evaluation should be done before the initial interview with the family, in order to rule out any organic problem.

Step 6: Communication of Findings and Treatment Recommendations

Following the assessment session(s), it is important for the child clinician to share information with the parents about the child's development and the ways in which the enuresis fits into the developmental process. This is particularly important, because the parents' and child's trust in the clinician and cooperation in the treatment process will depend on their understanding of the problem. The nature and possible etiology of the enuresis should be shared with the parents and child, and they should be given a rationale for the treatment recommendations. This process often involves explanations of the value of previously attempted methods and the reasons why they did not work.

The next section focuses on the most effective treatment approach to nocturnal enuresis as determined by empirical studies, and also includes the specific treatment protocol used in our clinic.

TREATMENT OF NOCTURNAL ENURESIS

Enuresis is a problem that *will* most likely get better simply with age, so should we even treat it? Although most children who are enuretic do not have emotional problems, we have found that those children who are referred for treatment of enuresis often appear to have more worries and lower self-esteem than children who are not enuretic. When children's enuresis is successfully treated, these troublesome problems also improve. All things taken into consideration, we believe that treatment should be offered for enuresis, but only if the child and family request help and are prepared to cooperate fully with the treatment program.

Most parents initially seek help from their pediatricians when there is a problem of enuresis. Physicians, however, tend to prescribe methods that have been shown to be of limited efficacy, such as drugs (especially imipramine), fluid restriction, rewards, and reassurance; some have even been known to suggest rather punitive methods, such as forcing the child to sleep in the bathtub. It is interesting that fewer than 5% of American primary care physicians recommend behavior modification procedures, although these methods are consistently associated with the highest reported cure rates and the lowest relapse rates (Foxman, Valdez, & Brock, 1986). In contrast, 32–50% of physicians prescribe drug therapy, which has limited effectiveness (Rushton, 1989).

It has been suggested that physicians do not use behavioral methods because they are too expensive and take too much time to carry out. However, the behavioral program for nocturnal enuresis used in our clinic costs $250 and involves a 1-hour initial interview and the provision of a urine alarm system, followed by biweekly phone contacts and letters to the child for a period of up to 3 months. Given that an initial course of treatment with desmopressin costs approximately $1,000 to $1,500 (Miller et al., 1989), there seems little reason for physicians not to use behavioral methods. Rather, the issue seems to be one of differences in professional training. Informing physicians of the availability of behavioral treatments and giving them feedback on the success of such programs for their patients should prove helpful in increasing physicians' recommendations for behavioral treatment.

Urine Alarm

The urine alarm or bell-and-pad method of treating enuresis was described in the literature as early as 1904 (Pfaundler, 1904), but became popular following the publication of an article by Mowrer and Mowrer (1938). The apparatus includes a urine-sensitive pad, which is placed under the child's buttocks; the pad is connected to a loud bell or buzzer. Urine, which contains salt and is an electrolyte, completes an electrical circuit in the pad, activating an alarm that continues to sound until manually turned off. Newer models use metal snaps that are attached to the crotch of the child's underpants and connected to a small wristwatch-type apparatus. This can be worn on the child's wrist or attached to the shoulder of the pajamas. The urine completes an electrical circuit between the snaps, which sounds the buzzer in the "wristwatch." We have found the wristwatch style to be the most efficient in ease of use and reliability. Moreover, Forsythe and Butler (1989) found that this type of alarm achieved a more rapid initial dry night rate than the more traditional bell-and-pad alarm. Figure 7.5 illustrates this device, which can be

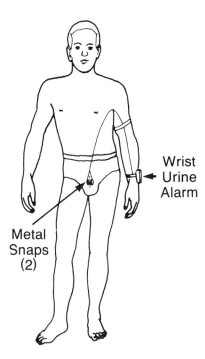

FIGURE 7.5.   Wrist urine alarm for treatment of enuresis.

obtained from Nytone Medical Products, Inc., 2424 South 900 West, Salt
Lake City, UT 84119.

Mowrer and Mowrer (1938) originally conceptualized the bell-and-
pad method as based on a classical conditioning paradigm, in which the
sensation of bladder distension becomes associated with the sound of the
alarm. Eventually, they believed, bladder distension becomes the cue for
the child to wake and go to the bathroom to urinate. However, this
conceptualization does not seem to reflect what actually happens, because most children using this method eventually learn to sleep through
the night without wetting or awakening to use the bathroom. Lovibond
(1964) suggested that an operant paradigm better explains the learning
process. The child learns to avoid the aversive alarm by retaining urine
and sleeping through the night, or by awakening and using the bathroom
before the alarm sounds. Other factors, such as positive reinforcement
from the parent and therapist, may also play an important role in treatment. Butler, Brewin, and Forsythe (1988) found that sibling teasing was
associated with successful treatment outcome with the urine alarm; however Butler et al. (1990) failed to replicate this finding. These conflicting

results, plus the obvious potential negative effects of sibling teasing, suggest that a supportive family environment is more conducive to effective treatment.

Walker et al. (1989) report on outcome studies from 1960 to 1975, which indicate success in 70–90% of cases. Although the relapse rate within 6 months of treatment has been reported to be as high as 41%, retreatment for a shorter length of time results in successful reconditioning for over 60% of these cases (Doleys, 1978). A number of studies have shown that the relapse rate can be significantly reduced by employing overlearning (increasing the liquid intake prior to bedtime after dryness has been achieved; Young & Morgan, 1972) and by using the alarm on an intermittent schedule after dryness has been achieved (Jehu, Morgan, Turner, & Jones, 1977).

Information gathered during the assessment can guide the clinician to potential problems in treatment (an uninterested child, a strong family history of enuresis) and can indicate the likely response to treatment. Given the empirically demonstrated effectiveness of the urine alarm system, its ease of implementation, and its relatively low cost, we begin almost all treatment for enuresis with this method. Data from the first 2 weeks provides important information about the child's wetting pattern. Our experience and that of others (Walker et al., 1989) indicates that the size of the wet spots and then the number of wets per night should decrease during the first 2 weeks, followed by intermittent dry nights for the next 2 weeks, with consistent dryness in 6–8 weeks. These data, along with information gathered in the assessment process, alert the clinician to potential problems and guide the treatment program; for example, they may indicate the need to add components such as urine retention or sphincter control exercises for the child who exhibits excessive frequency and urgency.

Treatment Protocol

We now outline the specific components of the treatment program used in our clinic, which is based on information derived from the empirical literature.

Sharing Information

The importance of sharing information and giving specific instructions in carrying out treatment programs for enuresis has been repeatedly emphasized in the literature (Rushton, 1989). Information provided in person by a professional has been shown to be superior to videotapes of the same material given by the same professional (Houts, Whelan, & Peterson, 1987), whether the information is given in a group or an individual session. Information on the frequency of enuresis and the general stages of learning to control the urine reflex should be shared with the parents and child in simple, understandable language. Most children are not aware of the prevalence of enuresis, and they and their parents find it reassuring that they are not the "only ones" with this problem.

The use of a diagram of the bladder, such as the one in Figure 7.3, helps both children and parents understand the process. The clinician should begin by describing how urine from the kidney fills the bladder, which functions like a storage bag. When the bladder expands to a certain point, the muscles contract to discharge urine into the tube at the lower end of the bladder, called the urethra. The sphincter muscles close the entrance to the urethra. The opening of the internal sphincter muscle is due to contraction of involuntary muscles of the bladder, but the external sphincter muscle is under voluntary control. When the bladder is full, it becomes distended; the internal sphincter muscle opens, and this is the signal that one has to go to the bathroom. Depending on the age of the child, the clinician can give as brief or as long a description of this process as necessary. The point is to give the child a picture of what he or she is trying to learn to do—that is, tune in to a distended (full) bladder and tighten the sphincter muscle until he or she wakes up and can get to the bathroom. Once children learn how to do this, they are usually able to sleep for longer periods of time without needing to use the bathroom. Children who wet frequently (eight or more times) during the day and many times during the night should be warned that it may take them a little longer to learn to stay dry.

Alarm System

The alarm system should be introduced at this time, with a rationale for how it can help the child learn to tighten the sphincter muscle and go to the bathroom before wetting the bed. The alarm acts as a "helper" by waking the child up as soon as he or she starts to wet. The goal is to "beat the buzzer"—that is, to get up before it goes off or sleep dry through the night. If possible, the alarm should be demonstrated on the child during the first treatment session. The snaps can be put on the outer clothing; a drop of water placed on the cloth near the snaps will set off the alarm. If the child does not want to have the alarm attached to his or her clothing in the office, then it should be demonstrated on the clinician or the parent. At night the alarm should be placed on the child's wrist or pinned to the shoulder, with the wires running up the child's arm, into the sleeve of the shirt, and down into the crotch of the pants. The parents can be shown how to shorten the wire by taping a length together with adhesive tape. This is an important step, so there is no chance that the child will become caught up in the wire or the leads will be disconnected.

This equipment can be unreliable, going off when it should not or not going off when it should, and we always keep backup alarms in the clinic. Parents are advised to exchange the equipment if there is the slightest problem. We use the alarm two or three times before sending it back to the factory for a maintenance check or a replacement. The family is loaned the alarm as part of the treatment package; an additional deposit increases the incentive to return the alarm after treatment is completed.

The procedure for using the alarm is as follows: The parents go to the child's room when the alarm rings and prompt the child to go to the bathroom, to empty the bladder completely, to change the bed, to put the soiled linen in the proper container, to change pajamas, to reconnect the alarm, and to record the data (Figure 7.6). The parents should be instructed to do this in a calm, matter-of-fact way without excessive praise or punishment.

The next step is to give the parents and child a description of the typical stages of treatment. The child should initially expect to wet with the same frequency, but the wet spots should become smaller. Then the frequency of the wets will decrease, with the first wet occurring later in the night. Next, the child will start to "beat the buzzer" and awaken to void before actually wetting the bed. Soon the child will be waking without the alarm with greater frequency and will no longer wet the bed. Finally, the child can expect to sleep longer and longer between awakenings, and will eventually sleep through the night without needing to void until he or she awakens in the morning. The time it takes to go through this process can vary from 1 to 3 months. The clinician should carefully monitor the data to determine whether the wet spots are getting smaller and the number of wets is decreasing at an acceptable rate. The goal is to get 14 consecutive dry nights.

After 14 consecutive dry nights, an overlearning procedure is implemented. This involves having the child drink 6–8 ounces of his or her favorite liquid (excluding drinks that are diuretic, such as cola, tea, etc.) before bed. The child and parents should be told that this is important, in order to make sure that the child has fully learned to tighten the sphincter muscle and to get up if necessary to go to the bathroom. They should be warned that there may be some accidents, but that this is to be expected at this stage of the training. This phase of the treatment is continued until there are 14 more consecutive dry nights.

The next phase of treatment is to use the alarm on an intermittent schedule to further strengthen the newly learned behavior of sleeping through the night dry. The child should be told that on *some* nights the parents will disconnect the alarm after he or she has gone to sleep. Because the child will not know when the alarm is connected, this will

Nighttime Wetting Chart
Treatment

Child's Name: _____   Age: _____

Address: _____

SAMPLE

Date/Day	Bedtime	Time up in A.M.	Time (wet/beat buzzer)	SIZE OF WET — Small	Medium	Large	Beat the Buzzer	Go to Bathroom	Change Sheets	Change P.J.'s	Dispose of Wet Clothing
3-22-90 / Thurs	9:00	7:00	11:30 P.M.			✓		✓	✓	✓	✓
			4:00 A.M.		✓			✓	✓	✓	
			6:30 A.M.				✓	✓			

FIGURE 7.6. Nighttime wetting chart for enuresis treatment data.

From *Assessment and Treatment of Childhood Problems: A Clinician's Guide* by Carolyn S. Schroeder and Betty N. Gordon. © 1991 by The Guilford Press.

help him or her to learn to sleep through the night without the alarm. The parents should be asked to disconnect the alarm two nights during the first week, and then to increase the number of nights after each completely dry week until the alarm is no longer connected. The alarm should be removed at this time. The parents and child should be reminded that relapses are not unusual, but if wetting occurs more than once a month (or once a month for 2 months) they should immediately call to borrow the alarm again until the child has 30 consecutive dry nights. We find that with the use of the overlearning procedure and the intermittent alarm schedule, relapses are rare; when they do occur, reinstituting the alarm resolves the problem quickly.

Parents are given addressed envelopes to mail the data to the clinic every week. The clinician should chart the data (see Figure 7.7), observe the course of treatment, mail a supportive letter to the child, and call the parents if necessary. (A phone call at least every 2 weeks is important to support the parents and answer any questions.) An example of an encouraging letter to a child follows:

May 25, 1990

Dear John:

Thank you for being so prompt in sending your chart to me. Wow! You must be very pleased with yourself! Four dry nights in one week and on the other nights the wet spots were small. Have you noticed that you are also sleeping longer before you "beat the buzzer" or wet? That is just what we want to happen.

Keep up the good work. After three weeks of using the buzzer you are already having dry nights, but remember to tell yourself to "beat the buzzer" before you fall asleep. Your mother said that you were doing a good job of remembering to start and stop your stream of urine when you have to go to the bathroom. Great!

I look forward to seeing your chart for this week. Enjoy your dry nights!

Sincerely,
Dr. Schroeder

Additional Treatment Strategies

Rewards

We generally have not found it necessary to use tangible rewards in conjunction with the alarm system. Praise from the parents and letters from the therapist are usually sufficient. With younger children, however, we have sometimes found that giving them a star for each night they follow the program and a fancy sticker for every dry night is helpful in

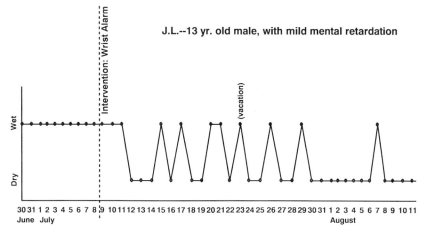

FIGURE 7.7.   Sample enuresis chart for use of wrist alarm.

acknowledging their efforts. Some parents offer social rewards, such as a sleepover, when the child has successfully completed the program.

Urine Retention and Sphincter Control Exercises

Walker et al. (1989) give a nice summary of urine retention and sphincter control exercises, and the reader is referred to their work for more information. These techniques are used to help the child gain control over the urination reflex and to increase functional bladder capacity. "Functional bladder capacity" refers to the bladder's ability to retain a given volume of urine without producing an urge to void, rather than the actual size of the bladder. A number of enuretic children have a small functional bladder capacity, causing increased frequency of daytime urination. Increasing bladder capacity alone, however, has not been demonstrated to be sufficient (or, for most children, necessary) to eliminate enuresis (Doleys, 1978). Urine retention training may be helpful, however, if the frequencyy of wets or awakenings during the night does not decrease as expected. This training involves giving the child increased liquids, and, when the urge to urinate occurs, having him or her refrain from urinating as long as possible. With practice, children can hold for several minutes to hours. Walker (1978) warns that the child should not be given excessive fluids (no more than 8–16 ounces per hour) or asked to retain fluids beyond 1–2 hours.

Another technique that has been used to strengthen the sphincter muscles and thus to increase bladder capacity is sphincter control training. This involves having the child practice starting and stopping the stream of urine when voiding. Walker (1978) suggests having the child do this three to five times during each voiding, and providing rewards to encourage this practice.

Dry Bed Training

No discussion of enuresis would be complete without mentioning Azrin, Sneed, and Foxx's (1974) "dry bed training" (DBT) approach to enuresis. Over the years, this method has undergone a number of changes, but it essentially involves the use of operant conditioning principles to teach the child the responses necessary to stay dry: (1) positive reinforcement for inhibiting urination; (2) urine retention control training; (3) positive practice (repeatedly getting out of bed to go to the bathroom); (4) nighttime waking; (5) full cleanliness training (cleaning the bed, including the mattress, for a period of up to 45 minutes); (6) negative reinforcement; (7) mild punishment (parent disapproval); (8) family encouragement; and (9) a urine alarm. This program has been the focus of much research. Bollard and Nettlebeck (1982), in a comparison of various components of the program, concluded that the only component that produced significant effects alone was the urine alarm. The effects of the other components were cumulative when added to the urine alarm. Thus, if the alarm alone is not working as expected, the clinician should consider what parts of DBT might be added to a particular child's treatment program (Azrin, Theines-Hontos, & Besalel-Azrin, 1979).

TREATMENT OF MIXED ENURESIS

Fielding (1980) states that children who are both diurnally and nocturnally enuretic may respond more slowly to treatment of nocturnal enuresis treatment and may relapse more quickly once continence is achieved. In the absence of a physical disorder, significant emotional/behavioral problems, or stress, daytime wetting is most often the result of poor toileting habits. We suggest first dealing with the daytime wetting by establishing good toileting habits, including (1) taking data on when the child wets, and having him or her sit on the toilet for 5 minutes at those times; (2) cleanliness training (including cleaning self, clothes, and the floor if wet) and sitting on the toilet for 5 minutes after accidents; (3) positive practice, such as practicing going to the bathroom from different parts of the house, yard, and neighborhood; (4) charting with rewards for dry days; and (5) parent and child support through regular therapist contact, however brief.

When the child appears to be having trouble recognizing when the bladder is full or waiting too long before going to the bathroom, we have used the urine alarm during the day. Sphincter control and urine retention exercises also can be added if necessary. Once continence is established, overlearning (the consumption of increased fluids) is added, and the reinforcement system is gradually faded by increasing the number of dry days necessary for rewards. When this is accomplished, if the child continues to wet the bed *and wants* a treatment program for the bedwetting, the alarm system should be used. The clinician should let the parent and child know that there may be some regression during the day, but with continuation of good toilet habits, daytime wets should decrease.

—————————————— *CASE EXAMPLE* ——————————————

Step 1: Initial Contact

Mrs. O'Dell, the single mother of a 7-year-old boy, Andrew, called to inquire about the feasibility of treating her son's bedwetting. Andrew had been seen in our clinic at age 5 regarding his readiness for school. An evaluation at that time indicated a verbally bright child with poor visual–motor organization skills. A referral to an occupational therapist resulted in a diagnosis of mild dyspraxia (i.e., difficulty in motor planning skills). The child had had a course of treatment with the occupational therapist, had gone on to kindergarten, and was currently doing quite well in the second grade.

Andrew had recently had a physical examination, and the physician had indicated that there was no organic basis for the bedwetting. The physician had suggested that he be made to sleep in his soiled sheets for a minimum of 2 weeks before washing them. When the child indicated that he wanted to have some friends spend the night, the physician encouraged him to do this and to be sure the friends slept in the same bed with him. Neither the mother nor the child was pleased with this advice, and the mother decided they would seek help from a psychologist.

To rule out the presence of significant emotional or behavioral problems, the mother was asked to complete the Parent Questionnaire, the CBCL, the ECBI, and the PSI. She was also asked to complete a nighttime wetting record (Figure 7.4) for 7 days prior to their appointment.

Step 2: Parent and Child Interview

Mrs. O'Dell and Andrew came in together for the initial interview. A review of the Parent Questionnaire indicated that Mrs. O'Dell was a licensed practical nurse who worked the day shift at a local nursing home. She had been divorced for 4 years. Andrew was described as a well-adjusted child who had a number of close friends, was doing well in school, and preferred quiet activities (such as rock collecting, reading, and playing computer games). Mrs. O'Dell confirmed the information on the rating scales by stating that she was quite pleased with Andrew and did not feel that the bedwetting was a problem for her. The request for treatment had come because Andrew wanted to have friends over, spend the night with friends, and go to a week-long overnight camp in the summer.

Bladder and bowel training during the day had been started at 2½ years of age and completed at age 4. Andrew was initially bowel-trained and then bladder-trained. Andrew reported that he still had occasional accidents during the day when he delayed going to the bathroom because he was playing. These accidents occurred approximately once a month. The only time Andrew had ever been dry at night was when he had spent the night at his grandmother's house 6 months earlier.

To the mother's knowledge, no one in her or her former husband's families had a history of enuresis. There had been no major changes for this family in the last year, and the atmosphere in the home was described as calm, with regular daily routines. A younger sister, age 4, was already sleeping dry through the night. Andrew enjoyed his twice a month week-end visits with his father and their relationship was described as warm and loving. The father was in agreement with Andrew and his mother's seeking help at this time as Andrew regularly wet his bed on his visits.

Step 3: Observation of Behavior

The primary observation data was provided by the Nighttime Wetting Chart. This chart indicated that Andrew went to bed around 8:30 P.M., had his first wet at 11 to 11:30 P.M., wet again between 3 A.M. and 5:30 A.M., and got up at 7 A.M. The size of the wets varied from medium to large. The record also indicated that Andrew would often put a blanket over the wet spot, or, if the wet was too large, he would change his clothes and spend the rest of the night in his mother's bed. During the interview Andrew was attentive; although he was initially reticent, he soon contributed information readily. Mrs. O'Dell was respectful of his input and often deferred to him in answering questions. He enjoyed the demonstration of the alarm and was enthusiastic about starting the program.

Step 4: Further Assessment

No further assessment appeared indicated at this time.

Step 5: Referral to Allied Health Professionals

The medical examination had been done prior to the initial contact.

Step 6: Communication of Findings and Treatment Recommendations

The findings were summarized for Andrew and his mother, and the rationale for the specific treatment recommendations was given. They were told that wetting the bed seemed to be an isolated problem for Andrew. He was well accepted by his family, had friends, had a variety of interests, and was doing well in school; in general, all the information indicated that he was a well-adjusted child. Although Mrs. O'Dell did not consider the bedwetting as a problem for her, and in fact had done nothing about it, she was supportive of Andrew and agreed to help with the program. Andrew was clearly interested in stopping the bedwetting for legitimate reasons. Next, information was shared on bladder functioning and enuresis, and the wrist alarm system was demonstrated. Nighttime wetting data forms and stamped envelopes were given to the mother and child to complete and return on a weekly basis.

Because Andrew had periodic difficulty making it to the bathroom during the day, he was instructed to start and stop the flow of urine three to five times each time he urinated. The purpose of this was to strengthen his sphincter muscle. He was also instructed not to change his consumption of liquids before bedtime and to increase fluids during the day, so that he would have more opportunity to practice sphincter control. Urine retention training was considered, but the mother felt that Andrew already was waiting too long before going to the bathroom.

Course of Treatment

In the first week, Andrew "beat the buzzer" one night, wet two times a night for three nights, and wet one time on the other three nights. The wets were all medium to large. During the second week, the wets were small to medium and the time of wetting was later. He "beat the buzzer" on two nights, wet two times on two nights, and had three nights with one wet. In the third week, he slept dry through one night, "beat the buzzer" two nights, and had one small wet on each of the remaining four nights. The course of treatment was unremarkable, and within 8 weeks Andrew had 14 consecutive dry nights. Overlearning and later intermittent use of the alarm were then instituted. After a period of slight regression, Andrew had 30 dry nights, 4 months from the start of treatment. He was delighted and had begun making plans for summer camp.

Chapter 8

Toileting:

Encopresis

"*E*ncopresis" is the term used for defecating in the pants in the absence of any organic pathology. Although this problem has been around for a very long time, it has received far less attention in the scientific literature than has enuresis. Traditionally, the psychiatric literature has viewed encopresis as a symptom of severe emotional problems, with psychological conflict as the primary catalyst for its onset (Halpern, 1977). Currently, however, there is a consensus that encopresis may be considered a "mental disorder" only by tradition, because children who are encopretic do not necessarily have severe emotional or behavioral disorders (American Psychiatric Association, 1980). Although encopretic children do present with more emotional problems than the normal population (Gabel, Hegedus, Wald, Chandra, & Chiponis, 1986), most encopretic children are not emotionally disturbed, nor are most emotionally disturbed children encopretic. It is frankly amazing that the foul odor of soiled pants and the painful cleanup process do not cause more emotional upset in children (and parents)! Recent treatment approaches that use a combination of behavioral and medical methods have proven to be the most successful (Walker, Milling, & Bonner, 1988). This chapter briefly reviews the definition and prevalence of encopresis, and then presents assessment and treatment procedures.

DEFINITION

The revised third edition of the *Diagnostic and Statistical Manual of Mental Disorders* (DSM-III-R; American Psychiatric Association, 1987) requires the following for a diagnosis of Functional Encopresis:

(A) Repeated passage of feces into places not appropriate for that purpose (e.g., clothing, floor) whether involuntary or intentional. . . .
(B) At least one such event a month for at least six months.
(C) Chronologic and mental age, at least four years.
(D) Not due to a physical disorder, such as aganglionic megacolon. (pp. 83–84)

"Primary encopresis" refers to fecal incontinence in children 4 years of age or older who have not been continent for at least a year; "secondary encopresis" refers to fecal incontinence in children who have been continent for at least a year. Although encopresis can be either diurnal or nocturnal, the latter is a rare occurrence.

Many pediatricians and child clinicians may quarrel with the DSM-III-R definition, especially with the age requirement, which does not account for the age at which toilet training was initiated. Nor does the definition give any clues as to the most effective treatment approach. We have come to define encopresis as primarily a "plumbing problem" that requires some medical intervention as well as systematic training in appropriate toileting habits. Walker (1978) supports this view. He further suggests that encopresis can be classified into three broad categories: (1) "retentive encopresis," which is the result of constipation; (2) "chronic diarrhea and irritable bowel syndrome," which appear to result from stress; and (3) "manipulative soiling," which is used by the child to control the environment.

A number of organic conditions involving structural anomalies or diseases of the bowel or sphincters (obstructing lesions or tumors), as well as of the nervous system (myelomeningocele, spina bifida), can cause fecal incontinence. Common in children is Hirschsprung's disease, which results from an absence of both the ganglion cells and the normal peristaltic waves in one segment of the bowel (Vaughan, McKay, & Behrman, 1979). Fecal material becomes impacted above this segment, resulting in an enlarged colon, or "megacolon." Severe cases are usually detected shortly after birth and must be corrected surgically by removing the portion of the bowel that is not functional and reconnecting the functional parts of the bowel. Some milder cases may not be discovered until much later, and it is not uncommon for these children to have only one bowel movement a month! The ratio of the incidence of Hirschsprung's disease to that of psychogenic megacolon caused by constipation is about 1:20. Other organic problems may result from dietary factors, allergic reactions to food, and infectious diseases of the large intestine (Vaughan et al., 1979). After corrective medical intervention for Hirschsprung's disease or other organic abnormalities, children may need special assistance in learning proper bowel control and appropriate toilet habits.

A recent study comparing the "defecation dynamics" (coordination of the reflexes and voluntary efforts necessary for stool expulsion) of healthy and chronically constipated children found that 46% of the chronically constipated children contracted instead of relaxing the external sphincter when they attempted to defecate (Loening-Baucke & Cruikshank, 1986). Constipated children who had this abnormal anal pressure were significantly less likely to improve with conventional laxative, diet, and toilet training treatment than constipated children who did not have this problem. The authors note that further study is necessary to determine whether the inability to defecate is the result of an unconsciously altered motor behavior or an anatomical abnormality of the pelvic floor. They suggest that biofeedback training may be an effective approach for constipated children with this inability to relax the external sphincter muscle.

PREVALENCE

There are few epidemiological studies on encopresis, and the differences in definitions, settings, and age ranges studied make it difficult to compare results. Estimates of occurrence range from 0.3% to 8% (Walker, Kenning, & Faust-Campanile, 1989). An epidemiological study in Sweden (Bellman, 1966, cited in Walker et al., 1989) found that 8.0% of 3-year-olds, 2.8% of 4-year-olds, and 2.2% of 5-year-olds were still soiling their clothes. The frequency of encopresis decreases with age; it is infrequent after the age of 7 (Knopf, 1979). The spontaneous remission rate is about 28% per year (Schaefer, 1979). These data indicate that the long-term prognosis for children with encopresis is good, even without treatment. Without treatment, however, soiling may last for several years, whereas with treatment it usually improves within a few weeks.

Referrals to psychiatric clinics for encopresis constitute about 5.7% of all referrals (Olatawura, 1973), whereas outpatient pediatric clinics indicate an encopresis referral rate of about 3% (Abrahamian & Lloyd-Still, 1984). The latter authors reported that 50% of their chronically constipated patients had a positive family history for encopresis, but there is little additional support for a genetic basis (Walker, Milling, & Bonner, 1988). Encopresis is more common in boys than girls (ratios vary from 5:1 to 6:1), with 50% to 60% of cases presenting with secondary encopresis (i.e., they were previously successfully trained). Levine (1975) found that approximately 25% of the children seen for one study reported that a stressful event, such as the loss of a parent or the birth of a sibling, immediately preceded the onset of soiling. Likewise, Abrahamian and Lloyd-Still (1984) found that the onset for 38% of 186 chronically consti-pated children could be traced to a specific event such as decreased food intake, illness with dehydration, or hospitalization. It is estimated that 80–95% of the children treated for encopresis have retentive encopresis, or chronic constipation (Christopherson & Rapoff, 1983; Levine, 1975). It is not surprising that approximately 25% of encopretic children are also enuretic, given the pressure that an impacted colon can put on the bladder. Levine (1975) states that common physical symptoms associated with encopresis include poor appetite, chronic abdominal pain, and lethargy.

There are no studies on the prevalence of encopresis in the general population. However, children who are encopretic are found at all socio-economic and intellectual levels, with the majority being developmen-tally normal and neurologically intact, according to Walker, Milling, and Bonner (1988). These authors also note that encopresis is probably under-reported, since most parents do not mention it as a problem unless they are specifically asked. The parents may be too embarrassed about the encopresis to report it, or, given the independence of toileting in older children, it may not become noticeable and/or annoying until it is a significant problem.

ASSESSMENT

General Considerations

The assessment process for encopresis is guided by one's theoretical position regarding the importance of factors influencing the develop-ment of this particular problem. Given the significant lack of empirical support for a psychodynamic approach, we focus our attention on the behavioral approach outlined by Walker, Milling, and Bonner (1988), which proposes that (1) children may not have acquired the prerequisite skills for toileting (recognizing body cues, undressing, going to the bath-room on cue, sitting on a toilet); (2) the physical condition of chronic constipation may have caused a breakdown in the learned cognitive control of the bowels; (3) the child's soiling may be reinforced through his or her manipulation of the environment; or (4) stress or anxiety may lead to impaired bowel control, with a consequent loss of successful performance of toileting behaviors. In addition, some children develop a phobia of the toilet as the result of a painful bowel movement, aggressive training techniques, punitive consequences following a soiling accident, or fearful fantasies regarding the toilet. Such a phobia can disrupt the training process or the use of appropriate toilet habits. Other children have diets that contain little fiber and/or a predominance of dairy products, which can result in constipation. A sedentary lifestyle can also promote constipation; exercise is an important element in keeping the body working properly.

The clinician must have a basic understanding of the digestive system in order to assess the encopretic child (see Figure 8.1). Portions of the following description of the gastrointestinal (GI) system and the process resulting in constipation have been distilled from works by Schaefer (1979) and Walker et al. (1989).

The GI tract is characterized by three different physiological functions: motility, vascularity, and secretion. These three functions are significantly affected by emotional factors (Schaefer, 1979) and can change in the direction of overactivity or underactivity. For example, intense feelings of anxiety, fear, or anger can lead to hypermobility, hypervascularity, and hypersecretion, whereas feelings of depression or apathy can

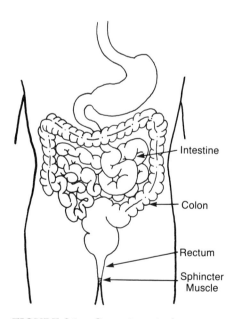

FIGURE 8.1. Gastrointestinal system.

lead to hypomotility, hypovascularity, and hyposecretion. Hypoactivity of these three functions in the upper GI tract can result in lack of appetite or weight loss, and hypoactivity of the lower GI tract can produce constipation, just as hyperactivity in the lower GI tract can produce diarrhea (Schaefer, 1979).

The digestive process is an active one that begins when food enters the mouth and is broken down in the stomach and small intestine. Nutrients are absorbed by the body as the food is digested. Wastes reach the large intestine, where water is reabsorbed and the waste material is formed into fecal material or "stools," which are excreted through the anus. The passage of feces through the intestinal tract is the result of a series of wave-like motions of the entire tract, termed "peristaltic contractions." During each contraction, the intestine above the fecal mass contracts and the portion of the intestine below the fecal mass relaxes, thus propelling the mass through the intestines toward the rectum. Distension of the rectum by the arrival of additional fecal material creates the urge to defecate. The peristaltic action resulting in the urge to defecate is usually strongest 15–30 minutes after breakfast, but some people experience a rush after each meal. On average, three-quarters of food waste is excreted within 96 hours, but there are wide individual differences. Although most people have a bowel movement every day, about 1% of the normal population have a bowel movement fewer than three times per week or more than three times per day. The normal stool should be soft, should be moist on the outside surface, and should have a distinct shape.

The ability to control defecation depends on adequate innervation of the colon and anus, as well as the child's ability to relax and contract the external sphincter purposively. The toilet training process teaches the child to recognize and respond to the stimulation of the colon, and then voluntarily to relax the external anal sphincter when seated on a toilet or potty chair (Walker, Milling, & Bonner, 1988). If for any reason the urge to defecate is not responded to, the fecal mass is reposited into the lower end of the colon by reverse peristalsis. When this process is repeated many times, the normally empty rectum tends to become accustomed to the increased pressure and the presence of stool; consequently, the urge to defecate diminishes. In the meantime, the colon is constantly absorbing water from its contents, and the stool becomes hard, dry, and difficult to pass. Children are reluctant to expel hard, large stools because they are painful, and constipation may result. With constipation, the feces becomes impacted in the bowel, and normal peristaltic and mass movements are not able to evacuate feces fully from the bowel.

As fecal material continues to accumulate, the intestine becomes enlarged (psychogenic megacolon; see Figure 8.2) and loses its muscle tone, and the intestinal wall becomes thin as a result of stretching caused

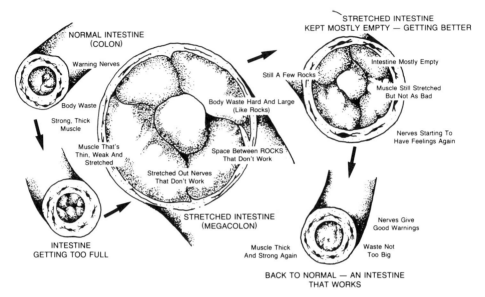

FIGURE 8.2. Megacolon: Patient training diagram. Copyright 1982, M. D. Levine, MD. Used by permission.

by the impacted fecal material. In some cases, the large intestine becomes so impacted with feces that the entire abdominal cavity is filled. With impaction, bowel function is compromised and there is a chronic state of constipation. Then, as fluid from the small intestine makes its way to the large intestine, it forms a pool above the impacted feces in the colon. This fluid material then seeps around the impacted mass and out through the anus, staining the child's clothes with a paste-like material. Because the passage of this material is not accompanied by the usual sensation of the urge to defecate, the child does not realize that it has happened until he or she feels wetness in the rectal area or on clothing. At other times large amounts of the impacted material may be explosively expelled, causing major soiling of the clothes. Given that neither the seepage nor the explosive bowel movements are under voluntary control, one can readily see that chronic constipation is likely to inhibit learning of bowel control or interfere with previously learned toileting skills.

The Assessment Process

The assessment process presented here follows the steps for gathering information in accordance with the Comprehensive Assessment-to-Intervention System (CAIS; see Chapter 3), with a focus on information pertinent to the problem of encopresis.

Step 1: Initial Contact

The first step in assessing an encopretic child is a thorough examination by a physician to rule out an organic basis for the problem and to determine whether there is an impacted colon. If the child is chronically constipated (which, as noted earlier, is the case for 80–95% of children with encopresis), then continued collaboration with the physician is necessary.

A general questionnaire (e.g., our Parent Questionnaire; see Appendix B) and checklists to rule out emotional or behavioral problems should be sent to the parents prior to the initial interview. The Child Behavior Checklist (CBCL; Achenbach & Edelbrock, 1983), the Parenting Stress Index (PSI; Abidin, 1990), and the Eyberg Child Behavior Inventory (ECBI; Eyberg & Ross, 1978) are recommended for this purpose. The parents should be asked to keep data on bowel and toilet activity for at least a week (see Figure 8.3), and data on food and liquid intake as well as physical activity (see Figure 8.4) for 3 days.

Step 2: Parent and Child Interview

The child and parents should be seen together for the initial interview. The child's perceptions of the problem and willingness to engage in a treatment program are important to assess, as well as the parent–child interaction in regard to this issue. The interview should focus on the following questions:

1. Are there behavioral or emotional problems? Information from the general questionnaire and rating scales should be reviewed to rule out significant emotional or behavioral problems. We have found that even if emotional and behavioral problems are present, treating the encopresis generally helps to improve these problems. If there is significant psychopathology, noncompliance, or serious parent–child conflict, however, the clinician should investigate the possibility that the encopresis is the result of manipulation on the child's part, and these issues should be treated before the encopresis.

2. Have there been recent stressful life events for the family or the child? A review of family history is important, with an emphasis on stressful life events such as a move, a new school, the birth of a sibling, parent separation, hospitalization, illness, death, and so forth. The clinician should determine whether any of these events occurred close to the time the encopresis started.

Bowel Movement
Baseline

Child's Name: _____ Age: _____

Address: _____

					SIZE			CONSISTENCY				
DATE	DAY	TIME	IN TOILET	IN PANTS	Small	Medium	Large	Paste-like	Hard	Runny/ Unformed	Soft/ Formed	WHAT HAPPENED?
							SAMPLE					
3-21	Thurs	10:00 A.M.		✔	✔			✔				Mother cleaned up
"	"	3:00 P.M.		✔	✔				✔			"
"	"	6:00 P.M.	✔		✔				✔			Painful BM

FIGURE 8.3. Bowel movement record for baseline data.

From *Assessment and Treatment of Childhood Problems: A Clinician's Guide* by Carolyn S. Schroeder and Betty N. Gordon. © 1991 by The Guilford Press.

Diet/Exercise Record

Child's Name: _____

	Day 1	Day 2	Day 3
Date/Day			
Breakfast			
Snack			
Lunch			
Snack			
Dinner			
Snack			
Exercise			
Comments			

From *Assessment and Treatment of Childhood Problems: A Clinician's Guide* by Carolyn S. Schroeder and Betty N. Gordon. © 1991 by The Guilford Press.

FIGURE 8.4.   Diet/exercise record for baseline data.

3. How did the toilet training process proceed? The parents should be asked to describe their child's toilet training process, including the age at which it was begun, methods used, responsiveness of the child, and the age at which both daytime and nighttime continence were achieved (if at all). Previous treatment attempts should also be described in detail. This information will help determine whether the child actually was taught and/or learned appropriate toileting skills.

4. What is the current status of toileting habits and bowel movements? A thorough review should be made of the bowel movement data and current toileting habits (time of day, length of sits), frequency of bowel movements (children can go several times a day in small amounts and still be constipated), and nature of the stool (size and form—e.g., runny, soft, paste-like stains; hard, small stools; or occasional enormous amounts).

5. What is the environmental context of the problem? Asking for a brief description of a typical day for the child and family is useful in getting a picture of the family's daily routine. A chaotic environment with irregular meals or a stressed time schedule can interfere with consistent toilet practices. The dietary and exercise data should also be reviewed at this time, to determine whether these might be factors contributing to the problem. A balanced diet—one with a variety of vegetables, fruits, whole wheat breads, fats, and at least six to eight glasses of water or juice—is optimal for normal bowel movements. A limited diet or large amounts of dairy products can promote constipation. The child should be engaged in some physical activity (e.g., bike riding, sports, walking) for at least an hour each day.

6. How do the child and parents perceive the problem? The child's beliefs, feelings, and concerns about the problem should be assessed. It is always important to ask, "Why are you seeking help now?" Treatment of encopresis requires considerable effort and vigilance on the part of both parents and child; without their full cooperation, treatment will fail. Thus it is important to assess their motivation for treatment.

Step 3: Observation of Behavior

Data on bowel habits and informal observation of parent–child interaction are usually all that are needed. If the parents report significant management problems, the clinician should engage in more detailed observation of parents and child, with the goal of identifying a treatment focus other than encopresis.

Step 4: Further Assessment

Further assessment is necessary only if other problems are suspected.

Step 5: Referral to Allied Health Professionals

The child should be seen by a physician prior to the initial interview. Collaboration with the physician is often necessary for children with encopresis, especially if cathartics are used in the treatment program.

Step 6: Communication of Findings and Treatment Recommendations

It is strongly recommended that the child be present to hear the findings and recommendations. In communicating the findings to the child and family, it is important to give them information about the GI system and the rationale for the treatment program. The influence of encopresis on the child's development in other areas should also be discussed. The family's clear understanding of the problem and the proposed treatment process, including the importance of consistency in carrying out its component parts, enhances the likelihood that the parents and child will cooperate with treatment. This cooperation is essential to resolving bowel problems.

TREATMENT

For a thorough review of the literature on treatment of encopresis, the reader is directed to Walker et al. (1989). Treatment approaches have involved (1) attention to the physical aspects of the problem, including medical procedures (i.e., the use of enemas, suppositories, and laxatives), exercise, and dietary changes; (2) psychotherapy, play therapy, and family therapy; (3) hypnosis (self-control through imagery); (4) biofeedback (teaching the child to exercise the external sphincter muscle, to discriminate rectal sensations, and to synchronize the internal and external sphincter responses); (5) behavioral programs (reinforcing appropriate behavior, mildly punishing inappropriate toileting); and (6) a combination of behavioral and medical interventions. Our approach to treatment of encopresis is a combination of behavioral and medical methods. Information is provided to the parents and child to change inappropriate beliefs or attitudes about the problem and to facilitate understanding and cooperation. Medical, dietary, and exercise interventions are used to correct the physical problems of chronic constipation. Appropriate toileting behaviors are taught or increased; environmental conditions are changed to facilitate the acquisition of the correct responses; and consequences for appropriate and inappropriate behaviors are changed. The particular components of the treatment program are now described in more detail.

Information Sharing

The parents and child should be told that encopresis is not an uncommon problem and that treatment can help to alleviate it. A brief description of the digestive system and of where the problem may lie for a particular child should be given in simple language appropriate to the child's level of understanding. The use of a diagram or simple drawing (Figure 8.1) showing the GI tract, with some discussion of where things can go wrong, has proven very helpful with our parents and children. If the child is diarrhetic or has irritable bowel syndrome, parents should be told that the digestive system responds to stress in particular ways, that each child's response is unique, and that the goal of treatment is to help the body respond in a way that decreases the likelihood of diarrhea. The retentive encopretic child should be shown (Figure 8.2) how constipation can cause the colon to get out of shape and not work properly, which then results in uncontrollable seepage (the paste-like stains) or uncontrollable large bowel movements. Constipation can also make it difficult to feel the urge to defecate and to empty the colon completely of feces. (Children who are manipulating the environment through their bowel movements do not need this explanation, because they obviously have good control of this function!)

The factors that can increase the likelihood of a healthy GI system, with regular and easily produced bowel movements, should also be discussed. These include a diet that is high in fiber and liquids (Table 8.1). The combination of fiber and water is what promotes bowel movements (Graham, Moser, & Estes, 1982). The diet should be *low* in milk products and in foods containing large amounts of refined sugars; these foods can promote constipation. Dairy intake should be limited to about 16 ounces of milk or its equivalent per day. The value of eating meals at a regular time and in a calm atmosphere, as well as the need for regular exercise, should be emphasized. Finally, the appearance of normal bowel movements (large, moist, well formed) should be described.

Proper toileting habits should be reviewed with the family, including (1) responding promptly to the urge to defecate, or sitting on the toilet at regular times (typically 20 minutes after breakfast); (2) having one's feet firmly planted on the floor or a stool to aid in expelling the feces; (3) sitting long enough (5–15 minutes) to evacuate all the feces; and (4) wiping the anus from front to back, using a clean tissue for each wipe (to avoid urinary tract infections in girls). The parents and child should understand that in addition to a proper diet and exercise, the colon has to be evacuated regularly in order for it to function properly. Ultimately, the child has to take responsibility for his or her own toileting behavior by tuning in to the urge to defecate and taking the time to sit on the toilet. It is the combination of these two things that eliminates bowel elimination problems.

TABLE 8.1. High-Fiber Diet

Vegetables:	Lettuce, spinach, cabbage, cauliflower, asparagus, tomatoes, onions, peas, celery, green pepper, carrots, corn, green beans.
	Raw vegetables are better than cooked.
Fruits:	Apples, pears, oranges, grapefruit, grapes, peaches, dried figs, dried apricots, prunes,° raisins, pineapple.
	Raw fruits are better than cooked. Fresh fruits are better than canned.
Breads:	Fresh Horizon™ bread°; bran cereal° (such as 100% Bran™, Honey Bran™, Cracklin' Bran™, Bran Chex™, 40% Bran Flakes™, or Raisin Bran™); Butternut™ Light, Wheat breads°; any whole-grain bread; graham crackers.
Drinks:	Six to eight glasses per day: water,° any fruit juice—prune,° pruneapple apricot,° pruneapple (Sunsweet).°

Miscellaneous Notes:

1. Honey and prunes have a chemical laxative effect.
2. Sufficient fluids (six to eight glasses per day), particularly water, help keep stools from becoming hard and dry.
3. Fats (butter, margarine, fried foods) aid the intestines in the evacuation of stool.
4. Give a balance of fiber foods and fats at each meal.
5. If mineral oil has been recommended, mix it in orange juice in a blender, then add soda water or 7-Up™ to it. It may also be mixed with any juice to make it more palatable, or mixed with canned fruit in heavy syrup.

Food Preparation Ideas:

1. Tossed salads.
2. Carrot, celery, green pepper sticks, raw cauliflower—may be dipped into salad dressing.
3. Celery with chunky peanut butter.
4. Stewed prunes with honey.
5. Stewed dried fruit with honey.
6. Bran muffins with prunes or raisins served with honey.
7. Homemade whole wheat bread with bran.
8. Glass of warm liquid with breakfast (example: apple juice with a cinnamon stick).
9. Fresh Horizon™ Bread with butter and honey.
10. Add soda water or 7-Up™ to any juice.
11. Substitute whole wheat flour for white flour in baking cookies.
12. Add ¼ to ½ cup of bran, cracked wheat, or wheat germ to cookies when baking. Add diced, dried fruit like prunes.
13. Cole slaw.
14. Popcorn.

° Highly recommended.

Physical Intervention

If the problem is chronic constipation, then the bowel will have to be cleansed of impacted feces with one or more enemas. Depending on how severely impacted the child is, the use of enemas may have to be repeated. The type of enema used should be one that is safe for repeated administration, such as Children's Fleet enemas (available without prescription), and enemas should always be given under the direction of a physician. Davidson, Kugler, and Bauer (1963) found that 92 of 119 patients required enemas to remove the impaction and that most children received two to four enemas in pairs. No case required more than four pairs.

Once the impacted mass is removed from the colon, it is important for the bowel to be evacuated regularly over a sufficient period of time, so that the colon can regain its normal shape and tone and begin to function properly. Suppositories, mineral oil, and milk of magnesia have each been used for this purpose. The idea is to promote several loose bowel movements daily and then gradually to decrease the use of cathartics over a period of several weeks as bowel movements come under the child's control. The dose should be enough to ensure the bowel movement, but at the same time should produce the urge to defecate, so that the child can learn to tune in to the cue. Davidson et al. (1963), reporting on the use of mineral oil, state that patients should be instructed to take a dose sufficient to produce several daily bowel movements, instead of a dose calculated according to body weight or a fixed dose. They note that most children initially require 4–5 tablespoons twice daily, and then the dose can be titrated to a smaller amount. We have also found this to be the case and have used a chocolate-flavored, pudding-like mineral oil, Neocultal, which is easier to administer (and tastier) than regular mineral oil. Giving the child a Life Saver candy after the mineral oil helps take away the bad taste. Mineral oil inhibits the absorption of fat-soluble vitamins, so if it is used for any length of time, a water-soluble vitamin (such as the liquid vitamins given to babies) should be used. Needless to say, none of these products should be used without consultation with a child's physician.

Wright (1975) has described a highly successful procedure, which has been repeatedly replicated (Christopherson & Rainey, 1976; Wright & Walker, 1976). It includes the use of suppositories and enemas as well as behavioral techniques. The first step in the program is to ensure that all fecal material is removed from the colon, usually through the use of enemas administered by the parent under a physician's direction. Then, in the morning immediately upon awakening, the child is told to sit on the toilet and attempt to have a bowel movement. If the child produces ¼ to ½ cup of feces, he or she is praised and given a reward. If the child produces less than that amount or nothing, the parent inserts a glycerine suppository and the child is instructed to dress, prepare for school, and have breakfast. After breakfast the child is instructed to sit on the toilet again; if this attempt is successful, the child is given a reward, but one smaller than the one for defecating independently. If the second attempt is unsuccessful, then an enema is given. No reward is given if an enema is needed to produce defecation. At the end of the day the child's clothing is examined for soiling. If it is clean, the child is given another reward; if it is soiled, a mild punishment (e.g., sitting on a chair for 10 minutes) is administered.

Training proceeds in this manner until the child has 2 consecutive weeks with no soiling. Then the cathartics are discontinued for 1 day of the week, and as each week is soil-free an additional cathartic-free day is added until the child is defecating completely independently (see Walker, Milling, & Bonner, 1988, pp. 388–391, for an in-depth description of this procedure). Walker et al. (1989) report that when properly applied, this program has resulted in cessation of soiling in 100% of the cases. We have also found this program to be the most effective method of treatment, especially for children who have had severely impacted bowels. However, we typically recommend the child first sit on the toilet after breakfast rather than on awakening, in order to maximize the chances of a successful, independent bowel movement.

Some physicians and parents resist using enemas and suppositories repeatedly. Moreover, most children who are encopretic have not developed good toileting habits, or their environment does not support good toileting habits. Thus, these areas will require some intervention, and so alternative treatment strategies are described.

Development of Toileting Skills

Many encopretic children have not learned proper toileting habits; even if they have, the onset of constipation usually disrupts these once-learned skills. In most cases of encopresis, it is necessary to institute daily practice of good toileting behaviors, especially if the supportory/enema treatment method is not used. We suggest a regimen of sitting on the toilet for 5–10 minutes, about 20 minutes after each meal (when the child is in school, he or she can sit upon returning home). A timer can be used so that the child can sit independently, and the child should be given a book or special "bathroom" toy to play with while he or she is on the toilet. (We have found that allowing the child to continue playing with the toy for 30 minutes after the successful defecation is a good reward.) It is imperative that the child's feet be firmly planted on the floor and that the toilet seat be comfortable. The use of a potty chair that sits on the floor or a toilet ring that fits into the toilet seat (we do not recommend the ones with a cup on the front, since children can hurt themselves getting on and off) are good for younger children. If a regular toilet seat is used, however, there should be a stool of the appropriate height under the child's feet. The requirement of sitting should be handled in a matter-of-fact way, and this should be practiced on a regular basis. As regularity increases, the sitting times will naturally move to the times when the child gets the urge to defecate.

If the child is successful in defecating ½ cup or more of feces, then he or she does not have to sit after the next meal. Keeping a chart in the bathroom is a good way to record sits and successful defecation. A star for each time the child complies with the routine, and fancy stickers for successful defecation, are good reinforcers for young children. For older children, a chart system (see Figure 8.5) can be used, with points exchanged for rewards at a later time.

A clean pants check should be instituted one to three times per day, depending on the nature of the child's problem. Times should be chosen that allow for consistent checks—for example, after school, after dinner, or at bedtime. At this time the child should be asked to show the parent his or her underpants (this can most easily be accomplished by having the child change his or her underpants). If they are clean, a small reward (or points) should be given, as well as praise (e.g., the parent can tell the child how good he or she smells or how nice it must feel to be clean). If the underpants are soiled, the child should be required to rinse the feces out of them in the toilet and then wash them in the sink. The child should undress and wash off, standing in the bathtub; put on clean underpants and outer clothing; and then sit on the toilet for 5 minutes. This should be seen as a natural consequence to soiling and handled in a matter-of-fact way, with little or no talking.

Environmental Interventions

The environment should be conducive to acquiring good toilet habits. All toileting activities should occur in a bathroom that is readily accessible to the child. Potty training chairs should only be used in the bathroom and not left in the family room or in front of the TV. Toileting charts and rewards should also be kept in the bathroom. Clothing should be easy to undo and remove. There should be time in the regular schedule for the child to use the toilet without feeling rushed.

The emotional atmosphere surrounding toileting should be calm and matter-of-fact, but the child's attempts at training should be praised, as well as the successes. Praise should not be effusive or unwarranted, and expressions of displeasure should be mild. The clinician's frequent contact with the family can be not only supportive to the parents, but also reinforcing to both the child and parents.

Bowel Movement
Treatment

Child's Name: _____ Age: _____

Address: _____

DATE	TIME SITS	CATHARTICS*	IN TOILET	IN PANTS	SIZE			CONSISTENCY				WHAT HAPPENED?
					Small	Medium	Large	Paste-like	Hard	Runny/ Unformed	Soft/ Formed	
						SAMPLE						
6-15	8-8:15	S	8:45			✔						
				10:00	✔						✔	

* Cathartics: Suppository (S); Enema (E); Oral—mineral oil or milk of magnesia (O).

FIGURE 8.5. Bowel movement record for treatment data.

From *Assessment and Treatment of Childhood Problems: A Clinician's Guide* by Carolyn S. Schroeder and Betty N. Gordon. © 1991 by The Guilford Press.

Changing the Consequences of the Behavior

Changing the consequences for the child's appropriate and inappropriate toileting behavior is usually necessary in a family with an encopretic child. The preceding sections have suggested ways to provide appropriate consequences for behavior. It is important that the clinician take the time to find out what is rewarding or punishing for a particular child and what are acceptable rewards and punishments in a particular family. Helping with charts, and giving specific information as to what type of consequence should be given and how, are also important.

CHOOSING A TREATMENT PLAN

In the treatment of encopresis, a program that meets the needs of the individual family and child must be designed. This section is intended to assist the clinician in choosing a treatment plan, depending on the type of problem that is presented.

Retentive Encopresis

A typical treatment plan for a child with retentive encopresis includes the following components:

1. The parents and child should be provided with information on the GI system and the mechanics of being constipated, with the goal of increasing understanding and cooperation.

2. Collaboration with a physician is necessary to determine the best approach to cleaning impacted material from the bowel and ensuring regular bowel movements. The approach to this will vary with the severity of the constipation and the treatment philosophy of the child's physician. We have found that providing information on effective treatments to physicians enhances their willingness to try the above-described methods. We have successfully treated many children with mineral oil after the physician or parent initially cleanses the colon with enemas, but Wright's (1975) method has a proven track record and should be considered for children who have been constipated for a long time or for whom a more conservative approach is not working. Regardless of the method that is used, dietary modifications and exercise are always recommended.

3. Teaching good toilet habits (with a regular toileting schedule; rewards for clean pants, good sitting, and successful defecation; and mild punishment for soiled pants) is an important part of any program for a constipated child.

4. Giving the parents data collection forms, helping them develop

charts and reward systems, and keeping in regular contact with the parents and child will ensure the much-needed consistency in carrying out the program. For some cases, we have had the parents mail in the data forms once a week and then called them at a set time to review the program and answer questions or concerns. For other families, we have found it necessary for the child and the parents to bring their data to the clinic for a more personal review. Children almost always respond well to written feedback from the clinician, as in this letter:

> Dear Steve,
>
> Good work! Your latest charts tell me that you are working very hard to keep clean pants and to have bowel movements every day. Last week you only needed one suppository and no enemas! Wow!
>
> It is also good that you are eating such healthy food and riding your bicycle or playing basketball every day. Remember that good food, six to eight glasses of water a day, and daily exercise will help keep your body in good shape.
>
> I liked the drawing of you and your dad playing basketball. It looked like you were getting lots of points! I've enclosed some basketball stickers that I thought you might like.
>
> Keep up the good work!!
>
> Sincerely,
> Dr. Schroeder

5. After treatment, these cases should be followed up on a monthly basis for a year. This helps prevent relapses and ensures that any relapses are immediately treated.

Diarrhetic Encopresis

Treatment for a diarrhetic problem generally includes (1) information sharing on the responsiveness of the GI tract to stress; (2) a discussion with the child's physician regarding potential medical intervention and diet modifications; and (3) ongoing data collection on the setting events for a diarrhetic episode and the consequences of the episode. In addition, on the basis of the stressors that the child encounters, the age of the child, and other individual characteristics, a stress reduction technique may be chosen (e.g., systematic desensitization, relaxation training, stress inoculation training, or assertiveness training). These techniques are described in Chapter 12. Hypnosis may also be considered.

Manipulative Encopresis

A child who soils to manipulate the environment will need further evaluation of the parent–child relationship. Instituting good toileting habits and a system of rewards and mild punishments may be helpful, but the success of this approach will depend on the severity of the problem. Teaching general behavior management skills to parents may be a better way to begin treatment. These techniques are described in Chapter 11.

CASE EXAMPLE

Step 1: Initial Contact

Mrs. Potter called about her 8-year-old son, Mark, who was soiling his pants one or two times a day. He had not had a physical examination within the last year, but previous medical examinations had indicated that there was no physiological basis for his soiling. Mrs. Potter was referred back to the physician for an updated physical, and permission to contact the pediatrician was obtained. Each parent was asked to complete checklists to rule out emotional and behavioral problems (the CBCL, the ECBI, and the PSI); together, they completed the Parent Questionnaire, a 3-day diet and exercise record (Figure 8.4), and a 7-day record of soiling that included how they handled these incidents (Figure 8.3).

The Parent Questionnaire indicated a middle-class family, with both parents in their late 40s. Mr. Potter was in a supervisory position at a local department store. Mrs. Potter was a former teacher who was currently a full-time homemaker. Mark was the only child of this marriage, which was the second for both parents. There were two half-siblings from the mother's previous marriage and three from the father's, none of whom were living in the home. The parents also indicated that although Mark was capable of achieving in school, he rarely completed his in-class work and often forgot his homework. The mother indicated that Mark's soiling was due to laziness and not wanting to take the time to go to the bathroom. Mr. Potter felt that Mark was just slow in learning good toileting habits.

The parents' responses to the rating scales differed dramatically in a number of areas. On the ECBI both mother and father had Intensity scores between 160 and 170, indicating that Mark engaged in many noncompliant and disruptive behaviors at a high frequency. The Problem scores, however, indicated that Mrs. Potter perceived significantly more of these behaviors as problematic (Problem score = 22) than Mr. Potter (Problem score = 6). On the CBCL, both parents indicated that Mark had only a few friends in the neighborhood; he had few chores at home, but was involved in organized sports activities in the community. Both parents rated Mark above the 98th percentile on Somatic Complaints and within the normal range on all other scales. The PSI described Mark as neither easy nor difficult; he was acceptable to both parents, but more reinforcing to the father than the mother. Mrs. Potter also had high scores (indicating problems) on the Social Isolation, Parent Health (she mentioned sleep difficulties and headaches), and Relationship with Spouse scales. Her Total Stress score was also very high. The father's responses placed him within the average range on all scales with the exception of Relationship with Spouse.

The 3-day diet and exercise record indicated low levels of fiber, and high intake of refined sugar and milk products. Exercise was limited to organized sports three times a week. The 7-day record of soiling indicated that while Mark had small paste-like soiling one or two times a day, he had large bowel movements in his pants about once a week.

Step 2: Parent and Child Interview

Mr. and Mrs. Potter and Mark came together for this interview. The parents presented as nervous, older parents who generally appeared unhappy. Although they described Mark as a very noncompliant child, they said the only reasons they came for help at this time were complaints from Mark's teacher about his odor, the fact that other children were starting to tease him, and the conflict they were having in handling the problem. Mr. Potter felt that his wife's nagging and pressuring Mark about his soiling was making it worse, and that if she would just leave him alone, it would go away. Mr. Potter admitted, however, that he felt the soiling was interfering with Mark's social development as well as being an annoyance for him and for Mark.

Mrs. Potter stated that Mark essentially toilet-trained himself for urine by age 4, although he still had accidents about once a month and had never been dry at night. Bowel training had never been fully accomplished. The soiling was described as an ongoing problem, and no particular stressful events had occurred that might have precipitated it. The parents had tried rewards (e.g., giving Mark a new watch if he was clean for a month), spanking, and threatening to remove privileges (e.g., not allowing Mark to go to the mall, not letting him watch TV for a week, etc.). When Mark complained of stomachaches and appeared constipated, they had also used enemas at the suggestion of their pediatrician. Currently, they were making Mark change his clothes when he smelled bad, and they had sent extra clothes to be kept at the school. Mrs. Potter, as a former teacher, was quite embarrassed about Mark's soiling at school.

The daily routine at home was chaotic. Mrs. Potter got up after Mr. Potter and Mark had left in the morning. Mark ate separate meals in front of the TV. His bedtime varied considerably from night to night, and he had no regular responsibilities or chores at home.

Mark appeared as a pleasant youngster who was rather lethargic and generally uninterested in the discussion. He denied any concern about soiling or feeling bad about being teased. He did, however, indicate (although rather unenthusiastically) that he would be willing to work with the psychologist to resolve the problem.

Step 3: Observation of Behavior

The parent–child interaction was quite warm and reinforcing. Mark frequently asked the parents to look at a Legos construction and drawing that he worked on as the clinician and parents talked. Mrs. Potter, however, asked Mark many questions for which an answer was not expected and made many requests to which Mark did not have an opportunity to comply. He seemed to tune out the mother's demands until she raised her voice, signaling, "Now is the time to listen."

Step 4: Further Assessment

The parents were seen both individually and together to explore marital issues and management skills further. The marriage problems all focused on disagreement in regard to handling Mark, and although there did not appear to be many parent-alone activities, both parents seemed content with their life together. Mrs. Potter felt stressed by the care of a young child, stating that she had few friends with children Mark's age, felt uncomfortable with the younger mothers, and therefore had decreased her social activities.

Mark's teacher was contacted to discuss soiling at school, and she was asked to complete a CBCL for teachers and the Elementary School Questionnaire (see Appendix B). Mark was also observed during a group activity, individual seatwork, and recess at school. The teacher described Mark as a quiet, generally compliant child (he did not always tune in to general directions given to the class), who was not actively disliked by other children but preferred to play alone. Although there was some teasing, she did not feel this was a major problem. She had him change clothes and wash himself at the first sign of soiling.

Step 5: Referral to Allied Health Professionals

A medical examination was completed prior to the initial interview. The pediatrician found Mark to be chronically constipated and recommended a course of treatment with enemas to cleanse the bowel. He also agreed to work with the psychologist in managing the problem.

Step 6: Communication of Findings and Treatment Recommendations

Following the assessment, the following information was shared with Mark and his parents. Mark was a youngster who had never learned appropriate toileting habits, had a poor diet, engaged in little exercise, and lived in an environment that provided little structure for normal daily routine activities. The parents' management skills were inconsistent at best. They provided few clear signals as to their expectations, and although threats were liberally used, they were rarely enforced. Mark appeared capable of engaging in expected developmental activities (schoolwork, personal hygiene, and social relationships), but he did not engage in any of these activities on a consistent basis. His encopresis was seen as due to long-standing, chronic constipation as a result of poor toilet training, poor diet, lack of exercise, and inconsistent management. Treatment recommendations included sharing information about the physiology of encopresis; medical intervention using mineral oil, enemas, and suppositories; diet changes; teaching good toileting habits; increased daily exercise; establishing a daily family routine; and parent training in management skills. These treatment strategies were implemented simultaneously.

Course of Treatment

The physician initially elected to cleanse the bowel with enemas and to try a course of treatment with mineral oil coupled with regular times for sitting on the toilet. After 3 weeks, it was evident that this was not enough to get Mark to have bowel movements on a daily basis without soiling accidents throughout the day. Thus, the Wright and Walker (1978) treatment program, which ensures daily bowel movements through the systematic use of suppositories and enemas, was begun. A high-fiber diet and daily exercise (riding his bicycle, swimming with Mom, shooting baskets with Dad) were recommended as lifestyle changes. Mark was initially rewarded every day; he earned 25 cents for clean pants and 25 cents for independent bowel movements. This was gradually faded into a weekly allowance. During the first week of this program, an enema was used on 3 days, suppositories were used alone on 3 days, and Mark had a bowel movement on his own 1 day. During the second week only one enema and three suppositories were necessary, and Mark had 4 days of independent toileting. By the fourth week, Mark was having bowel movements every morning after breakfast without the use of suppositories or enemas.

Parent training quickly brought about increased compliance and better listening skills on Mark's part. It was strongly recommended that

Mrs. Potter increase her social activities and that she and Mr. Potter do more things as a couple.

This case was followed through telephone contacts for 1 year following the completion of treatment. The parents indicated that they were not always as consistent as they should be, but that generally things were going very well. On vacations Mark's bowel movements tended to become less regular, but with the reinstitution of the normal daily routines, the problem was easily resolved. The parents and teacher reported that Mark was more energetic, had increased social interactions, was more independent, and seemed happier.

Chapter 9

Sleep

Sleep! Throughout our lifetimes this restorative activity is fought, manipulated, embraced, and finally accepted as a necessary part of our lives. Parents of infants have a front-row seat in learning to deal with interrupted sleep, and many go on to learn about bedtime struggles, night wakings, early risings of energetic toddlers, and the rather bizarre nocturnal occurrences (sleepwalking, sleeptalking, teeth grinding, head banging, rocking, night terrors, and nightmares) that are common among children. As children get older their repertoire of nighttime behaviors expands, and parental responses evolve and become more varied (Anders, 1979). The types of sleep disturbances seen in children seem to change with age, although sleep disturbances such as bedtime struggles, night wakings, and sleepwalking have been shown to persist over a number of years (Kataria, Swanson, & Trevathan, 1987). Thus, although sleep problems in children may be common, they do not always go away on their own.

When parents request help with sleep problems, the situation has usually reached a crisis point. It is important for the child clinician to be able to help these parents and their children (who may not be suffering!), as well as to be aware of the role that sleep problems can play in other disorders of childhood. This chapter reviews age differences in normal sleep states and patterns, and types of sleep disturbances seen in children; it then describes how to assess and treat these problems.

NORMAL SLEEP STATES AND PATTERNS

To understand sleep disturbances, one must first have a rudimentary understanding of the normal sleep process. A mature nervous system is necessary to regulate the sleep cycle over many hours, and thus children's sleep cycles follow a developmental course.

Sleep States and Stages

The sleeping person may appear inert, but his or her sleeping state is a complex, highly organized neurophysiological process. Sleep is divided into two distinctly different states: rapid-eye-movement (REM) sleep and non-rapid-eye-movement (NREM) sleep (Kales, 1969). REM sleep is characterized by irregular pulse and respiratory rate, in addition to rapid eye movements. There is a dramatic increase of blood flowing to the brain, the body uses more oxygen, and brain waves resemble a mixture of waking and drowsy patterns. Although dreams and nightmares occur during REM sleep, little happens behaviorally. Muscles become very relaxed, and nerve impulses are essentially blocked within the spinal cord; the body is thus effectively paralyzed, although there may be small twitches of the hands, legs, or face (Meyer, Sakai, & Naritomi, 1979; Ware & Orr, 1983).

NREM sleep is divided into four stages, which represent progressive levels of sleep from drowsiness to very deep sleep (Guilleminault & Anders, 1976). During the latter two stages, breathing and heart rate become very stable, and the muscles are very relaxed; although the person usually lies very quietly, he or she can move, often sweats profusely, and is very difficult to awaken. However, if the stimulus is important enough (e.g., a sick child crying), the person will promptly awaken but will be in a confused state (Kales, 1969).

A normal sleep cycle consists of a period of NREM sleep followed by REM sleep. In the adult, each cycle usually lasts about 90 minutes, with NREM and REM sleep alternating throughout the night. Deep sleep (NREM stages 3 and 4) is prominent during the first third of the night, and night terrors, sleepwalking, and sleeptalking usually occur at this time. REM sleep is more prominent during the last third of the night, and this is when dreams and nightmares usually occur (Zuckerman & Blitzer, 1981).

Ware and Orr (1983) describe the typical sleep pattern for children. Children usually fall asleep in 10–15 minutes, reach NREM stage 4 (via stages 1–3) 5–20 minutes after falling asleep, and have the first REM period (which lasts about 5 minutes) 1–2 hours after sleep onset. The NREM-REM sleep cycle is then repeated, with later REM periods lasting 15–20 minutes. Although full-term infants have a differentiated REM-NREM sleep cycle, the NREM period does not have differentiated stages. The infant enters sleep through REM rather than NREM, spends 50% of total sleep in REM sleep (compared to 20% in adults), and has sleep cycles about 50–60 minutes long (compared to the 90–100 minutes for adults). By 2–3 months of age, the four stages of NREM sleep are differentiated; by 3 months, the infant enters NREM sleep first; and by 12 months, the time in the REM sleep state is reduced to 30%. The normal adult sleep cycle is reached by about 8 years of age (Zuckerman & Blitzer, 1981).

It has been hypothesized that the function of REM sleep is to allow a person to process daytime emotional experiences, to transfer recent memories into long-term storage, and to integrate newly learned material (Ferber, 1985; Zuckerman & Blitzer, 1981). NREM sleep is thought to allow the person to restore the body and regain physical strength (Hartmann, 1973). Thus, a person appears to live in three distinct states. In the waking state, thoughts can be translated into action so that the necessary activity for survival can be maintained. In the NREM sleep state, mental processes are minimal, the body rests, and restoration occurs. In the REM sleep state the mind is active again and dreams occur, but the body, while receiving signals, does not carry them out.

Ferber (1985) suggests that REM sleep can be thought of as an intermediate state between NREM and waking, in which the mind wakes up before allowing signals to be received by the body. In evolutionary terms, sudden waking from NREM sleep would leave an animal confused and unable to protect itself; REM sleep allows the animal's brain to become more active without the accompanying body movements that could attract a predator. Once the animal is sufficiently alert, it can wake up fully, and the muscle "paralysis" of REM sleep disappears. Ferber (1985) states that this checking for danger may still be relevant for humans, because people wake up after each episode of dreaming, check the environment, and go back to sleep if all is well. Adults do not usually remember these wakings. Some children, however, may not return to sleep after these wakenings, perhaps sensing that something is wrong; they may need a bottle, need to be rocked, or need to feel the closeness of a parent to go back to sleep.

Sleep–Wake Cycles

The sleep–wake cycle changes considerably with age, and there are large individual differences among children of the same age. The newborn typically sleeps a total of 16 hours, with the longest time asleep being 2–4 hours. Although the total amount of sleep gradually decreases to 14 hours by the time the child is 12 months of age, the duration of each sleep period gradually increases from 4–8 hours at 3–4 months, to 8–12 hours plus two naps of about 2 hours each by 6–8 months. By age 2, children usually sleep 11–12 hours at night and have one 2-hour-long afternoon nap (Crowell, Keener, Ginsburg, & Anders, 1987). Most children continue an afternoon nap until age 3, but some continue until age 5, when the total amount of sleep is about 11 hours. Napping is rare after age 5, and there is a very gradual decrease in total sleep time to about 10 hours in preadolescence (Ferber, 1985).

Circadian Rhythms

It is important to have some understanding of the circadian rhythms that are associated with the sleep–wake cycle (Ware & Orr, 1983). "Circadian rhythms" are biological cycles that repeat themselves about every 25 hours; they include patterns of sleeping and waking, activity and rest, hunger and eating, and fluctuations in body temperature and hormone release. Not only is it important for a general sense of well-being that these cycles be in harmony during the day, but the ability to fall asleep and to stay asleep is closely tied to the timing of these cycles. For example, in adults, selection of bedtimes, self-rated alertness, the amount of time after falling asleep to REM onset, and the duration of the sleep period are all related to body temperature (Czeisler et al., 1981). A person falls asleep when body temperature is falling toward a daily minimum and wakes as it starts rising toward a peak; it is hard to wake up when the body temperature is still low, and, likewise, the person may have trouble falling asleep when the body temperature is at a peak (Ferber, 1985). These cycles are set each day by the daily routines of rising, eating, activity, going to bed, and so on. If the sleep–wake cycle gets out of rhythm, a person begins to feel bad. Jet lag is a good example of this.

If children's schedules are irregular, then their circadian rhythms may be off, and they may want to sleep when they should be awake and awake when they should sleep. Changing sleep routines (e.g., getting children to bed earlier, getting them up earlier, or having them sleep later in the morning) must take into account the children's normal body rhythms, and changes must occur gradually.

SLEEP DISTURBANCES

It is often difficult to understand what constitutes a sleep disorder, because of the many terms used to describe sleep problems, the varying definitions, and the lack of support for classifying certain behaviors as pathological. For example, "cosleeping" (child and parent sleeping together in the same bed) is widely viewed as a problem, even though the definition has included activities ranging from sharing the bed for a few minutes once or twice a year to regularly sleeping in the same bed (Crowell et al., 1987). The significance of a problem can also vary with the population studied. For example, cosleeping has been found to be more common in black families, where it is not associated with sleep problems; however, in white families cosleeping is associated with sleep problems (Lozoff, Wolf, & Davis, 1984). The revised third edition of the *Diagnostic and Statistical Manual of Mental Disorders* (DSM-III-R; American Psychiatric Association, 1987) does not have Sleep Disorders in the childhood-onset section, although Sleep Terror and Sleepwalking Disorders are generally considered to be childhood disorders. The diagnostic classification of sleep and arousal disorders published by the Association of Sleep Disorders Centers (1979), although based primarily on work with adults, appears to offer the best system for sorting out the disturbances of sleep in children. Children's sleep problems fall into the categories of (1) sleep–wake schedule disorders; (2) parasomnias—that is, abnormal events that occur during sleep or at the threshold between wakefulness and sleep (sleepwalking, sleep terrors, nightmares, rocking or head banging during sleep, sleep paralysis, sleep bruxism); (3) disorders of excessive sleepiness (narcolepsy and sleep-related respiratory problems); and (4) disorders of initiating and maintaining sleep (bedtime struggles, night wakings, getting up early).

Sleep–Wake Schedule Disorders

It is not until about 6 months of age that infants have sleep–wake patterns that are synchronized by the clock. Infants who are premature or have had perinatal problems tend to take longer to settle into a regular sleep–wake pattern (Moore & Ucko, 1957). Once a child has settled into a pattern, this pattern can be disturbed by a number of factors, including the inconsistency of the daily schedule, parental response to the waking child, illness, environmental changes, and emotional trauma (Guilleminault & Anders, 1976). Ferber, Boyle, and Belfer (1981) reported that 9% of the patients seen at their sleep disorders clinic had schedule problems. Prime clues to this problem are a child's not being sleepy at bedtime, getting up too early, and sleeping at irregular times. Other routines, such as eating or activity level, are also likely to be irregular. This problem is differentiated from bedtime struggles or night wakings, in that the child cannot fall asleep or go back to sleep no matter what a parent does, because the child is in the wake phase of the sleep–wake cycle (Ferber, 1985). A daily rhythm of waking in the morning, napping, going to sleep at night, eating at set times, and having activities connected with light and dark are important for the body to establish a circadian rhythm that goes along with daily living expectations. A consistent daily schedule is needed to solve this circadian rhythm disturbance, and most children respond fairly quickly, usually within a few weeks.

Some children have consistent schedules and still have problems with the distribution of their total amount of sleep throughout the 24-hour period (e.g., not sleeping through the night, waking very early in the morning, having too many or too few naps, or having a normal sleep–wake cycle that is out of phase with the rest of the household). Resolving these problems involves determining the total length of time a child sleeps per day, determining what factors may be interfering with a better pattern, and gradually changing the pattern (see Ferber, 1985, for a good discussion of this problem and treatment methods).

Parasomnias

"Parasomnias," as noted above, are disturbances during sleep or at the transition from sleep to wakefulness; they include sleepwalking, sleep terrors, nightmares, rocking or head banging during sleep, and sleep bruxism. Nocturnal enuresis has also been put in this category, but there is evidence to suggest that it is not a disturbance of sleep, and it is not discussed here (see Chapter 7). The disturbances in this category are most common among children; perhaps 20% of all children experience at least one of these disturbances (Ware & Orr, 1983). Although parasomnias get a lot of attention, they generally occur infrequently in individual children, have no clear etiology, are not associated with psychopathology, and usually disappear with maturation. Because parasomnias are so common in young children, a brief description of each disorder is given.

Sleepwalking

Sleepwalking occurs in the NREM stage of sleep (Anders & Weinstein, 1972), usually 3–4 hours after sleep onset, but can occur at other times (Fisher & Wilson, 1987). Most children sit up in bed with a glassy stare and may walk around the house for 5–30 minutes (Zuckerman & Blitzer, 1981). The child is not easily awakened and will not remember the incident. Prevalence is highest in children ages 9–12 years, with rates as high as 18.5%; however, most children have infrequent episodes (Fisher & Wilson, 1987; Klackenberg, 1982). Sleepwalking should be differentiated from a seizure disorder. If sleepwalking occurs in the early morning when stage 4 NREM sleep is less concentrated, it could be suggestive of a seizure disorder (Ware & Orr, 1983).

There is no evidence that sleepwalkers have an increased incidence of psychopathology, although Kales et al. (1980) found that mental stress, fatigue, and changes in the sleep environment increased the frequency of sleepwalking in adults. Management should consist of preventing accidents, calmly leading the child back to bed, and (if the child is agitated) doing nothing until he or she is calm.

Sleep Terrors

Sleep terrors usually occur within 15–90 minutes of sleep onset and are most common in preschool children, typically resolving with central nervous system maturation. DSM-III-R estimates a prevalence rate of 7% (American Psychiatric Association, 1987). Sleep terrors are characterized by intense sudden arousal, a loud panic-stricken scream, rapid pulse and respiration, profuse perspiration, a glassy stare, often strange fears, and inconsolability (Zuckerman & Blitzer, 1981). Sleep terrors can last up to 20 minutes, although they are usually over more quickly. It is difficult to awaken the child, and there is no memory of the episode. A sleep terror episode appears to be an abrupt partial transition from stage 4 NREM sleep to REM sleep (Zuckerman & Blitzer, 1981). Although sleep terrors are not associated with psychiatric disturbance, they may be precipitated by an illness with a high fever (Kales, Kales, Soldatos, Chamberlin, & Martin, 1979). Parents are usually very frightened when sleep terrors occur in their children, but the main treatment is to give them information and reassurance. If night terrors persist longer than 4 weeks, or the parents report that they are so frequent they are disrupting the family's sleep, parents and child should be referred for further assessment. It could be that there are additional problems in the family.

Nightmares

Nightmares occur in the REM stage of sleep and are frightening dreams that wake a person and leave him or her with a feeling of profound fear and anxiety. They usually occur in the last third of the sleep period. Nightmares are very different from night terrors of the NREM sleep stage; they can be easily distinguished by the recall of dream content and the lack of physical activity during the nightmare. Nightmares appear to be a reflection of stresses experienced during the day, and the content reflects a developmental sequence of fears and concerns, with more nightmares reported in the preschool and adolescent years than at ages 7–11 (Ferber, 1985). Support for the hypotheses that troubled sleep reflects emotional concerns is provided by case studies (Kellerman, 1979; Roberts & Gordon, 1979) and in an empirical study by Dollinger, Horn, and

Boarini (1988). The latter authors found nightmares to be more common among learning-disabled students who were concerned about their intellectual and academic adequacy. However, recent work with adults has found no relationship between nightmares and anxiety (Wood & Bootzin, 1990).

Almost all children will have a nightmare at some time in their lives, and 10.9% are reported to have them once a week or more (Fisher & Wilson, 1987). Frequent or persistent nightmares may reflect inordinate stress during the day and should prompt an inquiry about other problems. Although nightmares per se are not seen as pathological, they can result in disturbed sleep and fear of going to bed (Dollinger et al., 1988). Treatment approaches for nightmares are discussed later in this chapter.

Rocking and Head Banging

Rhythmical movements of the child's body during sleep usually begin at about 6 months of age, and head banging and head rolling at about 9 months (Ferber, 1985). These movements usually begin just prior to sleep (Baldy-Moulinier, Leny, & Passouant, 1970). Although they are uncommon after 3 years (Ferber, 1985), they occur in 15–20% of children under 2 years (Strauss, Rubinoff, & Atkeson, 1983). Ferber (1985) states that if the rhythmical patterns are strong, last longer than 10–15 minutes, and recur repeatedly during the night, there may be additional problems, such as parental attention to the behavior or (in the older child) other behavioral or emotional problems. The head banging, head rolling, and body rocking associated with blindness, mental retardation, and autism should be distinguished from these behaviors in normally developing children, who probably engage in this behavior to soothe themselves to sleep (Ferber, 1985). No treatment is suggested for the young child, but the parents may be advised to pad the crib or to have the child sleep on a mattress on the floor to decrease the noise of the rocking crib or bed.

Sleeptalking

"Somniloquy," or spontaneous speech during REM or NREM sleep, is a very common behavior, with reports in the general population as high as 50–60% (Coates & Thoresen, 1981; Fisher & Wilson, 1987). Sleeptalking appears to be associated with sleepwalking and nightmares (Fisher & Wilson, 1987) and is not associated with psychopathology.

Sleep Bruxism

The repetitive grinding of one's teeth or clenching of jaws during sleep ("bruxism") can occur at any age, with the highest incidence (15%) reported between 3 and 17 years (Reding, Zepelin, Robinson, Zimmerman, & Smith, 1968). This behavior can occur while the individual is awake or asleep, and severe bruxism may necessitate the use of a tooth-protective device. Although there is some evidence that anxiety may play a part in this problem (Clark, Rugh, & Handelman, 1975), it generally resolves with time. Consultation with a dentist is recommended if bruxism is damaging the teeth.

Familial Sleep Paralysis

Familial sleep paralysis occurs at the onset of sleep or upon awakening and is distinguished by the person's not being able to make voluntary movements. Ware and Orr (1983) explain this phenomenon as related to what happens after REM sleep, when the person actually awakens but the loss of muscle tone that accompanies REM sleep remains. Although sleep paralysis is temporary and not harmful, it can be a frightening experience. Movement can usually be restored by rapid eye movements or the touch of another person. No treatment other than reassurance is necessary.

Disorders of Excessive Sleepiness

Excessive sleepiness can be the result of illness, medication, depression, poor nighttime sleep, narcolepsy, or sleep apnea syndrome (Ware & Orr, 1983). If a child sleeps more than 2 hours longer than the average for his or her age, or requires daily naps beyond the preschool years, the child may be suffering from excessive sleepiness (Ferber, 1985). The behavioral signs of sleepiness usually include shorter attention span, reduced coordination, irritability, forgetfulness, fussiness, and general "laziness" (Ferber, 1985; Ware & Orr, 1983). Teachers are usually the first to notice these problems, and a child is often described as performing poorly because of inattention, laziness, or overactivity. Such concerns warrant investigation of the child's sleep patterns, especially if the child is both overactive and continuing to take naps after the age of 5 years.

Viral infections and illnesses with a high fever leave a child feeling tired and sleepy, but these feelings subside as the child recovers from the illness. Medications, such as antihistamines and those used to control seizures, can cause excessive sleepiness as a side effect. Inadequate sleep, poor-quality sleep, or inadequate deep sleep can also result in daytime sleepiness. Depression in children can also result in excessive sleepiness, but this should be only one of a number of other behavioral symptoms. Treatment would depend on the nature and cause of the excessive sleepiness. In the absence of medication or psychopathology, structuring the child's daily routines of sleep, eating, and exercise can be helpful to these children.

Narcolepsy

In narcolepsy, sleep is distributed across 24 hours instead of occurring in a single block at night; nighttime sleep is usually disturbed by many wakings, and short periods of uncontrollable daytime sleep occur in unstimulating or physically inactive situations (very similar to the sleep patterns of newborns). In narcolepsy, the REM state most often begins immediately or within 10 minutes after falling asleep, rather than after one complete cycle of NREM sleep. There are also episodes of partial activation of the REM system at bedtime, on waking, and during the day (Ferber, 1985; Ware & Orr, 1983). Narcolepsy occurs at the rate of 2–5 per 10,000 (Guilleminault & Anders, 1976); however, in families with a history of narcolepsy, the chances are 1 in 50 that a child will have the disorder (Ferber, 1985). Although narcolepsy is usually first diagnosed in adults, one-third of persons with this disorder date the onset of their sleepiness to adolescence or earlier (Anders, Carskadon, & Dement, 1980). This suggests that this disorder often goes undiagnosed in children.

Diagnosis of narcolepsy involves ruling out other possible problems that may cause sleepiness, determining the pattern of sleep, and documenting the appearance of REM sleep soon after sleep onset (Ware & Orr, 1983). The documentation of REM sleep is carried out by means of a multiple sleep latency test, performed in a sleep laboratory. Although there is no cure for narcolepsy, there is treatment in the form of medication for the various symptoms plus short naps throughout the day (Ware & Orr, 1983). However, the medications (methylphenidate hydrochloride for sleepiness, and imipramine or other tricyclic antidepressants for muscle weakness) can result in further sleep disturbances and should be used with caution.

Sleep-Related Breathing Disorders

Sleep apnea, or the absence of breathing during sleep, can produce a sleep disturbance resulting in sleepiness during the day. Although it was once thought to be rare in children, Ferber et al. (1981) reported that 14% of the children seen in their sleep disorders clinic had a primary diagnosis of sleep apnea. Sleep-related breathing disorders have been identified in conditions such as cystic fibrosis, sudden infant death syndrome (SIDS), enlarged tonsils and adenoids, and oral and facial abnormalities (Ferber, 1985; Ware & Orr, 1983). Once a person is asleep, the upper airway narrows or closes off so that the person cannot breathe properly. The obstruction usually occurs in the back of the throat behind the base of the tongue, where the airway can be blocked by collapse of the walls of the throat (which are floppy in this region) and by the tongue's falling backwards (Ferber, 1985). This process can occur up to several hundred times per night.

For children, the most common causes of sleep apnea are enlarged tonsils and adenoids, obesity, and (to a lesser extent) oral or facial abnormalities such as a markedly recessed chin or cleft palate (Ware & Orr, 1983). Children with sleep apnea present with very restless sleep, characterized by loud snoring or snorting with intervening silences. They may have morning headaches, and they are at risk for the development of hypertension. The disturbed sleep can have rather negative consequences for alertness and school performance (Ferber, 1985). Treatment usually involves removal of the tonsils and adenoids, weight reduction, or corrective oral or plastic surgery. In more severe cases, a tracheostomy, in which a tube is inserted into a hole made through the neck below the vocal cords (larynx) and into the windpipe (trachea), is performed (Ferber, 1985).

Sleep apnea in children should be taken seriously, but it should be recognized that it is not the same disorder as that which causes SIDS. In most SIDS cases, the stopping of breathing does not involve airway obstruction; rather, the baby simply stops breathing (Ferber, 1985). See Culbertson, Krous, and Bendell (1988) and Ware and Orr (1983) for further discussion of SIDS.

Disorders in Initiating and Maintaining Sleep

Delayed onset of sleep and/or frequent arousals during sleep are very common problems among preschool children. Frequent night waking occurs in approximately 20% of 1- to 2-year-olds, 4% of 3-year-olds, and 8% of 4-year-olds (Jenkins, Bax, & Hart, 1980; Richman, 1981; Richman, Stevenson, & Graham, 1975). Difficulties with getting to bed are also common, occurring in 12.5% of 3-year-olds and 5% of 4-year-olds. These two problems are often found together: 55% of 1- to 2-year-olds and 29% of 3-year-olds who wake in the night also have trouble going to bed (Richman, 1981; Richman et al., 1975). Crowell et al. (1987), in a study of 100 children ages 18–36 months, found that types of sleep problems seemed to follow a developmental progression even in this 1½-year age span. The youngest children (18–23 months) had the least difficulty with bedtime, but 21% of this group woke in the night. In the middle age group (24–29 months), bedtime problems increased; 20% fell asleep in their parents' arms, and 31% took more than 30 minutes to fall asleep. In the oldest group (30–36 months), both bedtime problems and night wakings increased; 16% called to their parents or came out of their room after being put to bed, and 24% expressed fear of the dark. In this group, 100% used a night light and 79% had a transitional object. It is interesting that few parents saw these problems as significant enough to justify seeking help. The behaviors that most concerned parents were cosleeping all or part of the night; a child's resisting being alone in such a way as to make bedtime difficult or unpleasant; and a parent's having to hold a child until he or she fell asleep. The authors concluded that the most prominent sleep problems—going to bed and going to sleep—mirror the developmental tasks of separation and independence.

Other work suggests that many factors contribute to the development of sleep behavior patterns and that these may not be the same factors contributing to the maintenance of the problems. Richman (1981) found that difficult temperament and difficult birth histories were associated with sleep problems, but that these associations were not evident by age 3. Ungerer, Sigman, Beckwith, Cohen, and Parmelee (1983) found an association between continuing sleep problems and a mother's going to a child's room in their sample of preterm children. Sleep problems do not simply "go away" with time. Richman, Stevenson, and Graham (1982), in a sample of 8-year-olds who were waking during the night, found that 40% had had the problem since at least age 3. Kataria et al. (1987) found that 84% of children with sleep problems at 15–18 months continued to have problems 3 years later. Persistent sleep problems were associated with increased stress in the environment, including unusual maternal absences, accidents and injuries of the child, family illnesses, and episodes of depressed maternal mood. In addition, 30% of these children had generalized behavior problems, as compared to 19% of non-sleep-disturbed children.

Problems of initiation and maintenance of sleep are difficult to treat for a number of reasons. First, they occur at home and at night so that they cannot be readily observed, and the clinician has to rely on the parents' reports of the problem and of treatment effectiveness. Second, parents are typically asked to keep a record and change their behavior in the middle of the night, when they are least alert. Third, the therapist cannot model the desired behavior. Finally, it is hard to use positive reinforcement to encourage development of new sleep-related behavior, especially with young children (Richman, Douglas, Hunt, Landsdown, & Levere, 1985).

Medication is the most widely used treatment. Ounsted and Hendrick (1977) reported that by 18 months of age, 25% of 59 first-born children had been given sedatives. In spite of this wide use of sedatives or hypnotics with children, there have been very few studies of their effectiveness. However, there is extensive literature on the limitations of drugs with adult insomniacs, which include deterioration in the quality of sleep and drug withdrawal insomnia (Kales, Bixler, Tan, Scharf, & Kales, 1974). The studies of drug effectiveness with children are no more encouraging. Richman (1985), in a double-blind trial of the hypnotic drug trimeprazine tartrate, found that one-third of 22 children with severe waking problems showed no improvement even on relatively high doses; improvement was only moderate in the other subjects, and no child started to sleep through the night after its use. It is interesting that although the parents reported improved sleep, their sleep records did not support their oral reports. Richman concluded that strong hypnotics have little effectiveness for most wakeful children. Ware and Orr (1983) point out that sedatives or hypnotics will suppress REM sleep, deep sleep, and wakefulness. Furthermore, as the use of a hypnotic continues, tolerance develops and a higher dose is required for the same effect. They caution that hypnotic-like drugs used in any context may produce significant sleep and behavioral disturbances. Both Ware and Orr (1983) and Richman (1985) advise against the use of drugs; if used, they should be monitored with a form such as the Sleep Diary (see below) and only given for a brief period of time (a few days to, at most, a few weeks).

Behavioral approaches are the most effective treatments and include a variety of techniques: gradual or rapid withdrawal of parental attention (Ferber, 1985; France & Hudson, 1990; Rapoff, Christophersen, & Rapoff, 1982); positive reinforcement of appropriate bedtime and sleep behavior (Kellerman, 1980); consistent bedtimes; shaping (making a gradually earlier bedtime); and cueing (making a clear distinction between day and nighttime activities) (Douglas & Richman, 1982; Ferber, 1985; Richman et al., 1985). Seymour, Brock, During, and Poole (1989) recently demonstrated the effectiveness of providing parents with written information on a standardized night waking program, which involved organized bedtime routines; procedures for settling the child; and instructions for handling crying, calling out, and getting out of bed. Although there is no one solution for all sleep problems, providing information to the parents about normal patterns of sleep and determining how they can change the environment and their responses to the behavior seem to constitute the most effective approach.

ASSESSMENT OF SLEEP PROBLEMS

A sleep disturbance may represent an isolated problem, or it may become evident in the process of evaluating other behavioral or emotional problems. The questions regarding sleep on screening questionnaires should be carefully reviewed and investigated, regardless of the presenting problem. The assessment process described here follows the steps for gathering information in accordance with the Comprehensive Assessment-to-Intervention System (CAIS) presented in Chapter 3; the emphasis here is on those factors particularly important in assessing and treating disturbances of initiating and maintaining sleep.

Step 1: Initial Contact

The parents should be asked to complete a general questionnaire (e.g., our Parent Questionnaire; see Appendix B) with demographic information, as well as their view of the problem and what they have been told and/or done thus far. The Child Behavior Checklist (CBCL; Achenbach & Edelbrock, 1983) will screen for general behavioral or emotional problems; the Eyberg Child Behavior Inventory (ECBI; Eyberg & Ross, 1978) will determine the extent of problems in daily activities, as well as difficulties occurring at bedtime; and the Parenting Stress Index (PSI; Abidin, 1990) will give information on the child's temperament and the parents' general levels of stress. In addition, parents should be asked to complete a Sleep Diary (Figure 9.1) for at least 1 week prior to the initial visit to gather specific information on the child's sleep pattern and the parents' response to it. The importance of the Sleep Diary for assessing the problem and determining the effectiveness of treatment cannot be overemphasized. When parents are tired or they have had a particularly bad night, their perception of the problem is not always an accurate reflection of the actual behavior (Ferber, 1985; Richman, 1985).

Step 2: Parent and Child Interview

Parent Interview

It is important that both parents attend the initial interview. Fathers and mothers are likely to handle sleep problems differently, with mothers tending to be more nurturant (taking children into their bed, feeding children at wakings) than fathers (Crowell et al., 1987). It is usually best not to have children accompany parents to the initial interview, especially older children (who may have their own perception of the problem and may also be able to describe more accurately how they feel and how they handle the situation).

The focus of the parent interview should be on the child's general development and behavior; a history of the sleep problem, as well as its current status; the environmental/social context of the problem; and the parents' level of stress. Specific questions include the following:

1. Development. What was the child's birth history? Was the child premature, or were there perinatal problems? Were developmental milestones achieved normally?

2. Behavior. The screening instruments will give information in this area, and the interview should follow up on any concerns, especially noncompliance. About one-third of children presenting with sleep problems also have more generalized behavior problems (Richman, 1981).

Sleep Diary

DATE	TIME AWAKE	MOOD	NAPTIME	BEDTIME	TIME ASLEEP	PARENT BEDTIME	NIGHT WAKINGS	WHAT DID	TIME ASLEEP	COMMENT
					SAMPLE					
7/6/90	6:00	Happy	1:00–3:00	9:00	10:20	11:00	12:00 3:00 5:00	Rocked Milk Talked	12:20 3:30 5:10	

From *Assessment and Treatment of Childhood Problems: A Clinician's Guide* by Carolyn S. Schroeder and Betty N. Gordon. © 1991 by The Guilford Press.

FIGURE 9.1. The sleep diary.

The clinician must determine whether these other behaviors should be treated first or whether treatment of the sleep problem will aid in the resolution of the other problems. Given the impact that sleep problems have on the child and family, and the parents' desire to get help with this problem, it is usually best to focus initially on the sleep problem unless the child is generally noncompliant. How the parents have handled behavior problems in general provides helpful information on how to structure the intervention. Most sleep problems are circumscribed, and daytime behavior is not highly correlated with nighttime behavior, especially after 3 years of age (Crowell et al., 1987). It should be remembered, however, that a disturbance such as sleep apnea can profoundly affect the child's daytime behavior, resulting in poor school performance, inattentiveness, fussiness, poor coordination, and complaints of laziness.

3. Medical history. What illnesses has the child had (e.g., chronic ear infections, asthma. seizures, chronic illness)? A history of medication use is especially important to obtain. Is the child taking (or has he or she recently stopped taking) medication, such as antihistamines, seizure medication, sedatives, or stimulants? Has the child ever had a head injury?

4. History of the sleep problem. Information about the onset of the sleep problem helps differentiate developmental from pathological problems and gives potential information on any associated events. Have there been changes in the child's daily routine (e.g., starting preschool or a new school, the birth of a sibling, moving to a new bed or bedroom)? Have there been changes in the family routines (e.g., an illness, hospitalization, unusual absences of the parent, a death, a divorce, overnight guests)?

5. Current sleep status. The Sleep Diary provides a good starting point for gathering information on a particular problem. Other areas to assess include (a) the frequency of occurrence (Has it increased and in what way?); (b) the time of occurrence (Does it happen in the first or last part of the night? Are there problems with initiating sleep, night wakings, early morning rising?); (c) nature of the sleep behavior (What does the child do while asleep? How does he or she look?); and (d) other sleep problems (What is the child's total sleep time? How is sleep distributed over 24 hours? Is the child easily awakened? How long to sleep onset? Is the child sleepy during the day, or are there complaints about inattentiveness or laziness?).

6. Sleep habits and schedule. Ware and Orr (1983) point out that just as most children develop predictable physiological patterns of sleep in infancy, most children develop presleep behavior patterns between the ages of 2 and 5 years. These serve the purpose of calming the child and avoiding sleep-related anxiety; they include the bedtime rituals of a story, prayers, saying good night to stuffed animals, cuddling with a special toy, and so on. What are the bedtime demands on the child? Is the

child expected to go to sleep when the house is full of activity? Are daytime activities sufficiently separated from nighttime activities? What is the temperature of the room, and how is it lit? What is the bedtime schedule? Are the times unrealistic for the child's age (too early or too late with regard to time of arising)?

7. Daytime activities. Does the child's schedule include regular exercise, and when does it occur? Are meals at regular times? Are meals or exercise occurring too close to bedtime? What snacks are given before bed (e.g., caffeinated beverages or chocolate and sweets, as opposed to a light snack that improves sleep)? How many naps does the child take and for how long? Are they taken at regular times? There is a negative correlation between the length of daytime sleep and nighttime sleep; thus as the child moves from the 16-hour daily sleep requirement of the infant to the 10-hour requirement for the adolescent, the naps should also decrease, although the child may still have a quiet time (Ferber, 1985).

8. Family sleep history. Do other members of the family have sleep problems? If other members of the family had similar sleep problems, what was their course, how were they treated, and how were the problems viewed?

9. Parents' response to the sleep problem. How do the parents handle the problem? What advice have they been given? What have they tried, and for how long? What have they told the child? How is the problem affecting other people in the family?

10. Parental/social/environmental issues. The Parent Questionnaire and the PSI should alert the clinician to potential contributing problems in these areas. Problems such as unaccustomed parental absences, maternal depression, marital conflict, hospitalization of a family member, and the birth of a sibling can precipitate or exacerbate a sleep disturbance. Information about the parents' mental and physical health status, support networks, the family's daily routine, and the home environment can shed light on what may be maintaining the problem.

Child Interview

Depending on the type of sleep problem, the age of the child, and the presence of other problems, a separate interview with the child may be warranted. Generally, it is not helpful to interview preschool children alone. School-age children who are having sleep problems, however, should be interviewed alone. The focus should be on their general adjustment to friends, school, and family, as well as their perception of the sleep problem (including a description of the problem, its frequency, how their parents have viewed and handled the problem, what the children themselves have done to resolve the problem, and how they themselves view the problem).

Step 3: Observation of Behavior

The parents' Sleep Diary serves as the source of observational data for sleep problems. If a referral is made to a sleep disorders center, then further observations will be made in that facility.

Step 4: Further Assessment

Further assessment is indicated if the child or family presents with problems beyond those associated with the sleep problem. For example, if the child has trouble in school or has other emotional or behavioral problems, it would be important to evaluate these areas further. If there are marital problems or if there is evidence of parental psychopathology, these should be evaluated or referred for evaluation.

Step 5: Referral to Allied Health Professionals

If there are medical problems, or the child is or has been taking medication, it is important for the clinician to contact the child's physician. If the child is taking sedatives for the sleep problem, then these should be discontinued before behavioral treatment begins. For problems such as allergies, asthma, or seizures, where treatment often involves medication that can cause sleep problems, it may be possible to make changes in the medication, the dose, the time of dose, or the medium in which it is delivered. For example, if the child has been taking antibiotics, the sleep problems may be caused by additives in the medium in which the antibiotics are given.

If there is any suspicion of narcolepsy or sleep apnea, the child should be referred to a sleep disorders center (see Ferber, 1985). A referral to a sleep disorders center is also appropriate if a severe sleep problem is persistent and not responsive to treatment.

Step 6: Communication of Findings and Treatment Recommendations

The nature of the sleep disturbance, the clinician's view of the problem, and potential treatment strategies should be shared with the parents. The clinician should also discuss the implications of the sleep problem for the child's development in other areas (e.g., independence, mastery). In the treatment of sleep disturbances, the clinician is primarily a consultant to the family members who must carry out the actual treatment program. Giving parents information on normal sleep states and patterns, with an emphasis on how their child's disturbance fits into this process, can both relieve parents' fears about the problem and ensure their understanding of and cooperation in selecting and carrying out appropriate treatment strategies. The parents' clear understanding of the nature of the problem and the rationale for the treatment plan is essential to gaining their trust and cooperation.

TREATMENT OF SLEEP PROBLEMS

Treatment of children's sleep disturbances will of course vary, depending on the nature of the problem. It is important to note, however, that factors related to the parents can influence the course of treatment. In many cases, it is clear that parents who seek help with their children's sleep disturbances have emotional or marital problems that contribute significantly to their children's problems. In these cases, treatment for the sleep disturbance per se is not likely to be effective. For example, a mother who is depressed or a parent who is recovering from a serious illness is not in the best position to insist that a 2-year-old sleep in his or her own bed when the child wakes in the middle of the night. To recommend that parents do this without consideration of the parents' emotional state is likely only to increase the problems. It would be best to support such parents in getting help for themselves or waiting until they are physically healthy before helping the child to sleep alone. With this in mind, this section focuses on treatment approaches that are appropriate for the more common sleep disturbances. In each case, the relevant information needed by parents is described first, and then specific techniques for treatment are provided.

Sleep-Wake Schedule Problems

Sleep–wake schedule problems can occur when daily routines are irregular, when the child naps at inappropriate times or for too long a time, or when the child's normal sleep–wake schedule does not fit into the family's routine. The parents should be given information on circadian rhythms, the average amount of sleep expected for the age of their child, the advantages and disadvantages of naps at various ages, and the importance of establishing regular routines throughout the day and night.

Parents should be helped to adjust the child's schedule gradually to the family's routine, or, conversely, to reorganize the family's routine in order to accommodate a routine for the child. Depending on the basis of the problem, changing the child's irregular sleep patterns can involve setting up regular daily schedules for going to bed, arising, eating, and exercise; clearly separating day and night activities; and providing cues for the child that it is time to sleep by establishing bedtime routines and rituals that are not stimulating. Treatment also may involve gradually establishing later or earlier bedtimes, and/or waking children earlier from naps and in the morning. Establishing or changing an inappropriate sleep–wake schedule must occur gradually and should be accomplished over a 1- to 3-week period.

Bedtime Struggles and Night Waking

For the 6- to 24-month-old who is still waking several times a night, the parents should be given information on the usual distribution of sleep at various ages, the reasons for the normal wakings every night (NREM-REM cycles), and an explanation of how the child may be relying on the parents to go back to sleep or how the parents' response is maintaining the behavior. Likewise, bedtime struggles can be understood in terms of the normal but often difficult separation that going to sleep alone involves. It should be explained how good bedtime routines and rituals help decrease the child's anxiety about going to sleep, and how parental responses can change the behavior without causing psychological problems for the child.

Treatment of bedtime struggles and night wakings involves techniques that focus on helping the child learn new and more independent bedtime behaviors. This essentially involves helping the child learn the task of falling asleep on his or her own. The most successful approaches to these problems include the following steps (see Douglas & Richman, 1982; Ferber, 1985):

1. Establishing good bedtime routines and rituals (including quiet activities, appropriate snack, a story, etc.) is an important way to cue the child that it is time to sleep.

2. The next step involves extinguishing the child's need for the parents. The parents do this by either gradually withdrawing their attention after saying good night, or going "cold turkey" through totally withdrawing all attention (i.e., closing the door and not going back to the child). Most parents find a gradual approach more tolerable, but it is important that they be given specific instructions on how to do this and follow an agreed-upon schedule of time spent with the child. For example, if the child is used to being nursed to sleep, the first step is to stop nursing before bed but to replace it with holding the child and reading a book or singing. The child should be put to bed just before he or she falls asleep. If the child cries when the parent leaves the room, the parent should return to the child on the schedule recommended by Ferber (1985), as shown in Table 9.1. For the older child who is capable of leaving the room, the parent should follow the schedule for closing the door as shown in Table 9.2 (Ferber, 1985).

TABLE 9.1.   Number of Minutes to Wait before Going in to Your Child Briefly

| Day | At first wait | If your child is still crying | | |
		Second wait	Third wait	Subsequent waits
1	5	10	15	15
2	10	15	20	20
3	15	20	25	25
4	20	25	30	30
5	25	30	35	35
6	30	35	40	40
7	35	40	45	45

Note. From *Solve Your Child's Sleep Problems* by R. Ferber, 1985, New York: Simon & Schuster. Copyright 1985 by Richard Ferber, M.D. Reprinted by permission.

1. This chart shows the number of minutes to wait before going in if your child is crying at bedtime or after nighttime wakings.

2. Each time you go in to your child, spend only 2 to 3 minutes. Remember, you are going in briefly to reassure him and yourself, not necessarily to help him stop crying and certainly not to help him fall asleep. The goal is for him to learn to fall asleep alone, without being held, rocked, nursed, or using a bottle or pacifier.

3. When you get to the maximum number of minutes to wait for that night, continue leaving for that amount of time until your child finally falls asleep during one of the periods you are out of the room.

4. If he wakes during the night, begin the waiting schedule at the minimum waiting time for that day and again work up to the maximum.

5. Continue this routine after all wakings until reaching a time in the morning (usually 5:30 to 7:30 A.M.) you have previously decided to be reasonable to start the day. If he wakes after that time, or if he is still awake then after waking earlier, get him up and begin the morning routines.

6. Use the same schedule for naps, but if your child has not fallen asleep after one hour, or if he is awake again and crying vigorously after getting some sleep, end that naptime period.

7. The number of minutes listed to wait are ones that most families find workable. If they seem too long for you, use the times shown on the chart in Table 9.2 (though without closing the door). In fact, any schedule will work as long as the times increase progressively.

8. Be sure to follow your schedule carefully and chart your child's sleep patterns daily so you can monitor his progress accurately.

9. By day 7 your child will most likely be sleeping very well, but if further work is necessary, just continue to add 5 minutes to each time on successive days.

The alternative "cold turkey" approach may be appropriate for parents who have tried many techniques without success, are able to tolerate crying, or want a fast cure. This involves letting the child know that the parent will not return to the room after saying good night. If necessary, the parent should be instructed to hold the door closed until the child is quiet. A chain lock that allows the child to see outside the room but not to get out is often helpful in extreme cases. In our experience, simply putting the lock on the door is enough to remind the child

TABLE 9.2. Number of Minutes to Close the Door if Your Child Will Not Stay in Bed

Day	First closing	If your child continues to get out of bed			
		Second closing	Third closing	Fourth closing	Subsequent closings
1	1	2	3	5	5
2	2	4	6	8	8
3	3	5	7	10	10
4	5	7	10	15	15
5	7	10	15	20	20
6	10	15	20	25	25
7	15	20	25	30	30

Note. From *Solve Your Child's Sleep Problems* by R. Ferber, 1985, New York: Simon & Schuster. Copyright 1985 by Richard Ferber, M.D. Reprinted by permission.

1. This chart shows the number of minutes to close your child's door if he will not stay in bed at bedtime or after nighttime wakings.

2. When you get to the maximum number of minutes for that night, continue closing the door for that amount of time until he finally stays in bed.

3. Keep the door closed for the number of minutes listed, even if your child goes back to bed sooner. However, you may talk to him through the door and tell him how much time remains.

4. When you open the door, speak to him briefly if he is in bed, offer encouragement, and leave. If he is still out of bed, restate the rules, put him back in bed (if it can be done easily), and shut the door for the next amount of time listed. If he lets you put him back easily and you are convinced he will stay there, you may try leaving the door open, but if you are wrong, do not keep making the same mistake.

5. If your child wakes during the night and won't stay in bed, begin the door-closing schedule at the minimum time for that day and again work up to the maximum.

6. Continue this routine as necessary after all wakings until reaching a time in the morning (usually 5:30 to 7:00 A.M.) previously decided to be reasonable to start the day.

7. Use the same routine at naptimes, but if your child has not fallen asleep after one hour, or if he is awake again and out of bed after getting some sleep, end that naptime period.

8. If he wakes and calls or cries but does not get out of bed, switch to the progressive routine described in Table 9.1.

9. The number of minutes listed to close the door are ones that most families find workable. However, you may change the schedule as you think best as long as the times increase progressively.

10. Be sure to follow your schedule carefully and chart your child's sleep patterns daily so you can monitor his progress accurately.

11. Remember, your goal is to help your child learn to sleep alone. You are using the door as a controlled way of enforcing this, not to scare or punish him. So reassure him by talking through the door; do not threaten or scream. By progressively increasing the time of door closure, starting with short periods, your child does not have to be shut behind a closed door unsure of when it will be opened. He will learn that having the door open is entirely under his control.

12. By day 7 your child will most likely be staying in bed, but if further work is necessary, just continue to add 5 minutes to each time on successive days.

13. If you prefer you may use a gate instead of a closed door as long as your child can't open or climb over it. In this case you must be out of his view during the periods of gate closure, but you can still talk to him reassuringly from another room.

that he or she must stay in the room. If the lock is used, the parents should be clearly instructed to open the door when the child is quiet or has gone to sleep. For children 2 years or older, reading a story about a child who has experienced a similar problem and what was done about it helps them understand what will happen, and also helps the parents and other caregivers to be consistent in carrying out the program. We use a book called *We Will See You in the Morning*, which is a revision of a book by Ann Spitznagel (1976). It can be obtained by sending $6.00 to Pediatric Psychology, 901 Willow Drive, Suite 2, Chapel Hill, NC 27514.

3. The child should be provided with praise for good nighttime behavior and a sticker for each night he or she goes to bed quietly and stays in bed. A sticker chart that is hung on the back of the child's door provides extra motivation.

4. Having the parents keep the Sleep Diary is very important. This allows them to see the progress that the child is making when it is difficult to "feel" the difference between 60 and 45 minutes of crying. This problem should resolve in a few days to 3 weeks if parents are consistent in carrying out the above-described treatment.

Bedtime Fears and Nightmares

The nature of nightmares can make some children afraid to go to bed for fear that the nightmare will reoccur. Other children may associate the content of the nightmare (monsters, etc.) with going to bed and night-time. Therefore, if a child is afraid to go to sleep, the clinician should determine whether this fear has been precipitated by nightmares. If the problem is one of nightmares, parents need to know when dreaming occurs during the sleep cycle. If parents are aware that nightmares can be the result of trying to understand or deal with new or frightening stimuli encountered during the day, they can then understand the need to support and desensitize the child to the feared stimuli, rather than insisting that the child avoid all potentially frightening material on TV or in daily activities (Kellerman, 1980).

As previously stated, dreams and nightmares reflect the resolution of daytime activities and the cognitive-developmental level of the child. The 1-year-old may be awakened by a frightening dream of something that happened during the day, such as falling down the stairs; the 2-year-old may have concerns about separation; and 3- to 5-year-olds often have nightmares of monsters' or creatures' doing harm to them. The last-mentioned type of nightmare is understandable when one considers the fears children at these ages have during the day and the socialization process of the preschool years. The child is expected to have greater control over his or her behavior and to express emotions appropriately, at the same time that he or she is exposed to many new and varied stimuli through preschool, social interactions, books, and television. Nightmares usually decrease between ages 7 and 11 and then show an increase during the adolescent years (mirroring the conflict and struggle of becoming more independent, as in the preschool years).

Children are able to describe the content of a nightmare as soon as they can talk; however, the understanding that a dream is not real, that it is invisible to others, that it comes from within and goes on inside the person, and that it is caused by one's own thought processes follows a developmental progression. By the age of 8 years, most children have a full understanding of dreams as thought processes (Kohlberg, 1969). Treatment techniques for children who have frequent and recurrent nightmares must thus take into account the children's developmental understanding of dreams. For example, although the clinician may tell a 4-year-old that his or her dream is not real, it is also important to give the child concrete reassurance (e.g., hugs, a night light). For older children, a discussion of the dream and its possible basis can facilitate the development of coping skills.

Although the parents and child must deal with the nightmare when it occurs, the treatment process must take into account what happens to the child during the day and must help the child gain a sense of control over difficult situations. In some instances, the child may have been exposed to situations that are too stressful or frightening to handle. Treatment in these cases involves removing the child from those situations (e.g., not allowing the child to watch monster movies, or stopping the physical and verbal battles to which the child is exposed in the home or the day care center). Allowing the young child to describe a nightmare, having a night light that allows the child to see that nothing is in the room, and being supportive but firm that nothing will happen to the child are always important. Treatment during the day can involve desensitizing the child to the frightening dream by having him or her draw or finger-paint the feared object, or dress up as the feared monster. The literature reports a number of successful treatment approaches, including teaching relaxation, using pleasant imagery, making statements about competence in regard to sleeping, and reinforcing the child for appropriate sleep behavior (Greening & Dollinger, 1989; Kellerman, 1980). Having the child replay the nightmare, with the child taking an active role in coping victoriously with the feared event or object in the replay, is also a good way for the child to gain a sense of competence. An excellent book that helps children cope with nightmares through storytelling is *Annie Stories: A Special Kind of Storytelling* by Doris Brett (see Appendix C). One should be careful not to decrease the child's exposure to all frightening movies or events, because part of learning to cope with fearful and stressful situations is being exposed to them in a gradual, age-appropriate fashion.

──────────── CASE EXAMPLE 1 ────────────

Step 1: Initial Contact

Mr. and Mrs. Knight, the parents of Amy, a 3-year-old girl, called for help in getting her to sleep through the night. Mr. Knight worked as a carpenter and Mrs. Knight did part-time work in a grocery store. Mrs. Knight explained that she was a very light sleeper, and the continual night wakings had left her exhausted. Although Mr. Knight helped in caring for Amy at night, he had a very strenuous job; the parents felt that of the two of them, he needed an uninterrupted night of sleep more. Both parents indicated that their sexual relationship had been almost nonexistent since Amy's birth, and they clearly wanted this to change. Amy's 8-year-old sister had not presented any sleep problems, and she did not wake up when Amy cried in the night. Mrs. Knight was clear that she would not be able to tolerate a lot of crying; this indicated that any program would have to be a gradual one.

The PSI, ECBI, and CBCL scores indicated a well-adjusted child during the day and parents who were stressed. The mother reported health problems, and both parents reported marital problems and disagreement about handling the sleep problem.

Step 2: Parent Interview

Amy had been born prematurely, after a complicated pregnancy that resulted in Mrs. Knight's being confined to bed for 5 months. Amy's sleep pattern was erratic until about age 16 months, when she slept for 8 hours during the night and took two 1½- to 2½-hour naps during the day. Her mother or father rocked her to sleep every night, and because of her early developmental history, one of them slept in the room with her. Amy woke two to four times throughout the night, at which times her mother or father changed her diaper, gave her a drink, and held her until she fell asleep again. All of this took about 5 minutes from the time of awakening. During the day, Amy was described as a happy child with a great deal of curiosity and a high activity level.

A 2-week Sleep Diary (Figure 9.1) indicated that it took Amy on the average 30 minutes to fall asleep at night and that she woke an average of four times per night, taking 5–10 minutes on each of these occasions to get back to sleep. The parents stated on the Sleep Diary that they tried not to respond to her nighttime cries, but within 10 minutes they would do so. They stated that it was easier to give in to her than to tolerate her crying and have a totally sleepless night. In the past they had let her cry up to 45 minutes before going to her; they had talked with her about the need for all of them to get a good night's sleep; and they had even screamed at her in the middle of the night to stop crying. They had also talked with their pediatrician, who recommended a sedative, but they did not want to use medication. Other advice had been to "let her cry it out." They were not able to follow this advice and were concerned about it's psychological effects on Amy.

Step 3: Observation of Behavior

The Sleep Diary served as the source of observational data for this case.

Step 4: Further Assessment

Further assessment was not needed in this case.

Step 5: Referral to Allied Health Professionals

Referral to other professionals was not necessary in this case.

Step 6: Communication of Findings and Treatment Recommendations

Mr. and Mrs. Knight were told that many children who are born prematurely take a longer time to develop a regular sleep pattern, and that their parents are understandably more reluctant to allow the child to cry for any extended period of time. Amy, however, appeared to be developing normally and was at an age when she should be able to fall asleep by herself and sleep through the night without the parents. Mr. and Mrs. Knight were resistant, however, to the idea of allowing Amy to cry herself to sleep, even though they were told that this would not result in any psychological harm to her. In fact, many children, by crying themselves to sleep, quickly learn that they are able to go to sleep independently and therefore feel better about themselves.

The parents insisted on a very gradual treatment approach, including fading a parent's sleeping in Amy's room. The clinician voiced concerns about their staying in the room with Amy, as well as the need for consistency over a long period of time to make the program effective. The intervention program that was eventually agreed upon included (1) establishing a clear nighttime ritual with a story and songs; (2) reading a story to Amy that described the planned treatment with another little girl; (3) patting Amy's back for a count of 100 initially, gradually decreasing the pats to a 1-minute back rub before saying good night; (4) not speaking to Amy after saying good night, and not talking to her during the middle of the night; (5) having a parent lie down on a cot in Amy's room without speaking to her until she fell asleep; (6) leaving Amy after she was asleep but returning to her room when they retired for the night; and (7) putting a chart with the days of the week on Amy's bedroom door and giving Amy a sticker for staying in her bed during the night.

Course of Treatment

Treatment occurred over a 6-month period with erratic progress. Within 2 weeks, Amy was going to sleep on her own while either Mr. or Mrs. Knight sat in a rocking chair placed at the doorway of the room, reading the newspaper. Mrs. Knight continued to sleep in Amy's room, but did not get out of bed or talk to Amy when she woke, and Amy soon went back to sleep on her own after calling out to her mother.

The plan for the next 2 weeks included telling Amy that her mother would no longer sleep in Amy's room, but that if she woke she could call to her mother, who would answer but not go into her room. Neither parent wanted to give up sitting in the rocking chair as Amy fell asleep. If Amy got out of bed, Mrs. Knight was instructed to take her back to bed, but not to talk to her or sleep in her room. Amy got a sticker for staying in her room during the night. The first night she came out twice, but by the seventh day, she was calling to the parents only once per night. The parents were comfortable with this, and follow-up a month later found that Amy was continuing to call to her parents one to two times per night. They did not feel that a change in procedure was necessary, however.

Several months later Mrs. Knight went away for a weekend. Amy did fine during her absence, but when she returned Amy was very clingy during the day and was described as "inconsolable" when she awoke at night. She was still going to bed on her own, with the parents sitting in the rocking chair for a few minutes, but she was waking four to five times each night and coming to the parents' room. By the time the parents contacted the clinician, Mrs. Knight was once more sleeping in Amy's room during the night.

Given Amy's increased insecurity, it was recommended that Mrs. Knight allow Amy to stay close by her throughout the day, even to the point of letting Amy know when she was going to another room. Mrs. Knight also continued to sleep in Amy's room, but did not talk or interact with her in any way when she awoke. Within 3 weeks, the parents indicated that Amy was no longer clingy during the day and seemed comfortable being away from the mother. At this point, Mrs. Knight went back to sleeping in her own room, but Amy repeatedly came into their room upon awakening; four out of seven nights, Amy spent the rest of the night in their bed or Mrs. Knight slept in Amy's room. During one of these nights, Mr. Knight became so angry with Amy that he turned the light on, got his coat, and walked out the front door!

The parents agreed with the clinician that the gradual approach they had helped design was no longer working. For their sake and Amy's, it was agreed that a "cold turkey" approach was needed at this time. Amy evidenced no separation anxiety during the day and was clearly capable of sleeping through the night without their assistance. The parents agreed that they had to respond consistently to her if she were ever to learn to sleep on her own. The parents put a chain lock on the door so that Amy could not get out of her room but could see into the hall. She was told that if she came out of the room after they said good night to her or during the night, she would be taken back to her room and the lock would be fastened until she was quiet and in bed. During the first and second nights, Amy only called out twice to her parents. By the third night she was going to bed on her own and sleeping through the night without disturbing her parents. The chain lock was never fastened.

At a follow-up 1 year later, Amy was continuing to sleep through the night. The parents indicated that after illnesses that required their attending to her during the night, they reminded Amy that she was now well and could manage on her own, and that if she did come out of her room they would return her and fasten the lock. They never actually had to do this, however.

―――――――――― CASE EXAMPLE 2 ――――――――――

Step 1: Initial Contact

Mr. and Mrs. Moon, the parents of 11-year-old Matthew, requested help in dealing with Matthew's recurrent nightmares. Screening instruments indicated that Matthew was doing well in school, was involved in many activities, and had friends. Although the parents described him as a rather sensitive and serious child, they saw him as quite happy. The Sleep Diary indicated that nightmares had occurred on 11 out of the last 14 nights. Matthew went to sleep in his own bed, but after having a nightmare he slept on the floor of his parents' bedroom or with his older brother. In the last 5 days, he had been taking longer to get to sleep at night, with repeated calling to the parents or staying up to read.

Step 2: Parent and Child Interviews

Parent Interview

The parents came alone for the initial interview, and a day later Matthew was seen. Mr. Moon was a security guard and Mrs. Moon cleaned houses. Matthew, the third of four children, was described as a healthy youngster who had never been hospitalized and had received only occasional antibiotics. His parents described a sleep history of occasional night terrors from ages 4 to 6. These had seemed to occur at about the time of the maternal grandfather's death and after a particularly difficult bout with the flu, including a very high fever. Night terrors had been especially frightening for the parents, but after talking with their pediatrician, they had been reassured. Matthew had had at least one nightmare a week during the preschool years, and only occasional nightmares up until 1 month prior to the initial contact.

The nightmares during the preschool years involved monsters chasing him and weird flying birds. The recent nightmares followed the theme of some tragic event happening to a member of the family, with Matthew feeling helpless to stop it. There was a great deal of focus on things happening to his youngest brother, age 5. Matthew complained of feeling tired during the day and becoming increasingly upset about the thought of going to sleep and having yet another nightmare. Matthew's parents and his older brother did not mind his coming into their rooms, but Matthew saw it as immature behavior. The parents indicated that the family situation was stable and that they were in good health. The only upsetting event that had occurred recently was that the paternal grandfather had had a heart attack 2 months previously, but he was currently at home and recovering.

Child Interview

In the interview with Matthew, it was interesting that he estimated having nightmares only every other night. He knew the nightmares were not real, but said that they were still very frightening. He described fairly stimulating and enjoyable daily routines. He also described a number of situations that caused him to be either very sad or very angry. For example, there were several bullies on the school bus who were constantly teasing and pushing the younger children (including him and his brothers); he was having trouble completing the requirements for a particular Scout badge; and he described his older brother as being particularly irritable with the entire family. He expressed affection toward his parents, particularly his mother, whom (he felt) was treated unfairly by his older brother. At the same time, however, Matthew felt that his mother did not always treat him fairly when he got into a fight with his older brother.

Step 3: Observation of Behavior

The Sleep Diary served as the source of observational data for this case.

Step 4: Further Assessment

Further assessment was not needed in this case.

Step 5: Referral to Allied Health Professionals

Referral to other professionals was not necessary in this case.

Step 6: Communication of Findings and Treatment Recommendations

Mr. and Mrs. Moon and Matthew were told that Matthew was a child with many strengths (good school performance, friends, and age-appropriate interests) but one who was also sensitive to injustices and to people being hurt or bullied by others. His nightmares seemed to be related to stresses that he was encountering at home from interactions with his older brother and from the bullies on the school bus who were particularly threatening to younger children (his 5-year-old brother rode the bus with him). Given the frequency and upsetting nature of Matthew's nightmares, it was understandable that going to bed was unpleasant for him. It was recommended that Matthew be seen for 4 to 6 sessions to learn ways to cope with his nightmares when they occurred as well as to learn more effective ways to deal with current and future stresses in his life.

Treatment Program

Matthew came in for four weekly appointments with the clinician. Phone contact was made with Mrs. Moon after each session. Matthew agreed to go to his parents' room when he had a nightmare. One of them was to take him back to his room, have him describe the nightmare to them, and reassure him that all was well. He was then to write the content of the nightmare in the Sleep Diary.

Matthew was taught to relax his body through first tensing his muscles and then letting them relax. As he was relaxing, he was to imagine one of two scenes that he particularly enjoyed. These were winning a basketball game and seeing himself get physically stronger and stronger as he rode his bike and engaged in other pleasurable activities. Matthew and the clinician went over his descriptions of the nightmares and role-played them, with responses from Matthew that resulted in a victory over the scary events.

Treatment also focused on the areas that were creating stress for Matthew during the day. He and the clinician took a problem-solving approach to the issue of the bullies on the bus. Matthew decided to ask his parents to inform the principal of his school about the bullies, and he planned to tell them to pick on someone their own size. Furthermore, he decided that if they physically attacked him, he was capable of defending himself. The family as a whole discussed sibling squabbles and agreed upon a program of time-out by isolation for everyone involved if the children could not resolve the problem themselves. The older brother was also encouraged to spend more time with his own friends, both inside and outside the home.

The decrease in nightmares over the next month coincided with Matthew's achieving greater control over daily events, and especially with the resolution of the problem with the bullies. The principal's investigation into this matter revealed real intimidation and physical aggression on the part of the bullies. They were suspended from riding the bus for a week. When they returned they made verbal threats to Matthew, which he handled by making the statement, "You must not feel very good about yourselves if you have to talk like that." Matthew recognized that he might have occasional nightmares as he tried to resolve and understand daytime activities, but that when he had *recurrent* nightmares, it was time for him to look for and cope with stressors in his environment.

Chapter 10

Sexuality

and

Sexual Abuse

*T*he nature and expression of sexuality in young children have received little attention in the professional literature, in part because of the widely accepted myth of the "sexual innocence" of children (Haroian, 1983) and the restrictive attitudes and values of our society (Martinson, 1981a). With current concerns about the sexual abuse of young children, however, interest in normal psychosexual development among young children has increased. This interest has focused on children's sexual behavior, as well as their knowledge and understanding of sexuality.

The child clinician is often confronted with questions from parents and teachers about the normality of a child's interest in sexual matters, sexual exploration, and masturbation. If these questions and concerns are to be placed in proper perspective, the clinician must have some understanding of the development of sexuality in children. This chapter first reviews what is known about the sexual development of young children. This is followed by a review of research on parents' attempts to provide sexuality education for their children, and the efficacy of sexual abuse prevention programs. Problems of sexuality, including gender identity disorder, precocious puberty, and excessive masturbation, are briefly discussed; this is followed by a summary of the extensive and ever-growing literature on child sexual abuse. Finally, outlines of the assessment and treatment programs for sexually abused children used in our clinic are presented.

NORMAL SEXUAL DEVELOPMENT

Sexual Behavior

It is now commonly accepted among professionals that the physiology for sexual arousal and orgasm, and the capacity for a variety of sexual behaviors, appear to be present in children from birth or even before birth (Kinsey, Pomeroy, & Martin, 1948; Langfeldt, 1981a; Martinson, 1981a). We know, for example, that fetuses suck their fingers and toes, and that newborn male babies have penile erections while female babies are capable of vaginal lubrication (Martinson, 1981a). Sexual arousal in infants and children, as well as in adults, is often associated with the rapid-eye-movement (REM) stage of sleep (Karacan, Rosenbloom, & Williams, 1970). However, infants and young children lack the cognitive capacity and experience that adults bring to sexual encounters; therefore, this autoerotic behavior is most appropriately thought of as "pleasure seeking" and is seen as primarily a reflex or a conditioned reflex (if it occurs repeatedly and appears nonaccidental) (Martinson, 1981a). Although the development of sexuality progresses throughout infancy and childhood, no developmental milestones have been clearly identified, with the exception of puberty (Haroian, 1983).

Masturbation is probably the first indication of sexual awareness in children; it has been observed in infants as young as 7 months (Martinson, 1981a). Masturbation is certainly a common occurrence among preschool children (Routh & Schroeder, 1981), and evidence suggests that even children as young as 2 or 3 (males especially) are capable of experiencing orgasm as a result of masturbation (Gundersen, Melas, & Skar, 1981; Kinsey et al., 1948).

The issue of when the awareness of sexuality as an interactive behavior begins is clouded by cultural attitudes and values about children and sexuality. Most of the work in this area has come from Scandinavian countries, where attitudes toward sexuality are quite permissive. Thus the conclusions resulting from this work may not apply to children in the United States, where there are significant societal and ethical restrictions on our ability to gather empirical data on children's sexual behavior. Nonetheless, we know that sensual and possibly erotic encounters between the infant and mother (and other caregivers) begin at birth and continue throughout the early years. Indeed, these experiences of touching and physical affection are critical to the healthy development of the child. It is also common knowledge that preschool children are very curious about their own and others' bodies, and that given the opportunity, they will engage in sexual exploration with other children. Gundersen et al. (1981) report a study of the sexual behavior of Norwegian children (ages 3–7) in a preschool setting where there were few restrictions on the children's sexual exploration; only coercive interaction and inserting objects into body openings were forbidden. The teachers reported that sexual play was very common among the children and involved body exploration, genital manipulation, and attempts at intercourse.

It has also been demonstrated that sexual exploration with adults is very common among children. In a survey of 576 families in the United States, Rosenfeld, Bailey, Siegel, and Bailey (1986) reported that nearly 90% of 2- to 4-year-olds had touched their mothers' genitals and/or breasts, and that approximately 60% had touched their fathers' genitals. They also found that although this behavior decreased with increasing child age, close to one-half of the 8- to 10-year-olds had recently touched their mothers' genitals and/or breasts, while 20–25% had touched their fathers' genitals.

Knowledge of Sexuality

Despite the fact that children are known to engage in sexual behavior alone and in interaction with others from an early age, their awareness of sexuality is in part a function of their knowledge of sexual facts and their understanding of sexual behavior. Again, research in this area is inevitably biased by the culture in which it is conducted. In societies where sexuality is treated openly, children have more sexual experience and are exposed to sexuality education earlier and to a greater extent than in societies with more restrictive attitudes. Thus these children would be expected to have more knowledge of sexuality. The research reviewed in this section was primarily conducted in the United States, and therefore reflects the prevailing attitudes (considered relatively restrictive) in this country.

Early studies of children's knowledge of sexuality focused on the development of gender identity (e.g., Slaby & Frey, 1975) and the extent of children's understanding of pregnancy and birth (e.g., Bernstein & Cowan, 1975). In general, these studies have found a developmental progression (related to Piagetian concepts of cognitive development) in children's understanding of gender and the birth process. Younger children tend to have incomplete and inaccurate concepts of these topics, whereas older children, who are more capable of thinking in the abstract, tend to have a more accurate understanding. More recent work indicates that children's knowledge of sexuality increases with age, but there are differences, depending on the area of sexuality assessed. Bem (1989), for example, found that girls knew as much about genitalia at 3 years as they knew at 5 years, whereas knowledge of genitalia among boys increased gradually with age. Moreover, significantly more girls knew what "vagina" meant than did boys (58% vs. 15%), but boys and girls knew "penis" equally well. We (Gordon, Schroeder, & Abrams, 1990a) assessed knowledge of a variety of sexual topics in 2- to 7-year-olds and found that knowledge of all areas increased with age. However, all children, even the youngest, were quite knowledgeable about certain aspects of sexuality (body parts and functions, gender differences). In contrast, even the oldest children knew very little about adult sexual behavior (sexual intercourse, pregnancy, and birth). Waterman (1986) reviewed a number of studies of children's sexual knowledge and concluded that "where babies come from" and gender differences are of primary interest to preschool children. She states that "concern about sexual intercourse or other adult sexual behaviors appears to be rare in children not involved in or exposed to such behaviors" (Waterman, 1986, p. 23).

The relationship between children's knowledge of sexuality and their sexual behavior is not clear. Gundersen et al. (1981), in their study of Norwegian preschool children, found that although the children were observed to engage in relatively sophisticated sexual behavior (including attempts at sexual intercourse), their questions focused on pregnancy, childbirth, and anatomical differences between boys and girls; understanding of sexual terminology was not demonstrated until at least 4 years of age. We (Gordon, Schroeder, & Abrams, 1990b) examined differences in the sexual knowledge of children who had been sexually abused (and thus were sexually experienced) and nonabused children who were matched for age and social class. We found no differences between the two groups in the children's knowledge of any area of sexuality assessed, including adult sexual behavior. Thus, it appears that in the area of sexuality, more experience is not necessarily accompanied by greater understanding.

Sexuality Education

Sexuality education in its broadest sense involves the teaching of attitudes, values, and feelings about being male and female, as well as learning about anatomical parts and functions of the body. Parents, because of their ongoing contact with children, are the primary sex educators of their children, especially in the early years. Thus, children's knowledge of sexuality is clearly going to be related to how parents and other adults have answered their questions and what information has been taught. Most parents, however, do not discuss all aspects of sexuality with their children (Finkelhor, 1984; Gordon & Snyder, 1983). A study of 1,400 parents with children at all ages (Roberts, Kline, & Gagnon, 1978, cited in Gordon & Snyder, 1983) indicated that only 25% of parents thought they were doing well in educating their children about sexuality, and 85–95% said they had never mentioned any aspect of erotic behavior. Pregnancy was the topic most discussed by parents; sexual intercourse, contraception, and sexually transmitted diseases were the least discussed. Finkelhor (1984) surveyed 517 parents and found that only 43% of them had discussed sexual intercourse with their children, whereas 84% had discussed pregnancy and birth. Furthermore, only 29% of parents had talked with their children about sexual abuse (the topic least likely to be discussed except for birth control), and among those who had discussed this topic, most emphasized "stranger danger."

Parents are uncomfortable discussing sexuality with their children for a variety of reasons, including their own attitudes about sexuality and their own experience of sexuality education as children. We (Gordon et al., 1990a) found that parents with more restrictive attitudes provided less sex education for their children and also had children with less sexual knowledge. Parents in the Finkelhor (1984) study gave a variety of reasons for not discussing sexual abuse with their children: 44% said their child was too young (9 or 10 years was considered an appropriate age), 55% said the child was in no danger, and 74% said it was too difficult a topic to discuss.

Gordon and Snyder (1983) suggest that two prevailing myths about sex education influence parents' decision not to provide information about sexuality to their children: (1) "Children already know all there is to know, so why teach them?" and (2) "Knowledge is harmful and will overstimulate children to participate in more sexual activity at an earlier age." The evidence contradicts both of these myths. The research cited above clearly indicates that children do not possess knowledge of many important aspects of sexuality. Furthermore, if children are told more than they want to know or are given information that they do not understand, they will simply "tune out" (Gordon & Snyder, 1983). Martinson (1981a) reports that in Scandinavia, where sex education is actively supported for young children, children do not remember all they are told (presumably because they do not understand it). This indicates that parents should view sex education as an ongoing process rather than a "one time effort." With regard to the second myth about sex education, provision of sexual information to children is associated with postponement of sexual activity by teenagers (Gordon & Snyder, 1983). Answering children's questions in a simple manner that is appropriate to their level of cognitive development can serve to satisfy their curiosity and decrease the need for sexual experimentation (Gordon & Snyder, 1983). Parents often become upset when they discover their children engaging in sexual exploration (alone or with peers), and do not know how to handle the situation. They should view the discovery of this exploration as an opportunity to have a "teachable moment." We have found it to be effective to say to the child "I can see you are curious about your body. I have a book that we can look at together, and then we can talk about it." In this way, parents can satisfy their children's normal curiosity about sexuality while setting appropriate limits on their behavior.

There are many excellent resources for parents and professionals on sexuality education for children. We have found the professional training manual *Sexuality Education for Parents of Young Children* (Koblinsky, 1983), and two books for parents, *Raising a Child Conservatively in a Sexually Permissive World* (Gordon & Gordon, 1983) and *The Family Book About Sexuality* (Calderone & Johnson, 1982), to be most helpful. These and other books for children of different ages are listed in Appendix C.

Sexual Abuse Prevention

Teaching children personal safety skills has become an increasingly important aspect of sexuality education. Unfortunately, most programs designed to do this do not take into account the cognitive-developmental level of the target children. The result is that children often do not understand key concepts and do not show long-term gains in knowledge or the ability to use preventive skills appropriately (Repucci & Haugaard, 1989). For example, preschoolers have difficulty understanding that someone they love could hurt them or discriminating when physical contact is good or bad. Interviews with sexual abuse offenders (Conte, Wolf, & Smith, 1989) have indicated that offenders are extremely sophisticated about desensitizing their young victims to touch before actually molesting them. Furthermore, offenders report typically using various kinds of threats to intimidate children. Conte et al. (1989) argue that most sex abuse prevention programs do not take these issues adequately into account. Some programs may even have negative effects, such as increasing the frequency with which children negatively interpret positive situations (bathing, cuddling, physical examinations) or insist that they can say "No" to anything and anyone (Repucci & Haugaard, 1989).

Sexual abuse prevention programs have also not consistently taken into account what children know or can understand about sexual abuse at different ages (Kolko, 1988). Just as research has documented age-related differences in children's knowledge of sexuality, younger children have been shown to have different conceptions of sexual abuse from those of older children. Wurtele and Miller (1987) found that 80% of children ages 5–7 were unsure about the nature of sexual abuse and were more likely to say that a perpetrator was a "bad person," a stranger, and someone close to their own age. In contrast, 50% of children ages 10–12 indicated that sexual abuse involved sexual touching, viewed the perpetrator as "mentally ill" or "sexually deviant," and indicated that the perpetrator was an older person. They conclude that programs for older children might appropriately incorporate less factual information and more problem-solving exercises and hypothetical situations, whereas younger children need simple facts in order to clear up misconceptions.

Most sexual abuse prevention programs have been designed for children of elementary school age, with few aimed at preschoolers or adolescents, few involving parents, and few based on developmental principles (Kolko, 1988; Miller-Perrin & Wurtele, 1988). Furthermore, it is only recently that studies evaluating the effectiveness of the multitude of available programs have been reported. Miller-Perrin and Wurtele (1988) suggest that programs for young children should focus on teaching the simple idea of protection of private parts, rather than "good touch, bad touch, and confusing touch." The latter concept is too confusing for young children. They also state that behavioral techniques such as modeling, guided practice, and reinforcement of appropriate responses are likely to make programs more effective, and this has been found to be true (Wurtele, 1990). Wurtele, Kast, Miller-Perrin, and Kondrick (1989) evaluated the effectiveness of a feelings-based program (good touch vs. bad touch vs. confusing touch) and a behavioral skills training program ("It's not OK for a bigger person to touch or look at my private parts, except for health or hygiene reasons") for preschool children. They found that behavioral skills training was more effective in teaching children about appropriate and inappropriate touching. Teaching the importance of disclosure ("Tell someone") is also considered a critical component of programs for young children, because it is unlikely that all children will be able to get away or say "No" (Kolko, 1988). The effectiveness of prevention programs for young children increases as the time, effort, and one-on-one practice provided increase (Garbarino, 1988). "Booster" sessions also appear to be essential for maintaining effectiveness. The involvement of parents in these programs would also appear to be an essential ingredient for success. In this way, the lessons learned in preschool or day care can be reinforced at home.

SEXUAL PROBLEMS

Human beings are capable of a broad range of sexual behaviors; what is considered normal or abnormal is, of course, a function of the prevailing values and attitudes of the society at any given time. Sexual problems in children "usually are public or semi-public behaviors that cause adults (usually the parents) embarrassment and concern because they are a departure from society's expectations" (Haroian, 1983, p. 574). Because of the lack of research in the area of children's sexuality, it is left to parents and professionals to decide which aspects of children's sexual behavior are normal and which are not. The following discussion of sexuality problems reflects these issues.

Excessive Masturbation

Masturbation is seen by most sexologists to be an important developmental step in becoming reliably orgasmic in adult partner sex (Haroian, 1983). Furthermore, it is seen as a viable sexual activity throughout the life span. The key clinical question regarding masturbation among children is not *why* children masturbate, because it is inherently pleasurable. Rather, *how much* and *where* the child masturbates are the important issues. There are large individual differences in the frequency of masturbation (Gundersen et al., 1981), and boys have been observed to masturbate earlier and more frequently than girls (Langfeldt, 1981a, 1981b). Whether or not masturbation constitutes a "behavior problem" is a function of family, societal, and cultural attitudes. A case example cited in Routh and Schroeder (1981, p. 387) clearly illustrates this. The mother of a 4-year-old girl wanted advice on how to stop her daughter from masturbating while she watched TV. When asked why she was concerned at this time, the mother stated, "Because my mother-in-law is coming to visit next week." This mother was not concerned about her child's masturbation per se, but was concerned about the social implications of the behavior for the child and family. Like most children, this child had to learn to manage personal needs, desires, and behaviors in socially acceptable ways.

Excessive masturbation, to the exclusion of or interference with other age-appropriate activities, may be a "red flag" for other problems. Children who have been sexually abused often engage in excessive masturbation, although excessive masturbation does not necessarily mean that a child has been sexually abused. Gundersen et al. (1981) reported that preschool children who were judged by their teachers to masturbate excessively were also considered to have other problems, such as being withdrawn, having conduct disorders, or coming from a poor home environment. Effective treatment of excessive masturbation should begin with a thorough assessment of the child's psychological status, the home situation, as well as a review of the child's daily routine, including interactions with children and adults in the community. Problems in these areas would have to be addressed in addition to treating the excessive masturbation per se, which would include reinforcement of incompatible behaviors, reinforcement for periods of time not engaged in masturbation, and teaching the child to masturbate only in private.

Gender Identity Disorder

Most child develop an understanding of themselves as boys or girls between the ages of 2 and 3 years, and same-sex preferences are usually reflected in children's behavior (choice of games, clothing) by the age of 4 or 5 (Rutter, 1971). Boys develop a same-sex preference earlier and more consistently than do girls (Rutter, 1975), and this probably reflects differential societal attitudes toward sex-typed behaviors for boys and girls.

Although there is a great deal of individual variation in the normal development of gender identity and gender-specific behaviors, for some children a significant incongruity between their biological and preferred gender persists and is pervasive. These children express a strong desire to be (or a belief that they are) of the opposite sex, and are preoccupied with activities that are strongly associated with the opposite sex. The revised third edition of the *Diagnostic and Statistical Manual of Mental Disorders* (DSM-III-R; American Psychiatric Association, 1987) differentiates these children from those who are simply "tomboys" or "sissies," and ascribes the diagnosis of Gender Identity Disorder of Childhood (GID) to them.

GID is a rare occurrence. Achenbach and Edelbrock (1981) found that 0–2% of boys and 2–5% of girls were reported by their parents to express a wish to be the opposite sex, but it is not known how many of these children would fulfill all the criteria for a DSM-III-R diagnosis of GID. Others have estimated prevalence rates of 1 in 24,000–37,000 males and 1 in 103,000–150,000 females (Meyer-Bahlburg, 1985). More boys than girls are referred for treatment of cross-gender behavior, but this most likely reflects our society's greater tolerance for cross-gender behavior in girls than in boys (Meyer-Bahlburg, 1985).

Although rare in occurrence, the significance of the disorder is pointed out in DSM-III-R, which indicates that one-third to two-thirds or more of boys with the disorder adopt a homosexual lifestyle in adolescence or early adulthood. The course of the disorder is less significant for girls, with spontaneous remission of symptoms in late childhood or early adolescence reported for the majority of cases (American Psychiatric Association, 1987). Most adult transsexuals and transvestites, and some homosexuals, report having had gender identity problems in early childhood (American Psychiatric Association, 1987; Rekers & Lovaas, 1974); many adults with cross-gender problems also have other serious emotional, social, and economic maladjustments (Rekers & Lovaas, 1974). However, there is no clear evidence regarding how many children with cross-gender behavior go on to have cross-gender problems as adults, or how changing attitudes toward sexual behaviors labeled as "deviant" might influence the degree of accompanying psychopathology (Winkler, 1977).

Although clinicians should be alert to the possibility of GID in children referred for cross-gender behavior, they should also be aware that current research supports the idea that healthy personality development depends in part on both masculine *and* feminine characteristics. Children who engage in cross-sex behavior, but are entirely comfortable with their own gender, may in fact be exhibiting quite adaptive behavior.

Treatment of GID in children primarily consists of behavioral approaches involving positive reinforcement for engaging in gender-appropriate behavior and choosing gender-appropriate toys and games; verbal feedback about appropriate and inappropriate gender behavior; and extinction of cross-gender behavior by ignoring (Rekers & Lovaas, 1974; Schaefer & Millman, 1981). Winkler (1977), however, suggests that clinicians should attempt to increase androgynous behaviors rather than those that are rigidly sex-typed. Consistency across settings and people is critical to the success of these programs, which in general appear to be quite successful, although long-term outcome has yet to be reported (Meyer-Bahlburg, 1985).

Precocious Puberty

Onset of puberty has been clearly associated with behavioral measures of adjustment, such as self-image, body image, peer relations, and parental relations (Brooks-Gunn & Warren, 1988). Onset of puberty is considered to be precocious if it occurs before age 9 in girls and age 10 in boys. Precocious puberty is caused by increased levels of sex steroids, which in turn can be caused by a variety of disorders, including central nervous system lesions, genetic disorders, neurofibromatosis, and so on (Sonis et al., 1986). Precocious puberty is associated with negative adjustment, particularly in the area of social relationships, and these negative effects are in part a function of the sex of the child (girls have more trouble adjusting than boys) and the degree of earliness (Haroian, 1983). Sonis et al. (1985) found that girls with precocious puberty exhibited 10 times more behavior problems in the areas of social withdrawal, depression, aggression, and social competence than did a group of matched controls. Treatment of precocious puberty should consist of referring the child for a thorough medical evaluation; helping parents to understand the potential lability in the child's moods; providing the child with opportunities for age-appropriate activities; and providing sexuality education, with emphasis on the bodily changes that are occurring.

CHILD SEXUAL ABUSE

The incidence of child sexual abuse has received so much attention in the professional literature that it would be remiss not to include this important topic in a chapter dealing with children's sexuality. Clinicians should be aware, however, that attitudes toward sexual contact between children and adults reflect the same cultural and subcultural values and practices that influence our thinking about the normal development of sexuality in children. Adult–child sexual contact that occurs in a context of mutual consent and societal acceptance has been shown to have no detrimental effects on children (Currier, 1981). Moreover, some argue that children have a right to express their sexuality behaviorally and that this right must be protected (Berger, 1981; Constantine, 1981; Martinson, 1981b). The question of when children's sexual experiences are part of normal development (perhaps reflecting the permissive practices of a particular family or culture), and when they should be considered abusive, is critical for clinicians working in this area.

Two factors are important in making this distinction: (1) informed consent and (2) exploitation. With regard to the first, one must seriously question, in light of the evidence concerning children's cognitive development and their relative lack of knowledge about sexuality, whether young children are truly capable of giving informed consent to sexual contact with a much older person. The age at which informed consent is possible is not yet known and thus is a matter for clinical judgment. Exploitation is perhaps more easily determined by examining the motivation for the sexual contact. The key issue here is whether the adult has considered the child's needs in *all* areas (not just with regard to sexual experience, which is often stated as a motivation) above his or her own need for sexual gratification.

Prevalence

Many investigators concur that the prevalence of sexual abuse is approximately 25% of girls and 10% of boys. Walker, Bonner, and Kaufman (1988) presented data from the American Association for Protecting Children indicating that the incidence of sexual abuse increases with age. Among children who were sexually abused, 25% were ages 0–5, 34.3% were ages 6–11, and 40.6% were ages 12–17. Faller (1989) has reported data indicating that for boys, the incidence of abuse may actually decrease with age. In her sample of sexually abused boys, 58.5% were 2–5 years old, 25.3% were 6–10 years old, and 17.2% were 11–17 years old when the abuse occurred. This may reflect the increased size and strength of boys as they become adolescents, which enable them to protect themselves better.

Boys are reported to be abused much less often (20% of cases) than girls, but this may reflect the fact that most of the information about cases of sexual abuse is gathered from child protective services. These agencies are responsible only for cases in which the perpetrator is a caregiver, and boys are more likely than girls to be abused by nonfamily members (Faller, 1989). Studies that survey other populations report a much higher percentage of male victims (30–50%; Faller, 1989). Faller (1989) examined differences in the characteristics of male and female victims of sexual abuse and found that females were more likely (1) to be from lower socioeconomic level homes (79.5% vs. 54%); (2) to be abused by someone within the family (86% vs. 51.7%); (3) to be abused by one person (33.6% vs. 14.9%); (4) to be abused by a male (81.7% vs. 63.2%); and (5) to be abused by a father or stepfather (60.3% vs. 52.4%). Pierce and Pierce (1985) reported that male victims were significantly less likely to have a father figure in the home and more likely to be subjected to the use of force or violence than were females. It seems clear that there are distinct differences in the sexual abuse of boys versus girls, although it is not yet clear why these differences exist.

Sexual Abuse in Day Care Settings

Sexual abuse that occurs in day care settings has received increasing media attention and is of particular concern during the preschool years. Finkelhor, Williams, and Burns (1988) gathered information on 270 day care settings in which sexual abuse was substantiated during 1983–1985. This information involved 1,639 victims under the age of 7, the majority of whom were 3 and 4 years old. From these data, they estimated the true incidence of sexual abuse cases in day care settings to be 500–550 centers involving 2,500 victims in a 3-year period. Although these are frightening statistics, Finkelhor et al. (1988) point out that when one considers that on average more children are cared for in day care centers than at home, young children are more likely to be abused in their own homes than in day care settings. Finkelhor et al. discuss the role that parents can play in the early detection, follow-up, and prevention of sexual abuse in day care centers. They state that parents should visit their child's day care center often; participate in the program as much as possible; and be suspicious about day care centers in "good" neighborhoods, as well as those in "high-risk" neighborhoods. Parents should also be informed about signs of abuse in young children, so that they can act quickly to protect their child if abuse is suspected. The book *No More Secrets: Protecting Your Child from Sexual Assault* by Caren Adams and Jennifer Fay (reviewed in Appendix C) is an excellent resource for parents.

Effects of Sexual Abuse

Short-Term Effects

Despite the suggestion that children's sexual encounters with adults do not necessarily lead to harmful effects, current research has clearly documented that victims of sexual abuse evidence a variety of significant problems. Browne and Finkelhor (1986), in a review of the empirical literature, found evidence for reactions of fear, anxiety, depression, anger, and hostility. In addition to these problems, most studies have found increases in sexual behaviors or preoccupation with sexual matters in children who have been abused (Browne & Finkelhor, 1986; Einbender & Friedrich, 1989; Friedrich, Urquiza, & Beilke, 1986; Purcell, Beilke, & Friedrich, 1986; White, Halpin, Strom, & Santilli, 1986). Increased sexual behavior has been related to the frequency of abuse and the number of perpetrators (Friedrich et al., 1986), but is not necessarily accompanied by an increase in knowledge or understanding of sexuality (Gordon et al., 1990b). The short-term effects of sexual abuse have also been shown to differ from the effects of physical abuse in a number of ways. In a group of child psychiatric inpatients, for example, Livingston (1987) reported more psychotic symptoms, depression, and somatic complaints among sexually abused children, and more conduct disorders among the physically abused children.

In addition to generalized behavior problems and sexual acting out, symptoms related to the DSM-III-R diagnosis of Post-traumatic Stress Disorder (PTSD) have been found in sexually abused children. PTSD involves the development of specific symptoms following a traumatic event and includes "re-experiencing the traumatic event, avoidance of stimuli associated with the event or numbing of general responsiveness, and increased arousal" (American Psychiatric Association, 1987, p. 247). Associated symptoms include depression, anxiety, guilt, and specific fears. McLeer, Deblinger, Atkins, Foa, and Ralphe (1988) found that 48.4% of sexually abused children in their sample met the DSM-III-R criteria for PTSD, and that the majority of others exhibited one or more of the symptoms.

The adjustment of sexually abused children is thought to be mediated by factors such as age and sex of the child, frequency and duration of the abuse, relationship to the perpetrator, and use of force. For all children, the effects of abuse are mediated by prior psychological adjustment; we have also found in our clinical work that the response of the parents (particularly the mother) and other close family members is critical, especially for young children. Children who are caught in the midst of family turmoil surrounding the abuse are clearly going to suffer more than children whose families provide support for them. Wolfe,

Gentile, and Wolfe (1989) add that, as in cases of PTSD, the attributional style of the child and specific attributions about the abuse experience are related to adjustment. Positive adjustment is thought to be mediated by internal, stable, and global attributions for positive events and by external, unstable, and specific attributions for negative events, although there is as yet no clear empirical support for this idea.

Although the evidence for short-term negative effects of sexual abuse seems clear, the clinician should be aware that most studies of the effects of sexual abuse have relied on clinical populations (i.e., children referred for evaluation and/or treatment) or have lacked adequate comparison groups. As Browne and Finkelhor (1986) conclude, "it is not clear that these findings reflect the experience of all child victims of sexual abuse or are even representative of those children currently being seen in clinical settings" (p. 69).

Long-Term Effects

Studies on the long-term effects of sexual abuse have been conducted with clinical populations, as well as through surveys of the general population. There is general agreement that women who have been sexually abused as children evidence a variety of significant problems as adults (for reviews, see Browne & Finkelhor, 1986; Walker, Bonner, & Kaufman, 1988). Detrimental effects noted include depression, self-destructive behavior, social isolation, eating disorders, anxiety, poor self-esteem, substance abuse, a tendency toward revictimization, relationship problems, and sexual dysfunction. Factors similar to those found to mediate adjustment in the short term have also been implicated in long-term adjustment. Abuse by fathers, genital contact, and use of force, for example, were reported by Browne and Finkelhor (1986) to result in poorer adjustment. Similarly, Gold (1986) found that attributional style for bad events (internal, stable, and global vs. external, unstable, and specific) was related to long-term adjustment in adult victims of child sexual abuse.

Despite the consistency of these findings, few studies note whether these women received treatment as children (and, if so, what kind or for how long). Thus, it is not possible to determine whether these long-term negative effects are inevitable or whether they may be alleviated by prompt intervention at the time of disclosure.

ASSESSMENT OF SEXUAL ABUSE

In view of the likelihood of involvement with the legal system, clinicians who engage in assessment of child sexual abuse cases must be clear about the purpose of assessment for any individual child. Assessment for purposes of determining treatment needs is very different from assessment for purposes of investigation (validating the abuse). In the former instance, the clinician need not necessarily focus on the specific circumstances of the abuse experience (in particular, getting the child to tell what happened), but may make a more global assessment of the child's functioning. Whether or not the sexual abuse actually occurred is not an immediate issue for these cases. Rather, the clinician accepts the facts as they are presented at the time of the assessment (although these may be proved wrong at a later time). For investigative assessment, paying careful attention to issues of the child's vulnerability to suggestion, documenting the facts of the sexual encounter(s), and making a judgment about the veracity of the child's report are required. In such a case, the clinician functions more as a "fact finder," gathering information and making his or her own judgment about the truth of those facts.

In this section, we follow the steps for gathering information in accordance with the Comprehensive Assessment-to-Intervention System (CAIS; see Chapter 3) and point out where the assessment process differs for treatment versus investigative purposes. We have also found a framework presented by Walker, Bonner, and Kaufman (1988) to be very helpful in assessing risk and planning intervention strategies for incestuous families. Table 10.1 presents many of the factors associated with poor outcome in incestuous families. The clinician should assess each of these prior to initiating treatment, as well as during the course of treatment when questions such as whether there is a need for further treatment or whether the child should be returned home must be answered. The presence of any one or two factors may not necessarily be of concern. Rather, the accumulation and interaction of risk factors determine outcome in each case.

Step 1: Initial Contact

Sexual abuse cases can be referred by a variety of people, including parents, protective services workers, police, physicians, attorneys, and others. In assessing sexual abuse cases, it is most important to clarify the referral question(s) so that the clinician and the referring person are in agreement about how the assessment will be focused. We have found that it is often necessary to help the referring person be specific about the information he or she is requesting, and we often request that the questions to be addressed by the assessment be written down. The clinician must then decide which questions can reasonably be answered according to the facts of each case (it is likely that the clinician will not have the expertise or the resources to address all questions) and should be careful to focus the assessment on only those questions.

TABLE 10.1.   Factors Associated with Poor Outcome in
Sexually Abusive Families

Child risk factors

Pre-existing behavioral or emotional problems

Age 13 years or older

Intellectual or physical handicaps

Abuse over a long time or many incidents

Abuse involving genital contact or intercourse

Use of threats or force, or injury to child

Family relationship to perpetrator

Social isolation

Poor relationship with nonabusing parent

Court appearance without adequate preparation

Nonabusing parent risk factors

Failure to believe child

History of inadequate parenting

Resistance to help, distrust

Inability or unwillingness to protect child

Excessive dependence on abusing spouse

Social isolation

Blaming others or child for abuse

Alcohol or drug abuse

Significant psychopathology

Intellectual handicaps

Perpetrator risk factors

Denial of abuse

Significant psychopathology

Alcohol or drug abuse

Significant life stress and poor coping skills

No normal sexual outlet

Blaming others or victim for abuse

Previous history of sexual abuse

History of antisocial behavior or criminal record

Lack of remorse, concerns only for self

History of inappropriate parenting

(*continued*)

TABLE 10.1. (*contintued*)

Social and environmental risk factors
Isolated family
Marital conflict or distress
Single-parent family
Stepparent family
Overly restrictive sexual attitudes
Environmental instability
Low socioeconomic status
Environmental stress (e.g., unemployment)

When investigation is requested, we have found that the questions usually center around four issues, although not all cases involve all four issues. These are (1) verifying the child's report of abuse; (2) determining the emotional/behavioral functioning of the child and the need for treatment; (3) determining the functioning of other family members, including their ability to provide protection for the child; and (4) making decisions about custody and placement. Depending on the specific questions to be addressed and on the availability of parents to complete them, questionnaires and checklists should be sent out prior to the initial session. Our Parent Questionnaire (see Appendix B) provides information about the family constellation and the parents' perceptions of the problem. The Child Behavior Checklist (CBCL; Achenbach & Edelbrock, 1983) has been used extensively in research with child sexual abuse victims and provides information on sexual behavior, PTSD, and other emotional or behavioral problems. In addition, the existence of sexual behavior problems can provide corroborative evidence for a child's report of abuse. Another measure of sexual behavior, the Child Sexual Behavior Inventory (Purcell et al., 1986), consists of questions about sexual education and experience, as well as about specific types and frequencies of sexual behavior exhibited by children. This instrument has been standardized and validated by comparing responses of parents of sexually abused children (ages 3–12) with those of parents of nonabused children of the same ages. Information about this measure is available from Janet Purcell, Department of Psychology, NI-25, University of Washington, Seattle, WA 98195. The Parenting Stress Index (PSI; Abidin, 1990) provides preliminary information about the sources of stress for the child's parent(s), apart from the abuse. Assessment for purposes of treatment should also include these questionnaires.

Before interviewing the child and family, the clinician should contact all persons who are involved in the case to determine their role in the case, to find out what information has already been gathered, and to promote collaboration. This is particularly important if the case will be prosecuted (which is likely in sexual abuse cases). The information necessary to assess sexual abuse cases is complex, and the assessment is likely to require several sessions.

Step 2: Parent and Child Interview

Parent Interview

When the purpose of the assessment is to determine the need for treatment, we typically conduct the parent interview with the child present. In order to decrease the pressure on the child, we ask the parent (or other adult) to tell us the details of the abuse, including how it was first disclosed, while checking periodically with the child to verify the information. Reactions of the parent(s) and other family members to the abuse should be noted as an indication of their ability to provide support for the child. The parent(s) should also be asked about any sex education the child has received and what terms for sexual body parts are used by the family. If the referral question concerns the ability of a parent to care for and protect the child, the parent's "parenting models," attitudes and values about parenting, and disciplinary practices should be assessed. Information about the child's day-to-day functioning at home and school, with an emphasis on changes in the child's behavior since the abuse occurred, should also be gathered at this time.

It is often relevant to briefly assess a parent's sexual history and sexual attitudes and values, although this is usually better done in the absence of the child. In some cases this area requires more in-depth assessment, and a separate session for the parent(s) alone may need to be scheduled. Questions should be asked about a parent's sex education and age at first sexual experience; it should also be determined whether the parent was ever molested as a child.

If the assessment is being conducted for the purpose of investigation, the initial parent interview is usually brief and the child is not present. The focus should be on parents' perceptions of the situation, the family's reactions, and the way in which the abuse was initially disclosed. Details of the child's disclosure are important, because it is often the most accurate account of the abuse; with young children especially, disclosure is often precipitated by an event associated with the circumstances of the abuse (bathing, watching TV, going to bed, etc.). The clinician should determine where and how the disclosure occurred, what the exact words used by the child were, and what was said and/or done in response.

Often one or both parents are not available during an investigation, because the child has been removed from the home or a parent is suspected of perpetrating the abuse. In these cases, the clinician should determine this information as well as the current living arrangement for the child prior to seeing the child.

Child Interview

There is some disagreement about whether the clinician investigating a child sexual abuse case should interview the child "blind" to what has occurred, in order to reduce potential bias in the interview (White, Strom, & Santilli, 1986). We find it more helpful to gather as much information as possible prior to the interview with the child, so that questions can be focused on essential information. Typically, by the time the child is referred to a psychologist, he or she has already been interviewed by a protective services worker or some other professional (often by many others), and the issue is to clear up questions resulting from those interviews. Garbarino, Stott, and the Faculty of the Erikson Institute (1989) have written an excellent book about interviewing children; it includes chapters on developmental factors influencing communication, ways to elicit accurate information from children, and methods of interpreting that information.

Several protocols for using anatomically correct dolls in conducting interviews with children about sexual abuse are available (Boat & Everson, 1986; White, Strom, & Santilli, 1986). Although the use of these dolls is widespread, it is quite controversial. We do not use a structured protocol for interviewing children, but focus instead on gathering specific kinds of information as it is relevant to the particular case; we use anatomically correct dolls only if necessary to help the child explain what happened. The following types of information are important for investigative assessment as well as assessment for treatment purposes.

1. Developmental level. Assessment of the child's development is critical to the interpretation of other information gathered during the assessment. Children perceive the world differently at different stages of development, and this will affect the impact of the abuse and the choice of intervention methods. The reader is referred to Chapter 1 for a discussion of normal developmental characteristics of children at different ages. The child's language, fine and gross motor, cognitive, and memory skills should be noted. Expressive language skills are limited in most children under 2 years and in older children with developmental problems. For these children, nonverbal means of obtaining information must be utilized.

2. Intellectual level. If formal testing of the child's intellectual level has recently been done, or if the clinician has information that the child is

performing at grade level in school and receiving no special services (and there are no specific questions about the child's intelligence), administration of an IQ test is probably not necessary. Intellectual testing of a child suspected of below-average intelligence is important, so that the child's statements about abuse can be put in the proper perspective and so that treatment can be geared to the appropriate level.

3. Memory skills. Assessment of children's memory skills plays an important role in determining the credibility of their statements about abuse. In general, research has shown that children as young as 3 years can remember experienced events quite accurately (Fundudis, 1989; Ornstein, Gordon, & Larus, in press), and older children have been shown to remember traumatic events that occurred before the age of 2 or 3 (Terr, 1988). Asking questions about the details of special events that can be verified by parents, such as a recent birthday or last Christmas, can elicit information in this area; however, the clinician should be aware that for younger children, free recall of details is more difficult than for older children. Specific questions such as "Tell me one thing you got for your last birthday" are easier for younger children to answer than open-ended questions such as "Tell me about your last birthday." Wehrspann, Steinhauer, and Klajner-Diamond (1987) suggest that the clinician next explore the child's susceptibility to suggestion by challenging some of the child's responses to questions about the details of such events. For example, the clinician could say, "You did not really get a bicycle for your birthday, did you?"

4. Reality monitoring. "Reality monitoring," or the ability to discriminate fact from fantasy, is another aspect of cognition that is relevant to determining the veracity of children's reports of abuse. Research suggests that there are age differences in this ability, but that children as young as 4 years can accurately remember things they did as opposed to things they imagined doing (Abrams, 1990; Jens, Gordon, & Shaddock, 1990). Furthermore, the nature of cognition in preoperational children makes them dependent on experience for the images of fantasy. Children's fantasies are usually about positive experiences, and reflect images of mastery rather than victimization (deYoung, 1987). The clinician can test this ability informally by asking the child to name some things that are real and some that are make-believe, or to sort examples of real and make-believe things into categories (Wehrspann et al., 1987).

5. Knowledge of sexuality. Children's knowledge of sexuality is another important area of development to assess. We assess knowledge in the following areas: body parts and functions (including sexual and nonsexual body parts), gender differences and gender identity, pregnancy and birth, sexual behavior (masturbation and sexual intercourse), and abuse prevention ("What are the private parts, and what should you do if someone tries to touch them?"). Young children respond better to

concrete stimuli, so we use pictures of nude boys and girls and men and women as we ask questions in these areas. This assessment often elicits unusual emotional reactions from a child who has been sexually abused, and sometimes spontaneously precipitates discussion of the child's sexual experience.

6. Locus of control or attributional style. Because recent research has shown locus of control to be an important mediator of children's adjustment to sexual abuse, it should be included in the child assessment. A suggested measure is the Locus of Control Scale for Children (Nowicki & Strickland, 1973), which can be found in Appendix B.

7. Emotional status. Although perhaps not directly related to assessment of the details of the abuse, the existence of emotional problems such as fears, anxiety, guilt, and poor self-esteem should also be assessed. This information provides guidelines for treatment and corroborative evidence regarding the veracity of the child's report of abuse. The Pictorial Scale of Perceived Competence and Social Acceptance for Young Children (Harter & Pike, 1984) and the Self-Perception Profile for Children (Harter, 1983b) are useful for assessing self-esteem, which is often very poor in sexually abused children (see Appendix A for descriptions of these measures). Maladaptive responses and poor coping skills can be assessed in children ages 6–15 with the Roberts Apperception Test for Children (see Appendix A). Additional information in this area can be gathered by observing the child's play and noting unusual themes (aggression, fear, guilt, etc.), over- or underactivity, and intense or unusual reactions to ordinary stimuli.

8. Differential perceptions of family members. A child's perceptions of members of the family can be assessed through a variety of methods. With young children, we use family drawings or doll house play and ask the children to describe what they like and dislike about each person and what kinds of things they do together. This information is especially important if a family member is suspected of the abuse. Extreme or intense reactions (fear, anger, hostility, etc.) to specific family members is especially important to assess. In one case, a 4-year-old girl was so afraid of her grandfather (who allegedly had molested her) that she could not draw a picture of him and refused to talk about him. At the same time, she was very open and expressed positive feelings about other members of the family.

9. Details of the sexual experience. In an investigative assessment, details of the sexual experience are central to the assessment process. The clinician must be cognizant of the possibility of contaminating the child's recall of abuse by asking leading questions, and should keep an audiotape or videotape record of this aspect of the interview. deYoung (1987) specifies some of the areas that are likely to be problematic for children in the preoperational stage of development (ages 2–7) because of their cognitive style. These include the following: (a) Descriptions may lack

clarity (e.g., young children may refer to sexual acts in terms of elimination rather than sexual functions, because this reflects their primary experience); (b) some essential elements of the description of abuse may be left out, resulting in a disjointed, disorganized account, and events may be connected in an illogical (at least to adults) manner; (c) children may also have been told they are to blame or that the sexual behavior is beneficial or desirable, and this may result in considerable confusion; and (d) children may tell different things to different people because of differences in the communication styles of the adults.

Recent work has been devoted to determining criteria for judging the credibility of children's reports of sexual abuse. These criteria can guide an interview and aid in interpretation, but the clinician should not expect every child to show evidence of all criteria. Wehrspann et al. (1987) suggest that the following are important to note: (a) spontaneity of the report, (b) repetitions or consistency over time, (c) spontaneous reactions to associated events, (d) amount and quality of detail, (e) a report that is consistent with the child's developmental level, (f) emotions consistent with disclosure, (g) evidence for the accommodation syndrome (Summit, 1983), (h) consistency in the face of challenge, and (i) sexually explicit details.

Faller (1988) suggests three criteria for determining credibility, which she validated by examining the reports of 103 children in cases where the perpetrators had admitted some aspects of the abuse. These criteria include "information about the context of the sexual abuse; the description or demonstration of the sexual victimization; and the victim's emotional state" (Faller, 1988, p. 391). Context of the abuse includes where and when it occurred, what clothing was worn and what was removed during the abuse, where other family members were when it occurred, what the perpetrator said, and any unusual events that occurred (e.g., "I always wore my pajamas backwards to make it harder for him"). Faller (1988) also suggests asking questions about the latest incident of abuse if there have been several, because the child's memory of the latest incident is likely to be clearest.

The child should be able to describe specific details of the sexual activity, although the vocabulary of a young child may not be adequate to do this. The descriptions may reflect sexual information that is not typically possessed by young children. Use of dolls to demonstrate sexual behavior or drawings can help children describe what happened to them.

Children who have been abused usually have difficulty recounting the details of the abuse without experiencing intense emotions, such as anxiety, embarrassment, anger, or even sexual arousal; the clinician should note such reactions. Questions about how the child felt during the abuse are also relevant.

Step 3: Observation of Behavior

Observation of the child's behavior during the interview is a critical component of the assessment, and has been covered to some extent above. In cases where the allegation of sexual abuse is made in the context of a custody dispute, it is wise to observe the child interacting with the mother and father separately as well as together. Green (1986) suggests noting fearfulness, inhibition, or seductive behavior in the father–child interaction, and excessive clinging to the mother in the presence of the father, as signs consistent with sexual abuse. Conversely, constant "checking" with the mother during the interview, hostility toward the father in the mother's presence but friendly behavior in her absence, and easy telling of the sexual activity in the father's presence are thought to be signs that abuse has not occurred. Further observation of parent–child interaction is indicated in cases where this is to be a focus of treatment.

Step 4: Further Assessment

Further assessment is necessary only if other specific problems are noted.

Step 5: Referral to Allied Health Professionals

If the child has not had a complete medical examination, this should be done before or soon after the first session with the child clinician. Although physical evidence of sexual abuse is not frequently found, it can be critical in cases that are prosecuted. When the referral question involves determining the adequacy of parents to care for and protect the child, particularly if one parent is suspected of the abuse, it is necessary to obtain a complete psychological evaluation of each parent. If the child clinician is not trained to do this, the family should be referred to an appropriate agency. We often make this referral at the start of the assessment process and then work with that agency to coordinate the assessments.

Step 6: Communication of Findings and Treatment Recommendations

Communication of assessment findings in sexual abuse cases is a very important part of the process. The clinician must first decide who is to receive the results. In an investigative assessment, a protective services worker or district attorney may be the appropriate person. If at all possible, the parent(s) should be included in this feedback conference, so that intervention recommendations and planning for the management of the case can be coordinated. A parent should be given general information on the impact of sexual abuse on children's development and children's typical reactions to sexual abuse, so that he or she will have some idea of what to expect. Ways of handling inappropriate behaviors, such as sexual acting out or increased irritability or fears, should also be discussed.

TREATMENT OF SEXUAL ABUSE

A developmental perspective is essential in treating victims of sexual abuse. Developmental factors influence all aspects of treatment, including the effects of abuse and prognosis for treatment, treatment issues and approaches, placement and protection decisions, and expectations for the child as a witness in legal proceedings. Because children understand the world differently at different ages, their understanding of sexual experiences is a function of their developmental level and will change as they develop new cognitive abilities. Thus a sexually abused child will probably "reprocess" his or her experience of sexual abuse as cognitive capacity increases. Furthermore, developmental issues interact with treatment issues. Trust, for example, is a critical developmental issue for preschoolers and is likely to be a focus of treatment for this age group, whereas issues involving interpersonal and intimate relationships are more important for adolescents.

Finkelhor and Browne (1986) have outlined four treatment issues for victims of sexual abuse, which clinicians should have in mind as they treat these children. These are traumatic sexualization, stigmatization, betrayal of trust, and powerlessness. Walker, Bonner, and Kaufman (1988) discuss these issues, their manifestations in children's behavior, and possible treatment strategies. The four issues are presented in Table 10.2, along with suggestions for treatment strategies we have used with children at different ages. Based on the work of Finkelhor and Browne (1986) and Walker, Bonner, and Kaufman (1988), we briefly discuss each of these issues and a fifth, case management, that we have found central to treatment of sexual abuse. Finally, we present a format for immediate or short-term treatment of sexually abused children that we have found effective in our practice.

Treatment Issues

Traumatic Sexualization

"Traumatic sexualization" refers to the distortion of the child's normal sexuality by the experience of abuse. A perpetrator of abuse often rein-

TABLE 10.2. Treatment Issues and Intervention Strategies for Sexually Abused Children

Age group	Traumatic sexualization	Stigmatization	Betrayal of trust	Powerlessness
			*Key Issue	
0–6 years	• Sex education • Limits on sexual acting out • Reinforcement of appropriate interactions • Role plays	• *Something Happened to Me* (book and activities)** • Reinforcement of positive characteristics	• Setting and keeping routines • Reinforcement of independence	• Treatment of nightmares and sleep problems • Prevention skills • "What if" exercises • Role plays • Identifying feelings
		*Key Issue		*Key Issue
7–11 years	• Sex education • Cognitive–behavioral techniques for assertiveness training and gaining control • Reinforcement of age-appropriate sexual behavior • Social skills training	• *No More Secrets* (book)** • *Liking Myself* (book and activities)** • Group treatment • Age-appropriate activities	• Making a book—"Whom can I trust?" • Cognitive restructuring for depression • Teaching problem-solving skills regarding trust issues	• Prevention skills • "What if" exercises • Assertiveness training • *The Mouse, The Monster and Me* (book and activities)** • Letter to abuser • Channeling aggression • Relaxation training for fears

256

12–18 years	*Key Issue	°Key Issue		°Key Issue
	• Sex education	• Group treatment	• Cognitive restructuring for depression	• Prevention skills
	• Cognitive–behavioral techniques for assertiveness training and gaining control	• Age-appropriate activities	• Group trust exercises	• Assertiveness training
	• Role plays of relationship skills		• Using problem-solving skills regarding trust issues	• Letter to abuser
	• Social skills training		• Listing of people who can be trusted and why	• Role plays of relationship skills
	• Relaxation training			

Note. "°Key Issue" means that this is a significant treatment issue for a particular age group.

°°See Appendix C.

forces a child for inappropriate sexual behavior, or pays inordinate attention to and distorts the importance of sexual parts of the child's body. Misconceptions about sexuality and morality are also often conveyed to the child. Moreover, if the abuse involves violence, sexuality is likely to become associated with fear and anxiety. Sexuality is likely to be more traumatized when the abuser attempts to arouse sexual responses in the child or entices the child to participate actively, and when the child is older and has a greater understanding of the implications of the abuse. Boys often have concerns about homosexuality if the abuser is a male. The manifestations of traumatic sexualization include sexual acting out (preoccupation with sexual matters, promiscuity, compulsive sexual behavior), confusion about sexual identity (especially true for boys), distorted views of normal sexuality or active avoidance or fear of sexual matters.

Treatment of traumatic sexualization should involve sex education for all children, including information about what is normal sexual activity at different ages. Parents are often confused about what constitutes normal sexual behavior in children and may also need basic sex education. We have found the series of books by Sol Gordon (listed in Appendix C) to be excellent resources in this regard. For a young child, parents should be helped to set limits on inappropriate sexual behavior, and the therapist should do the same during the treatment sessions. This can be done at the same time that the child's natural curiosity is satisfied (by reading a sex education book, looking at pictures, etc.) Acceptable means of obtaining affection and attention can be taught using behavioral techniques, such as shaping, modeling, and reinforcement. Appropriate child–child and child–adult interaction can be role-played in regard to issues of friendship, affection, and caregiving.

Stigmatization

Children who have been sexually abused often feel that they are different or stigmatized in some way. This results from an abuser's blaming or denigrating a child, making him or her feel like "damaged goods." A child also often feels guilty for causing the disruptions to the family that may result from the disclosure. The manifestations of stigmatization include poor self-esteem, withdrawal from social interactions and isolation from peers, and (in older children) delinquent activity, drug or alcohol abuse, and/or suicide attempts.

Children should be helped to identify and clarify their feelings of guilt or responsibility. Although a child is never responsible for the abuse, some guilt feelings may be realistic if, for example, the child was placed in a favored position by the perpetrator and then used that status to manipulate others in the family. Building self-esteem by identifying and reinforcing the child's competencies is also an important focus for treatment of stigmatization. Group treatment is especially effective in dealing with issues of blame and responsibility, as well as of isolation from peers. Group discussions can concretely demonstrate that sexual abuse happens to other children, and group members can reinforce the assignment of blame to the perpetrator, where it rightly belongs. Books such as *No More Secrets for Me* (Wachter, 1983) or *Something Happened to Me* (Sweet, 1981) can help the child assign responsibility for the abuse to the perpetrator. It has also been suggested (M. Everson, personal communication, November 16, 1988) that a child who is experiencing particular difficulty with feelings of being different be taken to a public place and asked to point out other people who have been abused. (Because this is impossible to do without talking to the people, the message is dramatically clear to the child that others cannot know he or she was abused.) Finally, social skills training is effective for socially isolated children, and they (and their parents) can be encouraged to join age-appropriate groups and activities.

Betrayal of Trust

Loss of a sense of security and trust in people is a significant problem when the perpetrator is a family member or other familiar person. Preschool children, especially, have the expectation that they will be cared for and protected by adults, and this expectation is betrayed when an adult exploits such a child without regard for the child's needs. A young child may also feel betrayed by other family members as well as by the perpetrator. For example, a 5-year-old girl who was abused by her uncle expressed intense feelings of having been betrayed by her parents because they had failed to protect her. Betrayal of trust can result in an impaired ability to judge the trustworthiness of others; some children become indiscriminately and overly attached to adults, while others show pervasive mistrust of adults and discomfort in close relationships. Significant depression, hostility, aggression, and delinquency can also result from betrayal of trust.

Treatment for this issue will vary, depending on the age of the child. Preschool children need parental reassurance that they will be safe, and concrete demonstrations of security such as regular routines, a nightlight, a security blanket, being allowed to cling to parents for a while, and so on. Older children can benefit from practicing problem-solving and decision-making skills in regard to specific problematic situations. Making a list of people who can be trusted and talking about why they can be trusted is another activity helpful for older children. In group treatment, "trust exercises" are fun and effective.

Powerlessness

Feelings of vulnerability and powerlessness reflect children's anxiety, fear, and helplessness because they were unable to stop the abuse. These feelings can be exacerbated if the disclosure of the abuse is not believed or if a child is not informed about decisions being made regarding the case (e.g., whether the child will have to go to court and when, whether the child will be allowed to return home, etc.). Feeling a loss of control can result in excessive fears, nightmares, eating and sleeping disturbances, depression, and (in older children) running away and truancy. Many children show an inordinate need to control things in their lives and become extremely bossy, noncompliant, and stubborn. Some children will also attempt to molest other children sexually as a way of regaining control. The demonstrated vulnerability of abused children to revictimization is thought to be a result of these intense feelings of loss of control and powerlessness.

Treatment of this component must involve finding appropriate ways for the child to regain a sense of control. Training in abuse prevention skills, including role-playing "what if" situations, is one strategy we have found effective with most children. Group treatment lends itself well to teaching personal safety skills. Children can be asked to generate various strategies to deal with future abuse attempts, and then to evaluate which are safe and which are risky. The group leader can also present self-protective and nonprotective vignettes that the children can evaluate. Assertiveness skills training is also effective, especially with older children. Younger children can be allowed to choose some of the activities included in their treatment sessions and can control the structure of the session ("We have four things to do today; which would you like to do first?"). Sleep disturbances and fears should be treated as for any child (see Chapters 9 and 12).

Case Management

Case management is a critical issue in treatment for sexually abused children and their families, and clinicians who work with these children often find themselves forced into this role. Case management involves several components, including (1) assessing the needs of the child and family; (2) providing information about and coordinating services for the family; (3) consulting with other professionals (e.g., police, protective services workers, district attorneys, school personnel) involved with the child; and (4) periodically re-evaluating the family's status and needs. The child victim of sexual abuse is part of an extensive system and cannot be treated effectively in isolation. Failure to consider the system can lead to many problems, including duplication of services, confusion for the family, unnecessary delays in legal proceedings, and even a lack of progress in the child's treatment.

Format for Immediate Short-Term Treatment

Providing immediate help for a sexually abused child, so that he or she can begin to understand and deal with the abuse, is crucial to the child's adjustment. Unfortunately, many children never receive treatment or do not receive help for months, because therapists with skills in this area cannot take more patients and/or some clinicians feel that the task is overwhelming. To provide immediate and potentially time-limited treatment, we have developed a protocol that covers many of the issues for the young sexually abused child and helps determine the need for long-term treatment (see Table 10.3). In following this format, the clinician should be flexible. Although we have found all the components to be essential, the order in which they are included in treatment (with the exception of the first two components) is not fixed. Furthermore, the number of treatment sessions can vary greatly, depending on the needs of the individual child. It usually takes six to eight sessions, but we have done it all in one marathon session (when we had only one chance to see a child). A discussion of various aspects of this treatment format follows.

1. Setting the Stage

There are several ways in which clinicians can set the stage for treatment of child victims of sexual abuse. One of these is to become knowledgeable about the area and to be aware of their own feelings and responses to sexual abuse and sexuality. Sex is inevitably a critical issue for treatment, and a clinician must be comfortable talking about it.

A second task is to gather all the relevant background information. This typically involves contacting other professionals who are involved with a family to determine (1) what their role in the case has been, (2) what has been done or still needs to be done, (3) who will do what, and (4) how information will be shared. It is important to determine exactly how and to whom the abuse was disclosed, what was done at that time, and whether or not the abuse has been substantiated. Among other things, the current status of the family (who is the primary caregiver, where is the perpetrator living, what steps have been taken to protect the child); the child's living arrangements (foster care, living with a relative, etc.); and an estimate of the child's developmental status should be determined. The information gathered in this first step can help the clinician to plan the first contact with the child and family, as well as to make decisions about whom to see, what questions to ask, what materials to have available, and how much consultation/coordination is needed.

TABLE 10.3. Format for Short-Term Treatment of the Young Sexually Abused Child (Preschool–Age 10)

I. *Setting the stage*

   A. Become knowledgeable about sexual abuse and own feelings about it in order to remain calm and nonjudgmental.

   B. Gather *all* background information before starting (department of social services, district attorney's office, medical). Know family composition, child's environment, and living arrangements.

   C. Obtain estimate of child's developmental level in cognitive, emotional, social, and physical areas, in order to gear work to that level.

II. *Initial interview*

   A. Acknowledge abuse with parents and/or other important people (e.g., social worker) in child's presence. Reassure child regarding abuse.

   B. Establish a relationship by taking time, allowing parent to be present, having enjoyable activities, and talking to child about interests.

   C. Further assessment of developmental level of child if needed.

III. *Steps for treatment*

   A. Assess sexual knowledge of the child. Assess the family's attitudes, behavior, and beliefs regarding sexuality. Determine what and how sexuality information is shared with child. Provide appropriate sexuality education.

   B. Assess knowledge of feelings and coping skills. Talk about thoughts and feelings. Teach coping skills.

   C. Teach personal safety skills.

   D. Include parent (or parent figure) in all aspects of treatment. Parents need information *and* support. Parenting skills are also often needed. These sometimes must be taught before there is focus on the sexual abuse, or they can be taught simultaneously with the child's treatment.

   E. Prepare for court.

IV. *Indicators of short-term versus long-term treatment*

   A. Age of child

   B. Duration and severity of abuse

   C. Parental denial of abuse

   D. Environmental stability

   E. Concomitant emotional/behavioral problems

2. Initial Interview

The primary purpose of the initial contact with the child and family is to develop good rapport with the child. The clinician should introduce himself or herself to the child and explain why the child has been brought to the clinic. For the initial interview, the child and primary caregiver are usually seen together. (If the child is in foster care, the protective services worker often accompanies the child.) The parent or other caregiver is asked to tell the details of the abuse in front of the child (young children often like to play with a toy as they listen), while the child is asked periodically for confirmation. This serves to acknowledge the abuse openly without placing demands on the child, and allows the clinician to begin to provide the child with important information and reassurance ("It is never your fault," "We will protect you," "You can ask any questions," "It's OK to talk about it," etc.). At this time, the clinician can also briefly discuss the parent's or caregiver's concerns, but it should be communicated clearly to the child that he or she is the most important focus of the session.

Making the child feel important and in control is a primary goal, so the clinician should take considerable time with the child, talking about the child's interests and activities, playing games, drawing, and having fun. Use of reflective comments and praise instead of asking many questions is essential to making the child feel comfortable. One way of communicating to the child that he or she is an important, valued person is for the clinician to keep all contracts and appointments consistently, and to be on time. Although the parent or caregiver is invited to stay in the room if the child wishes, the clinician must be careful not to let the adult monopolize the session. It is not unusual for parents to need time and attention from the clinician, but this can be provided at other times (by scheduling a separate session or telephone contact).

3. Steps for Treatment

Sexuality Education. Giving children information about sexuality helps them to develop a sense of power and the ability to protect themselves. We typically begin by assessing what a child already knows about normal sexuality (body parts and functions, private parts, sexual behaviors) and what the child has been taught. Then we provide the child with appropriate information, keeping in mind that because of their precocious sexual experience, abused children will often need information that would ordinarily be more appropriate for older children. Reading a book about sexuality often elicits further questions and comments from the child that allow the clinician to provide reassurance and information directly related to the child's experience. Sharing the sex education information with the parent(s) or caregiver before the session is important, so that the clinician can clarify any concerns they may have about the material. It is equally important after the session for the clinician and child to review briefly the material covered with the parent or caregiver. This confirms to the child that it is acceptable to talk about these things. It is good if the material or book used can be sent home with the child.

Feelings. Children's understanding of feelings is dependent on their developmental status, so assessment of what they currently understand and experience is essential prior to attempting to deal with their feelings about the abuse. We may begin by making a "feelings book" in which various feelings are described and illustrated. Older children enjoy making lists of things that make them happy, sad, angry, and so on, as well as how they cope with these feelings. Younger children can cut out pictures depicting various feelings and paste them on each page. A variety of techniques are effective in helping children deal with feelings about the abuse, including story telling, doll play, drawings, and writing letters to the perpetrator. As an example, a 6-year-old girl who was not able to talk about her feelings demonstrated them each week in doll play, and the clinician then wrote a short story dealing with each issue, to read to her the following week.

Personal Safety Skills. Teaching sexually abused children self-protection skills is essential to restoring a sense of personal control and power. There are many programs available that are appropriate for group treatment. For individual work, we have found that *A Better Safe Than Sorry Book* (Gordon & Gordon, 1984) is excellent for children ages 6–11, while *My Very Own Book About Me* (Stowell & Dietzel, 1982) is good for younger children. In addition, a child should be provided with the opportunity to practice skills in role-play situations. The importance of telling someone should be emphasized.

Parent Work. Because the response of parents to the abuse of their children is closely tied to the children's adjustment, parent work is a central part of treatment for these children. Parents often need basic instruction in parenting skills, or at least help in appropriately managing the behavioral sequelae of the abuse. We provide parents information about normal sexuality and abuse prevention skills, usually sending home the materials used in treatment with the children. Parents who are extremely upset, to the extent that they are temporarily unable to meet their children's needs, may need separate sessions with the clinician in which they can express and work through their feelings about the abuse and receive support from the therapist. If one-way mirrors are available, allowing parents to observe their children's sessions can help them come to terms with the abuse. Finally, most parents appreciate help with the many decisions that must be made, especially if the case will be prosecuted.

Preparation for Court. Although testifying in court can be a very stressful experience for children, many children with whom we have worked have found that it is actually beneficial, especially if a child's testimony is believed and a perpetrator is found guilty. Good preparation helps children and parents handle the experience as well as possible. Both parents and children need to know what to expect from a court appearance. A visit to the courtroom should be arranged some time shortly before the start of a trial; the child should be told who will be there, where these people will sit, what will happen and in what order, and what is expected of the child. In the weeks prior to the trial, the child can be prepared to testify by role-playing various situations that are likely to occur during the trial. Having the child assume a variety of roles (including those of the judge, prosecutor, and witness) helps to develop a sense of control and relieve anxiety. (The actual incident of abuse under examination should not be used as content for these role plays, lest the clinician be accused of biasing the child's testimony).

There are a few books for children about being a witness at a trial, and these are listed in the bibliography of books for parents and children in Appendix C. We have found, however, that "homemade" books with simple line drawings that are specific to an individual child's experience are just as effective. The parent(s) and child should be aware that parents may not be allowed into the courtroom during the child's testimony. Another person who is well known and liked by the child (a teacher, family friend, neighbor, social worker, etc.) should be designated as a special support person and should sit in the front of the courtroom where the child can see him or her. The child should also be prepared to wait for what may be a very long time before being called to testify. Materials for quiet play should be provided. Finally, the child should be prepared for either a "guilty" or "not guilty" decision by the jury. It is likely that the child will have ambivalent feelings about a verdict of "guilty," especially if the perpetrator is a family member, and these feelings should be explored. In the case of a "not guilty" verdict, the child needs to know that this does not mean that the abuse did not happen and that the clinician still believes the child.

4. Indicators for Long-Term Treatment

Although the above-described treatment program is sufficient for many children and provides a good starting place for most cases of sexual abuse, some children will continue to need treatment beyond six to eight sessions. The clinician must assess each child's and family's status at the end of these sessions, taking into account factors that have been identified in the empirical literature as contributing to the need for longer-term treatment. These factors are those that have been shown to be associated with poorer adjustment on the part of child victims of sexual abuse. They include (1) the age of the child (an older child is at greater risk); (2) the duration and severity of the abuse (longer duration means a poorer prognosis); (3) parental denial of the abuse; (4) environmental instability; and (5) current emotional, behavioral, or learning problems. The age of the child and duration of abuse are somewhat confounded, in that older children are more likely to have been exposed to abuse over longer periods of time. Older children and especially adolescents are also likely to need longer treatment, because they are more cognizant of the implications of the abuse for their own developing social and sexual relationships. Furthermore, the longer the abuse has gone on, the more likely the child is to have suffered damage to self-esteem and personal identity— both key issues in adolescent development. Similarly, abuse involving anal, oral, or genital intercourse, or abuse that results in injury to the child is related to poorer adjustment.

Parents who deny the possibility of abuse in spite of a child's disclosure of abuse, or who minimize the potential negative effects, make it difficult for the child to feel accepted and safe. These parents will need help in understanding the reasons for their denial (we have found that many of these parents were themselves molested as children and have not come to terms with their own experience) and to meet their child's needs for emotional support.

Children who live in unstable environments, especially those who are in foster care, experience considerable stress in addition to the experience of sexual abuse. These children will need help in coping with these stresses. Children who have other problems that either predate the abuse or are results of the abuse will need further treatment focused on dealing specifically with these problems. Finally, we have found that most children need a "booster" session from time to time as they progress through developmental stages. This is because with increasing cognitive skills children come to a different, more complex understanding of their experience and often have new questions.

———————————————— CASE EXAMPLE ————————————————

Step 1: Initial Contact

The district attorney called to request treatment and possible court preparation for two brothers, ages 9 and 5. Two weeks prior to this contact, the 9-year-old, John, had told his maternal grandmother, Mrs. Comfort, that his father had been sexually abusing him and his little brother, Jimmy. John described oral and anal sex as well as mutual masturbation; he also reported that his father had said he would kill him, his brother, and his grandmother if John told. The child had recently returned home from a 6-month inpatient stay for severe depression. During hospitalization, no one had asked him about the sexual abuse, nor did he tell anyone. He told his grandmother that he "got better" so he could come home to protect his little brother from his father. Mrs. Comfort took the child to the department of social services, and an investigation substantiated the abuse.

The two boys had been living with their father, who was a local magistrate, and their stepmother. The boys' mother had died 2 years previously. Given the father's position in the community and the lack of evidence for abuse of Jimmy, he remained in the home while John was placed in the custody of Mrs. Comfort. The department of social services asked that the 5-year-old be brought to our clinic, which was in a neighboring county, for medical and psychological evaluation. The stepmother brought Jimmy, who was found to have anal lacerations and venereal disease. During the course of this evaluation, the stepmother admitted that the father had indeed abused the children and had been doing so over a long period of time. Both children were then placed in the custody of Mrs. Comfort, and the father was charged with sexual abuse but released on bail. Although he was not a lawyer, the father planned to defend himself in court.

The purposes of referral were to determine the emotional status of both children; to provide the children and the grandmother with short-term treatment; and to determine the probable effects on the children of going to court to testify against their father, who would be cross-examining them.

The children's teachers and Mrs. Comfort were asked to complete the CBCL. Prior to the initial interview, phone calls were also made to the teachers to determine the boys' academic and social functioning within the school setting. Both boys had significantly high scores on the Internalizing scales of the CBCL, with significant fears and physical complaints indicated as specific problems. They were reported, however, to be well liked by their peers and "no problem" to their teachers. The teachers indicated that the boys often came to school very tired, appeared sad, and on many days did not want to join in on academic tasks or social activities. They had noticed a dramatic change in the boys' affect, alertness, and willingness to participate in activities in the short time since they had begun living with their grandmother.

Step 2: Caregiver and Child Interviews

Caregiver Interview

Mrs. Comfort, the social worker, and both boys were present for the initial interview. The social worker, at Mrs. Comfort's request, related what had been done and what was known about the abuse. The boys were given some toys to play with during the interview. As they were playing, they often added information to the social worker's report. Both boys expressed a great deal of anger at their father, but they were also quite fearful that he would come to the grandmother's house and kill all of them. Mrs. Comfort assured them that the house was secure and that she was quite capable of protecting them. She transported the children to and from school, and outside of school they rarely left her side. Because they were both having nightmares, she also allowed them to sleep with her. Mrs. Comfort presented as a warm, loving supportive person who had struggled, against the father's wishes, to keep contact with her grandchildren since the death of her daughter.

Child Interviews

The boys were seen separately for their initial interview. John was able to share difficult information easily. He described with great sadness the death of his mother, who had been rushed to the hospital in a diabetic coma. John felt she had protected him from his father. It was after her death that the father began to abuse him. Until he was hospitalized, John did not feel that his younger brother had been abused. He found it difficult to discuss the specifics of the abuse, and he was not pressured to do so. Although John was afraid of what his father might do, he said he felt safe both at school and with his grandmother. He obviously was relieved by having told about the abuse and was able to express his anger toward his father, despite his fear of him. Although he admitted it would be "scary," John stated that he wanted to testify in court so that his father would never be able to do this again.

Assessment of John's knowledge of sexuality revealed that he used slang terms for sexual body parts and was very knowledgeable about adult sexual behavior. He also knew about private parts and was forceful in stating that he would tell his grandmother or teacher if anyone tried to touch his private parts.

Five-year-old Jimmy refused to separate from his grandmother; as a result, she was included in this session. Jimmy was active and easily distracted by any noise or sudden movement on the part of the clinician. He was reluctant to talk about his father, but stated that he missed being at home and playing with his toys. In playing with the doll house, Jimmy carefully avoided including the father doll in his play. When the clinician introduced the father doll, he turned away and refused to continue his play. Further attempts to get him to play with the family dolls resulted in his hiding behind a chair and refusing to come out until the father doll was put away.

Assessment of knowledge of sexuality indicated that Jimmy used slang terms for sexual body parts and did not know about private parts or what to do if someone tried to touch them. He also did not have any knowledge of adult sexual behavior, pregnancy, or birth. It was significant that he became very quiet or left the table when he saw pictures of nude adult males or males engaging in child care activities (bathing, putting to bed, etc.).

Step 3: Observation of Behavior

Only observations during clinic sessions were made in this case.

Step 4: Further Assessment

Additional assessment of emotional status in order to determine the need for longer-term treatment was done as part of the immediate treatment process.

Step 5: Referral to Allied Health Professionals

The boys had already had a medical evaluation, and Jimmy was being treated for venereal disease.

Step 6: Communication of Findings and Treatment Recommendations

Prior to beginning treatment, the clinician met with Mrs. Comfort and the social worker to summarize the assessment findings. They were told that John appeared to be resilient and was using a lot of good skills to cope with a very difficult situation. He felt well loved and protected by his grandmother, and was clearly very attached to his brother. Jimmy, on the other hand, was seen as emotionally vulnerable, with few coping skills available with which to deal with the trauma. Unlike John, he needed a great deal of support from his grandmother. Mrs. Comfort was described as having a good grasp of the children's needs and interacting with them in a very appropriate manner. The boys obviously cared for her, were affectionate with her, and responded well to her requests and discipline. In a phone call, the district attorney was told that although John was frightened, he was willing to testify against his father and we felt that with support and preparation, he was emotionally capable of dealing with the legal process. Although the district attorney was told that the younger boy was not as well able to handle court as his brother, he was eventually required to appear.

Course of Treatment

John and Jimmy were seen together for treatment, and Mrs. Comfort participated in the last 15 minutes of each 1-hour session. The course of six sessions followed the short-term treatment program outlined earlier in this chapter. The children made "feelings books" to identify and talk about feelings and to learn appropriate ways to express their feelings. They also were engaged in a sexuality education program that taught them the correct names for body parts and functions, their private parts and who may touch them and when, and personal safety skills. During this time both boys were able to talk more openly about the abuse and to give details of what had happened to them, how they felt, and what they would do in the future if anyone tried to abuse them.

Mrs. Comfort had a good support system in the community and was handling the situation well. She needed little help from the clinician. She was given sex education and abuse prevention books, as well as the children's "feeling" exercises to take home, so that she could talk with the boys about them throughout the week. She was also given information on sexual abuse and its effects on children. The clinician supported her good parenting skills.

Court Preparation

Although both children were prepared to testify in court, it was felt that only the 9-year-old would be able to do so. With treatment, Jimmy was able to talk about his father and the abuse, but he still demonstrated significant fear about potential interactions with his father. This was particularly significant in this case because the father would be cross-examining the boys. The district attorney met with both children, described to them what would happen in court, and took them to visit the actual courtroom in which the trial would take place. Preparation in the clinic involved the use of role plays to practice court procedures; a booklet was also written for the boys to describe what would happen and what would be expected of them. The clinician was very careful not to tell them what to say. The children knew that the therapist and their grandmother would be in the courtroom with them, and that they could look to them for reassurance. The children were also prepared for the possibility that their father might not be convicted. They were told that this did not mean that he had not been abusive, but rather that the court would not punish him for this. With the support of the department of social services, Mrs. Comfort had already engaged a lawyer to take permanent custody of the children, regardless of the outcome of the trial.

John was able to testify, although he was visibly upset with his father's cross-examination and attempts to confuse him. Jimmy clung to the district attorney; even when he was allowed to sit on the courtroom floor rather than in the witness box, he was not able to talk. Nonetheless, the father was found guilty and sentenced to two consecutive life terms. Given the trauma these boys had experienced, and unresolved issues regarding the death of their mother, both children were referred for further treatment.

Chapter 11

Negative

Behavior

A major goal for parents is to socialize their children, and, as part of this process, to teach them to cope with the stresses of life in socially acceptable ways. As children become more autonomous and independent, their desires and frustrations often come into conflict with those of their parents; the result is typically a display of negative behavior on the part of the children (and often also the parents!). These negative behaviors are usually transient and considered "normal" at certain ages (e.g., toddler temper tantrums or adolescent rebellion). Some children, however, exhibit negative behaviors with greater intensity and/or frequency than would be expected, and these behaviors tend to persist throughout childhood and into adult life. Thus, a considerable problem for clinicians is determining when negative behaviors exhibited by children referred for treatment are "normal" and transient, and when they are clinically significant.

The term "negative behavior" embraces a diverse set of behaviors, including temper tantrums, excessive whining or crying, demanding attention, noncompliance, defiance, aggressive acts against self or others, stealing, lying, destruction of property, and delinquency. Children exhibiting a pattern of these negative behaviors have been variously labeled as "acting out," "externalizing," "oppositional," "noncompliant," "antisocial," or "conduct-disordered." Because of the use of these different labels, determination of the incidence and prevalence of negative behavior problems in children has been difficult. Nonetheless, negative behaviors of one sort or another are the most frequent causes of concern for parents of normal children, and some form of negative behavior is the primary problem for a substantial percentage of children referred for mental health services. This chapter focuses on the developmental course and correlates of negative behavior; classification, prevalence, and persistence of negative behavior; and issues and methods for assessment and treatment. In the section on treatment, research on the efficacy of parent–child interaction training and other treatment approaches for negative behavior is reviewed, and the program used in our clinic is described.

DEVELOPMENT OF NEGATIVE BEHAVIOR

The two types of negative behavior that have received most attention in the empirical literature are noncompliance and aggression. "Noncompliance" is narrowly defined as not following directions, disregarding requests, or doing the opposite of what is asked (Forehand & McMahon, 1981). More broadly defined, noncompliance can include almost any negative behavior, including tantrums, whining, breath holding, and physical or verbal aggression. Noncompliance is seen as soon as children have the cognitive capacity to understand parental requests and the physical capabilities to carry them out; however, it typically begins to be perceived as a problem at about 2 years of age, when children assert their need for autonomy and control.

According to the broader definition, noncompliance encompasses aggressive behavior. "Aggression" includes physically aggressive acts against another person (hitting, kicking, biting, fighting), verbal aggression (threats, tattling, teasing, name calling), and nonverbal or symbolic aggression (threatening gestures, chasing, making faces). Temper tantrums are probably the first real expression of aggression, and these can be seen in very young infants.

Given the high rates of negative behavior seen in the normal population, as well as the prevalence and stability of serious conduct problems among children, the following questions are of interest: How and when do these behaviors originate, and why do they persist and become more severe in some children while decreasing in others? We now review the literature on the development of noncompliance and aggression.

Compliance–Noncompliance

Developmental research into the origins of compliance–noncompliance in normal children suggests that very young children may be predisposed to comply with adult commands. Rheingold, Cook, and Kolowitz (1987) found that adult commands were associated with increased enthusiasm and compliance in the play of 18- to 24-month-old children. These authors speculate that compliance with adult commands provides children with some inherent pleasure and motivation. They note that "the achievement of fitting their actions to the words of another was enjoyable; the pleasure resided in the accomplishment" (p. 151). Although temperamental differences were not taken into account, this study suggests that given a predisposition to compliance, compliance should increase and persist as a behavioral style if it is rewarded rather than ignored or punished.

Other work has linked maternal responsiveness with individual differences in children's compliance–noncompliance. Rocissano, Slade, and Lynch (1987) found that toddlers were more likely to comply when the mothers' commands were consistent with the children's ongoing activity. This study and others (e.g., Parpal & Maccoby, 1985) suggest that mothers who are able to allow their children a degree of control in the interaction by following their lead and modeling compliance to child requests will have children who are more likely to be compliant to their demands.

Children's compliance–noncompliance has also been found to be mediated by situational factors and to change with age. Schneider-Rosen and Wenz-Gross (1990) studied 18- to 30-month-old children and found that levels of compliance were strongly related to the situations in which commands were given (e.g., free play, picking up toys, reading a book). Furthermore, compliance did not increase linearly with age. Rather, in some situations 2-year-olds were less compliant than older and younger children, and in other situations they were more compliant. Kuczynski, Kochanska, Radke-Yarrow, and Girnius-Brown (1987) found developmental changes both in mothers' strategies for gaining compliance and in children's responses to control. As the age of the children increased, mothers relied less on distraction and more on explanations, bargaining, and reprimands. Among the children, passive noncompliance (ignoring the request) and direct defiance decreased with age, while negotiation increased. Mothers who relied on more direct control strategies (e.g., issuing orders and commands vs. negotiating) had children who were more likely to be actively defiant.

Since most children are noncompliant to some extent, documenting differences between "normal" and "deviant" noncompliance is important. "Normal" child compliance to maternal commands ranges from 51%

to 74% (Forehand, Gardner, & Roberts, 1978; Johnson, Wahl, Martin, & Johansson, 1973), whereas children referred to clinics for treatment of noncompliance exhibit compliance to only about 41% of parental commands (Forehand et al., 1978). Although these differences are statistically significant, there is considerable overlap in rates of compliance between children referred for treatment and nonreferred children.

Parents often perceive their children's behavior as being more deviant than it may actually be. Observational studies indicate that clinic-referred children cannot always be distinguished from normal children. Thus factors other than children's behavior may be contributing to negative parent perceptions and to subsequent referral for treatment (Griest & Wells, 1983). Some of these factors include parental and marital adjustment (Oltmanns, Broderick, & O'Leary, 1977), high parental standards (Atkeson & Forehand, 1978), and aversive relationships outside the family (Wahler, 1980).

Differences in parenting styles of normal and clinic-referred children's parents have also been documented. Mothers of clinic-referred children tend to issue more commands and use more criticism that do mothers of non-clinic-referred children (Forehand, King, Peed, & Yoder, 1975). Furthermore, clinic-referred children's parents frequently interrupt behavioral sequences by repeating a command, giving help, retrieving the command, and so forth, so that compliance on the part of the children is not possible. Thus to some extent, "problem" noncompliance may be more a function of the parents' behavior than of the children's characteristics.

Evidence for a biological basis for negative behavior lies in the fact that boys are consistently found to be more aggressive than girls (Maccoby & Jacklin, 1974, 1980). Moreover, individual differences in the expression of negative behavior exist from birth, and these appear to be reflections of children's temperamental characteristics. Some children are placid, are happy, and have well-regulated patterns of sleep, eating, and elimination; others are irritable, colicky, easily overstimulated, and totally unpredictable. The behavior of these latter infants will clearly be seen as more negative and difficult than the behavior of the former. Some parents, however, are better equipped to manage difficult infants than others, so here again the interplay between an infant's characteristics and those of the parents is a critical factor. For some parents, difficult infants' negative behavior may set the stage for mother–infant conflict, which may in turn lead mothers to become less responsive to their infants (Campbell, 1990). And maternal responsiveness and sensitivity to an infant's needs and signals are strongly implicated in optimal developmental outcomes. Although the developmental process is not entirely clear, a relationship between difficult temperamental characteristics (particularly low distractibility, high persistence, high intensity, and low adaptability) and a generalized oppositional style of responding has been documented (Garrison & Earls, 1987).

Aggression

Although parental reactions to children's aggressive outbursts clearly provide feedback to the children about the efficacy of aggressive behaviors, evidence indicates that early peer relationships are the arena in which children first learn to master their aggressive behavior and to cope with the affective and other outcomes of aggressive interaction. Hartup (1976) suggests that the unique egalitarian relationship with age mates permits aggressive acts to be successful at some times and unsuccessful at other times. This balance has the effect of making the child neither excessively aggressive nor excessively permissive.

Hartup (1976) has documented the changes in aggressive behavior during the years from 2 to 6:

1. The form of the aggression changes from more physical acts to increased verbal attacks.

2. The frequency of "afterreaction," including sulking, whining, and brooding, increases markedly after age 4, even though there is little change in the duration of angry outbursts.

3. The stimuli eliciting aggression change from habit training to peer interactions; furthermore, while instrumental aggression (for possession or loss of object) predominates, there is an increase in person-oriented retaliatory hostile outbursts.

4. The frequency of aggression decreases after 6 years, primarily due to a decrease in instrumental aggression.

5. When younger children are insulted, they are more likely to retaliate with hitting than are older children, who reciprocate with insults.

6. Boys engage in more hostile (person-oriented) aggression than girls, with no sex differences in rates of instrumental aggression.

7. Levels of aggression appear to stabilize earlier for boys than for girls.

8. Aggressive behavior in preschool children is initially positively reinforced (the children get what they want), but if it continues unchecked, it is negatively reinforced (others use aggressive behavior to stop an aggressor), and this operates to increase the aggressive behavior (Patterson, 1976). In this age group, children with higher rates of physical aggression are also more likely to show higher rates of verbal aggression (McCabe & Lipscomb, 1988).

Spivack and Shure's (1974) work sheds light on the social-cognitive skills that develop in the preschool years and are associated with aggressive behavior. "Alternative-solutions thinking" (i.e., the generation of alternative solutions to a social problem such as conflict over a toy) and "consequential thinking" (or accurate recognition of the likely results of different social behaviors such as hitting) increase with age. Spivack and Shure (1974) found that both aggressive children and more withdrawn children had marked deficits in alternative-solutions thinking, by comparison with other children. In contrast, Gouze (1987) compared aggressive and nonaggressive preschool boys and demonstrated that aggressive boys generated a greater number of solutions to hypothetical interpersonal problem situations, but that these solutions were primarily aggressive. Gouze also found that the aggressive boys attended more to aggressive than to nonaggressive social interactions. She concluded that this attention is likely to affect the types of social information that aggressive children take in and retain over time, with the result that these children increasingly see the social world as hostile; this further narrows their focus to the hostile or aggressive aspects of their environment and interactions.

Developmental Process

As a whole, this work suggests that complex interactions between parents and children and between children and peers (which are functions of the characteristics of parents, children, and the environment) contribute to the development of clinically significant levels of negative behaviors. Loeber (1990) suggests that there are critical periods during development, at which times children are more vulnerable to adverse conditions and more likely to develop patterns of negative behaviors that have the potential to persist and become more severe with age. He cites as an example the period of early childhood (between birth and about 3–4 years), when children typically form affectionate bonds with significant adults. During this period, children are particularly vulnerable to disruptions in their social environment, such as marital separation and divorce, parental illness or death, physical and/or emotional neglect, or poor-quality parenting. Research has linked early social loss or deprivation to later delinquency and has documented that the more adverse factors experienced, the higher the rate of delinquent behavior (Kolvin, Miller, Fletting, & Kolvin, 1988). Loeber (1990) further argues that negative behavior can also develop in association with events that occur in the normal course of development. These events may include the birth of a sibling, beginning school, associating with peers, and moving from elementary to junior high school. As discussed in Chapter 4 on siblings, research in this area demonstrates that the birth of a sibling does have the potential to shift a child's developmental path toward more maladaptive behavior. It would not be surprising to find that other major transitions could function in the same way.

Patterson (1976) has examined parent–child relationships as the source of antisocial behavior; he argues that children's negative behaviors are maintained and exacerbated through the operation of aversive stimuli and negative reinforcement cycles. Early mother–infant conflict—due to difficult temperamental characteristics in the child, poor parenting skills in the parent, or both—may begin the coercive cycle that is so clearly seen in families of older children with antisocial behavior problems. In the coercive cycle, the child's negative behavior is increased by removal of an aversive parent behavior, and vice versa. For example, the parent tells the child to pick up the toys (aversive stimulus), the child whines and cries, and the parent withdraws the request. Thus, the child's noncompliance is successful in removing the aversive stimulus and consequently is negatively reinforced. Moreover, the parent is negatively reinforced for withdrawing the request by the cessation of the child's whining. Patterson (1986; Patterson, DeBaryshe, & Ramsey, 1989) further suggests that ongoing poor management on the part of parents—characterized by ignoring or punishing the child's prosocial behavior, and positive or negative reinforcement of negative behavior—contributes to the child's increasing use of aversive behaviors. When the child enters school, this behavior results in rejection by peers and poor academic progress. Both peer rejection and learning problems have been shown to be strongly associated with antisocial behavior (Loeber, 1990; Patterson et al., 1989). Peer rejection and academic problems, in turn, lead to increased problems with antisocial behavior and possible delinquency.

Patterson's (1976) theory suggests that aversive interchanges between parent and child are initiated primarily by the parent, who presents an aversive stimulus such as a command. In contrast to this conceptualization, Wahler and Dumas (1986) argue that children's negative behavior is related to the *lack of predictability* of parental behavior, rather than to systematic use of negative reinforcement. They present data indicating that 90% of aversive parent–child interactions are initiated by the child and that aversive child behaviors are positively associated with the mother's indiscriminate attention (positive parent response to a negative child behavior or negative parent response to a positive child behavior). This unpredictability of the mother's response to the child's positive and/or negative behavior increases the likelihood that the child will engage in more aversive behavior. This forces the mother to become more discriminate or predictable in her attention, which generally results in matching aversive child behavior to aversive responses. Thus, the child engages in negative behaviors because the mother's aversive responses to that behavior are more predictable than her responses to prosocial or neutral behavior. Consistent with this theory, others (Forehand et al., 1975; Lobitz & Johnson, 1975) have found that parents of conduct problem children are less contingent in their responses to child behavior, providing more negative responses to deviant as well as nondeviant behavior.

Regardless of which process operates, some children engage in a variety of negative behaviors in many settings. For these children, the negative behaviors often persist and become more severe as the child grows older, and a diagnosis of Oppositional Defiant Disorder or Conduct Disorder is often warranted. The next section highlights the differentiation and prevalence of these two clusters of negative behavior.

NEGATIVE BEHAVIOR DISORDERS

The *Diagnostic and Statistical Manual of Mental Disorders* (DSM-III-R; American Psychiatric Association, 1987) includes three disorders in the group called Disruptive Behavior Disorders: Conduct Disorder, Oppositional Defiant Disorder, and Attention-deficit Hyperactivity Disorder (ADHD). Although these three disorders are interrelated, we focus only on Conduct Disorder and Oppositional Defiant Disorder here. The reader is referred to Russell Barkley's (1990) excellent book on ADHD for an in-depth discussion of this disorder.

Oppositional Defiant Disorder

Noncompliance is an important criterion in the definition of Oppositional Defiant Disorder as described in DSM-III-R, but aggression is not necessarily a component of this disorder. According to DSM-III-R, children with Oppositional Defiant Disorder exhibit a pattern of negativistic, hostile, and defiant behavior, which in young children is typically directed toward parents. This pattern of behaviors must be evident for at least 6 months in order to warrant the diagnosis, and the child must evidence at least five of the following behaviors more frequently than would be expected for children of the same mental age:

(1) often loses temper
(2) often argues with adults
(3) often actively defies or refuses adult requests or rules . . .
(4) often deliberately does things that annoy other people . . .
(5) often blames others for his or her own mistakes
(6) is often touchy or easily annoyed by others
(7) is often angry and resentful
(8) is often spiteful or vindictive
(9) often swears or uses obscene language (American Psychiatric Association, 1987, p. 57)

DSM-III-R states that while precursors of this disorder can be seen in early childhood, it typically begins by 8 years and not later than early adolescence.

The clinician should be aware, however, that there is some controversy as to whether a diagnosis of Oppositional Defiant Disorder is ever warranted. Rutter and Shaffer (1980), for example, have suggested that the criteria proposed by DSM-III (which do not differ greatly from those outlined in DSM-III-R) do not enable the clinician to differentiate children with a psychiatric disturbance from those who are merely exhibiting normal oppositional behavior. Rey et al. (1988), however, provide empirical evidence that Oppositional Defiant Disorder does result in significant disability. In a study of inpatient adolescents, they found that those diagnosed as having Oppositional Defiant Disorder were within the clinical range on the Social Competence scale of the Child Behavior Checklist (CBCL; Achenbach & Edelbrock, 1983) and had significantly elevated scores on the Externalizing and Total Behavior Problems scales. Werry, Reeves, and Elkind (1987) argue that Oppositional Defiant Disorder as described in DSM-III-R is a mild form of Conduct Disorder, and the Rey et al. (1988) data are consistent with this notion.

Conduct Disorder

Many of the features of Oppositional Defiant Disorder are seen in children with Conduct Disorder. DSM-III-R distinguishes the two diagnoses by whether or not the basic rights of others and major age-appropriate societal norms or rules are violated. These two features are essential for a diagnosis of Conduct Disorder, but not for one of Oppositional Defiant Disorder. Conduct-disordered children exhibit a pattern of behavior that includes aggression, theft, vandalism, fire setting, opposition to authority, and other antisocial behaviors (Kazdin, 1987a). The DSM-III-R criteria for a diagnosis of Conduct Disorder (American Psychiatric Association, 1987, p. 55) include a pattern of antisocial behavior lasting at least 6 months that features at least three of the following behaviors: stealing (with or without confrontation of a victim), running away, lying, fire setting, truancy, breaking and entering, destroying property, cruelty to animals or people, forced sexual activity, using a weapon in fights, and initiating fights.

It appears that the more serious antisocial behaviors typical of Conduct Disorder do not emerge until later in childhood or even adolescence (Loeber & Lahey, 1989), and that a diagnosis of Oppositional Defiant Disorder is more likely than one of Conduct Disorder for young children. Although DSM-III-R differentiates three types of Conduct Disorders (group, solitary aggressive, and undifferentiated), empirical studies have differentiated only two: aggressive (arguing, attacking people, fighting, irritability) and nonaggressive (alcohol and/or drug use, truancy, theft, fire setting) Conduct Disorder (Loeber & Lahey, 1989).

Children with conduct-disordered behavior also often have symptoms of ADHD (and vice versa); as a result, the distinction between these two disorders is often not clear. However, it has been clearly demonstrated that the two disorders are distinct in having different etiologies and prognoses. Children who have symptoms of both disorders will display far more serious antisocial behaviors and are at increased risk for delinquent behavior and Antisocial Personality Disorder in adulthood than children with a single diagnosis of either Conduct Disorder or ADHD (Loeber & Lahey, 1989).

PREVALENCE AND PERSISTENCE

Epidemiological research has shown that negative or antisocial behavior is a major problem for children and results in enormous costs to society (Patterson et al., 1989). Although the prevalence of Conduct Disorder is estimated to be 4–10% (Rutter, Cox, Tupling, Berger, & Yule, 1975), self-reports of specific antisocial behaviors provide much higher estimates, with as many as 60% of 13- to 18-year-olds admitting to more than one type of antisocial behavior (e.g., drug abuse, arson, vandalism, or aggression; Kazdin, 1987a). Similarly, Achenbach and Edelbrock (1981) reported that 50% of 4- and 5-year-olds exhibited disobedience and 26% exhibited destruction of possessions. Elsewhere (Schroeder, Gordon, Kanoy, & Routh, 1983), we have reported data from a call-in service wherein parents could talk with a professional about their children's behavior or developmental problems. Over a 9-year period, negative behavior (defined as "won't listen to parents, doesn't obey, has tantrums, bossy and demanding, cries, whines") consistently accounted for more concerns than any other problem (15% of calls). In general, noncompliance is the most frequent presenting problem for children referred for mental health services (Bernal, Klinnert, & Schultz, 1980) and is the most frequent "deviant" behavior seen among nonreferred children (Johnson et al., 1973).

Boys are more often described as exhibiting negative behaviors, particularly noncompliance and aggression, than are girls (Campbell, 1990; Kuczynski et al., 1987). Among conduct-disordered boys, theft and aggression are the most common behaviors; among girls, sexual misconduct is more frequent (Kazdin, 1987a). Furthermore, Conduct Disorder is most frequently diagnosed prior to age 10 for boys and between 14 and 16 years for girls.

Research in behavioral genetics suggests that there is a substantial genetic component to adult antisocial behavior and criminality, although the evidence for heritability of antisocial behavior in children is not strong (Plomin, 1989; Rutter et al., 1990). Antisocial behavior in children is clearly associated with parental antisocial behavior (especially that of fathers), and appears to be stable across generations (Kazdin, 1987a). In reviewing the available data, Rutter et al. (1990) argue that a genetic link is more likely to be found in those cases in which the antisocial behavior persists into adulthood, whereas cases in which the antisocial behavior decreases with age are more likely to be environmentally based.

Other work has demonstrated that negative behavior in children is quite stable. In a random sample of parents from a primary health care setting, negative behavior was reported to be a significant problem by 50–80% of parents of children ages 2–4, and also by parents of children ages 7–10 (Schroeder, Gordon, Kanoy, & Routh, 1983). Cairns, Cairns, Neckerman, Ferguson, and Gariepy (1989) followed fourth-grade children for 6 years and found that individual differences in aggression tended to remain stable.

Although early negative behavior is not necessarily clinically significant, children who exhibit *clusters* of antisocial behaviors at *high rates across settings* and *early in life* appear to be particularly at risk for an eventual diagnosis of Conduct Disorder and tend to continue to be antisocial into adult life (Loeber, 1990; Patterson, 1986; Patterson et al., 1989). Richman, Stevenson, and Graham (1982) reported that in a sample of 3-year-olds with clusters of negative behaviors (overactivity, tantrums, noncompliance, irritability), 67% (and especially boys) continued to have clinically significant problems at age 8. Ongoing problems among the children were associated with family problems, marital dysfunction, maternal illness or depression, and environmental stress. In a study reported by Campbell (1990), preschool children with symptoms of Oppositional Defiant Disorder tended to have persistent problems; at age 9, over 60% of these children met the DSM-III criteria for Attention Deficit Disorder, Conduct Disorder, or Oppositional Defiant Disorder.

School-age children diagnosed as having Conduct Disorder also tend to remain disturbed as they grow into adolescence and adulthood. Esser, Schmidt, and Woerner (1990) found, for example, that all children described as conduct-disordered at age 8 had psychiatric problems at age 13, with the majority of them (75%) continuing to be described as conduct-disordered.

ASSESSMENT

When children are referred for treatment of negative behaviors, an important task for the clinician is to differentiate those children whose conduct problems are likely to persist from those whose problems are more likely to be transient. This involves careful assessment of the factors reported in the literature that place children at risk for persistent conduct problems. These are summarized in Table 11.1 (Dadds, Schwartz, & Sanders, 1987; Esser et al., 1990; Holden, Lavigne, & Cameron, 1990; Kazdin, 1987a; Kazdin, 1990; McMahon, Forehand, Griest, & Wells, 1981; Webster-Stratton, 1985a). Barkley (1987) and Forehand and McMahon (1981) provide detailed assessment procedures for conduct problems. The present outline follows the steps for gathering information in accordance with the Comprehensive Assessment-to-Intervention System (CAIS; see Chapter 3), which enable the clinician to obtain the necessary data systematically and efficiently.

Step 1: Initial Contact

At the time of the initial referral, parents should be asked to complete a general questionnaire (e.g., our Parent Questionnaire; see Appendix B) giving demographic information and their perception of the problem. Standardized questionnaires specific to child conduct problems, such as the Child Behavior Checklist (CBCL; Achenbach & Edelbrock, 1983) and the Eyberg Child Behavior Inventory (ECBI; Eyberg & Ross, 1978), also provide essential information about the extent of the child's behavior problems (from the parents' point of view) relative to other children of the same age. It is important to have both parents complete each measure, as there are often significant differences between mothers' and fathers' perceptions of the severity and frequency of the child's problems. The Conners Parent Rating Scale (Goyette, Conners, & Ulrich, 1978) can help the clinician screen for the presence of problems with attention and/or hyperactivity.

Parents of children under the age of 12 should complete the Parenting Stress Index (PSI; Abidin, 1990) to provide information about the marital relationship, parental depression, child temperament, and life stress. Parents may also be asked to complete other questionnaires, such as the Dyadic Adjustment Scale (Spanier, 1976; Spanier & Thompson, 1982) and the Beck Depression Inventory (Beck, Ward, Mendelson, Mock, & Erbaugh, 1961). The Home Situations Questionnaire (Barkley, 1987) gives information on the number of problem settings (e.g., playing alone, when visitors are in the home, when parents are on the telephone, at recess, when arriving at school, etc.) and the severity of the problems. This questionnaire can also be used to assess changes in behavior during and after treatment. A copy is included in Appendix B. Finally, parents can be asked to keep a daily record of the child's negative behaviors (e.g., our Daily Log; see Chapter 3 and Appendix B). This record helps the clinician determine what the child is actually doing (in contrast to what the parents *think* he or she is doing), and gives preliminary information about the frequency and intensity of the problem behaviors.

TABLE 11.1. Factors Influencing the Persistence of Conduct Problems

- Attention-deficit Hyperactivity Disorder
- School problems
- Antisocial behavior onset earlier than 10 years of age
- Large number of socially deviant behaviors
- Frequent episodes of antisocial behavior
- Severe antisocial behavior
- Specific antisocial behaviors
    Lying
    Impulsivity
    Truancy
    Running away
    Theft
    Violating curfew
    High rate of noncompliance

- Parent psychopathology
    Paternal antisocial behavior
    Paternal alcoholism
    Maternal depression
- Parenting practices
    Poor supervision
    Excessive permissiveness
    Excessive punitiveness
    Inconsistency
- Marital discord

- Frequent negative life events
- Poor social support
- Aversive extrafamilial relationships
- Low socioeconomic status
- Large family
- Deteriorating family circumstances

It also provides a baseline against which to measure changes with treatment.

In our clinic, the child is typically included in the initial interview with the parents (see below). This enables the clinician to observe the parent–child interaction, and also ensures that everyone hears the same information. We have found that children have a good idea of the problems and will often offer their own opinions about topics the parents bring up. Parents are informed of this arrangement during the initial phone contact, and are asked to make a list of the child's positive qualities and behaviors. They are asked to refer frequently to this list when talking with the clinician about the child's troublesome behaviors; if they do not do so, the clinician asks about the child's strengths directly. If parents are uncomfortable with the child's being present, a separate time is scheduled for them without the child, and the child is seen at a later time. The interview with the child is, however, begun with the parents present and with a discussion of both the problems and the child's positive qualities.

Step 2: Parent and Child Interview

Parent Interview

It is important that both parents attend the initial interview. Fathers and mothers often have very different perceptions of the child's behaviors and may handle discipline very differently (and inconsistently). The clinician should determine whether this is a source of conflict for them that will need to be resolved with treatment. Having both parents present also increases the chances that both parents will participate in treatment. Although the presence of both parents is not always necessary for effective treatment (Martin, 1977), the cooperation and support of the absent parent is important. The parent interview necessarily covers a great deal of information, and the clinician should allow 1½–2 hours for this first appointment. The following areas should be assessed:

1. Developmental history and current status. The clinician should focus on the child's early development, particularly in regard to issues of control and independence, because negative behaviors often originate in early childhood. Early medical history should also be explored, as parents often have difficulty providing effective and consistent discipline for children who have been seriously ill. As an example, a 4-year-old girl was unable to be tested for intellectual problems because her behavior was so out of control. Her parents admitted that they had been afraid to discipline her, because the first time they had sent her to her room for being bad she had had a seizure! Questions should also be asked about the child's temperamental characteristics as they were manifested during

infancy and early childhood. Current developmental status is important to assess, particularly for young children. Delays in language, cognition, or other areas can excerbate children's negative behavior and also can influence the focus of treatment.

2. Parent and family characteristics. Information gathered from the screening instruments provides a basis for discussion of these issues. If, for example, marital conflict, maternal depression, or other types of psychopathology appear to be problems, these should be addressed directly; the clinician should assess their severity, as well as the extent to which they are likely to interfere with treatment for the child's problems. In some cases marital conflict and parent psychological problems decrease as the child's behavior improves, although in other cases these problems are associated with premature termination of treatment or ineffective treatment. The parents should be advised about the necessity of seeking treatment for these problems prior to or in conjunction with treatment for the child's conduct problems. Single parents have been shown to have difficulty maintaining the effects of treatment over time, and are also more likely to drop out of treatment prematurely (Webster-Stratton, 1985b). Webster-Stratton (1985b) suggests that single parents be encouraged to involve a close friend, relative, or regular child care provider in the treatment process in order to enhance effectiveness.

3. Parenting styles and techniques. General information about the parents' attitudes and expectations for themselves as parents and for their children can inform the clinician about aspects of the parent–child relationship that will affect the parents' abilities to follow through with treatment. Asking questions about the parents' own parenting history is often revealing. It is also critical to assess the parents' responses to their child's behavior as it occurs in day-to-day life. Barkley (1987) suggests assessing specific situations (e.g., playing alone or with other children, mealtimes, visiting others, bedtimes, or bathtimes) that may involve misbehavior by asking parents the following: (a) "Is it a problem?" (b) "What does the child do?" (c) "What is your response?" (d) "What does the child do next?" (e) "What is the outcome of the interaction?" (f) "How often do problems occur in this situation?" and (g) "How do you feel about these problems?" Finally, parents are asked to rate the severity of the problem on a scale of 1 ("no problem") to 9 ("severe problem"). The Home Situations Questionnaire (Barkley, 1987) or the Daily Log can help to guide and thus shorten the interview.

Another method of getting this type of information is to ask parents to describe in detail their typical daily routines. This usually reveals the situations that are most problematic for the parents, and gives the clinician the opportunity to determine what the child does and how the parents handle it. This method also reveals the "rhythm" of the family's life and the strengths as well as the weaknesses of the child and parents.

The clinician will need to ask very specific questions ("Who gets up first?" "What happens next?" "Who fixes breakfast?" "What time is dinner usually served?") in order to get the necessary detail. Specific questions about the antecedents and consequences of the negative behavior should be asked. Negative behavior is maintained, strengthened, or decreased by its consequences; therefore, identification and manipulation of these consequences are important aspects of treatment. Likewise, environmental conditions can set the stage for increased negative behavior (e.g., parents may come home tired and try to fix dinner while the child needs parental attention) and can be an effective focus for treatment. Parents' attempts to manage the child's negative behaviors should be examined in detail, in order to determine the various techniques the parents have tried and their relative effectiveness. Parents will typically indicate that they "have tried everything, and it doesn't work"!

4. Recent and ongoing stresses. A simple question such as "Has anything happened in your family lately that might be related to your child's behavior problems?" often reveals startling and important information. It is not unusual for a parent to mention in an offhand manner that he or she has just lost a job, or that an important family member has recently died. Sources of ongoing stress (financial problems, job-related stress, stressful family relationships, etc.) are very important to assess, as these will influence treatment effectiveness.

5. Persistence of problem behaviors. Specific information about the child's problem behaviors is obtained when the parents are asked about a typical day. However, the clinician should also assess the persistence of the behavior and the number of situations in which it occurs. Children who are exhibiting negative behavior at home but nowhere else ("street angels, house devils") have a better prognosis than children who are having conduct problems in school and in the community as well as at home. Moreover, children for whom negative behavior has been a characteristic pattern for a long time will be more difficult to treat than those for whom the negative behavior is relatively recent.

Child Interview

Having the child present while the clinician talks with the parents provides an opportunity to begin to observe the child's behavior and to assess his or her perceptions of the problem vis-à-vis those of the parents. Age-appropriate toys should be provided for the child, and the clinician can informally assess the child's attention span and ability to play alone, as well as the parents' management skills. The clinician can also begin to model appropriate methods of interacting with the child as the situation permits.

A short period of time alone with the child following the interview with the parents is always a good idea, as this gives the clinician the opportunity to assess the child's behavior with someone other than the parents and to determine more closely the child's perceptions of the problem and of his or her parents. With a child 6 years of age or older, the child's perceptions of his or her role in the negative behavior, its consequences, and/or setting conditions can be assessed. General areas to assess include family ("What do you like best about your father, mother, brother, or sister?" "What do you like least?"), friends ("Who is your best friend?" "What do you like to do with him/her?"), school ("What do you like best/least about school?" "What is your best/worst subject?"), and personal strengths and weaknesses ("What do you like to do best/least?" "What are your favorite games/sports?" "What do you like best about yourself?").

Step 3: Observation of Behavior

Direct observation of the parent–child interaction is a central feature of the assessment of conduct problems, and a variety of systematic methods have been proposed. Barkley (1987) suggests having the parent and child play together "as they would at home" for about 5 minutes, and then giving the parent a list of 10 simple tasks (e.g., "Stand up," "Open the door," "Take off your shoes," "Do these math problems") to do with the child. The observer records the parent behavior (command, repeated command), the child's response (comply, noncomply, negative), and the parent's reaction to the child's behavior (attend or praise, negative) for about 10 minutes. Forehand and McMahon (1981) instruct parents to play with the child in two situations for 5 minutes each. During the "Child's Game," the child is allowed to determine the play activities and rules; during the "Parent's Game," the parents determine the rules and activities. Behavior is recorded as it occurs in 30-second intervals. Parent behaviors coded consist of rewards, attends, questions, commands, warnings, and time-out. Child behaviors coded include compliance, noncompliance, and deviant behavior.

We use a modification of Forehand and McMahon's observational system. We record parental commands (C), questions (Q), praise (P), and attention (A), and child compliance (C), noncompliance (N), and other deviant behavior (D), as they occur in two 5-minute situations: the Child's Game and the Parent's Game. Age-appropriate toys are provided for younger children; older children and their parents are asked to play a game together and to solve a family problem (e.g., to plan a family vacation). Figure 11.1 illustrates the data sheet we use.

Although observations most typically take place in the clinic, home or school observations are also useful if the clinician needs a more complete picture of the child's functioning. In the school, the observer can simply keep a running account, divided into 1-minute segments (this indicates when in the observation period a behavior occurred and for

Parent–Child Interaction Data Sheet

Name: _____   Recorder: _____

Date: _____   Time: _____

Parent:	Attention	(A)		**Child:**	Compliance	(C)
	Praise	(P)			Non-Compliance	(N)
	Question	(Q)			Other deviant behavior	(D)
	Command	(C)				

P																							
C																							
P																							

P																							
C																							
P																							

P																							
C																							
P																							

P																							
C																							
P																							

P																							
C																							
P																							

P																							
C																							
P																							

P																							
C																							
P																							

From *Assessment and Treatment of Childhood Problems: A Clinician's Guide* by Carolyn S. Schroeder and Betty N. Gordon. © 1991 by The Guilford Press.

FIGURE 11.1. Data sheet for recording parent–child interaction in the clinic.

how long), of the child's behavior and responses to it; or the observer can focus on the frequency, antecedents, and consequences of target behaviors if these are identified in advance. Home observations should occur at times identified as being problematic for families. Dinnertime or just before is typically a good time to observe negative behaviors. Again, a running account of the interactions is usually the most efficient method.

Step 4: Further Assessment

At this point, the clinician will have a good idea of the nature and severity of the child's conduct problems. Further assessment is warranted if there are concerns about the child's developmental status or performance in school, or about the parents' ability to meet the demands of the treatment program. Because learning problems are positively associated with conduct problems in school-age children, psychoeducational assessment may be necessary. If the child's behavior is a problem in school as well as in the home, permission should be obtained to contact the child's teacher, and behavioral questionnaires such as those described in Chapter 3 should be sent out. The Sutter–Eyberg Student Behavior Inventory (SESBI; Sutter & Eyberg, 1984), the School Situations Questionnaire (Barkley, 1987), the Teacher Report Form of the CBCL (Achenbach & Edelbrock, 1983), and the Conners Teacher Rating Scale (Goyette et al., 1978) are particularly helpful. Copies of the SESBI and the School Situations Questionnaire are included in Appendix B. Descriptions of the CBCL Teacher Report Form and the Conners Teacher Rating Scale are included in Appendix A.

Step 5: Referral to Allied Health Professionals

The clinician should be alert to the possibility that ADHD may coexist with conduct problems, and should refer the family to an appropriate professional for assessment of the possibility of a medication trial if this is relevant. Management of ADHD as well as the negative behaviors will be necessary in these cases. It is often the case that children with conduct problems also have significant developmental or medical problems that require the use of medication (e.g., seizures). In these cases, contact should be made with the child's physician to discuss the proposed treatment program and to ensure appropriate coordination of medical and behavioral treatment. Finally, children who engage in severe aggressive behaviors that are potentially dangerous to themselves or others may need to be referred to an inpatient facility until their coercive behaviors are brought under better control. In these cases, behavioral management training should be recommended in conjunction with inpatient treatment or immediately following the child's release.

Step 6: Communication of Findings and
Treatment Recommendations

The clinician's understanding of the nature, etiology, and severity of the child's negative behavior, and potential treatment approaches, should be discussed with the parents. A clear understanding of these issues, as well as of how the negative behavior fits into the child's developmental picture, will help the parents and child to trust the clinician and maximize the possibility of their cooperation with treatment. Some discussion about the prognosis for the child's problem is also warranted, although this must be done carefully (particularly when the child is young) to avoid setting up a "self-fulfilling prophecy." In some cases, it is clear that a course of parent training will eliminate the child's problem behaviors. In other cases, however, the prognosis is less positive. The risk factors for continuing conduct problems are well known. In particular, when the child is older; when the antisocial behavior has begun early in life; when it is severe, is frequent, and occurs across situations; and/or when the parents or environmental characteristics exacerbate the child's problems, there is little chance of a "cure." Kazdin (1987a, 1987b) recommends that these cases of severe conduct problems be viewed from the perspective of a "chronic illness" model. Treatment can bring the behavior under sufficient control that the family can function reasonably well, but the child is likely to need continual monitoring, and the parents will need ongoing or periodic help and support from the clinician.

TREATMENT

Clinical and developmental research supports the idea that contingent, appropriate maternal responses to child behaviors constitute a key factor in the development and maintenance of positive child behaviors. This research has stimulated the development of programs designed to train parents in principles of social learning and in effective parent–child interaction and child management skills. This and a number of other treatment approaches for negative behavior, including early education, social skills training, cognitive skills training, and family therapy, are reviewed by Dumas (1989) and Kazdin (1987b). Each of these approaches is discussed briefly here, but the focus of this section is on behavioral parent training, because this approach has accumulated the most proof of effectiveness.

Other Treatment Approaches

Early education programs are based on the assumption that antisocial children have school and learning problems, and that early educational opportunities will reduce school failure and thus indirectly decrease the occurrence of antisocial behaviors. Unfortunately, while these programs do seem to result in academic improvement among their participants, there is only limited evidence that they are effective in reducing antisocial behavior. However, it should be noted that these programs were not designed specifically for the purpose of preventing antisocial behavior problems, and it is possible that early intervention programs could be designed that would be more effective in reducing conduct problems, particularly in multiproblem families (see Chapter 2). In particular, Kazdin (1987a) recommends a short course of parent training for parents of preschool children who are oppositional or noncompliant, as a possible means of preventing more serious conduct problems from developing.

Social skills training programs are based on the assumption that antisocial behaviors are learned, and that faulty learning leads to deficits in the social skills necessary for interacting effectively and appropriately with others. Although social skills training results in gains in social skills, there is no evidence that this type of treatment modifies antisocial behavior to a clinically significant degree.

Antisocial children have demonstrated deficits in social cognition. They attend more to aggressive stimuli, overattribute hostile intent, lack empathy, are deficient in social problem-solving skills, and lack awareness of the consequences of their behaviors (Dumas, 1989). Cognitive skills training programs are aimed at remediating these deficits; although they do seem to improve social-cognitive skills, again there is little evidence for their long-term effectiveness in reducing antisocial behavior.

Family therapy programs are based on the assumption that conduct problem children come from dysfunctional families wherein the children's deviant behavior serves an adaptive function. Treatment is focused on identifying the issues that maintain a child's deviant behavior and then teaching family members more adaptive ways to interact and communicate. Evaluation of this approach to treatment of conduct problems suggests that it can be effective if families have the resources necessary to undergo the change process and the therapists have the requisite relationship and structuring skills (Dumas, 1989; Kazdin, 1987b).

Behavioral Parent Training

Parent–child interaction training programs are the most common and successful treatments for negative behavior among young children cited in the literature, and most parents report satisfaction with these programs (Eyberg & Robinson, 1982; Forehand, Steffe, Furey, & Walley, 1983; McMahon, Tiedemann, Forehand, & Griest, 1984; Webster-Stratton, 1989). Current research, however, has found a lack of long-term effectiveness for some families, particularly low-income, socially isolated, multiproblem families (Kazdin, 1987b). Other work suggests that parent training combined with other therapies designed to meet the specific needs of individual families may be more effective (Griest & Wells, 1983; Kazdin, 1987a, 1987b). Kazdin and his colleagues (Kazdin, Esveldt-Dawson, French, & Unis, 1987) combined parent training with problem-solving skills training for the children and found it more effective in reducing the children's antisocial behavior and in increasing prosocial and overall adjustment than parent training alone. In addition to parent training, Griest et al. (1982) provided mothers with treatment focused on parental perceptions of child behavior, parents' personal adjustment, marital adjustment, and extrafamilial relationships. The combination of this "parent enhancement therapy" with parent training was found to be more effective in changing children's and parents' behavior than parent training alone.

Wahler and Dumas (1984) combine parent–child training with training the parents to attend to and observe their children's behavior accurately. They then teach mothers how their interpretations of the children's behavior as appropriate or inappropriate may vary in relation to the mothers' coercive interactions with persons outside the family. This approach, called "mand review," has proven effective in maintaining the behavior changes resulting from parent training in isolated, multiply stressed families. Acknowledging that parent training is not successful for all families, Blechman (1984) recommends three other adjunct treatment approaches, depending on the individual needs of the family. These include self-control training, for parents who have trouble with impulse control; self-sufficiency training, for parents who have problems managing the basic necessities of life; and marital problem-solving training, for parents with marital conflict. Finally, treatment involving problem solving (problem identification, generating alternative solutions, implementing solutions, and evaluating effectiveness) focused on problems other than child management has been found to enhance the long-term effectiveness of parent training for single parents (Pfiffner, Jouriles, Brown, Etscheidt, & Kelly, 1990).

Behavioral parent training is based on the assumption that a child's behavior (normal, deviant, or delayed) is related to past and current interactions with significant others, particularly parents, and that the behavior of these significant people must be changed in order to change the child's behavior (Bijou, 1984). The strategies employed include objectively defining goals for treatment; teaching parents principles of social learning; shaping the child's behavior, using behaviorally based techniques; monitoring progress with systematic records and adjusting teaching accordingly; and modifying environmental conditions so that changes are maintained and generalized (Bijou, 1984). The specific process is described in the next section. In a review of research evaluating parent training programs, Kazdin (1987a) concluded that the characteristics associated with good outcomes for families with severely conduct-disordered children were (1) more sessions (up to 50–60 hours); (2) training in specific techniques such as time-out; (3) training in principles of social learning; (4) therapist training and skill; and (5) broad-based therapy designed to ameliorate a variety of problems associated with conduct problems in children.

The Parent Training Program

A highly effective program, used in our clinic, is that developed by Hanf (1969) and modified by Sheila Eyberg (Eyberg & Boggs, 1989) and others (Barkley, 1987; Forehand & McMahon 1981). This is a two-part program, in which parents are first trained to attend to and praise their child's appropriate behavior. Once this skill is polished (indeed, over-learned), parents are taught to give simple, clear commands and to use time-out by isolation. The parents are also helped to generalize their new skills to specific problem situations such as visiting friends or shopping. Although the program is most suited to younger children (about 2–7 years of age), it can be easily modified for older children by adding features such as token systems (Barkley, 1987) or contingency contracting and family problem solving (Blechman, 1984). The following is a brief outline of how this program is used in our clinic. For greater detail, the reader is referred to books by Forehand and McMahon (1981) and Barkley (1987).

Step 1: Attending and Praising

In the first session, the clinician explains the rationale for the parent training program and presents basic social learning principles. We emphasize how children learn by drawing a diagram for parents (Figure 11.2). Simply put, behavior can be increased or decreased by providing something or taking something away. If, contingent on a specific behavior, positives are presented (positive reinforcement) or negatives are taken away (negative reinforcement), that behavior will increase. Similarly, if negatives are presented (punishment) or positives are taken away (time-out, response cost), the behavior will decrease. Next, a presentation of developmental expectations for children of the target child's age is given, with a discussion of the child's strengths and weaknesses within this developmental framework. Specific behaviors are targeted to be increased and decreased.

The parent training program is based on a system of presenting and taking away positives. The rationale for attending and praising is discussed as one way of presenting positives. There are many reasons why parents should learn to attend and praise a child's appropriate behavior.

	Present	Take Away
Increase Behavior	Positive Reinforcement + (tokens, privileges, praise)	Negative Reinforcement — (nagging, yelling)
Decrease Behavior	Punishment — (yelling, spanking)	Punishment + (removing privileges, logical and natural consequences, time out by isolation)

FIGURE 11.2.   How children learn.

These are described in Table 11.2, which is a handout for parents that we use in our clinic. It should be emphasized that simply eliminating negative behaviors is never successful, because the child will find some other way (usually aversive) to gain parental attention. Teaching appropriate behaviors fulfills this need effectively. Moreover, the technique of following, attending, and praising is remarkably similar to observations in the research literature of maternal responsiveness or synchrony, which has been demonstrated to be related to increased levels of child compliance (Parpal & Maccoby, 1985; Rocissano et al., 1983). These skills also provide the basis for active listening, which is crucial to good communication with adolescents (Ginott, 1969; Gordon, 1970). Teaching following, attending, and praising skills to parents also helps to break the aversive parent–child interaction cycle that is common when the child has been exhibiting high levels of negative behavior. Finally, parents should know that time-out will not be effective unless the child's experience is largely positive. Time-out works by removing the child from opportunities to receive positive reinforcement, which is only possible if the child experiences large doses of reinforcing interactions with family members. If these interactions are largely negative, time-out will be experienced as a relief by the child and may actually serve as a reinforcer for negative behavior.

The idea behind attending is to watch the child carefully and to describe enthusiastically what he or she is doing, in a "play-by-play"

TABLE 11.2.   Parent Handout for Teaching Self-Control: Part 1—Child's Game

The goal of "Child's Game" is to increase your child's appropriate and desired behavior by following, attending, and praising it. The benefits of the "Child's Game" for both you and your child are many.

- It will help your child learn the behaviors that you find acceptable and appropriate. If you want to stop certain behaviors, it is important to teach your child what behaviors you *do* want.

- Following your child's lead by attending to and praising appropriate behavior sets the stage for a pleasant, positive relationship. This will increase the likelihood that your child will naturally want to please you.

- You will learn to monitor your child's behavior more accurately, so that you can be more consistent in both rewarding good behavior and ignoring or punishing undesirable behavior.

- Children learn by watching their parents. Child's Game will teach your child how to follow, attend, and praise behavior he or she likes in other people. Your child may even begin to praise your behavior!

- Punishment of undesirable behavior works best when there are many positive interactions with the child. A positive relationship also decreases the need for punishment!

- The skills of reflective listening, along with attending and praising your child's behavior, are ones that can be used throughout your child's development. These skills let your child know that you are interested in what he or she is doing or thinking, and therefore your child will naturally want to share more with you. What you have to say will also become more important to your child.

- Your child will feel good about himself or herself, because you have let the child know what you like about him or her.

STEPS FOR SUCCESS

1. *Time*

   Find a time every day when you can give full attention to your child. It is often best to choose a regular time of the day so that it becomes a part of your daily routine. Plan for 5 to 20 minutes. The use of a timer also helps, especially when you are first learning to follow, attend, reflect, and praise.

2. *Child's Activity*

   Allow your child to choose the activity. Activities such as building blocks, drawing, puzzles, or Legos™ that allow free expression are good. Try to avoid games that require following rules, such as table games. Avoid reading stories. Let your child know that this is his or her special time and that you will play with the child for the next 5 to 20 minutes.

(continued)

TABLE 11.2.   (*continued*)

3. *Follow*

This simply means that you should watch closely and with interest what your child is doing. You should not be reading the newspaper or thinking about something else during this time.

4. *Attend*

Think of yourself as a baseball announcer on the radio. You want to give an enthusiastic and detailed running commentary on your child's activity. You can describe:

- Your child's activity:

  "You are building a high tower."
  "You're driving your car very carefully."
  "You're using a red crayon and making a circle."

- Where your child is:

  "You are sitting on the floor."
  "You are showing me your picture of a house."
  "You are on your stomach checking out your tower."

- Your child's mood or appearance

  "You are smiling."
  "You are wearing a green shirt."
  "You are trying very hard and being very careful."

5. *Reflective Listening*

This lets your child know that you are hearing and are interested in what he or she says. You can listen reflectively by:

- Simply repeating back what the child has said

  Child: "I want a green block."
  Parent: "You want a green block."

  Child: "I like playing with you."
  Parent: "You like playing with me."

  Child: "I hate these blocks."
  Parent: "You hate those blocks."

- Elaborating on what the child says

  Child: "I want a green block."
  Parent: "You want a green block for your house."

  Child: "I like playing with you."
  Parent: "You are enjoying our special time."

  Child: "I hate these blocks."
  Parent: "You are really angry."

6. *Praise*

You can praise by *labeling* what it is you like ("I like the way you used yellow to draw the sun," or "You are putting the cars in the box so carefully"), or you

(*continued*)

TABLE 11.2. (continued)

can give *unlabeled* praise ("Good work!"). Labeled praise has the advantage of letting your child know specifically what you like and thus gives your child more information. This will take some practice, but it will get easier. Another way to praise your child is to give hugs, kisses, and smiles.

7. *Ignore*

   When your child engages in behavior that is undesirable but *not* harmful or destructive, withhold your attention (i.e., stop following, attending, or praising). This lets the child know that you don't like the behavior. Ignoring is difficult, but practicing ignoring during Child's Game will make it easier in day-to-day activities. If your child engages in destructive behavior, then it is time to stop the game.

8. *No Questions or Commands*

   It is very important not to ask questions ("What are you doing?" "You are happy, aren't you?" "What are you drawing?") or give commands ("Give me the car," "Put this on top"). This interferes with the flow of your child's play and structures the play unnecessarily.

9. *No Teaching*

   This is not a time to teach your child or to find out what he or she knows. It is a time to follow your child's lead, so that you can see how much your child does know and can do by himself or herself!

10. *Parent Participation*

    It is important that your child's activity is the focus of your time together. You can participate in the activity by handing your child things and imitating his or her play, but be sure to continue describing and praising what your child is doing. Be careful not to lead the activity or structure it in any way.

11. *Homework*

    Play the Child's Game with your child every day for 5 to 20 minutes, but no less than 5 minutes. This is a time to practice the attending, reflective listening, and praising skills, but it is also a time to enjoy and get to know your child. Keep a record of each time you play the game on the attached record sheet. Remember that you can also practice using these skills throughout the day. The goal is to make them a natural part of your everyday interactions with your child.

    Have fun!! You can make a difference in your child's life!!

manner (see Table 11.2 for examples). Parents should be taught to use "labeled praise" (which specifies the desired behavior) whenever possible, because this lets the child know clearly what is acceptable behavior. Forms of physical affection, such as hugs, kisses, or pats on the back, are also good ways to praise the child.

The clinician should model following, attending, and praising with the child in play. The parents are then given an opportunity to try out this new skill. It is awkward and difficult for most parents at first, and the clinician should coach the parents by offering suggestions for descriptive statements or praise as appropriate and by praising their efforts. The clinician should remember to tell parents that behaviors described and praised will increase, so they need to be careful to ignore any behaviors that are not considered appropriate. At this point in treatment, behaviors that cannot be ignored (hitting, throwing toys, etc.) should be handled as the parent typically does; however, these behaviors should serve to terminate the play session. Parents should also be reminded not to ask questions, give any commands, or teach the child during this playtime. Questions are perceived by the child as demands, while commands and teaching interrupt and structure the child's play. Because these are typical ways in which adults interact with children, parents usually need to be gently reminded about this from time to time ("Oops, that was a question! Try to restate it as a descriptor" or "That was a command; did you really mean it?").

Parents should be instructed to set aside a short period of time each day to play with their child and practice attending and praising, and each session should be recorded on a record chart (Figure 11.3). We recommend 15–20 minutes, although Eyberg and Boggs (1989) argue that 5 minutes is sufficient and effective. If two parents are involved in treatment, they can take turns coaching each other. If there are other children in the family, or both parents work, the clinician will have to help parents determine how this special time will fit into the family schedule. Although attending and praising are specifically practiced during these special play sessions with the child, parents should be encouraged to apply these skills at other times during the day. The way to do this is to check periodically (e.g., once every 30 minutes) on the child, decide whether the behavior in which he or she is engaging is appropriate, and if so, then praise or describe it. Describing behavior during daily activities is also effective—for example, "I like the way you are staying close to me in the mall." The handout describing the procedure (Table 11.2) is given to the parents, plus the chart to record each time the Child's Game is played and the child's reaction to it (Figure 11.3).

At the beginning of the next session (and all subsequent sessions), the clinician should check with the parents to determine what has happened during the preceding week. Reviewing the parents' Daily Log provides

Child's Game

Date	Time	Activity	Child's Response

FIGURE 11.3.   Chart for recording sessions of the "Child's Game."

a structured way to do this. Parents should then each be asked to demonstrate attending and praising, and the clinician should record these behaviors for about 5 minutes for each parent. The goal is to reach a rate of about 12 attends and several labeled praises per minute and to ignore low-level inappropriate behaviors before beginning the next step of the program. The remainder of this session (and succeeding sessions until the criteria are reached) should be spent in reviewing the rationale for attending and praising, coaching the parents, and discussing their progress. The clinician should be sure to praise the parents' efforts, especially if they are having difficulty mastering the techniques. Remember, behavior that is reinforced will increase! Some parents will need to increase their rates, whereas others may lack enthusiasm. In the latter case, the clinician will need to model enthusiastic statements.

Step 2: Giving Good Commands and Using Time-Out

The second step of the parent training program consists of teaching parents how to give good, clear, age-appropriate commands and then to provide consistent consequences for compliance and noncompliance to those commands. Good commands have four characteristics: (1) They are given one at a time rather than in a string; (2) they are stated in a way that the child knows exactly what behavior is expected (e.g., instead of saying "Be good," the parent should specify what is meant by "good" in the specific situation); (3) they ask the child to do something the child is capable of doing; and (4) they are not questions or suggestions. Questions or suggestions offer the child a choice, and the parents should be prepared to accept a "No" response.

The procedure for giving commands and using time-out for noncompliance is described in Table 11.3. Important parameters of time-out are duration (a period of 1–4 minutes appears to be effective) and contingent release (time-out should be terminated only after a period of quiet) (Hobbs & Forehand, 1975). In addition, the parent should be instructed to ignore any low-level annoying behavior (crying, whining, kicking the wall, complaining) that occurs while the child is in time-out. A kitchen timer should be used so that both parent and child know when time-out is over. If the child cries excessively, screams, or is otherwise disruptive in time-out, the parent should reset the timer each time this occurs.

Some children will not stay in time-out. A recent study by Roberts and Powers (1990) on four time-out enforcement procedures gives valuable information on how to deal with this behavior. They compared the effectiveness of (1) spanking (two spanks on the buttocks with an open hand), (2) holding a child in the chair for a count of 10, (3) putting the child in a room closed by a partial barrier or door, and (4) allowing the child to leave time-out when he or she decided to do as told. Holding

TABLE 11.3.   Parent Handout for Teaching Self-Control: Part 2—Parent's Game

The goal of "Parent's Game" is to learn how to give commands and to punish undesirable behavior by using time-out. "Time out" refers to "time away from ongoing positive reinforcement." Most young children like to be around people, so time-out from attention and ongoing activities can be an effective punishment. Time-out is only effective if there are a lot of positive "time-in" opportunities.

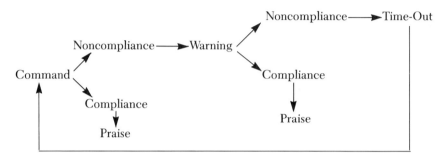

STEPS FOR SUCCESS

1. *Commands*

   Good commands are:

   - GIVEN ONE AT A TIME
     "John, please pick up your coat."
     versus
     "John, you know you are to put your coat in the closet, your lunch bag in the kitchen, and your books on the table when you get home."

   - CLEAR AND CONCISE
     "I want you to sit quietly in the cart. Don't touch anything in the store."
     versus
     "I want you to be good."

   - SOMETHING THE CHILD CAN DO IMMEDIATELY
     "Please get ready for bed now."
     versus
     "Tomorrow I want you to go to bed on time."

2. *No Questions or Suggestions*

   Do not ask a question when you want your child to do something ("Would you feed the cat now?"). When you ask your child a question, you give him or her a choice, and you must be willing to accept "No" as an answer. If you give a suggestion ("Let's go outside"), you should also be prepared to allow your child to say "No." Be sure to give your child true choices as much as possible, but not when you want him or her to do what you say.

3. *Praise Compliance*

   After you give a command, *stop* and *wait* 5 seconds for your child's response (count silently, never out loud). If your child does what you want, immediately

   (continued)

TABLE 11.3.   (*continued*)

praise or attend to him or her ("I appreciate your hanging up your coat"). As you learned in the Child's Game, you can increase compliance by giving it attention after its occurrence. You can also increase compliance by describing your child's actions as he or she starts to obey ("You are picking up the blocks").

4. *Warning*

If your child does not comply with your command after a (silent) count of 5 seconds, give a warning. *Do not repeat the command.* Warnings are "if–then" statements ("If you don't pick up your coat, then you will have to sit on the chair!"). Warnings should be given in a stern voice so that your child knows that you are serious.

5. *Praise Compliance*

If your child complies following a warning, immediately praise or attend to him or her.

6. *Time-Out*

If your child does not start to comply within 5 seconds after a warning, you should use time-out. Time-out by isolation is best carried out by putting your child in a chair facing a corner or in his or her room. Take your child firmly by the hand and place him or her on the chair. Say, "Since you did not _____, you will have to sit in the chair (or stay in your room)." The length of time-out should be 2 to 4 minutes for preschool children and about 5 minutes for school-age children. Use the same length of time-out for both major and minor offenses.

Do not talk to your child on the way to time-out or while the child is in time-out. Completely ignore your child's temper tantrums, shoutings, protesting, or promises to behave. Go about your activities.

Use a kitchen timer so the child knows he or she has to sit until the timer rings. *A very important rule is that your child must sit quietly; in the chair for 30 seconds before being released from time-out.* If your child is not quiet when the bell rings, say, "You will have to stay until you are quiet."

If you are using a chair for time-out and your child gets off the chair without your permission (buttocks leave the seat or the chair is moved), immediately use one of the following procedures:

- Take your child to an uninteresting and safe room, and close the door for 60 seconds. Take the child back to the chair and say, "Sit there and be quiet." If your child still does not stay in the chair, take him or her back to the room and again close the door. Say "You must stay here until you are quiet."

- Simply take your child back to the chair EVERY time the child gets out of the chair. Do not talk to the child. Be prepared for 10 to 20 trips.

After your child has been quiet for at least 30 seconds (preferably for the entire length of the time-out period) and the timer rings, the child may come out of

(*continued*)

TABLE 11.3. (*continued*)

time-out ("You may come out now"). Repeat the command that resulted in time-out. Then repeat giving a warning and time-out as many times as necessary until your child complies. Be sure to praise compliance.

DO NOT REASON WITH A YOUNG CHILD IMMEDIATELY AFTER MIS-BEHAVIOR

Explanations and reasoning about rules and consequences are important, especially as your child gets older, but if you reason immediately after misbehavior you may actually increase the undesirable behavior. Reason with your child when he or she is doing something you like ("When you get ready for bed so quickly, it gives us more time to talk and read stories").

DO NOT GIVE A COMMAND UNLESS YOU ARE PREPARED TO USE TIME-OUT

This will help you reduce the number of demands to those that are REALLY important!

Be affectionate and praise your child for desirable behaviors that occur after the time-out.

When time-out is not working, ask yourself the following questions.

1. Are you giving more than one command or warning?
2. Is everyone in the house who is responsible for the child using time-out appropriately and consistently?
3. Are there plenty of opportunities to praise the child (and are you praising desired behavior)? Is the general atmosphere in the home pleasant?
4. Are you falling for the trick, "I like to go to time-out?" Don't be fooled! Or is your child putting himself or herself in time-out? If this is happening, be sure to make your child stay there for the required length of time.
5. Is your child getting attention while in time-out, or can he or she see the TV or other enjoyable sights?
6. Is the child aware of the rules? Is time-out used consistently?

---

the child in the chair was associated with less compliance and excessive escape from time-out efforts; allowing the child to determine when to leave time-out was associated with excessive time-outs. Therefore, neither of these procedures is recommended to keep a child in time-out. Use of a barrier or spanking appeared to be equally effective and significantly better than either of the other two procedures for increased compliance (they resulted in fewer time-outs and fewer escape efforts). Roberts and Powers also found that children who refused to stay in time-out when spanked accepted the use of a barrier, and vice versa. For children who resisted both spanking and use of a barrier, the barrier procedure was modified so that the children stayed behind the barrier or door until they were quiet for the required length of time-out (e.g., 2 minutes).

These procedures should be discussed with parents to determine which would work best for them. If spanking is chosen, the parents can be instructed to warn the child once and only once, "If you come out of time-out again, I will spank you." If the child comes out of time-out after this warning, the parents are instructed to administer two spanks on the child's bottom, using only an open hand (Barkley, 1987; Eyberg & Boggs, 1989; Forehand & McMahon, 1981; Roberts & Powers, 1990). The child is then placed back in time-out. If the child comes out of time-out again, he or she is told, "Since you left the chair, you must be spanked!"; after two spanks are administered, the child is once again placed back in time-out. In using a barrier, the parents are instructed to say, "Since you left the chair, you will have to stay by yourself," and the child should be put in a room closed by a partial barrier or door (Roberts & Powers, 1990). Roberts and Powers (1990) indicate that after 60 seconds the barrier should be removed or the door opened, and the child should be taken back to the time-out chair with the instruction, "Now stay there and be quiet." If the child continues to leave the time-out chair, he or she should be put back behind the barrier and told, 'You must stay here until you are quiet."

We have also found that repeatedly taking a resistant child back to the time-out chair can be an effective procedure; however, it takes considerable amounts of parents' time and energy. Parents need to assess whether they can do this repeatedly without becoming unduly upset or angry.

The clinician should model the command/time-out sequence with one parent, and then should have the parents take turns practicing with each other while the clinician coaches them. We typically include children in this session and explain the new rules to them while the parents demonstrate. Children are usually very interested in watching Mom put Dad in time-out, and the concrete demonstration helps them understand the consequences of noncompliance. At the end of this session, parents are given a handout (Table 11.3) describing the procedure in detail, and a chart on which to record all instances of time-out for the coming week (Figure 11.4). They are instructed to call the clinician if they have questions or problems in implementing the procedures. Some parents will need help deciding where to locate the time-out chair in their home. The best place is in a corner of a seldom-used room, such as a dining room or laundry room, where the child is out of the mainstream of family life (no TV, toys, etc.) but can be watched.

Reasoning about rules and consequences with children is important, but parents should not do this at the time the child is misbehaving, because this will reinforce the child's inappropriate behavior. Rather, parents can reason with the child when he or she is behaving appropriately, discussing why they like the child's behavior. Finally, it is impor-

Time-Out (TO)

Date	Time	Duration of TO	Reason for TO	Child's Response

From *Assessment and Treatment of Childhood Problems: A Clinician's Guide* by Carolyn S. Schroeder and Betty N. Gordon. © 1991 by The Guilford Press.

FIGURE 11.4.   Chart for recording instances of time-out.

tant for parents to be sure to be affectionate and to attend to and praise the child's appropriate behaviors as soon as these occur after the time-out is over.

Succeeding sessions focus on troubleshooting the time-out procedure, generalizing the new skills to other situations, and dealing with any specific problems that have not been resolved. Parents are taught the value of anticipating troublesome situations by providing children with the rules (and consequences of breaking the rules) ahead of time. As new problems occur, parents are helped to use problem-solving skills to decide how they can apply what they have learned and resolve the problem on their own.

Adaptations for Older Children

In the parent training program described above, control is largely external. Although this is appropriate for younger children, the long-range goal is for children to internalize control. For this reason, as children grow older it is important that they participate actively in the training. Contingency contracting, with a system of tokens or points, can accomplish this goal. We suggest weekly family meetings (which can occur at the clinic until everyone has a clear idea of how these work), during which parents and children negotiate together what behaviors or chores are expected, what the rewards will be for engaging in these behaviors or completing chores, and what the consequences will be for failing to do so. A response cost system is implemented, wherein tokens or points are earned for appropriate behavior and taken away for inappropriate behavior. Points or tokens are accumulated and traded in at regular intervals for privileges (e.g., having a friend stay overnight, watching extra TV, dinner out, special time with a parent, etc.). The program is reviewed and adjusted each week at the family meeting. An example of a token system for sibling rivalry is illustrated in Chapter 4 (see Figure 4.1). The response cost method has been demonstrated to be very effective in managing children's negative behavior (Little & Kelley, 1989), and parents perceive it as a highly acceptable method (Frentz & Kelley, 1986; Heffer & Kelley, 1987). Barkley (1987) provides a detailed description of such a system.

—————————— *CASE EXAMPLE* ——————————

Step 1: Initial Contact

Mrs. Sweet, who called at the suggestion of her friends, said that her 3½-year-old son, Henry, was causing a "few" problems and that the problems occurred primarily with her. The mother stated that she viewed much of Henry's behavior as normal for an active, bright boy, but recent comments from her friends and family about his escalating negative behavior had pushed her to talk with a professional. She asked to come in for an appointment to get some specific suggestions on handling his negative and oppositional behavior. She further indicated that she was hoping to get confirmation that everything was really OK with Henry.

Prior to the initial interview, the parents were asked to complete the Parent Questionnaire. They were also each asked to complete the ECBI and the PSI, and the mother was asked to keep the Daily Log for 1 week prior to the initial interview. Mrs. Sweet returned the completed forms and checklists before her appointment so that they could be scored and reviewed by the clinician. Although Mr. Sweet completed the forms and supported his wife in seeking help, he elected not to come to the interview, since he saw it as primarily "my wife's problem."

The Parent Questionnaire indicated that Mr. Sweet was a construction worker and his wife was a full-time homemaker. Henry was the older of two children, having a 9-month-old sister. On the ECBI, Mrs. Sweet gave Henry an Intensity score of 189 and a Problem score of 5, indicating that she perceived Henry as engaging in a significant amount of negative behavior but did not consider the behavior to be problematic for her. In contrast, Mr. Sweet described Henry within the normal range on both the Intensity and Problem scales. On the PSI, the responses of both mother and father were within the normal limits, with the exception that the father's score for Child Adaptability and the mother's score for Sense of Competence were both above the 90th percentile (high scores on the PSI are problematic). The Daily Log contained such descriptions of inappropriate behaviors such as "Henry hit his grandfather on the shin with a baseball bat" and "Henry scraped a knife across the kitchen wall."

Step 2: Parent and Child Interview

Mrs. Sweet and Henry came together for the initial interview. Mrs. Sweet stated that Henry's developmental milestones were within normal limits, with speaking in sentences occurring by 24 months. He was described, however, as being a "difficult" child from birth. Henry was cared for primarily by the mother; babysitters were limited to the occasional evening out, and no problems were reported during those times. Likewise, his three mornings a week at a preschool were problem-free, although the teachers initially reported that they had to be rather "firm" in their expectations for him. He was often invited to spend time with friends in their homes; although this went well, difficulties were reported when friends visited him. At these times, Henry was described as very active, getting into things that were forbidden and in general creating chaos. Henry's father, who was 15 years older than the mother, thoroughly enjoyed Henry, often taking him on full-day outings with only minor problems. He felt that the mother simply was "too nice" and should be firmer with Henry. The major problems, according to Mrs. Sweet, were "not listening," "refusing to do as requested," and "talking back." All of these behaviors occurred primarily with the mother, but they were beginning to occur with other people in the family.

In order to determine the extent of the problems and the frequency of their occurrence, Mrs. Sweet was asked to describe a typical day for Henry, from the time he got up in the morning to the time he went to bed. She described Henry as managing many routine events such as eating and bathing with ease, but when any demands were placed on him, he would refuse to comply. Mrs. Sweet spent much of her time rearranging her schedule in order to avoid confrontations. This was becoming increasingly difficult as her 9-month-old baby demanded more attention. Although she was clearly exhausted from the effort of caring for her children, she felt that this was simply part of being a mother.

Step 3: Observation of Behavior

Henry appeared in the clinic wearing an army camouflage outfit, cowboy hat, and boots; he was toting two six-shooters and a toy machine gun. He greeted the clinician with "I'm going to shoot your eyes out." The clinician responded with a firm "We don't talk like that in my office," to which Henry quickly responded in a contrite voice, "Oh, I'm sorry."

Observation of parent–child interaction indicated a mother who gave a high rate of noncontingent positive reinforcement, placed few demands on Henry, and tried to get compliance through reasoning. Henry placed many demands on his mother and rarely complied with her requests. There were also many positive interactions between Henry and his mother, and they seemed to enjoy playing together. Henry's play was observed to be age-appropriate; interactions with the clinician after the initial negative statement were positive; and although he refused to comply with the mother's requests to pick up the toys or change activities, he readily complied with the clinician's requests to clean up the toys.

On the basis of the information gathered thus far, the clinician decided that further assessment (Step 4) and referral to an allied health professional (Step 5) were not necessary.

Step 6: Communication of Findings and Treatment Recommendations

In determining where things were going wrong for this mother and child, the clinician told Mrs. Sweet that Henry appeared physically to be in good health, that developmentally he was on target, but that his mother's expectations for him and for herself were creating and maintaining much of the inappropriate behavior. Furthermore, her management techniques were actually increasing the problem behavior. The fact that the behavior occurred primarily with the mother and was just beginning to generalize to other adults close to him indicated a rather circumscribed problem. Although Mrs. Sweet indicated that she was not suffering personally from the behavior, she was told that the continuation of the behavior could only have a negative effect on their relationship and on the child's development. The generalization of negative behaviors with other adults could lead to decreased interactions with Henry, and consequently fewer opportunities for him to learn.

It was recommended that both parents attend classes on child development and management, and that they both be involved with Henry in a series of treatment sessions to increase the positive parent–child interactions, to set age-appropriate limits, to increase compliance on Henry's part, and to determine a consistent method of discipline. Mr. Sweet was asked to come in for an interview prior to giving these recommendations, so that his view of the problem could be further explored. He agreed to this as well as to the recommendations. He felt that coming to an agreement on management techniques would ultimately decrease the conflict between him and his wife over Henry's behavior.

Course of Treatment

The parent training program described earlier in this chapter was carried out over a 6-week period, with follow-up appointments 1 and 3 months after treatment. After treatment, although Henry was described as "headstrong," both parents felt that his behavior was acceptable and for the most part easily managed. Both parents rated him within normal limits on the ECBI and PSI.

Chapter 12

Fears

and

Anxieties

*I*n the normal course of events, everyone from birth to death experiences fear or anxiety at one time or another. These emotions help mediate behaviors essential to survival and can increase the motivation for learning adaptive skills. The stimuli that provoke fear and anxiety change developmentally in a way that corresponds with the child's increasing cognitive and physical abilities and the consequent expectations and experiences. Given the frequency and developmental sequence of fears and anxieties in childhood, some investigators argue that the *absence* of these reactions signals abnormalities in development (Miller, 1983). Indeed, fears and anxieties appear to be such "normal" aspects of a child's life that, according to Miller (1983), even excessive fears will not be brought to the attention of mental health professionals unless they seriously interfere with the child's development or the parents' lives.

Our understanding of the origins of and developmental changes in children's fears has been hindered by the lack of clear definitions of the constructs of "fear" and "anxiety"; problems in measuring constructs that change with age and cannot be readily observed; and the complex contextual issues that come to bear on the behavioral manifestations of fear and anxiety (Campbell, 1986; Miller, 1983). The fear process is especially complex for children. It can vary with age, sex, cognitive level, physical status, past learning history, socioeconomic status (SES), environmental setting, social support system, and the response to the behavior. It is thus not surprising that as recently as 1979, Graziano and DeGiovanni stated that "despite some sixty years of psychological research in children's fears, little is known in any systematic way about the development, response characteristics, maintenance and reduction of children's fears and phobias" (p. 161).

There is little empirical work in this area, and the bulk of the literature focuses on case reports of treatment approaches. Books by Gittelman (1986a) and King, Hamilton, and Ollendick (1988) help to clarify major issues for research and theory, as well as to outline current assessment and treatment procedures; they are recommended for an in-depth discussion of the "state of the art" concerning anxieties and fears in children. This chapter briefly reviews definitions, developmental aspects of fear, the prevalence and nature of fears, classification of fears and anxieties, and finally what is known about the assessment and treatment of these disorders.

DEFINITIONS

The terms "anxiety" and "fear" reflect hypothetical constructs for subjective events that must be inferred by behavioral signs and responses, physiological responses, and self-reports. The terms are often used interchangeably because of their similiar cognitive, affective, and physiological response patterns. These response patterns include thoughts of imminent danger; feelings of apprehension, tension, or uneasiness; and autonomic nervous system reactions such as sweating, trembling, and gastrointestinal distress (American Psychiatric Association, 1987). The differentiation of "fear," "anxiety," and "phobia" focuses on the origin of threat (i.e., external or internal) and the behavioral or physiological response to the perceived real or imagined threat. However, significant problems with the definitions of these concepts remain.

Fear

"Fear" is defined as a normal physiological reaction to a real or perceived threat, which disappears with the withdrawal of the danger (Miller, 1983). Fear appears to prepare the person to evade a danger or to withstand injury or stress when the danger cannot be avoided. It is so closely tied to the external environment that individual differences in perception and understanding greatly influence a fear's appearance and intensity. For example, stimuli that evoke fear in toddlers may not be feared by school-age children.

Anxiety

"Anxiety" is defined as an internally cued aversive emotional state (subjective discomfort and physiological arousal) with no specific focus or obvious external trigger. The literature often refers to anxiety as "manifest" anxiety (i.e., anxiety that is overt and readily inferred) or "latent" anxiety (i.e., anxiety that is covert and hypothesized to be causing other behavior such as aggressive behavior).

Some people appear to be predisposed to experience anxiety in response to a wide range of stimuli, whereas others have more transitory moments of anxiety that fluctuate in duration and intensity. These conditions are often referred to as "chronic" and "acute" anxiety, respectively. The term "chronic" in this context can be misleading, however; it does not mean that the person has a continuing state of low anxiety, but rather is more susceptible to experiencing anxiety. Spielberger (1972) more appropriately describes these conditions as "trait" and "state" anxiety. "Trait" anxiety is defined as a relatively stable individual condition that makes the person more likely to perceive a wide range of stimulus situations as dangerous or threatening. A person with high trait anxiety is thus more likely to react with "state" anxiety, which is characterized by subjective, consciously perceived feelings of tension and apprehension, and activation of the autonomic nervous system.

Given that for children there are developmental stages in which certain types of fears are frequent and can last for a long period of time, Miller (1983) suggests that the concept of trait anxiety in childhood should "refer to a condition characterized by a high frequency of manifest anxiety to a variety of stimuli that are not age specific" (p. 342). Behavioral manifestations of state anxiety among children are motor restlessness, compulsions, and escape-avoidant behaviors such as shyness or school refusal (Werry, 1986).

Phobia

"Phobia" is an extreme, persistent, maladaptive fear attached to an external, nondangerous object or situation. Phobias are usually restricted to objects or situations that *could* threaten survival, such as strangers, being left alone, the dark, animals, and so on. Children often learn to fear a specific object or situation after having an extremely unpleasant experience or injury, such as a painful visit to the dentist, a dog bite, or an accident. Unless the trauma is very severe or highly reinforced, however, these fears usually remit spontaneously and thus would not be considered phobias. Miller (1983) defines a phobia as "anxiety" that:

1. Is attached to a specific nonthreatening stimulus.
2. Is out of proportion to the demands of the situation.
3. Cannot be explained or reasoned away.
4. Is beyond voluntary control.
5. Leads to avoidance of the feared situation.
6. Persists over an extended period of time.
7. Is unadaptive.
8. Is not age- or stage-specific. (p. 338)

Because many people have fears that meet these criteria but remit spontaneously, Graziano, DeGiovanni, and Garcia (1979) have proposed that clinically significant phobias be defined as those that last for 2 or more years and are debilitating to the person's everyday functioning. Miller (1983), however, points out that children are rarely referred for treatment unless the phobia is significantly interfering with their functioning; and therefore, it would be inappropriate for a child to experience a fear for 2 years before receiving treatment.

DEVELOPMENT OF FEARS

Among children, fears are generally seen as mild, age-specific, and transitory (King et al., 1988). There are patterns of fears that increase and decrease over the normal course of development (Miller, 1983). Table 12.1 shows the predominant fears at different ages. The specific content, expression, and intensity of these fears at any given age, however, depend on the learning and experiential history of the individual child. Campbell (1986) states that with increased cognitive development and experience, the child has more resources to evaluate new situations as less novel or threatening, and children's responses to these situations change accordingly with age.

In infancy, responses to novel stimuli—specifically, to strangers— have been shown to be very dependent on a multitude of contextual factors, such as the presence or absence of familiar people, the proximity of familiar people, familiarity of the setting, past experience, arousal level, the response options available to the infant (can the child move to the mother or another familiar person?), the infant's characteristic reaction to heightened arousal, characteristics of the stranger, and the way in which the stranger approaches the infant (Rheingold & Eckerman, 1973). This work raises questions about the universality of the fear of strangers. It would appear that in one situation an infant may react negatively to a

TABLE 12.1. Sources of Fears for Children at Different Ages

Age	Source of fear
0–6 months	Loud noises Loss of support
6–9 months	Strangers Novel stimuli (masks) Heights
12–24 months	Separation
2 years	Auditory stimuli (trains, thunder) Imaginary creatures Burglars Spatial stimuli (large approaching objects)
3 years	Visual stimuli (masks) Animals Dark Being alone Burglars
4 years	Auditory stimuli (fire engines) Dark Wild animals Parents leaving at night
5 years	Visual stimuli Concrete stimuli (injury, falling, dogs) Dark
6 years	Auditory stimuli (ugly tone of voice) Ghosts, witches Someone under the bed Natural disasters (fire, flood, thunder)
7–10 years	Failure and criticism Unknown (shadows, ghosts, dark) Minor injuries Danger (getting lost, burglars) Death Medical and dental procedures

Note. Adapted from "Fears and Anxiety in Children" by L. C. Miller, 1983. In C. E. Walker and M. C. Roberts (Eds.), *Handbook of Clinical Child Psychology* (337–380). New York: Wiley. Copyright 1982 by John Wiley & Sons, Inc. Adapted by permission.

stranger by crying or avoiding the stranger, whereas in another he or she may show interest and make social overtures.

Distress at separation from the primary caregiver, which is at its peak between 18 and 24 months of age, is a universal reaction. The individual child's response once again depends on a number of factors, including age, past experience with separation, the amount of control the child has over the situation, cognitive level, temperamental characteristics, the quality of the mother–child relationship, and specific maternal behaviors during separation (Campbell, 1986). As the child enters the preschool years, separation from the primary caregiver is additionally influenced by the presence of familiar people (including peers and siblings), familiarity with the setting, and the child's general level of social competence (Campbell, 1986). Distress over separation appears to decrease as the securely attached child learns what to do in the mother's absence, experiences the mother's return, and is in an appropriate setting during the mother's absence.

By their second year, children's fears become more individualized. Fear responses to concrete stimuli give way to fears of imaginary creatures and anticipatory fears of the unknown, such as being alone, the dark, death, kidnappers, and robbers (MacFarlane, Allen, & Honzik, 1954). These fears tend to increase up to the age of 4, are predominant between 4 and 6 years, and then begin to decrease (Bowlby, 1973). Between 6 and 12 years, fears become associated with school, bodily injury, and natural events; the more abstract social anxiety and performance anxiety also arise (Miller, 1983). Fears of injury, natural events, and social anxiety appear to remain throughout the life span (Graziano et al., 1979; King et al., 1988).

CLASSIFICATION AND DIAGNOSIS

Classification and diagnosis of all types of childhood disorders must take into account the severity and developmental timing of the behavior. In the case of fears and anxieties, certain fears are considered to be "normal" at a particular age or stage of development, whereas the same fears occurring at a different time in life would be considered abnormal. For example, separation anxiety is expected in toddlers, but is unusual in school-age children. Moreover, expected fears can be abnormal if they are severe enough to interfere with a child's functioning or development. Given the lack of empirical work on children's fears and anxieties, it is understandable that there is not a satisfactory classification system for these problems. Although the current *Diagnostic and Statistical Manual of Mental Disorders* (DSM-III-R; American Psychiatric Association, 1987) classification of children's anxiety disorders leaves a great deal to be desired, it does summarize the knowledge, however limited, about the main clinical, epidemiological, and differential diagnostic and prognostic features of each category (Werry, 1986). A problem in categorizing children's anxiety disorders is that children can present with overlapping symptoms. Hence, it is not uncommon for children to meet the criteria for more than one diagnostic category.

DSM-III-R lists three types of anxiety disorders that apply to children: Separation Anxiety Disorder, Avoidant Disorder of Childhood and Adolescence, and Overanxious Disorder. Two diagnostic categories in the adult section on Anxiety Disorders would also seem to fit the clinical data for young children: Social Phobia and Simple Phobia. The DSM-III-R categories relevant to children's fears and anxieties are briefly reviewed here, followed by a discussion of diagnostic issues.

Separation Anxiety Disorder

According to DSM-III-R, the diagnostic category of Separation Anxiety Disorder is distinguished by the following;

1. Excessive anxiety (which in its severe form could be panic) upon separation from major attachment figures. The reaction is beyond that expected for the child's developmental level.
2. Morbid worries about potential dangers, such as accidents or illness that threaten the integrity of the family.
3. Severe homesickness, to the point of misery and panic, when away from home and a yearning to return home that interferes with participation in activities.

These behavioral manifestations can occur independently or concurrently and are considered clinically significant when they are severe enough to interfere with the child's functioning or emotional well-being, and last for a period of at least 2 weeks (American Psychiatric Association, 1987). The disorder can begin in the preschool years, and the child can have periods of exacerbation and remission over several years. Further, the anxiety reaction can be pervasive or limited to a specific situation; it is often precipitated by a stressful life event, such as a death, a move, or a change of school.

According to DSM-III-R, when separation is anticipated or occurs, children with this disorder may exhibit other fears, such as fear of the dark, burglars, and death and dying. They may also be unable to stay in a room by themselves, may display "clinging" behavior, and may have physical complaints. When no demands for separation are made, children with this disorder usually do not evidence interpersonal difficulties. The families of children with Separation Anxiety Disorder tend to be close-knit and caring (American Psychiatric Association, 1987). Francis, Last, and Strauss (1987), in a study of children ages 5–16 with Separation Anxiety Disorder, found age differences in the manifestation of the disorder. The adolescents (ages 13–16) had more anxiety symptoms and had more somatic complaints on days involving separation, but did not evidence stress upon separation. The middle group (ages 9–12) evidenced withdrawal, apathy, sadness, and poor concentration when separated. Two equally likely symptoms were seen among younger children: worry about attachment figures *and* worry about calamitous events *or* school refusal. Over half of the young children reported nightmares involving separation.

The issue of gender differences in separation anxiety is not clear. Although DSM-III-R indicates an equal sex distribution in the disorder, and the data of Francis et al. (1987) are consistent with this, another study (Last, Hersen, Kazdin, Finkelstein, & Strauss, 1987) found more girls than boys among children with a diagnosis of Separation Anxiety Disorder.

Avoidant Disorder of Childhood

According to DSM-III-R, the essential feature of Avoidant Disorder of Childhood is extreme shyness that interferes with age-appropriate social functioning and peer relationships, lasting for a period of at least 6 months. Another key feature is that the child often has genuinely warm and satisfying relationships with family members and well-known peers and wants social involvement with these people. DSM-III-R states that the child must be at least 2½ years old to exhibit this problem and the behavior must be expressed in all aspects of the child's life. Children with Avoidant Disorder are distinguished from children who are slow to warm up. The latter typically adjust well to new situations and people after a brief period of time. Gittelman (1986b) points out, however, that no evidence exists for the validity of this disorder's criteria, because there could be many reasons besides shyness why children may avoid age-appropriate social interactions. She argues that social avoidance in children should not be classified as a distinct disorder.

Although it is not clear when or whether shyness should be considered clinically significant, there is evidence for a stable characteristic of inhibition that has a significant genetic component (Plomin, 1989). Others have found physiological correlates of shyness. Kagan, Reznick, and Snidman (1987) followed two groups of children—extremely cautious and shy children (inhibited) and fearless, outgoing children (uninhibited—from 2–3 years of age to age 6. They found that these characteristics remained the same over time; furthermore, on physiological measures the inhibited children showed signs of activation in one or more of the physiological circuits that usually respond to novelty and challenge (i.e., a fearful or wary response), whereas the uninhibited children did not.

Shyness is also dependent, to a large extent, on the situation. Buss (1984) suggests that shyness is provoked by situations that involve novelty, formality, extremes of attention, and breaches of privacy. Thus, it is not surprising to find that many children exhibit shyness when entering a new school or classroom. Honig (1987) suggests that elective mutism in school may be an extreme form of shyness. In our experience shyness is best treated by preparing the child for new or different experiences (i.e., the situation, the people present, and any expectations should be discussed). It also helps to have a familiar person initially accompanying the child to the new situation, teaching him or her coping skills (cognitive–behavioral self statements, stress innoculation, social skills), and participant modeling.

Overanxious Disorder

According to DSM-III-R, Overanxious Disorder is characterized by multiple excessive or unrealistic fears that persist for a period of 6 months or more. Anxieties usually include self-consciousness, performance anxiety, worry about future events, and worries about past behaviors. There also can be an excessive need for reassurance, somatic complaints, and feelings of an inability to relax. Perfectionistic tendencies can result in obsession with details of homework or chores. Preoccupation with an adult figure who seems "mean" or critical, and with aspects of performance such as grades or athletic abilities, are common. This category is thus a "mixed bag"; as with Separation Anxiety Disorder, no single form of anxiety defines Overanxious Disorder. The onset can be sudden or gradual, and exacerbations may be associated with stress.

Overanxious Disorder is more common among oldest children from small, high-SES white families, and when there is a concern about achievement even when the children are performing well (APA, 1987). Strauss, Lease, Last, and Francis (1988) found developmental differences for children ages 5–11 and 12–19 who were diagnosed with Overanxious Disorder. The older children had a higher total number of anxious symptoms, more frequent concurrent Major Depression or Simple Phobia, and higher intensity levels of anxiety and depression. The younger children were more likely to have concurrent Separation Anxiety Disorder or Attention-deficit Hyperactivity Disorder.

Campbell (1986) reviewed studies of the development of test anxiety, which is thought of as a specific instance of performance anxiety (i.e., anxiety about personal adequacy and achievement). She concluded that child-rearing practices (punitive and less supportive in achievement situations), parental expectations (unrealistically high), and negative experiences in evaluative contexts contribute to the development of test anxiety. This anxiety leads to lower performance, which in turn increases the anxiety level, setting in motion a cycle that can significantly interfere with the child's development of coping skills (Campbell, 1986).

Phobias

Social Phobia

The key feature of Social Phobia, which is listed in DSM-III-R as an adult anxiety disorder, is a persistent fear of one or more situations in which the person is exposed to possible scrutiny by others and fears that he or she may do something that will be humiliating or embarrassing (e.g., fear of not being able to talk while speaking in public, choking on food in public, vomiting in front of others, etc.). Although the person recognizes the unreasonableness of the fear, he or she has marked anticipatory anxiety if it is necessary to enter the social situation, has high anxiety in the situation, and avoids the situation if at all possible. This disorder is chronic and often associated with other anxiety disorders. It usually begins in late childhood or early adolescence, and is described as rarely incapacitating but considerably inconvenient (APA, 1987).

Simple Phobia

Another DSM-III-R anxiety disorder, Simple Phobia, is characterized by a persistent fear of a specific stimulus (object or situation). The most common fears involve animals (e.g., dogs, snakes, insects, and mice); other feared situations include witnessing blood or tissue injury, closed spaces (claustrophobia), heights (acrophobia), and air travel. To be classified as a disorder, the fear must significantly interfere with a person's functioning or result in marked distress about having the fear. The onset of the animal phobias is in childhood; the blood/injury phobias begin in adolescence or early adulthood; and the other phobias begin most frequently after age 30 (APA, 1987). Simple phobias are very common in children and should be diagnosed as disorders only if they significantly interfere with children's functioning or development.

School Phobia

One of the more common phobias seen by clinicians, but not described as a disorder in the DSM-III-R classification system, is school phobia or school avoidance. Ollendick and Mayer (1984) recommend using the Berg, Nichols, and Pritchard (1969) guidelines for defining school phobia:

1. Severe difficulty attending school, resulting in prolonged absence;
2. Severe emotional upset including fearfulness, temper outbursts, or complaints of feeling ill when faced with the prospect of going to school;

3. Staying at home with the knowledge of the parent when the young-ster should be in school; and
4. Absence of antisocial characteristics such as stealing, lying, and destructiveness. (Ollendick & Mayer, 1984, p. 370)

School phobia can be the result of a variety of conditions, and as such may be a symptom of any one of the other anxiety disorders (Miller et al., 1974). Separation Anxiety Disorder is often felt to be the basis for school phobia, but a fear of attending school can reflect either separation anxiety or a phobic reaction to school itself. Furthermore, not all children with Separation Anxiety Disorder show school refusal (Ollendick & Mayer, 1984). The prognosis for younger children with school phobia is very good, and there is evidence that a careful coordination of the school and family resources can produce effective results with older children (Blagg & Yule, 1984).

DIAGNOSTIC ISSUES

In making a diagnosis of one or another anxiety disorder for a child, it is important to recognize that children can evidence more than one of these disorders at a time and that the number of anxieties exhibited within a particular disorder can vary greatly. Last, Hersen et al. (1987) studied 69 children who had been referred to an outpatient anxiety disorder clinic and found that nearly one-third of these children met the DSM-III criteria for both Separation Anxiety Disorder and Overanxious Disorder. The children presenting with only Overanxious Disorder were significantly more likely to receive an additional anxiety diagnosis (predominantly Simple Phobia or Panic Disorder) than children with only Separation Anxiety Disorder. Furthermore, they found that one-third of the children in their sample met the criteria for Major Depression, and that another third presented with Attention Deficit Disorder, Oppositional Defiant Disorder, or both.

The age differences found by Last, Hersen et al. (1987) were also interesting. Almost all of the children with Separation Anxiety Disorder alone were prepubertal, whereas the diagnosis of Overanxious Disorder occurred at or after puberty. Children with both diagnoses fell between these two groups with respect to age. Thus, as children with Separation Anxiety Disorder grow older, they may be at risk for Overanxious Disorder.

In another study, Last, Strauss, and Francis (1987) studied the co-morbidity among childhood anxiety disorders in a sample of 73 consecutive admissions to an outpatient clinic. Children with a primary diagnosis of Separation Anxiety Disorder were also likely to have Overanxious

Disorder; a primary diagnosis of Overanxious Disorder was likely to include the additional diagnosis of a social anxiety problem (either Social Phobia or Avoidant Disorder of Childhood). There was no clear-cut pattern of comorbidity for those with a primary diagnosis of Social Phobia.

A related diagnostic issue is the extent to which an anxiety disorder is seen as the primary diagnosis or as a secondary diagnosis. This is of importance, because anxiety can be a symptom of almost every psychopathological disorder of childhood, although it is less likely to be seen in the aggressive disorders (Miller, 1983). Depending on the population and on who reports the data, the percentage of children given a primary diagnosis of anxiety disorder varies from 40% (Miller, 1983) to 6.8% (Graziano & DeGiovanni, 1979). There are no clear guidelines or rules for specifying anxiety as the primary problem, and at this point it is obviously a clinical judgment.

Clinicians must also be concerned about the covariation between anxiety disorders and other forms of psychopathology—in particular, obsessive–compulsive and depressive disorders. Berg, Zahn, Behar, and Rapoport (1986), in a review of the literature on the role of anxiety in childhood Obsessive–Compulsive Disorder, concluded that the data at present are insufficient to support childhood Obsessive–Compulsive Disorder as being an anxiety disorder. Although children indicate a subjective state of worry or apprehension concurrent with obsessive symptoms, physiological measures do not suggest that high autonomic activity is a primary etiological factor in childhood Obsessive–Compulsive Disorder. It is interesting that boys with Obsessive–Compulsive Disorder were found to be consistently higher on arousal measures than controls, whereas girls with the same diagnosis were not higher on these physiological measures. Berg et al. (1986) propose the interesting hypothesis that if obsessive–compulsive symptoms are assumed to develop to alleviate feelings of discomfort, then the feelings are more likely to be fear and anxiety in boys, but perhaps shame and guilt in girls. It could also be that girls are more successful in using obsessive–compulsive behavior to control their anxiety, if indeed they are anxious.

Studies indicate that anxiety and depressive disorders are closely linked, but the nature of the association between these disorders is not fully understood. Puig-Antich and Rabinovich (1986) report that for children with Major Depression and/or Dysthymic Disorder, the overlap between depressive and anxiety symptoms is high: About one-third of prepubertal children with Major Depression have a coexisting diagnosis of some anxiety disorder, most frequently Separation Anxiety Disorder. Strauss, Last, Hersen, and Kazdin (1988) found that 28% of 106 children (ages 5-18) who were diagnosed with an anxiety disorder displayed concurrent Major Depression. These children had a mean age of 12.9 years, demonstrated severe anxiety, and tended to have multiple anxiety disorders. It is interesting that the children with only an anxiety disorder could not be distinguished from a control group of children with other forms of psychopathology in trait anxiety and the number of fears reported. The only difference between these two groups was that the anxiety disorders group had a higher state anxiety score; that is, the intensity of their anxiety was higher.

In a study of the peer status of 6- to 13-year-old children with anxiety disorders, Strauss, Lahey, Frick, Frame, and Hynd (1988) found that these children were likely to fall into the socially neglected category, especially if they had a concurrent depressive disorder.

Taken together, these studies indicate to clinicians that children can and often do evidence more than one of these anxiety disorders at a time, and that the number of anxiety symptoms exhibited by children with a particular disorder can vary greatly. Separation Anxiety Disorder appears to be more prominant in prepubertal children, and these children are likely to have Overanxious Disorder as well, especially as they enter the adolescent years. Children with Overanxious Disorder are likely to have an additional diagnosis of Simple Phobia, Panic Disorder, or Social Phobia. Moreover, children with a primary diagnosis of Major Depression in the prepubertal years have a good chance of also having Separation Anxiety Disorder; older depressed children tend to have multiple anxiety disorders.

PREVALENCE AND ETIOLOGY

In a review of the research on parental reports of fears, Miller (1983) concluded that children ages 2-6 have an average of three fears and that 40% of children ages 6-12 have as many as seven fears. Ollendick and colleagues (Ollendick, King, & Frary, 1989; Ollendick, Matson, & Helsel, 1985) found that children reported significantly more fears than indicated by studies using parent reports, with an average of 11-13 fears for children ages 7-18 years. The younger children in this age range had more fears about specific events (e.g., dark room, strange dog), whereas fears of injury, natural events, and social fears were characteristic of all ages. Table 12.2 shows the percentages of children ages 7-18 who reported the 10 most common fears within this age group. Ollendick et al. (1985) also found that in the 7-18 age group, girls reported more fears than boys (16 vs. 8), as well as a higher intensity of fear; these are similar to other findings (King et al., 1988).

Because fears and anxieties are common in children, an important question for clinicians is this: How many children have fears or anxieties that are excessive, or severe enough to interfere significantly with their development? Excessive fears are estimated to be present in 3-8% of the

TABLE 12.2. Most Frequent Fears of Children Ages 7–18

Fear	Percentage reporting
Being hit by car or truck	42%
Not being able to breathe	38%
Fire or getting burned	38%
Death or dead people	36%
Bombs, being attacked	34%
Getting poor grades	34%
Burglars	33%
Parents arguing	33%
Looking foolish	31%
Falling from high places	30%
Being sent to principal	30%

Note. The data are from Ollendick, Matson, and Helsel (1985).

population (King et al., 1988). The number of children referred for fears and anxieties is smaller than the number of adults seen for these disorders, and King et al. (1988) hypothesize that this is due to the relative lack of treatment services for children, as well as to parents' and professionals' lack of information regarding these services. The work of Ollendick and colleagues also suggests that parents are simply not aware of the extent to which their children experience fears.

Although it is generally believed that most children's fears are transient and will remit without treatment, few studies have examined the natural history of extreme fears or phobias. Those studies that have followed referred but untreated children indicate that the fears do tend to improve over time, but the time period may be from 1 to 5 years (Agras, Chapin, & Oliveau, 1972; Hampe, Noble, Miller, & Barrett, 1973). Treatment appears to hasten the recovery period; given the distress caused by extreme fears, there does not seem to be any justification to withhold treatment on the basis of a potential spontaneous remission in the distant future.

What causes children to experience clinically significant fears? There is some support for SES differences in children's fears that reflect the realities of life experiences. Lower-SES children reportedly have more specific fears, such as fear of switchblades, guns, and killers; upper-SES children have more nebulous fears, such as fear of heights or disasters (King et al., 1988).

In a review of the limited literature on the effects of traumatic experiences on anxiety and fear responses, Gittelman (1986b) concluded that traumatic and catastrophic events, such as school desegregation and cyclones, do not appear to make children more susceptible to anxiety symptoms. Her own work (Gittelman-Klein & Klein, 1980), however, points to the importance of attachment in anxiety responses. She found that in 80% of cases of Separation Anxiety Disorder, onset had occurred after the pattern of a child's attachment changed (e.g., after an illness or death in the family, a move of the child's home, or a change of school).

The question of a genetic component to certain anxiety disorders has received some study, but it is difficult to tease out the effects of environment and learning. It appears that children of mothers who have anxiety disorders are more likely to have anxiety symptoms than children of mothers with other psychiatric disorders (Gittelman, 1986b). Last, Phillips, and Statfield (1987) found that mothers of children who were diagnosed as having Overanxious Disorder reported an increased prevalence (42%) of overanxious behavior among themselves as children, but mothers of children who were diagnosed as having Separation Anxiety Disorder did not report a higher rate of separation anxiety as children. Gittelman-Klein (1975) compared parents of hyperactive and school-phobic children and found that the parents of school-phobic children did not report more simple phobias as children, but that they did evidence a greater history of separation anxiety.

In summary, a genetic basis for fears and anxieties is not clearly substantiated, but there is evidence that anxieties and fears tend to run in families. In general, the expression of fears and anxieties can vary with age, sex, cognitive level, environmental setting, past learning history, SES, and the social support system. Thus, fears and anxieties are complex constructs. Although certain treatment methods have been found useful with fears and anxieties, the empirical basis for these clinical interventions is sorely lacking.

ASSESSMENT

Given the complexity of the fear process, and the lack of a systematic way to define and measure fear and anxiety responses, the assessment process for these disorders is not well refined. Graziano et al. (1979) give an excellent summary of the important issues that the child clinician should take into consideration in the assessment and treatment of these disorders. They point out that the identification of the fear stimuli is only a small part of the fear process. The fear reaction can be the result of a complex system, including the following:

1. Fear stimuli that vary in number, type, and intensity, and that may be internal, external, or both.

2. Emotional and cognitive reactions within the child.
3. Overt fear responses that may act upon and modify the social and physical environment, and that themselves may occasion variations in any part of the fear process.
4. Developmental factors.

Furthermore, one must determine how a child in his or her natural environment typically deals with fearful events, and how these strategies vary with factors such as developmental level and sex. Questions about the conditions under which the child's natural coping processes fail and fear processes become debilitating are also important. Finally, one must determine the optimum conditions for reducing the fear (Graziano et al., 1979).

Werry (1986), in a review of assessment techniques for childhood anxiety disorders, concludes that none of the current assessment methods—including unstructured and structured interviews, rating scales, psychological tests, behavioral assessment methods, and physiological measures—are comprehensive, efficient, reliable, and valid ways for the clinician to gather information about these problems. For example, behavioral assessments often ignore the child's social ecology and internal state, whereas physiological measures are too complex for most clinicians to implement and are often difficult to interpret. Miller (1983) cogently points out that, given the complex problems associated with the assessment of childhood fears and anxieties plus our limited understanding of these disorders, the best approach to assessment is an intensive clinical case study. This would include interviews with the parents and child, plus the use of rating scales that give information on the frequency and intensity of the fear or anxiety. Indeed, the most reasonable approach would seem to be a multimethod one that attempts to assess those factors outlined by Graziano et al. (1979). The remainder of this section thus follows the steps for gathering information in accordance with the Comprehensive Assessment-to-Intervention System (CAIS; see Chapter 3), with emphasis on the factors most relevant to fears and anxieties.

Step 1: Initial Contact

The parents should be asked to complete a general questionnaire (e.g., our Parent Questionnaire; see Appendix B), plus a number of other questionnaires that focus on general behavior as well as anxieties and fears. The Child Behavior Checklist (CBCL; Achenbach & Edelbrock, 1983) screens for coexisting behavioral or emotional problems, and gives the clinician information about the extent to which the child's fears and anxieties are greater than those of other children the same age. The

Parenting Stress Index (PSI; Abidin, 1990) provides information about the child's temperament, the parents' general level of stress, and the parents' attachment to the child.

In addition, rating scales focusing on anxiety in general or a specific anxiety or fear can provide a structured way of identifying the specific stimuli that elicit fear in the child. The reader is referred to Barrios, Hartmann, and Shigetomi (1981) for a review of the available scales. Most of the rating scales are self-report measures, but they may be answered by either the child or the parent. The parent–child correlations on the ratings, however, are low (Barrios et al., 1981). The Louisville Fear Survey Schedule for Children (Miller, Barrett, Hampe, & Noble, 1972) is useful for assessment of specific fears, as well as of the generalized effects of fears, relative to those of a normal population. Having the parents keep the Daily Log (see Chapter 3 and Appendix B) on the child's behavior provides information on the child's daily activities to determine whether the fear is interfering with the child's functioning. The reverse side of the Daily Log, Specific Events Causing Concern (see Appendix B), records the antecedents, behaviors, and consequences in specific instances of observed fear and anxiety. This chart can be very helpful in guiding the interview and also in measuring the effects of treatment. Depending on the age of the child, this chart may be kept by both the parents and the child for a week prior to the initial appointment.

Step 2: Parent and Child Interview

Parent Interview

Children's self-reports of fear and anxiety do not correlate well with parents' observations of their children's behavior. Including the child in the initial interview with the parents, regardless of age, has the advantage of clarifying discrepant views of the problem; it also provides an opportunity for observation of the parent–child interaction concerning the problem. If the parents feel that a joint interview would be unsatisfactory for either themselves or the child, then the child should be seen at a later time. (It is usually not wise to leave an anxious or fearful child alone in the waiting room while the parents are interviewed!)

Clinicians often find structured interviews cumbersome, but they can at times be helpful in sorting out anxiety disorders. The Anxiety Disorders Interview Schedule for Children (Silverman & Nelles, 1988) is a structured interview designed for diagnosis of anxiety disorders that uses both parent and child report. It is consistent with the DSM-III-R and can help to screen out other disorders. The clinician can also use the section of the Child Assessment Schedule (Hodges, Kline, Stern, Cytryn,

& McKnew, 1982) that focuses on anxious responding and fearful behavior. Information should be gathered in the following areas:

1. Developmental and medical history. A brief review of the child's developmental milestones can give information on the child's resources, and a review of the child's general pattern of coping with events such as sleep, toileting, eating, and child care can give information about the child's responses to everyday events. Attention should also be given to any medical problems or medications. Behar and Stewart (1981) describe a number of physical conditions that may produce anxiety, including (a) reactions to caffeine, psychostimulants, sedatives/hypnotics, inhalants, and neuroleptics; (b) central nervous system problems, including partial seizures, lesions of the limbic system and frontal lobes, and post-concussion syndrome; (c) metabolic and endocrine disorders, including hypoglycemia, hyperthyroidism, carcinoid tumor, and hypocalcemia; and (d) cardiac problems, including mitral valve prolapse, arrhythmias, and valvular diseases causing palpitations.

2. History of the presenting symptoms and current status. The clinician should clarify the parents' (and child's) perceptions of the problem, as well as define the specific problem behaviors (e.g., avoidant behavior, agitated behavior, reports of feeling upset or sick, crying, specific worries, etc.). The goal here is to try to define the fear—its frequency, intensity, duration, persistence, and situation specificity, plus the antecedents and consequences of the fear-related behavior. The clinician should also determine whether there are conditions under which the fear is not exhibited. For example, a child may show no fear of the dark when he or she is with a sibling or parent.

Mooney, Graziano, and Katz (1985) discuss the need to look at events or meanings associated with the fear responses and the child's coping strategies. For example, fear of going to bed may be associated with fear of ghosts, fear of a recurrent nightmare, or fear that the parents may leave the child. The fear also may be maintained by the coping strategies of the child (e.g., avoidance, escape, immature or dependent behavior).

3. Family history. It is important to determine whether any members of the family have had or continue to have similiar or related problems. Information on the course of the problem may give insight into the antecedents of the fear or the parents' handling of it.

4. Changes in the family or environment. A change in the environment or the child's attachment figures can precipitate fear or anxiety; thus, the clinician should explore recent changes in the family situation or changes at about the time the fears first occurred.

5. Impact on functioning. It is important to gather information on the extent to which the family members have changed their routines to accommodate the problem or to protect the child from exposure to the

feared stimuli, as well as the extent to which the problem interferes with the child's activities.

6. Efforts to help the child. Finding out what has been done thus far to help the child and the child's response to these efforts gives information of the family's bias about certain treatment techniques, as well as efforts that may have inadvertently strengthened the fear (e.g., making the child avoid all TV shows with imaginary figures, "rescuing" the child when confronted by a friendly dog, etc.).

7. Family and community resources. Parents often are ambivalent about having the child confront a feared stimulus, and most children will *not* want to confront it. The clinician should try to determine who in the family is best suited to help the child through the treatment process, as well as how well the family will be able to carry out a particular procedure. The clinician should also find out what support can be offered by neighbors, school personnel, or other community resources. This is particularly important for school-avoidant behavior, where specific information should be gathered on the nature of the parents' relationship to the school and what has been done previously at the school.

Child Interview

The child should be seen alone, either at the time of the initial interview with the parents or shortly after this interview. The clinician should generally assess the child's cognitive-developmental level, verbal skills, and compliance. The child interview also gives the clinician an opportunity to observe the child's emotional reactions, as well as to get a subjective idea of the fear or anxiety. It is important to ask the child about the nature of the distressing behavioral, physiological, and/or cognitive responses that result from the actual or anticipated exposure to the feared stimulus or situation. Determining the response (e.g., avoidance, increased heart rate, diffuse muscle tension, maladaptive thoughts and images, etc.) will have a direct impact on the treatment strategy.

It is often difficult to get a good estimate of the child's experience of fear, especially with a younger child. The fear survey scales appear to offer the most valid method, although they should be used in combination with other assessment methods to provide a comprehensive view of the problem. There are a number of self-report instruments available for children, of which the State–Trait Anxiety Inventory for Children (Spielberger, 1973); the Revised Children's Manifest Anxiety Scale, called "What I Think and Feel" (Reynolds & Richmond, 1978); and the Fear Survey Schedule for Children—Revised (Ollendick, 1983) are the most promising, given their reliability, validity, and practicality. Descriptions of these measures are included in Appendix A. There are also a number of self-report measures that focus on specific fears, including hospitalization (Vernon, 1973), and snakes (Kornhaber & Schroeder, 1975). The reader is referred to Barrios et al. (1981) for a critical review of these and other self-report instruments. It is recommended that these instruments be completed during the child's interview with the clinician or considered for use in further assessment.

Another method for assessing children's experience of fear is a "fear thermometer" (with 0 representing no fear and the top of the thermometer representing extreme fear or anxiety). Fear thermometers are not very reliable, but asking the child to rate the intensity of his or her fears does allow the clinician to establish a fear hierarchy and enables the child to distinguish among different levels of fear. A drawing of the thermometer is helpful for younger children. The clinician can also give young children a concrete way to describe fear or anxiety (e.g., "It feels a lot or just a little like bees or butterflies"), or can have them draw themselves and indicate how different parts of the body feel, as well as give colors to their feelings. Projective tests such as the Roberts Apperception Test for Children (McArthur & Roberts, 1982) can also help clarify a child's fears, particularly if the child has difficulty talking about situations eliciting fears.

Step 3: Observation of Behavior

Observation of the child's reactions to discussions of the fear or anxiety, as well as the parent–child interactions, can often give information about the nature of the fear reaction and what may be maintaining it. Although fears of specific objects or situations are best observed in the natural setting, this is often difficult to accomplish. It should be considered, however, if the parents or child cannot give enough information about the problem to enable the clinician to define it or the variables that may be maintaining the fear. Observations by the clinician can also help code the fear response in a way that will allow parents to observe the behavior more accurately as treatment progresses.

Step 4: Further Assessment

A psychoeducational assessment is warranted for a case of school-related fears when there is a question about the child's actual abilities and performance level.

Step 5: Referral to Allied Health Professionals

When there is suspicion that a medical problem may be precipitating the anxiety symptoms, a referral should be made to a physician. The clinician may be tempted to refer the child for medication to treat the anxiety.

There has been very little research on this treatment method, however. The little evidence that exists suggests that tricyclic drugs may be effective for severe, early Separation Anxiety Disorder (Gittelman & Koplewicz, 1986).

Step 6: Communication of Findings and Treatment Recommendations

As with all childhood problems, it is important for the child clinician to share information with the parent(s) about the child's development and the way in which the problem behavior fits into the developmental process. This can then lead to discussion of the clinician's hypothesis about the process by which a particular fear or anxiety may have become established and/or what may be maintaining it. The parents' and child's trust in the clinician and cooperation in the treatment process will depend on their understanding of the problem. The next section focuses on various treatment strategies for fears and anxieties.

TREATMENT

The goal of treatment for anxieties and fears is to desensitize the child to the feared or anxiety-producing stimulus. This can be done in a number of ways, but the treatment process must involve a gradual and eventually successful confrontation of the stimulus by the child. The child has to learn to cope with the situation or learn that he or she is no longer anxious (Miller, 1983). Case studies indicate that behavioral treatment strategies are generally the most effective with fearful and anxious children, although there is little empirical work demonstrating the effectiveness of different methods. Escape or avoidant responses are treated by participant modeling and operant procedures. Physiological arousal is treated by inducing competing emotional responses through the use of systematic desensitization or emotive imagery; maladaptive thoughts or images are treated with cognitive–behavioral procedures such as self-instruction. A child may have problems in one or all of these areas, so a combination of these techniques that takes into account the developmental level of the child, the resources available to the child and family, and the expertise of the clinician usually makes up the treatment program.

For all the potential difficulties in defining, assessing, and treating fears and anxieties, it is interesting that typical treatment, especially for phobic children, is relatively brief (four to five sessions; Ollendick, 1979). Even for the more complex Overanxious Disorder, treatment can average between 16 and 20 sessions (Kane & Kendall, 1989). The clinician should be aware, however, that a number of children and families will need rather intensive treatment over a long period. Phillips and Wolpe's (1981) work with a particularly complex case, which required 88 sessions over a 2-year period, points out the need for careful assessment and data collection throughout treatment (to ensure the continuation of slow but successful methods and the discontinuation of ineffective techniques).

An in-depth coverage of all the possible treatment strategies used with phobic and anxious children is beyond the scope of this chapter; the reader is referred to other works for overviews of specific procedures (Barrios & O'Dell, 1989; Kendall, Howard, & Epps, 1988; King et al., 1988; Morris & Kratochwill, 1983; Ollendick & Cerny, 1981; Strauss, 1988). This section briefly covers the use of systematic desensitization, emotive imagery, thought stopping, participant modeling, reinforced practice of approach responses and coping skills, and cognitive–behavioral techniques. Specific treatments for school refusal are also discussed.

Systematic Desensitization

"Systematic desensitization," originally developed by Wolpe (1958), involves first training the person in a response that is incompatible or antagonistic to anxiety, and then requiring the person to imagine a hierarchy of anxiety-provoking scenes or actually gradually to confront the fear-evoking stimuli (the latter is called "*in vivo* desensitization"). The incompatible response used most often is muscle relaxation, but laughter (e.g., having the child imagine the feared monster dressed in red flannel underwear!), engaging in play with toys or games, eating food, or interacting with a favorite person can also be used with children. The anxiety hierarchy usually consists of 15–25 stimuli or situations listed from least to most anxiety-provoking. Older children can help make up the hierarchies by rating fears from 0 to 10; parents and clinical observations can provide data for the hierarchies for younger children. King et al. (1988) give examples of hierarchies for common fears such as injections, dentist, darkness, dogs, tests, and reading, but each child's hierarchy will have to be individually determined.

A number of muscle relaxation training procedures have been developed for use with children (Cautela & Groden, 1978; Koeppen, 1974; Ollendick & Cerny, 1981). It is generally suggested that training sessions be limited to 15–20 minutes, with no more than three muscle groups (e.g., face, arms, and legs) introduced in a training session. It is often difficult to use muscle relaxation with children under 6 years of age, and some older children are too fidgety or giggly, so the use of other incompatible responses may be more suitable.

The type of problem plus the child's ability to imagine the fear-evoking stimuli will determine whether *in vivo* or imagery-based desensitization is employed. If possible, it is best to use real-life or *in vivo* exposures. In setting up the real-life situation, the clinician must be sure that he or she has control over the feared stimuli (e.g., a cooperative dentist, a friendly but slow dog, etc.). If real-life exposure is not feasible, imagery should proceed by having the child relax for several minutes and then imagine the least feared scene for 10–15 seconds; when no anxiety is evoked, the child can move up the hierarchy. Pictures or slides can be used to help with the imagery. According to Wolpe's (1958) reciprocal inhibition hypothesis, the therapist should remove an anxiety-provoking stimulus if the child becomes anxious. Goldfried (1971), however, describes systematic desensitization as an active, cognitively mediated process of learning to cope with anxiety. So, instead of removing the scene when the child shows anxiety, the clinician may encourage the child to apply relaxation or other learned coping skills to manage the feared image or real situation. Clinically, Goldfried's (1971) approach is recommended over removing the anxiety-provoking stimulus. An example of this approach is given in a study with dental-phobic 3- to 6-year-old children (Allen & Stokes, 1987). The children were negatively reinforced to be calm in the dental chair by being allowed to escape after increasingly longer periods of calm behavior. The new coping skill, calmness, was then positively reinforced.

Many questions remain about the usefulness of systematic desensitization as described by Wolpe, but relaxation and graduated stimulus presentations are especially useful with phobic reactions involving a high level of physiological reactivity and extreme avoidance, or in cases when it is not advisable to use more confrontational methods (King et al., 1988). King et al. correctly state that systematic desensitization is not the treatment of choice for phobias that are due primarily to a lack of skills, or for fears that are being inadvertently reinforced by significant others.

Emotive Imagery

A variation of systematic desensitization developed by Lazarus and Abramovitz (1962) is emotive imagery. The term "emotive imagery" is used to describe "those classes of imagery which are assumed to arouse feelings of self-assertion, pride, affection, mirth and similar anxiety-inhibiting responses" (p. 191). The therapist evokes these images by incorporating the child's hero image (e.g., Batman, Care Bears, Superman) into a fantasy that includes the child. Through this "emotive imagery," the therapist induces positive affect and then gradually introduces the feared stimuli into the narrative. Rosenstiel and Scott (1977) suggest that the imagery scenes should be tailored to the age of the child, should incorporate the child's existing fantasies and cognitions, and should include language that the child has used to describe his or her fears. They also indicate that the therapist should be alert to nonverbal cues (muscular tension, facial expressions) that may indicate anxiety, so that the therapist can continue the scene until there is no evidence of anxiety. The procedure is similar to systematic desensitization, but the emotive imagery is used as the incompatible response to the feared stimuli. This procedure involves developing anxiety hierarchies, determining a hero and theme that the child enjoys, and interweaving the feared stimuli into scripts in a graduated fashion.

Although the mechanisms underlying this technique have not been well studied, it has been successfully used with children as young as age 4. It has been especially successful with nighttime fears (King, Cranstoun, & Josephs, 1989), which represent about 15% of the total referrals for childhood phobias (Graziano & DeGiovanni, 1979).

Thought Stopping

Jones and Davey (1990), in an experimental analogue of "worry" (i.e., thinking about feared stimuli in the absence of the feared stimuli), found that worry can increase the persistence of a fear. Borkovec and Inz (1990) found that worry decreased the ability to use imagery. They hypothesized that worry can function as a motivated avoidance of emotional imagery, and indeed found that treatment through systematic desensitization increased the imagery and decreased the number of thoughts or worries.

This interesting work may have some bearing on another technique described by Wolpe (1958), called "thought stopping." A case report by Campbell (1973) demonstrates the potential power of this technique with children. He treated a 12-year-old boy who experienced distressing and persistent negative thoughts related to the violent death of a younger sister. The child spent so much time ruminating about the experience that he stopped eating and sleeping and performed poorly in school. In a slight variation of the procedure described by Wolpe (1958), Campbell (1973) trained the boy first to evoke a negative thought, then to stop the thought pattern by counting backwards from 10 to 0 as rapidly as possible. After counting, the boy was to imagine a preselected pleasant scene. The boy was then instructed to use this technique (including a subvocal "No") every time he began to think of the negative experience, and to practice it every night before he went to bed. Within 4 weeks the boy was free of the negative thoughts; he was also able to talk about his sister without undue distress. We have found this technique to be very useful with children who engage in excessive fantasy about a situation that is out of their control (e.g., wishing divorced parents would reunite) or who ruminate about a concern to such an extent that it interferes with effective coping (e.g., worrying about studying so much that they cannot concentrate).

Some children indicate that they do not want to use thought stopping because they like to engage in fantasy about a situation or are afraid that if they stop worrying, the feared event will occur. For these children, we have successfully decreased the intrusive nature of the worry or unproductive thoughts by having them worry for a set period of time each day. The child is told, for example, "You must think about your parents' remarrying for 30 minutes after you get home from school." A timer is used, and the child is not to engage in any other activity until it rings. They are instructed to use the thought-stopping technique at all other times. We have found that children are soon calling the therapist to ask whether the timer can be set for shorter periods of time!

Positive Reinforcement

Positive reinforcement is an integral part of almost every treatment program for fears and anxieties. The systematic use of reinforcement involves specifying a target behavior, determining a naturally occurring reinforcer, and making the reinforcement contingent on the occurrence of the targeted behavior. It is important that the behavior be readily observable, and that both the child and parent understand how and when the behavior is to be reinforced. It is also important to be able to fade the reinforcement gradually as the target behavior becomes more robust.

The use of a chart system that specifies the desired behavior and rewards is often the best way to ensure that the reinforcement is given in a systematic manner. For example, for a child who is fearful of the dark, a chart can specify getting to bed within a certain number of minutes after being told to do so, no complaining about bedtime, staying in bed without calling to the parents, and staying in one's own bed all night. A reinforcement system has the benefits of letting the child and parent know what behaviors are expected and of specifically rewarding the appropriate behavior. The child's behavior also can be shaped by rewarding successive approximations to the final desired behavior. This technique has been successfully used with medical and dental phobias (Hermecz & Melamed, 1984).

Another important part of a reinforcement program is that it can change the child's attitudes about himself or herself relative to a feared stimulus. For example, rewarding the child for sleeping in his or her own room and not allowing the child to come into the parents' room teach the child that there is nothing to fear in his or her own room and that he or she is capable of handling the situation. Moreover, the feared response is not negatively reinforced by avoidance. Positive reinforcement programs are most often used in combination with other techniques, such as relaxation training, modeling, and cognitive self-instructions (Friedman & Ollendick, 1989; Klesges, Malott, & Ugland, 1984).

Modeling

Modeling is a well-researched behavioral method that has been used extensively to help fearful and anxious children. Based on an observational learning paradigm, modeling provides a number of important therapeutic features for the fearful child: (1) vicarious extinction of the feared response by observing a model engage in the feared response without negative consequences; (2) the acquisition of information about the feared stimulus and coping strategies to effectively deal with it; and (3) response facilitation that results in engaging in the expected behavior. Perry and Furukawa (1980) provide the clinician with a very helpful checklist of factors that enhance acquisition of responses and performance via modeling (see Table 12.3).

One of the best features of modeling is that it provides an opportunity for children to learn skills to deal effectively with a feared situation. King et al. (1988) point out that if skill acquisition is to be a major goal of modeling, then a list of the desired skills should be made so that they can be systematically demonstrated, practiced, and reinforced. A graduated exposure to the feared stimulus or situation can also be part of a modeling program. "Participant modeling" is a widely used procedure that involves direct interaction between the model and the child observer, with the model guiding the child through the steps involved in confronting the feared stimulus and offering immediate feedback and reinforcement (Osborn, 1986). Ollendick and Cerny (1981) describe the advantages of a model who explicitly demonstrates coping with the feared stimulus. For example, the model is initially reluctant to have his or her teeth cleaned; then the model complies and says, "That wasn't so bad after all." Modeling via the use of films has been used successfully in the treatment of medical and dental fears (Hermecz & Melamed, 1984). "Symbolic modeling," in the form of stories that describe models coping with feared stimuli, has been shown to increase the frequency of coping statements in kindergarteners (Klingman, 1988). Other promising work uses both a story and games that allow the child to practice the coping skills presented in the book (Mikulas & Coffman, 1989). We have successfully used a story from the book *Annie Stories: A Special Kind of Storytelling* (Brett, 1988) to help children cope with general fears and nightmares (see Appendix C).

Cognitive-Behavioral Approaches

The premise of the cognitive–behavioral approach to treatment is that emotional and behavioral problems are the result of maladaptive thinking. Thus the goal of treatment is to change the maladaptive thoughts, and consequently to change the inappropriate behavior. There are a

TABLE 12.3. Factors That Enhance Modeling

Factors enhancing acquisition (learning and retention)	Factors enhancing performance
Characteristics of the model 1. Similarity in sex, age, race, and attitudes 2. Prestige 3. Competence 4. Warmth and nurturance 5. Reward value	*Factors providing incentive for performance* 1. Vicarious reinforcement (reward to model) 2. Vicarious extinction of fear of responding (no negative consequences to model) 3. Direct reinforcement 4. Imitation of children
Characteristics of the observer 1. Capacity to process and retain information 2. Uncertainty 3. Level of anxiety 4. Other personality factors	*Factors affecting quality of performance* 1. Rehearsal 2. Participant modeling
Characteristics of the modeling presentation 1. Live or symbolic model 2. Multiple models 3. Slider model 4. Graduated modeling procedures 5. Instructions 6. Commentary on features and rules 7. Summarization by observer 8. Rehearsal 9. Minimization of distracting stimuli	*Transfer and generalization of performance* 1. Similarity of training setting to everyday environment 2. Repeated practice affecting response hicrarchy 3. Incentives for performance in natural setting 4. Learning principles governing a class of behaviors 5. Provision of variation in training situations

Note. From "Modeling Methods" by M. A. Perry and M. J. Furukawa, 1980, in F. H. Kanfer and A. P. Goldstein (Eds.), *Helping People Change: A Textbook of Methods* (3rd ed., pp. 66–110). Elmsford, NY: Pergamon Press. Copyright 1980 by Pergamon Press, Inc. Reprinted by permission.

variety of such procedures, including changing irrational beliefs (Ellis, 1970), self-instructional training (Meichenbaum, 1977), and self-control training (Kanfer & Karoly, 1972). There is little evidence that cognitive procedures alone change a child's anxious or fearful behavior, and it is often difficult for young children to identify specific maladaptive thoughts. Positive self-statements in conjunction with other behavioral techniques, however, do appear to help the child cope with stressful situations. Self-statements can emphasize a number of coping strategies:

1. Active control ("I can go inside the house when I like" or "I can get out of the pool any time I like").
2. Reducing aversive aspects ("I will be able to visit friends who have dogs" or "I will be able to go on the school trip").

3. Reinforcing statements ("I am brave; I can take care of myself").
4. Reality-testing statements ("A big bear could never hide in my closet" or "No one has ever died as a result of a bad grade").

A cognitive–behavioral treatment approach that was used with four children (ages 9–13 years) diagnosed with Overanxious Disorder demonstrates the use of these techniques (Kane & Kendall, 1989). There were four major components of the treatment: (1) The children were taught to recognize anxiety feelings and somatic reactions to anxiety; (2) cognitions (unrealistic or negative attributions or expectations) that occurred in the anxiety-provoking situation were clarified; (3) a plan to help cope with the situation was developed (e.g., anxious self-talk was changed to coping self-talk, and the coping actions that might be effective were determined); and (4) success of the coping strategies was evaluated and self-reinforcement given as appropriate. The younger children were reported to have more difficulty using this cognitive approach. In addition to the cognitive techniques, a variety of behavioral strategies were used, including modeling, *in vivo* exposure, role play, relaxation training, and contingent reinforcement; as a result, it is hard to know exactly what was effective. The training tasks and assignments were presented in a graduated sequence, and the children practiced coping skills in imagery and *in vivo*. Treatment took 16–20 sessions lasting 1 hour each, and follow-up reports (no time period given) indicated that treatment gains were maintained for two of the four children.

Wilson, Hoffner, and Cantor (1987) did an interesting study of the perceived effectiveness of coping strategies for dealing with scary television programs. They found that among 3- to 11-year-olds, effective cognitive strategies ("Tell yourself it is not real") increased with age and noncognitive strategies ("Get something to eat or drink") decreased with age. Three- to 5-year-olds chose the "Sit with Mom and Dad" strategy; 6- to 8-year-olds chose "Sit with Mom and Dad" and "Leave the room"; and 9- to 11-year-olds chose "Sit with Mom and Dad" and "Tell yourself it is not real"). This study indicates that the use of self-statements may be most effective for older children, and that the use of social support (and perhaps, transitional objects) may be the most effective for younger children.

Treatments for School Refusal

School refusal is a behavior that every child clinician will encounter at one time or other. It can be precipitated by a host of factors, including a change of school, death of a parent, illness, hospitalization, or an accident. Factors within the school, such as academic failure, a mean teacher, bullying by other children, or fear of ridicule or failure, can also precipitate school refusal. As previously stated, separation anxiety is not necessarily the most important variable in school refusal. A careful assessment of the home and school situation is needed to determine the most appropriate treatment approach. Kennedy (1965) describes a straightforward approach in which the clinician projects an optimistic attitude about success. Other components are as follows: (1) The problem is handled matter-of-factly; (2) there is no further discussion of school; (3) there is a decreased discussion of somatic complaints; (4) the child is taken back to school, forcefully if necessary; and (5) the child is verbally reinforced for staying in school.

Successful treatment of children over age 11 who have school phobia has been limited. Blagg and Yule (1984), however, reported on the successful treatment of 11- to 16-year-olds by a psychologist working in the school system. The program involved the children, parents, and teachers, with specific plans on what was expected of the children and what would be done if the expectations were not met. A contingency plan to ensure maintaining the children in school was developed, with praise for attendance, ignoring complaints, taking the children back to school with an escort (or two, if necessary), and careful follow-up. The point to be made here is that school phobia is a problem that takes a great deal of cooperation (and frequent contact) among the home, school, and clinician, as well as a great deal of clinical skill and careful planning. Without this careful management, these procedures may actually increase the school phobia. If a child is extremely anxious, then the use of hypnosis, systematic desensitization, and cognitive coping skills may be necessary, as well as greater support from the school in maintaining the child in school.

CASE EXAMPLE

Step 1: Initial Contact

Kenny, age 7, was referred by his pediatrician after his complaints of leg paralysis, stomach pains, and headaches were found to have no organic basis. These psychosomatic complaints had begun 2 weeks prior to the initial contact, and Kenny's parents, Mr. and Mrs. Craven, were having great difficulty in getting him to go to school, although the doctor had reassured him that he was fine. Kenny and his mother were seen the day after the initial contact, and thus questionnaires were not completed prior to the first interview.

Step 2: Parent and Child Interviews

Parent Interview

Kenny and his mother were seen together for the initial interview. Mrs. Craven presented as a warm, nurturing person who was obviously very worried about her son and said that she still wondered whether his pains had a physical basis. She stated that she was a full-time wife and mother, and that her husband was a university professor. Kenny was the youngest of three children, with a brother age 10 and a sister age 13. Mrs. Craven indicated that neither of her other children had exhibited any unusual fears or anxieties, but that she herself was always hesitant to join new groups and preferred being with her family and close friends. She stated that all of the children, including Kenny, did well in school, were involved in after-school activities, and had satisfactory relationships with friends. Kenny tended to enjoy a small circle of friends and had always been reluctant to play with unknown children. Up until this time, Kenny had been healthy, was currently taking no medications, and had not taken any medication for the past 7 weeks.

Shortly before the referral, the family had moved two blocks down the street into a larger home. Everyone was pleased with the location and Kenny had his own room for the first time, which he said he enjoyed. When asked whether any other events had recently occurred in the family, the mother recalled after some thought that 3 weeks ago she had gone to the hospital for day surgery to remove a cyst. She felt that perhaps Kenny's problems had begun at that time and had progressively gotten worse. Currently, he became upset at bedtime, saying that he did not want to go to school in the morning. He was also having difficulty getting out of bed in the morning (he said that he couldn't walk, his stomach had shooting pains, and his head hurt). After the physical examination, Mr. and Mrs. Craven had tried to insist that he go to school. Kenny's teacher had recommended that Mrs. Craven stay with Kenny for a half hour in the morning and return to have lunch with him every day. This worked fairly well the first week, but during the second week it seemed to make matters worse: Kenny clung to his mother when she tried to leave the class in the morning, and the teacher said that shortly before lunch, he became agitated and worried that his mother might not show up. In the last week, Mrs. Craven had stayed three afternoons in his classroom helping the teacher.

Although the mother reported no other behavioral or emotional problems for Kenny, she and Mr. Craven were asked to complete the Parent Questionnaire, the CBCL, and the PSI. Mrs. Craven was also given the Daily Log and the Specific Events Causing Concern chart to keep track of Kenny's behavior for the following week. The CBCL scores were within the normal range on all scales, except for the Anxiety scale, which was significantly elevated. The scores on the PSI indicated that Kenny's parents saw him as an easy going child who was very reinforcing to the parents but significantly overly attached to the mother.

Child Interview

Kenny easily separated from his mother, who indicated that she would wait in the waiting room, and readily engaged in activities with the clinician. He drew a picture of himself and was asked to show where he hurt. He chose a red crayon to illustrate a hot, burning pain in his leg when he awoke in the morning; a green crayon with red streaked through it to show his stomach pain; and a black crayon to show the pain in his head. He said he had these pains only in the morning and then, as an afterthought, said he also felt some of them when he went to bed at night. He was not sure when and how the pains went away, but he was not feeling them at the present time. He said he enjoyed his teacher, liked his classmates, and usually got all A's and B's in school. For the last 2 weeks, however, he said he had not been able to do much work because he felt so bad; he only felt good when his mother was in school with him or when he was home.

Kenny was helped to complete the State–Trait Anxiety Scale for Children (Spielberger, 1973) which indicated very high scores on the Trait Anxiety scale. In other words, Kenny was a child who tended to react to a variety of stimuli with an anxious or fearful response. Kenny said that he wanted to go to school, but he just felt awful when he left home, though he couldn't explain why. He had no trouble going to Boy Scouts or Little League.

Step 3: Observation of Behavior

The fear record that the mother kept over the next week indicated only minor complaints about going to school, but anxiety when Kenny did not know where his mother was going to be or when she went out at night. Kenny was pleasant during the parent interview, but chose to sit on the floor beside his mother and to play independently with toys. He exhibited no observable signs of anxiety even when specific fear situations were discussed and questions about his behavior were directed to him.

Step 4: Further Assessment

The Roberts Apperception Test for Children was administered. Kenny's responses to this measure indicated a child with high anxiety and poor coping skills.

Step 5: Referral to Allied Health Professionals

Referral to another professional was not needed, as Kenny had been seen by his pediatrician.

Step 6: Communication of Findings and Treatment Recommendations

Given the nature of Kenny's problem of school refusal, a treatment plan was developed during the initial interview. Mrs. Craven and Kenny were told that although more information needed to be gathered, it was important for everyone to help Kenny feel better as soon as possible. The clinician reviewed Kenny's many strengths and indicated that it was not unusual for some children his age to have worries or scary feelings about leaving home, especially after a move or after someone in the family had been in the hospital. The clinician communicated optimism about resolving the problem with some effort on everyone's part. It was strongly recommended that Kenny be helped to get back to school as soon as possible.

Kenny and his mother agreed to a reward system that specified the steps to get back to school and rewards for completing these steps (see Figure 12.1). Kenny thought it would be hard to get all the points, but he was willing to try, and Mrs. Craven was relieved to have a specific plan of action. Kenny was to go to school as usual on the school bus; his mother was not to accompany him or have lunch with him; and he was to return home on the bus. Mrs. Craven agreed to ask the teacher, who had been quite supportive thus far, to keep Kenny in school. If he was too sick to remain in class, he was to be sent to the nurse's office until the end of the day. Points for engaging in the appropriate behaviors were exchanged each week for having friends spend the night and family activities that Kenny thoroughly enjoyed (e.g., dinner out, a picnic in the park, etc.). All of the steps were carefully written down and agreed upon by both Kenny and his mother. Mrs. Craven was told to call the clinician if she had any difficulty in getting Kenny to school. She felt that her husband would help, and Kenny indicated that he "could make it." The clinician agreed to call Mrs. Craven the following evening to make any necessary changes in the program. After the initial interview, the clinician called Kenny's pediatrician to share her findings and recommendations.

Course of Treatment

Kenny returned to school the next day, and within a week was earning all of his points on the chart. He said that he was feeling a lot better. It was clear from the assessment data, however, that Kenny would benefit from

Going Back to School Chart

	Pts.	Monday	Tuesday	Wednesday	Thursday	Friday	Sun. Nite
I. Getting up in the morning when called and without fuss	1						
II. Eating breakfast and being ready for the bus on time	1						
III. No crying or fussing when leaving for school	2						
IV. Staying in school all day	1						
V. Happy day report from teachers	1						
VI. Report on two good things that happened in school	1 1						
VII. No tears or fussing at bedtime	1						
VIII. BONUS	1						

Total Points   10
Possible Points   50

1st Prize   85%   (43–50) _____   (Dinner out, friends spend the night, or go to movie with friends)
2nd Prize   75%   (38–42) _____   (Rent video)
3rd Prize   65%   (33–37) _____   (Trip to frozen yogurt shop)

FIGURE 12.1.   A record chart for a reward system in the treatment of school phobia.

further treatment. Both parents were asked to come in for a feedback session.

In this session, the parents were told that Kenny was a child who obviously had many strengths, as well as a warm and loving relationship with his family; however, it also appeared that he tended to react to a variety of stimuli in an anxious manner. Given the many stresses of childhood, it was recommended that he enter into some preventive treatment that would help him learn to cope with these stresses more effectively. Specifically, he would be helped to identify a wide range of emotional responses and the situations in which these emotions occurred; to develop skills to cope effectively with his anxious or fearful responses, especially in response to separation from his family; and to become more self-sufficient. The parents agreed with this recommendation, and in subsequent sessions Kenny was taught problem-solving skills. (These are illustrated in Chapter 6, Table 6.1.) Mrs. Craven also agreed to two sessions to discuss how she might best prepare Kenny for new situations, in order to prevent anxious behavior in the future. She was advised to inform him of events well ahead of time, to allow him to engage in increasingly mature and independent behavior (including more activities apart from the family), and to present a rather casual "I know you can do it" response rather than a concerned or solicitous one.

Kenny responded well to this treatment approach, which was carried out over the next 4 weeks. Not unexpectedly, he later returned to the clinic at age 10 when his grandfather died, and at age 12 when he was about to enter junior high school. On the first occasion, his mother requested the appointment because she could see that Kenny was having a difficult time with the death and was becoming increasingly clingy. On the latter occasion, Kenny asked for the appointment on his own. Treatment at these times consisted of three to six sessions, focused on his developing age-appropriate coping skills. Kenny indicated that stresses were getting easier for him to manage, given that he was more easily aware of when he was beginning to feel anxious or fearful and was developing a number of techniques to deal with these situations (relaxation, self-instruction, modeling of peers).

Chapter 13

Habits

and

Tics

*I*n the course of growing up, most children will display at least one fixed repetitive behavior that is not always under voluntary control, called a "habit." For most children, these habits are responses to temporary physical or emotional needs. They seem to help children cope with the stresses of growing up, and appear and disappear in the normal course of development. For example, children are observed sucking their fists within an hour after birth, then primarily after a feeding; by the preschool years, however, most children suck only at bedtime or at other relaxed moments. Similarly, the use of a transitional object (eg., a blanket, teddy bear, or doll) increases after age 2, at just about the time when separation and individuation issues peak; however, the need for these objects begins to decrease after the preschool years. Body rocking begins to occur at about 6 months when a child is beginning to sleep for longer periods of time, but it is usually gone by 2–3 years of age. Movement tics (e.g., blinking, shoulder shrugs, etc.) peak between 6 and 8 years of age, when demands to "sit still and learn" increase; yet these tics diminish rather quickly for most children.

For some children "old" habits may reappear with new stresses, such as the birth of a sibling, a parental divorce, a move to a new school, or the prolonged absence of a parent. Other children "hang on" to a particular behavior for no apparent reason, and it becomes an automatic, involuntary response. These behaviors or habits are not usually symptomatic of underlying pathology, and only become problems under certain circumstances: (1) The behavior continues longer than is typical; (2) the behavior becomes severe or chronic enough to cause physical damage; and/or (3) the behavior is engaged in so frequently that it interferes with ongoing physical, social, and/or cognitive development. This chapter reviews a number of habits that have been known to create problems for children or their families, including oral habits (thumb sucking, nail biting, etc.), hair pulling, and other habits (e.g., breath holding). Motor and vocal tics are most often transient problems, but can persist and/or be indicative of a more serious problem, Tourette's Disorder, and thus are reviewed in some depth.

ORAL HABITS

Thumb Sucking

Thumb sucking, which can include sucking the thumbs, fingers, or fist, is a common behavior among children; there is evidence that some children begin to suck while in the womb! For others, 20% begin sucking their thumbs between 3 and 5 months of age, 15% begin between 6 and 9 months of age, and 10% begin after 9 months of age (Matthews, Leibowitz, & Matthews, 1983). Usually by age 2 sucking is primarily associated with hunger, sleep, frustration, or fatigue. By age 2½ to 3 years, when transitional objects become important, thumb sucking is likely to become associated with the object. It can also be associated with some other behavior, such as twisting or pulling the hair or ear, rubbing a cheek, or sucking on a blanket. With the advent of pacifiers, many children may choose this method of sucking as opposed to sucking the thumb; for our purposes these children are considered with the more "natural" thumb suckers.

There is no evidence that children who suck their thumbs have increased behavioral or emotional problems. Rather, Ilg and Ames (1955) point out the value of this early thumb sucking: It decreases crying, makes teething easier, helps the child get to sleep, and generally acts to soothe the child. As can be seen from Figure 13.1, almost half of all children suck their thumbs or fingers during the preschool years, with a fair number persisting beyond this time (Klackenberg, 1949).

Unless it is so chronic that it interferes with the child's involvement in other activities, thumb sucking is usually not viewed as a problem until dental concerns arise (between 4 and 6 years of age), although some parents find it very annoying or offensive and can make it into a problem through negative attention. Dental concerns include malocclusions, gingi-

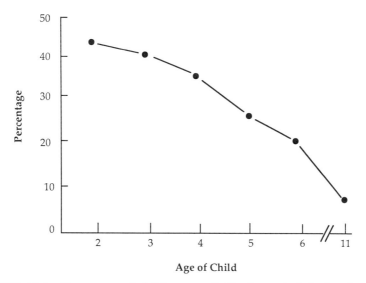

FIGURE 13.1.   Percentage of children ages 2–11 who suck their thumbs. Data from "Thumbsucking: Frequency and Etiology" by G. Klackenberg, 1949, *Pediatrics, 4,* 418–424.

vitis, and facial deformities. There is some difference of opinion on when thumb sucking results in serious dental problems. Hargett, Hansen, and Davidson (1970) state that no harm is done if it is stopped by age 4, and Popovich and Thompson (1973) found that the incidence of malocclusion did not increase if thumb sucking was stopped by age 6 years. Thus, concerns about thumb sucking are dependent on the chronicity of the habit, its effect on the parent, and its effect on the oral structure of an individual child (which would have to be determined through a dental examination).

Friman and Leibowitz (1990) advocate a conservative approach to the treatment of thumb sucking that takes into consideration the child's age, parental attitudes about thumb sucking, risk of unhealthy correlates, and the child's interest in quitting. Many parents help their children give up thumb sucking by removing the associated object, and a recent study supports this action. Friman (1988) successfully decreased thumb sucking in a little girl by preventing the covarying response of doll holding. When the child was sucking her thumb, she always held a crocheted doll in the opposite hand. When the doll was removed (the child was told that she had outgrown it), the thumb sucking stopped almost immediately. When the doll was reintroduced, the thumb sucking increased to baseline, but after 3 days the child angrily told her parents that she was too old for the doll and no longer wanted it! All thumb sucking stopped.

A commonly used dental treatment for thumb sucking has involved the use of an intraoral device, a palatal crib with spurs. With this device, insertion of the thumb in the mouth is difficult and painful. Treatment results, particularly if the device is in place for at least 6 months, are good; however, some authors also note the potential negative side effects of emotional problems and difficulties in eating and speech (Hargett et al., 1970). Given these problems, dentists and most parents are understandably reluctant to use this treatment except as a last resort.

Fortunately, there are a number of behavioral treatments far less intrusive than a dental crib that have been demonstrated to be effective in treating thumb sucking. Habit reversal is a very effective treatment for this problem, as well as for other habits; it is discussed in detail in the "Treatment" section of this chapter.

The efficacy of using a bad-tasting substance and a reward system to treat thumb sucking was demonstrated by Friman and Leibowitz (1990) with 22 children ages 4–11 who were chronic diurnal and nocturnal thumb suckers. Parents coated their child's thumbnail or fingernail with a commercially available substance, Stop-zit (Purepac Pharmaceutical Co.; cost about $3.00), in the morning when the child awoke, each time thumb sucking was observed during the day, and once just before bed. The reward system consisted of a grab bag with 50–100 slips of paper on which parents had written a variety of tangible and intangible rewards (e.g., nutritious snacks, privileges, special time with parents, etc.). By 3 months, 12 children had stopped sucking their thumbs; after 1 year, 20 of the 22 children had ceased all thumb sucking. The parents rated the treatment as very acceptable. Friman has shown in previous work (Friman, Barone, & Christophersen, 1986; Friman & Hove, 1987) that although the aversive-tasting treatment is sufficient to reduce the thumb sucking, the reward system is important because of its positive effect on treatment acceptance.

Several methods of reducing the use of oral pacifiers have been tried, including simply removing the pacifier, allowing it to be used only at certain times and places, putting an aversive-tasting substance on the pacifier, and gradually decreasing the size and form of the nipple by trimming it back (McReynolds, 1972). A positive approach to this problem was reported by Schloss and Johann (1982). The parents of a 15-month-old child modeled the desired response (giving up the pacifier) with a doll, and then reinforced the subsequent appropriate response from the child with praise and a raisin.

Nail Biting

Nail biting (biting on or chewing the nails) and the often associated behavior of picking at nails with fingers is a common habit of children, especially between the ages of 6 years and puberty (Matthews et al., 1983). The prevalence rates vary between 33% and 50%, with a peak for girls estimated at 8–9 years and for boys at 12–13 years (Warme, 1977). Nail biting is primarily viewed as a learned behavior that reduces tension. Habit reversal, with its emphasis on self-awareness and a competing behavior, has effectively reduced nail biting (Azrin & Nunn, 1977), as have self-monitoring plus regularly scheduled nail measurements (Matthews et al., 1983) and reinforcing alternative behaviors (Mulick, Hoyt, Rojahn, & Shroeder, 1978).

Other Oral Habits

Other oral habits (e.g., lip picking, lip biting, lip licking, tongue sucking, tongue biting, sucking the roof of the mouth, and cheek biting) are primarily problems with children or adults who are developmentally disabled. People with Lesch–Nyhan syndrome, for example, are known to mutilate parts of their bodies (including the tongue, lips, and oral cavity) by biting. For children and adults who are developing normally, the habit reversal procedure has been demonstrated to be effective. Azrin, Nunn, and Frantz-Renshaw (1982) successfully treated a 9-year-old boy, who pushed and flicked his tongue on his upper teeth and the roof of his mouth while making audible flicking noises, by using habit reversal; the competing responses were clenching the teeth lightly, pressing the tongue lightly on the roof of the mouth, and keeping the lips closed. In an innovative treatment program for a bright 12-year-old who engaged in mutilating lip biting and wiping his face on his sleeve, Lyon (1983) used tracking (self-recording with a knitting counter), response substitution (dabbing Vaseline on the lips in place of biting the lips), response prevention (attaching sandpaper to the wrist to deter face wiping), and relaxation training to reduce the behaviors to zero in 5 weeks and after 7 months.

TRICHOTILLOMANIA

"Trichotillomania" refers to chronic hair pulling that results in baldness. Although it usually involves pulling hair from the head, hair can be plucked from eyebrows, eyelashes, the pubic region, and the armpit (Risch & Ferguson, 1981). In assessing trichotillomania, it is important to rule out other factors that could cause hair loss, such as vigorous brushing, tight braids, eczema with resultant rubbing, seborrhea, and fungal infections. Alopecia areata, a disorder found in children, results in nonscarring sudden loss of hair in smooth single or multiple spots about the size of a nickel. The etiology of noninflammatory alopecia areata is unknown, but it has been shown to develop a few weeks after severe emotional insult (Owen & Fliegelman, 1978). Trichotillomania is easily distinguishable from alopecia areata because it presents as a combination of inflamed areas with missing hair, broken hair, and intact hair with normal hair follicles (Matthews et al., 1983).

Estimates of the prevalence of trichotillomania vary from less than 1% in psychiatric populations (Mannino & Delgado, 1969) to about 10% in the general population (Azrin & Nunn, 1977). The disorder generally appears between 1½ and 5 years of age, but it can start in adolescence and can persist for a number of years (Matthews et al. 1983). It is more common among girls than among boys (Adam & Kashani, 1990).

The psychoanalytic literature argues that trichotillomania is a disorder of seriously disturbed individuals that is multiply determined. Parent–child conflict and/or disrupted psychosexual development is thought to be symbolically displayed in the hair pulling (Greenberg, 1969; Mannino & Delgado, 1969). On the other hand, Friman, Finney, and Christophersen (1984) state that the behavioral literature views trichotillomania as a learned behavior that can present as a relatively isolated symptom, comparable to other habit disorders such as thumb sucking or nail biting.

Although studies of treatment effectiveness have primarily involved single cases, there are enough good examples using single-subject designs to provide guidelines for the treatment of this problematic behavior. (See Friman et al., 1984, for a review of this literature.) Habit reversal has been found to be a very effective treatment for this problem. For example, the use of a competing response (fist clenching) plus relaxation was effective in treating a 17-year-old female with a 14-year history of hair pulling and nail biting (DeLuca & Holborn, 1984). Three separate case studies have reported a relationship between finger sucking and hair pulling in preschoolers. Hair pulling was eliminated by preventing (taping fingers) or punishing (putting a bad-tasting substance on the thumb) the finger-sucking response (Altman, Grahs, & Friman, 1982; Knell & Moore, 1988; Sanchez, 1979). Knell and Moore (1988) point out that although the temporal order of thumb sucking varied in the three cases (before, during, and after hair pulling), treatment of the thumb sucking eliminated hair pulling in all the cases.

Dahlquist and Kalfus (1984) used praise, ignoring hair loss, education in hair hygiene, response prevention at night (mittens), and a variable schedule of material rewards to stop hair pulling in a 9-year-old girl who denied pulling out her hair. Other studies have focused on improving the parent–child interaction, but have also used punishment or response prevention to eliminate the behavior (Altman et al., 1982; Massong, Edwards, Range-Sitton, & Hailey, 1980). Most of the successful treatment reports with children have used either response prevention or some type of punishment for hair pulling along with positive reinforcement for not pulling out or for an incompatible behavior.

OTHER HABITS

Other childhood habits that occasionally come to the attention of the child clinician include head banging, bruxism, and breath holding. The reader is referred to Chapter 9 on sleep problems for a review of head banging and bruxism. Breath holding consists of holding the breath for more than 30 seconds, with resultant signs of cyanosis and possible unconsciousness to end the attack. Episodes occur primarily when a child is frustrated and angry, with the onset reported to be as early as 4 months of age. Breath holding usually spontaneously disappears at about age 4 years, when periods of violent crying decrease. Matthews et al. (1983) report that the etiology appears to be either learned and inadvertently reinforced by parents, or constitutional (with increased instances of breath holding in families with a history of the problem). Parents should be reassured that these frightening breath-holding episodes appear to be benign and are best handled by ignoring the behavior and reinforcing calm behavior.

TICS

It is important for the child clinician to be aware of the nature of childhood tics and to be alert to the potential diagnosis of Tourette's Disorder, which is typically first seen at about the age of 7–8 years. This section covers the various tic disorders as defined by the revised third edition of the *Diagnostic and Statistical Manual of Mental Disorders* (DSM-III-R; American Psychiatric Association, 1987, pp. 78–82), with an emphasis on Tourette's Disorder.

A "tic" is a sudden, rapid, and intermittent but recurrent, nonrhythmic, and stereotyped motor movement or vocalization that is usually involuntary. DSM-III-R classifies tics into four groups:

Transient Tic Disorder: Single or multiple motor and/or vocal tics of varying frequency and intensity, occuring every day for at least 2 weeks and not for more than 12 consecutive months.

Chronic Motor or Vocal Tic Disorder: Either motor or vocal tics, but not both, occurring throughout a period of more than 1 year.

Tourette's Disorder: Usually a lifelong disorder, with both multiple motor and one or more vocal tics present (but not necessarily concurrently). The anatomical location, frequency, severity, and complexity of the tics change over time.

Tick Disorder Not Otherwise Specified: Tics not meeting the criteria for a specific Tic Disorder.

Although the etiology may be different, these disorders appear to represent a continuum, ranging from a mild transient problem such as throat clearing or eye blinking that lasts only 1 or 2 months, to the more severe and lifelong Tourette's Disorder, with its waxing and waning of multiple motor and vocal tics. According to DSM-III-R, tic disorders share a number of common characteristics, including the following:

Age of onset is before 21 years.
Tic symptoms can be suppressed for minutes to hours and attenuated during an absorbing activity.
Tics can be exacerbated by stress or fatigue.
Tics are markedly diminished or absent during sleep.
Male–female ratio is 3:1.
Vocal tics can occur in each disorder.

The tics can appear as simple motor movements (e.g., eye blinking, nose twitching, pursing of lips, neck jerking, shoulder shrugging) or simple vocalizations (e.g., coughing, grunting, throat clearing, sniffing, snorting, or barking). More complex motor tics can involve a number of muscle movements (such as raising the arm and shrugging the shoulder), facial gestures, grooming behaviors, jumping, stomping, touching and smelling objects or people, or echokinesis (imitating observed movements). Complex vocal tics can include repeating words or phrases out of context, coprolalia (obscene words), palilalia (repeating one's own sounds or words), and echolalia (repeating the last heard word or phrase of another person). Many people with tics indicate that they have a sensory experience like an "itch," which is relieved by the tic movement (Bliss, 1980; Levine & Ramirez, 1989).

Transient and Chronic Tics

Given the transient nature of some tics, it is difficult to determine the exact prevalence of the problem. Estimates range from 1% to 24% (American Psychiatric Association, 1987; Azrin & Nunn, 1977). Age of onset is typically about 5–7 years. MacFarlane, Honzik, and Allen (1954) reported that 4% of the children in the Berkeley Growth Study showed tics, with a peak frequency reached at 6–7 years. A lower prevalence was found in the Isle of Wight Study (Rutter, Tizard, Yule, Graham, & Whitmore, 1976), but these researchers used the criterion that the tic had to interfere significantly with the child's life. Teachers in the same study reported that 5–6% of school-age boys and 1–2% of the girls had "twitches." Thus tics are not unusual in children, especially between the ages of 5 and 8 years.

Chronic Motor or Vocal Tic Disorder is thought to be similar to but less severe than Tourette's Disorder. In Chronic Tic Disorder, the person does not present simultaneously with both motor and vocal tics; also, persons with Tourette's Disorder present with more variability in frequency and type of tics. Transient Tic Disorder may initially be difficult to differentiate from Tourette's Disorder, but the duration of the tics, the progression to different tics, and a family history of tics should make a clinician suspect Tourette's Disorder. Such suspicions should result in an immediate referral to a child neurologist.

There is little agreement on the etiology of Transient and Chronic Tic Disorders. Psychodynamic theories stress that tics represent repressed feelings or conflicts expressed in a symbolic manner (Cavenar, Spaulding, & Sullivan, 1979). Environmental etiologies include emotional tension (Bakwin & Bakwin, 1972) and serious home conflicts (Feldman & Werry, 1966). Some behavioral theorists assert that both chronic and transitory tics are learned responses that are maintained by operant conditioning (Azrin & Peterson, 1988; Yates, 1970). Azrin and Nunn (1973) argue that tics may start as a normal reaction to physical or psychological trauma and continue long after the initial event, or they may originate from normal movements that over time gradually assume an unusual form and high frequency. This can then result in strengthening particular skeletal muscle groups and weakening the antagonistic muscles, thus making it harder to inhibit the tic. Genetic factors may also pay an important role in the development of tics, as a family history of tics is found in 10–30% of all cases (Matthews et al., 1983). It also appears that some tics can be precipitated by phenothiazines, head trauma, and central nervous system stimulants (American Psychiatric Association, 1987). Given the frequency of transient tics in children, and the nature and severity of Tourette's Disorder, it would seem that there is no one etiology for all tics. Some do appear to be learned behaviors, and some appear to have a primary organic basis.

Behavioral treatments have been used successfully for single and multiple tics in children, including habit reversal (Azrin & Nunn, 1973; Finney, Rapoff, Hall, & Christophersen, 1983); negative practice (Yates, 1958); contingent negative practice (Levine & Ramirez, 1989); assertiveness training (Mansdorf, 1986); reinforcement (Schulman, 1974); time-out (Lahey, McNees, & McNees, 1973); self-monitoring (Friedman, 1980); and a combination of self-monitoring, external reinforcement, and time-out (Varni, Boyd, & Cataldo, 1978). Although most behavioral approaches use techniques that focus directly on the tic by reinforcing a motor response incompatible with the tic and decreasing the tic by punishment, techniques have also been used that focus on modifying an emotional state (e.g., anxiety) that is mediating the tic behavior. A study by Mansdorf (1986) is a good example of the use of self-control techniques, assertiveness, and cognitive training to eliminate a series of facial tics in a 10-year-old boy. In 10 weekly sessions lasting 1 hour each, the child was taught assertive responses to heretofore threatening situations (e.g., requesting to join a group, handling teasing, etc.) and given self-instruction training in the form of positive self-statements (e.g., "I can say just what I want," "I'm just as good as Nate," "I'll tell him just what I feel," etc.). The one-to-one treatment with the child was supplemented by contact with the mother for general guidance and feedback. She was instructed to avoid criticizing the child for his tics and to reinforce tic-free behavior with praise. The treatment was successful within eight sessions and after 1 year.

Overall, the most successful procedures for the treatment of tics appear to be habit reversal (or variations of this procedure) and contingent negative practice. Habit reversal procedures are based on the premise that tic behaviors are maintained by response chaining (linking by reinforcement, a sequence of conditioned responses), limited awareness of engaging in the behavior, excessive practice, and social tolerance of the tics. Contingent negative practice as described by Levine and Ramirez (1989) involves having the person repeatedly perform the tic, exactly as it occurs, for 30 seconds contingent upon its occurrence. The habit reversal and contingent negative practice procedures are described in greater detail later in this chapter.

Tourette's Disorder

Tourette's Disorder, or Gilles de la Tourette syndrome, was first described by Itard in 1825; although it is one of the rarer tic disorders, it has received a great deal of attention because of its lifelong course and bizarre manifestations. Although simple, nonpurposeful, rapid movements and noises are the hallmark of Tourette's Disorder, these symptoms convey only a partial view of the disorder and the complexities of its clinical expression. Symptoms can appear as early as 12 months but typically begin at about 7 or 8 years, with the great majority occurring before age 14 (American Psychiatric Association, 1987). Although the disorder can be quite severe, the majority of cases fall in the mild range. There is increasing evidence for a genetic link with an autosomal dominant transmission (Leckman & Cohen, 1988).

Prevalence rates for Tourette's Disorder vary from 0.5 per 1,000 (American Psychiatric Association, 1987) to 1 per 1,000 psychiatric patients (Woodrow, 1974). In 50% of the cases, the disorder starts with a single tic (most frequently eye blinking), but can include other tics of the face or body and sniffing, barking, throat clearing, and other noises.

Eventually all cases have involuntary movements and some vocal tics (Bruun & Shapiro, 1972). There is some evidence for a cephalocaudal (head-to-toe) progression of tics, but this is not always the case. There also appears to be a progression of symptoms from simple motor tics to vocal tics, with coprolalia beginning 3½ to 7½ years after the onset of motor tics (Comings & Comings, 1988). The median age of onset for Tourette's Disorder is 7 years, but diagnosis is often delayed because of the erratic symptoms and the fact that transient tics are at their peak near this age. Unlike transient tics, the Tourette's Disorder tics change in intensity and type, and the presence of throat clearing, grunts, or noises with facial tics should raise suspicion of Tourette's Disorder.

The course of this disorder is usually lifelong, with periods of remission lasting for weeks or years. For a great many cases, the symptoms are not as frequent or severe by adolescence or adulthood (Bruun, 1988). Symptoms can be exacerbated during periods of high emotional stress, excitement, or fatigue (Bruun, 1988). It is estimated that in one-third of the cases, the severity of the tics is exacerbated by the administration of a central nervous system stimulant (American Psychiatric Association, 1987), and Tourette's Disorder has been precipitated in some children as a result of their being given methylphenidate (Denckla, Bemporad, & MacKay, 1976). Given the common use of this drug for Attention-deficit Hyperactivity Disorder (ADHD), clinicians should be aware of this potential problem, especially if the child is anxious or exhibits minor tics, or if there is a family history of tics.

Several other symptoms are associated with Tourette's Disorder (Leckman & Cohen, 1988). Fifty percent of all patients with tic disorders have characteristics of ADHD. Some argue that ADHD is a component of the tic disorder and generally precedes the actual appearance of tics (Comings & Comings, 1988); others view it as a comorbid condition that complicates the course and management of the tic disorder (Pauls et al., 1986), as well as the treatment of ADHD. In any case, an ADHD disorder makes a child with Tourette's Disorder even more vulnerable to the stresses of development and societal expectations. Barkley (1990) states that stimulant medication for ADHD should *not* be used if a child also has tics, or should be stopped immediately if a child develops tics. A more conservative approach to the treatment of ADHD that focuses on changing the environment and the behavior is recommended (Towbin, Riddle, Leckman, Bruun, & Cohen, 1988).

Children with Tourette's Disorder are at high risk for educational problems, given the primary problem implicit in the disorder itself. The potential indirect effects of impaired attention, behavioral problems, and problems with adjustment and acceptance all set the stage for problems in learning. Learning disabilities, particularly in math and the motor control area (as demonstrated by specific weakness on the Coding subtest of the Wechsler Intelligence Scale for Children—Revised and in writing samples; Hagin & Kugler, 1988), are reported at a higher rate for children with Tourette's Disorder.

Children with Tourette's Disorder also have a greater incidence of behavioral problems than other populations (Comings & Comings, 1988). Diminished frustration tolerance, argumentativeness, mood lability, and periods of extreme temper tantrums or aggressive behaviors are reported to occur more frequently in children with Tourette's Disorder (Riddle, Hardin, Ort, Leckman, & Cohen, 1988). From 10% to 40% of Tourette's Disorder patients report obsessional thoughts and exhibit compulsive behaviors and rituals (Towbin, 1988). Recent family interview data support the hypothesis that tic disorders and some forms of obsessive-compulsive disorders are linked etiologically (Pauls & Leckman, 1986). Treatment for Tourette's Disorder reflects the complexity of the disorder in including a variety of approaches. These are discussed later in this chapter.

ASSESSMENT

Habits or tics may present as isolated problems or may be part of a larger constellation of problems. As noted at the beginning of this chapter, referral for clinical evaluation and treatment of a habit or tic usually indicates that the behavior has continued longer than is typical; has become severe or chronic enough to cause physical damage; or is engaged in so frequently that it interferes with ongoing physical, social, and/or cognitive development. A physician or dentist may also refer for evaluation and treatment a child who has been diagnosed as having Tourette's Disorder or for whom thumb sucking is resulting in oral problems. The assessment outline presented here follows the steps for gathering information in accordance with the Comprehensive Assessment-to-Intervention System (CAIS; see Chapter 3), with an emphasis on those factors particularly important in assessing and treating habits and tics.

Step 1: Initial Contact

The parents should be asked to complete a general questionnaire (e.g., our Parent Questionnaire; see Appendix B). Other questionnaires that should be completed by each parent include the Child Behavior Checklist (CBCL; Achenbach & Edelbrock, 1983), to screen for coexisting behavioral or emotional problems; the Eyberg Child Behavior Inventory (ECBI; Eyberg & Ross, 1978), to determine the level of compliance to parents requests in daily activities; and the Parenting Stress Index (PSI; Abidin, 1990), to provide information on the child's temperament and the parents' general level of stress. In addition, the parents should be asked to complete the Habit Diary (see Figure 13.2) for at least 1 week prior to the initial interview, to gather specific information on the frequency, typography, antecedents, and consequences of the behavior. It is usually best to ask the parents to gather this information at the time of day when the frequency of the behavior is likely to be at its highest level. The length of the observation period should be set to fit the parents' and child's schedule; this will increase the likelihood of getting consistent data. Gathering this information is a difficult task, especially if the child is exhibiting complex tics or the behavior is affected by environmental changes. Yet, even if the data are not entirely accurate, they give the clinician some information about the behavior and the parents' response to it.

A number of rating scales have been developed to assess the severity of tic disorders, but their reliability is questionable. The Tourette Syndrome Questionnaire (Jagger et al., 1982) provides information on the developmental history, the course of tic behaviors, and the impact of Tourette's Disorder on the individual's life; it can provide useful information to explore in a clinical interview.

Step 2: Parent and Child Interview

It is important to have an opportunity to interview both the parent and the child on the first contact. The child can be included in the interview with the parent, but there should also be an opportunity to interview the child alone.

Parent Interview

The parent interview should focus on the following areas:

1. Developmental and medical history. Were there any prenatal, perinatal, or postnatal risk factors? Have there been major illnesses or hospitalizations? For tics, the clinician should pay particular attention to potential neurological insults (e.g., adverse perinatal events, serious head injuries, or exposure to medications affecting the central nervous system).

2. Course of the behavior and current status. When was the behavior first noticed? Has it changed in topography (e.g., initially just sucking the thumb and now sucking and pulling the hair), frequency, or intensity? Is it situation- or time-specific? Is it exacerbated by emotional stress, heightened emotional expression (e.g., anger, excitement), or particular situations? It will be important to review the Habit Diary to determine whether the data represent "typical" behavior and responses to the behavior. What have parents been told about the behavior? What have they done about the behavior thus far?

Habit Diary

Child's Name: _____ Date: _____

Behavior: _____

Day	Observation Time	Antecedents (What's Happening)	Behavior (Frequency or Duration)	Consequences	Comments
			SAMPLE		
Monday	5–5:30 P.M.	Watching TV	Checked 6 times and thumb sucking 5/6	Told to take out of mouth	He was really tired from school and fell asleep for 10 minutes.

From *Assessment and Treatment of Childhood Problems: A Clinician's Guide* by Carolyn S. Schroeder and Betty N. Gordon. © 1991 by The Guilford Press.

FIGURE 13.2. The habit diary, used to record the frequency with which habits and tics occur.

3. Family history. A family history of similar behavior is important in the assessment of habit and tic disorders. Whether environmental or genetic factors play a part is not always clear, but a family history of similiar problems often dictates how the parents respond to the behavior. Children with tics are more likely to have parents or extended family members with a history of tics than are other children; for Tourette's Disorder, obsessive–compulsive behaviors are also more prevalent among family members.

4. Impact of behavior. Is the behavior adversely affecting the child's academic learning, the child's social relationships or participation in social activities, or the child's self-esteem? The parents' views of the problematic behavior and of the impact it is having on them, their relationship with the child, and their relationships with other significant people in the child's life are often the determining factors in seeking treatment for habits or tics.

5. Associated behaviors. Determining the presence of other behavioral or emotional problems that could be associated with or occurring simultaneously with the behavior in question is important in deciding on the advisability of treating the presenting problem or initially focusing on areas that exacerbate the problem. Other problems (e.g., a poor parent–child relationship, an unassertive child in a stressful situation, etc.) may make it difficult to treat the habit or tic successfully. Intervention in these areas does not mean that the habit or tic will decrease in intensity or stop, but it sets the stage for more effective treatment of the habit or tic.

For Tourette's Disorder and tics in general, it is important to gather information on inattention, impulsivity, motoric hyperactivity, irritability, and mood lability, as well as obsessions or compulsions (see Step 4, below).

Child Interview

The child should be seen alone sometime during the initial contact. The focus of the interview should be on the child's general adjustment to the family, school, and friends, as well as on his or her perception of the presenting problem. Is the child aware of when and where the problem occurs? Why does the child think the behavior occurs? Is the behavior a concern to the child? Does the child perceive it as interfering in his or her life? Is it being commented on by others? What has the child done to resolve the problem? What is the child's perception of the parents' response to the problem? Does the child want treatment for the problem?

Step 3: Observation of Behavior

The Habit Diary provides initial observational data on the behavior. For oral habits, trichotillomania, or breath holding, it is useful to have the parents continue to keep a record of the behavior, in order to monitor treatment and determine treatment effectiveness. Additional observational methods, such as taking pictures of the nails, measuring their length, counting the number of hairs in bald spots, and recording the number of times the behavior occurs in the treatment session, can also be effective ways to measure progress.

A number of instruments have been developed to make clinical judgments about the frequency and disruption of tic behaviors after observing the child and reviewing details of the child's progress over a time interval. Leckman, Towbin, Ort, and Cohen (1988) review these instruments; the reader is referred to their chapter, which also contains the actual rating scales.

Step 4: Further Assessment

For most isolated habits, there is no need for an assessment to include standardized tests or costly in-home or school observations. For Tourette's Disorder, the clinician should evaluate the child for learning disabilities; should have teachers and parents fill out the appropriate Conners Rating Scales (see Appendix A) to screen for ADHD; should have the teacher complete the Sutter–Eyberg Student Behavior Inventory (see Appendices A and B); and should assess the child for anxiety or obsessive-compulsive disorders.

Step 5: Referral to Allied Health Professionals

If there is any suspicion of Tourette's Disorder, an immediate referral to a neurologist should be made. It will be important for the child clinician and the neurologist to work together in the treatment and monitoring of Tourette's Disorder. Likewise, oral habits that are causing physical damage should be referred to a dentist.

Step 6: Communication of Findings and Treatment Recommendations

The clinician plays an important role in sharing information about a particular habit, the advisability of treatment, and the available treatment options. Although the clinician can teach the child and parents intervention strategies, the child and parents are responsible for carrying out the treatment. It is thus very important for them to understand the rationale and steps for successful treatment and be committed to the treatment program. An inconsistent approach to eliminating troublesome habits is sure to fail.

TREATMENT

In the overview of the various habits, a number of treatment approaches have been discussed. This section focuses on the specific techniques of habit reversal and contingent negative practice. Treatment approaches for Tourette's Disorder are outlined in a separate section.

Habit Reversal

Habit reversal has proven to be an effective treatment for thumb sucking and other oral habits, trichotillomania, and chronic and transient tics. There is also some evidence that it can decrease the number and severity of tics in Tourette's Disorder. The number, length, and type of sessions needed for successful implementation of the habit reversal procedure have varied from one 2-hour group session to 12 individual sessions lasting 1 hour each. Although the habit reversal procedure outlined by Azrin and Nunn (1973) has many components, all of them may not be necessary in the treatment of a particular habit or tic. The clinician, however, should be aware of the specific components of the procedure as used in the original studies; for a particular child or situation, one or another component may be useful. The components include awareness training (response description, response detection, early warning, situation awareness), competing-response training, relaxation training, contingency management (inconvenience review, social support, public display), generalized training, and symbolic rehearsal. In an attempt to simplify this multicomponent procedure, a number of studies have identified overall awareness training and competing-response training as the crucial components of the procedure.

Awareness Training or Self-Monitoring

The purpose of awareness training is to increase the child's awareness of the frequency and severity of the habit, the environmental variables influencing the behavior, and the specific movements involved in the habit. The child or the parents should record the incidence of the habit or the tic for a specified duration each day. The length of recording time is dependent on the frequency of the behavior (i.e., higher-frequency behavior can be recorded for a shorter period of time than lower-frequency behaviors). A 10- to 30-minute recording period at the same time each day is usually sufficient. The use of a counter is often helpful, and the Habit Diary (Figure 13.2) can be used to record the data.

As part of the awareness training, a response description procedure is used. The child verbally and/or physically describes the details of the habit to the therapist, using a mirror or videotape if necessary. This makes the child more aware of the habit and increases motivation to stop the habit. A third part of the awareness training is response detection, in which the therapist alerts the child to each occurrence of the habit. The child is also taught to recognize the earliest sign (early-warning procedure) that the habit is about to occur (e.g., touching the lips in thumb sucking or feeling the urge to engage in a tic). Finally, the child should be helped to become more aware of the situations (situation awareness training) in which the habit occurs most frequently, and to identify situations associated with making the habit better or worse. The child can then be prepared to implement the appropriate procedures or even to practice them upon entering the situation (e.g., the child who sucks a thumb at bedtime can practice fist clenching upon going to bed).

Competing-Response Training

Competing-response training typically requires the person to engage in a response that is incompatible with the habit, contingent on the occurrence of the habit (e.g., opening the eyes wide contingent on eye blinking, or clenching the fist contingent on thumb sucking or nail picking). Azrin suggests that the competing response (1) be opposite to or incompatible with the habit response; (2) be capable of being maintained for several minutes; (3) be socially inconspicuous, so that it is compatible with ongoing activities; and (4) be able to strengthen the muscle antagonistic to the habit and to produce a heightened awareness through tensing of the muscle (Azrin & Nunn, 1973; Azrin & Peterson, 1988). For tic movements, the isometric tensing of the muscles opposite to those involved in the tic movement is recommended. For example, a competing response for shoulder jerking is the isometric contraction of the shoulder depressors (to strengthen the muscles that work in opposition to the upward jerking movements). A competing response for barking is slow, rhythmic, deep breathing through the nose while keeping the mouth closed. For thumb sucking or trichotillomania, clenching of the fists has been shown to be an effective competing response. For tics, the child should be instructed to tense the muscles just tight enough so that the tic movement cannot occur, even when he or she is instructed to attempt to perform the movement intentionally. The competing response should be engaged in for about 2 minutes whenever there is an urge to have a tic or engage in a habit, or immediately after the actual occurrence of a tic or habit. For tics, the most frequent and disruptive one should be treated first, with one training session devoted to working on each tic.

Sharenow, Fuqua, and Miltenberger (1989) demonstrated that the contingent competing response did not have to be a response that was incompatible with the habit. For example, a child could tighten a muscle not related to the habit, such as clenching the left fist contingent on a mouth twitch. Their study suggests that the competing-response intervention is essentially a punishment procedure. Although the small number of subjects ($n = 3$) should make one cautious, the potential to use competing responses that are not as obvious is of clinical importance.

As an example of habit reversal for thumb sucking, Azrin, Nunn, and Frantz-Renshaw (1980) taught the use of a competing response (grasping and clenching the fist for 1–3 minutes), parental support for not sucking the thumb, and stimulus identification (determining the conditions under which the behavior occurs) to 18 parents and children during one 1- to 2-hour session with telephone follow-up. The immediate results were striking, with 92% not sucking the thumb after 1 week and 89% not doing so at a 20-month follow-up.

Relaxation Training

Relaxation training is taught to reduce tension and decrease the frequency and severity of the habit or tics. A combination of methods is recommended, including progressive muscle relaxation (Jacobson, 1962), deep breathing (Cappo & Holmes, 1984), visual imagery (Suinn, 1975), and self-statements of relaxation (Schultz & Luthe, 1959). The imagery helps the child imagine that he or she is in the ideal situation for relaxation. Self-statements to "relax" or "be calm" during relaxation exercises help the child to relax at other times upon verbalizing the "calm" statement. Deep breathing is a form of relaxation that can be easily taught to children. It is most effective when exhalation is slightly longer than inhalation (5 vs. 7 seconds) and the child inhales and exhales slowly without pausing (Cappo & Holmes, 1984). The goal of the training is that the child should be able to relax upon cue in stressful situations. Although relaxation has not always been found to be a necessary component of the habit reversal procedure, it may be very helpful when the habit or tic occurs in particular stressful settings or situations.

Contingency Management

Contingency management is used to ensure that the child is highly motivated to engage in the treatment. The goal is to increase the motivation first by a habit inconvenience review, in which the child and therapist discuss in detail the inconveniences, embarrassment, and suffering that result from the tic or habit, as well as the positive aspects and advantages of reducing or eliminating the tic or habit. Azrin and Peterson (1988) recommend that these inconveniences and positive aspects be written on an index card so that they can be carried and reviewed frequently, as a cognitive strategy to increase the motivation to use the treatment procedures. Next, they suggest that the parents and teachers offer social support by praising the child for performing the prescribed exercises and for not engaging in the tic or habit. A token or chart system can also be used to reward the young or unmotivated child more concretely. If the habit or tic occurs at a high rate, the reward system can be dependent upon observation for a specified period of the day, and the time period can be increased as the frequency of the behavior decreases. Azrin and Peterson (1988) further indicate that in some cases it is necessary for a parent or teacher to prompt or guide a child through the exercises. If the child or family do not believe that the child has voluntary control over the habit then a *public display* procedure can be used. This involves having family members observe the child's ability to control the behavior in the presence of the therapist, as well as having them inform other significant people in the child's life (teachers, siblings, relatives) that the behavior is under his or her control.

Generalized Training and Symbolic Rehearsal

In generalized training, the child is given practice and instruction on how to control the habit or tics in everyday situations. In symbolic rehearsal, children are asked to imagine the situations that are likely to be associated with the habit or tick and cue themselves to relax or engage in the required exercise. Also during the treatment session, if the child fails to detect a tic or habit response, the therapist prompts him or her to engage in the appropriate procedure.

Contingent Negative Practice

Levine and Ramirez (1989) describe contingent negative practice as a relatively simple home-based treatment for involuntary motor responses, tics, and stuttering. This method has a reported success rate (i.e., responses are eliminated or reduced to normal limits) of approximately 80%. Levine and Ramirez have used the procedure clinically and in research since 1973 with 60 people of varying ages. The procedure involves having the child engage in the tic rather than fighting the urge to have it. Once the tic has occurred, the child engages in contingent negative practice of the tic for a period of 30 seconds. The child is encouraged to engage in the contingent negative practice every day at home, during which time the tic is to be repeated as exactly as possible for 30 seconds immediately after every occurrence of the tic. Levine and Ramirez report that some people stop the tic within a few days. According to these authors, some of the underlying principles that may be plausible explanations for the behavioral change produced by contingent negative practice include the following:

1. Practicing the motor response involved in a tic increases the voluntary control over the involuntary response of a tic. This was the basis for the massed-negative-practice procedure used by Yates (1958); although tics were reduced, improvement was not always maintained over time. The difference between contingent negative practice and massed practice is that the practice is contingent upon the tic response and practiced for a much shorter time (30 seconds vs. 30 minutes with 1-minute rest periods every 4 minutes).

2. Contingent negative practice may be a desensitization or habituation procedure when the involuntary response is required and there are no negative social consequences. Thus, it is analogous to a desensitization procedure in which anxiety-producing stimuli are presented and the child remains calm. Producing the involuntary response without any negative consequences means that a respondent extinction paradigm is produced to the tic itself as well as to the social situation.

3. Punishment may be an active ingredient in contingent negative practice, just as it is in the competing response of habit reversal. Voluntary repetition of an involuntary response contingent upon its occurrence punishes the involuntary response immediately.

4. Paradoxical intention may play a role, given that people are required to engage in the very response that they have worked so hard to inhibit. A rule of contingent negative practice is not to fight the tic but to go with it.

As Levine and Ramirez (1989) state, contingent negative practice appears to be a simple method to apply. It is cost-effective, and has been demonstrated to generalize to situations outside the treatment setting.

TREATMENT FOR TOURETTE'S DISORDER

Treatment of Tourette's Disorder must take into account the "whole" child, with a focus on the interaction of the biological, psychological, and social components of the disorder as opposed to a focus on specific behavioral manifestations (i.e., tics). Furthermore, because the disorder is a lifelong problem, a developmental perspective to treatment must be taken. Treatment approaches should focus on the specific needs of the child and family, including reassurance, education, and guidance; advocacy in the school; and the use of behavioral techniques, psychotherapy, and pharmacotherapy (Towbin et al., 1988). Behavioral treatment has included the use of habit reversal, contingent negative practice, contingency management, relaxation training, and self-monitoring (Azrin & Peterson, 1988; Levine & Ramirez, 1989). Psychotherapeutic approaches to Tourette's Disorder generally focus on helping the child to recognize circumstances that are associated with the exacerbation of the symptoms, to understand how such circumstances arise, and to select ways to diffuse or avoid them.

Neuroleptic Drugs

The most widely used and successful treatment for Tourette's Disorder has included the use of the neuroleptic drugs haloperidol, clonidine, and pimozide. (See Cohen, Bruun, & Leckman, 1988, for an excellent review of the risks and benefits of using pharmacological interventions.) Golden (1982) used haloperidol successfully to treat three-fourths of 61 children with Tourette's Disorder, but one-half of this group experienced side effects when using the drug. The negative side effects of neuroleptics can be substantial; they include cognitive impairment, drowsiness, lethargy, extreme anxiety, depression, and Parkinson-like effects (drooling, tremors, rigidity, and loss of associated movements) (Hagin, 1984; Matthews et al., 1983). Lidsky, Labuszewski, and Levine (1981) found that for some people, prolonged use of neuroleptics resulted in sensory, attentional, memory, and intellectual losses.

Although stimulants have been used to counteract the side effects of neuroleptics (Golden, 1988; Towbin et al., 1988), the potential problems of stimulants as well as the problems of using multiple medications make this a questionable choice of treatment. Given the adverse side effects, the risk–benefit factors for using neuroleptics should be very carefully weighed. In general, their use should be considered only for cases where the tics are significantly interfering with development. If medication is used, it should be gradually stopped after a period of time to determine whether it continues to be needed. Abrupt stopping of the medication can result in increased symptoms lasting for several months (Towbin et al., 1988).

In addition to medication, treatment for Tourette's Disorder should always include providing information and counseling for the child and parents to help them understand and adjust to the stresses of the disorder, as well as working with the school and community to facilitate that adjustment. The Tourette Syndrome Association provides excellent information that can be used to inform the child's teachers and classmates about the disorder, and there are support groups in most urban areas. The Tourette Syndrome Association can be contacted at 42-40 Bell Boulevard, Bayside NY 11361; the telephone number is (718) 224-2999.

School Modifications

The direct and indirect effects of Tourette's Disorder on the child's functioning in the school should be of concern to clinicians. Hagin and Kugler (1988) outline a number of modifications in the school that should help children with Tourette's Disorder to learn and adjust more effectively:

1. Educational setting. The ideal setting is one in which children are permitted the freedom of physical movement when their symptoms require it, but one that also offers appropriate environmental cues to guide learning. Thus, a moderate amount of structure seems important. When a child's symptoms are especially severe, it is recommended that the child be able to leave the classroom without special permission and go to a place of "refuge" to continue his or her work (e.g., a resource room, the nurse's office, etc.).

2. Reasonable goals. Giving small segments of work seems to help the child with Tourette's Disorder set reasonable goals and to prevent him or her from being overwhelmed by the complexity of a task or the length of an assignment.

3. Timing. Children with Tourette's Disorder should be allowed to work at their own pace with the least amount of time pressure. The untimed administration of tests in private is especially important, as is allowing rest breaks during long examinations. All of these modifications can help reduce the stress level and allow the child with Tourette's Disorder to perform well.

4. Directions. Most children with Tourette's Disorder need help with directions; having directions repeated, underlining significant words, and sequencing steps for a task can help with this problem.

5. Support. Informing the school personnel, teachers, and peers about Tourette's Disorder is extremely important and relieves the child of having continually to explain his or her behavior. The Tourette Syndrome Association has a number of excellent films and publications that can be used for this purpose. The clinician should be aware, however, that even with the best information and explanations, some school personnel do not believe that the child cannot control the behavior. Moreover, many believe that it is the result of parents' mishandling of the child. Persistence is needed, and sometimes a change in schools may be necessary. If the child is taking medication, it is important to provide the school with information on the potential side effects of the medication. It may also be necessary to help teachers to understand that homework assignments may need to be adjusted for a child who may be relatively symptom-free during the school day but has explosive rates of tics at home.

CASE EXAMPLE

Step 1: Initial Contact

Mrs. Fox called for an appointment for her 7-year-old son, Steve, who had exhibited a recent increase in eye blinking and head jerking. At Steve's last physical examination, she had discussed these behaviors with the pediatrician, who assured her that they were typical for children Steve's age but that they might have gotten worse because of her recent marital separation and the resultant conflict over visitation. The clinician sent Mrs. Fox the Parent Questionnaire, the ECBI, the CBCL, the PSI, and the Habit Diary (Figure 13.2) to complete and return prior to the initial interview. The Parent Questionnaire indicated that Mr. and Mrs. Fox had separated 4 months previously and that Mrs. Fox had returned to school for her teaching degree. This had resulted in a recent move away from the family home near her large extended family, as well as a significant decrease in income. Steve was in second grade at a local elementary school, and his 4-year-old sister was in a day care program. Steve was involved in many after-school activities and had responsibility for age-appropriate chores, which he completed without problems. Mrs. Fox's responses to the other questionnaires indicated that Steve was a compliant child who had an easy temperament and was quite reinforcing to his mother. On the parent domain of the PSI, the only significant score was on the Depression scale, which Mrs. Fox later related to the separation and move. The only problems noted on the CBCL were a high frequency of tics, some worries about these, and a very high activity level.

Step 2: Parent and Child Interview

Parent Interview

Mrs. Fox said that she and Steve had openly discussed his tics and that he was as eager to resolve them as she was. She felt there was no reason not to include him in the interview. Mrs. Fox said that Steve had no significant developmental or medical problems and had not taken any medication in the recent past. Furthermore, Mrs. Fox said that no one else in the family exhibited tics, although her mother had told her that one of her brothers had had similar tics at about the same age as Steve. Mrs. Fox stated that Steve had engaged in some eye blinking at about the age of 4, but that the frequency had decreased up until the present time. She had not noticed any vocal tics. The mother's current concern about the tics resulted from a phone call from the teacher to ask her about them. The teacher felt that other children were beginning to notice the tics and tease Steve. The teacher was also concerned that they might begin to interfere with Steve's ability to sustain attention. Moreover, Steve had asked his mother whether there was anything he could do to stop the tics.

Steve was described as physically active, but this did not bother Mrs. Fox; because he was in an "open" classroom, his high activity level did not cause problems in school. Although he had trouble completing written assignments and attending to academic work beyond 10 minutes, he was doing relatively well in school.

The recent move had been difficult for all of the family, because they had enjoyed close relationships with the extended family and the children's primary playmates had been cousins. They did, however, visit the maternal grandparents every weekend. The parents' separation had occurred after many unhappy years of marriage, although there had been no open parental conflict prior to the separation because Mr. Fox had spent very little time at home. Visitation problems centered around the father's complaints that he was not able to see the children often enough, but Mrs. Fox said he refused to follow a set visitation schedule. The children did not feel they got to see enough of their father, and Mrs. Fox was at a loss as to how to increase their contact with their father.

Child Interview

Steve presented as a pleasant child who interacted freely with the clinician. He readily described family activities and said that he already had made a lot of friends in school. He said that while school was not hard, he sometimes found it difficult to work "all day." It was hard for him to talk about his parents' separation, and he said he wished he could see his father more often. Steve said that the family's daily routine had not changed much since the separation, except that his mother had to study after she put them to bed at night.

Steve said that he wanted to stop blinking and jerking his head because some of the children at school teased him and it embarrassed him. He also felt that the tics made it more difficult for him to complete his work in school. Steve also reported increased compulsive behaviors (e.g., putting his pencil to his mouth and then laying it on the desk before picking it up to write). During the interview, Steve's eye blinks increased when he was talking about the parental separation, and they decreased when he was involved in a game that required concentration.

Step 3: Observation of Behavior

The Habit Diary, which was completed for the half hour after dinner each evening, indicated that Steve blinked 20–30 times on average and that this was often followed by head jerking. There was no specific antecedent to these behaviors; they occurred across a variety of activities; and the mother did not respond to them. Mrs. Fox later admitted that her lack of response was the result of her having made an appointment with the clinician, and that normally (but not consistently) she told Steve to stop. Mrs. Fox was asked to continue to keep track of Steve's tics with the Habit Diary throughout treatment.

During the parent interview, Steve played with cars on the floor, and his tics were quite obvious to the clinician. The mother–child interaction was positive; Mrs. Fox also proudly described Steve's many activities, athletic skills, and good relationship with his 4-year-old sister, who was described as "fun but firey."

Step 4: Further Assessment

At this time there were no major concerns about other areas of development. The mother and teacher, however, were asked to complete the Conners Parent and Teacher Rating Scales to gather further information on possible ADHD.

Step 5: Referral to Allied Health Professionals

Steve had had a recent physical examination, and at this time there was insufficient evidence to suspect Tourette's Disorder.

Step 6: Communication of Findings and Treatment Recommendations

The following information was shared with Mrs. Fox. In general, Steve appeared to be well adjusted in school, with his peers, and at home. It was felt that the recent move and parental separation might have precipitated the tics, which have a high incidence among children Steve's age. It seemed important to decrease Steve's stress in regard to visitation with his father, as well as to provide him with ways to decrease the frequency of tics.

Mrs. Fox was open to the possibility of regular and frequent visitation, and she agreed to ask Steve's father to make an appointment with the clinician or at least to contact her by phone. Mr. Fox refused to do so, however; he said that Steve's problems were all related to the mother's desire to separate, and that if she would return to the marriage Steve would be fine. Mr. Fox also refused to set up a regular visitation schedule. With the clinician's encouragement, Mrs. Fox decided on a visitation schedule that included Mr. Fox's having the children every other weekend and at any other time with 1 day's notice. She further agreed to transport the children to see their father one weekend a month. Mr. Fox was to let them know on the Wednesday before the weekend whether he planned to see the children. Mrs. Fox told the children about this plan; she said that she would send it in writing to their father, but that it was up to him to carry it out. The clinician also wrote a letter to Mr. Fox encouraging him to visit the children on a regular basis. Unfortunately, over the next 4 months, Mr. Fox saw the children for only one full day and several evenings.

Because of his high activity level, Steve was not able to engage in muscle relaxation. Thus he was taught relaxation by deep breathing. He was also taught habit reversal, with the competing response of opening his eyes wide for 30 seconds after each blink or before entering situations that were likely to result in blinking. This was successful in decreasing the blinks to an average of 1–2 in the 30-minute home recording period. The head jerk was also treated through habit reversal by having him tense his neck in response to each head jerk. This tic also decreased within a 2-week period to a frequency of 0–1 during the 30-minute home observation period. Both the mother and teacher indicated that they rarely observed either tic over the next 2 months.

Two months after treatment, Mrs. Fox called to report that Steve was once again engaging in tics, but that this time they involved the jerking of his arm and leg as well as eye blinking. When Steve was seen by the clinician, he was easily taught habit reversal for these new tics. It was significant, however, that the mother reported that Steve would engage in the tics at a very high rate after periods of no tic behavior. Furthermore, though Steve engaged in very low levels of tics during two treatment sessions (apparently in order to please the clinician), the rate of tics increased dramatically after he left the clinic. It was also noted during the treatment sessions that Steve was clearing his throat a great deal, and he offhandedly told the clinician that he had "a tickle in his throat" and probably just needed a cough drop. At this point the clinician began to suspect Tourette's Disorder and referred Steve to a neurologist, who confirmed this diagnosis.

The clinician had the opportunity to work with Steve and his mother over the next 4 years. During this time, Steve's sister was also diagnosed with Tourette's Disorder. The focus of treatment was on helping the family cope with this chronic disorder; it included consultation with the school, psychoeducational evaluations of both children (the sister also proved to have a learning disability), and teaching the children coping skills (defining stressful situations, using relaxation, engaging in habit reversal, and avoiding stressful situations). Mrs. Fox was put in contact with the Tourette Syndrome Association, and both she and the children participated in local chapter meetings. Mrs. Fox became a strong advocate for her children, and provided teachers and the children's classmates with films and handouts describing Tourette's Disorder.

PART IV

CLINICAL

PRACTICE

Chapter 14

A Model

for Clinical

Child Practice

CAROLYN S. SCHROEDER
JUDY MANN

Providing mental health services to children and their families has generally been given a low priority in federal, state, and local funding, as well as in the private sector. Although there are a few notable exceptions (e.g., Head Start), the focus on primary prevention, screening, and early intervention programs is disappointing, especially given the available information on the factors that put children at risk for significant emotional and behavioral problems (see Chapter 2). In addition to the lack of financial resources to provide these preventive services, the number of professionals trained to work with children who evidence significant behavioral or emotional problems is equally small. Fewer than 1% of psychologists focus primarily on serving children (VandenBos et al., 1979), and Tuma (1989) estimates that 70–80% of the children needing mental health services do not get them. There is, therefore, a significant gap between existing needs and services presently provided for children.

Pediatricians are the professionals most likely to encounter children's behavior problems first; indeed, most parents are likely to talk initially to a pediatrician when they have concerns about their children's behavior or development (Clarke-Stewart, 1978; Schroeder & Wool, 1979). Pediatricians are thus in a unique position to provide preventive services, as well as to identify those children and families who are in need of mental health services. It has been estimated that 20% of pediatric primary care patients have biosocial or developmental problems, which, for the pediatrician seeing 27 patients a day, translates into 4 patients per day (American Academy of Pediatrics, 1978). Although the American Academy of Pediatrics (1978) has recommended radical changes in pediatric training that would emphasize the biosocial aspects of patient care, the reality is that pediatricians rarely have the time or the resources to meet these needs.

Another approach to meeting the mental health needs of children is to include mental health workers in the primary care setting. Indeed, as early as 1964 (in his presidential address to the American Academy of Pediatrics), Wilson stated that "one of the things I would do if I could control the practice of pediatrics would be to encourage groups of pediatricians to employ their own clinical psychologists" (p. 988). Work in a primary health care setting does, however, require a shift in the way that mental health services have traditionally been offered: (1) More clients are seen; (2) less time is spent with each client; and (3) clients generally present with less debilitating disorders (Wright & Burns, 1986). The focus is thus on prevention and early intervention rather than on treatment of severe psychopathology. Although this approach is especially reasonable for parents and children, it is not widely practiced and has not received a great deal of attention in the literature or in the training of child mental health workers.

The model to be described in this chapter is based on our work in a primary pediatric practice that has evolved over a period of 19 years. By working in a setting in which children are followed over the course of their development, and a setting that has the trust of both parents and children, we have had the opportunity to help change children's lives at many levels. In addition to developing a variety of preventive programs and clinical services, we have been able to coordinate our work with other community agencies that serve children, as well as to engage in professional training and research. These activities have been described, in part, in other publications (e.g., Hawk, Schroeder, & Martin, 1987; Kanoy & Schroeder, 1985; Mesibov, Schroeder, & Wesson, 1977; Routh, Schroeder, & Koocher, 1983; Schroeder, 1979; Schroeder, Gordon, Kanoy, & Routh, 1983). Because this book has been written as a result of our clinical, training, and research experiences within this practice, we feel that it is appropriate to end it with a summary of the various professional activities, as well as the business aspects of the practice. It is our hope that more child clinicians will see the value and feasibility of serving children within the primary care setting, and that our experiences will provide some guidance to them on how to do this most effectively.

THE CHAPEL HILL PEDIATRICS PROGRAM

Chapel Hill Pediatrics is a private group practice with six pediatricians serving 14,000–16,000 patients in a small university town. Mental health professionals have been involved with the practice since 1973, offering services that have evolved out of the needs of the children and their parents. Although our clients are primarily from the pediatric practice, anyone in the community may use our services, and no referral from a pediatrician is necessary. The primary location of the psychological services is in the pediatric setting, with five offices, a reception/record room, and waiting area. Because of the growth of the practice, we recently acquired space in a building next door, with a large room for group treatment and several offices for diagnostics, research, and administrative purposes.

In 1973, a randomly selected group of parents from the pediatric practice was surveyed, in order to assess the need for mental health services and the types of services desired. As a result of that survey, three services were developed: (1) a "Call-In Hour" twice a week, when parents could ask questions about child development and behavior; (2) weekly evening parent groups, which focused on different ages and stages of development; and (3) a "Come-In" time 2–4 hours a week, to give parents an opportunity to discuss their child-related concerns in greater depth. These services were provided free by psychologists, social workers, nurses, and their students from a developmental clinic at the University of North Carolina Medical School.

In 1982, as a result of requests for more in-depth assessment of school-related problems and short-term treatment for behavioral or emotional problems, Carolyn Schroeder joined the practice on a full-time basis to develop a wider range of services. Currently there are two full-time psychologists and several part-time staff members, including three psychologists, a psychiatrist who does both child and adult work, a clinical social worker, and a child development specialist. The office staff includes a group administrator, an office manager, and several part-time workers to help with filing, scoring of questionnaires, typing, and so forth. Professionals have been selected to join the practice on the basis of identified needs for services. For example, with an increased number of parents being referred for individual work, we added the clinical social worker. The child development specialist was added for her expertise in parent education, and the psychiatrist was added in response to the need for a physician knowledgeable in psychotropic drugs. The group administrator, who shares the authorship of this chapter, recently joined the practice to streamline the business aspects of the practice and to determine more accurately the financial issues involved in providing a full array of free and paid services.

Given that we work in a pediatric setting, and that we focus as much on prevention and early intervention as we do on treating the more traditional mental health concerns for children, we call ourselves "pediatric psychologists." It could be argued that we do what most clinical child psychologists do and that "pediatric psychology" should refer to work that interfaces more closely with medical issues. Fortunately, most children do not have major medical or developmental problems; our goal as psychologists, like that of pediatricians, is to enhance the development of all children and to reduce the number of children with significant emotional and behavioral problems through early identification and intervention. The emphasis should be less on what we call ourselves than on the type of training required to work effectively in a primary health care setting. The question of training can be answered only when we more fully understand the parameters of this work.

Clinical services, community consultation, training, and research have always been integral parts of the practice, with each part stimulating the activities of the other parts. With this recognition, we describe each of these aspects of the practice separately.

Clinical Services

Although our clinical approach has a behavioral orientation, we attempt to take the transactional–developmental perspective that is emphasized throughout this book. The clinical services cover a range of preventive work, screening, assessment, and short- and long-term treatment.

Preventive Services

Preventive services offered include the evening parent groups, a parent library, the Call-In Hour, and parent handouts. The evening parent groups are 1½-hour sessions that focus on different ages and stages in development (Figure 14.1). They are limited to 20 parents each and are organized to include a didactic presentation of material, an opportunity for questions and answers, and the use of handouts that focus on the presented material. These sessions are advertised in the community as well as in the pediatric exam rooms; parents must register in advance, and there is a charge for them. We have not formally evaluated the effectiveness of these groups, but their popularity often results in two separate sessions on the same topic in order to accommodate the number of parents who wish to attend. The pediatricians offer prenatal parent groups, and an ongoing group for mothers of newborns to 6-month-olds is offered by a nurse. The nurse is also available every morning to talk with parents on the telephone about infant and child health and development.

A parent library is another preventive service offered. Parents' first choice of an information source is books or reading material (Clarke-

Parent Group on Child Development and Management

Presented by
Pediatric Psychology of Chapel Hill Pediatrics
at the Pediatric Psychology Annex, 110 Conner Drive, Suite 4, Chapel Hill

FALL EVENING PROGRAM 1990
Thursday Nights 7:30–9:00 PM

Living with Toddlers (18 mo–3 yr)
September 13, 20, 27

9/13 Ages and Stages
9/20 Toilet Training
9/27 Preventing Power Struggles

The Preschooler (3–5 yr)
October 4, 11, 18, 25

10/4 Assessing Your Preschooler's Development
10/11 Sibling Rivalry
10/18 Family Discipline Part I
10/25 Family Discipline Part II

The School-Age Child (6–9 yr)
November 1, 8, 15

11/1 Setting Realistic Expectations
11/8 Developing Cooperation: Chores, Homework, and Relationships
11/15 Discipline Without Shouting or Threatening

The Challenging Adolescent (10–15 yr)
November 29, December 6

11/29 Tips for Parenting during the Adolescent Years
12/6 Balancing Their Needs: Indepence and Rules

FALL LUNCH & LEARN PROGRAM *
Tuesdays, 11:30–12:30

10/30 Tips on Limit Setting   11/27 Building Self-Esteem   12/11 Children and Holidays: Meeting Expectations

SPRING EVENING PROGRAM 1991
Thursday Nights, 7:30–9:00 PM

Living with Toddlers (18 mo–3 yr)
January 10, 17, 24, 31

1/10 Toddler Struggles
1/17 Survival Tactics: Dinner through Bedtime
1/24 Toilet Training
1/31 Discipline: When to Begin

The Preschooler (3–5 yr)
February 7, 14, 21, 28

2/7 Developmental Stages
2/14 Self-Esteem
2/21 Dealing with Your Child's Anger
2/28 Discipline: Being Firm and Consistent

The School Age Child (6–9 yr)
March 7, 14, 21, 28

3/7 Developing Their Sense of Self
3/14 Sibling Rivalry
3/21 Family Discipline Part I
3/28 Family Discipline Part II

The Changing Adolescent (10–15 yr)
April 18, 25

4/18 Adolescence: What to Expect
4/25 Establishing Effective Rules

SPRING LUNCH & LEARN PROGRAM *
Tuesdays, 11:30–12:30

1/29 Building Family Cohesiveness   2/26 Sibling Rivalry   3/19 Balancing Work and Family
4/23 Toilet Training   5/14 Preventing Misbehavior   6/4 Traveling with Children

* Bring a bag lunch; drinks provided.

FIGURE 14.1.   Flyer advertising evening parent groups.

Stewart, 1978), although there is little empirical evidence on the usefulness of books (Bernal & North, 1978). Our parent library was developed in response to the continual requests of parents for reading material on child related issues. The parent library is located in the receptionist's office, and an annotated list of books (organized by topic) in a three-ring notebook is kept in the waiting area. The books can be checked out for 2 weeks at no charge. The books that are included in the library have been selected from the "Books for Parents and Children" section of the *Journal of Clinical Child Psychology* (see, e.g., Schroeder, Gordon, & McConnell, 1987). This section has been published several times a year since 1984 and includes reviews of books on divorce, sexuality education, sexual abuse prevention, learning disabilities, developmental disabilities, general parenting, behavior management, stepparenting, single parenting, death, medical problems, and other topics. These books are widely used by the general pediatric clientele, in addition to being used as adjuncts to treatment. Some of our favorites are described in Appendix C.

The Call-In Hour, offered twice a week, is a time when parents can ask psychologists about common child development and management concerns. From the inception of this program in 1973, a log has been kept of the phone calls received, the nature of the parents' concerns, and the advice given to them. Reports on the types and frequency of problems, as well as the effectiveness of the advice given, have been published in a number of sources (Kanoy & Schroeder, 1985; Mesibov et al., 1977; Schroeder, Gordon, Kanoy, & Routh, 1983). Chapters 2 and 3 include tables summarizing the types and frequency of problems reported by parents of children at different ages. The Comprehensive Assessment-to-Intervention System (CAIS), described in Chapter 3, was developed as a systematic way to assess and offer suggestions to parents who called. Examples of how the CAIS is used are given in Chapter 3 and in Gordon and Schroeder (1990). In general, the suggestions given to parents usually focus on environmental changes, punishing (using time-out or removing privileges) or ignoring inappropriate behavior, and rewarding and encouraging appropriate behavior. An important part of the program is to share information on appropriate developmental expectations and behaviors, so that the parents can put their children's behavior in perspective.

Telephone follow-up indicated that in general the Call-In Hour and specific suggestions were rated highly by parents (Kanoy & Schroeder, 1985). Suggestions for socialization problems (e.g., negative behavior, sibling/peer difficulties, personality/emotional problems) were rated as more effective than those for developmental problems (e.g., toileting, sleep, developmental delays). Only about 25% of the suggestions for sleep and toileting difficulties were rated between 4 and 5 on a 5-point scale (1 = "not helpful" and 5 = "very helpful"), whereas about 75% of those for socialization problems were rated between 4 and 5. Table 14.1 summarizes the types of advice for negative behaviors and toileting problems, and parent ratings of this advice.

Kanoy and Schroeder (1985) found that parents were much more likely to use both the Come-In Service and the Call-In Hour when they had concerns about socialization (about 50% used both services) as compared to developmental problems (fewer than 30% used both services). The increased contact with professionals could account for the parents' finding the suggestions for socialization concerns more helpful. With developmental problems, the parents were concerned about a skill or

TABLE 14.1. Advice Given for Negative Behavior and Toileting, and Parents' Ratings of Effectiveness

	Negative behavior	
Advice	Mean ratings	No. of suggestions
Reward appropriate behavior with stars or charts	4.57	13
Focus more on positive behaviors by giving more praise and special time	4.78	21
Punish inappropriate behavior using time out	4.24	23
Ignore inappropriate behavior	3.58	14
Reassurance to parents that behavior represents a normal developmental stage	4.80	10
Parental consistency, environmental changes, and recommended books	3.65	10
Toileting		
Reward appropriate behaviors such as sitting on toilet or successfully eliminating	3.39	33
Do not be overly punitive when child has accidents	3.85	15
Have child clean up when he or she has accidents	3.10	10
Collect data on number, time, and place of accidents	3.28	11
Provide more consistency (e.g. get the child up at night, use training pants, have the child on a schedule)	3.63	11
Referral for treatment	5.00	3

Note. From "Suggestions to Parents about Common Behavior Problems in a Pediatric Primary Care Office: Five Years of Follow-up" by K. Kanoy and C. S. Schroeder, 1985, *Journal of Pediatric Psychology, 10*, 21–22. Copyright 1985 by Plenum Press, Inc. Reprinted by permission.

ability their children had failed to acquire by the age the parents believed was normal. We found that providing only support and developmental information did not decrease parents' concerns, but that when this information was combined with suggestions for specific actions, the ratings for both information and suggestions increased. The effectiveness of giving specific suggestions was evident for socialization problems (behaviors children *had* acquired that were undesirable). Suggestions such as time-out and rewarding appropriate behaviors with stars gave parents specific strategies to use. These findings led to the development of a series of handouts that are sent to parents who use the Call-In Hour to reinforce specific suggestions. Further follow-up studies will now have to be done to determine parents' perceptions of the effectiveness of these handouts.

One concern that we had with the Call-In Hour was determining when a parent should be referred for more in-depth assessment and/or treatment. If a problem or concern did not remit after two or three contacts, the parents and child were referred elsewhere. In addition, referrals were made when any of the following constellation of problems was evident:

1. A parent had serious personal problems (e.g., depression, marital problems).
2. A child had multiple emotional and behavioral problems that occurred across settings (e.g., home, school, neighborhood).
3. A family had multiple psychological problems or stress events (e.g., several children with problems).
4. The child exhibited behavior that had caused (or could cause) significant physical harm to self or others, or serious property damage.
5. There was evidence or suspicion of child abuse, which was reported to appropriate authorities for further investigation.
6. An infant or preschool child showed delayed development that had been targeted through standardized developmental screening tests and had not responded to stimulation recommendations within a 3- to 6-month period.
7. A child's general development or academic achievement was below the child's, parents', or teacher's expectations.

Over the years, about 17% of the parents using the Call-In Hour have been referred for further assessment/treatment. Those parents who did follow through with the referral rated the suggestion very highly, but 33% of the parents who had been referred did not use the referral suggestion. Now that more clinical services are being offered in the pediatric setting, it is rare that a parent does not follow through with a referral suggestion.

The number of parents who called in with concerns regarding developmental delays led to the routine use of the Denver Developmental Screening Test (Frankenburg & Dodds, 1967) for all children at their 3-year-old checkup. In this way, parents could get direct feedback on how their children were developing, and the number of calls regarding this concern has accordingly dropped.

It had been planned that the handouts developed for the Call-In Hour also would be used in conjunction with well-child physical examinations. For example, the toilet training handout was to be included in the 18-month physical examination. We have discovered, however, that unless the nurses remember to include it with the chart, the pediatricians do not routinely give these to the parents. It is usually at a parent's request for the information that a handout is given. Although this has been rather disappointing, particularly given this group of pediatricians' interest in and support for anticipatory guidance, it is not an atypical problem. One observational study (Reisinger & Bires, 1980) of 23 pediatricians found that the time spent on anticipatory guidance averaged a high of 97 seconds for children under 5 months and a low of 7 seconds for adolescents! One way to ensure that certain areas are discussed with parents both before and after the birth of a baby is to include forms in the patient's medical chart that include the physical and psychosocial areas to be covered at each well-child visit (Christophersen & Rapoff, 1979). Without such a system, it is not likely that this information will be shared with parents at the proper "anticipatory" time.

Direct Clinical Services

In 1982, when the services offered were expanded to include more in-depth assessment and short-term treatment, we were not quite certain about the types of problems that would be referred for these services. The number of referrals made from the Call-In Hour was small and primarily focused on developmental delays, learning problems, and negative behavior. Hawk et al. (1987) did a descriptive study of a random sample of clients seen from 1982 to 1987. At that time our patient data were not computerized, and therefore only rather general statements can be made about the findings. During that 5-year period of time, 681 clients were seen for treatment or diagnostic services. The random sample consisted of 304 (45%) of these parents and children. In that sample, 48% were boys and 52% were girls. The percentages of referrals by age were as follows: birth to 5 years, 34%; 6 to 11 years, 45%; and 12 to 20 years, 20%. The ages with the highest number of referrals were 7 years (11.4%) and 5 years (10.8%). The most frequent problems were negative behavior and child management issues (24.4%); learning problems (18.4%); divorce, stepparenting, and adoption issues (11.5%); and developmental or medical problems (11.4%). There were also a substantial number of children who had suffered a sudden loss of a parent and/or sibling through death or disappearance. These data were fairly consistent with those from the Call-In Hour.

The number of hours spent with families varied rather significantly, depending on the problem. Developmental issues such as sleep, toilet training, enuresis, and encopresis took an average of 2.19 hours; negative behaviors required an average of 5.35 hours; and specific fears and anxieties took an average of 6.75 hours. Children with multiple problems required more sessions: For example, a child who had a sleep problem as well as negative behavior was seen for an average of seven sessions. A child who exhibited problems that were more pervasive and occurred across a number of settings required an average of 54 hours spent with child, parents, school, and other community agencies!

When we began the extended services, our goal was to provide short-term treatment; given the sheer number of referrals, a quick turn-over of clients was required. We have thus been faced with the dilemma of deciding what types of problems are best suited to the primary care setting as opposed to a setting geared to handling longer term clients. Although we could try to focus only on the short-term clients, the reality is that in a population of 14,000–16,000 patients there are probably 140–160 children at any one time who have serious emotional, behavioral, and/or developmental problems. We have discovered that neither the parents nor the pediatricians want us to refer these children out of the practice. They argue for continuity of care and working with people whom they have come to trust.

In addition to new referrals, we have discovered that a number of children and parents return for help repeatedly at different points in the children's development. Initially, we felt that perhaps we had not done a thorough enough assessment and/or treatment the first time around, but the clinical and behavioral data on these cases have all indicated that the initial treatment goals were accomplished. Indeed, these children appear to be more vulnerable to the occurrence of stressful events, and their parents periodically seek help in managing a developmental stage or particular event in their lives. The stresses can be developmental problems, traumatic experiences such as sexual abuse or the death of a parent, environmental instability, parental psychopathology, or behavioral or emotional problems that persist at a subclinical level but are exacerbated by a certain developmental stage. We have come to accept that successful treatment at one point in time does not automatically mean a "cure" for these children, nor does it mean that continued long-term treatment is necessary. As in the moving-risk model described by Gordon and Jens (1988), these children appear to need help at different points in their lives; with this periodic help, they are able to cope with the stresses of life.

Assessment. Assessment is recognized as an integral part of every contact, whether it be talking to a parent who has called for a suggestion on how to handle a specific problem, determining the need for treatment, or gathering and integrating information from multiple sources and with multiple methods to answer specific questions about a child and/or family.

A routine part of the practice is to evaluate children for specific learning disabilities and developmental delays, as well as for purposes of class placement. At one time an educational specialist was part of our group. There are certain advantages to having such a professional within the practice (e.g., ease of communication); however, we found that, given the number of children seen for tutoring, the type of space needed, overhead costs, and so forth, these services did not easily fit into the primary health care setting. Both the educational specialist and our staff have found that referring children out of the clinic for these services is a more feasible solution.

Some assessment procedures that have developed out of our association with the pediatricians include follow-up for children who are on seizure medication, with yearly assessments of cognitive, educational, and behavioral/emotional functioning, as well as assessments before and after changes in medication. If a child is suspected of having Attention-deficit Hyperactivity Disorder (ADHD), we work not only with the child but also with the school and parents to assess the behavior. If medication is used, we collaborate with the child's physician to determine and monitor dosage effectiveness. Every 3–6 months, the teacher is asked to complete the short form of the Conners Teacher Rating Scale (Goyette, Conners, & Ulrich, 1978) for a period of 5–10 days when he or she is blind to the child's medication level. The child's performance on math and written work is also monitored during this time. We are currently developing a more comprehensive assessment and monitoring protocol, based on recent work in the area of ADHD. This protocol will include a more thorough assessment of the child's actual performance on different medication dosage levels (Barkley, 1990).

The pediatric clinic serves as the county medical evaluation center for children who have been neglected or abused. As part of this program, we began assessing the emotional and behavioral status of the children for whom abuse or neglect had been substantiated. This led us to develop the short-term treatment program for sexual abuse described in Chapter 10, as well as to perform the research that is presented in this chapter. One of the pediatricians in the practice (Dr. Charles Sheaffer) is responsible for much of the work on behalf of physically and sexually abused children in North Carolina, and he has been instrumental in getting the state to fund psychological evaluations for children for whom abuse or neglect is suspected or has been substantiated. We are now part of the statewide Child Mental Health Evaluation Program, which involves answering a wide range of referral questions. We may be asked, for example, "Has the child been abused?" "What are the effects of the abuse?" "Is the mother or father capable of protecting the child?" "Does the child need treatment?" "How would the child be affected by going to court?"

Treatment. The child clinician can play a number of roles in the process of providing intervention services to children and families (Gordon & Schroeder, 1990). These may include the following:

1. Educator: Giving specific information, sharing books and other written material, offering parent groups, or helping to develop more realistic expectations.
2. Advocate: Speaking for the child in court, helping the parents negotiate with the educational system, or advocating for the child's needs within the family system.
3. Treatment provider: Giving direct treatment to the child or family, or providing indirect treatment (e.g., intervention in the environment).
4. Case manager: Accessing and networking services to meet the needs of the child and family.

We have found ourselves involved in all of these roles. The role of case manager is particularly pertinent to the primary care setting. This involves networking the often fragmented and specialized services of the community, in order to meet the individual needs of the child and family. This approach, as described by Hobbs (1975), involves looking for unique ways to use the available services as well as for creative ways to develop services that are needed but unavailable. Children with developmental disabilities are most often thought of as in need of case managers, but this is an important role in work with most children and parents. It requires the clinician to be very familiar with the resources available in the community and to become skilled in negotiating cooperation between agencies.

The individual treatment strategies described in this book are the ones most often used in our practice. We also offer group treatment services. In cooperation with the local department of social services, we have developed a group treatment program for children who have been sexually abused and their parents. The goal is to help the children and families deal with the complex emotional sequelae of the abuse and to find ways to cope effectively with the aftermath of the abuse. The children's groups are divided into preschool, elementary school, and adolescent ages, and meet for 10 weekly sessions with a focus on the issues outlined in Chapter 10. The parents meet separately and focus on the effects of abuse, the role of the legal system in abuse cases, problem solving for ways to meet their individual needs, and learning about ways to prevent the abuse from recurring. At the end of these sessions, a determination is made for each child and family regarding the need for further treatment.

Currently, we are developing a number of parent and child treatment groups that focus on specific problem areas or life events, such as ADHD, divorce, social skills, noncompliance, and stepparenting. The empirical literature indicates that we should be able to meet the needs of parents and children in a more cost-effective and efficient manner through groups. Groups also have the advantage of being able to provide support and perspective from parents and children who have experienced similar problems or life events. The goals of these groups will be to provide information, teach principles of learning and behavior management, build parenting and communication skills, and develop problem-solving skills. For some parents and children, this may be the only treatment necessary; for others, group participation may be followed by individual parent or family work.

Community Consultation

Being in a primary health care setting gives the professional a great deal of visibility in the community, and also a great deal of responsibility to advocate for children. We have discovered that when the newspaper wants information about a particular issue (e.g., is it morally right to tell children there is a Santa Claus?) or the court system wants information on a particular problem, they are just as likely to call the pediatric office as parents are to ask the pediatrician for advice on a whole array of issues. We have thus increasingly found ourselves in the position of having to interface with the community on a number of levels.

In the late 1960s and early 1970s, the pediatric office became the coordinator for all the community agencies involved with children who were physically or sexually abused. Regular meetings were held with representatives from the pediatric office, the police department, the schools, and the department of social services, together with mental health professionals from the community. The focus of the meetings was initially educational, but it quickly moved to case management issues. Problems of roles and responsibilities were worked out (sometimes hammered out!), and the result has been an ongoing coordinated community effort on behalf of these children. At times the system falters, especially when new people are added to one of the agencies or new regulations change the nature of the services. However, the short- and long-term benefits of this work cannot be underestimated, as is demonstrated by the statewide Child Mental Health Evaluation Program and the contract with the local department of social services to provide group treatment for all children who have been sexually abused.

Another example of our community involvement is that we first convinced and then consulted with the school system to include sex education and sexual abuse prevention at all grade levels. This involved collaboration with school personnel to develop the program, train the teachers, and inform parents. In addition, both pediatricians and psychologists have been asked to provide training for the North Carolina Guardian Ad Litem program, district court judges, district attorneys, the department of social services, the rape crisis center, the YMCA, day care centers, and many of the other community groups that are involved in the lives of children. We have discovered, however, that all of this work is made possible by the community interaction concerning a particular child or family, which identifies problems and solutions that can then be applied to the benefit of all our children. In the real world, where one must juggle time, economic issues, and altruism, this is as it should be.

Training

Training has always been part of the work in the pediatric office. From 1973 to 1982, graduate students, interns, and postdoctoral fellows in psychology; graduate social work students; and medical students and residents participated in all aspects of the program. In 1982, the Division of Community Pediatrics at the University of North Carolina at Chapel Hill Medical School began a training program for all first-year pediatric residents and fourth-year medical students taking an ambulatory pediatrics elective (Sharp & Lorch, 1988). The goals of the program are to introduce the pediatric trainees to community resources for children and to increase their knowledge of the factors affecting child development. The pediatric psychology practice is one of 25 community agencies involved in this training. This is a unique approach to training pediatricians in the biosocial aspects of development, and in 1984 the program won the prestigious American Academy of Ambulatory Pediatrics Excellence of Teaching Award. The residents and medical students each spend 1 day a week for a month in our office; they learn about the types of developmental and behavioral problems parents bring to the pediatric office, are trained to interview parents and to develop intervention strategies for common problems, and learn what a psychologist has to offer in a primary health care setting and when children should be referred to them. It is our hope that we will alert these residents at an early stage in their careers to the value of psychologists! In the very near future, we plan to do a survey of the graduates of this program to determine how they interface with psychologists. We already know of a number of them who have psychologists in their practices.

Clinical psychology graduate students have continued to participate in the Call-In Hour and to provide treatment one afternoon a week. Most recently, we had our first 2-year postdoctoral fellow in psychology, who was jointly sponsored by our practice and the University of North Carolina Medical School Department of Pediatrics.

Training in a busy private clinic takes time and effort, which in part can be recouped by the trainees' work in the community or with families who cannot afford the full fee for service. The ultimate benefit is having more professionals trained to integrate knowledge from the child development literature into clinical practice.

Research

The primary health care setting is a fertile ground for psychological research. The sheer number of available children who are developing along a normal continuum offers opportunities for interesting developmental research, and the smaller number of children who have chronic physical and behavioral or emotional disorders encourages research on treatment effectiveness as well as longitudinal research on these problems. The primary health care setting also offers the opportunity to evaluate the effectiveness of primary and secondary prevention programs. To do this work, one has to demonstrate credibility within the system by offering a range of high-quality services.

The first 5 years of the expanded practice (1982–1987) were devoted to developing the clinical services, and as we entered another 5-year era we began to look at research issues that were raised by the clinical practice. One study, done as a doctoral dissertation in the University of North Carolina School of Public Health Department of Epidemiology, compared a group of 2- to 7-year-old children who received treatment for noncompliance with a control group matched for age and level of noncompliance (Martin, 1988). In view of the number of children identified with this potentially persistent problem, and the desire to provide early intervention to change the course of the behavior, the research questions were whether the treatment would be effective and (given the age of the children) whether the behavior of the untreated control group would improve without intervention. The parent training program for negative behavior presented in Chapter 11 was used. Martin found that at a 3-month follow-up, the 31 treated children showed clinically and statistically significant decreases in both the number and frequency of behavior problems. The behavior of the 22 untreated control children did not improve over the same time period. Further follow-up of these children will provide more information about the course of this behavior.

Current work involves the collaboration of developmental and clinical psychologists in the study of questions raised by our work with sexually abused children. We quickly discovered that questions asked by the legal system exceeded our knowledge in this area. We were asked, for example, "Can we believe what young children tell us about what has happened to them?" "Can children remember and report events as completely and as accurately as adults, especially when the events may have been traumatic?" "Are children particularly vulnerable to suggestive and leading questions?" "What are the effects of repeated questioning on children's abilities to remember particular events?"

To begin answering these questions, we first looked at the role of prior knowledge. A common belief among professionals who testify in court on behalf of preschoolers who have been abused is that young children's knowledge of sexuality is limited, and therefore that these children cannot describe sexual acts unless they have actually experienced them. To provide empirical evidence for this belief, we studied 192 nonabused children (ages 2–7) to determine their knowledge of gender identity, body parts and functioning, pregnancy and birth, adult sexual behavior, private parts, and personal safety skills (Gordon, Schroeder, & Abrams, 1990a). There were significant age differences in children's knowledge of all areas of sexuality, but under the age of 6 or 7, children had little knowledge of adult sexual behavior. The children's sexual knowledge was directly related to their parents' attitudes about sexuality: Parents with more restrictive attitudes had children who knew less about sexuality than parents who had more liberal attitudes. A second study examined the sexual knowledge of children for whom sexual abuse had been substantiated and an age-matched control group of nonabused children (Gordon, Schroeder, & Abrams, 1990b). This study indicated that sexually abused children do not necessarily have greater knowledge of sexuality than nonabused children of the same age. The children who were sexually abused, however, gave qualitatively unusual responses to the stimulus materials. For example, a 3-year-old withdrew in fright when presented with a picture of a child being put to bed by an adult.

A second line of research focuses on factors that influence the accuracy of children's testimony. This research is supported by a National Institute of Mental Health grant and examines children's memory for a personally experienced event, a physical examination (an analogue to sexual abuse). The purpose of this research is to establish baseline data for children's memory over varying periods of time, and to examine factors that influence children's memory (e.g., repeated interviews, use of props in interviews, and prior knowledge of visits to the doctor). Preliminary data (Ornstein, Gordon, & Larus, in press) indicate that even 3-year-olds remember approximately 80% of the features of a physical examination, with only a slight decay in recall after 6 weeks. Children ages 6 and 7 years remember 90–95% of the features with no decay up to 6 weeks after the event. Furthermore, both younger and older children are able to respond accurately to questions about events that did not occur during the physical examination.

This basic research, born out of our clinical work and carried out by necessity in the primary health care setting, is an excellent example of the type of research that can be done in natural settings. With the advent of computerization, we will be able to track our patient population and our assessment and treatment procedures more effectively. Better evaluation procedures should enable us to report more conclusive findings on the effectiveness of particular mental health services in the primary health care setting.

PRACTICE ADMINISTRATION

Structure of the Practice

An often-asked question is "How does one set up a pediatric psychology practice in a primary health care setting?" It is not dissimilar to establishing a private practice, but the options available to the psychologist in a primary health care setting will depend on the particular health care setting and the relationship the psychologist wants with the other professionals in that setting. It is usually not possible for a psychologist to be a partner in another professional group (e.g., pediatrics); thus, other options for association must be considered. A psychologist may be employed by a pediatric practice, with a fixed salary or a salary based on a percentage of the collected receipts. The amount charged for overhead will vary with the services offered (e.g., telephone, equipment, space, billing, etc.). Another option is for the psychologist to establish an independent practice within the health care setting, with overhead paid for by the psychologist. The administrative functions may be contracted to the pediatric practice or handled independently by the psychologist. Establishing an independent practice within the health care setting gives the psychologist the options of sole proprietorship, a partnership (if more than one psychologist is involved), or a corporation.

A sole proprietorship is owned entirely by one person who gains all the profits and bears the full amount of any losses—to the full extent of personal net worth. All income from the practice is considered personal income and taxed accordingly. A partnership is an association of two or more people who agree to share the ownership of the practice. Each partner may act on behalf of the partnership and bind it contractually, and each is entitled to participate in the day-to-day decisions, subject to the rights and obligations of each partner as defined by a "partnership agreement" drawn up to form the organization. Like a sole proprietorship, a partnership does not pay taxes, but each partner is taxed on his or her share of the profits. The partner is responsible not only for his or her own business decisions and losses, but also for those of all the copartners.

A corporation of any kind is the most flexible business form, providing shareholders (owners) with almost total protection from personal liability and with the most latitude in tax planning. The risks incurred by a corporation encompass only those assets that are in the practice. In other words, the liability of the owners is limited to the assets of the corporation. The corporate structure consists of a board of directors, a president, and the owners. There are federal laws related to corporations, as well as individual state laws. Both the state and federal governments treat a corporation as a separate taxable and legal entity from its owners. In deciding whether to form a professional corporation, the clinician should have the advice of appropriate professionals, including a financial consultant, a lawyer, and a certified public accountant.

In our practice, we chose to form a corporation and for the first 2 years paid the pediatric practice for overhead costs. As the pediatric psychology staff grew, we hired a secretary, obtained separate phone numbers, did our own billing, paid a fixed rent, and so forth, while still being physically located within the pediatric setting.

The space available in a primary health care setting is geared to medical rather than psychological needs; it is therefore important to negotiate for space that will permit privacy, as well as flexibility to serve small children and families for diagnosis and treatment. It has been our experience that private pediatric offices are under renovation every 5–8 years, so although the clinician may have to start with less than optimal space, a goal to improve the space options as the value of the practice is demonstrated is usually realistic.

The practitioner will need to consult an insurance agent for advice concerning insurance against loss and liability. Professional organizations such as the American Psychological Association often offer liability insurance to their members at a reasonable rate. For other insurance needs, such as disability, health, and property insurance, a Certified Life Underwriter (CLU) or Certified Liability and Casuality Underwriter (CLCU) is recommended. These underwriters have met standards to be certified in their fields and have pledged themselves to a strict professional code of ethics. Most insurance agents admit that to serve clients most effectively, the agent must concentrate on only one or two types of coverage; thus, it is wise to get bids on insurance needs and possibly to split coverage between agents. It is important that insurance needs be evaluated at least on a yearly basis.

Careful thought should be given to the model used to handle the accounting functions of a practice. A combination of an accountant for advice and tax preparation, and a bookkeeper for day-to-day accounting needs, usually provides maximum benefit at the lowest cost. Whatever model is used, we recommend that the practitioner have someone who can assist in budget planning and financial projections.

Another important issue in establishing a private practice is obtaining the appropriate state licensure. It is likewise important to know the requirements for licensing/certification of every practitioner in the practice, especially if supervision is necessary. Each state has legislation governing the issuance of licenses from the state's regulatory boards. A business license is also necessary and can be obtained from state or city government. Licenses must be displayed in the practice office and renewed annually.

The Internal Revenue Service (IRS) requires an employer to have a federal employment identification number (FEIN) in order to collect employee taxes; this number is also used in many business transactions. The clinician should contact the nearest IRS office and ask for Form SS-4. Without a FEIN, a clinician's business transactions will be associated with his or her Social Security number, and this could cause problems at tax time.

Personnel and Service

One of the most important decisions made in establishing a private practice concerns the people hired to help carry out the work and provide services to clients. The office personnel must be not only technically competent, but also able to put the clients at ease. Written job descriptions for office personnel are important and should be specific enough to facilitate the evaluation of any employee, yet not so specific as to create an arena for dispute over less important issues. We recommend that the job description make it clear that the employee is expected to maintain an inviting and friendly atmosphere for both clients and practitioners.

All the practitioners in our practice were originally under contract to the corporation, which was set up by Carolyn Schroeder. The practitioners set their own hours and were paid a percentage of the charges generated. Payment was guaranteed regardless of collections, which kept the bookkeeping simple and did not penalize any individual providing a service. Currently, the full-time or near-full-time staff are employees of the corporation but continue to be paid on the basis of charges.

Interdisciplinary Networking

It is imperative to have ongoing interactions with the pediatricians and nurses and in the health care setting. This involves having "down" times during the day, which coincide with times the medical staff members are free and available to "curbside" consultations. This can be difficult if the clinician works on a 30- or 50-minute schedule and the medical staffers work on a 15-minute schedule, but it is possible with careful planning. It is important that the medical staffers know what the clinician is doing and receive timely feedback from the clinician concerning each referral. It is also important to be visible in the community. Talking to parent groups, day care centers, and so forth gives the community an opportunity to know the clinician and the services provided.

Financial Planning and Budgeting

The control and management of income and operating costs are fundamental to the efficient operation of any practice. This involves establishing priorities and objectives, determining a budget, and making a variety of financial projections. Making financial projections is briefly discussed here.

Start-Up Expenses

The costs of setting up a practice go far beyond renting space and buying furniture and equipment. We recommend using a worksheet (see Appendix D) to estimate the costs of starting a practice. Some of the items on the worksheet may not apply to all practices, but careful thought should be given to each item before it is eliminated. A cash fund will be necessary even when money starts coming in from clients.

Operating Expenses

Operating costs include the day-to-day income and expenses of running a practice, as well as estimates on profit or loss. Income is comprised of client and third-party payments (and may also include interest from a savings or checking account). We use a worksheet (see Appendix D) to estimate the profit or loss; we calculate this projection by the quarter and by the year. In the early stages of a practice, we recommend a monthly projection, as it is easy to overestimate the income for the first year and to underestimate the expenses.

Cash Flow

In addition to estimating the profit or loss, we recommend making a month-by-month estimate of cash flow. A cash flow projection gives the practitioner information about when cash comes into and goes out of the practice. It is possible to be making a profit and yet to be short of cash. A cash flow worksheet (see Appendix D) allows an estimate of how much money the practice will have at any given time, and enables the practitioner to pinpoint areas that need attention before danger points are reached. The best guide for this estimate is the historical pattern of receipts. There may be peaks and valleys within the billing and receipts generated in the practice. If there is a cash flow problem, the practitioner may want to consider the following:

1. Develop specific payment policies and communicate them in writing to the staff and clients. For example, have clients sign a contract to make payments on a regular basis.

2. Review the accounts receivable at least monthly. Develop a plan to deal with aging accounts.

3. Learn as much as possible about third-party payers and their reimbursement policies. Be sure to complete the insurance forms accurately and quickly.

4. Advocate payment at the time of service. This is our policy.

5. Charge interest to clients for balances not paid within the contract established for payment. It is essential that the client receive a full explanation of the interest charges. Instead of an interest charge we charge $5.00 for billing that is sent out at the end of the month.

6. Establish a line of credit with a bank.

Balance Sheet

To complete the financial planning, a balance sheet (see Appendix D) should be prepared. This computation shows the properties owned by the practice; the debts owed; and the difference between the two, which constitutes the net worth of the practice. An accountant or bookkeeper can prepare this report. The practitioner should keep in mind, however, that these people may or may not be able to give advice concerning measuring goals and developing contingency plans to correct for financial difficulties.

Business Record System

Although computerization of business records is common, it is not necessary for all practices, as long as a manual system provides all the needed information. If automation is desired, the clinician must consider what system to purchase and its cost. There is a confusing array of hardware and software systems on the market, and the clinician must put some effort into determining specific needs (including short- and long-range goals) before selecting a system. The second author of this chapter, Judy Mann, who is our group administrator found no packaged medical management software system that could provide exactly what we wanted. After consulting with computer experts at a local university, we decided to purchase a data base management system and create our own application. We contracted with a computer specialist in the community for the application development. Our software system runs on an IBM-compatible "clone," a 386 SX processor with an 80-megabyte hard drive, and a Laserjet III printer. The system performs the following functions:

1. Billing system, including record keeping and processing of bills.

2. Practice management statistics, including analysis of various parameters about our practice (e.g., cash flow, referral sources, number of visits, demographics).

3. Practice management reports, including individual practitioner accounts receivable summaries. This report reflects the charges, payments, and "writeoffs" based on month-to-date and year-to-date data. It provides the information needed to pay each practitioner. The report indicates the clients seen, dates of service, procedures, charges, and the amount to be paid to the practitioner.

4. Business bookkeeping, including monthly budget analysis.

5. Budget planning, including constructing spread sheets and "what if" tables.

Policies and Procedures

Appointments

The clinical staff members work a variety of hours, offering an appointment schedule that accommodates most client needs. Each staff person makes his or her own appointments and, on a regular basis, gives these appointments to the secretary to be entered in the central appointment book. We charge for missed appointments unless notice of cancellation is received 24 hours in advance or unless the last-minute cancellation is made necessary by a genuine emergency.

Messages

During regular office hours (8:30 A.M. to 5:00 P.M.), calls are answered by the secretary or office assistant; during evenings and weekends, the calls are answered electronically. Each day, each practitioner schedules a time known as the "Call-Back Hour," and the secretary informs the caller of this schedule for returning calls. We have discovered the advantage of using a telephone record system that provides two copies of the telephone message. One copy is given to the staff person, and the other is retained in the telephone record book. The copy given to the staff becomes a part of the client's record. The system we use has adhesive on the message sheet so that it can easily be attached to a clinical record sheet. Notes are then handwritten on the record sheet concerning the clinician's conversation with the client. This system can be purchased from MILCOM, a division of Hollister, P.O. Box 250, Libertyville, IL 60048; the toll-free number is (800) 243-5546.

Emergency Services

We rotate being "on call" for emergency situations on a daily basis. The person on call makes a decision regarding the best course of action in each situation. If the client's regular clinician is not available, the on-call person either sees the client or arranges for someone else to see him or her. If a client is facing an emergency at the time of the initial contact, we either see the client as soon as possible or arrange for someone outside our practice to do so.

Referrals

When someone is referred to our practice, the secretary obtains the name of the person making the referral, the client's name and age, and a brief explanation of the problem. We have one psychologist who calls all referrals and makes decisions as to the appropriateness of each referral to our practice. If the referral is deemed appropriate, this psychologist works with the other staff members to arrange an appointment, and the secretary then acknowledges the appointment with a letter. If the referral is not appropriate for our practice, the psychologist will recommend several other options to the client. We maintain a file of all referrals not seen in our practice.

Informed Consent

Before their second visit, clients are given a written "informed consent" document to read and sign. In this document we describe our policies regarding appointments, messages, fees and payments, missed or late-cancelled appointments, confidentiality, insurance filing, and release of information. The purpose is to provide the client with all the information that might potentially affect his or her decision to participate in the clinical services offered. The signed informed consent document is part of the client's clinical record.

Fees and Payments

A two-part bill is given to each client at the end of each visit. This bill includes all the information routinely needed for record keeping and for filing health insurance claims. It is our policy that the person who initiates services for a child is the person responsible for payment. We do not bill another person or an estranged spouse unless that individual informs us in writing of his or her willingness to pay for services. Unless coverage is provided by a health maintenance organization (HMO), we do not routinely file insurance claims from our office. We do not accept the responsibility of negotiating settlement on a disputed insurance claim. Fees are payable in full at the end of each visit. As noted earlier, a monthly billing fee of $5.00 is charged against any balance requiring a bill to be mailed at the end of the month.

Clients' Rights and Confidentiality

At any time, our clients may question and/or refuse therapeutic or diagnostic procedures or methods, or gain whatever information they wish to know about the process and course of treatment. Child clients are entitled to the same right of confidentiality as adult clients; however, parents have the right and responsibility to question and understand the nature of our activities and progress with their children.

We let our clients know that we are a collaborative practice of professionals, and that in order to provide them with the best care possible, we consult with one another frequently. On our Parent Questionnaire, which is sent out after the initial contact, we ask parents to give us permission to give and receive information from a child's pediatrician. If permission is granted, a note is placed in the child's medical chart indicating that he or she is being seen by our staff. A brief oral or written report of assessment findings or treatment progress is given to the pediatrician, and this information is put in the child's medical chart at the discretion of the pediatrician.

After the first visit, the client is given a postage-paid questionnaire that assesses the client's experience from reception through therapist's recommendations (the Initial Contact Satisfaction Questionnaire; see Appendix D). Another postage-paid questionnaire (the Parent Satisfaction Questionnaire; see Appendix D) is used near the end of treatment to assess a parent's view of the entire treatment process. As a result of client feedback, continual improvements in the practice are made.

APPENDIX A

Description of
Assessment Instruments

CHILD BEHAVIOR INSTRUMENTS

Child Behavior Checklist (CBCL; Achenbach & Edelbrock, 1983)

The CBCL consists of two forms for children ages 2–3 years and 4–16 years. Parents rate a number of child behaviors (negative) on a 3-point rating scale as "not true," "somewhat or sometimes true," or "very true or often true" for their child. The scores provide a profile of the child's behavior relative to other children of the same age and sex. In addition, summary scores representing Internalizing and Externalizing problems are calculated. There is also a scale measuring Social Competence. The CBCL has been carefully constructed and has generated considerable research, which has indicated its validity for screening for problems in children and measuring the effects of treatment. The CBCL can be obtained from Thomas Achenbach, PhD, University Associates in Psychiatry, Department of Psychiatry, University of Vermont, 1 South Prospect Street, Burlington, VT 05401; (802) 656–4563.

Conners Parent Rating Scale (Goyette, Conners, & Ulrich, 1978)

This rating scale requires parents of children ages 3–17 to rate 48 behaviors on a 4-point scale. Although designed for use in assessing hyperactivity in children, this scale provides a profile of child behavior in five categories: Conduct Problems, Learning Problems, Psychosomatic Problems, Impulsivity–Hyperactivity, and Anxiety. There is also a cluster of items comprising a Hyperactivity Index. Scores on this measure have been shown to discriminate hyperactive from normal children (Conners, 1970) and to be sensitive to the effects of drug treatment (Barkley, 1981). The Conners Parent Rating Scale is available from Multi Health

Systems, 908 Niagara Falls Boulevard, North Tonawanda, NY 14120-2060; (800) 456-3003.

Eyberg Child Behavior Inventory (ECBI; Eyberg & Ross, 1978)

The ECBI consists of 36 common behaviors that are problematic for parents. Parents rate each behavior on a 7-point Intensity scale, and also indicate whether each behavior is a problem for them. Scores indicating clinical significance are 127 or above for the Intensity score and 11 or above for the Problem score. The ECBI is very simple and quick to complete, and thus is appropriate for use with any parents, including those with poor reading skills. Research has provided considerable evidence of its reliability and validity in screening for behavior problems (Eyberg & Ross, 1978) and evaluating the effects of treatment (Eyberg & Robinson, 1982). A copy of the ECBI is included in Appendix B.

PARENT CHARACTERISTICS QUESTIONNAIRES

Parenting Stress Index (PSI; Abidin, 1990)

The PSI provides a measure of the degree of stress in the parent–child relationship. Parents rate 101 items on a 5-point scale, and scores are summed to form 13 subscale scores in two broad domains: stress that results from characteristics of the parent, and stress that results from characteristics of the child. In the parent domain, items cover such areas as Depression, Attachment to Child, Restriction of Role, Sense of Competence, Social Isolation, Relationship with Spouse, and Parent Health. In the child domain, items cover such areas as aspects of the child's temperament (Adaptibility, Demandingness, Mood, Distractibility/Hyperactivity) and the degree to which the child is Acceptable to Parent and Reinforces Parent. The PSI has generated considerable research, and its validity in discriminating clinic-referred from non-clinic-referred children has been demonstrated (Martin, 1988; Mash & Johnston, 1983; Mash, Johnston, & Kovitz, 1983). This measure is particularly helpful in screening for problems in the child's family that may be related to the child's behavior problems and that can be further evaluated as the assessment progresses. The PSI is available from Pediatric Psychology Press, 320 Terrell Road West, Charlottesville, VA 22901.

Dyadic Adjustment Scale (DAS; Spanier, 1976; Spanier & Thompson, 1982)

The DAS consists of 32 items that assess the quality of a marriage. Most items are rated on a 6-point scale; there are a few yes–no questions, and some are rated on a 4-point scale. Research (Spanier, 1976) has shown that married couples differ significantly from divorced couples on each of four factors as well as the total score; means and standard deviations for these two groups are provided. The

DAS is available from Multi Health Systems, 908 Niagara Falls Boulevard, North Towanda, NY 14120–2060; (800) 456–3003.

Beck Depression Inventory (Beck, Ward, Mendelson, Mock, & Erbaugh, 1961)

Because of the extent of the influence of parental depression on child functioning, further assessment of this disorder in parents may be warranted. The Beck Depression Inventory is the measure most commonly used for this purpose. It consists of 21 items assessing "the way you feel today, that is, right now." Reliability and validity have been demonstrated. This instrument is available from the Psychological Corporation, 555 Academic Court, San Antonio, TX 78204-9990.

DEVELOPMENTAL STATUS INSTRUMENTS

Minnesota Child Development Inventory (MCDI; Ireton & Thwing, 1972)

The MCDI was developed for pediatricians and other health care professionals as a means of evaluating the developmental, self-help, and personal–social status of preschool children. It is completed by the parents of children ages 1–6 years, and consists of 320 yes–no questions concerning the child's development. The scores are plotted on a profile giving the child's standing in relationship to children the same age in the areas of General Development, Gross and Fine Motor, Expressive Language, Comprehension–Conceptual, Situation Comprehension, Self-Help, and Personal–Social. Developmental inventories such as this one are given when the referral question raises questions about the developmental status of the child (e.g., inability to perform a specific task, or an expression of concern by the preschool teacher about the child's development). Information from the screening instrument gives an overview of the child's skills in relation to a normative sample. This information, in turn, may lead the clinician to conduct a more in-depth assessment of specific areas of development. The MCDI is available from Behavior Science Systems, Box 1108, Minneapolis, MN 55440.

Vineland Adaptive Behavior Scales (VABS; Sparrow, Balla, & Cicchetti, 1984)

The VABS measures the personal and social sufficiency of individuals from birth to adulthood. It is commonly used with mentally retarded and handicapped individuals, but provides useful information about the development of young children. It is administered through a semistructured interview with parents or primary caregivers; it covers the areas of Communication, Daily Living Skills,

Socialization, and Motor Skills. Scores yield a profile of development relative to children the same age. The VABS is available from American Guidance Service, Inc., Circle Pines, MN 55014-1796.

SCHOOL QUESTIONNAIRES

Preschool Behavior Questionnaire (PBQ; Behar & Stringfield, 1974)

The PBQ is a 30-item checklist designed for use by preschool teachers. Each item is rated on a 3-point scale, and scores are obtained for three subscales: Hostile–Aggressive, Anxious–Fearful, and Hyperactive–Distractible. This questionnaire was standardized on a large population of children ages 3–6, and has been shown to discriminate clinic-referred from non-clinic-referred children. The PBQ is available from Lenore Behar, PhD, 1821 Woodburn Road, Durham, NC 27705.

Sutter–Eyberg Student Behavior Inventory (SESBI; Sutter & Eyberg, 1984)

The SESBI was designed for use with the school-age child, but has recently been standardized for use with preschool children (ages 3–5) as well (Funderburk & Eyberg, 1989). It follows the format of the ECBI in requiring teachers to rate 36 child behaviors on two dimensions, Intensity (of occurrence) and (number of) Problems. On the basis of preliminary data, specific cutoff scores have not been recommended. A score of one standard deviation above the mean (Intensity = 147) may alert the clinician to significant problems in the classroom. Some items are similar to those on the ECBI; others reflect behaviors typically reported as problems by teachers. The SESBI has been shown to discriminate between normal children and those referred for behavior problems. A copy of the SESBI is included in Appendix B.

Child Behavior Checklist—Teacher Report Form (Edelbrock & Achenbach, 1984)

This measure is similar to the parent version of the CBCL, except that in place of the Social Competence scale, an Adaptive Functioning scale has been added. The measure consists of 126 items scored 0 ("none"), 1 ("a little"), or 2 ("a lot"), which yields scores for various factors (variations depend on age and sex) within the two broad dimensions of Externalizing and Internalizing. The measure is well standardized and has demonstrated good reliability and validity. The CBCL for teachers is available from Thomas Achenbach, PhD, University Associates in Psychiatry, Department of Psychiatry, University of Vermont, 1 South Prospect Street, Burlington, VT 05401; (802) 656-4563.

Conners Teacher Rating Scale—Revised (Goyette et al., 1978)

This rating scale consists of 28 items designed to measure hyperactivity and conduct problems in children ages 3–17. This measure has proven reliability and validity, and provides an efficient method for assessing the effects of stimulant medication and other treatment programs in the classroom. The Conners Teacher Rating Scale—Revised is available from Multi Health Systems, 908 Niagara Falls Boulevard, North Towanda, NY 14120-2060; (800) 456-3003.

PERSONALITY AND EMOTIONAL ASSESSMENT INSTRUMENTS

Personality Inventory for Children (PIC; Wirt, Lachar, Klinedinst, & Seat, 1977)

The PIC is the childhood equivalent of the Minnesota Multiphasic Personality Inventory (MMPI). It consists of 600 true–false items that are completed by parents. Separate norms and profiles are available for boys and girls ages 3–5 and 6–16 for 14 clinical subscales and two validity subscales. Although this is an extremely well-constructed and standardized measure, its length makes it less useful than some other shorter instruments. The PIC is available from Western Psychological Services, 12031 Wilshire Boulevard, Los Angeles, CA 90025; (800) 222-2670.

Children's Depression Inventory (CDI; Kovacs, 1981)

The CDI is designed for children ages 7–17 years, and includes 27 items that assess the cognitive, affective, and behavioral signs of depression. For each item, children select one of three alternatives that characterized them during the last 2 weeks. Items are scored 0, 1, or 2, with higher scores indicative of more severe depression. In general, this instrument has demonstrated reliability and validity (Finch, Saylor, & Edwards, 1985), and can be used as one source of information to discriminate clinic-referred from non-clinic-referred children in the area of depression. The CDI is available from Maria Kovacs, 144 North Dethridge Street, Pittsburgh, PA 15213; (412) 624-2043.

Roberts Apperception Test for Children (RATC; McArthur & Roberts, 1982)

The RATC represents an advance in the field of projective testing. This instrument consists of a series of 27 picture cards (only 16 are administered to a child) illustrating common scenes of daily life. Children (ages 6–15) are instructed to tell a story about each picture. The stories are then scored according to eight adaptive scales and five clinical scales. The measure was standardized on a small group of children, and information on reliability and validity is provided in the manual. The RATC is available from Western Psychological Services, 12031 Wilshire Boulevard, Los Angeles, CA 90025; (800) 222-2670.

Child Assessment Schedule (CAS; Hodges, Kline, Stern, Cytryn, & McKnew, 1982; Hodges, McKnew, Cytryn, Stern, & Kline, 1982)

The CAS is a semistructured interview for use with children ages 7–12. It consists of 75 items about school, friends, family, self-concept, behavior, mood and thought disorders; these are scored "yes," "no," "ambiguous," "no response," or "not applicable." Items are designed to coordinate with *Diagnostic and Statistical Manual of Mental Disorders*, third edition (DSM-III) diagnoses. Reasonable reliability and validity have been reported. A modified version of the CAS, developed for use with the DSM-III-R (American Psychiatric Association, 1987), is available from Dr. Kay Hodges, Eastern Michigan University, 537 Mark Jefferson, Ypsilanti, MI 48197.

Semistructured Clinical Interview for Children Aged 6–11 (SCIC; McConaughy & Achenbach, 1990)

The SCIC consists of questions and tasks covering seven areas of child functioning: (1) Activities, School, Friends; (2) Family Relations; (3) Fantasies; (4) Self-Perception, Feelings; (5) Parent/Teacher-Reported Problems; (6) Achievement Tests; and (7) Screen for Fine and Gross Motor Abnormalities. Forms are also provided for scoring interviewer observations of the child's behvior and the child's self report of his or her own behavior and feelings. The entire interview is scored according to Achenbach's Conceptualization of two broad-band scales (Internalizing, Externalizing) and eight narrow-band scales (Inept, Unpopular, Anxious, Withdrawn/Depressed, Inattentive/Hyperactive, Resistant, Family Problems, Aggressive). Scales were derived by factor analysis of interviews with 108 clinic-referred children. Reliability and validity data are provided but normative data are not yet available. The SCIC can be obtained from Thomas Achenbach, PhD, University Associates in Psychiatry, University of Vermont, 1 South Prospect Street, Burlington, VT 05401; (802) 656-4563.

Children's sentence completion tasks

There are many versions of children's sentence completion tasks; the one used in our practice is provided in Appendix B. Although these are not typically standardized, they do provide one means of gathering important information from children. Older children can write their answers, and younger children can respond orally. The clinician can then go back over some of the responses to clarify or expand on the information provided. We have found it best not to do this while a child is completing the task, as the constant interruption tends to disrupt the child's responses.

Pictorial Scale of Perceived Competence and Social Acceptance for Young Children (Harter & Pike, 1984); Self-Perception Profile for Children (Harter, 1983b)

These two instruments are efficient measures of children's self-concept. There are two versions of the former scale—one for preschool and kindergarten children, and one for first- and second-graders. Both consist of 24 items in two scales. The child is asked to choose which of two pictures is more like himself or herself, and to indicate whether he or she is always like that or usually like that. The latter scale is for children in third through seventh grades and consists of 36 items in six scales. The format is similar to the measure for younger children, in that the child is presented with two statements and asked to choose which is more like him or her. Teacher rating scales that are comparable to both the younger and older versions are also available. Reliability and validity of these two measures have been documented. Copies are available from Susan Harter, PhD, HD 09613, University of Denver, 2040 South York Street, Denver, CO 80208.

Nowicki–Strickland Locus of Control Scale for Children

This scale consists of 40 questions that measure internal–external locus of control. The child responds "yes" or "no" to each item, and a total score is obtained that indicates degree of externality (high scores indicate external locus of control; low scores indicate internal locus of control). Split-half and test–retest reliabilities are adequate (Nowicki & Strickland, 1973). The scale correlates significantly with measures of achievement; higher scores are related to lower achievement. A copy of the scale, with norms and scoring instructions, is included in Appendix B.

ANXIETY AND FEAR INVENTORIES

Fear Survey Schedule for Children—Revised (FSSC-R; Ollendick, 1983; Ollendick, King, & Frary, 1989)

The FSSC-R is an 80-item questionnaire revised from the original scale published by Scherer and Nakamura (1968). It is used with children ages 7–18 (and can also be used with developmentally delayed children). The FSSC-R documents both the number and intensity of fears on a 3-point scale ("none," "some," "a lot"). The FSSC-R is a well-normed, reliable, and valid instrument that provides a good pre- and posttreatment outcome measure and is helpful in identifying specific fears for individual children. A copy, with norms and scoring instructions, is included in Appendix B.

Revised Children's Manifest Anxiety Scale
(Reynolds & Richmond, 1978)

Also called "What I Think and Feel," this measure is a 37-item scale that uses a true–false format to measure anxiety in children ages 6–19 years. The items are written at a third-grade reading level, and children can complete it independently or have it read to them. The scale is reliable, and age norms are available. The scale is available from Western Psychological Services, 12031 Wilshire Boulevard, Los Angeles, CA 90025; (800) 222-2670.

State–Trait Anxiety Inventory for Children
(STAIC; Spielberger, 1973)

The STAIC includes two 20-item self-report scales for children ages 9–12 years, although the manual states that is can be used with younger children who are average or above in reading ability and with older children who are below average in reading ability. Norms are provided for fourth-, fifth-, and sixth-graders. The STAIC measures enduring tendencies to experience anxiety (Trait Anxiety) and temporal or situational variations in levels of anxiety (State Anxiety). Test–retest reliability coefficients for the Trait Anxiety scale are moderate, but considerably higher than those for the State Anxiety scale. Evidence for concurrent and construct validity is provided in the manual. The STAIC is available from Consulting Psychologists Press, 577 College Avenue, Palo Alto, CA 94306.

Louisville Fear Survey Schedule for Children
(Miller, Barrett, Hampe, & Noble, 1972)

This is an 81-item inventory, with intensity rated on a 3-point scale ("no fear," "reasonable fear," "excessive fear"), for children ages 4–18 years. It can be completed by children or caregivers, but there is little congruence between child and parent ratings. Internal consistency is high, but there are no data on temporal stability or validity, and there are no norms. It is useful in screening and in the assessment of the generalized effects of fears. It can be obtained from Lovick C. Miller, Child Psychiatry Research Center, 608 South Jackson Street, Louisville, KY 40202.

APPENDIX B

Assessment Instruments

APPENDIX B.1
Parent Questionnaire

DATE _____ FORM COMPLETED BY _____

CHILD'S NAME _____ M □ F □ BIRTHDATE _____

ADDRESS _____
      Street   City   State   County   Zip
Code

HOME TELEPHONE _____ BUSINESS PHONE (Mother) _____ (Father) _____

WHO REFERRED THE CHILD? _____
                      Name   Address

CHILD'S PRIMARY PHYSICIAN _____ INSURANCE COMPANY _____

FAMILY

Father's Name _____ Birthdate: _____

Occupation: _____ Educational level: _____ No. of Dependents: _____

Mother's Name _____ Birthdate: _____

Occupation: _____ Educational level: _____ No. of Dependents: _____

Date of Marriage: _____ Present Marital Status: _____

With whom does the child live: Birth Parents? _____ Adoptive Parents? _____

    Foster Parents? _____ Other (Specify) _____

List all *other* persons living in the home.

Name	Age	Relationship to child	Present health

List any other people who care for the child a significant amount of time.

Name	Relationship to child (grandmother, neighbor, etc.)

CHILD

Pregnancy and Birth: any complications? _____

If yes, briefly explain: _____

_____

Developmental Milestones: (Ages) Sitting _____ Walking _____ Talking _____
Toilet-Trained _____

Medical Problems: _____ Yes _____ No

If yes, briefly explain: _____

_____

_____

What are your child's favorite recreational or extracurricular activities? _____

_____

_____

Comments: _____

_____

_____

_____

_____

Who generally disciplines the child? _____

What methods are used? _____

_____

_____

_____

_____

_____

_____

Do parents agree on methods of discipline? _____ Elaborate, if no: _____

_____

_____

_____

_____

SCHOOL HISTORY

Has child been enrolled in nursery or day care? _____ At what age? _____

Has child attended kindergarten? _____ At what age? _____

Has child begun elementary school? _____ At what age did he/she enter first
grade? _____

What is present grade?_____

If your child has ever been to school (including nursery, kindergarten, and grade school), complete the following for all classes beginning with nursery and ending with current placement. Please indicate if your child repeated or is in a special class (gifted, learning-disabled, emotionally handicapped, etc.)

Grade	School	Comments
_____	_____	_____
_____	_____	_____
_____	_____	_____
_____	_____	_____
_____	_____	_____

Current school performance—for children aged 6 and older:

_____ Does not go to school

	Failing	Below Average	Average	Above Average
a. Reading	_____	_____	_____	_____
b. Writing	_____	_____	_____	_____
c. Arithmetic or math	_____	_____	_____	_____
d. Spelling	_____	_____	_____	_____

Other academic subjects (history, science, foreign language, geography, etc.)

e. _____	_____	_____	_____	_____
f. _____	_____	_____	_____	_____
g. _____	_____	_____	_____	_____

PARENTAL CONCERNS

What do you feel is your child's main problem? _____

_____

_____

What do you feel caused your child's problem? _____

_____

_____

_____

_____

What have you been told by doctors, teachers, and/or others about your child's problems? _____

_____

_____

_____

Has this child had any other mental health evaluations or treatment? _____

_____

_____

Has any other member of child's immediate family had mental health treatment?

_____

_____

Other comments: _____

_____

_____

May we contact the child's primary physician?

_____ to receive information

_____ to give information

                                             _____

                                             (Signed) Parent or Guardian

APPENDIX B.2
Daily Log

Record a brief summary of both appropriate and inappropriate behavior each day. Give each day's overall behavior a rating from 0 to 10, with 0 being "dreadful" and 10 being "fantastic!"

Date	Appropriate Behavior	Inappropriate Behavior	Overall Rating (0 to 10)

From *Assessment and Treatment of Childhood Problems: A Clinician's Guide* by Carolyn S. Schroeder and Betty N. Gordon. © 1991 by The Guilford Press.

APPENDIX B.3
Specific Events Causing Concern

Child's Name: _____

Initial	Date	Time	What happened?	What did you do?	Child's reaction?

From Assessment and Treatment of Childhood Problems: A Clinician's Guide by Carolyn S. Schroeder and Betty N. Gordon. © 1991 by The Guilford Press.

Elementary School Questionnaire

DATE FORM COMPLETED: _____

CHILD: _____
     (Name)   (Age)   (Grade)

SCHOOL INFORMATION

SCHOOL: _____ ADDRESS: _____
                       (Street)   (City)   (Zip)

TEACHERS AND SCHOOL PERSONNEL WHO WORK WITH THE CHILD:

_____   _____
          (Name)   (Subject)

_____   _____
          (Name)   (Subject)

_____   _____
          (Name)   (Subject)

PRINCIPAL: _____ Telephone: _____

COUNSELOR OR SCHOOL PSYCHOLOGIST: _____

Is the child enrolled in any special programs? _____ If so, please specify: _____

BEHAVIOR INFORMATION

Please rank the following behaviors on a 1–4 scale: 1 = "no problem," 4 = "severe problem."

	1	2	3	4
1. Behavior				
2. Speech				
3. Language				
4. Reading				
5. Writing				
6. Arithmetic				
7. Home Background				
8. Intelligence Level				
9. Physical Problem (please list)				
10. Other (specify) _____				

Do you feel the child is functioning grade-appropriately in:

	Yes	No	Comments
Academics			
Behavior			
Social Adjustment w/peers			
Social Adjustment w/adults			

Please list the child's strengths and weaknesses as you see them in the *classroom*.

Strengths:

Weaknesses:

SCHOLASTIC INFORMATION

Check known problem areas; cross out skills not yet taught.

READING

Listening Comprehension and Speech
_____ Comprehension of orally
     presented material
_____ Expressive language
_____ Speech (intelligibility)
_____ Other _____
Visual Perception
_____ Matching letters
_____ Copying letters
_____ Identifying letters
Word Analysis Abilities
_____ Using phonic skills
_____ Using structural analysis (syllables,
     root words, etc.)
_____ Using context clues
_____ Sight vocabulary
Reading Comprehension
_____ Gets main idea
_____ Singles out details
_____ Sequences events
_____ Draws inferences
_____ Follows written directions
_____ Recall of material
_____ Other _____

Present level: _____

Book: _____

Publisher: _____

Note any significant reading behaviors
(slow, reversals, loses place easily, etc.):

_____

_____

_____

SPELLING AND WRITTEN LANGUAGE

____ Letter–sound relationships
  (phonics)
____ Irregular words (nonphonetic)
____ Oral spelling
____ Written spelling
____ Syntax
____ Sequencing events
____ Other _____

ARITHMETIC

Present level: _____

Number Concepts

Book: _____

____ Meaning of bigger (more), smaller
  (less,) same as (number
  vocabulary)
____ Number recognition
____ Counting orally
____ Counting objects
____ Sequencing alternate numbers (by
  2's, 5's, 100's, etc.)
____ Meaning of +, −, = signs
Computation
____ Meaning of place values (ones,
  tens, hundreds, etc.)
____ Simple addition facts
____ Simple subtraction facts
____ Regrouping (borrowing and
  carrying)
____ Multiplication tables
____ Division tables
____ Telling time
____ Fractions
____ Decimals
____ Word problems
____ Money values
____ Other _____

What remedial and/or behavioral techniques have been attempted with the child?
(Please be as specific as possible)

If the child has an IEP, please send us a copy.

SCHOOL EXPECTATIONS

What information from our evaluation would be helpful in planning for the child?

_____ Specific academic suggestions, particularly _____
(this is not an individual prescription)
_____ Behavioral management suggestions
_____ Intellectual functioning
_____ Suggestions for class placement
_____ Materials suggestions
_____ None
_____ Other (specify) _____

Please sign:

_____   _____
              (Principal)   (Teacher[s] completing this form)

                                         _____

                                         _____

                                         _____

From *Assessment and Treatment of Childhood Problems: A Clinician's Guide* by Carolyn S. Schroeder and Betty N. Gordon. © 1991 by The Guilford Press.

Eyberg Child Behavior Inventory
(Reprinted by permission of Sheila Eyberg)

Parent: _____
Child: _____
Date: _____

Below are a series of phrases that describe children's behavior.

How often does this occur with your child?

	Never	Seldom	Sometimes	Often	Always		Is this a problem for you?
1. Dawdles in getting dressed	1	2	3	4	5	6	7	Yes	No
2. Dawdles or lingers at mealtime	1	2	3	4	5	6	7	Yes	No
3. Has poor table manners	1	2	3	4	5	6	7	Yes	No
4. Refuses to eat food presented	1	2	3	4	5	6	7	Yes	No
5. Refuses to do chores when asked	1	2	3	4	5	6	7	Yes	No
6. Slow in getting ready for bed	1	2	3	4	5	6	7	Yes	No
7. Refuses to go to bed on time	1	2	3	4	5	6	7	Yes	No
8. Does not obey house rules on his own	1	2	3	4	5	6	7	Yes	No
9. Refuses to obey until threatened with punishment	1	2	3	4	5	6	7	Yes	No
10. Acts defiant when told to do something	1	2	3	4	5	6	7	Yes	No
11. Argues with parents about rules	1	2	3	4	5	6	7	Yes	No
12. Gets angry when doesn't get his own way	1	2	3	4	5	6	7	Yes	No
13. Has temper tantrums	1	2	3	4	5	6	7	Yes	No
14. Sasses adults	1	2	3	4	5	6	7	Yes	No

15. Whines	1	2	3	4	5	6	7	Yes	No
16. Cries easily	1	2	3	4	5	6	7	Yes	No
17. Yells or screams	1	2	3	4	5	6	7	Yes	No
18. Hits parents	1	2	3	4	5	6	7	Yes	No
19. Destroys toys and other objects	1	2	3	4	5	6	7	Yes	No
20. Is careless with toys and other objects	1	2	3	4	5	6	7	Yes	No
21. Steals	1	2	3	4	5	6	7	Yes	No
22. Lies	1	2	3	4	5	6	7	Yes	No
23. Teases or provokes other children	1	2	3	4	5	6	7	Yes	No
24. Verbally fights with friends his own age	1	2	3	4	5	6	7	Yes	No
25. Verbally fights with sisters and brothers	1	2	3	4	5	6	7	Yes	No
26. Physically fights with friends his own age	1	2	3	4	5	6	7	Yes	No
27. Physically fights with sisters and brothers	1	2	3	4	5	6	7	Yes	No
28. Constantly seeks attention	1	2	3	4	5	6	7	Yes	No
29. Interrupts	1	2	3	4	5	6	7	Yes	No
30. Is easily distracted	1	2	3	4	5	6	7	Yes	No
31. Has short attention span	1	2	3	4	5	6	7	Yes	No
32. Fails to finish tasks or projects	1	2	3	4	5	6	7	Yes	No
33. Has difficulty entertaining himself alone	1	2	3	4	5	6	7	Yes	No
34. Has difficulty concentrating on one thing	1	2	3	4	5	6	7	Yes	No
35. Is overactive or restless	1	2	3	4	5	6	7	Yes	No
36. Wets the bed	1	2	3	4	5	6	7	Yes	No

APPENDIX B.6
Sutter–Eyberg Student Behavior Inventory
(Reprinted by permission of Sheila Eyberg.)

Rater's Name _____   Child's Name _____
Relationship to Child _____   Child's Age _____
Date of Rating _____   Child's Sex _____

Directions: Below are a series of phrases that describe children's behavior. Please (1) circle the number describing *how often* the behavior currently occurs with this student, and (2) circle either "yes" or "no" to indicate whether the behavior is *currently a problem*.

	How often does this occur with this student?							Is this a problem for you?	
	Never	Seldom		Sometimes		Often	Always		
1. Dawdles in obeying rules or instructions	1	2	3	4	5	6	7	Yes	No
2. Argues with teachers about rules or instructions	1	2	3	4	5	6	7	Yes	No
3. Has difficulty accepting criticism or correction	1	2	3	4	5	6	7	Yes	No
4. Does not obey school rules on his/her own	1	2	3	4	5	6	7	Yes	No
5. Refuses to obey until threatened with punishment	1	2	3	4	5	6	7	Yes	No
6. Gets angry when doesn't get his/her own way	1	2	3	4	5	6	7	Yes	No
7. Acts defiant when told to do something	1	2	3	4	5	6	7	Yes	No
8. Has temper tantrums	1	2	3	4	5	6	7	Yes	No
9. Sasses teacher(s)	1	2	3	4	5	6	7	Yes	No
10. Whines	1	2	3	4	5	6	7	Yes	No
11. Cries	1	2	3	4	5	6	7	Yes	No

	1	2	3	4	5	6	7		
12. Pouts	1	2	3	4	5	6	7	Yes	No
13. Yells or screams	1	2	3	4	5	6	7	Yes	No
14. Hits teacher(s)	1	2	3	4	5	6	7	Yes	No
15. Is careless with books and other objects	1	2	3	4	5	6	7	Yes	No
16. Destroys books and other objects	1	2	3	4	5	6	7	Yes	No
17. Steals	1	2	3	4	5	6	7	Yes	No
18. Lies	1	2	3	4	5	6	7	Yes	No
19. Makes noises in class	1	2	3	4	5	6	7	Yes	No
20. Teases or provokes other students	1	2	3	4	5	6	7	Yes	No
21. Acts bossy with other students	1	2	3	4	5	6	7	Yes	No
22. Verbally fights with other students	1	2	3	4	5	6	7	Yes	No
23. Physically fights with other students	1	2	3	4	5	6	7	Yes	No
24. Demands teacher attention	1	2	3	4	5	6	7	Yes	No
25. Interrupts teachers	1	2	3	4	5	6	7	Yes	No
26. Interrupts other students	1	2	3	4	5	6	7	Yes	No
27. Has difficulty entering groups	1	2	3	4	5	6	7	Yes	No
28. Has difficulty sharing materials	1	2	3	4	5	6	7	Yes	No
29. Is uncooperative in group activities	1	2	3	4	5	6	7	Yes	No
30. Blames others for problem behaviors	1	2	3	4	5	6	7	Yes	No
31. Is easily distracted	1	2	3	4	5	6	7	Yes	No
32. Has difficulty staying on task	1	2	3	4	5	6	7	Yes	No
33. Acts frustrated with difficult tasks	1	2	3	4	5	6	7	Yes	No
34. Fails to finish tasks or projects	1	2	3	4	5	6	7	Yes	No
35. Impulsive, acts before thinking	1	2	3	4	5	6	7	Yes	No
36. Is overactive or restless	1	2	3	4	5	6	7	Yes	No

APPENDIX B.7
Children's Sentence Completion Form
(the sentence completion task used in our clinic)

Name _____ Date _____ Age _____ Grade _____

Finish all the following sentences. Write down the first thing you think of.

1. I would like to _____
2. My neighborhood _____
3. I wish that I _____
4. School is _____
5. I cannot _____
6. I get mad when _____
7. I think girls are _____
8. My greatest fear is _____
9. My mother _____
10. I worry _____
11. There are times when _____
12. I think boys are _____
13. I hate _____
14. When I grow up _____
15. It isn't nice to _____
16. My father _____
17. I don't like _____
18. People think that I _____
19. Mother should _____
20. I need _____
21. My teacher _____
22. When I was younger _____
23. Father should _____
24. Sometimes I think about _____
25. Sex is _____
26. I feel lonesome _____
27. At night when I can't sleep I _____
28. I love _____
29. Nobody knows that _____
30. If I could change one thing about myself I would _____
31. The last dream I remember was about _____
32. The best thing that ever happened to me was _____
33. The worst thing that ever happened to me was _____
34. The earliest thing I remember _____
    (How old were you?) _____
35. I feel sad _____
36. If I could have three wishes I would wish for:
    a. _____
    b. _____
    c. _____
37. The thing I do best is _____
38. The thing I do worst is _____
39. It is fun to _____
40. My favorite joke is _____

From *Assessment and Treatment of Childhood Problems: A Clinician's Guide* by Carolyn S. Schroeder and Betty W. Gordon. © 1991 by The Guilford Press.

Fear Survey Schedule for Children—Revised (FSSC-R), with scoring procedures and normative data

NAME: _____ AGE: _____ DATE: _____

DIRECTIONS: A number of statements which boys and girls use to describe the fears they have are given below. Read each fear carefully and put an X in the box in front of the words that describe your fear. There are no right or wrong answers. Remember, find the words which best describe how much fear you have.

1. Giving an oral report	☐ None	☐ Some	☐ A lot
2. Riding in the car or bus	☐ None	☐ Some	☐ A lot
3. Getting punished by mother	☐ None	☐ Some	☐ A lot
4. Lizards	☐ None	☐ Some	☐ A lot
5. Looking foolish	☐ None	☐ Some	☐ A lot
6. Ghosts or spooky things	☐ None	☐ Some	☐ A lot
7. Sharp objects	☐ None	☐ Some	☐ A lot
8. Having to go to the hospital	☐ None	☐ Some	☐ A lot
9. Death or dead people	☐ None	☐ Some	☐ A lot
10. Getting lost in a strange place	☐ None	☐ Some	☐ A lot
11. Snakes	☐ None	☐ Some	☐ A lot
12. Talking on the telephone	☐ None	☐ Some	☐ A lot
13. Roller coaster or carnival rides	☐ None	☐ Some	☐ A lot
14. Getting sick at school	☐ None	☐ Some	☐ A lot
15. Being sent to the principal	☐ None	☐ Some	☐ A lot
16. Riding on the train	☐ None	☐ Some	☐ A lot
17. Being left at home with a sitter	☐ None	☐ Some	☐ A lot
18. Bears or wolves	☐ None	☐ Some	☐ A lot
19. Meeting someone for the first time	☐ None	☐ Some	☐ A lot
20. Bombing attacks—being invaded	☐ None	☐ Some	☐ A lot
21. Getting a shot from the nurse or doctor	☐ None	☐ Some	☐ A lot
22. Going to the dentist	☐ None	☐ Some	☐ A lot
23. High places like mountains	☐ None	☐ Some	☐ A lot
24. Being teased	☐ None	☐ Some	☐ A lot
25. Spiders	☐ None	☐ Some	☐ A lot

26. A burglar breaking into our house	☐ None	☐ Some	☐ A lot
27. Flying in a plane	☐ None	☐ Some	☐ A lot
28. Being called on by the teacher	☐ None	☐ Some	☐ A lot
29. Getting poor grades	☐ None	☐ Some	☐ A lot
30. Bats or birds	☐ None	☐ Some	☐ A lot
31. My parents criticizing me	☐ None	☐ Some	☐ A lot
32. Guns	☐ None	☐ Some	☐ A lot
33. Being in a fight	☐ None	☐ Some	☐ A lot
34. Fire—getting burned	☐ None	☐ Some	☐ A lot
35. Getting a cut or injury	☐ None	☐ Some	☐ A lot
36. Being in a big crowd	☐ None	☐ Some	☐ A lot
37. Thunderstorms	☐ None	☐ Some	☐ A lot
38. Having to eat some food I don't like	☐ None	☐ Some	☐ A lot
39. Cats	☐ None	☐ Some	☐ A lot
40. Failing a test	☐ None	☐ Some	☐ A lot
41. Being hit by a car or truck	☐ None	☐ Some	☐ A lot
42. Having to go to school	☐ None	☐ Some	☐ A lot
43. Playing rough games during recess	☐ None	☐ Some	☐ A lot
44. Having my parents argue	☐ None	☐ Some	☐ A lot
45. Dark rooms or closets	☐ None	☐ Some	☐ A lot
46. Having to put on a recital	☐ None	☐ Some	☐ A lot
47. Ants or beetles	☐ None	☐ Some	☐ A lot
48. Being criticized by others	☐ None	☐ Some	☐ A lot
49. Strange-looking people	☐ None	☐ Some	☐ A lot
50. The sight of blood	☐ None	☐ Some	☐ A lot
51. Going to the doctor	☐ None	☐ Some	☐ A lot
52. Strange or mean-looking dogs	☐ None	☐ Some	☐ A lot
53. Cemeteries	☐ None	☐ Some	☐ A lot
54. Getting a report card	☐ None	☐ Some	☐ A lot
55. Getting a haircut	☐ None	☐ Some	☐ A lot
56. Deep water or the ocean	☐ None	☐ Some	☐ A lot
57. Nightmares	☐ None	☐ Some	☐ A lot
58. Falling from high places	☐ None	☐ Some	☐ A lot
59. Getting a shock from electricity	☐ None	☐ Some	☐ A lot
60. Going to bed in the dark	☐ None	☐ Some	☐ A lot

61. Getting carsick	☐ None	☐ Some	☐ A lot
62. Being alone	☐ None	☐ Some	☐ A lot
63. Having to wear clothes different from others	☐ None	☐ Some	☐ A lot
64. Getting punished by my father	☐ None	☐ Some	☐ A lot
65. Having to stay after school	☐ None	☐ Some	☐ A lot
66. Making mistakes	☐ None	☐ Some	☐ A lot
67. Mystery movies	☐ None	☐ Some	☐ A lot
68. Loud sirens	☐ None	☐ Some	☐ A lot
69. Doing something new	☐ None	☐ Some	☐ A lot
70. Germs or getting a serious illness	☐ None	☐ Some	☐ A lot
71. Closed places	☐ None	☐ Some	☐ A lot
72. Earthquakes	☐ None	☐ Some	☐ A lot
73. Russia	☐ None	☐ Some	☐ A lot
74. Elevators	☐ None	☐ Some	☐ A lot
75. Dark places	☐ None	☐ Some	☐ A lot
76. Not being able to breathe	☐ None	☐ Some	☐ A lot
77. Getting a bee sting	☐ None	☐ Some	☐ A lot
78. Worms or snails	☐ None	☐ Some	☐ A lot
79. Rats or mice	☐ None	☐ Some	☐ A lot
80. Taking a test	☐ None	☐ Some	☐ A lot

Scoring Procedures

Record 1 ("none"), 2 ("some"), or 3 ("a lot") for each item. To determine intensity scores for each factor, sum across items within each factor. To determine total intensity scores, sum across factors. To determine frequency scores, total the number of items scored 3 across the five factors.

Failure and Criticism

1 ___	15 ___	29 ___	42 ___	54 ___	66 ___
3 ___	19 ___	31 ___	44 ___	63 ___	69 ___
5 ___	24 ___	38 ___	46 ___	64 ___	80 ___
14 ___	28 ___	40 ___	48 ___	65 ___	Total _____

The Unknown

6 ___	17 ___	45 ___	56 ___	62 ___	71 ___
9 ___	36 ___	49 ___	57 ___	67 ___	74 ___
13 ___	37 ___	53 ___	60 ___	68 ___	75 ___	Total _____

Minor Injury and Small Animals

4 ___	18 ___	32 ___	39 ___	50 ___	78 ___
7 ___	25 ___	33 ___	43 ___	52 ___	79 ___
11 ___	30 ___	35 ___	47 ___	77___	

Total _____

Danger and Death

10 ___	26 ___	58 ___	72 ___
20 ___	34 ___	59 ___	73 ___
23 ___	41 ___	70 ___	76 ___

Total _____

Medical Fears

8 ___	22 ___
21 ___	51

Total _____

Intensity Total _____

Normative Data

Age and sex	Frequency of fears (range = 0–74)	Intensity of fears (range = 74–222)
7–10	17	139
11–13	13	133
14–16	12	129
Boys	10	125
Girls	18	144

Means and Standard Deviations of Intensity Scores for Categories of Fears

Factor	7–10		11–13		14–16		Boys		Girls	
	$\bar{X}$	SD	$\bar{X}$	SD	$\bar{X}$	SD	$\bar{X}$	SD	$\bar{X}$	SD
Failure and Criticism	39	(8.3)	39	(7.6)	37	(7.9)	36	(7.8)	40	(7.6)
The Unknown	29	(7.5)	27	(6.4)	26	(6.2)	25	(6.3)	30	(6.8)
Minor Injury and Small Animals	28	(7.5)	27	(6.4)	26	(6.1)	24	(5.8)	30	(6.6)
Danger and Death	26	(6.4)	25	(6.0)	24	(6.0)	23	(5.9)	27	(5.8)
Medical Fears	7	(2.1)	7	(2.2)	7	(2.1)	6	(2.0)	7	(2.2)

Normative data are from "Fears in Children and Adolescents: Reliability and Generalizability across Gender, Age and Nationality" by T. H. Ollendick, N. J. King, and R. B. Frary, 1989, *Behaviour Research and Therapy, 27*, 19–26. Copyright 1989 by Pergamon Press. Reprinted by permission.

Nowicki–Strickland Locus of Control
Scale for Children, with scoring
instructions and normative data

Child's Name _____   Date _____

Child's Grade _____

Child's Sex _____

Read each sentence and circle "Yes" if you think it is true for you or "No" if you think it is *not true* for you.

1. Do you believe that most problems will solve themselves if you just don't fool with them?   Yes   No

2. Do you believe that you can stop yourself from catching a cold?   Yes   No

3. Are some kids just born lucky?   Yes   No

4. Most of the time, do you feel that getting good grades means a great deal to you?   Yes   No

5. Are you often blamed for things that just aren't your fault?   Yes   No

6. Do you believe that if somebody studies hard enough he or she can pass any subject?   Yes   No

7. Do you feel that most of the time it doesn't pay to try hard because things never turn out right anyway?   Yes   No

8. Do you feel that if things start out well in the morning, it's going to be a good day no matter what you do?   Yes   No

9. Do you feel that most of the time parents listen to what their children have to say?   Yes   No

10. Do you believe that wishing can make good things happen?   Yes   No

11. When you get punished, does it usually seem it's for no good reason at all?   Yes   No

12. Most of the time, do you find it hard to change a friend's (mind) opinion?   Yes   No

13. Do you think that cheering more than luck helps a team to win?   Yes   No

14. Do you feel that it's nearly impossible to change your parents' mind about anything?   Yes   No

15. Do you believe that your parents should allow you to make most of your own decisions?   Yes   No

16. Do you feel that when you do something wrong there's very little you can do to make it right?   Yes   No

17. Do you believe that most kids are just born good at sports?   Yes   No

18. Are most of the other kids your age stronger than you?   Yes   No

19. Do you feel that one of the best ways to handle most problems is just not to think about them?   Yes   No

20. Do you feel that you have a lot of choice in deciding who your friends are?   Yes   No

21. If you find a four-leaf clover, do you believe that it might bring you good luck?   Yes   No

22. Do you often feel that whether you do your homework has much to do with what kind of grades you get?   Yes   No

23. Do you feel that when a kid your age decides to hit you, there's little you can do to stop him or her?   Yes   No

24. Have you ever had a good-luck charm?   Yes   No

25. Do you believe that whether or not people like you depends on how you act?   Yes   No

26. Will your parents usually help you if you ask them?   Yes   No

27. Have you felt that when people were mean to you it was for no reason at all?   Yes   No

28. Most of the time, do you feel that you can change what might happen tomorrow by what you do today?   Yes   No

29. Do you believe that when bad things are going to happen, they just are going to happen no matter what you try to do to stop them?   Yes   No

30. Do you think that kids can get their own way if they just keep trying?   Yes   No

31. Most of the time, do you find it useless to try to get your own way at home?   Yes   No

32. Do you feel that when good things happen they happen because of hard work?   Yes   No

33. Do you feel that when somebody your age wants to be your enemy, there's little you can do to change matters?   Yes   No

34. Do you feel that it's easy to get friends to do what you want them to?   Yes   No

35. Do you usually feel that you have little to say about what you get to eat at home?   Yes   No

36. Do you feel that when someone doesn't like you, there's little you can do about it?   Yes   No

37. Do you usually feel that it's almost useless to try in school because most other children are just plain smarter than you are?   Yes   No

38. Are you the kind of person who believes that planning ahead makes things turn out better?   Yes   No

39. Most of the time, do you feel that you have little to say about what your family decides to do?   Yes   No

40. Do you think it's better to be smart than to be lucky?   Yes   No

Scoring Key

Part I: For each item, record 1 if the response is "Yes" and 0 if the response is "No."

1 __	10 __	17 __	24 __	35 __	
3 __	11 __	18 __	27 __	36 __	
5 __	12 __	19 __	29 __	37 __	
7 __	14 __	21 __	31 __	38 __	
8 __	16 __	23 __	33 __	39 __	Sum _____

Part II: For each item, record 1 if the response is "No" and 0 if the response is "Yes."

2 __	15 __	28 __		
4 __	20 __	30 __		
6 __	22 __	32 __		
9 __	25 __	34 __		
13 __	26 __	40 __	Sum __	Total I & II _____

Means and Standard Deviations*

	Males		Females	
Grade	*M*	*SD*	*M*	*SD*
3	17.97	4.67	17.38	3.06
4	18.44	3.58	18.80	3.63
5	18.32	4.38	17.00	4.03
6	13.73	5.16	13.32	4.58
7	13.15	4.87	13.94	4.23
8	14.73	4.35	12.29	3.58
9	13.81	4.06	12.25	3.75
10	13.05	5.34	12.98	5.31
11	12.48	4.81	12.01	5.15
12	11.38	4.74	12.37	5.05

Note. From "A Locus of Control Scale for Children" by S. Nowicki, Jr., and B. R. Strickland, 1973, *Journal of Consulting and Clinical Psychology, 40*, 148–154. Copyright 1973 by the American Psychological Association. Adapted by permission.

*Higher scores indicate more external locus of control.

APPENDIX B.10
Home Situations Questionnaire

Child's name _____ Date _____

Name of person completing this form _____

Instructions: Does your child present any problems with compliance to instructions, commands, or rules for you in any of these situations? If so, please circle the word "Yes" and then circle a number beside that situation that describes how severe the problem is for you. If your child is not a problem in a situation, circle "No" and go on to the next situation on the form.

Situations	Yes/No (Circle one)		If yes, how severe? Mild (Circle one) Severe								
Playing alone	Yes	No	1	2	3	4	5	6	7	8	9
Playing with other children	Yes	No	1	2	3	4	5	6	7	8	9
Mealtimes	Yes	No	1	2	3	4	5	6	7	8	9
Getting dressed/undressed	Yes	No	1	2	3	4	5	6	7	8	9
Washing and bathing	Yes	No	1	2	3	4	5	6	7	8	9
When you are on the telephone	Yes	No	1	2	3	4	5	6	7	8	9
Watching television	Yes	No	1	2	3	4	5	6	7	8	9
When visitors are in your home	Yes	No	1	2	3	4	5	6	7	8	9
When you are visiting someone's home	Yes	No	1	2	3	4	5	6	7	8	9
In public places (restaurants, stores, church, etc.)	Yes	No	1	2	3	4	5	6	7	8	9
When father is home	Yes	No	1	2	3	4	5	6	7	8	9
When asked to do chores	Yes	No	1	2	3	4	5	6	7	8	9
When asked to do homework	Yes	No	1	2	3	4	5	6	7	8	9
At bedtime	Yes	No	1	2	3	4	5	6	7	8	9
While in the car	Yes	No	1	2	3	4	5	6	7	8	9
When with a babysitter	Yes	No	1	2	3	4	5	6	7	8	9

.... For Office Use Only ....

Total number of problem settings_____ Mean severity score _____

Note. From *Hyperactive Children: A Handbook for Diagnosis and Treatment* (p. 133) by R. A. Barkley, 1981, New York: Guilford Press. Copyright 1981 by The Guilford Press. Reprinted by permission.

APPENDIX B.11
School Situations Questionnaire

Child's name _____ Date _____

Name of person completing this form _____

Does this child present any behavior problems for you in any of these situations? If so, indicate how severe they are.

Situations	Yes/No (Circle one)		If yes, how severe? Mild (Circle one) Severe
While arriving at school	Yes	No	1 2 3 4 5 6 7 8 9
During individual desk work	Yes	No	1 2 3 4 5 6 7 8 9
During small-group activities	Yes	No	1 2 3 4 5 6 7 8 9
During free playtime in class	Yes	No	1 2 3 4 5 6 7 8 9
During lectures to the class	Yes	No	1 2 3 4 5 6 7 8 9
At recess	Yes	No	1 2 3 4 5 6 7 8 9
At lunch	Yes	No	1 2 3 4 5 6 7 8 9
In the hallways	Yes	No	1 2 3 4 5 6 7 8 9
In the bathroom	Yes	No	1 2 3 4 5 6 7 8 9
On field trips	Yes	No	1 2 3 4 5 6 7 8 9
During special assemblies	Yes	No	1 2 3 4 5 6 7 8 9
On the bus	Yes	No	1 2 3 4 5 6 7 8 9

.... For Office Use Only ....

Total number of problem settings_____ Mean severity score _____

Note. From *Hyperactive Children: A Handbook for Diagnosis and Treatment* (p. 142) by R. A. Barkley, 1981, New York: Guilford Press. Copyright 1981 by The Guilford Press. Reprinted by permission.

432

APPENDIX C

Books for Parents and Children

GENERAL PARENTING

The Process of Parenting. Jane B. Brooks. Palo Alto, CA: Mayfield, 1981.

This book provides excellent information on child development and behavior for sophisticated parents. The author integrates various ideas about common child-rearing problems into a general approach to parenting from birth through adolescence.

The Essentials of Parenting in the First Years of Life. Barbara Danzger Gross and Bernard J. Shuman. New York: Child Welfare League of America, 1979.

This small book provides information about child development research and is packed with information about critical features in the development of young infants and children. Topics covered include attachment, stimulation, consistency, parental expectations, and impact of experiences of pregnancy and delivery.

Baby Owner's Manual: What to Expect and How to Survive the First Year. Edward R. Christophersen. Kansas City, MO: Westport, 1988.

New parents will appreciate this humorous yet factual book about taking care of a new baby. The book begins with some simple exercises that enable parents to assess the skills with which infants are born (e.g., hearing, vision, self-soothing, etc.). Other chapters cover the basics of infant care, bathing, safety, sleeping, crying, feeding, bonding, and more. A good book to include in prenatal classes.

Your Child at Play: Birth to One Year. Marilyn Segal. New York: Newmarket Press, 1985.

Your Child at Play: One to Two Years. Marilyn Segal and Don Adcock. New York: Newmarket Press, 1985.

Your Child at Play: Two to Three Years. Marilyn Segal and Don Adcock. New York: Newmarket Press, 1985.

Your Child at Play: Three to Five Years. Marilyn Segal and Don Adcock. New York: Newmarket Press, 1986.

The volumes in the *Your Child at Play* series are based on research and observation at the Family Center at Nova University in Florida. The authors' goal is to enhance communication between the child and parents, teachers, and caregivers. Each book traces the developmental stages of a particular age, describes routine behavior, gives ideas on child rearing, and provides suggestions for encouraging and enhancing development.

Rattle Fatique: And You Thought You Were Busy before You Had Children. Linda Lewis Griffith. San Luis Obispo, CA: Impact, 1986.

Rattle Fatique provides a wealth of practical advice and suggestions on how to survive the first 3 years as a parent. The book is divided into two sections. Typical problems encountered at each stage of development are covered in the first section, along with common-sense suggestions for dealing with them. More general strategies for coping with the stresses of parenting are discussed in the second section.

Creative Parenting. William Sears. New York: Dodd, Mead, 1983.

This book provides a comprehensive guide to physical growth and development of children from before birth through adolescence. Sections on pregnancy and infancy include the latest research information.

No Fault Parenting. Helen Neville and Mona Halaby. New York: Facts on File, 1984.

This book is a compendium of child care information for parents of children from birth through about 5 or 6 years of age. It includes general principles of behavior, arguments pro and con for various child-rearing techniques, and specific useful practical advice.

The Critical Years: A Guide for Dedicated Parents. Doris E. Durrell. Oakland, CA: New Harbinger, 1984.

The purpose of this book is to "translate research findings into practical terms" for parents of children from birth to 3 years of age. Topics covered include temperament, attachment, language development, and behavior modification.

The Magic Years: Understanding and Handling the Problems of Early Childhood.
Selma H. Fraiberg. New York: Charles Scribner's Sons, 1984.

This classic book on child rearing is still in print and remains a valuable resource
for parents. The unique value of this book is in the integration of development
and behavior: how the capabilities of children at different stages naturally lead to
specific behaviors that can cause problems for parents. Child-rearing advice is
always firmly based in developmental theory.

Between Parent and Child. Haim G. Ginott. New York: Avon, 1959.
Between Parent and Teenager. Haim G. Ginott. New York: Avon, 1971.

Although these books were first published many years ago, they contain information and advice that is still very relevant today. Ginott's focus is on learning to
communicate with children and teenagers in ways that will build self-esteem, as
well as increase appropriate behavior.

Child Behavior from Birth to Ten (rev. ed.). Frances L. Ilg and Louise Bates
Ames. New York: Harper & Row, 1981 (hardcover); New York: Barnes & Noble,
1982 (paperback).

This book is another classic that has withstood the test of time. The authors
present vivid descriptions of what children are like at different stages in development, coupled with discussion of individual differences. Topics include eating,
sleeping, fears, sexuality, siblings, school, divorce, death, and discipline.

SIBLING RIVALRY

Kids Can Cooperate: A Practical Guide to Teaching Problem Solving. Elizabeth
Crary. Seattle, WA: Parenting Press, 1984.

This is an excellent book offering specific, practical suggestions for dealing with
sibling conflict in an easy-to-follow format.

The New Baby at Your House. Joanna Cole. Photographs by Hella Hammid. New
York: William Morrow, 1985.

This excellent book for preschool children includes a preface for parents, which
covers most of the critical things parents need to know to prepare a child for the
arrival of a new baby. The story itself provides information about infants,
discusses the advantages of being the older brother or sister, and illustrates
appropriate interactions between the older child and the infant.

Just like Me. Jan Ormerod. New York: Lothrop, Lee & Shepard, 1986.

This book will appeal to very young children or beginning readers. The simple point is made that older children are different from babies but were once babies too.

Our New Baby: A Picture Story for Parents and Children. Grethe Fagerstrom and Gunilla Hansson. Woodbury, NY: Barron's, 1982.

This book for children from preschool to 10 years of age tells the story of a family that is expecting a baby. It describes how babies are made, as well as how the new baby sister is accepted by her older siblings.

When the New Baby Comes, I'm Moving Out. Martha Alexander. New York: Dial Press, 1981.

This amusing little book for preschoolers successfully captures the feelings of the older child and will undoubtedly spark some good questions and discussion between parent and child.

Jack and Jake. Aliki. New York: Greenwillow Books, 1986.

Twins and siblings of twins will enjoy this short story for children ages 3–5 years about identical twins, Jack and Jake, and the way people constantly confuse them.

DIVORCE

Mom and Dad Are Divorced but I'm Not: Parenting after Divorce. Hal W. Anderson and Gail S. Anderson. Chicago: Nelson-Hall, 1981.

This book covers all aspects of parenting through the divorce process. It includes how and what to tell children; how to restructure the home; how to handle visitation, stepparenting, and noncustodial parenting; and more. The emphasis is on viewing the situation from the children's perspective and meeting children's needs.

What Every Child Would Like His Parents to Know about Divorce. Lee Salk. New York: Harper & Row, 1978.

Lee Salk covers all the important issues of divorce from the point of view of how best to meet children's needs. Included are thoughtful discussions of what the impact of divorce on children can be; how to determine custody and visitation; how and what to tell children; how to maintain good communication with children; and when to seek professional help.

Divorced Dads: Their Kids, Ex-Wives, and New Lives. Morris A. Shepard and Gerald Soldma. New York: Berkley Books, 1979.

Written by two divorced fathers, this book focuses on how to maintain meaningful involvement with children after divorce. They stress getting out of the mold of being a "Sunday hero" or "Disneyland Dad," and having a plan for caring for children that is predictable and works for everyone.

The Good Step-Mother: A Practical Guide. Karen Savage and Patricia Adams. New York: Crown, 1988.

This book covers a wide range of important stepfamily issues, including money, sex, the ex-wife, and stages of stepfamily development. Examples of common problems are given, along with practical guidelines on how to deal with them.

Stepmotherhood: How to Survive without Feeling Frustrated, Left Out, or Wicked. Cherie Burns. New York: Harper & Row, 1985.

Adjustment to stepparenting is the focus of this book, which covers topics such as common problems and conflicts, feelings, unrealistic expectations, planning holidays, managing money, and occasions to seek professional help.

Making It as a Stepparent: New Roles, New Rules. Clair Berman. New York: Harper & Row, 1986.

Among other topics, sexuality (including incest) is dealt with in an open, constructive manner in this book. Also included is advice from experts such as Emily and John Visher, Lee Salk, and Richard Gardner.

How to Win as a Stepfamily. Emily and John Visher. New York: Dembner, 1982.

This book is organized as a chronology of events leading up to remarriage and stepparenting. The focus is an adjustment to living in a stepfamily.

Mom's House, Dad's House: Making Shared Custody Work. Isolina Rieci. New York: Collier Books, 1982.

The focus of this book is on meeting children's needs after divorce through negotiating a working relationship with the other parent. Topics covered include coping with stress, stages of the divorce process, and legal issues.

The Divorce Workbook: A Guide for Kids and Families. Sally B. Ives, David Fassler, and Michele Lash. Burlington, VT: Waterfront Books, 1985.

This book is designed to help children understand and cope with parental divorce. Its format allows for drawing, coloring, and other activities that will involve children in learning how to cope.

Changing Families: A Guide for Kids and Grown-ups. David Fassler, Michele Lash, and Sally B. Ives. Burlington, VT: Waterfront Books, 1988.

This book covers issues related to separation, divorce, and stepfamilies. Its format is similar to that of *The Divorce Workbook*, allowing children to participate in activities designed to facilitate the expression of feelings.

Divorce Is a Grown Up Problem: A Book about Divorce for Young Children and Their Parents. Janet Sinberg. New York: Avon, 1979.

This book promotes an atmosphere of open communication about divorce between parents and children. The preface contains important information for parents; the story for children is sensitive to the feelings experienced by children and offers good suggestions for coping.

What's Going to Happen to Me: When Parents Separate or Divorce (rev. ed.). Eda LeShan. New York: Macmillan, 1986.

This is an excellent book for children 8 years of age and older. The author covers a variety of divorce-related topics and provides examples of situations that other children have experienced. Ways of talking with parents are suggested.

Mommy and Daddy Are Divorced. Patricia Perry and Marietta Lynch. New York: Dial Press, 1978.

This story for children ages 3–7 illustrates the feelings experienced by children whose parents are divorcing. Common questions are asked and answered, and reassurance is given that children will begin to feel better with time.

Divorce Is . . .: A Kids' Coloring Book. Den Magid and Walt Schriebman. Gretna, LA: Pelican, 1980.

The guide for parents at the beginning of this coloring book covers most of the major issues that children must deal with in coping with the divorce process. Parents are encouraged to read this first and then to use the child's portion of the book as a vehicle for open discussion about fears, negative feelings, parental dating, remarriage, and other topics.

DEATH

How Do We Tell the Children? Dan Schaefer and Christine Lyons. New York: Newmarket Press, 1986.

This easy-to-read book provides guidance for parents who are helping their children understand and cope with death. It includes a comprehensive discussion of the questions that are most often asked by children and their typical concerns about death.

What about the Children: Dealing with Death. Rose Helms and Doris Blazer. Raleigh, NC: Project Enlightenment.

This booklet provides practical answers to many of the questions parents have about helping their children deal with death. Included are suggestions about attending the funeral, ways to explain death, and ways in which young children are likely to respond.

On Children and Death. Elisabeth Kübler-Ross. New York: Macmillan, 1983.

This book is written for parents whose children have died or are terminally ill. It covers a wide range of topics, including the funeral, dealing with the siblings of the terminally ill child, and the fear of having more children.

A Little Death. Mary-Jane Creel. New York: Vantage Press, 1987.

This book is based on the author's own experience of the death of her infant daughter. There are several excellent chapters with information on siblings of the deceased child, answers to common religious questions, things *not* to say to bereaved parents, and ways to be a good friend to a bereaved parent.

Kids Grieve Too! Victor S. Lombardo and Edith Foran Lombardo. Springfield, IL: Charles C Thomas, 1986.

Topics covered in this book include ways in which children of different ages view death; ways in which children are likely to experience death (e.g., television, books, and real-life situations); children's reactions to death; and commonly asked questions about children and death.

Afraid to Ask: A Book for Families to Share about Cancer. Judylaine Fine. New York: Lothrop, Lee & Shepard, 1984.

The author has compiled very technical and complex information about the nature of cancer and its causes and cures by talking to experts in Canada and the United States, and has translated this information into a very readable book. Chapters cover the biology of cancer, prevention, treatment approaches and their side effects, the experience of dying of cancer, and a reference guide to all the various types of cancer (what each is, who is at risk, treatment approaches, and more).

Home Care for Seriously Ill Children: A Manual for Parents. D. Gay Moldow and Ida M. Martinson. Alexandria, VA: Children's Hospice International, 1984.

This is a superb manual for parents of children with cancer or other life-threatening diseases who want to care for their dying children at home. All the practical issues of how to do this are covered, including specifics of physical care; necessary equipment; emotional issues, such as dealing with siblings; discipline; marital relationships; the special concerns of the teenage child; financial considerations and resources; community resources; a table describing medications; helpful information on deciding when it is time to stop treatment; and an appendix, with recommended readings for children and parents, plus a list of "dos and don'ts" for helping bereaved parents.

Whole Parent Whole Child: A Parents' Guide to Raising a Child with a Chronic Illness. Patricia M. Moynihan and Broatch Haig. Wayzata, MN: DCI, 1989.

The goal of this book is to help parents put their children's chronic illness in perspective so that it is not the entire focus of their lives or their children's lives. It covers the many issues that parents face, including understanding the concept of chronic illness, roles parents play, developing confidence in oneself and the child, developmental issues, dealing with everyday concerns, caregivers, and the school.

Lifetimes: The Beautiful Way to Explain Death to Children. Bryan Mellonie and Robert Ingpen. New York: Bantam Books, 1983.

The ideas that death is a natural part of life and that every living thing has a special lifetime, whether it is short or long, are the central themes of this small book. The text, which is very simple and yet is appropriate for children of all ages, is accompanied by lovely illustrations.

A Present for Jessica. Teddi Doleski. Mahwah, NJ: Paulist Press, 1986.

This book tells the story of the death of Jessica's beloved pet dog, Penny. The grieving process is accurately and sensitively depicted, and the writing is simple enough that the complex emotions associated with death can be easily understood by young children.

Harry's Mom. Barbara Ann Porte. Illustrated by Yossi Abolafia. New York: Greenwillow Books, 1985.

Harry's mother died when he was 1 year old and he does not remember her. The focus of this story is on Harry's attempts to get information about his mother from his father and grandparents, and his incorporation of this information into his sense of identity.

Thumpy's Story: A Story of Love and Grief Shared by Thumpy, the Bunny. Nancy C. Dodge. Springfield, IL: Prairie Lark Press, 1984.
Sharing with Thumpy: My Story of Love and Grief. Sister Jane Marie Lamb and Nancy C. Dodge. Springfield, IL: Prairie Lark Press, 1985.

Thumpy's Story tells the story of the death of Thumpy's sister, Bun, and illustrates typical feelings experienced by children. The accompanying workbook, *Sharing with Thumpy*, encourages children to tell their own stories about their experience with death.

Cancer: The Whispered Word. Judy Harris Swenson and Roxane Brown Kunz. Minneapolis: Dillon Press, 1986.

This story about a young mother with breast cancer is told through the eyes of a young boy, and is well written and comprehensive in its coverage of medical terminology and psychological issues. As well as exploring the child's feelings about his mother's illness, the book provides specific suggestions for both the child and the family in helping each other to deal with this threatening disease.

TOILETING

Toilet Training in Less Than a Day. Nathan H. Azrin and Richard M. Foxx. New York: Simon & Schuster, 1974.

Although the intense training procedure described in this easy-to-read book is not for everyone, the methods are based on sound principles. If parents are having difficulty training their child, the step-by-step instructions may be helpful.

No More Diapers. Joae Graham Brooks. New York: Delacorte Press/Seymour Lawrence, 1981.

This is a pleasantly illustrated book for children with an introduction for parents. It is easy to change the text to fit the program described in this chapter. Note that this book proposes that children stay in diapers until they are trained and are ready to give them up. We suggest that diapers not be used at all (except at naptime and at night) once the training process is started.

SLEEP

Solve Your Child's Sleep Problems. Richard Ferber. New York: Simon & Schuster, 1985.

This book is one of our favorite resources for helping parents deal with sleep problems. Ferber, who is director of the Center for Pediatric Sleep Disorders at Children's Hospital in Boston, has provided parents and professionals with basic information about sleep (e.g., stages of sleep, sleep needs at different ages), the causes of most sleep problems in childhood, and detailed advice on how to handle these problems.

Goodnight Moon. Margaret Wise Brown. New York: Harper & Row, 1947.

This classic book for toddlers is the story of a bunny saying good night to everything as darkness falls and sleep comes.

I Hate to Go to Bed. Judi Barrett. New York: Four Winds Press, 1977.

A good book for preschoolers about a child who thinks first about why he hates to go to bed and then about why he likes to, as he tries to gain mastery over bedtime.

SEXUALITY EDUCATION

Raising a Child Conservatively in a Sexually Permissive World. Sol and Judith Gordon. New York: Simon & Schuster, 1983.

This book is written for parents with children of any age. It covers all areas of sexuality, with an emphasis on being an "askable" parent. Topics covered include building self-esteem, what and when to tell children of various ages, values, sex roles, family life, and sexually transmitted diseases.

The Family Book about Sexuality (rev. ed.). Mary S. Calderone and Eric W. Johnson. New York: Bantam Books, 1983.

This book is a comprehensive encyclopedia of sexual information for parents and children. Topics include sexual anatomy and physiology, marriage, families, family planning, sexuality and aging, sexual problems, and sexual decision making.

The Parent's Guide to Raising Sexually Healthy Children. Lynn Leight. New York: Rawson Associates, 1988.

In addition to facts about sexuality, the author discusses self-esteem, nurturance, limit setting, and physical development as aspects of human development that affect sexuality. This information is neatly woven into discussions of typical sexual topics, such as nudity, masturbation, and birth control.

Sexuality Education for Parents of Young Children: A Facilitator Training Manual. Sally Koblinsky. Fayetteville, NY: Ed-U-Press, 1983.

This book provides *everything* needed to run parent groups on sexuality education for young children (up to 8 years) and to train leaders for these groups. The book includes sample letters to parents, suggestions for advertising groups, lesson plans, parent handouts, a variety of group exercises, and more.

Did the Sun Shine before You Were Born?: A Sex Education Primer. Sol and Judith Gordon. New York: Joseph Okpaku, 1974.

Girls Are Girls and Boys Are Boys, So What's the Difference: A Nonsexist Sexuality Education Book for Children Age 6 to 10 (rev. ed.). Sol Gordon. Fayetteville, NY: Ed-U-Press, 1983.
Facts about Sex for Today's Youth. Sol Gordon. Fayetteville, NY: Ed-U-Press, 1978.

Sol Gordon's series of three books is an excellent source of general information for children and teenagers about sex and sexuality. Each book carefully selects information appropriate for children in a particular age range.

Our New Baby: A Picture Story for Parents and Children. Grethe Fagerstrom and Gunilla Hansson. Woodbury, NY: Barron's, 1982.

This book tells the story of a family that is expecting a baby; cartoons describe "how babies are made," including sexual intercourse and the birth process. A good book for children from 3 to 10 years of age.

A Kid's Book about Sex. Joani Blank. Burlingame, CA: Yes Press, 1983.

This book focuses on sexual attitudes and values rather than on facts. It is appropriate for children ages 6–10.

As Boys Grow Up (Pamphlet). South Deerfield, MA: Channing L. Bete, 1987.

Information about growth, sexual changes, intercourse, pregnancy, venereal diseases, relationships, and ways to be healthy is given in a straightforward and simple manner that can be easily understood by most 10-year-olds. The pamphlet would, however, be valuable for any teenage boy who does not like to read yet wants or needs facts about his body.

How You Were Born. Joanna Cole. New York: William Morrow, 1985.

This book provides simple, clear, factual information about the birth process. Illustrations include actual photographs of fetuses at different stages of development and drawings of other aspects of pregnancy (male and female anatomy, a baby coming through the birth canal, etc.). There is no discussion of sexual intercourse.

What Is a Girl? What Is a Boy? Stephanie Waxman. New York: Harper & Row Junior Books, 1989.

Sexual identity is an important issue for preschoolers, and this book is a good source of information on the topic. With simple text and photographs of boys and girls, the author explains that external features (hair, clothing, play activities, etc.) do not really differentiate boys and girls. Gender is determined by one's genitalia and remains the same throughout one's life.

The Boy Toy. Phyllis Hacken Johnson. Illustrated by Lena Shiffman. Carrboro, NC: Lollipop Power Books, 1988.

This book for older preschoolers and beginning readers explores issues of sexual stereotyping. The point is clearly made that dolls can be boy toys, girls can be doctors, and so on.

SEXUAL ABUSE PREVENTION

No More Secrets: Protecting Your Child from Sexual Assault. Caren Adams and Jennifer Fay. San Luis Obispo, CA: Impact, 1981.

This book for parents gives very specific suggestions for what to say to children about sexual abuse. It also provides information on disclosure of sexual abuse and things parents can do to help a child who has been molested.

Sexual Abuse: Let's Talk about It. Margaret O. Hyde. Philadelphia: Westminster, 1984.

Contains much information about sexual abuse of children, ways children can protect themselves, the types of help available, and ways to increase public awareness of the problem. One chapter provides insight into the characteristics and motivation of perpetrators.

The Silent Children: A Parent's Guide to the Prevention of Child Sexual Abuse. Linda Tschirhart Sanford. New York: McGraw-Hill, 1980.

This book combines information about the theory and dynamics of child sexual abuse with practical suggestions for prevention. Exercises and role plays are included.

Protect Your Children from Sexual Abuse: A Parent's Guide. Janie Hart-Rossi. Seattle, WA: Parenting Press, 1984.

This guide accompanies the children's book *It's My Body* (see below), and includes exercises and activities for families to supplement the information in the child's book. Topics include what to do if abuse is suspected and how to prevent abuse; preparation is also provided for parents, to help them feel more comfortable talking with children about this topic.

No More Secrets for Me. Oralee Wachter. Boston: Little, Brown, 1983.

Written for school-aged children, this book contains stories of four children who experienced sexual abuse. The reader is told how each child sought help to stop the abuse. It is an excellent resource for parents and clinicians.

It's My Body: A Book to Teach Young Children How to Resist Uncomfortable Touch. Tory Freeman. Seattle, WA: Parenting Press, 1982.

This book is written for 2- to 4-year-old children and introduces the topic of sexual abuse very gently and sensitively. The emphasis is on self-reliance and open communication, with the main message that it's OK to say, "Don't touch me, I don't like it."

A *Better Safe Than Sorry Book: A Family Guide for Sexual Assault Prevention*. Sol and Judith Gordon. Fayetteville, NY: Ed-U-Press, 1984.

This is one of our favorite books on sexual abuse prevention for children ages 3–9. It includes an excellent section for parents about sexual abuse and sexuality education.

My Very Own Book about Me. Jo Stowell and Mary Dietzel. Spokane, WA: Lutheran Social Services of Washington, 1982.

This is an excellent workbook for children ages 4–9 years that helps them prevent and/or deal with sexual abuse. Teacher and therapist guides are also available; together, these constitute the basis for an entire educational and therapeutic program for use at home, at school, and in treatment. Data on the effectiveness of the program is included.

Red Flag, Green Flag People. Joy Williams. Fargo, ND: Rape and Abuse Crisis Center, 1980.

Using the format of a coloring book, this book teaches children the prevention message that some people and some kinds of touch are bad, confusing, or exploitative. A program guide is also available that outlines learning activities, using the coloring book as a focus.

I Like You to Make Jokes with Me, but I Don't Want You to Touch Me. Ellen Bass and Marti Betz. Carrboro, NC: Lollipop Power, 1985.

This book contains an excellent message about being sensitive to children's feelings/concerns and giving them permission to appropriately control adults' interactions with them. The short story describes an adult male who interacts in a pleasant and positive way with a little girl, but does some things that make her uncomfortable. With the mother's help, the child tells the adult how she feels and what she likes and does not like. The man responds in a positive manner. This is a good book for preschoolers.

You're in Charge. South Deerfield, MA: Channing L. Bete, 1986.
What Every Kid Should Know about Sexual Abuse. South Deerfield, MA: Channing L. Bete, 1986.

Designed for children of elementary school age, these excellent coloring/activity books focus on the prevention of sexual abuse. The message presented in *You're in Charge* is that children's bodies belong to themselves and nobody has the right to touch them in ways that feel strange or upsetting. Guidelines are presented about how to stay in charge of one's body. *What Every Kid Should Know about Sexual Abuse* provides more extensive and detailed information about sexual abuse, including anatomical details, appropriate touching and the child's rights for privacy, examples of sexual abuse and potential abusers, things to do if someone tries to sexually abuse the child, and the importance of telling someone what happened.

SEXUAL ABUSE

The Mother's Book: How to Survive the Incest of Your Child. Carolyn M. Byerly. Dubuque, IA: Kendall/Hunt, 1985.

The Mother's Book is written specifically for mothers whose children have experienced incest. A wealth of information addresses the unique needs of the mother living in an incestuous household. Topics covered include the dynamics of incest; disclosure and the feelings that follow; the effects on various relationships; guidelines for reporting the abuse and what to expect throughout the investigative process; ways to find support; and parenting, cultural, and religious issues.

Something Happened and I'm Scared to Tell. Patricia Kehoe. Seattle, WA: Parenting Press, 1987.

This book, written in a story format for the very young child (ages 3–7), focuses on "rebuilding the very fragile self-image of the young child" who has been physically or sexually abused. It encourages the abused child to talk to someone safe about what happened. The book provides correct labels for body parts, explains to the child that he or she was not to blame for the abuse, and talks about reasons why an adult might abuse a child.

Something Happened to Me. Phyllis E. Sweet. Racine, WI: Mother Courage Press, 1981.

This book is designed to reassure children who have been abused and to give them permission to talk about what has happened to them. We have used it extensively in the treatment of abuse victims.

Chris Tells the Truth. Kent R. Caruso and Richard J. Pulcini. Redding, CA: Northwest Psychological, 1988.

This book was designed for children ages 4–12 to help them understand and cope with the legal process. It tells about the sexual abuse of Chris (who may be either male or female, as the authors carefully avoid the use of personal pronouns) by his or her stepfather, and follows him or her through the process of disclosure, investigation, treatment, and court appearance. Terminology and procedures are explained throughout the book, and black-and-white drawings illustrate many aspects of the legal process and court room.

Margaret's Story: Sexual Abuse and Going to Court. Deborah Anderson and Martha Finne. Minneapolis, MN: Dillon Press, 1986.

Margaret's Story is another book designed to help children who must testify in court about sexual abuse. It does a good job of explaining legal procedures, although descriptions of the child's fears are excessive and may encourage children to feel more afraid than they might otherwise. The book includes information for children about sexual abuse, as well as a note to adults on how to use the book and what to do if a child reports abuse.

Carla Goes to Court. Jo Beaudry and Lynne Ketchum. New York: Human Sciences Press, 1987.

Carla is a "Latchkey" child who witnesses a burglary and then must go to court to testify about what she saw. This book provides the details of the legal process in which Carla is involved, following her through the police lineup, the pretrial hearing, and finally the jury trial. The text weaves definitions for some very complicated legal terms into the story, and the child's feelings at different times during the process are also presented. Black-and-white photographs illustrate actual courtroom scenes.

BEHAVIOR MANAGEMENT

Parent Power: A Guide to Responsible Childrearing. Logan Wright. New York: Psychological Dimensions, 1978.

The author translates empirically based information into sensible advice for parents, presenting the behavioral techniques of rewards, shaping, modeling, time out, reflective listening, and more. The appendix covers special topics (single parenting, sibling rivalry, death, etc.).

Surviving with Kids: A Lifeline for Overwhelmed Parents. Wayne R. Bartz and Richard A. Rasor. San Luis Obispo, CA: Impact, 1978.

This is one of our favorite books for parents. Based on behavioral principles, it focuses on how children learn to behave appropriately or inappropriately and how to teach them through parental attention and other consequences, modeling, clear messages, and consistency.

Sensitive Parenting: From Infancy to Adulthood. Katherine Kersey. Washington, DC: Acropolis, 1983.

This book provides a general review of behavioral principles, with an emphasis on the emotional aspects of the parent–child relationship and on anticipating and preventing problems. Ten steps to "sensitive" parenting are illustrated (e.g., treat the child with respect, reward appropriate behavior, make sure privileges are earned, etc.).

Without Spanking or Spoiling: A Practical Approach to Toddlers and Preschool Guidance. Elizabeth Crary. Seattle, WA: Parenting Press, 1979.

This excellent child management book includes useful techniques from parent effectiveness training, transactional analysis, and Adlerian–Dreikurs approaches. Some basics of effective parenting are discussed (e.g., defining values, developing reasonable expectations, and increasing parental self-esteem), and behaviorally based guidelines for solving common problems are provided.

How to Help Children with Common Problems. Charles E. Schaefer and Howard L. Millman. New York: Van Nostrand Reinhold, 1984.

This comprehensive book is organized by specific concerns (e.g., hyperactivity, shyness, sleep, and temper tantrums) and covers all the problems with which parents may be confronted. Each section includes a discussion of the possible causes of the behavior, how to prevent it, and what to do if it is a problem.

What Do I Do When: A Handbook for Parents and Other Beleaguered Adults. Juliet V. Allen. San Luis Obispo, CA: Impact, 1983.

This is a handy, practical book designed to provide quick solutions to common child-rearing problems. The introduction covers behavioral principles, while the remainder is organized alphabetically by problem for easy reference.

SOS! Help for Parents. Lynn Clark. Bowling Green, KY: Parents Press, 1985.

SOS is based on the work of Gerald Patterson, Rex Forehand, and others who have developed and researched parent training programs for noncompliant children. It describes basic behavioral principles, ways to increase appropriate behavior, ways to use time out, and generalization of skills to specific behavior problems. It also covers other techniques, such as token systems, contracting, and use of logical consequences.

Families: Applications of Social Learning to Family Life. Gerald Patterson. Champaign, IL: Research Press, 1975.

This book must be considered a classic. It teaches parents to apply social learning principles to family situations, including many significant behavioral problems (e.g., stealing or aggression).

MISCELLANEOUS

A Children's Problem Solving Book Series: My Name Is Not Dummy; Mommy Don't Go; I Can't Wait; I'm Lost; I Want It; I Want to Play. Elizabeth Crary. Seattle, WA: Parenting Press, 1982–1986.

This series of books is designed to help children learn to solve social problems. The author does this by helping children think about a problem before they act; offering a variety of ways to handle a situation; showing how their behavior affects others; talking about choices and feelings; and reinforcing thinking before acting. The books invite listener participation by letting the child decide what the book's character will do and then turning to the part of the book that describes the consequences of that choice.

Liking Myself. Pat Palmer. San Luis Obispo, CA: Impact, 1977.

This book provides exercises and activities for children (ages 5–9) that are designed to raise self-esteem and promote good coping skills. We use it with many children during the course of treatment.

The Mouse, the Monster, and Me. Pat Palmer. San Luis Obispo, CA: Impact, 1977.

Written for children ages 8–12 years, this book provides activities aimed at teaching assertiveness skills and raising self-esteem. We have used it effectively in treatment with many children.

How to Raise Children's Self-Esteem. Harris Clemes and Reynold Bean. Los Angeles: Price/Stern/Sloan, 1980.

This book provides very helpful information on how to enhance children's self-esteem. It begins with a discussion of the characteristics of self-esteem and reasons why it is important in a child's development. Next, the conditions that are required for self-esteem are defined and discussed, with concrete examples of how to recognize when children are having problems in each area and what to do about them.

Stress and Your Child (Pamphlet). South Deerfield, MA: Channing L. Bete, 1987.

This pamphlet defines stress; gives reasons to be concerned about stress and children; clearly describes what happens to the body during stress; gives warning signs of harmful stress; describes sources of stress for children and ways to deal with them; offers techniques that children, parents, and the family can use to reduce stress; and lists sources of additional help.

Helping Your Child Handle Stress: The Parent's Guide to Recognizing and Solving Childhood Problems. Katherine Kersey (Ed.). Washington, DC: Acropolis, 1986.

This book presents a variety of common and not-so-common problems that parents and children may encounter, along with suggestions for dealing with those problems. Topics covered include toilet training, eating habits, siblings, school, moving, independence and letting go, depression, illness, handicapped children, adoption, "latchkey" children, divorce and single parenting, stepfamilies, alcoholism, crimes against children, and death. Each section presents a discussion of the problem, some examples of how *not* to handle the situation, and some good suggestions for possible solutions.

Annie Stories: A Special Kind of Storytelling. Doris Brett. New York: Workman Publishing, 1988.

The stories in this book are designed to help children deal with stressful events and common problems, including nightmares, a new baby, death, going to the hospital, and starting school. Each story can be adapted to a child's unique experience and includes activities related to mastering the troublesome event.

APPENDIX D

Clinical Practice Forms

APPENDIX D.1
Start-Up Costs Worksheet

Decorating and remodeling $ _____

Equipment/furniture $ _____

Legal fees, accounting fees $ _____

Licenses and permits $ _____

Lease deposit $ _____

Office supplies $ _____

Operating cash $ _____

Reserve for unexpected costs $ _____

Test materials $ _____

Utility deposits $ _____

Other (list each item) $ _____

TOTAL $ _____

From *Assessment and Treatment of Childhood Problems: A Clinician's Guide* by Carolyn S. Schroeder and Betty N. Gordon. © 1991 by The Guilford Press.

Profit–Loss Worksheet
(Anticipated Monthly Operating Statement)

Income:

Client receipts	$ _____
Interest (checking/saving accounts)	$ _____
Other miscellaneous income	$ _____

Total Gross Profit $ _____

Expenses:

Wages, salaries, benefits	$ _____
Rent	$ _____
Taxes and licenses	$ _____
Utiities: gas, electric, sewer, water	$ _____
Telephone	$ _____
Supplies	$ _____
Postage	$ _____
Travel	$ _____
Dues, subscriptions	$ _____
Insurance	$ _____
Maintenance, trash removal	$ _____
Advertising	$ _____
Legal and accounting fees	$ _____
Employee taxes: FICA, unemployment	$ _____
Depreciation and/or equipment leases	$ _____
Miscellaneous	$ _____

Total Expenses   − $ _____

Net Profit before Taxes $ _____

   Less estimated local, state, and federal business taxes   − $ _____

Net Profit after Taxes $ _____

	Jan.	Feb.	Mar.	April	May	June	July	Aug.	Sept.	Oct.	Nov.	Dec.
1. Cash in bank (start of month)												
2. Expected client receipts												
3. Other money expected												
4. Total receipts (add 2 and 3)												
5. Total cash and receipts (add 1 and 4)												
6. All disbursements (for month)												
7. Cash balance at end of month in bank acct. (subtract 6 from 5)*												

*This balance is the starting cash balance for the next month.

From *Assessment and Treatment of Childhood Problems: A Clinician's Guide* by Carolyn S. Schroeder and Betty N. Gordon. © 1991 by The Guilford Press.

APPENDIX D.4
Current Balance Sheet

_____

(Name of your practice)

As of _____

(Date)

ASSETS			LIABILITIES AND STOCKHOLDER EQUITY	
Current Assets:			*Current Liabilities*:	
Cash in bank	$ ___		Accounts payable	$ ___
Petty cash	$ ___		Payroll taxes and withheld taxes	$ ___
Accounts receivable	$ ___		Total current liabilities	$ ___
Less allowance for doubtful accounts	$ ___		*Stockholder Equity*:	
Profit-sharing Plan	$ ___		Common stock	$ ___
Total Current Assets	$ ___		Profit sharing	$ ___
			Net Profit or (loss)	$ ___
Fixed Assets:			TOTAL LIABILITIES AND STOCKHOLDER EQUITY	$ ___
Automobile	$ ___			
Office equipment	$ ___			
Furniture and fixtures	$ ___			
Books	$ ___			
Leasehold improve-ments	$ ___			
Less allowance for depreciation	$ (___)			
Less amortization	$ (___)			
Total Fixed Assets	$ ___			
TOTAL ASSETS	$ ___			

From *Assessment and Treatment of Childhood Problems: A Clinician's Guide* by Carolyn S. Schroeder and Betty N. Gordon. © 1991 by The Guilford Press.

APPENDIX D.5
Initial Contact
Satisfaction Questionnaire

Our records indicate that you were a first-time client in our practice, and we would like to know how you feel about your visit. We would appreciate your answering the questions and returning it in the enclosed envelope.

It is our intention to use your response along with others to improve our services. You may sign your name or remain anonymous.

Thank you for your help.

CIRCLE ONE

1. My original contact with the telephone receptionist was	Excellent	Good	Fair	Poor
2. The therapist who returned my call was	Excellent	Good	Fair	Poor
3. The length of time it took to return my call was	Excellent	Good	Fair	Poor
4. The new patient registration process was	Excellent	Good	Fair	Poor
5. My experience with the office staff other than the therapist was	Excellent	Good	Fair	Poor
6. I found your waiting areas to be	Excellent	Good	Fair	Poor
7. The therapist's sensitivity to my needs was	Excellent	Good	Fair	Poor
8. The therapist's recommendations were	Excellent	Good	Fair	Poor
Indicate, if you want to, your therapist's name:	_____			
9. I found the therapist's office to be	Excellent	Good	Fair	Poor
10. My overall rating of your services was	Excellent	Good	Fair	Poor

Please list any general comments or suggestions that you feel will help us improve our services or quality of care.

_____

_____

_____

_____   _____

Date   Signature (if desired)

From *Assessment and Treatment of Childhood Problems: A Clinician's Guide* by Carolyn S. Schroeder and Betty N. Gordon. © 1991 by The Guilford Press.

APPENDIX D.6
Parent Satisfaction Questionnaire

Parent's Name _____ Date _____

The following questionnaire is part of our evaluation of the treatment program that you have received. It is important that you answer as honestly as possible. The information obtained will help us to evaluate and continually improve the program we offer. Your cooperation is greatly appreciated.

A. The Overall Program

Please circle the responses that best expresses how you honestly feel.

1. The major problem(s) that originally prompted me to begin treatment for my child is (are) at this point

Considerably worse	Worse	Slightly worse	The same	Slightly improved	Improved	Greatly improved

2. My child's problems that have been treated at the clinic are at this point

Considerably worse	Worse	Slightly worse	The same	Slightly improved	Improved	Greatly improved

3. My child's problems that have not been treated at the clinic are

Considerably worse	Worse	Slightly worse	The same	Slightly improved	Improved	Greatly improved

4. My feelings at this point about my child's progress are that I am

Very dissatisfied	Dissatisfied	Slightly dissatisfied	Neutral	Slightly satisfied	Satisfied	Very satisfied

5. To what degree has the treatment program helped with other general personal or family problems not directly related to your child?

Hindered much more than helped	Hindered	Hindered slightly	Neither helped nor hindered	Helped slightly	Helped	Helped very much

6. At this point, my expectation for a satisfactory outcome of the treatment is

Very pessimistic	Pessimistic	Slightly pessimistic	Neutral	Slightly optimistic	Optimistic	Very optimistic

7. I feel the approach taken to treating my child's behavior problems in the home has been

Very inappropriate	Inappropriate	Slightly inappropriate	Neutral	Slightly appropriate	Appropriate	Very appropriate

8. Would you recommend the program to a friend or relative?

Strongly recommend	Recommend	Slightly recommend	Neutral	Slightly not recommend	Not recommend	Strongly not recommend

458

9. How confident are you in managing current behavioral problems in the home on your own?

Very confident	Confident	Somewhat confident	Neutral	Somewhat unconfident	Unconfident	Very unconfident

10. How confident are you in your ability to manage future behavior problems in the home, using what you learned from this program?

Very unconfident	Unconfident	Somewhat unconfident	Neutral	Somewhat confident	Confident	Very confident

11. My overall feeling about the treatment program for my child and family is

Very negative	Negative	Somewhat negative	Neutral	Slightly positive	Positive	Very positive

B. Therapist(s)

In this section we'd like to get your ideas about your therapist(s). Please circle the response to each question that best expresses how you feel.

1. I feel that the therapist's skills were

Very poor	Fair	Slightly below average	Average	Slightly above average	Good	Superior

2. The therapist's preparation was

Poor	Fair	Slightly below average	Average	Slightly above average	Good	Superior

3. Concerning the therapist's interest and concern in me and my problems with my child, I was

Extremely dissatisfied	Dissatisfied	Slightly dissatisfied	Neutral	Slightly satisfied	Satisfied	Extremely satisfied

4. At this point, I feel that the therapist was

Extremely not helpful	Not helpful	Slightly not helpful	Neutral	Slightly helpful	Helpful	Extremely helpful

5. My personal feelings toward the therapist:

I dislike him/her very much	I dislike him/her	I dislike him/her slightly	I have a neutral attitude toward him/her	I like him/her slightly	I like him/her	I like him/her very much

C. Your Opinion, Please

1. What part of the treatment program was most helpful to you?

2. What did you like most about the treatment program?

3. What did you like least about the treatment program?

4. What part of the treatment program was least helpful to you?

5. How could the treatment program have been improved to help you move?

D. Environment

1. I feel my experience with the office staff other than the therapist was

Very poor	Fair	Average	Good	Superior

2. The length of time it took the therapist to return my calls was

Poor	Fair	Average	Superior

3. I feel your waiting areas are

Poor	Fair	Average	Superior

4. The therapist's office was

Poor	Fair	Average	Superior

Thank you. Please enclose this questionnaire in the attached envelope and drop it in the mail.

Note. Adapted from *Helping the Noncompliant Child: A Clinician's Guide to Parent Training* by R. L. Forehand and R. J. McMahon, 1981, New York: Guilford Press. Copyright 1981 by the Guilford Press. Adapted by permission.

References

Abidin, R. R. (1989, August). *The determinants of parenting: What variables do we need to look at?* Paper presented at the meeting of the American Psychological Association, New Orleans.

Abidin, R. R. (1990). *Parenting Stress Index manual* (3rd ed.). Charlottesville, VA: Pediatric Psychology Press.

Abrahamian, R. P., & Lloyd-Still, J. D. (1984). Chronic constipation in childhood: A longitudinal study of 186 patients. *Journal of Pediatric Gastroenterology and Nutrition, 3*, 460–467.

Abrams, J. M. (1990). *Reality monitoring in young children: Implications for testimony.* Unpublished master's thesis. University of North Carolina–Chapel Hill.

Achenbach, T. M. (1980). DSM-III in light of empirical research on the classification of child psychopathology. *Journal of the American Academy of Child Psychiatry, 19*, 395–412.

Achenbach, T. M. (1985). *Assessment and taxonomy of child and adolescent psychopathology.* Beverly Hills, CA: Sage.

Achenbach, T. M., & Edelbrock, C. (1978). The classification of childhood pathology: A review and analysis of empirical efforts. *Psychological Bulletin, 85*, 1273–1301.

Achenbach, T. M., & Edelbrock, C. S. (1981). Behavioral problems and competencies reported by parents of normal and disturbed children aged 4 through

16. *Monographs of the Society for Research in Child Development, 46*(1, Serial No. 188).

Achenbach, T. M., & Edelbrock, C. (1983). *Manual for the Child Behavior Checklist and Revised Child Behavior Profile.* Burlington, VT: University Associates in Psychiatry.

Adam, B. S., & Kashani, J. H. (1990). Trichotillomania in children and adolescents: Review of the literature and case report. *Child Psychiatry and Human Development, 20,* 159-168.

Adams, C., & Fay, J. (1981). *No more secrets: Protecting your child from sexual assault.* San Luis Obispo, CA: Impact Press.

Agras, W. S., Chapin, N. H., & Oliveau, D. C. (1972). The natural history of phobias: Course and prognosis. *Archives of General Psychiatry, 26,* 315-317.

Ainsworth, M., Blehar, M., Waters, E., & Wall, S. (1978). *Patterns of attachment.* Hillsdale, NJ: Erlbaum.

Allen, K. D., & Stokes, T. F. (1987). The use of escape and reward in the management of young children during dental treatment. *Journal of Applied Behavior Analysis, 20,* 381-390.

Allen, L., & Zigler, E. (1986). Psychological adjustment of seriously ill children. *Journal of the American Academy of Child Psychiatry, 25,* 708-712.

Allison, P. D., & Furstenberg, F. F., Jr. (1989). How marital dissolution affects children: Variations by age and sex. *Developmental Psychology, 25,* 540-549.

Alpert-Gillis, L. J., Pedro-Carroll, J. L., & Cowen, E. L. (1989). The Children of Divorce Intervention Program: Development, implementation, and evaluation of a program for young urban children. *Journal of Consulting and Clinical Psychology, 57,* 583-589.

Altman, R., Grahs, C., & Friman, P. C. (1982). Treatment of unobserved trichotillomania by attention–reflection and punishment of an operant covariant. *Journal of Behavior Therapy and Experimental Psychiatry, 13,* 337-340.

American Academy of Pediatrics, Task Force on Pediatric Education. (1978). *The future of pediatric education.* Evanston, IL: American Academy of Pediatrics.

American Psychiatric Association. (1980). *Diagnostic and statistical manual of mental disorders* (3rd ed.). Washington, DC: Author.

American Psychiatric Association. (1987). *Diagnostic and statistical manual of mental disorders* (3rd ed., rev.). Washington, DC: Author.

Anders, T. (1979). Night waking in infants during the first year of life. *Pediatrics, 63,* 860-864.

Anders, T., Carskadon, M. A., & Dement, W. C. (1980). Sleep and sleepiness in children and adolescents. *Pediatric Clinics of North America, 27,* 29-42.

Anders, T., & Weinstein, P. (1972). Sleep and its disorders in infants and children: A review. *Pediatrics, 50,* 312-324.

Armistead, L., McCombs, A., Forehand, R., Wierson, M., Long, N., & Fauber, R. (1990). Coping with divorce: A study of young adolescents. *Journal of Clinical Child Psychology, 19,* 79-84.

Association of Sleep Disorders Centers. (1979). Diagnostic classification of sleep and arousal disorders (1st ed.): Prepared by the Sleep Disorders Classification Committee, H. P. Roffworg, Chairman. *Sleep, 2,* 1-37.

Atkeson, B. M., & Forehand, R. (1978). Parent behavior training for problem children: An examination of studies using multiple outcome measures. *Journal
of Abnormal Child Psychology, 6,* 449–460.

Azrin, N. H., & Foxx, R. M. (1974). *Toilet training in less than a day.* New York:
Simon & Schuster.

Azrin, N. H., & Nunn, R. G. (1973). Habit reversal: A method of eliminating
nervous habits and tics. *Behaviour Research and Therapy, 11,* 619–628.

Azrin, N. H., & Nunn, R. G. (1977). *Habit control in a day.* New York: Simon &
Schuster.

Azrin, N. H., Nunn, R. G., & Frantz-Renshaw, R. S. (1980). Habit reversal
treatment of thumbsucking. *Behaviour Research and Therapy, 18,* 395–399.

Azrin, N. H., Nunn, R. G., & Frantz-Renshaw, R. S. (1982). Habit reversal vs.
negative practice treatment of self-destructive oral habits (biting, chewing
or licking of the lips, cheeks, tongue or palate). *Journal of Behavior Therapy
and Experimental Psychiatry, 13,* 49–54.

Azrin, N. H., & Peterson, A. L. (1988). Behavior therapy for Tourette syndrome
and tic disorders. In D. J. Cohen, R. D. Bruun, & J. F. Leckman (Eds.),
Tourette syndrome and tic disorders (pp. 237–256). New York: Wiley.

Azrin, N. H., Sneed, T. J., & Foxx, R. M. (1974). Dry-bed training: Rapid
elimination of childhood enuresis. *Behaviour Research and Therapy, 12,*
147–156.

Azrin, N. H., Theines-Hontos, P. T., & Besalel-Azrin, V. (1979). Elimination of
enuresis without a conditioning apparatus: An extension of office instruction
of the child and parents. *Behavior Therapy, 10,* 14–19.

Bailey, D. B., Jr. (1987). Collaborative goal-setting with families: Resolving differences in values and priorities for services. *Topics in Early Childhood
Special Education, 5,* 59–71.

Baker, L., & Cantwell, D. P. (1985). Psychiatric and learning disorders in children
with speech and language disorders: A critical review. *Advances in Learning
and Behavioral Disabilities, 4,* 1–28.

Bakwin, H. (1973). The genetics of enuresis. In I. Kolvin, R. C. MacKeith, & S. R.
Meadow (Eds.), *Bladder control and enuresis* (pp. 73–77). Philadelphia:
J. B. Lippincott.

Bakwin, H., & Bakwin, R. M. (1972). *Behavior disorders in children* (4th ed.).
Philadelphia: W. B. Saunders.

Baldy-Moulinier, M., Leny, M., & Passouant, P. A. (1970). A study of jactatio
capitis during sleep. *Electroencephalography and Clinical Neurology, 23,*
87.

Barkley, R. A. (1981). *Hyperactive children: A handbook for diagnosis and
treatment.* New York: Guilford Press.

Barkley, R. A. (1987). *Defiant children: A clinician's manual for parent training.*
New York: Guilford Press.

Barkley, R. A. (1990). *Attention deficit hyperactivity disorder: A handbook for
diagnosis and treatment.* New York: Guilford Press.

Barrios, B. A., Hartmann, D. P., & Shigetomi, C. (1981). Fears and anxieties in
children. In E. J. Mash & L. G. Terdal (Eds.), *Behavioral assessment of
childhood disorders* (pp. 259–304). New York: Guilford Press.

Barrios, B. A., & O'Dell, S. L. (1989). Fears and anxieties. In E. J. Mash & R. A. Barkley (Eds.), *Treatment of childhood disorders* (pp. 167–221). New York: Guilford Press.

Barton, E. J., & Ascione, F. R. (1984). Direct observation. In T. H. Ollendick & M. Hersen (Eds.), *Child behavioral assessment: Principles and procedures* (pp. 166–194). Elmsford, NY: Pergamon Press.

Bates, J. E., & Bayles, K. (1988). The role of attachment in the development of behavior problems. In J. Belsky & T. Nezworski (Eds.), *Clinical implications of attachment* (pp. 253–299). Hillsdale, NJ: Erlbaum.

Bauer, P. J., & Mandler, J. M. (1989). One thing follows another: Effects of temporal structure on 1- to 2-year olds' recall of events. *Developmental Psychology, 25,* 197–206.

Baumrind, D. (1967). Child care practices anteceding three patterns of preschool behavior. *Genetic Psychology Monographs, 75,* 43–88.

Baumrind, D. (1971). Current patterns of parental authority. *Developmental Psychology Monographs, 4*(1, Pt. 2).

Beck, A. T., Ward, C. H., Mendelson, M., Mock, J., & Erbaugh, J. (1961). An inventory for measuring depression. *Archives of General Psychiatry, 4,* 561–571.

Behar, D., & Stewart, M. A. (1981). Fears and phobias. In S. Gabel (Ed.), *Behavior problems in childhood: A primary care approach* (pp. 333–340). New York: Grune & Stratton.

Behar, L., & Stringfield, S. (1974). A behavior rating scale for the preschool child. *Developmental Psychology, 10,* 601–610.

Belsky, J. (1984). The determinants of parenting: A process model. *Child Development, 55,* 83–96.

Belsky, J. (1986). Infant day care: A cause of concern? *Zero to Three, 6,* 1–9.

Bem, S. L. (1989). Genital knowledge and gender constancy in preschool children. *Child Development, 60,* 649–662.

Berg, C. J., Zahn, T. A., Behar, D., & Rapoport, J. L. (1986). Childhood obsessive–compulsive disorder: An anxiety disorder. In R. Gittelman (Ed.), *Anxiety disorders of childhood* (pp. 126–135). New York: Guilford Press.

Berg, I., Nichols, K., & Pritchard, C. (1969). School phobia—its classification and relationship to dependency. *Journal of Child Psychology and Psychiatry, 10,* 123–141.

Berger, B. M. (1981). Liberating child sexuality. In L. L. Constantine & F. M. Martinson (Eds.), *Children and sex: New findings, new perspectives* (pp. 247–254). Boston: Little, Brown.

Bernal, M. E., Klinnert, M. D., & Schultz, L. A. (1980). Outcome evaluation of behavioral parent training and client-centered parent counseling for children with conduct problems. *Journal of Applied Behavior Analysis, 13,* 677–691.

Bernal, M. E., & North, J. A. (1978). A survey of parent training manuals. *Journal of Applied Behavior Analysis, 11,* 533–544.

Berndt, T. J. (1981). Effects of friendship on prosocial intentions and behavior. *Child Development, 52,* 636–643.

Berndt, T. J., & Bulleit, T. N. (1985). Effects of sibling relationships on preschoolers' behavior at home and at school. *Developmental Psychology, 21,* 761–767.

Bernstein, A. C., & Cowan, P. A. (1975). Children's concepts of how people get babies. *Child Development, 46*, 77–91.

Bierman, K. L. (1983). Cognitive development and clinical interviews with children. In B. B. Lahey & A. E. Kazdin (Eds.), *Advances in clinical child psychology* (Vol. 6, pp. 217–251). New York: Plenum Press.

Bierman, K. L., & Schwartz, L. A. (1988). Clinical child interviews: Approaches and developmental considerations. *Journal of Child and Adolescent Psychotherapy, 3*, 267–278.

Bijou, S. W. (1984). Parent training: Actualizing the critical conditions of early childhood development. In R. F. Dangel & R. A. Polster (Eds.), *Parent training* (pp. 15–26). New York: Guilford Press.

Black, D., & Urbanowicz, M. A. (1987). Family intervention with bereaved children. *Journal of Child Psychology and Psychiatry, 28*, 467–476.

Blagg, N. R., & Yule, W. (1984). The behavioural treatment of school refusals: A comparative study. *Behaviour Research and Therapy, 22*, 119–127.

Blechman, E. A. (1984). Competent parents, competent children: Behavioral objectives of parent training. In R. F. Dangel & R. A. Polster (Eds.), *Parent training* (pp. 34–66). New York: Guilford Press.

Bliss, J. (1980). Sensory experiences of Gilles de la Tourette syndrome. *Archives of General Psychiatry, 37*, 1343–1347.

Block, J. H., Block, J., & Gjerde, P. F. (1986). The personality of children prior to divorce: A prospective study. *Child Development, 57*, 827–840.

Block, J., Block, J. H., & Gjerde, P. F. (1988). Parental functioning and the home environment in families of divorce: Prospective and concurrent analyses. *Journal of the American Academy of Child and Adolescent Psychiatry, 27*, 207–213.

Blomfield, J. M., & Douglas, J. W. B. (1956). Bedwetting: Prevalence among children age 4–7 years. *Lancet, i*, 850–852.

Blount, R. L., Corbin, S. M., Sturges, J. W., Wolfe, V. Y., Prater, J. M., & James, L. D. (1989). The relationship between adults' behavior and child coping and distress during BMA/LP procedures: A sequential analysis. *Behavior Therapy, 20*, 585–601.

Blum, H. M., Boyle, M. H., & Offord, D. R. (1988). Single-parent families: Child psychiatric disorder and school performance. *Journal of the American Academy of Child and Adolescent Psychiatry, 27*, 214–219.

Boat, B. W., & Everson, M. D. (1986). *Using anatomical dolls: Guidelines for interviewing young children in sexual abuse investigations.* Unpublished manuscript, School of Medicine, University of North Carolina–Chapel Hill.

Boggs, S. R., & Eyberg, S. M. (1988). Interviewing techniques and establishing rapport. In A. La Greca (Ed.), *Childhood assessment: Through the eyes of a child* (pp. 85–108). Newton, MA: Allyn & Bacon.

Bollard, J., & Nettlebeck, T. (1982). A component analysis of dry-bed training for treatment of bed wetting. *Behaviour Research and Therapy, 20*, 383–390.

Borkovec, T. D., & Inz, J. (1990). The nature of worry in generalized disorder: A predominance of thought activity. *Behaviour Research and Therapy, 28*, 153–158.

Bornstein, P. H., Bornstein, M. R., & Dawson, B. (1984). Integrated assessment and treatment. In T. H. Ollendick & M. Hersen (Eds.), *Child behavioral assessment: Principles and procedures* (pp. 223-243). Elmsford, NY: Pergamon Press.

Bowlby, J. (1973). *Attachment and loss: Vol. 2. Separation, anxiety and anger.* New York: Basic Books.

Brazelton, T. B. (1962). A child oriented approach to toilet training. *Pediatrics, 29,* 121-128.

Brazelton, T. B. (1989, February 13). Working parents: How to give your kids what they need. *Time,* pp. 66-70.

Brazelton, T. B., & Yogman, M. (1986). *Affective development to infancy.* Norwood, NJ: Ablex.

Brett, D. (1988). *Annie Stories: A special kind of story telling.* New York: Workman Publishing.

Brody, G. H., Pillegrini, A. D., & Sigel, I. E. (1986). Marital quality and mother-child and father-child interactions with school-aged children. *Developmental Psychology, 22,* 291-296.

Brody, G. H., & Stoneman, Z. (1983). Children with atypical siblings: Socialization outcomes and clinical participation. In B. J. Lahey & A. E. Kazdin (Eds.), *Advances in clinical child psychology* (Vol. 6, pp. 285-326). New York: Plenum Press.

Brody, G. H., & Stoneman, Z. (1987). Sibling conflict: Contributions of the siblings themselves, the parent-sibling relationship, and the broader family system. *Journal of Children in Contemporary Society, 19,* 39-53.

Brody, G. H., Stoneman, Z., & Burke, M. (1987). Child temperaments, maternal differential behavior, and sibling relationships. *Developmental Psychology, 23,* 354-362.

Brody, G. H., Stoneman, Z., & Burke, M. (1988). Child temperament and parental perceptions of individual child adjustment: An intrafamilial analysis. *American Journal of Orthopsychiatry, 58,* 532-542.

Brooks-Gunn, J., & Warren, M. P. (1988). The psychological significance of secondary sexual characteristics in nine- to eleven-year-old girls. *Child Development, 59,* 1061-1069.

Brown, R. (1973). *A first language: The early stages.* Cambridge, MA: Harvard University Press.

Browne, A., & Finkelhor, D. (1986). Impact of child sexual abuse: A review of the research. *Psychological Bulletin, 99,* 66-77.

Bruun, R. D. (1988). The natural history of Tourette's syndrome. In D. J. Cohen, R. D. Bruun, & J. R. Leckman (Eds.), *Tourette's syndrome and tic disorders* (pp. 21-41). New York: Wiley.

Bruun, R. D., & Shapiro, A. K. (1972). Differential diagnosis of Gilles de la Tourette syndrome. *Journal of Nervous and Mental Disease, 155,* 328-334.

Burger, A. L., & Jacobson, N. S. (1979). The relationship between sex role characteristics, couple satisfaction and problem-solving skills. *American Journal of Family Therapy, 7,* 52-61.

Bush, J. P., & Cockrell, C. S. (1987). Maternal factors predicting parenting behaviors in the pediatric clinic. *Journal of Pediatric Psychology, 12,* 505-518.

Buss, A. H. (1984). A conception of shyness. In J. Daly & J. C. McCrosky (Eds.), *Avoiding communication: Shyness, reticence, and communication apprehension* (pp. 39–49). Beverly Hills, CA: Sage.

Buss, A. H., & Plomin, R. (1984). *Temperament: Early developing personality traits*. Hillside, NJ: Erlbaum.

Butler, J. F. (1976). The toilet training success of parents after reading *Toilet training in less than a day. Behavior Therapy, 7,* 185–191.

Butler, R. J., Brewin, C. R., & Forsythe, W. I. (1988). A comparison of two approaches to treatment of nocturnal enuresis and the prediction of effectiveness using pre-treatment variables. *Journal of Child Psychology and Psychiatry, 29,* 501–509.

Butler, R. J., Redfern, E. J., & Forsythe, W. I. (1990). The child's construing of nocturnal enuresis: A method of inquiry and prediction of outcome. *Journal of Child Psychology and Psychiatry, 31,* 447–454.

Cairns, R. B., Cairns, B. D., Neckerman, H. J., Ferguson, L. L., & Gariepy, J. L. (1989). Growth and aggression: 1. Childhood to early adolescence. *Developmental Psychology, 25,* 320–330.

Calderone, M. S., & Johnson, E. W. (1983). *The family book about sexuality* (rev. ed.). New York: Bantam Books.

Caldwell, E. C., & Hall, V. C. (1970). Concept learning in discrimination tasks. *Developmental Psychology, 2,* 41–48.

Campbell, L. M., III. (1973). A variation of thought-stopping in a twelve-year-old boy: A case report. *Journal of Behavior Therapy and Experimental Psychiatry, 4,* 69–70.

Campbell, S. B. (1986). Developmental issues in childhood anxiety. In R. Gittelman (Ed.), *Anxiety disorders of childhood* (pp. 24–57). New York: Guilford Press.

Campbell, S. B. (1987). Parent-referred problem three-year-olds: Developmental changes in symptoms. *Journal of Child Psychology and Psychiatry, 28,* 835–845.

Campbell, S. B. (1990). *Behavior problems in preschool children.* New York: Guilford Press.

Campbell, S. B., & Ewing, L. J. (1990). Follow-up of hard-to-manage preschoolers: Adjustment at age 9 and prediction of continuing symptoms. *Journal of Child Psychology and Psychiatry, 31,* 871–890.

Campbell, S. B., Ewing, L. J., Breaux, A. M., & Szumowski, E. K. (1986). Parent-identified behavior problem toddlers: Follow-up at school entry. *Journal of Child Psychology and Psychiatry, 27,* 473–488.

Cantwell, D. P. (1988). DSM-III studies. In M. Rutter, A. H. Tuma, & L. S. Lann (Eds.), *Assessment and diagnosis in child psychopathology* (pp. 3–36). New York: Guilford Press.

Caplan, M. G., & Douglas, V. I. (1969). Incidence of parental loss in children with depressed mood. *Journal of Psychology and Psychiatry, 10,* 225–244.

Caplan, M. G., & Hay, D. G. (1989). Preschoolers responses to peers distress and beliefs about bystander intervention. *Journal of Child Psychology and Psychiatry, 30,* 231–242.

Cappo, B. M., & Holmes, D. S. (1984). The utility of prolonged respiratory exhalation for reducing physiological and psychological arousal in non-threatening and threatening situations. *Journal of Psychosomatic Research, 28*, 265–273.

Carey, W. B., & McDevitt, S. C. (1978). Stability and change in individual temperament diagnoses from infancy to early childhood. *Journal of the American Academy of Child Psychiatry, 17*, 331–337.

Cassidy, J. (1988). Child–mother attachment and the self in six-year-olds. *Child Development, 59*, 121–134.

Cautela, J. R., & Groden, J. (1978). *Relaxation: A comprehensive manual for adults, children, and children with special needs.* Champaign, IL: Research Press.

Cavenar, J. O., Spaulding, J. G., & Sullivan, J. L. (1979). Child's reaction to mother's abortion: Case report. *Military Medicine, 144*, 412–413.

Cebollero, A. M., Cruise, K., & Stollak, G. (1986). The long-term effects of divorce: Mothers and children in concurrent support groups. *Journal of Divorce, 10*, 219–228.

Chamberlin, R. W. (1974). Management of preschool behavior problems. *Pediatric Clinics of North America, 21*, 33–47.

Chamrad, D. L., & Robinson, N. M. (1986). Parenting the intellectually gifted preschool child. *Topics in Early Childhood Special Education, 6*, 74–87.

Christoffel, K. K., & Liu, K. (1983). Homicide death rates in childhood in 23 developed countries: U.S. rates atypically high. *Child Abuse and Neglect, 7*, 339–345.

Christophersen, E. R. (1989). Injury control. *American Psychologist, 44*, 237–241.

Christophersen, E. R., Barrish, H. H., Barrish, I. J., & Christophersen, M. R. (1984). Continuing education for parents of infants and toddlers. In R. F. Dangel & R. A. Polster (Eds.), *Parent training* (pp. 127–143). New York: Guilford Press.

Christophersen, E. R., & Rainey, S. K. (1976). Management of encopresis through a pediatric outpatient clinic. *Journal of Pediatric Psychology, 1*, 38–41.

Christophersen, E. R., & Rapoff, M. A. (1979). Behavioral pediatrics. In O. F. Pomerleau & J. P. Brady (Eds.), *Behavioral medicine: Theory and practice* (pp. 99–123). Baltimore: Williams & Wilkins.

Christophersen, E. R., & Rapoff, M. A. (1983). Toileting problems in children. In C. E. Walker & M. C. Roberts (Eds.), *Handbook of clinical child psychology* (pp. 593–615). New York: Wiley.

Cicchetti, D. (1984). The emergence of developmental psychopathology. *Child Development, 58*, 1–7.

Clark, G. T., Rugh, J. D., & Handelman, S. L. (1975). Nocturnal masseter activity and urinary catecholamine levels in bruxers. *Journal of Dental Research, 59*, 1571–1576.

Clarke-Stewart, K. A. (1978). Popular primers for parents. *American Psychologist, 33*, 359–369.

Clarke-Stewart, K. A. (1988). Parents' effects on children's development: A decade of progress? *Journal of Applied Developmental Psychology, 9*, 41–84.

Clarke-Stewart, K. A. (1989). Infant day care: Maligned or malignant? *American Psychologist, 44*, 266–273.

Coates, T. J., & Thoresen, C. E. (1981). Sleep disturbances in children and adolescents. In E. J. Mash & L. G. Terdal (Eds.), *Behavioral assessment of childhood disorders* (pp. 639–678). New York: Guilford Press.

Cohen, D. J., Bruun, R. D., & Leckman, J. F. (Eds.). (1988). *Tourette's syndrome and tic disorders.* New York: Wiley.

Comings, D. E., & Comings, B. G. (1988). Tourette's syndrome and attention-deficit disorders. In D. J. Cohen, R. D. Bruun, & J. F. Leckman (Eds.), *Tourette's syndrome and tic disorders* (pp. 119–136). New York: Wiley.

Conners, C. K. (1970). Symptom patterns in hyperactive, neurotic, and normal children. *Child Development, 41,* 667–682.

Conte, J. R., Wolf, S., & Smith, T. (1989). What sexual offenders tell us about prevention strategies. *Child Abuse and Neglect, 13,* 293–301.

Constantine, L. L. (1981). The sexual rights of children. In L. L. Constantine & F. M. Martinson (Eds.), *Children and sex: New findings, new perspectives* (pp. 255–264). Boston: Little, Brown.

Covell, K., & Abramovitch, R. (1987). Understanding emotion in the family: Children's and parents' attributions of happiness, sadness, and anger. *Child Development, 58,* 985–991.

Crawford, J. D. (1989). Introductory comments. *Journal of Pediatrics, 114,* 687–690.

Crnic, K. A., Friedrich, W. N., & Greenberg, M. T. (1983). Adaptation of families with mentally retarded children: A model of stress, coping, and family ecology. *American Journal of Mental Deficiency, 88,* 125–138.

Crnic, K. A., Greenberg, M. T., Ragozin, A. S., Robinson, N. M., & Basham, R. (1983). Effects of stress and social support on mothers and premature and full-term infants. *Child Development, 54,* 209–217.

Crockenberg, S. (1987). Predictors and correlates of anger towards and punitive control of toddlers by adolescent mothers. *Child Development, 58,* 964–975.

Crowell, J., Keener, M., Ginsburg, N., & Anders, T. (1987). Sleep habits in toddlers 18 to 36 months old. *Journal of the American Academy of Child and Adolescent Psychiatry, 26,* 510–515.

Cruickshank, W. M. (1977). Myths and realities in learning disabilities. *Journal of Learning Disabilities, 10,* 51–58.

Culbertson, J. L., Krous, H. S., & Bendell, R. D. (Eds.). (1988). *Sudden infant death syndrome: Medical aspects and psychological management.* Baltimore: Johns Hopkins University Press.

Cummings, E. M. (1987). Coping with background anger in early childhood. *Child Development, 58,* 976–984.

Currier, R. L. (1981). Juvenile sexuality in global perspective. In L. L. Constantine & F. M. Martinson (Eds.), *Children and sex: New findings, new perspectives* (pp. 9–19). Boston: Little, Brown.

Cutrona, C. E. (1984). Social support and stress in the transition to parenthood. *Journal of Abnormal Psychology, 93,* 378–390.

Czeisler, C. A., Richardson, G. S., Coleman, R. M., Zimmerman, J. C., Moore-Ede, M. C., Dement, W. C., & Weitzman, E. D. (1981). Chronotherapy and resetting the circadian clocks of patients with delayed sleep phase insomnia. *Sleep, 4,* 1–21.

Dadds, M. R., Schwartz, S., & Sanders, M. R. (1987). Marital discord and treatment outcome in behavioral treatment of child conduct disorders. *Journal of Consulting and Clinical Psychology, 55,* 396-403.

Dahlquist, L. M., & Kalfus, G. R. (1984). A novel approach to assessment in the treatment of childhood trichotillomania. *Journal of Behavior Therapy and Experimental Psychiatry, 15,* 47-50.

Dangel, R. F., & Polster, R. A. (Eds.). (1984). *Parent training.* New York: Guilford Press.

Daniel, J. H., Hampton, R. L., & Newberger, E. H. (1983). Child abuse and accidents in black families: A controlled study. *American Journal of Orthopsychiatry, 53,* 645-653.

Davidson, M., Kugler, M. M., & Bauer, C. H. (1963). Diagnosis and management in children with severe and protracted constipation and obstipation. *Journal of Pediatrics, 62,* 261-265.

DeJonge, D. A. (1973). Epidemiology of enuresis: A survey of the literature. In I. Kolvin, R. C. MacKeith, & S. R. Meadow (Eds.), *Bladder control and enuresis* (pp. 39-46). Philadelphia: J. B. Lippincott.

DeLoache, J. S., Cassidy, D. J., & Brown, A. L. (1985). Precursors of mnemonic strategies in very young children. *Child Development, 56,* 125-137.

DeLuca, R. V., & Holborn, S. W. (1984). A comparison of relaxation training and competing response training to eliminate hair pulling and nail biting. *Journal of Behavior Therapy and Experimental Psychiatry, 15,* 67-70.

Denckla, M., Bemporad, J., & MacKay, M. (1976). Tics following methylphenidate administration: A report of 20 cases. *Journal of the American Medical Association, 235,* 1349-1351.

deYoung, M. (1987). Disclosing sexual abuse: The impact of developmental variables. *Child Welfare, 66,* 217-223.

Doleys, D. M. (1978). Assessment and treatment of enuresis and encopresis in children. In M. Hersen, R. Eisler, & P. M. Miller (Eds.), *Progress in behavior modification* (Vol. 6, pp. 85-121). New York: Academic Press.

Doleys, D. M., & Dolce, J. D. (1982). Toilet training and enuresis. *Pediatric Clinics of North America, 29,* 297-313.

Dollinger, S. J., Horn, J. L., & Boarini, D. (1988). Disturbed sleep and worries among learning disabled adolescents. *American Journal of Orthopsychiatry, 58,* 428-434.

Douglas, J., & Richman, N. (1982). *Sleep management manual.* (Available from the Department of Psychological Medicine, Hospital for Sick Children, Great Ormond Street, London WC1, England).

Douglas, J. W. B. (1973). Early disturbing events and later enuresis. In I. Kolvin, R. C. MacKeith, & S. R. Meadow (Eds.), *Bladder control and enuresis* (pp. 109-117). Philadelphia: J. B. Lippincott.

Dreikurs, R. (1964). *Children: The challenge.* New York: Hawthorne Books.

Dumas, J. E. (1989). Treating antisocial behavior in children: Child and family approaches. *Clinical Psychology Review, 9,* 197-222.

Dunn, J. (1988). Sibling influences on childhood development. *Journal of Child Psychology and Psychiatry, 29,* 119-127.

Dunn, J., & Kendrick, C. (1982). *Siblings: Love, envy, and understanding.* Cambridge, MA: Harvard University Press.

Dunn, J., & Munn, P. (1985). Becoming a family member: Family conflict and the development of social understanding in the second year. *Child Development, 56,* 480–492.

Dunn, J., & Munn, P. (1986a). Sibling quarrels and maternal intervention: Individual differences in understanding and aggression. *Journal of Child Psychology and Psychiatry, 27,* 583–595.

Dunn, J., & Munn, P. (1986b). Siblings and the development of prosocial behavior. *International Journal of Behavioral Development, 9,* 265–284.

Dunn, J., Plomin, R., & Nettles, M. (1985). Consistency of mother's behavior towards infant siblings. *Developmental Psychology, 21,* 1188–1195.

Earls, F. J. (1983). An epidemiological approach to the study of behavior problems in young children. In S. B. Guze, F. J. Earls, & J. E. Barrett (Eds.), *Childhood psychopathology and development* (pp. 1–15). New York: Raven Press.

Earls, F. J., & Jung, K. G. (1987). Temperament and home environment characteristics as causal factors in the early development of childhood psychopathology. *Journal of the American Academy of Child and Adolescent Psychiatry, 26,* 491–498.

Edelbrock, C., & Achenbach, T. A. (1984). The teacher version of the Child Behavior Profile: I. Boys aged 6–11. *Journal of Clinical and Consulting Psychology, 52,* 207–217.

Edelbrock, C., & Costello, A. J. (1988). Structured psychiatric interviews for children. In M. Rutter, A. H. Tuma, & I. S. Lann (Eds.), *Assessment and diagnosis in child psychopathology* (pp. 87–112). New York: Guilford Press.

Egeland, B., Kalkoski, M., Gottesman, N., & Erickson, M. R. (1990). Preschool behavior problems: Stability and factors accounting for change. *Journal of Child Psychology and Psychiatry, 31,* 891–910.

Einbender, A. J., & Friedrich, W. N. (1989). Psychological functioning and behavior of sexually abused girls. *Journal of Consulting and Clinical Psychology, 57,* 155–157.

Elizur, E., & Kaffman, M. (1982). Children's bereavement reactions: II. *Journal of the American Academy of Child Psychiatry, 140,* 23–29.

Ellis, A. (1970). *The essence of rational psychotherapy: A comprehensive approach to treatment.* New York: Institute for Rational Living.

Esser, G., Schmidt, M. H., & Woerner, W. (1990). Epidemiology and course of psychiatric disorders in school-age children: Results of a longitudinal study. *Journal of Child Psychology and Psychiatry, 31,* 243–263.

Estrada, P., Arsenio, W. F., Hess, R. D., & Holloway, S. D. (1987). Affective quality of the mother–child relationship: Longitudinal consequences for children's school-relevant cognitive functioning. *Developmental Psychology, 23,* 210–215.

Eyberg, S. M. (1985). Behavioral assessment: Advancing methodology in pediatric psychology. *Journal of Pediatric Psychology, 10,* 123–139.

Eyberg, S. M., & Boggs, S. R. (1989). Parent training for oppositional-defiant preschoolers. In C. E. Schaefer & J. M. Briesmeister (Eds.), *Handbook of parent training: Parents as co-therapists for children's behavior problems* (pp. 105–132). New York: Wiley.

Eyberg, S. M., & Robinson, E. A. (1982). Parent–child interaction training: Effects on family functioning. *Journal of Clinical Child Psychology, 11*, 130–137.

Eyberg, S. M., & Robinson, E. A. (1983). Dyadic Parent-Child Interaction Coding System: A manual. *Psychological Documents, 13*, (Ms. No. 2582).

Eyberg, S. M., & Ross, A. W. (1978). Assessment of child behavior problems: The validation of a new inventory. *Journal of Clinical Child Psychology, 7*, 113–116.

Faller, K. C. (1988). Criteria for judging the credibility of children's statements about their sexual abuse. *Child Welfare, 67*, 389–401.

Faller, K. C. (1989). Characteristics of a clinical sample of sexually abused children: How boy and girl victims differ. *Child Abuse and Neglect, 13*, 281–291.

Feagans, L., Sanyal, M., Henderson, F., Collier, A., & Appelbaum, M. (1987). Relationship of middle ear disease in early childhood to later narrative and attentional skills. *Journal of Pediatric Psychology, 12*, 581–594.

Fein, G., & Fox, N. (1988). Infant day care: A special issue. *Early Childhood Research Quarterly, 3*.

Feldman, R. B., & Werry, J. S. (1966). An unsuccessful attempt to treat a tiquer by massed practice. *Behaviour Research and Therapy, 4*, 111–117.

Felner, R. D., Stolberg, A., & Cowen, E. L. (1975). Crisis events and school mental health patterns of young children. *Journal of Consulting and Clinical Psychology, 43*, 305–310.

Felner, R. D., & Terre, L. (1987). Child custody dispositions and children's adaptation following divorce. In L. A. Weithorn (Ed.), *Psychology and child custody determinations: Knowledge, roles and expertise* (pp. 106–153). Lincoln: University of Nebraska Press.

Ferber, R. (1985). *Solve your child's sleep problems.* New York: Simon & Schuster.

Ferber, R., Boyle, M. R., & Belfer, M. (1981, June). *Initial experience of a pediatrics sleep disorder clinic.* Paper presented at the 21st Annual Meeting of the Association of the Psychophysiological Study of Sleep, Hyannis, MA.

Feshbach, S. (1970). Aggression. In P. H. Mussen (Ed.), *Carmichael's manual of child psychology* (3rd ed., Vol. 2, pp. 159–259). New York: Wiley.

Fidler, B. J., & Saunders, E. B. (1988). Children's adjustment during custody/access disputes: Relation to custody arrangement, gender, and age of child. *Canadian Journal of Psychiatry, 33*, 517–523.

Field, T., & Reite, M. (1984). Children's responses to separation from mother during the birth of another child. *Child Development, 55*, 1308–1316.

Fielding, D. (1980). The response of day and night wetting children and children who wet only at night to retention control training and enuresis alarm. *Behaviour Research and Therapy, 18*, 305–317.

Finch, A. J., Saylor, C. R., & Edwards, G. L. (1985). Children's Depression

Inventory: Sex and grade norms for normal children. *Journal of Consulting and Clinical Psychology, 53*, 424-425.

Finkelhor, D. (1984). What parents tell their children about sexual abuse. In D. Finkelhor (Ed.), *Child sexual abuse: New theory and research* (pp. 134-149). New York: Free Press.

Finkelhor, D., & Browne, A. (1986). Initial and long-term effects: A conceptual framework. In D. Finkelhor & Associates (Eds.), *A sourcebook on child sexual abuse* (pp. 180-198). Beverly Hills, CA: Sage.

Finkelhor, D., Williams, L. M., & Burns, N. (1988). *Nursery crimes: Sexual abuse in day care*. Newbury Park, CA: Sage.

Finkelstein, N. (1982). Aggression: Is it stimulated by day care? *Young Children, 37*, 3-9.

Finney, J. W., Rapoff, M. A., Hall, C. L., & Christophersen, E. R. (1983). Replication and social validation of habit reversal treatment of tics. *Behavior Therapy, 14*, 116-127.

Fischer, M., Rolf, J. E., Hasazi, J. E., & Cummings, L. (1984). Follow-up of a preschool epidemiological sample: Cross-age continuities and predictions of later adjustment with internalizing and externalizing dimensions of behavior. *Child Development, 55*, 137-150.

Fisher, B. E., & Wilson, A. E. (1987). Selected sleep disturbances in school children reported by parents: Prevalence, interrelationships, behavioral correlates and parental attributions. *Perceptual and Motor Skills, 64*, 1147-1157.

Flavell, J. (1977). *Cognitive development*. Englewood Cliffs, NJ: Prentice-Hall.

Forehand, R. L., Gardner, H., & Roberts, M. (1978). Maternal response to child compliance and noncompliance: Some normative data. *Journal of Clinical Child Psychology, 7*, 121-124.

Forehand, R. L., King, H. E., Peed, S., & Yoder, P. (1975). Mother-child interactions: Comparisons of a non-compliant clinic group and non-clinic group. *Behaviour Research and Therapy, 13*, 79-84.

Forehand, R. L., Lautenschlager, G. J., Faust, J., & Graziano, W. G. (1986). Parent perceptions and parent-child interactions in clinic-referred children: A preliminary investigation of the effects of maternal depressive moods. *Behaviour Research and Therapy, 24*, 73-75.

Forehand, R. L., McCombs, A., Long, N., Brody, G., & Fauber, R. (1988). Early adolescent adjustment to recent parental divorce: The role of interparental conflict and adolescent sex as mediating variables. *Journal of Consulting and Clinical Psychology, 56*, 624-627.

Forehand, R. L., & McMahon, R. J. (1981). *Helping the noncompliant child: A clinician's guide to parent training*. New York: Guilford Press.

Forehand, R. L., Steffe, M. A., Furey, W. M., & Walley, P. B. (1983). Mothers' evaluation of a parent training program completed three and one-half years earlier. *Journal of Behaviour Therapy and Experimental Psychiatry, 14*, 339-342.

Forsythe, W. I., & Butler, R. J. (1989). Fifty years of enuretic alarms. *Archives of Disease in Childhood, 64*, 879-885.

Forsythe, W. I., & Redmond, A. (1974). Enuresis and spontaneous cure rate: A study of 1129 enuretics. *Archives of Disease in Childhood, 49*, 259-276.

Foxman, B., Valdez, R. B., & Brock, R. H. (1986). Childhood enuresis: Prevalence, perceived impact and prescribed treatments. *Pediatrics, 77*, 482–487.

Foxx, R. M., & Azrin, N. H. (1973). Dry pants: A rapid method of toilet training children. *Behaviour Research and Therapy, 11*, 435–442.

France, K. G., & Hudson, S. M. (1990). Behavior management of infant sleep disturbance. *Journal of Applied Behavior Analysis, 23*, 91–98.

Francis, G., Last, C. G., & Strauss, C. C. (1987). Expression of separation anxiety disorder: The role of age and gender. *Child Psychiatry and Human Development, 18*, 82–89.

Frankenburg, W. K., & Dodds, J. B. (1967). The Denver Developmental Screening Test. *Journal of Pediatrics, 71*, 181–191.

Frentz, C., & Kelley, M. L. (1986). Parents' acceptance of reductive treatment methods: The influence of problem severity and perception of child behavior. *Behavior Therapy, 17*, 75–81.

Friedman, A. G., & Ollendick, T. H. (1989). Treatment programs for severe nighttime fears: A methodological note. *Journal of Behavior Therapy and Experimental Psychiatry, 20*, 171–178.

Friedman, S. (1980). Self-control in the treatment of Gilles de la Tourette's syndrome: Case study with 18 month follow-up. *Journal of Consulting and Clinical Psychology, 48*, 400–402.

Friedrich, W. N., Urquiza, A. J., & Beilke, R. L. (1986). Behavior problems in sexually abused young children. *Journal of Pediatric Psychology, 11*, 47–57.

Friman, P. C. (1988). Eliminating chronic thumb sucking by preventing a covarying response. *Journal of Behavior Therapy and Experimental Psychiatry, 19*, 301–304.

Friman, P. C., Barone, V. J., & Christophersen, E. R. (1986). Aversive taste treatment of finger and thumb sucking. *Pediatrics, 78*, 174–176.

Friman, P. C., Finney, J. W., & Christophersen, E. R. (1984). Behavioral treatment of trichotillomania: An evaluative review. *Behavior Therapy, 15*, 249–266.

Friman, R. C., & Hove, G. (1987). Apparent covariation between child habit disorders: Effects of successful treatment for thumb sucking on untargeted chronic hair pulling. *Journal of Applied Behavior Analysis, 20*, 421–427.

Friman, P. C., & Leibowitz, J. M. (1990). An effective and acceptable treatment alternative for chronic thumb- and finger-sucking. *Journal of Pediatric Psychology, 15*, 57–65.

Funderburk, B. W., & Eyberg, S. M. (1989). Psychometric characteristics of Sutter–Eyberg Student Behavior Inventory: A school behavior rating scale for use with preschool children. *Behavioral Assessment, 11*, 297–313.

Fundudis, T. (1989). Children's memory and the assessment of possible child sex abuse. *Journal of Child Psychology and Psychiatry, 30*, 337–346.

Furman, E. (1976). Commentary. *Journal of Pediatrics, 89*, 143–145.

Furman, W. (1980). Promoting social development: Developmental implications for treatment. In B. B. Lahey & A. E. Kazdin (Eds.), *Advances in clinical child psychology* (Vol. 3, pp. 1–40). New York: Plenum.

Gabel, S., Hegedus, A. M., Wald, A., Chandra, R., & Chiponis, D. (1986). Prevalence of behavior problems and mental health utilization among encopretic children: Implications for behavioral pediatrics. *Journal of Developmental and Behavioral Pediatrics, 7,* 293–297.

Garbarino, J. (1988). Preventing childhood injury: Developmental and mental health issues. *American Journal of Orthopsychiatry, 58,* 25–45.

Garbarino, J., Stott, F. M., & Faculty of the Erikson Institute. (Eds.). (1989) *What children can tell us.* San Francisco: Jossey-Bass.

Gardner, R. A. (1982). *Family evaluation in child custody litigation.* Cresskill, NJ: Creative Therapeutics.

Garmezy, N. (1983). Stressors of childhood. In N. Garmezy & M. Rutter (Eds.), *Stress, coping and development in children* (pp. 43–84). New York: McGraw-Hill.

Garmezy, N. (1985). Stress-resistant children: The search for protective factors. In J. E. Stevenson (Eds.), *Recent research in developmental psychopathology (Journal of Child Psychology and Psychiatry* Book Supplement No. 4, pp. 213–233). Oxford: Pergamon Press.

Garmezy, N., & Masten, A. S. (1986). Stress, competence, and resilience: Common frontiers for therapist and psychopathologist. *Behavior Therapy, 89,* 500–521.

Garmezy, N., & Rutter, M. (1985). Acute reactions to stress. In M. Rutter & L. Hersov (Eds.), *Child and adolescent psychiatry: Modern approaches* (2nd ed., pp. 152–176). Oxford: Blackwell Scientific.

Garrison, W. T., & Earls, F. J. (1987). *Temperament and child psychopathology.* Newbury Park, CA: Sage.

Gelfand, D., & Peterson, L. (1985). *Child development and psychopathology.* Beverly Hills, CA: Sage.

Gelman, R. & Baillargeon, R. (1983). A review of some Piagetian concepts. In J. H. Flavell & E. M. Markman (Vol. Eds.), *Handbook of child psychology (4th ed.): Vol. 3. Cognitive development* (pp. 167–230). New York: Wiley.

Gibson, E. J. (1969). *Principles of perceptual learning and development.* Englewood Cliffs, NJ: Prentice-Hall.

Ginott, H. G. (1969). *Between parent and teenager.* New York: Avon.

Gittelman, R. (Ed.). (1986a). *Anxiety disorders of childhood.* New York: Guilford Press.

Gittelman, R. (1986b). Childhood anxiety disorders: Correlates and outcome. In R. Gittelman (Eds.), *Anxiety disorders of childhood* (pp. 101–125). New York: Guilford Press.

Gittelman, R., & Koplewicz, H. S. (1986). Pharmacotherapy of childhood anxiety disorders. In R. Gittelman (Ed.), *Anxiety disorders of childhood* (pp. 188–203). New York: Guilford Press.

Gittelman-Klein, R. (1975). Psychiatric characteristics of the relatives of school phobic children. In D. V. S. Sankar (Ed.), *Mental health in children* (pp. 325–334). New York: PJD.

Gittelman-Klein, R., & Klein, D. F. (1980). Separation anxiety in school refusal and its treatment with drugs. In L. Hersov & I. Berg (Eds.), *Out of school* (pp. 321–341). New York: Wiley.

Glicklich, L. B. (1951). An historical account of enuresis. *Pediatrics, 8,* 859–876.

Gold, E. R. (1986). Long-term effects of sexual victimization in childhood: An attributional approach. *Journal of Consulting and Clinical Psychology, 54,* 471–473.

Goldberg, I. D., Roghmann, K. J., McInery, T. K., & Burke, J. D. (1984). Mental health problems among children seen in pediatric practice: Prevalence and management. *Pediatrics, 73,* 278–293.

Golden, G. S. (1982). Movement disorders in children: Tourette syndrome. *Journal of Developmental and Behavioral Pediatrics, 3,* 209–216.

Golden, G. S. (1988). The use of stimulants in the treatment of Tourette's syndrome. In D. J. Cohen, R. D. Bruun, & J. F. Leckman (Eds.), *Tourette's syndrome and tic disorders* (pp. 317–325). New York: Wiley.

Goldfried, M. R. (1971). Systematic desensitization in training in self-control. *Journal of Consulting and Clinical Psychology, 37,* 228–234.

Goldsmith, J. J., Buss, A. H., Plomin, R., Rothbart, M. K., Thomas, A., Chess, S., Hinde, R. A., & McCall, R. B. (1987). Roundtable: What is temperament? Four approaches. *Child Development, 58,* 505–529.

Goodnow, J. J., & Levine, R. A. (1973). "The grammar of action": Sequence and syntax in children's copying. *Cognitive Psychology, 4,* 82–98.

Gordon, B. N., & Jens, K. G. (1988). A conceptual model for tracking high-risk infants and making early service decisions. *Developmental and Behavioral Pediatrics, 9,* 279–286.

Gordon, B. N., & Schroeder, C. S. (1990). Clinical practice: From assessment to intervention. In J. H. Johnson & J. Goldman (Eds.), *Developmental assessment in clinical child psychology* (pp. 251–267). Elmsford, NY: Pergamon Press.

Gordon, B. N., Schroeder, C. S., & Abrams, J. M. (1990a). Children's knowledge of sexuality: Age and social class differences. *Journal of Clinical Child Psychology, 19,* 33–43.

Gordon, B. N., Schroeder, C. S., & Abrams, J. M. (1990b). Children's knowledge of sexuality: A comparison of sexually abused and nonabused children. *American Journal of Orthopsychiatry, 60,* 250–257.

Gordon, S., & Snyder, S. V. (1983). Sex education. In C. E. Walker & M. C. Roberts (Eds.), *Handbook of clinical child psychology* (pp. 1154–1173). New York: Wiley.

Gordon, S., & Gordon, J. (1983). *Raising a child conservatively in a sexually permissive world.* New York: Simon & Schuster.

Gordon, S., & Gordon, J. (1984). *A better safe than sorry book: A family guide for sexual assault prevention.* Fayetteville, NY: Ed-U-Press.

Gordon, T. (1970). *Parent effectiveness training.* New York: Plume Books.

Gouze, K. (1987). Attention and social problem solving as correlates of aggression in preschool males. *Journal of Abnormal Child Psychology, 15,* 181–197.

Goyette, C. H., Conners, C. K., & Ulrich, R. F. (1978). Normative data on the revised Conners Parent and Teacher Rating Scales. *Journal of Abnormal Child Psychology, 6,* 221–236.

Graham, D. Y., Moser, S. E., & Estes, M. K. (1982). The effect of bran on bowel function in constipation. *American Journal of Gastroenterology, 77,* 599–603.

Graziano, A. M., & DeGiovanni, I. A. (1979). The clinical significance of childhood phobias: A note of the proportion of child-clinical referrals for the treatment of children's fears. *Behaviour Research and Therapy, 17,* 161–162.

Graziano, A. M., DeGiovanni, I. A., & Garcia, K. A. (1979). Behavioral treatment of children's fears: A review. *Psychological Bulletin, 86,* 804–830.

Green, A. H. (1986). True and false allegations of sexual abuse in child custody disputes. *Journal of the American Academy of Child Psychiatry, 25,* 449–456.

Greenberg, H. R. (1969). Transaction of a hair pulling symbiosis. *Psychiatry Quarterly, 43,* 662–674.

Greening, L., & Dollinger, S. J. (1989). Treatment of a child's sleep disturbance and related phobias in the family. In M. C. Roberts & C. E. Walker (Eds.) *Casebook of child and pediatric psychology* (pp. 94–111). New York: Guilford Press.

Griest, D. L., Forehand, R., Rogers, T., Breiner, J., Furey, W., & Williams, C. A. (1982). Effects of parent enhancement therapy on the treatment outcome and generalization of a parent training program. *Behaviour Research and Therapy, 20,* 429–436.

Griest, D. L., & Wells, K. C. (1983). Behavioral family therapy with conduct disorders in children. *Behavior Therapy, 14,* 37–53.

Gross, A. M. (1984). Behavioral interviewing. In T. H. Ollendick & M. Hersen (Eds.), *Child behavioral assessment: Principles and procedures* (pp. 61–79). Elmsford, NY: Pergamon Press.

Gruen, G. E. (1985). Genetic epistemology and the development of intelligence. In B. B. Wolman (Ed.). *Handbook of intelligence: Theories, measurements and applications* (pp. 159–200). New York: Wiley.

Guidubaldi, J., & Perry, J. D. (1985). Divorce and mental health sequelae for children: A two-year follow-up of a nationwide sample. *Journal of the American Academy of Child Psychiatry, 24,* 531–537.

Guilleminault, C., & Anders, T. (1976). Sleep disorders in children: Part II. *Advances in Pediatrics, 22,* 151–174.

Gundersen, B. H., Melas, P. S., & Skar, J. E. (1981). Sexual behavior of preschool children: Teachers' observations. In L. L. Constantine & F. M. Martinson (Eds.), *Children and sex: New findings, new perspectives* (pp. 45–61). Boston: Little, Brown.

Hagin, R. A. (1984). *Tourette syndrome and the school psychologist.* New York: Tourette Syndrome Association.

Hagin, R. A., & Kugler, J. (1988). School problems associated with Tourette's syndrome. In D. J. Cohen, R. D. Bruun, & J. F. Leckman (Eds.), *Tourette's syndrome and tic disorders* (pp. 223–236). New York: Wiley.

Hallgren, B. (1956). Enuresis: I. A study with reference to morbidity risk and symptomatology. II. A study with reference to certain physical, mental and social factors possibly associated with enuresis. *Acta Psychiatric Scandinavica, 31,* 379–436.

Halpern, E., & Palic, L. (1984). Developmental changes in death anxiety in childhood. *Journal of Applied Developmental Psychology, 5,* 163–172.

Halpern, W. I. (1977). The treatment of encopretic children. *Journal of the American Academy of Child Psychiatry, 16,* 478–499.

Hampe, E., Noble, H., Miller, L. C., & Barrett, C. L. (1973). Phobic children one and two years post treatment. *Journal of Abnormal Psychology, 82,* 446-453.

Hanf, C. (1969). *A two-stage program for modifying maternal controlling during mother-child (M-C) interaction.* Paper presented at the meeting of the Western Psychological Association, Vancouver, British Columbia.

Hargett, R. D., Hansen, F. G., & Davidson, P. O. (1970). Chronic thumbsucking: A second report on treatment and its psychological effects. *American Journal of Orthodontics, 57,* 164-178.

Haroian, L. M. (1983). Sexual problems of children. In C. E. Walker & M. C. Roberts (Eds.), *Handbook of clinical child psychology* (pp. 573-592). New York: Wiley.

Harter, S. (1983a). Developmental perspectives on the self system. In E. M. Hetherington (Vol. Ed.), *Handbook of child psychology (4th ed.): Vol. 4. Socialization, personality, and social development* (pp. 275-385). New York: Wiley.

Harter, S. (1983b). *Supplementary description of the Self-Perception Profile for Children: Revision of the Perceived Competence Scale for Children.* Unpublished manuscript, University of Denver.

Harter, S., & Pike, R. (1984). The Pictorial Scale of Perceived Competence and Social Acceptance for Young Children. *Child Development, 55,* 1969-1982.

Hartmann, E. L. (1973). *The functions of sleep.* New Haven, CT: Yale University Press.

Hartup, W. W. (1976). Peer reactions and the behavioral development of the individual child. In E. Schopler & R. J. Reichler (Eds.), *Psychopathology and child development* (pp. 203-218). New York: Plenum Press.

Hartup, W. W. (1989). Social relationships and their developmental significance. *American Psychologist, 44,* 120-126.

Haskins, R. (1985). Public school aggression among children with varying day care experience. *Child Development, 56,* 689-703.

Haskins, R. (1989). Beyond metaphor: The efficacy of early childhood education. *American Psychologist, 44,* 274-282.

Hawk, B. A., Schroeder, C. S., & Martin, S. (1987). Pediatric psychology in a primary care setting. *Newsletter of the Society of Pediatric Psychology, 11,* 13-18.

Heffer, R. W., & Kelley, M. L. (1987). Mother's acceptance of behavior interventions for children: The influence of parent race and income. *Behavior Therapy, 18,* 153-163.

Heinicke, C. M., Beckwith, L., & Thompson, A. (1988). Early intervention in the family system: A framework and review. *Infant Mental Health Journal, 9,* 111-141.

Heller, K., & Swindle, R. W. (1983). Social networks, perceived social support, and coping with stress. In R. D. Felner, L. A. Jason, J. N. Moritsugu, & S. S. Farber (Eds.), *Preventive psychology: Theory, research, and practice* (pp. 87-103). Elmsford, NY: Pergamon Press.

Hermecz, D. A., & Melamed, B. G. (1984). The assessment of emotional imagery training in fearful children. *Behavior Therapy, 15,* 156-172.

Hetherington, E. M. (1989). Coping with family transitions: Winner, losers, and survivors. *Child Development, 60,* 1-14.

Hetherington, E. M., Cox, M., & Cox, R. (1976). Divorced fathers. *Family Coordinator, 25,* 417-428.

Hetherington, E. M., Cox, M., & Cox, R. (1978). The aftermath of divorce. In J. H. Stevens, Jr., & M. Mathews (Eds.), *Mother-child, father-child relationships* (pp. 149-176). Washington, DC: National Association for the Education of Young Children.

Hetherington, E. M., Cox, M., & Cox, R. (1985). Long-term effects of divorce and remarriage on the adjustment of children. *Journal of the American Academy of Child Psychiatry, 24,* 518-530.

Himmelfarb, S., Hock, E., & Wenar, C. (1985). Infant temperament and noncompliant behavior at four years: A longitudinal study. *Genetic, Social, and General Psychology Monographs, 111,* 7-21.

Hindley, C. B., Fillozat, A. M., Klackenberg, G., Nicolet-Meister, D., & Sand, E. A. (1965). Some differences in infant feeding and elimination training in five European longitudinal samples. *Journal of Child Psychology and Psychiatry, 6,* 179-201.

Hobbs, N. (1975). *The futures of children.* San Francisco: Jossey-Bass.

Hobbs, S. A., & Forehand, R. (1975). Differential effects of contingent and noncontingent release from time-out on noncompliance and disruptive behavior of children. *Journal of Behavior Therapy and Experimental Psychiatry, 6,* 256-257.

Hodges, K., Kline, L., Stern, L., Cytryn, L., & McKnew, D. (1982). The development of a child assessment interview for research and clinical use. *Journal of Abnormal Child Psychology, 10,* 173-189.

Hodges, K., McKnew, D., Cytryn, L., Stern, L., & Kline, J. (1982). The Child Assessment Schedule (CAS) diagnostic interview: A report on reliability and validity. *Journal of the American Academy of Child Psychiatry, 21,* 468-473.

Hodges, W. F., Buchsbaum, H. K., & Tierney, C. W. (1983). Parent-child relationships and adjustment in preschool children in divorced and intact families. *Journal of Divorce, 7,* 43-58.

Hoffman, L. W. (1989). Effects of maternal employment in the two-parent family. *American Psychologist, 44,* 283-292.

Hoffman, M. L. (1977). Empathy, its development and prosocial implications. In B. Keasy (Ed.), *Nebraska Symposium on Motivation* (Vol. 25, pp. 169-217). Lincoln: University of Nebraska Press.

Hoffman, M. L. (1979). Development of moral thought, feeling, and behavior. *American Psychologist, 10,* 958-966.

Holden, G. W., Lavigne, V. V., & Camerson, A. M. (1990). Probing the continuum of effectiveness in parent training: Characteristics of parents and preschoolers. *Journal of Clinical Child Psychology, 19,* 2-8.

Honig, A. S. (1987). The shy child. *Young Children, 42,* 54-64.

Horacek, H. J., Ramey, C. T., Campbell, F. A., Hoffmann, K. P., & Fletcher, R. H. (1987). Predicting school failure and assessing early intervention with high-risk children. *Journal of the American Academy of Child and Adolescent Psychiatry, 26,* 758-763.

Houts, A. C., Whelan, J. P., & Peterson, J. K. (1987). Filmed versus live delivery of full-spectrum home training for primary enuresis: Presenting the information is not enough. *Journal of Consulting and Clinical Psychology, 55,* 902–906.

Howes, C. (1987). Social competence with peers in young children: Developmental sequences. *Developmental Review, 7,* 252–272.

Howes, C. (1988). Relations between early child care and schooling. *Developmental Psychology, 24,* 53–57.

Howes, P., & Markman, H. J. (1989). Marital quality and child functioning: A longitudinal investigation. *Child Development, 60,* 1044–1051.

Ilg, F. L., & Ames, L. B. (1955). *Child behavior.* New York: Harper.

Ireton, H., & Thwing, E. (1972). *Minnesota Child Development Inventory.* Minneapolis: Authors.

Jacobson, D. (1978). The impact of marital separation/divorce on children: I. Parent–child separation and child adjustment. *Journal of Divorce, 1,* 341–360.

Jacobson, E. (1962). *You must relax.* New York: McGraw-Hill.

Jacobson, J. L., & Willie, D. E. (1986). The influence of attachment pattern on developmental changes in peer interaction from the toddler to the preschool period. *Child Development, 57,* 338–347.

Jacobson, J. W. (1982a). Problem behavior and psychiatric impairment within a developmentally disabled population: I. Behavior frequency. *Applied Research in Mental Retardation, 3,* 121–139.

Jacobson, J. W. (1982b). Problem behavior and psychiatric impairment within a developmentally disabled population: II. Behavior severity. *Applied Research in Mental Retardation, 3,* 369–381.

Jagger, J., Prusoff, B., Cohen, D. J., Kidd, K. K., Carbonari, C., & John, K. (1982). The epidemiology of Tourette's syndrome. *Schizophrenia Bulletin, 8,* 267–278.

Jay, S. M. (1988). Invasive medical procedures: Psychological intervention and assessment. In D. K. Routh (Ed.), *Handbook of pediatric psychology* (pp. 401–425). New York: Guilford Press.

Jay, S. M., Green, V., Johnson, S., Caldwell, S., & Nitschke, R. (1987). Differences in death concepts between children with cancer and physically healthy children. *Journal of Clinical Child Psychology, 16,* 301–306.

Jehu, D., Morgan, R., Turner, R., & Jones, A. (1977). A controlled trial of the treatment of enuresis in residential homes for children. *Behaviour Research and Therapy, 15,* 1–16.

Jenkins, S., Bax, M., & Hart, H. (1980). Behavior problems in preschool children. *Journal of Child Psychology and Psychiatry, 21,* 5–17.

Jens, K. G., Gordon, B. N., & Shaddock, A. J. (1990). Remembering activities performed vs. imagined: A comparison of children with mental retardation and children with normal intelligence. *International Journal of Disability, Development and Education, 37,* 201–214.

Johnson, S. M., Wahl, G., Martin, S., & Johansson, S. (1973). How deviant is the normal child? A behavioral analysis of the preschool child and his family. In R. D. Rubin, J. P. Brady, & J. D. Henderson (Eds.), *Advances in behavior therapy* (Vol. 4, pp. 37–54). New York: Academic Press.

Johnston, J. R., Campbell, L. E. G., & Mayes, S. S. (1985). Latency children in post-separation and divorce disputes. *Journal of the American Academy of Child Psychiatry, 24*, 563–574.

Johnston, J. R., Gonzalez, R., & Campbell, L. E. G. (1987). Ongoing post divorce conflict and child disturbance. *Journal of Abnormal Child Psychology, 15*, 493–509.

Jones, T., & Davey, G. C. (1990). The effects of cued UCS rehearsal on the retention of differential "fear" conditioning: An experimental analogue of the "worry" process. *Behaviour Research and Therapy, 28*, 159–164.

Kaffman, M., & Elizur, E. (1983). Bereavement responses of kibbutz and non-kibbutz children following death of father. *Journal of Child Psychology and Psychiatry, 24*, 435–442.

Kagan, J., Reznick, J. S., & Snidman, N. (1987). The physiology and psychology of behavioral inhibition in children. *Child Development, 58*, 1459–1473.

Kales, A. (Ed.). (1969). *Sleep: Physiology and pathology*. Philadelphia: J. B. Lippincott.

Kales, A., Bixler, E. O., Tan, T. L., Scharf, M. B., & Kales, J. D. (1974). Chronic hypnotic drug use: Ineffectiveness, drug withdrawal insomnia and dependence. *Journal of the American Medical Association, 5*, 573–577.

Kales, J. D., Kales, A., Soldatos, C. R., Caldwell, A., Charney, D. S., & Martin, E. D. (1980). Night terrors: Clinical characteristics and personality patterns. *Archives of General Psychiatry, 37*, 1413–1417.

Kales, J. D., Kales, A., Soldatos, C. R., Chamberlin, K., & Martin, E. D. (1979). Sleepwalking and night terrors related to febrile illness. *American Journal of Psychiatry, 136*, 1214–1215.

Kalter, N. (1977). Children of divorce in an outpatient psychiatric population. *American Journal of Orthopsychiatry, 47*, 40–51.

Kalter, N., Riemer, R., Brickman, A., & Chen, J. W. (1985). Implications of parental divorce for female development. *Journal of the American Academy of Child Psychiatry, 24*, 538–544.

Kane, M. T., & Kendall, P. C. (1989). Anxiety disorders in children: A multiple-baseline evaluation. *Behavior Therapy, 20*, 499–508.

Kanfer, F. H., & Karoly, P. (1972). Self-control: A behavioristic excursion into the lion's den. *Behavior Therapy, 3*, 398–416.

Kanfer, R., Eyberg, S. M., & Krahn, G. L. (1983). Interviewing strategies in child assessment. In C. E. Walker & M. C. Roberts (Eds.), *Handbook of clinical child psychology* (pp. 95–108). New York: Wiley.

Kanoy, K., Cunningham, J. L., White, P., & Adams, S. J. (1984). Is family structure that critical? Family relationships of children with divorced and married parents. *Journal of Divorce, 8*, 97–105.

Kanoy, K., & Schroeder, C. S. (1985). Suggestions to parents about common behavior problems in a pediatric primary care office: Five years of follow-up. *Journal of Pediatric Psychology, 10*, 15–30.

Karacan, I., Rosenbloom, A. L., & Williams, R. L. (1970). The clitoral erection cycle during sleep. *Psychophysiology, 7*, 338.

Kastenbaum, R., & Costa, P. T. (1977). Psychological perspectives on death. *Annual Review of Psychology, 28*, 225–249.

Kataria, S., Swanson, M. S., & Trevathan, G. E. (1987). Persistence of sleep disturbances in preschool children. *Journal of Pediatrics, 110*, 642–646.

Kazdin, A. E. (1987a). *Conduct disorders in childhood and adolescence.* Newbury Park, CA: Sage.

Kazdin, A. E. (1987b). Treatment of antisocial behavior in children: Current status and future directions. *Psychological Bulletin, 102*, 187–203.

Kazdin, A. E. (1989). Developmental psychopathology: Current research, issues and directions. *American Psychologist, 44*, 180–187.

Kazdin, A. E. (1990). Premature termination from treatment among children referred for antisocial behavior. *Journal of Child Psychology and Psychiatry, 31*, 415–425.

Kazdin, A. E., Esveldt-Dawson, K., French, N. H., & Unis, A. S. (1987). Effects of parent management training and problem-solving skills training combined in the treatment of antisocial child behavior. *Journal of the American Academy of Child and Adolescent Psychiatry, 26*, 416–424.

Kellerman, J. (1979). Behavioral treatment of night terrors in a child with acute leukemia. *Journal of Nervous and Mental Disease, 167*, 182–185.

Kellerman, J. (1980). Rapid treatment of nocturnal anxiety in children. *Journal of Behavior Therapy and Experimental Psychiatry, 11*, 9–11.

Kempe, C. H., & Helfer, R. E. (1972). *Helping the battered child and his family.* Philadelphia: J. B. Lippincott.

Kendall, P. C., Howard, B., & Epps, J. (1988). The anxious child: Cognitive-behavioral treatment strategies. *Behavior Modification, 12*, 281–310.

Kennedy, W. A. (1965). School phobia: Rapid treatment of fifty cases. *Journal of Abnormal Psychology, 70*, 285–289.

Keogh, B. K., & Burstein, N. D. (1988). Relationship of temperament to preschoolers' interactions with peers and teachers. *Exceptional Children, 54*, 456–461.

Kimmel, H. D. (1974). [Review of *Toilet training in less than a day: How to do it*]. *Journal of Behavior Therapy and Experimental Psychiatry, 5*, 113.

King, H. E., & Kleemeier, C. P. (1983). The effect of divorce on parents and children. In C. E. Walker & M. C. Roberts (Eds.), *Handbook of clinical child psychology* (pp. 1249–1272). New York: Wiley.

King, N. J., Cranstoun, F., & Josephs, A. (1989). Emotive imagery and children's night-time fears: A multiple baseline design evaluation. *Journal of Behavior Therapy and Experimental Psychiatry, 20*, 125–135.

King, N. J., Hamilton, D. H., & Ollendick, T. H. (1988). *Children's phobias: A behavioral perspective.* New York: Wiley.

Kinsey, A. C., Pomeroy, W. B., & Martin, C. E. (1948). *Sexual behavior in the human male.* Philadelphia: W. B. Saunders.

Klackenberg, G. (1949). Thumbsucking: Frequency and etiology. *Pediatrics, 4*, 418–424.

Klackenberg, G. (1982). Somnambulism in children: Prevalence, course and behavioral correlations. *Acta Paediatrica Scandinavica, 71*, 495–499.

Klauber, G. T. (1989). Clinical efficacy and safety of desmopressin in the treatment of nocturnal enuresis. *Journal of Pediatrics, 114*, 719–722.

Klesges, R. C., Malott, J. M., & Ugland, M. (1984). The effects of graded exposure and parent modeling on the dental phobias of a four-year-old girl and her mother. *Journal of Behavior Therapy and Experimental Psychiatry*, *15*, 161–164.

Kline, M., Tschann, J. M., Johnston, J. R., & Wallerstein, J. S. (1989). Children's adjustment in joint and sole physical custody families. *Developmental Psychology*, *25*, 430–438.

Klingman, A. (1988). Biblioguidance with kindergartners: Evaluation of a primary prevention program to reduce fear of the dark. *Journal of Clinical Child Psychology*, *17*, 237–241.

Knell, S. M., & Moore, D. J. (1988). Childhood trichotillomania treated indirectly by punishing thumb sucking. *Journal of Behavior Therapy and Experimental Psychiatry*, *19*, 305–310.

Knoff, H. M. (1986). The personality assessment report and the feedback and planning conference. In H. M. Knoff (Ed.), *The assessment of child and adolescent personality* (pp. 547–582). New York: Guilford Press.

Knopf, I. J. (1979). *Childhood psychopathology: A developmental approach*. Englewood Cliffs, NJ: Prentice-Hall.

Koblinsky, S. A. (1983). *Sexuality education for parents of young children: A facilitator training manual*. Fayetteville, NY: Ed-U-Press.

Kochanska, G., Kuczynski, L., Radke-Yarrow, M., & Welsh, J. D. (1987). Resolutions of control episodes between well and affectively ill mothers and their young children. *Journal of Abnormal Psychology*, *15*, 441–456.

Koeppen, A. S. (1974). Relaxation training for children. *Elementary School Guidance and Counseling*, *9*, 14–21.

Kohlberg, L. (1969). Stage and sequence: The cognitive–developmental approach to socialization. In D. A. Goslin (Ed.), *Handbook of socialization theory and research* (pp. 347–480). Chicago: Rand McNally.

Kolko, D. J. (1988). Educational programs to promote awareness and prevention of child sexual victimization: A review and methodological critique. *Clinical Psychology Review*, *8*, 195–209.

Kolvin, I., Miller, F. J. W., Fletting, M., & Kolvin, P. A. (1988). Social and parenting factors affecting criminal-offense rates: Findings from the Newcastle Thousand Family Study. *British Journal of Psychiatry*, *152*, 80–90.

Koocher, G. P. (1973). Childhood, death, and cognitive development. *Developmental Psychology*, *9*, 369–375.

Koocher, G. P. (1983). Grief and loss in childhood. In C. E. Walker & M. C. Roberts (Eds.), *Handbook of clinical child psychology* (pp. 1273–1284). New York: Wiley.

Kopp, C. V. (1982). Antecedents of self regulation: A developmental perspective. *Developmental Psychology*, *18*, 199–214.

Kopp, C. V. (1983). Risk factors in development. In M. M. Haith & J. J. Campos (Vol. Eds.), *Handbook of child psychology* (4th ed.): *Vol. 2. Infancy and developmental psychobiology* (pp. 1081–1181). New York: Wiley.

Kopp, C. V. (1989). Regulation of distress and negative emotions: A developmental view. *Developmental Psychology*, *25*, 343–354.

Kornhaber, R. C., & Schroeder, H. E. (1975). Importance of model similarity in extinction of avoidance behavior in children. *Journal of Consulting and Clinical Psychology*, *43*, 601–607.

Kovacs, M. (1981). Rating scales to assess depression in school-aged children. *Acta Paedopsychiatrica, 46*, 305–315.

Kübler-Ross, E. (1969). *On death and dying.* New York: Macmillan.

Kuczynski, L., Kochanska, G., Radke-Yarrow, M., & Girnius-Brown, O. (1987). A developmental interpretation of young children's noncompliance. *Developmental Psychology, 23*, 799–806.

Kuperman, W., & Stewart, M. A. (1981). Grief and depression. In S. Gabel (Ed.), *Behavioral problems in childhood: A primary care approach* (pp. 393–398). New York: Grune & Stratton.

Kupst, M. J., & Schulman, J. L. (1988). Long-term coping with pediatric leukemia: A six-year follow-up study. *Journal of Pediatric Psychology, 13*, 7–22.

Kurdek, L. A. (1986). Custodial mothers' perceptions of visitations and payment of child support by noncustodial fathers in families with low and high levels of preseparation interparent conflict. *Journal of Applied Developmental Psychology, 7*, 307–323.

Kurdek, L. A. (1988). A 1-year follow-up study of children's divorce adjustment, custodial mothers' divorce adjustment and postdivorce parenting. *Journal of Applied Developmental Psychology, 9*, 315–328.

Kurdek, L. A., & Sinclair, R. J. (1988). Adjustment of young adolescents in two-parent nuclear, stepfather, and mother-custody families. *Journal of Consulting and Clinical Psychology, 56*, 91–96.

Lahey, B. B., McNees, M. P., & McNees, M. C. (1973). Control of an obscene "verbal tic" through timeout in an elementary school classroom. *Journal of Applied Behavior Analysis, 6*, 101–104.

Langfeldt, T. (1981a). Processes in sexual development. In L. L. Constantine & F. M. Martinson (Eds.), *Children and sex: New findings, new perspectives* (pp. 37–44). Boston: Little, Brown.

Langfeldt, T. (1981b). Masturbation: Individual and social organization. In L. L. Constantine & F. M. Martinson (Eds.), *Children and sex: New findings, new perspectives* (pp. 63–72). Boston: Little, Brown.

Last, C. G., Hersen, M., Kazdin, A. E., Finkelstein, R., & Strauss, C. C. (1987). Comparison of DSM-III separation anxiety and overanxious disorders: Demographic characteristics and patterns of comorbidity. *Journal of the American Academy of Child Psychiatry, 26*, 527–531.

Last, C. G., Phillips, J. E., & Statfield, A. (1987). Childhood anxiety disorders in mothers and their children. *Child Psychiatry and Human Development, 18*, 103–112.

Last, C. G., Strauss, C. C., & Francis, G. (1987). Comorbidity among childhood anxiety disorders. *Journal of Nervous and Mental Disease, 175*, 726–730.

Lazarus, A. A., & Abramovitz, A. (1962). The use of emotive imagery in the treatment of children's phobias. *Journal of Medical Science, 108*, 191–195.

Leckman, J. F., & Cohen, D. J. (1988). Descriptive and diagnostic classification of tic disorders. In D. J. Cohen, R. D. Bruun, & J. F. Leckman (Eds.), *Tourette's syndrome and tic disorders* (pp. 3–19). New York: Wiley.

Leckman, J. F., Towbin, K. E., Ort, S. I., & Cohen, D. J. (1988). Clinical assessment of tic disorder severity. In D. J. Cohen, R. D. Bruun, & J. F.

Leckman (Eds.), *Tourette's syndrome and tic disorders* (pp. 55–78). New York: Wiley.

Legg, C., Sherrick, L., & Wadland, W. (1974). Reactions of preschool children to the birth of a sibling. *Child Psychiatry and Human Development, 5,* 3–39.

Levine, F. M., & Ramirez, R. (1989). Contingent negative practice as a home-based treatment of tics and stuttering. In C. E. Schaefer & J. M. Briesmeister (Eds.), *Handbook of parent training: Parents as co-therapists for children's behavior problems* (pp. 38–59). New York: Wiley.

Levine, M. D. (1975). Children with encopresis: A descriptive analysis. *Pediatrics, 56,* 412–416.

Lidsky, T., Labuszewski, J., & Levine, R. M. (1981). Are movement disorders the most serious side effects of maintenance therapy with antipsychotic drugs? *Biological Psychiatry, 16,* 1189–1194.

Lillywhite, H. S., Young, N. B., & Olmstead, R. W. (1970). *Pediatrician's handbook of communication disorders.* Philadelphia: Lea & Febiger.

Little, L. M., & Kelley, M. L. (1989). The efficacy of response cost procedures for reducing children's noncompliance to parental instructions. *Behavior Therapy, 20,* 525–534.

Livingston, R. (1987). Sexually and physically abused children. *Journal of the American Academy of Child and Adolescent Psychiatry, 26,* 413–415.

Lobitz, G. K., & Johnson, S. M. (1975). Normal vs. deviant children: A multimethod comparison. *Journal of Abnormal Child Psychology, 3,* 353–374.

Loeber, R. (1990). Development and risk factors of juvenile antisocial behavior and delinquency. *Clinical Psychology Review, 10,* 1–41.

Loeber, R., & Lahey, B. B. (1989). Recommendations for research on disruptive behavior disorders of childhood and adolescence. In B. B. Lahey & A. E. Kazdin (Eds.), *Advances in clinical child psychology* (Vol. 12, pp. 221–251). New York: Plenum Press.

Loening-Baucke, V. A., & Cruikshank, B. M. (1986). Abnormal defecation dynamics in chronically constipated children with encopresis. *Journal of Pediatrics, 108,* 562–566.

Long, N., & Forehand, R. (1987). The effects of parental divorce and parental conflict on children: An overview. *Developmental and Behavioral Pediatrics, 8,* 292–296.

Lovibond, S. H. (1964). *Conditioning and enuresis.* New York: Macmillan.

Lozoff, B., Wolf, A. W., & Davis, N. S. (1984). Co-sleeping in urban families with young children in the United States. *Pediatrics, 74,* 171–182.

Lyon, J. B., & Vanderberg, B. R. (1989). Father death, family relationships and subsequent psychological functioning in women. *Journal of Clinical Child Psychology, 18,* 327–335.

Lyon, L. S. (1983). A behavioral treatment of compulsive lipbiting. *Journal of Behavior Therapy and Experimental Psychiatry, 14,* 275–276.

Maccoby, E. E., & Jacklin, C. N. (1974). *The psychology of sex differences.* Stanford, CA: Stanford University Press.

Maccoby, E. E., & Jacklin, C. N. (1980). Sex differences in aggression: A rejoinder and reprise. *Child Development, 51,* 964–980.

MacFarlane, J. W., Allen, L., & Honzik, M. P. (1954). *A developmental study of the behavior problems of normal children between twenty-one months and fourteen years.* Berkeley: University of California Press.

MacKeith, R. C., Meadow, S. R., & Turner, R. K. (1973). How children become dry. In I. Kolvin, R. C. MacKeith, & S. R. Meadow (Eds.), *Bladder control and enuresis* (pp. 3–22). Philadelphia: J. B. Lippincott.

Mahalski, P. A., Silva, P. A., & Spears, G. R. S. (1985). Children's attachment to soft objects at bedtime, child rearing, and child development. *Journal of the American Academy of Child Psychiatry, 24,* 442–446.

Main, M., Kaplan, N., & Cassidy, J. (1985). Security in infancy, childhood, and adulthood: A move to the level of representation. in I. Bretherton & E. Waters (Eds.), Growing points of attachment theory and research: *Monographs of the Society for Research in Child Development, 50*(1–2, Serial No. 209).

Mannino, F. V., & Delgado, R. A. (1969). Trichotillomania in children: A review. *American Journal of Psychiatry, 26,* 505–511.

Mansdorf, I. J. (1986). Assertiveness training in the treatment of a child's tics. *Journal of Behavior Therapy and Experimental Psychiatry, 17,* 29–32.

Martin, B. (1975). Parent–child relations. In F. D. Horowitz (Ed.), *Review of child development research* (Vol. 4, pp. 463–540). Chicago: University of Chicago Press.

Martin, B. (1977). Brief family intervention: Effectiveness and the importance of including the father. *Journal of Consulting and Clinical Psychology, 45,* 1002–1010.

Martin, S. L. (1988). *The effectiveness of a multidisciplinary primary health care model in the prevention of children's mental health problems.* Unpublished doctoral dissertation, University of North Carolina–Chapel Hill.

Martinson, F. M. (1981a). Eroticism in infancy and childhood. In L. L. Constantine & F. M. Martinson (Eds.), *Children and sex: New findings, new perspectives* (pp. 23–35). Boston: Little, Brown.

Martinson, F. M. (1981b). Childhood and the institutionalization of sexuality. In L. L. Constantine & F. M. Martinson (Eds.), *Children and sex: New findings, new perspectives* (pp. 265–278). Boston: Little, Brown.

Mash, E. J., & Johnston, C. (1983). Parental perceptions of child behavior problems, parenting self-esteem and mothers' reported stress in younger and older hyperactive and normal children. *Journal of Consulting and Clinical Psychology, 51,* 86–99.

Mash, E. J., Johnston, C., & Kovitz, K. (1983). A comparison of the mother–child interactions of physically abused and non-abused children during play and task situations. *Journal of Clinical Child Psychology, 12,* 337–346.

Mash, E. J., & Terdal, L. G. (1988). Behavioral assessment of child and family disturbance. In E. J. Mash & L. G. Terdal (Eds.), *Behavioral assessment of childhood disorders: Selected core problems* (2nd ed., pp. 3–68). New York: Guilford Press.

Mash, E. J., Terdal, L. G., & Anderson, K. (1973). The Response Class Matrix: A procedure for recording parent–child interactions. *Journal of Consulting and Clinical Psychology, 40,* 163–164.

Massong, S. R., Edwards, R. P., Range-Sitton, L., & Hailey, B. J. (1980). A case of trichotillomania in a three year old treated by response prevention. *Journal of Behavior Therapy and Experimental Psychiatry, 11,* 223–225.

Masten, A. S., & Garmezy, N. (1985). Risk, vulnerability, and protective factors in developmental psychopathology. In B. B. Lahey & A. E. Kazdin (Eds.), *Advances in clinical child psychology* (Vol. 8, pp. 1–52). New York: Plenum Press.

Masterman, S. H., & Reams, R. (1988). Support groups for bereaved preschool and school-aged children. *American Journal of Orthopsychiatry, 58,* 562–570.

Matas, L., Arend, R. A., & Sroufe, L. A. (1978). Continuity of adaptation in the second year: The relationship between quality of attachment and later competence. *Child Development, 49,* 547–556.

Matheny, A. P. (1986). Injuries among toddlers: Contributions from child, mother, and family. *Journal of Pediatric Psychology, 11,* 163–176.

Matson, J. L., & Mulick, J. A. (Eds.). (1983). *Handbook of mental retardation.* Elmsford, NY: Pergamon Press.

Matson, J. L., & Ollendick, T. H. (1977). Issues in toilet training normal children. *Behavior Therapy, 8,* 549–558.

Matthews, J. R., Friman, P. C., Barone, V. J., Ross, L. V., & Christophersen, E. R. (1987). Parental management of infants: Increasing positive maternal interactions and decreasing dangerous infant behaviors. *Journal of Applied Behavior Analysis, 20,* 165–169.

Matthews, L. H., Leibowitz, J. M., & Matthews, J. R. (1983). Tics, habits, and mannerisms. In C. E. Walker & M. C. Roberts (Eds.), *Handbook of clinical child psychology* (pp. 406–436). New York: Wiley.

McArthur, D. S., & Roberts, G. E. (1982). *Roberts Apperception Test for Children.* Los Angeles: Western Psychological Services.

McCabe, A., & Lipscomb, T. (1988). Sex differences in children's verbal aggression. *Merrill–Palmer Quarterly, 34,* 389–401.

McConaughy, S. H., & Achenbach, T. M. (1990). *Guide for the Semistructured Clinical Interview for Children Aged 6–11.* Burlington, VT: University Associates in Psychiatry.

McCown, D. E., & Pratt, C. (1985). Impact of sibling death on children's behavior. *Death Studies, 9,* 323–335.

McDevitt, S. C., & Carey, W. B. (1978). The measurement of temperament in 3–7 year old children. *Journal of Child Psychology and Psychiatry, 19,* 245–253.

McGurk, H., & Glachan, M. (1987). Children's conception of the continuity of parenthood following divorce. *Journal of Child Psychology and Psychiatry, 28,* 427–435.

McLeer, S. V., Deblinger, E., Atkins, M. S., Foa, E. B., & Ralphe, D. L. (1988). Post-traumatic stress disorder in sexually abused children. *Journal of the American Academy of Child and Adolescent Psychiatry, 27,* 650–654.

McMahon, R. J., Forehand, R., Griest, D. L., & Wells, K. C. (1981). Who drops out of therapy during behavioral training? *Behavior Counseling Quarterly, 1,* 79–85.

McMahon, R. J., Tiedemann, S. L., Forehand, R., & Griest, D. L. (1984). Parental satisfaction with parent training to modify child noncompliance. *Behavior Therapy*, *15*, 295–303.

McReynolds, M. T. (1972). A procedure for the withdrawal of an infant oral pacifier. *Journal of Applied Behavior Analysis*, *5*, 65–66.

Meichenbaum, D. H. (1977). *Cognitive-behavior modification*. New York: Plenum Press.

Mesibov, G. B., Schroeder, C. S., & Wesson, L. (1977). Parental concerns about their children. *Journal of Pediatric Psychology*, *2*, 13–17.

Meyer, J. S., Sakai, R., & Naritomi, H. (1979). Regional cerebral blood flow in man during different stages of wakefulness and sleep. In B. B. Mršulja, Lj. M. Rakić, I. Klatzo, & M. Spatz (Eds.), *Pathophysiology of cerebral energy metabolism* (pp. 433–440). New York: Plenum Press.

Meyer-Bahlburg, H. F. L. (1985). Gender identity disorder of childhood. *Journal of the American Academy of Child Psychiatry*, *24*, 681–683.

Mikulas, W. L., & Coffman, M. F. (1989). Home-based treatment of children's fear of the dark. In C. E. Schaefer & J. M. Briesmeister (Eds.), *Handbook of parent training: Parents as co-therapists for children's behavior problems* (pp. 177–202). New York: Wiley.

Miller, K., Goldberg, S., & Atkin, B. (1989). Nocturnal enuresis: Experience with long-term use of intranasally administered desmopressin. *Journal of Pediatrics*, *114*, 723–726.

Miller, L. C. (1983). Fears and anxiety in children. In C. E. Walker & M. C. Roberts (Eds.), *Handbook of clinical child psychology* (pp. 337–380). New York: Wiley.

Miller, L. C., Barrett, C. L., & Hampe, E. (1974). Phobias of childhood in a prescientific era. In A. Davids (Ed.), *Child personality and psychopathology: Current topics* (Vol. 1, pp. 89–134). New York: Wiley.

Miller, L. C., Barrett, C. L., Hampe, E., & Noble, H. (1972). Factor structure of childhood fears. *Journal of Consulting and Clinical Psychology*, *39*, 264–268.

Miller-Perrin, C. L., & Wurtele, S. K. (1988). The child sexual abuse prevention movement: A critical analysis of primary and secondary approaches. *Clinical Psychology Review*, *8*, 313–329.

Moffatt, M. E. K. (1989). Nocturnal enuresis: Psychologic implications of treatment and nontreatment. *Journal of Pediatrics*, *114*, 697–704.

Mooney, K., Graziano, A. M., & Katz, J. N. (1985). A factor analytic investigation of children's nighttime fear and coping responses. *Journal of Genetic Psychology*, *146*, 205–215.

Moore, T., & Ucko, C. (1957). Night waking in early infancy: Part I. *Archives of Disease in Childhood*, *33*, 333–342.

Morris, R. J., & Kratochwill, T. R. (1983). *Treating children's fears and phobias: A behavioral approach*. Elmsford, NY: Pergamon Press.

Mowrer, O. H., & Mowrer, W. M. (1938). Enuresis: A method for its study and treatment. *American Journal of Orthopsychiatry*, *8*, 436–459.

Mulick, J. A., Hoyt, P., Rojahn, J., & Schroeder, S. R. (1978). Reduction of a nervous habit in a profoundly retarded youth by increasing toy play. *Journal of Behavior Therapy and Experimental Psychiatry*, *9*, 381–385.

National Center for Health Statistics. (1985). *Advance report of final divorce statistics* (Vol. 33, No. 11; DHHS Publication No. PHS 85-1120). Washington, DC: U.S. Government Printing Office.

Neeper, R., & Lahey, B. B. (1983). Learning disabilities of children. In C. E. Walker & M. C. Roberts (Eds.), *Handbook of child clinical psychology* (pp. 680–696). New York: Wiley.

Nelson, K. (1973). Structure and strategy in learning to talk. *Monographs of the Society for Research in Child Development*, *38*(1–2, Serial No. 149).

Norgaard, J. R., Rittig, S., & Djurhuus, J. C. (1989). Nocturnal enuresis: An approach to treatment based on pathogenesis. *Journal of Pediatrics*, *114*, 705–710.

Nowicki, S., Jr., & Strickland, B. R. (1973). A locus of control scale for children. *Journal of Consulting and Clinical Psychology*, *40*, 148–154.

O'Brian, M., & Huston, A. C. (1986). Activity level and sex-stereotyped toy choice in toddler boys and girls. *Journal of Genetic Psychology*, *146*, 527–533.

O'Grady, D., & Metz, J. R. (1987). Resilance in children at high risk for psychological disorder. *Journal of Pediatric Psychology*, *12*, 3–23.

Offord, D. R. (1987). Prevention of behavioral and emotional disorders in children. *Journal of Child Psychology and Psychiatry*, *28*, 9–19.

Olatawura, M. D. (1973). Encopresis: A review of thirty-two cases. *Acta Paediatrica Scandinavica*, *62*, 358–364.

Ollendick, T. H. (1979). Fear reduction techniques with children. In M. Hersen, R. M. Eisler, & P. M. Miller (Eds.), *Progress in behavior modification* (Vol. 8, pp. 127–168). New York: Academic Press.

Ollendick, T. H. (1983). Reliability and validity of the revised Fear Survey Schedule for Children (FSSC-R). *Behaviour Research and Therapy*, *21*, 685–692.

Ollendick, T. H., & Cerny, J. A. (1981). *Clinical behavior therapy with children*. New York: Plenum Press.

Ollendick, T. H., & Hersen, M. (1984). An overview of child behavioral assessment. In T. H. Ollendick & M. Hersen (Eds.), *Child behavioral assessment: Principles and procedures* (pp. 3–19). Elmsford, NY: Pergamon Press.

Ollendick, T. H., King, H. J., & Frary, R. D. (1989). Fears in children and adolescents: Reliability and generalizability across gender, age and nationality. *Behaviour Research and Therapy*, *27*, 19–26.

Ollendick, T. H., Matson, J. L., & Helsel, W. J. (1985). Fears in children and adolescents: Normative data. *Behaviour Reesearch and Therapy*, *23*, 465–467.

Ollendick, T. H., & Mayer, J. A. (1984). School phobia. In S. M. Turner (Ed.), *Behavior theories and treatment of anxiety* (pp. 367–411). New York: Plenum Press.

Olson, R. L., & Roberts, M. W. (1987). Alternative treatments for sibling aggression. *Behavior Therapy*, *18*, 243–250.

Oltmanns, T. F., Broderick, J. E., & O'Leary, K. D. (1977). Marital adjustment and the efficacy of behavior therapy with children. *Journal of Consulting and Clinical Psychology*, *45*, 724–729.

Oppel, W. C., Harper, P. A., & Rider, R. V. (1968). Social, psychological, and neurological factors associated with nocturnal enuresis. *Pediatrics*, *42*, 627–641.

Ornstein, P. A. (1978). The study of children's memory. In P. A. Ornstein (Ed.), *Memory development in children* (pp. 1-20). Hillsdale, NJ: Erlbaum.

Ornstein, P. A., Gordon, B. N., & Larus, D. B. (in press). Children's memory for a personally experienced event: Implications for testimony. *Applied Cognitive Psychology.*

Osborn, E. L. (1986). Effects of participant modeling and desensitization on childhood warm water phobia. *Journal of Behavior Therapy and Experimental Psychiatry, 17,* 117-119.

Ounsted, M. C., & Hendrick, A. M. (1977). The first born child: Patterns of development. *Developmental Medicine and Child Neurology, 19,* 446-453.

Owen, L. G., & Fliegelman, M. T. (1978). Diseases of the hair and scalp. In S. S. Gellis & B. K. Kagan (Eds.), *Current pediatric therapy* (Vol. 8, pp. 504-506). Philadelphia: W. B. Saunders.

Palisin, H. (1986). Preschool temperament and performance of achievement tests. *Developmental Psychology, 22,* 766-770.

Panaccione, V. F., & Wahler, R. G. (1986). Child behavior, maternal depression, and social coercion as factors in quality of child care. *Journal of Abnormal Child Psychology, 14,* 263-278.

Park, K. A., & Waters, E. (1989). Security of attachment and preschool friendships. *Child Development, 60,* 1076-1081.

Parker, J. G., & Asher, S. R. (1987). Peer relations and later adjustment: Are low-accepted children "at risk"? *Psychological Bulletin, 102,* 357-389.

Parker-Cohen, N. Y., & Bell, R. Q. (1988). The relationship between temperament and social adjustment to peers. *Early Childhood Research Quarterly, 3,* 179-192.

Parpal, M., & Maccoby, E. (1985). Maternal responsiveness and subsequent child compliance. *Child Development, 56,* 1326-1334.

Passman, R. H. (1987). Attachments to inanimate objects: Are children who have security blankets insecure? *Journal of Consulting and Clinical Psychology, 55,* 825-830.

Patterson, G. R. (1976). The aggressive child: Victim and architect of a coercive system. In E. J. Mash, L. A. Hamerlynck, & L. C. Handy (Eds.), *Behavior modification and families: Vol. 1. Theory and research* (pp. 267-316). New York: Brunner/Mazel.

Patterson, G. R. (1980). Mothers: The unacknowledged victims. *Monographs of the Society for Research in Child Development, 45*(5, Serial No. 186).

Patterson, G. R. (1986). Performance models for antisocial boys. *American Psychologist, 41,* 432-444.

Patterson, G. R., DeBaryshe, B. D., & Ramsey, E. (1989). A developmental perspective on antisocial behavior. *American Psychologist, 44,* 329-335.

Patterson, G. R., Ray, R. S., Shaw, D. A., & Cobb, J. A. (1969). *A manual for coding family interactions.* New York: Microfiche.

Pauls, D. L., Hurst, C. R., Kruger, S. D., Leckman, J. F., Kidd, K. K., & Cohen, D. J. (1986). Gilles de la Tourette's syndrome and attention deficit disorder with hyperactivity. *Archives of General Psychiatry, 43,* 1177-1179.

Pauls, D. L., & Leckman, J. F. (1986). The inheritance of Gilles de la Tourette syndrome and associated behaviors. *New England Journal of Medicine, 315*, 993–997.

Pedro-Carroll, J. L., & Cowen, E. L. (1985). The Children of Divorce Intervention Program: An investigation of the efficacy of a school-based prevention program. *Journal of Consulting and Clinical Psychology, 53*, 603–611.

Pedro-Carroll, J. L., Cowen, E. L., Hightower, A. D., & Guare, J. E. (1986). Preventive intervention with latency-aged children of divorce: A replication study. *American Journal of Community Psychology, 14*, 277–289.

Perlmutter, D. (1985). Enuresis. In P. D. Kelalis, L. R. King, & A. B. Belman (Eds.), *Clinical pediatric urology* (2nd ed., pp. 311–325). Philadelphia: W. B. Saunders.

Perry, M. A., & Furukawa, M. J. (1980). Modeling methods. In F. H. Kanfer & A. P. Goldstein (Eds.), *Helping people change: A textbook of methods* (3rd ed., pp. 66–110). New York: Pergamon Press.

Peterson, C., & Peterson, R. (1986). Parent–child interaction and day care: Does quality of day care matter? *Journal of Applied Developmental Psychology, 7*, 1–15.

Peterson, L. (1989). Coping by children undergoing stressful medical procedures: Some conceptual, methodological, and therapeutic issues. *Journal of Consulting and Clinical Psychology, 57*, 380–387.

Peterson, L., Hartmann, D. P., & Gelfand, D. M. (1980). Prevention of child behavior disorders: A lifestyle change for child psychologists. In P. O. Davidson & S. M. Davidson (Eds.), *Behavioral medicine: Changing health lifestyles* (pp. 195–221). New York: Brunner/Mazel.

Peterson, L., & Ridley-Johnson, R. (1983). Prevention of disorders in children. In C. E. Walker & M. C. Roberts (Eds.), *Handbook of clinical child psychology* (pp. 1174–1197). New York: Wiley.

Pettit, G. S., & Bates, J. E. (1989). Family interaction patterns and children's behavior problems from infancy to 4 years. *Developmental Psychology, 25*, 413–420.

Pfaundler, M. (1904). Demonstration of an apparatus for automatic warning of the occurrence of bedwetting. *Verhandlungen der Gesellschaft für Kinderheilpundl, 21*, 219–220.

Pfiffner, L. H., Jouriles, E. N., Brown, M. M., Etscheidt, M. A., & Kelly, J. A. (1990). Effects of problem-solving therapy on outcomes of parent training for single-parent families. *Child and Family Behavior Therapy, 12*, 1–12.

Phillips, D., & Wolpe, S. (1981). Multiple behavioral techniques in severe separation anxiety of a twelve-year-old girl. *Journal of Behaivor Therapy and Experimental Psychiatry, 12*, 329–332.

Physicians' Desk Reference (PDR) (44th ed.). (1990). Oradell, NJ: Medical Economics.

Piacentini, J. C. (1987). Language dysfunction and childhood behavior disorders. In B. B. Lahey & A. E. Kazdin (Eds.), *Advances in clinical child psychology* (Vol. 10, pp. 259–287). New York: Plenum Press.

Piaget, J., & Inhelder, B. (1969). *The psychology of the child.* New York: Basic Books.

Pierce, C. M. (1971). Enuresis. In A. M. Friedman & H. I. Kaplan (Eds.), *The child: His psychological and cultural development* (Vol. 1, pp. 203–209). New York: Atheneum.

Pierce, R., & Pierce, L. H. (1985). The sexually abused child: A comparison of male and female victims. *Child Abuse and Neglect, 8,* 191–198.

Piersel, W. C., & Gutkin, R. B. (1983). Resistance to school-based consultation: A behavioral analysis of the problem. *Psychology in the Schools, 20,* 311–320.

Plomin, R. (1989). Environment and genes: Determinants of behavior. *American Psychologist, 44,* 105–111.

Pope, A. W., McHale, S. M., & Craighead, W. E. (1988). *Self-esteem enhancement with children and adolescents.* Elmsford, NY: Pergamon Press.

Popovich, F., & Thompson, G. W. (1973). Thumb- and finger-sucking: Its relation to malocclusion. *American Journal of Orthodontics, 63,* 148–155.

Price, R. H., Cowen, E. L., Lorion, R. P., & Ramos-McKay, J. (1989). The search for effective prevention programs: What we learned along the way. *American Journal of Orthopsychiatry, 59,* 49–58.

Prochaska, J. M., & Prochaska, J. O. (1985). Children's views of the causes and "cures" of sibling rivalry. *Child Welfare, 64,* 427–433.

Puig-Antich, J., & Rabinovich, H. (1986). Relationship between affective and anxiety disorders in childhood. In R. Gittelman (Ed.), *Anxiety disorders of childhood* (pp. 136–156). New York: Guilford Press.

Purcell, J., Beilke, R. L., & Friedrich, W. N. (1986, May). *Sexualized behavior in sexually abused and non-sexually abused children.* Paper presented at the Fourth National Conference on the Sexual Victimization of Children, New Orleans.

Putallaz, M. (1987). Maternal behavior and children's sociometric status. *Child Development, 58,* 324–340.

Quay, H. C. (1979). Classification. In H. C. Quay & J. S. Werry (Eds.), *Psychopathological disorders of childhood* (2nd ed., pp. 1–42). New York: Wiley.

Ragan, P. V., & McGlashan, T. H. (1986). Childhood parental death and adult psychopathology. *American Journal of Psychiatry, 143,* 153–157.

Ramey, C. T., & Campbell, F. A. (1984). Preventive education for high risk children: Cognitive consequences of the Carolina Abecedarian Project. *American Journal of Mental Deficiency, 88,* 515–523.

Rand, C. W. (1973). Copying in drawing: The importance of adequate visual analysis versus the ability to utilize drawing rules. *Child Development, 44,* 47–53.

Rando, T. A. (1984). *Grief, dying and death: Clinical interventions for caregivers.* Champaign, IL: Research Press.

Rapoff, M. A., Christophersen, E. R., & Rapoff, K. E. (1982). The management of common childhood bedtime problems by pediatric nurse practitioners. *Journal of Pediatric Psychology, 7,* 179–196.

Reding, G. R., Zepelin, H., Robinson, J. E., Zimmerman, S. O., & Smith, V. H. (1968). Nocturnal teeth grinding: All-night psychophysiologic studies. *Journal of Dental Research, 47,* 786–797.

Reid, W. J., & Crisafulli, A. (1990). Marital discord and child behavior problems: A meta-analysis. *Journal of Abnormal Child Psychology, 18,* 105–117.

Reilly, T. P., Hasazi, J. E., & Bond, L. A. (1983). Children's conceptions of death and personal mortality. *Journal of Pediatric Psychology, 8,* 21–31.

Reisinger, K. S., & Bires, J. A. (1980). Anticipatory guidance in pediatric practice. *Pediatrics, 66,* 889–892.

Rekers, G. A., & Lovaas, O. I. (1974). Behavioral treatment of deviant sex-role behaviors in a male child. *Journal of Applied Behavior Analysis, 7,* 173–190.

Repucci, N. D., & Haugaard, J. J. (1989). Prevention of child sexual abuse: Myth or reality? *American Psychologist, 44,* 1266–1275.

Rey, J. M., Bashir, M. R., Schwarz, M., Richards, I. N., Plapp, J. M., & Stewart, G. W. (1988). Oppositional disorder: Fact or fiction? *Journal of the American Academy of Child and Adolescent Psychiatry, 27,* 157–162.

Reynolds, C. R., & Richmond, B. O. (1978). What I Think and Feel: A revised measure of children's manifest anxiety. *Journal of Abnormal Child Psychology, 6,* 271–280.

Rheingold, H. L., Cook, K. V., & Kolowitz, V. (1987). Commands activate the behavior and pleasure of 2-year-old children. *Developmental Psychology, 23,* 146–151.

Rheingold, H. L., & Eckerman, C. O. (1973). Fear of the stranger: A critical examination. In H. W. Reese (Ed.). *Advances in child development and behavior* (Vol. 8, pp. 186–222). New York: Academic Press.

Rice, M. L. (1989). Children's language acquisition. *American Psychologist, 44,* 149–156.

Richman, N. (1981). A community survey of characteristics of one- to two-year-olds with sleep disruptions. *Journal of the American Academy of Child Psychiatry, 20,* 281–291.

Richman, N. (1985). A double-blind drug trial of treatment in young children with sleep disruptions. *American Academy of Child Psychiatry, 20,* 281–291.

Richman, N., Douglas, J., Hunt, H., Landsdown, R., & Levere, R. (1985). Behavioural methods in the treatment of sleep disorders: A pilot study. *Journal of Child Psychology and Psychiatry, 26,* 581–590.

Richman, N., Stevenson, J., & Graham, P. (1975). Prevalence of behaviour problems in three-year-old children: An epidemiological study in a London borough. *Journal of Child Psychology and Psychiatry, 26,* 272–287.

Richman, N., Stevenson, J., & Graham, P. (1982). *Preschool to school: A behavioural study.* London: Academic Press.

Rickel, A. W., & Allen, L. (1987). *Preventing maladjustment from infancy through adolescence.* Newbury Park, CA: Sage.

Riddle, M. A., Hardin, M. T., Ort, S. I., Leckman, J. F., & Cohen, D. J. (1988). Behavioral symptoms in Tourette's syndrome. In D. J. Cohen, R. D. Bruun, & J. F. Leckman (Eds.), *Tourette's syndrome and tic disorders* (pp. 179–196). New York: Wiley.

Risch, C. R., & Ferguson, J. M. (1981). Behavioral treatment of skin disorders. In J. M. Ferguson & C. B. Taylor (Eds.), *The comprehensive handbook of behavioral medicine* (Vol. 2, pp. 263–278). New York: Spectrum.

Roberts, M. C., & Powers, S. W. (1990). Adjusting chair timeout enforcement procedures for oppositional children. *Behavior Therapy, 21,* 257–271.

Roberts, M. C., & Turner, D. S. (1986). Rewarding parents for their children's use of safety seats. *Journal of Pediatric Psychology, 11*, 25–36.

Roberts, R. N., & Gordon, S. B. (1979). Reducing childhood nightmares subsequent to a burn trauma. *Child Behavior Therapy, 1*, 373–381.

Rocissano, L., Slade, A., & Lynch, V. (1987). Dyadic synchrony and toddler compliance. *Developmental Psychology, 23*, 698–704.

Roedell, W. C., Jackson, N. E., & Robinson, H. B. (1980). *Gifted young children.* New York: Teachers College Press.

Rohman, W., Sales, B. D., & Lou, M. (1987). The best interests of the child in custody disputes. In L. A. Weithorn (Ed.), *Psychology and child custody determinations: Knowledge, roles and expertise* (pp. 59–105). Lincoln: University of Nebraska Press.

Rosenfeld, A., Bailey, R., Siegel, B., & Bailey, G. (1986). Determining incestuous contact between parent and child: Frequency of children touching parents' genitals in a nonclinical population. *Journal of the American Academy of Child Psychiatry, 25*, 481–484.

Rosenstiel, A. K., & Scott, D. S. (1977). Four considerations in using imagery techniques with children. *Journal of Behavior Therapy and Experimental Psychiatry, 8*, 287–290.

Rotenberg, K. J. (1988). Causes, intensity, motives, and consequences of children's anger from self-reports. *Journal of Genetic Psychology, 146*, 101–106.

Routh, D. K., & Schroeder, C. S. (1981). Masturbation and other sexual behaviors. In S. Gabel (Ed.), *Behavior problems of childhood* (pp. 387–392). New York: Grune & Stratton.

Routh, D. K., Schroeder, C. S., & Koocher, G. P. (1983). Psychology and primary health care for children. *American Psychologist, 38*, 95–98.

Routh, D. K., Schroeder, C. S., & O'Tuma, L. A. (1974). Development of activity level in children. *Developmental Psychology, 10*, 163–168.

Rushton, H. G. (1989). Nocturnal enuresis: Epidemological, evaluation, and currently available treatment options. *Journal of Pediatrics, 114*, 691–696.

Rutter, M. (1971). Normal psychosexual development. *Journal of Child Psychology and Psychiatry and Allied Professions, 11*, 259–283.

Rutter, M. (1975). *Helping troubled children.* New York: Plenum Press.

Rutter, M. (1979). Protective factors in children's responses to stress and disadvantage. In M. W. Kent & J. E. Rolf (Eds.), *Social competence in children* (pp. 49–74). Hanover, NH: University Press of New England.

Rutter, M. (1983). Stress, coping, and development: Some issues and some questions. In N. Garmezy & M. Rutter (Eds.), *Stress, coping, and development in children* (pp. 1–41). New York: McGraw-Hill.

Rutter, M., Cox, A., Tupling, C., Berger, M., & Yule, W. (1975). Attainment and adjustment in two geographical areas: I. Prevalence of psychiatric disorder. *British Journal of Psychiatry, 126*, 493–509.

Rutter, M., Macdonald, H., LeCouteur, A., Harrington, R., Bolton, P., & Bailey, A. (1990). Genetic factors in child psychiatric disorders: II. Empirical findings. *Journal of Child Psychology and Psychiatry, 31*, 39–83.

Rutter, M., & Shaffer, D. (1980). DSM-III: A step forward or back in terms of the classification of child psychiatric disorders? *Journal of the American Academy of Child and Adolescent Psychiatry, 19*, 371–394.

Rutter, M., Tizard, J., Yule, W., Graham, P., & Whitmore, K. (1976). Isle of Wight studies, 1964–1974. *Psychological Medicine, 6*, 313–332.

Rutter, M., & Tuma, A. H. (1988). Diagnosis and classification: Some outstanding issues. In M. Rutter, A. H. Tuma, & I. S. Lann (Eds.), *Assessment and diagnosis in child psychopathology* (pp. 437–452). New York: Guilford Press.

Rutter, M., Tuma, A. H., & Lann, I. S. (Eds.). (1988). *Assessment and diagnosis in child psychopathology*. New York: Guilford Press.

Sallis, J. F., Patterson, T. L., McKenzie, T. L., & Nader, P. R. (1988). Family variables and physical activity in preschool children. *Developmental and Behavioral Pediatrics, 9*, 57–61.

Sameroff, A. J. (1985). Environmental factors in the early screening of children at risk. In W. K. Frankenburg, R. N. Emde, & J. W. Sullivan (Eds.), *Early identification of children at risk: An international perspective* (pp. 21–44). New York: Plenum Press.

Sameroff, A. J., & Chandler, M. J. (1975). Reproductive risk and the continuum of caretaking casualty. In F. D. Horowitz, M. Hetherington, S. Scarr-Salaptek, & G. Siegel (Eds.), *Review of child development research* (Vol. 4, pp. 187–244). Chicago: University of Chicago Press.

Sanchez, V. (1979). Behavioral treatment of chronic hair pulling in a two-year-old. *Journal of Behavior Therapy and Experimental Psychiatry, 10*, 241–245.

Sattler, J. M. (1988). *Assessment of children* (3rd ed.). San Diego, CA: Author.

Scarr, S., Phillips, D., & McCartney, K. (1990). Facts, fantasies and the future of child care in the United States. *Psychological Science, 1*, 26–35.

Schaefer, C. E. (1979). *Childhood encopresis and enuresis*. New York: Van Nostrand Reinhold.

Schaefer, C. E., & Briesmeister, J. M. (Eds.). (1989). *Handbook of parent training: Parents as co-therapists for children's behavior problems*. New York: Wiley.

Schaefer, C. E., & Millman, H. L. (1981). *How to help children with common problems*. New York: Van Nostrand Reinhold.

Schaefer, D., & Lyons, C. (1986). *How do we tell the children?* New York: Newmarket Press.

Schaughency, E. A., & Lahey, B. B. (1985). Mothers' and fathers' perceptions of child deviance: Roles of child behavior, parental depression, and marital satisfaction. *Journal of Consulting and Clinical Psychology, 53*, 718–723.

Scherer, M. W., & Nakamura, C. Y. (1968). Fear Survey Schedule for Children (FSS-FC): A factor analytic comparison with manifest anxiety (CMAS). *Behaviour Research and Therapy, 6*, 173–182.

Schloss, P. J., & Johann, M. (1982). A modeling and contingency management approach to pacifier withdrawal. *Behavior Therapy, 13*, 254–257.

Schneider-Rosen, K., & Wenz-Gross, M. (1990). Patterns of compliance from eighteen to thirty months of age. *Child Development, 61*, 104–112.

Schnell, R. R. (1982). The psychologist's role in the parent conference. In G. Ulrey & S. J. Rogers (Eds.), *Psychological assessment of handicapped infants and young children* (pp. 179–187). New York: Thieme-Stratton.

Schowalter, J. E. (1976). How do children and functions mix? *Journal of Pediatrics, 89,* 139–142.

Schroeder, C. S. (1979). Psychologist in a private pediatrics office. *Journal of Pediatric Psychology, 1,* 5–18.

Schroeder, C. S., & Gordon, B. N. (in press). Behavioral assessment of young children. In D. J. Willis & J. L. Culbertson (Eds.), *Testing young children.* Austin, TX: Pro-Ed.

Schroeder, C. S., Gordon, B. N., Kanoy, K., & Routh, D. K. (1983). Managing children's behavior problems in pediatric practice. In M. Wolraich & D. K. Routh (Eds.), *Advances in developmental and behavioral pediatrics* (Vol. 4, pp. 25–86). Greenwich, CT: JAI Press.

Schroeder, C. S., Gordon, B. N., & McConnell, P. (1987). Books for parents and children on behavior management. *Journal of Clinical Child Psychology, 16,* 89–94.

Schroeder, C. S., Mesibov, G., Eastman, J., & Goolsby, E. (1981). Preventive services for children: A model. In A. W. Burgess & B. A. Baldwin (Eds.), *Crisis intervention theory and practice: A clinical handbook* (pp. 128–135). Englewood Cliffs, NJ: Prentice-Hall.

Schroeder, C. S., & Wool, R. (1979, March). *Parental concerns for children one month to 10 years and the informational sources desired to answer these concerns.* Paper presented at the meeting of the Southeastern Psychological Association, New Orleans.

Schulman, M. (1974). Control of tics by maternal reinforcement. *Journal of Behavior Therapy and Experimental Psychiatry, 5,* 95–96.

Schultz, J., & Luthe, W. (1959). *Autogenic training: A psychophysiologic approach in psychotherapy.* New York: Grune & Stratton.

Seymour, F. W., Brock, P., During, M., & Poole, G. (1989). Reducing sleep disruptions in young children: Evaluation of therapist-guided and written information approaches. A brief report. *Journal of Child Psychology and Psychiatry, 30,* 913–918.

Shaffer, D. (1973). The association between enuresis and emotional disorder: A review of the literature. In I. Kolvin, R. C. MacKeith, & S. R. Meadow (Eds.), *Bladder control and enuresis* (pp. 118–136). Philadelphia: J. B. Lippincott.

Shafii, T. (1986). The prevalence and use of transitional objects: A study of 230 adolescents. *Journal of the American Academy of Child Psychiatry, 25,* 805–808.

Shantz, C. V. (1983). Social cognition. In J. H. Flavell & E. M. Markman (Vol. Eds.), *Handbook of child psychology* (4th ed.): *Vol. 3. Cognitive development* (pp. 495–555). New York: Wiley.

Shantz, C. V. (1987). Conflicts between children. *Child Development, 58,* 283–305.

Sharenow, E. L., Fuqua, R. W., & Miltenberger, R. G. (1989). The treatment of muscle tics with dissimiliar competing response practice. *Journal of Applied Behavior Analysis, 22,* 35–42.

Sharp, M. C., & Lorch, S. C. (1988). A community outreach training program for pediatrics residents and medical students. *Journal of Medical Education, 63,* 316–322.

Shaw, D. S., & Emery, R. E. (1987). Parental conflict and other correlates of the adjustment of school-age children whose parents have separated. *Journal of Abnormal Child Psychology, 15,* 269–281.

Shea, V. (1984). Explaining mental retardation and autism to parents. In E. S. Schopler & G. B. Mesibov (Eds.), *The effects of autism on the family* (pp. 265–283). New York: Plenum.

Sheras, P. L. (1983). Suicide in adolescence. In C. E. Walker & M. C. Roberts (Eds.), *Handbook of clinical child psychology* (pp. 759–784). New York: Wiley.

Silverman, W. K., & Nelles, W. B. (1988). The Anxiety Disorders Interview Schedule for Children. *Journal of the American Academy of Child and Adolescent Psychiatry, 27,* 772–778.

Simon, J., Larson, C., & Lehrer, R. (1988). Preschool screening: Relations among audiometric and developmental measures. *Journal of Applied Developmental Psychology, 9,* 107–123.

Simonds, J. D. (1977). Enuresis: A brief review of current thinking with respect to pathogenesis and management. *Clinical Pediatrics, 16,* 79–82.

Skarpness, L. R., & Carson, D. K. (1987). Correlates of kindergarten adjustment: Temperament and communicative competence. *Early Childhood Research Quarterly, 2,* 367–376.

Slaby, R. G., & Frey, K. S. (1975). Development of gender constancy and selective attention to same-sex models. *Child Development, 46,* 849–856.

Sonis, W. A., Comite, R., Blue, F. J., Pescovitz, O. H., Rahn, C., Hench, K., Cutler, G. B., Loriaux, D. L., & Klein, R. P. (1985). Behavior problems and social competence in girls with true precocious puberty. *Journal of Pediatrics, 106,* 156–160.

Sonis, W. A., Comite, R., Pescovitz, O. H., Hench, K., Rahn, C. W., Cutler, G. B., Loriaux, D. L., & Klein, R. P. (1986). Biobehavioral aspects of precocious puberty. *Journal of the American Academy of Child Psychiatry, 25,* 674–679.

Spanier, G. B. (1976). Measuring dyadic adjustment: New scales for assessing the quality of marriage and similar dyads. *Journal of Marriage and the Family, 38,* 15–38.

Spanier, G. B., & Filsinger, E. E. (1983). The Dyadic Adjustment Scale. In E. E. Filsinger (Ed.), *Marriage and family assessment: A source book for family therapy* (pp. 155–168). Beverly Hills, CA: Sage.

Spanier, G. B., & Thompson, L. (1982). A confirmatory analysis of the Dyadic Adjustment Scale. *Journal of Marriage and the Family, 44,* 731–738.

Sparrow, S. S., Balla, D. A., & Cicchetti, D. V. (1984). *Vineland Adaptive Behavior Scales.* Circle Pines, MN: American Guidance Service.

Speece, M. W., & Brent, S. B. (1984). Children's understanding of death: A review of three components of a death concept. *Child Development, 55,* 1671–1686.

Spielberger, C. D. (Ed.). (1972). *Anxiety: Current trends in theory and research* (Vol. 1). New York: Academic Press.

Spielberger, C. D. (1973). *Manual for the State–Trait Anxiety Inventory for Children.* Palo Alto, CA: Consulting Psychologists Press.

Spinetta, J. J. (1978). Communication patterns in families dealing with life-threatening illness. In O. J. Z. Sahler (Ed.), *The child and death* (pp. 43–51). St. Louis, MO: C. V. Mosby.

Spinetta, J. J. (1982). Psychosocial issues in childhood cancer: How the professional can help. In M. Wolraich & D. K. Routh (Eds.), *Advances in developmental and behavioral pediatrics* (Vol. 3, pp. 51–72). Greenwich, CT: JAI Press.

Spinetta, J. J., & Maloney, L. J. (1975). Death anxiety in the outpatient leukemic child. *Pediatrics, 65,* 1034–1037.

Spitznagel, A. (1976). *We will see you in the morning.* Unpublished manuscript, Chapel Hill, NC.

Spivack, G., & Shure, M. B. (1974). *Social adjustment of young children: A cognitive approach to solving real-life problems.* San Francisco: Jossey-Bass.

Sprigle, J. E., & Schaefer, L. (1985). Longitudinal evaluation of the effects of two compensatory preschool programs on fourth- through sixth-grade students. *Developmental Psychology, 21,* 702–708.

Sroufe, L. A., & Fleeson, J. (1986). Attachment and the construction of relationships. In W. W. Hartup & Z. Rubin (Eds.), *Relationships and development* (pp. 51–72). Hillsdale, NJ: Erlbaum.

Sroufe, L. A., & Rutter, M. (1984). The domain of developmental psychopathology. *Child Development, 55,* 17–29.

Stambrook, M., & Parker, K. C. H. (1987). The development of the concept of death in childhood: A review of the literature. *Merrill–Palmer Quaterly, 33,* 133–157.

Stanhope, L., Bell, R. Q., & Parker-Cohen, N. Y. (1987). Temperament and helping behavior in preschool children. *Developmental Psychology, 23,* 347–353.

Starfield, B., Gross, E., Wood, M., Pantell, R., Allen, C., Gordon, B., Moffatt, P., Drachman, R., & Katz, H. (1980). Psychosocial and psychosomatic diagnoses in primary care of children. *Pediatrics, 66,* 159–167.

Stehbens, J. A. (1988). Childhood cancer. In D. K. Routh (Ed.), *Handbook of pediatric psychology* (pp. 135–161). New York: Guilford Press.

Steinman, S. (1981). The experience of children in a joint-custody arrangement: A report of a study. *American Journal of Orthopsychiatry, 51,* 403–414.

Stephens, J. A., & Silber, D. L. (1974). Parental expectations versus outcome in toilet training. *Pediatrics, 48,* 451–454.

Stewart, R. B., & Marvin, R. S. (1984). Sibling relations: The role of conceptual perspective-taking in the ontogeny of sibling caregiving. *Child Development, 55,* 1322–1332.

Stewart, R. B., Mobley, L. A., Van Tuyl, S. S., & Salvador, R. A. (1987). The firstborn's adjustment to the birth of a sibling: A longitudinal assessment. *Child Development, 58,* 341–355.

Stillwell, R., & Dunn, J. (1985). Continuities in sibling relationships: Patterns of aggression and friendliness. *Journal of Child Psychology and Psychiatry, 26,* 627–637.

Stocker, C., Dunn, J., & Plomin, R. (1989). Sibling relationships: Links with child temperament, maternal behavior, and family structure. *Child Development, 60,* 715–727.

Stoneman, Z., Brody, G. H., & Burke, M. (1989). Marital quality, depression, and inconsistent parenting: Relationship with observed mother–child conflict. *American Journal of Orthopsychiatry, 59,* 105–117.

Strauss, C. C. (1988). Behavioral assessment and treatment of overanxious disorder in children and adolescents. *Behavior Modification, 12,* 234–251.

Strauss, C. C., Lahey, B. B., Frick, P., Frame, C. L., & Hynd, G. W. (1988). Peer social status of children with anxiety disorders. *Journal of Consulting and Clinical Psychology, 56,* 137–141.

Strauss, C. C., Last, C. G., Hersen, M., & Kazdin, A. E. (1988). Association between anxiety and depression in children and adolescents with anxiety disorders. *Journal of Abnormal Child Psychology, 16,* 57–68.

Strauss, C. C., Lease, C. A., Last, C. G., & Francis, G. (1988). Overanxious disorder: An examination of developmental differences. *Journal of Abnormal Child Psychology, 16,* 433–443.

Strauss, C. C., Rubinoff, A., & Atkeson, B. M. (1983). Elimination of nocturnal headbanging in a normal seven-year-old girl using overcorrection plus rewards. *Journal of Behavior Therapy and Experimental Psychiatry, 14,* 269–273.

Strayer, J. (1986). Children's attributes regarding the situational determinants of emotion in self and others. *Developmental Psychology, 22,* 649–654.

Suinn, R. M. (1975). Anxiety management training for general anxiety. In R. M. Suinn & R. G. Weigel (Eds.), *The innovative psychological therapies: Critical and creative contributions* (pp. 66–70). New York: Harper and Row.

Summit, R. C. (1983). The child sexual abuse accommodation syndrome. *Child Abuse & Neglect, 7,* 177–193.

Sutter, J., & Eyberg, S. (1984). Sutter–Eyberg Student Behavior Inventory. Unpublished manuscript, University of Florida, Gainsville.

Sweet, P. E. (1981). *Something happened to me.* Racine, WI: Mother Courage Press.

Teele, D. W., Klein, J., & Rosner, B. (1984). Otitus media with effusion during the first three years of life and development of speech and language. *Pediatrics, 74,* 282–287.

Terr, L. (1988). What happens to early memories of trauma: A study of twenty children under age five at the time of documented traumatic events. *Journal of the American Academy of Child and Adolescent Psychiatry, 27,* 96–104.

Thomas, A., & Chess, S. (1977). *Temperament and development.* New York: Brunner/Mazel.

Thomas, A., Chess, S., & Birch, H. B. (1968). *Temperament and behavior disorders in children.* New York: New York University Press.

Thompson, R., & Hoffman, M. L. (1980). Empathic arousal and guilt feelings in children. *Developmental Psychology, 16,* 155–156.

Towbin, K. E. (1988). Obsessive–compulsive symptoms in Tourette's syndrome. In D. J. Cohen, R. D. Bruun, & J. F. Leckman (Eds.), *Tourette syndrome and tic disorders* (pp. 137–149). New York: Wiley.

Towbin, K. E., Riddle, M. A., Leckman, J. F., Bruun, R. D., & Cohen, D. I. (1988). The clinical care of individuals with Tourette's syndrome. In D. J. Cohen, R. D. Bruun, & J. F. Leckman (eds.), *Tourette's syndrome and tic disorders* (pp. 329–352). New York: Wiley.

Tuma, J. M. (1989). Mental health services for children. *American Psychologist*, *44*, 188–199.

U.S. Bureau of the Census. (1985). *Statistical abstract of the United States: 1986* (10th ed.). Washington, DC: U.S. Government Printing Office.

Ungerer, J., Sigman, M., Beckwith, L., Cohen, S., & Parmelee, A. (1983). Sleep problems of pre-term children at 3 years of age. *Developmental Medicine and Child Neurology*, *25*, 297–304.

Vandell, D. L. (1987). Baby sister/baby brother: Reaction to the birth of a sibling and patterns of early sibling relations. *Journal of Children in Contemporary Society*, *19*, 13–37.

VandenBos, G. R., Nelson, S., Stapps, J., Olmedo, E., Coates, D., & Batchelor, W. (1979). *APA input to NIMH regarding planning for mental health personnel development*. Washington, DC: American Psychological Association.

Varni, J. W., Boyd, E. F., & Cataldo, M. F. (1978). Self-monitoring, external reinforcement, and time-out procedures in the control of high rate tic behaviors in a hyperactive child. *Journal of Behavior Therapy and Experimental Psychiatry*, *9*, 353–358.

Vaughan, V. C., McKay, R. J., & Behrman, R. E. (1979). *Nelson textbook of pediatrics* (11th ed.). Philadelphia: W. B. Saunders.

Verhulst, F. C., Van Der Lee, J. H., Akkerhuis, G. W., Sandersj-Woudstna, J. A., Timmer, F. C., & Donkhorst, J. D. (1985). The prevalence of nocturnal enuresis: Do DSM-III criteria need to be changed? A brief research report. *Journal of Child Psychology and Psychiatry*, *26*, 989–993.

Vernon, D. T. A. (1973). Use of modeling to modify children's responses to a natural, potentially stressful situation. *Journal of Applied Psychology*, *58*, 351–356.

Vetter, D. K. (1980). Speech and language disorders. In S. Gabel & M. T. Erickson (Eds.), *Child development and developmental disabilities* (pp. 303–320). Boston: Little, Brown.

Wachter, O. (1983). *No more secrets for me*. Boston: Little, Brown.

Wahler, R. G. (1980). The insular mother: Her problems in parent–child treatment. *Journal of Applied Behavior Analysis*, *13*, 207–219.

Wahler, R. G., & Dumas, J. E. (1984). Changing the observational coding styles of insular and noninsular mothers. In R. F. Dangel & R. A. Polster, (Eds.), *Parent training* (pp. 379–416). New York: Guilford Press.

Wahler, R. G., & Dumas, J. E. (1986). Maintenance factors in coercive mother–child interactions: The compliance and predictiability hypotheses. *Journal of Applied Behavior Analysis*, *19*, 13–22.

Walker, C. E. (1978). Toilet training, enuresis, and encopresis. In P. R. Magrab (Ed.), *Psychological management of pediatric problems* (Vol. 1, pp. 129–189). Baltimore: University Park Press.

Walker, C. E., Bonner, B. L., & Kaufman, K. L. (1988). *The physically and sexually abused child: Evaluation and treatment*. Elmsford, NY: Pergamon Press.

Walker, C. E., Kenning, M., & Faust-Campanile, J. (1989). Enuresis and encopresis. In E. J. Mash & R. A. Barkley (Eds.), *Treatment of childhood disorders* (pp. 423–448). New York: Guilford Press.

Walker, C. E., Milling, L. S., & Bonner, B. L. (1988). Incontinence disorders: Enuresis and encopresis. In D. K. Routh (Ed.), *Handbook of pediatric psychology* (pp. 363–397). New York: Guilford Press.

Wallace, I. F., Gravel, J. S., McCarton, C. M., & Ruben, R. J. (1988). Otitis media and language delays at 1 year of age. *Journal of Speech and Hearing Disorders, 53*, 245–251.

Wallerstein, J. (1985). Children of divorce: A preliminary report of a ten-year follow-up of older children and adolescents. *Journal of the American Academy of Child Psychiatry, 24*, 545–553.

Wallerstein, J., & Kelly, J. (1980). *Surviving the breakup: How children and parents cope with divorce.* New York: Basic Books.

Ware, J. C., & Orr, W. C. (1983). Sleep disorders in children. In C. E. Walker & M. C. Roberts (Eds.), *Handbook of clinical child psychology* (pp. 381–405). New York: Wiley.

Warme, G. (1977). Childhood developmental problems. In P. D. Steinhauer & Q. Rae-Grant (Eds.), *Psychological problems of the child and his family* (pp. 100–125). Toronto: Macmillan.

Waterman, J. (1986). Developmental considerations. In K. MacFarlane & J. Waterman (Eds.), *Sexual abuse of young children: Evaluation and treatment* (pp. 15–29). New York: Guilford Press.

Weaver, S. J. (Ed.). (1985). *Testing children: A reference guide for effective clinical and psychoeducational assessments.* Kansas City, MO: Test Corporation of America.

Webster-Stratton, C. (1981). Modification of mother's behaviors and attitudes through a videotape modeling group discussion program. *Behavior Therapy, 12*, 634–642.

Webster-Stratton, C. (1985a). Predictors of treatment outcome in parent training for conduct disordered children. *Behavior Therapy, 16*, 223–243.

Webster-Stratton, C. (1985b). The effects of father involvement in parent training for conduct problem children. *Journal of Child Psychology and Psychiatry, 26*, 801–810.

Webster-Stratton, C. (1989). Systematic comparison of consumer satisfaction of three cost-effective parent training programs for conduct problem children. *Behavior Therapy, 20*, 103–115.

Webster-Stratton, C., & Hammond, M. (1988). Maternal depression and its relationship to life stress, perceptions of child behavior problems, parenting behaviors, and child conduct problems. *Journal of Abnormal Child Psychology, 16*, 299–315.

Weddig, R. R. (1984). Parental interpretation of psychoeducational reports. *Psychology in the Schools, 21*, 477–481.

Wehrspann, W. H., Steinhauer, P. D., & Klajner-Diamond, H. K. (1987). Criteria and methodology for assessing credibility of sexual abuse allegation. *Canadian Journal of Psychiatry, 32*, 615–623.

Weithorn, L. A. (1987). Psychological consultation in divorce custody litigation: Ethical considerations. In L. A. Weithorn (Ed.), *Psychology and child custody determinations: Knowledge, roles and expertise* (pp. 182–210). Lincoln: University of Nebraska Press.

Weithorn, L. A., & Grisso, T. (1987). Psychological evaluations in divorce custody: Problems, principles, and procedures. In L. A. Weithorn (Ed.), *Psychology and child custody determinations: Knowledge, roles and expertise* (pp. 157–181). Lincoln: University of Nebraska Press.

Weller, E. B., Weller, R. A., Fristad, M. A., Cain, S. E., & Bowes, J. M. (1988). Should children attend their parent's funeral? *Journal of the American Academy of Child and Adolescent Psychiatry, 27,* 559–562.

Werner, E. E., & Smith, R. S. (1982). *Vulnerable but invincible: A longitudinal study of resilient children and youth.* New York: McGraw-Hill.

Werry, J. S. (1986). Diagnosis and assessment. In R. Gittelman (Ed.), *Anxiety disorders of childhood* (pp. 73–100). New York: Guilford Press.

Werry, J. S., Reeves, J. C., & Elkind, G. S. (1987). Attention deficit, conduct, oppositional, and anxiety disorders in children: I. A review of research on differentiating characteristics. *Journal of the American Academy of Child and Adolescent Psychiatry, 26,* 133–143.

White, E. A., Elsom, B., & Prawat, R. (1978). Children's conceptions of death. *Child Development, 49,* 307–310.

White, S., Halpin, B. M., Strom, G. A., & Santilli, G. (1986, May). *Behavioral comparisons of young sexually abused, neglected, and nonreferred children.* Paper presented at the Fourth National Conference on the Sexual Victimization of Children, New Orleans.

White, S., Strom, G. A., & Santilli, G. (1986). *A clinical protocol for interviewing young children with the sexually anatomically correct dolls.* Unpublished manuscript, Case Western Reserve University School of Medicine.

Wilson, B. J., Hoffner, C., & Cantor, J. (1987). Children's perceptions of the effectiveness of techniques to reduce fear from mass media. *Journal of Applied Developmental Psychology, 8,* 39–52.

Wilson, J. L. (1964). Growth and development of pediatrics. *Journal of Pediatrics, 65,* 984–991.

Wilson, R. S. (1985). Risk and resilience in early mental development. *Developmental Psychology, 21,* 795–805.

Winkler, R. C. (1977). What types of sex-role behavior should behavior modifiers promote? *Journal of Applied Behavior Analysis, 10,* 549–552.

Wirt, R. D., Lachar, D., Klinedinst, J. D., & Seat, P. D. (1977). *Multidimensional description of child personality: A manual for the Personality Inventory for Children.* Los Angeles: Western Psychological Services.

Wolfe, D. A., Edwards, B., Manion, I., & Koverola, C. (1988). Early intervention for parents at risk of child abuse and neglect: A preliminary investigation. *Journal of Consulting and Clinical Psychology, 56,* 40–47.

Wolfe, V. V., Gentile, C., & Wolfe, D. A. (1989). The impact of sexual abuse on children: A PTSD formulation. *Behavior Therapy, 20,* 215–228.

Wolman, B. B. (Ed.). (1985). *Handbook of intelligence: Theories, measurements and applications.* New York: Wiley.

Wolpe, J. (1958). *Psychotherapy by reciprocal inhibition.* Stanford, CA: Stanford University Press.

Wood, J. M., & Bootzin, R. R. (1990). The prevalence of nightmares and their independence from anxiety. *Journal of Abnormal Psychology, 99,* 64–68.

Woodrow, K. M. (1974). Gilles de la Tourette's disease: A review. *American Journal of Psychiatry, 131*, 1000–1003.

Wright, L. (1975). Outcome of a standardized program for treating psychogenic encopresis. *Professional Psychology, 6*, 453–456.

Wright, L., & Burns, B. J. (1986). Primary mental health care: A "find" for psychology. *Professional Psychology: Research and Practice, 17*, 560–564.

Wright, L., & Walker, C. E. (1976). Behavioral treatment of encopresis. *Journal of Pediatric Psychology, 4*, 35–37.

Wurtele, S. K. (1990). Teaching personal safety skills to four-year-old children: A behavioral approach. *Behavior Therapy, 21*, 25–32.

Wurtele, S. K., Kast, L. C., Miller-Perrin, C. L., & Kondrick, P. A. (1989). Comparison of programs for teaching personal safety skills to preschoolers. *Journal of Consulting and Clinical Psychology, 57*, 505–511.

Wurtele, S. K., & Miller, C. L. (1987). Children's conceptions of sexual abuse. *Journal of Clinical Child Psychology, 16*, 184–191.

Wyer, M. M., Gaylord, S. J., & Grove, E. T. (1987). The legal context of child custody evaluations. In L. A. Weithorn (Ed.), *Psychology and child custody determinations: Knowledge, roles and expertise* (pp. 3–22). Lincoln: University of Nebraska Press.

Yates, A. J. (1958). The application of learning theory to the treatment of tics. *Journal of Abnormal and Social Psychology, 56*, 175–182.

Yates, A. J. (1970). *Behavior therapy.* New York: Wiley.

Young, G. C., & Morgan, R. T. T. (1972). Overlearning in the conditioning treatment of enuresis. *Behaviour Research and Therapy, 10*, 419–420.

Zahn-Waxler, C., Radke-Yarrow, M., & King, R. M. (1979). Childrearing and children's prosocial imitations toward victims of distress. *Child Development, 50*, 319–330.

Zaslow, M. J. (1988). Sex differences in children's response to parental divorce: 1. Research methodology and post-divorce family forms. *American Journal of Orthopsychiatry, 58*, 353–378.

Zaslow, M. J. (1989). Sex differences in children's response to parental divorce: 2. Samples, variables, ages, and sources. *American Journal of Orthopsychiatry, 59*, 118–141.

Zuckerman, B. S., & Blitzer, E. C. (1981). Sleep disorders. In S. Gabel (Ed.), *Behavioral problems in childhood: A primary care approach* (pp. 257–272). New York: Grune & Stratton.

Index